"WHAT MADE MURROW TICK...A FASCINATING STUDY OF A FASCINATING AND REMARKABLE MAN."
—UPI

"Edward R. Murrow was such a giant the man is in danger of being lost in the myth. . . . Persico sees Murrow whole and human."
—Harry Reasoner

"This book is both history and biography, richly researched and very well written."
—Dan Rather

"Persico's book digs beneath the sometimes impenetrable surface to reveal what made this man tick. This is a new dimension of Ed Murrow."
—Daniel Schorr

"Fascinating, penetrating. I knew Ed Murrow well. But I never knew him as clearly as I do now, after reading Joe Persico's book."
—Howard K. Smith

"Revelatory . . . adds telling detail to Murrow's career."
—*Kirkus Reviews*

"Besides being wonderfully readable, *An American Original* is thorough. Persico puts Murrow's achievements in a historical and professional context."
—*The Boston Herald*

EDWARD R. MURROW

An American Original

JOSEPH E. PERSICO

LAUREL

A LAUREL TRADE PAPERBACK

Published by
Dell Publishing
a division of
Bantam Doubleday Dell Publishing Group, Inc.
666 Fifth Avenue
New York, New York 10103

ISBN: 0-440-50301-9

Reprinted by arrangement with McGraw-Hill Publishing Company

Printed in the United States of America
Published simultaneously in Canada

April 1990

10 9 8 7 6 5 4 3 2 1

BVG

To Vanya and Andrea

Contents

Foreword

Edward R. Murrow crossed my life at three points.

As a boy growing up in the forties, I heard his voice from London, cutting through the whine and crackle of shortwave radio, and it was to me the very sound of the war. I can close my eyes now and turn on that sound in my memory, hear the mournful wail of the sirens, the crumple of distant bombs, and that somber voice intoning, "It's a bomber's moon tonight."

In the fifties, I was a college student, a card-carrying member of the silent generation. I recall only two political activists during my college years. One was a seedy looking sophomore who wore a rumpled, double-breasted suit with an unclean white shirt, in the era of khakis and white bucks. The other was a stunningly beautiful Communist. Her commitment must have been ardent indeed, since this was the era of the witch hunts and Joe McCarthy when there were probably more FBI undercover agents at her cell meetings than bona fide Reds.

I hated the suffocating conformity of that era. I hated the idea, not so much that a McCarthy existed, they always do, but that he could prosper, that his ilk wielded power, struck fear, choked off healthy dissent, and destroyed the lives of innocent people. And then, in March of 1954, with McCarthy at the peak of his power, Murrow used the relatively young medium of television to take the bully on. I was drawn not only by what Murrow did, but how skillfully he did it. What he managed in the course of a half hour was virtually to have McCarthy stand before millions of Americans, place a rope woven of his own demagoguery around his neck, and hang himself.

In 1961, I was abroad with the U.S. Information Agency. At that point, the USIA was a stepchild of government, an organization with a poorly understood, even suspect, propaganda mission, no domestic power base, and an anemic budget. The agency was the whipping boy on Capitol Hill of certain small-bore politicians who would never have dared lift a finger against the tobacco lobby or the military-industrial complex, but who cut the small USIA appropriation with impunity.

And then President John F. Kennedy announced that he was appointing Edward R. Murrow as director of the U.S. Information Agency. One could feel an adrenalin surge throughout the agency. Suddenly we felt better about our mission and ourselves. If Kennedy had wanted a man of Murrow's stature heading the agency, if Murrow had found the USIA worthy of his gifts, then a new era had dawned for the USIA.

Back in Washington on home leave, I saw Ed Murrow for the only time in my life. We were riding the same elevator with a half-dozen other USIA employees at the headquarters on Pennsylvania Avenue. I thought of introducing myself. But I was more interested in studying him, because there is so little point in those ten-second interchanges between the layman and the famous. Furthermore, though there was a twinkling in the eye and suppressed bemusement in the set of his mouth, something about the man did not invite casual intrusion.

The image of him, however, remains as sharp as a daguerreotype—a haggard handsomeness (he was then 53), Lincolnian moles and crevices in skin the color of a sidewalk, and the thick, quizzical eyebrows of a cross-examiner. His suit, a gray pinstripe, draped in the way that only good tailoring achieves. My eye went automatically to his hand, where indeed there was a cigarette. I remember thinking that Ed Murrow looked the way Ed Murrow was supposed to look, save for an unexpected homburg, which he removed in the elevator. I remember too an electrical field around the man that the others in the elevator pretended not to feel, the stiff silence merely heightening the voltage.

I admired the public man, but I was, then as now, more curious about what lay beneath the surface. There was an aura of mystery about Murrow. My publishers, happily, shared my curiosity in this man whose life was really two stories, his own and the history of broadcast journalism. The two are inseparable.

And so I began the biographer's peculiar manhunt. I spent years pursuing a specter, bent on cloaking it in flesh, blood, and spirit, reconstructing, as nearly as possible, the man as he was. In this pursuit, an honest biographer suffers from a gnawing sense of inadequacy, even fraudulence. What we set out to do is inherently presumptuous. Any person's life is the sum of a hundred thousand mosaic pieces. The most assiduous biographer unearths perhaps ten thousand pieces and tries to convince not only the reader, but himself, that he has captured the whole man. I sometimes imagined Murrow hovering above me; he is in the classic Murrow pose, jacket off, suspenders exposed, collar open, tie pulled down, perched on the edge of a chair, his elbows planted on his knees, his face wreathed in cigarette smoke. His head is lowered, and he is looking at me over the tops of his eyes, as I struggle to capture him on paper. And he is saying, "Good luck, Buster." The eyes and the small, amused smile also seem to say that if I fail to get it right, it is all the same to him.

A man who is dead lives on in the memories of those who knew him, in what has been written about him, and in Murrow's case, in his papers and coils of celluloid that he left behind. I have gone to all these sources in writing his life.

Fortunately, the vast majority of his colleagues were still alive while I was working on this project. I interviewed 109 of them, most personally, a few by telephone, fewer still through letters. To discuss Murrow with his colleagues, particularly Murrow's Boys, was the most rewarding part of this undertaking. What struck me most was the remarkable degree of consistency in their feelings about the man. These were impressive figures in their own right, people respected for their acute perceptions of the world around them, Eric Sevareid, Charles Collingwood, Howard K. Smith, and Robert Trout among them. The man, invariably, that they looked up to was Murrow. Often, they spoke of him wistfully, as though the bright summer of their own careers had passed with his passing. They also spoke of him with a certain puzzlement. Not one of them, no matter how long or how close the exposure, seemed to feel that he truly understood Murrow. Murrow remained a figure of mystery, forever out of reach. There was something uncapturable in the Murrow persona, something at the core of the man, like a bead of mercury, that could not be grasped or held.

As I slowly penetrated this resistant figure in my research, one of my major concerns was dispelled. He had seemed, when I knew little, too good to be true. He was on the side of right in all the political controversies of his time, at least as I reckoned the right side. He was courageous, generous, and well loved. But as I talked to those who knew him, read his letters, studied his broadcasts, it became apparent that here was a man possessing the requisite foibles, failings, and inconsistencies for membership in that flawed species, the human race.

I was relieved to find that so gallant a man could occasionally be petty and unfair. I was pleased to find that a man whose name is constantly invoked to condemn commercialism in broadcasting was not above doing a mediocre television program that made him modestly rich. It was somehow comforting to know that a man who exuded such total confidence felt insecure enough early in his career to embellish his résumé. It was a surprise to discover that behind that coolly confident delivery was a man who, when broadcasting, would drip with sweat, his leg bouncing like a metronome gone mad. It was perhaps less surprising to learn that a man who was a natural leader could be a peevish coequal, as Walter Cronkite was to find out. It was unsettling to find that a man who inspired much love in other men was almost incapable of returning it.

Murrow was a cut stone with an astonishing number of facets. He was born in a cabin with an outhouse, and behaved like an English squire, when he was not acting like a lumberjack, or an intellectual gadfly, or a cowboy, or a philosopher, or a daredevil, or a social crusader, or a raconteur, or a hermit. He could be found firing at metal ducks in a Times Square shooting gallery or shooting at grouse on the moors of an English country estate. He could spin dialect stories at a crowded bar or go for twenty-four hours without uttering a word to a house guest. He could send his son to the most prestigious schools, all the while telling the boy that college was not important to a successful life. He was either telling friends how humble his own origins were or insinuating into the conversation that his wife's ancestors came over on the Mayflower. He was a handsome man and an elegant dresser who bristled at anyone who made mention of his striking appearance. He was impervious, even oblivious, to the charms of most women, yet became involved with an aristocratic beauty and nearly destroyed his marriage. He spent his professional life in world capitals, yet liked to imagine that he would be happier at a small-town college. He made a good deal of money, yet felt guilty about it and was so openhanded that it seemed at times that he was trying to give it all away. His pastimes were those of the he-man, yet he was a favorite of intellectuals. He had everything to live for, but he gambled his life dozens of times flying unnecessary combat missions. He could condemn a war, as he did in Korea, yet find it irresistible. He was modest, even flip, with colleagues about his physical bravery, but wrote letters to his parents presenting an almost maudlinly heroic self-image. He had every reason to be a happy man. He was not.

I was drawn to his life because he was the preeminent figure in a profession that he essentially fathered. It is difficult for any thinking person not to be simultaneously mesmerized and repelled by the hold of mass communications over the modern world. Murrow's story is integral to that phenomenon. This writer is of sufficient age to have watched television rise from nothing to the most pervasive cultural force in most of the world. A concomitant of that phenomenon, at least in this country, has been a seasonal condemnation of much of what appears on the commercial networks, a jeremiad as predictable as winter following the fall. As these words are being written, Murrow's network, CBS, is at the center of, as one newsmagazine cover story describes it, a "struggle for the soul of a legendary network." Critics within and without the walls of television are again bemoaning the triumph of pap over substance. A Gresham's law of television is spied once again, with bad programming presumably driving out the good.

Yet, everything complained of this season, and the season before, and the season before that, was said by Murrow in his speech before the Radio and Television News Directors Association thirty years ago. I thus leave to mass communications sociologists the diagnosis and prescription for the ills of television. My emphasis in this work is on the man. In following his life, we inescapably learn most of what went right and what went wrong in broadcasting. His career, the triumphs and the frustrations, his rise and fall, will stand as this author's commentary on the medium.

If the emphasis is on the man, this begs the question: how do we adduce him? A mass of biographical facts is no more a person than a pile of stone is a cathedral. Indeed, in a work of any length it is inevitable to get some facts wrong. The important thing is to get the spirit right. The former is an act of excavation, and the latter must be, to a degree, a leap of faith. My search has been for the Murrow character. If the character is revealed, the behavior becomes coherent.

The author who attempts this journey into character risks the complaint that he is not objective and pretends to be a mind reader. But to attempt anything less penetrating is to write merely an extended encyclopedia entry. In this biography, where I deal with Murrow's interior thoughts and motivations, my statements are based on what he revealed of himself in his personal correspondence and his attitudes as reported by his friends and family.

If the biographer succeeds, what the reader ought to feel, after investing his mental energies in several hundreds of pages, is "Ah, so that was Leonardo?" or "Now I feel that I've met Orwell." Or unhappily, "Sorry, you missed the boat." In this attempted journey inside the subject's psyche, the author is inevitably troubled by contradictions. The temptation is somehow to reconcile them, to iron them out or even omit them, or else to risk having the character solution appear incorrect because it is inconsistent. But what we realize in the end is that the contradictions are the character. To seek to render Murrow, or anyone else, whole in motive and constant in behavior is to rob him of his humanity. To accept what does not make sense is to admit how much of another human being is as forever hidden from us as the dark side of the moon.

CHAPTER 1

The Peak or the Precipice

At 10:30 p.m. on the night of March 9, 1954, a CBS thriller, "The First Hold-Up," with Ben Gazzara and Bethel Leslie, faded from the black and white screen. The network went into "system," thirty seconds given to local stations to identify themselves and run their commercials. The system break over, there appeared on the screen a man sitting in a control room. There was something dark and arresting about him. The head was large and handsome, the visage somber, the brows thick and black; and the eyes, peering upward through the brows, were both baleful and riveting. When he spoke, the voice too had a dark timbre and projected total authority. The man was Edward R. Murrow, the program *See It Now*, a documentary series then in its third year.[1]

"Good evening," Murrow began. "Tonight, *See It Now* devotes its entire half hour to a report on Senator Joseph R. McCarthy, told mainly in his own words and pictures...."[2]

Five months had passed since Murrow had decided to turn the essentially untried power of television on McCarthy. At the time, both men were at their peak, Murrow the preeminent broadcaster in America, McCarthy, the most successful demagogue in America's history. Murrow's outward air of composure belied his anxiety. Moments before, the makeup woman had been swabbing away the sweat that beaded his face and dripped off the point of his chin. He was mindful of Emerson's dictum: "When you strike at a king, you must kill him." For McCarthy's path was littered with the political corpses of those who had dared oppose him.

As Murrow spoke, he was like a man climbing a mountain in a dense fog. He could not tell if his next steps were going to take him higher, or if he was already at the summit and another step would begin his descent, even his fall.

1

His decision to take on McCarthy had been long in the making, too long, he later confessed. The incident that had finally triggered him to act illuminates much about both Murrow and the times. It had occurred in November, five months before. The United States Senate was then preparing to investigate charges that the previous President, Harry S. Truman, had committed treason. There is no more delicate way to put it. In the climate of that era, however, the charge was hardly as sensational as it seems at first blush. Allegations of treachery and spying, of disloyalty and subversion, were thick in the air that season. And even a former President was not spared.

Murrow had assigned Joe Wershba, a young *See It Now* reporter, to cover the investigation. Wershba was a bear of a man, more precisely, an oversized teddy bear, for he was an amiable soul, as well as a gifted reporter. His assignment this November day was to cover the testimony of FBI Director J. Edgar Hoover before the Senate's Internal Security Subcommittee. Hoover presumably held the answer to the treasonous point at issue: Did Harry Truman, as President, knowingly keep Harry Dexter White, an alleged Communist agent, in a high post at the Treasury Department?

On his arrival in Washington, Wershba had gone directly to the Senate Caucus Room, where he found Hoover already testifying. He rushed outside, looking frantically for his cameraman, when he felt an arm restraining him. He turned to see Donald Surine. Surine, an investigator for Joe McCarthy, was a shadowy figure who had earlier been fired by the FBI for, word had it, keeping a whore at the taxpayers' expense. "Hey, Joe," Surine asked Wershba, sounding disappointed, "what's this Radwich junk you're putting out?"

Surine had mangled the name. But Wershba knew instantly what he meant. The month before, Ed Murrow had devoted a full broadcast of *See It Now* to the plight of an Air Force Reserve lieutenant named Milo Radulovich. The Air Force had called Radulovich a "security risk," not because he was disloyal, since his patriotism was beyond question. Radulovich could not be trusted, the Air Force feared, because his sister was allegedly a Communist, and his father was said to read subversive Serbian-language newspapers. Radulovich had been asked to resign his commission. When he refused, an Air Force board ordered his separation from the service.

To Murrow, the Radulovich case reeked of a sickness abroad in the land. A man was being punished without due process of law, without being permitted to know the evidence against him, indeed without having committed a crime. His ordeal was being shared by hundreds of other Americans. While responsibility for the sickness could not be blamed entirely on one man, "McCarthyism," in Murrow's reckoning, fully summed up the disease.

The Air Force had pressured Murrow to kill the Radulovich story, but he had pressed ahead and broadcast it anyway. This broadcast was the "Radwich junk" bothering Donald Surine. Wershba told Surine that he was in a hurry, that he had no time to gab, and began to leave. But as he started to go, Surine said something that stopped him cold. "What would you say if I told you Murrow was on the Soviet payroll in 1934?" Before Wershba could react, Surine cocked his head and said, "Come on up to the office. I'll show you."

Surine's charge struck Wershba as ludicrous. But given McCarthy's genius for mischief, no threat from him or his agents could be dismissed out of hand. Wershba momentarily forgot about finding his cameraman and followed Surine to McCarthy's fourth-floor office in the Senate Office Building. Surine ordered the reporter to wait outside. When he returned, he handed Wershba a photostat of a newspaper story. Wershba read it and then asked Surine if he could show a copy to Murrow. Surine agreed. As Wershba was leaving, Surine said, "It's a terrible shame. Murrow's brother being a general in the Air Force." Murrow's older brother, Lacey, was in fact an Air Force Reserve officer. Surine gave Wershba a friendly wave, confident that Wershba would carry his barely veiled warning to his boss.

When Wershba got back to CBS in New York the next night, he went immediately to see Murrow, who was just wrapping up his nightly radio newscast. He handed him the photostated clipping. Murrow, he was later to recall, "reddened and a weak grin came to his face." "So that's what they've got," Murrow said quietly.

Joe Wershba idolized Ed Murrow, and he sought to put himself at ease in the man's presence by playing court jester. "You've had a long and honorable career," he said, "enough to enable any man to retire to the role of country gentleman." Murrow had in fact just bought an expensive home in the country.

Murrow, seated, head bent, looked up at Wershba through the heavy brows with a stare that made clear he was in no mood to be humored. Wershba started to leave. As he did, the annoyance suddenly vanished from Murrow's face. He looked drained, Wershba remembered thinking, "Like a fallen warrior."

The following morning, Wershba ran into Murrow again at the water fountain. He was happily astonished. The gloom had faded. Murrow was aggressively chipper. "The only question now," he said, with a teeth-baring smile, "is when do I go up against those guys?"[3]

Attacking bureaucratic bone-headedness in the Air Force on *See It Now* was one thing; taking on Joe McCarthy was a risk of another order of magnitude. The man was, on his own peculiar terms, a quintessential American success story. Joseph Raymond McCarthy was the fifth of seven children of a dirt-poor Wisconsin farm family. He had been yanked out of school at 14 and did not make it back to high school until he was 20. He then proceeded to breeze through four years of high school in one. He went on to the Jesuit's Marquette University in Milwaukee, where he was best remembered as a boxer who seemed to relish taking punishment as much as giving it, the kind of fighter who blocks punches with his head.[4]

Joe McCarthy became a lawyer and at the age of 32 was elected to a local judgeship. During World War II, he enlisted and was commissioned in the Marine Corps. He came home from the war and proceeded to accomplish a seeming political miracle. In the 1946 Wisconsin Republican primary he brought down a Wisconsin dynasty, defeating Robert LaFollette, twenty-one years in the U.S. Senate, whose father had served there for twenty years before him. McCarthy went on to win the general election in the fall.[5]

His Senate colleagues came to know a man at once simplistic and complex, an ugly bully one instant, a raffish charmer the next. He just missed being handsome. The eyes were a trifle too narrow, the brow too frowning, the mouth too thin-lipped, the needle-sharp nose planted in a face too broad, the beard too heavy. He had grown narrower in the shoulders and broader in the beam with middle age. Like an aging bull, his body now suggested power going slack. He walked with a slouching gait that gave a certain menace to his movements. He was an indifferent dresser, rumpled, careless, willing to let a white shirt go another day. His appearance suggested a very tough, very smart old con.

Joe McCarthy became the avatar of anticommunism much the way other men choose a new suit. Up for reelection in 1952, he was shopping around for a campaign issue. He had tried on a couple of issues—the St. Lawrence Seaway, giving every American over 65 a hundred dollars a month—and had discarded them. A priest-academic from Georgetown University had suggested Communist subversion. McCarthy's eyes danced. That was it. "The government," he exclaimed, "is full of Communists."[6]

On February 10, 1950, McCarthy found the first occasion to wear the new suit. He had drawn a second-rung speaking assignment from the Republican Campaign Committee for the annual round of Lincoln Day fundraising dinners—Wheeling, West Virginia.

McCarthy that night, hunched over a lectern in the ballroom of the McClure Hotel, waving a never-identified document purportedly listing 205 Communists "working and shaping policy in the State Department," has become by now a part of American political demonology. The charge was spectacular. Overnight, Joe McCarthy found himself catapulted ahead of the Senate pack to the front rank of political celebrity. He had tried on the new suit. It not only fit; it looked good, it felt great, and it was obviously going to do wonders for his career.[7]

It mattered not that his original charge of 205 Communists at the State Department had fluctuated almost from news cycle to news cycle—eighty-one, to sixty-one, to fifty-seven. It mattered not that he promised to expose the "top Soviet agent in the State Department" and came up with Owen Lattimore, who was not a spy, not a Communist, and not in the State Department. It mattered not that on serious measures to halt the spread of communism Joe McCarthy voted no—no to the Marshall

Plan, no to Point IV aid to underdeveloped countries, no to military aid for non-Communist states. Nothing fazed Joe McCarthy as he went on hurling his charges against Communists in government like a pitcher with dazzling speed but no control.[8]

Many of his Senate colleagues saw Joe McCarthy as a publicity-besotted buffoon, a politically lewd figure whose membership in their club was an embarrassment. Millard Tydings of Maryland, a pillar of the Senate establishment, investigated McCarthy's accusations. McCarthy campaigned against him, and Millard Tydings was defeated for reelection. Scott Lucas of Illinois, the Democratic floor leader, challenged McCarthy, and Lucas was defeated for reelection. Senator William Benton succeeded Lucas as floor leader and introduced a resolution to have McCarthy expelled from the Senate. McCarthy went to Connecticut where Benton was campaigning for reelection, and Benton was defeated. Ernest MacFarland of Arizona succeeded Benton as floor leader. McCarthy campaigned against him, and MacFarland was defeated for reelection. In the Senate, contempt for Joe McCarthy continued, but the nature of it changed. Ridicule largely gave way to caution, or silence, or even grudging admiration.[9]

Joe McCarthy had started his anti-Communist crusade virtually from nothing, from an assignment of almost embarrassingly low status, a seat on the Senate Operations Committee, a housekeeping body that looked into government motor pool abuses and jacked-up office furniture contracts in federal agencies. McCarthy had managed to transform this unlikely base into a fearsome instrument of political inquisition.[10]

He took on seemingly untouchable targets. George C. Marshall was one of the most respected figures in America—chief of staff and an architect of victory during World War II, and later Truman's secretary of state, father of the plan that bore his name and that saved a prostrate Western Europe from a genuine threat of Communism. Joe McCarthy called General Marshall, "A man steeped in falsehood, part of a conspiracy so immense and an infamy so black as to dwarf any previous venture in the history of man." And McCarthy got away with it.

McCarthy's staffers drew up a list of "subversive" American authors—Stephen Vincent Benét, Theodore Dreiser, Edna Ferber, Henry Steele Commager, and John Dewey among them—and U.S. information libraries abroad started yanking books by these people off their shelves.

McCarthy cowed the State Department into scrapping the two most powerful radio transmitters ever built, costing $815 million. Disloyal officials of the Voice of America had sabotaged the transmitters he said, by locating them where their signals would not work.[11]

Ohio's conservative John Bricker came off the Senate floor one day and met McCarthy in the cloakroom. "Joe," Bricker said, "you're a dirty son of a bitch. But there are times when you've got to have a son of a bitch around. And this is one of them." The proud teller of this story was Joe McCarthy.[12]

The shanty Irish kid had achieved what he had hungered for all his life. He was somebody, a figure to be taken seriously, to be reckoned with, to be played up to and stood aside for. He mattered. No matter the route, he had arrived.

Obviously, he had not achieved his success-through-excess in a vacuum. Joe McCarthy had cast the seed of his ambition on fertile soil. World War II had been over barely five years when he gave the Wheeling speech. When the war had ended in 1945, America stood unscathed and unrivaled, the sole possessor of the atomic bomb, the most powerful nation on earth. Her victorious armies were quickly demobilized and came home to cities that were intact, to factories that were undamaged, and to an economy readying itself to meet enormous pent-up consumer demand. The United States, her people believed, stood on the threshold of a new age of peace and prosperity. And deservedly so. They had fought the good fight, and they had won.

Too soon it started to unravel. The defeat of nazism had saved western democracy, but it also saved Russian communism. And communism, in its global reach and appeal to the earth's disinherited, began to loom as a more formidable long-term enemy than nazism. In 1946, China went Communist, because of, some Americans believed, traitorous officials shaping Asian policy, people like Secretary of State George C. Marshall. In 1949, the Soviet Union, thought to be war-ravaged and backward, exploded an atomic bomb. How? Through secrets given to Russians by western spies and traitors. Just one month before the Wheeling speech, Alger Hiss, who had held sensitive State Department positions at Yalta and at the birth of the United Nations, was convicted of perjury for denying his past connections to Communists. And five months after Wheeling, the United States was actually at war against Communists in North Korea.[13]

How could it all have gone so wrong so fast? Why had the United States, so recently unassailable, found herself competing with communism for world leadership and bogged down in an ugly war with a fourth-rate Communist pawn. The conspiracy theory had the appeal of all great simplifications, an understandable answer to the inexplicable. Traitors, spies, and soft-headed liberal dupes in government, boring from within, had obviously achieved what no external enemy had been able to do to America. And as for those who criticized this explanation as simplistic and paranoid, what exactly were their motives? Whose side were they on? Which were precisely the questions that Joe McCarthy asked.[14]

To Ed Murrow, a man already inclined to pessimism and dark forebodings, the era of McCarthyism was a nightmare coming true. As a student leader in Europe, and later as a broadcaster, he had watched the Germans trade unruly Weimar democracy for Nazi order. He had witnessed home-grown Fascist movements in England, France, and Poland. He knew how the Fascists made their excesses palatable: anticommunism was the respectable cloak they wore. When Murrow and his wife, Janet, were flying home from England in 1946, as the American coast came into view, she recalled Ed saying, "We saw it happen in Europe. There's no reason to suppose it can't happen here."[15]

He had taken stands. He had spoken out against the circus-style anticommunism of the House Un-American Activities Committee. McCarthy's victim, Owen Lattimore, thanked Murrow for defending him on the air "even when the hysteria was at its height." Murrow helped save the careers of CBS colleagues who had been blacklisted.

Still, some of Murrow's friends had been asking aloud why he was not doing more, not using his unrivaled position, that bully pulpit of microphone and camera with its audience of millions, to challenge McCarthy head-on. Bill Downs, a gruff, much valued friend came up from CBS's Washington bureau to have dinner with the Murrows at their Park Avenue apartment. Afterward, over drinks, Downs warned, "You'd better do something about that guy."

Murrow hedged. "Fred Friendly says it isn't time yet," he said, referring to the coproducer of *See It Now.*

"It is time," Downs insisted. "The effect that McCarthy is having is nothing short of devastating."[16]

Another friend taunted Murrow that he was avoiding a confrontation with McCarthy because he had too much to lose, his programs, his sponsors, the Park Avenue apartment, the new country estate. Murrow answered with the stock dodge that he used to conceal his private thoughts: "You may be right." Joe Wershba gingerly asked Murrow, was he interested in a "let's-you-and-him-fight-it-out" scrap with McCarthy? Murrow answered, "We ain't." Another acquaintance criticized him for being unfair to McCarthy in his broadcasts. "His methods may be a little harsh," the man said, "but he's doing a job that needs doing." Murrow replied, "You may be right."[17]

Still, underneath the caution, the stalling, the you-may-be-rights, the matter of McCarthy rankled. At times, Murrow's restraint wore through. Struve Hensel, the Pentagon's counsel in the Eisenhower administration, and his wife were having dinner at Murrow's country home one Sunday. Also present was Murrow's weekend guest, the British ambassador to the United States. Murrow proposed a snide toast mocking President Eisenhower for his fear of offending McCarthy. Mrs. Hensel got up and started to march out. Murrow went after her. "You simply cannot speak that way about the President," she said, "especially not in front of foreigners." Murrow apologized and led the woman back to the table.[18]

He began thinking about using television to deal with McCarthy, to make the public see the man, as it were, with the naked eye. After work one day he was having a drink with the cartoonist Walt Kelley. "You know," Murrow said, "the best man to destroy McCarthy is Joe himself."

"Yes," the creator of Pogo agreed. "But will he take the job?"[19]

Murrow was driving one day to the Astoria film studios on Long Island with Sam Goldwyn, Jr., to narrate a film. As they drove, Murrow began thinking out loud. Nobody in the press, he speculated, was going to nail McCarthy simply by attacking him, even with the truth. McCarthy was too smart for that. He could counterpunch faster and harder than any of them. "It has to be done," Ed concluded, "through his own deeds and words." Conventional reporting, he thought, actually played into McCarthy's hands.[20]

Indeed it did. McCarthy was a U.S. senator, and he was making charges of such gravity that they could not be ignored. Even as respected a liberal voice as Walter Lippmann conceded: "When he makes such attacks against the State Department, the Defense Department, it is news which has to be published." *The New York Times* concluded: "It is difficult if not impossible to ignore charges by Senator McCarthy just because they are usually proved false." *The Times* then proceeded to put the responsibility for separating innuendo from truth and accusation from guilt in a strange place. "The remedy," said *The Times*, "lies with the reader."[21]

What saved McCarthy from his own recklessness was the lack of any continuing context in which his behavior could be judged. He tossed out the day's accusations like a keeper feeding the animals at the zoo. The reporters snapped up his charges, reported them, and waited for the next day's feeding. Yesterday's victim was forgotten in the dash for tomorrow's headline. However contemptible many journalists found him, Joe McCarthy was great copy. And so the press, the government, and the public continued to gape like spectators at a circus watching the man on the high wire, wondering, spellbound, what he would dare next.

It was this question, where McCarthy might strike next, that appears to have triggered Murrow's decision to take him on. Murrow knew, in a normal climate, that the flimsy information McCarthy had on him, based on an old newspaper clipping, could be explained to fair minds. But these were not normal times, and Joe McCarthy had not achieved his success through fair play.

He tried later to analyze his motives for attacking McCarthy. "I wouldn't say it was liberalism," he told an interviewer. "...I think it stems from my feeling about the sacredness of due process of law. I saw in Germany and Czechoslovakia that the law is destroyed first and then, after the law is gone, the freedom of the people is destroyed. The thing about McCarthy that bothers me is his disrespect for the due process of law." And his motive may have been to strike before McCarthy struck him—the belief that a good offense is indeed the best defense.[22]

Whatever the motive or the unknowable amalgam of motives, immediately after Surine delivered McCarthy's threat through Joe Wershba, Murrow asked Fred Friendly how much film they had on McCarthy. He was especially eager to know if anyone had shot the Wheeling speech. To his disappointment, no one had. He also began to fire off memos to Fred Friendly to make sure that *See It Now* crews covered future McCarthy appearances. He dispatched reporters to McCarthy's home town of Appleton, Wisconsin, to talk to the senator's relatives, friends, old schoolmates, and former employers.[23]

Still, he was dissatisfied. The conventional documentary-making process was too slow. He also feared that the usual piecing together of a documentary portrait would fail to capture the essence of Joe McCarthy. He found himself drawn back again to his earlier gut instinct. As he told Charles Collingwood: "The thing to do is to let the man damn himself out of his own mouth."[24]

As 1954 opened, Joe McCarthy was on to fresh game—Communists and Communist influence in the Army. As in his other crusades, McCarthy was using a time-tested approach. If he could not find a big Communist and bring him low, he would find a small fish and inflate his importance. On the hook this time was a draftee Army dentist named Irving Peress, stationed at Camp Kilmer, New Jersey. Just as he was about to be discharged, Peress had been routinely mass-promoted, along with 7,000 other Army doctors and dentists, to the rank of major. McCarthy charged that Peress's promotion revealed "Communist influence" at Camp Kilmer. McCarthy acted with a zeal suggesting that he had cornered Rosa Luxembourg in the Pentagon. His insistent demand was to become the caricature battle cry of this bizarre era: "Who promoted Peress?"[25]

Brigadier General Ralph Zwicker, a decorated hero of the Battle of the Bulge, was the Camp Kilmer commandant and hence Peress's commanding officer. McCarthy hauled General Zwicker before his subcommittee in executive session. His treatment of the war hero was brutal even by McCarthy standards. "You are," he said, "a disgrace to the uniform. You're shielding Communist conspirators. You are not fit to be an officer. You are ignorant. You are going to be put on public display next Tuesday."[26]

Joe McCarthy was not known to read the classics. But his life now paralleled Aristophanes's *The Knights,* in which Demosthenes says of a sausage-maker who has become a powerful demagogue: "You shall trample down the Senate underfoot, confound them and crush the generals and the commanders." Walter Lippmann watched McCarthy's Senate colleagues remaining silent or profiting politically from his excesses and wrote: "This is the year that the Senate of the United States, in order not to appear red decided to be yellow."[27]

In February of 1954, Joe McCarthy was at his zenith. Never had he been stronger or looked more invincible. If he could browbeat a genuine war hero, brand him a fool and a dupe, and have Senate conservatives pressure the Army to put up with it, what could be denied him?

Yet Murrow thought he sensed something different in McCarthy's Zwicker performance, the crossing of an invisible line that separated audacity from rashness, boldness from self-destructiveness. The time to strike, he decided, had come. Early in March, he told Friendly to splice together every foot of film that they had on McCarthy. The two men then disappeared into a projection room and spent three hours reviewing five miles of film. Murrow pulled *See It Now* reporters off other assignments and put them to work full-time on the McCarthy project. He chose a tentative air date, March 9, just one week away.[28]

He had an obligation, he knew, to tell his network and his sponsors his intentions. The problem was how much to say, and to whom and when. Up until now, Murrow had enjoyed virtual autonomy at CBS. He and Fred Friendly did not ask approval for the subjects they covered, and no one in the corporation had ever attempted to censor them. Murrow's sponsor, the Aluminum Company of America, had proved the most tolerant of patrons. ALCOA had scrupulously respected Murrow's iron rule—no sponsor interference. ALCOA let him do what he wanted and paid the bills. Still, if he intended to take on McCarthy, he knew that CBS and ALCOA deserved some warning.

Five days before the broadcast date, Murrow informed Sig Mickelson, the CBS vice president for news and public affairs and hence Murrow's nominal boss, of his plan. Murrow and Friendly had agreed that if Mickelson asked to see the program in advance, they would screen it for him. But they would not initiate the offer.[29]

Sig Mickelson well knew that at CBS the power line ran directly from Murrow to Chairman William S. Paley, cutting out not only a news bureaucrat like himself, but bypassing the company's president, Frank Stanton, too. Mickelson had never exercised a shred of control over Murrow. He was not about to assume responsibility for a broadcast over which he had no authority, particularly one on Joe McCarthy. He did not ask to see the program.[30]

Distancing became the pattern in the upper echelons of CBS as word of the program spread. When Friendly tried to place a newspaper ad to run on the day of the program, the head of the CBS television network vetoed the request. Thereupon, Murrow and Friendly decided to run the ad at their own expense using prize money that they had won for *See It Now*. No connection to CBS, not even use of the company's logo, they were warned, was to appear in the ad.

Murrow and Friendly were virtually living in the studio now, as they pared the mass of film from three hours, down to two hours, down to an hour, and finally to thirty-seven minutes, still too long. Yet, for all the feverish preparation, Murrow had left himself an escape hatch. He had two other *See It Now* broadcasts standing by in case he changed his mind at the last minute.[31]

The arguments favoring prudence, delay, even retreat, were powerful. Four U.S. senators had directly challenged McCarthy, and all four had paid with their political careers. The President of the United States had watched McCarthy slander George C. Marshall, Eisenhower's wartime chief, and had essentially looked the other way. As Eisenhower explained his inaction to his brother Milton: "I just won't get into a pissing contest with that skunk." McCarthy had destroyed the professional lives of scores of people as innocent and honorable as Edward R. Murrow. And Murrow himself was employed in an industry then practicing its own form of McCarthyism with blacklists and loyalty oaths. He was laying his career on the line along with those of all the men and women who had hitched their future to his.[32]

Joe McCarthy was not going to be an easy target. It mattered not that he had led a stained and soiled life; that he had won his first judgeship by tacking twenty years onto the age of his 66-year-old opponent and then ran as the youth candidate; that he had campaigned for the U.S. Senate as "tail-gunner Joe" with thirty combat missions, when actually he had had a desk job, fired guns only at coconut trees, and flew no combat missions; that he had wangled a purple heart for "ten pounds of shrapnel" that he claimed he carried in his leg when actually he had hurt himself falling down a ship's gangway during an equator-crossing hazing ceremony; that as a freshman senator, in order to placate German-American voters in his state, he had defended Nazi SS troops on trial for the Malmedy Massacre of over eighty defenseless American prisoners of war; that he had taken so many favors from American soft-drink makers in return for helpful legislation that he was called "the senator from Pepsi Cola"; that a poll of Washington news correspondents had chosen him the worst member of the U.S. Senate; that despite all the fuss, he had never found a single Communist in the State Department.[33]

None of his deformities of character were known, or remembered, or seemed to matter to the public at large. Murrow was taking on a man who, at this point, enjoyed far-reaching popular support. The most recent Gallup poll had revealed that 50 percent of the American people surveyed had a "favorable" opinion of Senator McCarthy, 29 percent an "unfavorable" opinion, and 21 percent "no opinion." Thus 71 percent of the American people had no quarrel with Joe McCarthy. In the eyes of millions of his countrymen, McCarthy, whatever his failings, was fighting Communists, and who could criticize that? Murrow might have a minority of liberals, intellectuals, and civil libertarians in his corner. But Joe McCarthy had the people.[34]

Janet Murrow recalls the night that her husband came home, red-eyed and exhausted. "I've definitely decided," he said. "We're going with it." As he spoke, she remembered "cold shivers going up and down my spine."

With one day left before the broadcast, Murrow finally went up to the CBS executive offices on the twentieth floor of 485 Madison Avenue to see Bill Paley. He had previously told Paley in general terms that he was planning a *See It Now* broadcast on McCarthy. Now he told him that the program would be done the following night.[35]

Paley offered no objection. Murrow then asked Paley if he wanted to see the program in advance. Paley asked him, "Are you sure of your facts? Are you on safe ground?" Murrow assured him that he was. Then, said Paley, there was no need for him to see the program. Paley's decision may be seen as a touching confidence in Murrow. Then again, it may have been another evidence of that distancing, an effort even by the chairman of the board to detach the network from what it carried, as though it were a telephone line indifferent to and unaccountable for what people said over it.

Paley did set one condition. He told Murrow to offer McCarthy equal time for a rebuttal. Murrow was upset. "He became rather emotional about certain things," Paley was later to recall of that moment. Offering the resources of the CBS television network to Joe McCarthy was, in Murrow's view, "to give Jesus and Judas equal time." Murrow may also have been understandably concerned with what McCarthy might do with that time, given the information that McCarthy had on him.

Nevertheless, he went back and announced, without apology or explanation, to a disappointed *See It Now* crew that he was going to offer McCarthy equal time to rebut. He was not about to bad-mouth Paley, one of the few heros in his personal pantheon.[36]

During those last days, his in-laws were staying with him and recalled hearing Murrow pacing the apartment until the small hours, and when he finally did go to bed, they could hear him grinding his teeth in his sleep.[37]

On the day of the broadcast, Murrow finally informed Frank Stanton, the CBS president, of what he was doing. Stanton remembers that it was not until 4:30 in the afternoon that Murrow came to his office. Stanton was later to claim that this was the first time that he had heard about the McCarthy program. It is hard to believe that the president of CBS did not read the television section of *The New York Times* that day, which carried a quarter-page ad announcing: "Tonight at 10:30 *See It Now* presents a report on Senator Joseph R. McCarthy...." It is harder to believe that Sig Mickelson had not informed his boss, Stanton, instantly upon getting the word days before. And it is doubtful that Stanton and Bill Paley would not have discussed the possible consequences for a government-licensed corporation of incurring the wrath of a vengeful McCarthy. And it seems more than a coincidence that on this occasion Stanton also repeated Paley's warning that Murrow give McCarthy equal time. Still, years later, Stanton was to recall that the McCarthy broadcast was news to him.

During the visit, Murrow also offered to screen the program in advance for Stanton. Frank Stanton was a proud man and no fool. He knew that Murrow disliked him. He saw Murrow's present offer for the empty gesture that it was. It was far too late to change anything, even in the unlikely event that Murrow sincerely wanted his advice. And so Stanton also distanced himself and declined to see the program. He did not express his true feeling at the moment, which was bitter resentment at this perfunctory last-minute treatment of the chief executive of the corporation concerning a critical broadcast already past the point of no return.[38]

Murrow could obviously have been more forthcoming about his intentions. Perhaps he should have been. But if you are going to strike at a king, you must kill him, and it does not pay to alert him in advance. Murrow was convinced, in the prevailing climate, that to be too open too soon would have meant that the network might stop him.

That night, Murrow had to make his regular nightly newscast on radio before doing *See It Now* on television. There was fresh McCarthy news to report. The senator had threatened the networks that they must give him equal time to answer a recent attack on him by Adlai Stevenson. That afternoon, Senator Ralph Flanders of Vermont had denounced McCarthy on the floor of the Senate, a brave and lonely gesture by the elderly Vermonter. Murrow reported it all, straight and without comment, folded in with the other news about a tax reform bill before Ways and Means and French-German talks on the Saar.[39]

After the news, he left the radio studios at 485 Madison Avenue and went to the Grand Central Station building, where CBS had its television studios. The atmosphere on his arrival was electric. Amid the chaos of last-minute preparations, one of the film projectors had broken down and the technicians were working frantically to have it ready by air time. Murrow barely had time to get in one last rehearsal. Minutes before 10:30, he picked up his script and headed for Studio 41. In the hallway he passed Joe Wershba. "I've made out my will," he said, giving the reporter a gallows smile, "and I'm resolved to do my duty." Murrow disappeared into the studio.[40]

One of the moving stories in broadcasting legend is the phone call that Bill Paley made to Ed Murrow that day. It is a tale frequently told, and it is true. Paley called Murrow and said, "I'll be with you tonight, Ed. And I'll be with you tomorrow as well." It was a noble sentiment and doubtless sincere in spirit, though not quite literally true. Bill Paley did not watch *See It Now* that night.[41]

Don Hewitt was Murrow's director for the McCarthy program. Hewitt was a brash talent who would one day make his own television history as the creator of CBS's *60 Minutes*. He had set up his camera that night on a high hat, almost at floor level, to catch Murrow at his most effective angle. Fred Friendly sat on the floor at Murrow's feet, out of camera range, ready to signal Murrow with a tap on the leg when he was to begin reading his script. When it was time for Murrow to stop and let the film segments roll, Friendly would give him a light jab with his pencil point. On the studio wall was a clock with a reverse face to tell them how much time was left in the program. Hewitt watched the second hand sweep across the clock's face. The story with Ben Gazzara and Bethel Leslie faded from the monitor. The local stations identified themselves. Commercials ran. Hewitt gave the cue.[42]

The man that viewers saw on the screen looked like a casting director's ideal of exactly what he had been, a famous war correspondent, strikingly handsome, but without the pretty-boy Hollywood perfection. His teeth were not quite regular. The face was deeply furrowed, with a mole here and there giving his good looks a Lincolnesque believability. He would not let the make-up woman conceal the moles. They were him, he said. His forehead and brow had the heavy bone structure that boxers dislike because they cannot get at the eyes. He was a man of somber mien, rescued by a dazzling smile that he could flash on and off in an instant. The eyes, however, did not always smile when he did.

His voice was of a piece with the appearance of the man. As Godfrey Talbot, an English friend who had heard a good deal of Murrow during the war, described it: "There was no honey, or wine or cigars about Ed's voice. It punched through. It was the voice of doom, but not the end, a voice of dire tidings. It was one of those good, virile North American voices which wake you out of any sleep you might have...." To Murrow's broadcast colleague, Howard K. Smith, "Ed could say 'twenty-six' and it sounded like the most important declaration ever made by man."[43]

The sweat that the make-up woman had just swabbed from his brow was a better clue to the nature of this man than the picture of total control that he presented to the camera. Beneath the cool veneer, he was a man perpetually at war with himself, incurably dissatisfied, torn by contradictory impulses, a public persona recognized by millions, yet an almost inaccessible human being. He once told an interviewer, "I've never had any intimate friends. If I were in serious trouble, I could have trouble knowing where to turn." Ed Bliss, who edited the radio news for Murrow, had once said to him, "You and Eric Sevareid are two of the shyest people I know. Yet you both make your living speaking to millions of people." "Yes, I know," Murrow nodded moodily. Then his face broke into that engaging grin. "But I hide it better than Eric."

Television, the instrument that had brought him fame and wealth and what he sought most, a pulpit for his well-modulated furies, left him uneasy. "It's a mystery to me," he once had said, "why a person, any civilized person, would be sitting at home on a Sunday afternoon watching television."[44]

The urbanity, the cultivated speech, the impeccable grooming, the sheer class that Murrow exuded, were genuine enough, but also misleading. They had been earned, not inherited through privileged birth. For Ed Murrow had been born and raised in circumstances not unlike those of Joe McCarthy. The contradictions between the world that he had been raised in and the life that he now led—and what attracted and repelled him in both these worlds—were at the heart of an inner conflict that he was never entirely to compose.

The opening commercial ended. The cameras returned to Murrow. He felt Friendly's tap on his leg and plunged ahead: "Because a report on Senator McCarthy is by definition controversial, we want to say exactly what we mean to say...." He resumed his steps along that fog-shrouded mountain—toward the summit or toward a precipice, he could not tell.

CHAPTER 2

A Child of Polecat Creek

He was born at Polecat Creek. It was not a city or town, not a hamlet or even a crossroads, but rather an obscure feature on the North Carolina landscape. Though he was born in the twentieth century, he was born of the nineteenth.

It was April 24, 1908, a damp, dreary night when Ethel Murrow told her husband, Roscoe, that her time had come. Ethel retreated to her bed in their large log cabin, a home lacking electricity, running water, indoor plumbing, and heat, except from a fireplace.

Roscoe Murrow hurried over to his parent's nearby farm and woke up his 13-year-old brother, Edgar, and sent him to Pleasant Garden, five miles away, to fetch the doctor. By the time Edgar got there, the doctor was already gone, off delivering another baby. It was not until four o'clock in the morning that the boy and the doctor returned to Polecat Creek.

They were greeted by a lusty wail. The baby had already been delivered by his grandmother. He was long, with a tuft of dark hair on his head, a remarkably large head, which had made the delivery excruciating for his mother. She named him Egbert Roscoe Murrow.[1]

The child's father, Roscoe Murrow, was working 120 acres of bottomland on Polecat Creek at the time his son was born, land given to him by his father when Roscoe reached 21. Tobacco was king along the Durham–Winston-Salem axis, and Roscoe planted a little. But his cash crops were corn and hay.

He stood 6 feet tall and weighed over 200 pounds. Everything about Roscoe was thick, solid, sturdy. He was broad-shouldered and thick-chested. His arms were thickly muscled from hard labor. He had a broad, open face, laughing eyes, and black hair like a sheet of coal. He was handsome, but in a pleasant rather than a striking way. The face was too placid

15

to possess any magnetism or mystery. He was of that breed of big men who are liked because there is no menace in their size and strength. Their power is unexercised. He had the appeal of a tame bear, one whom people approach gingerly at first and, in time, carelessly. He was easygoing, imperturbable, slow to anger, and quick to forgive; a teller of funny stories—a quintessential good ole boy.[2]

The Murrows were Quakers. They had originally settled in Guilford County near Greensboro shortly after the Revolution in a fertile stretch of the Piedmont between the Tidewater and the Blue Ridge Mountains. Where they came from before is lost in the mists of time. Ed Murrow would later describe his family's American roots with a jest. They descended, he liked to say, from "a couple of Scotch-Irish who jumped overboard."

There may have been some truth in the jest. The name Murrow first appears in America in 1651 in the manifest of the *John and Sara,* a British merchantman. The *John and Sara* left England for Boston in November of that year carrying "Ironworke, household stuffe & other provisions for planters and Scotch prisoners freed by ordinance of parliament date 20th of October 1651." Among the Scottish prisoners who had been released to become indentured servants in New England were Neile, Jonas, James, and John Murrow.

The Murrows appear to have taken up the Quaker faith after arriving in America. They became part of a Quaker migration that edged down from New England to Pennsylvania and, ultimately, settled in the Piedmont. In 1750, a Pennsylvania Quaker, William Hackett, tied his pony to a sapling near Polecat Creek, and founded the Centre Community of Friends. It was here that Ed Murrow's ancestors eventually settled.

They were not much for pedigree, but the family did take an ironic American pride in one blood line. The white man might scorn the Indian, steal his land, and slaughter him with impunity. But a romantic conceit caused him to prize Indian blood in his veins. Part of the cherished Murrow family legend was that Roscoe's grandfather had married a woman who was half Cherokee.[3]

The Murrows were farmers for generations. The first of them to make a mark more lasting than the furrow of plow through the soil was Roscoe's father, Joshua. He was born in 1851 and came into a considerable patrimony for those parts, 750 acres. Joshua bought an interest in a gold mine. He became the first of the family to put the Murrow gift for affability to political ends. At the age of 36, Joshua Murrow reached the summit of his ambition. He was elected to the North Carolina State Senate on the Republican ticket during Reconstruction. His idol, for unknown reasons, was Roscoe Conkling, the U.S. senator from New York. He had named his son after his hero.[4]

Joshua Murrow did not, however, transmit the gene of ambition to Roscoe. Not that Roscoe Murrow was lazy. Among his neighbors he had a fabled appetite for bulling that huge body through twelve-hour days of backbreaking toil. But Roscoe's labors were at the level of sheer muscular output, the sort of work that enabled a man to live, but did not allow him to rise. For all the sweat with which he irrigated his acres along Polecat Creek, $700 was the most that he ever earned from farming in one year.

Underneath the placid surface of Roscoe's nature swirled currents of discontent. He believed that somewhere, around the bend, over the ridge, in some other place, in some other trade, life could be made to deliver more handsomely.

For a time it looked as though baseball might be his escape from the plow. Roscoe was big, strong, and fleet, the qualities of the successful athlete. He loved the game. He was good, good enough to excel among the pickup teams playing around Guilford County during the mid-nineties. But not good enough for much more. And so he remained a farmer.

When America went to war against Spain in 1898, Roscoe seized another chance to escape Polecat Creek. He enlisted in the First North Carolina Regiment. When the war ended, his regiment marched into Havana, hailed as the liberators of Cuba. But Roscoe was not among them. He was denied even this shred of glory because a childhood eye injury had kept him in a noncombatant billet in Jacksonville, Florida. He soon found himself back in Polecat Creek telling his friends that one of these days he would be moving on to something better. Somewhere. Anywhere.[5]

The farm next to the Murrows' was owned by George Van Buren Lamb, father of five daughters. Around Polecat Creek, Lamb was much revered as a Civil War hero and still deferred to as "Captain Van." His daughter Ethel was no great beauty, pert rather than pretty, plain of face and plain of dress, a tiny thing, barely over 5 feet tall who never weighed a hundred pounds in her life. She had thick brown hair that fell halfway down her back when loose. But she usually wore it braided and severely coiled around her head. Ethel was a teacher in the Centre Friends schoolhouse built the year after her father came home from the war.

Plain face and plain clothes aside, plainness was the last word that anyone ever associated with Ethel Lamb. She virtually throbbed with uncontained vitality. Her blue eyes had an electric quality. She was forever in motion, always fussing, an engine too small to consume all the energy it generated in a single day. She could, when it suited her, adopt the fluttery, sweetly cloying manner of the southern belle. But for all her daintiness and sweetly drawled phrases, she was a formidable young woman. The petals were soft; the stem was iron. She was also afflicted by that ailment common to tightly strung personalities; Ethel Lamb suffered breath-robbing sieges of asthma.

Had such things counted with them, Ethel and her sisters could lay claim to two badges of social acceptability much prized in certain circles at the time. The Lamb girls had an ancestor who fought in the Revolution and a father who had served in the Civil War. They were thus eligible for membership in both the Daughters of the American Revolution and the United Daughters of the Confederacy. But farm life along Polecat Creek left scant time for social climbing. Ethel Lamb did have, nevertheless, strong, if self-taught and rather idiosyncratic, ideas of what constituted well-bred behavior. Ed Murrow once told his colleague Howard K. Smith, "My mother wouldn't answer the telephone with 'Hello.' She'd say 'Hi ya.'" When the puzzled Smith asked why, Murrow responded, "She wouldn't allow herself to utter the word 'Hell.'"[6]

She was three years older than Roscoe. They made an odd couple, this fussy little woman and her outsized, stolid suitor. It was, nevertheless, a complementary match, though the pliant Roscoe was expected to do most of the complementing. Ethel had found in Roscoe Murrow precisely what she wanted in a husband. He was a fine figure of a man, hardworking, dependable, reasonably temperate; and most important, this bear could be bridled and led by his tiny trainer. She loved him dearly, though it was not her way to express affection in word or deed. Roscoe loved Ethel too, simply and unrestrainedly.

They were married on March 27, 1900. Part of Ethel's dowry was a horse. Though the Lambs were Methodists, Ethel was willing to adopt her husband's Quaker faith. She had already taught in the Quaker school, and now she took to wearing a shawl Quaker style. But behind the doors of the little house on Polecat Creek, it was Ethel Murrow's personal convictions that prevailed.[7]

Their first child was born the year after they were married. They named him Roscoe, Jr. The child lived only a few hours. Three years later, Lacey Van Buren Murrow arrived. The name appears to have been taken from a character whom Ethel had encountered in her voracious reading of romantic novels. Another boy, Dewey Joshua, was born two years later. His first name celebrated the victor of Manila Bay, and his middle name honored Roscoe's father. Ethel hoped that one of her boys would enter the ministry, and she had known and admired a man of the cloth named Egbert. Thus she had fastened the minister's name on her youngest son.[8]

For all her restless energy, Ethel Murrow looked upon herself as a sickly woman. Her asthma had grown worse, and she had begun to suffer from allergies. Around Polecat Creek it was commonly accepted that Ethel Murrow had "poor lungs." She was a compulsively dutiful wife and mother, but a passionless woman. By the eighth year of her marriage, the pleasures of the marriage bed, if indeed they had ever pleased her, held little further appeal. The birth of Egbert had been particularly hard for her, suggesting to this deeply religious woman the passage in Romans 8:22: "creation groaneth and travaileth in pain together...."

After Egbert was born, Ethel informed Roscoe that she was suffering from some undefined female trouble, and that she would have to "get it fixed" before they could resume marital relations. If, in fact, she did have a gynecological disorder, Ethel never did get it fixed. Roscoe thereafter may have fallen victim to the ultimate form of birth control. As one relative put it, "Ethel shut him off."[9]

Egbert Murrow's earliest memories were of the feel of the rich red clay of the Piedmont, damp and cool against a child's bare feet. His earliest recollected emotion was frustration at trying to make smaller hands and a shorter stride keep up with two older brothers. The child's fierce will to catch up was to harden in time into a competitiveness that became the fuel of his character long after the original reason was forgotten.

In those early years, his world was bounded by a creek, a dirt road, and a hill. From his front door the boy looked down 300 sloping feet to Polecat Creek. Off to the right, on a hill, was the Centre Friends Community meetinghouse and the Quaker cemetery. Directly in front of the house, a dirt road ran up to the city of Greensboro and the larger world beyond. It was, to a child's eye, an infinite universe.

The Piedmont was formed of round hills and low ridges, not spectacular, but pretty in a ragged, unfinished way. Apart from the tilled fields, this stretch of country had barely changed from the time when it was the hunting grounds of the Catawba Indians. In winter the red earth became hard and encrusted with frost. When spring came, the rains turned the unpaved roads and paths into a crimson sea of mud, to the delight of the young Murrows. Spring also brought an explosion of white dogwood and wildflowers. Sycamores, white ash, maples, and evergreens covered Roscoe Murrow's land. Polecat Creek still teemed with game, bobcats, racoons, rabbits, wild turkey, and deer. Roscoe Murrow hunted not for sport, but to put food on the table. When his eldest son, Lacey, turned 8 Roscoe taught him to shoot.

The creek was the boys' playground. Young Egbert tagged after Lacey and Dewey, who knew every eddy and embankment where pike, suckers, and catfish lurked. They showed Egbert how to catch frogs, green, glistening, and slick, with his bare hands. They taught him how to trap rabbits in the surrounding woods. He had a favorite retreat—he liked to slip off by himself to the drying shed; in the winter it was cavernous and gray, and late in the summer it became a pungent cave where a child could become lost for one terrifying instant among the drying tobacco leaves.[10]

The house in which Egbert Murrow was raised had been built when George Washington was President. It was small and sturdy, constructed of stout poplar planks secured by oak pegs and chinked with clay. The floors were planed logs, rough on a boy's bare feet. The fireplace had been built from stones culled from the surrounding fields and covered the entire side of one wall. Downstairs was one large room; upstairs Roscoe and Ethel slept in one bed and the three boys in another.[11]

Egbert Murrow came into the world on the cusp of a new age. The modern world was emerging but had not touched Polecat Creek. Electric street lighting had been in use in American cities for nearly thirty years. The General Electric Company was making electric irons, toasters, and washing machines. But there was still no electricity in Polecat Creek. Henry Ford had originated the assembly line, and over 19,000 Model T's rolled off the line the year that Egbert was born. There were no cars in Polecat Creek. In the county seat of Greensboro, a phone was no longer a luxury, and in the year that Egbert was born, the governor of North Carolina saved a man from the gallows with an eleventh-hour phone call. But there were no telephones in Polecat Creek. All over the United States, builders, manufacturers, and farmers were harnessing engines to machines to do their work. In Polecat Creek, though, horsepower retained its literal meaning. America was a beckoning shore when Egbert Murrow was born. More than eight million immigrants who had arrived in the previous ten years, mostly from eastern Russia and Southern Europe, had swelled the nation's population to 92 million. Few of these exotically named arrivals found their way to Guilford County and none to Polecat Creek. Here, the blood stock remained essentially what it had been for a century and a half, English, Scotch-Irish, and German.

It was a bucolic backwater; yet Polecat Creek and surrounding Guilford County had produced a respectable share of the country's *illuminati*. Dolley Payne, a Quaker widow from Guilford County married James Madison and became the nation's First Lady. Andrew Jackson practiced law in Guilford County. The virtual dictator of the House of Representatives at the time of Murrow's birth, Uncle Joe Cannon, was a Guilford County boy. And the country's most popular author of the moment, O. Henry, was born William Sidney Porter at Polecat Creek—in a house, however, much grander than the Murrows'. There were Milhous and Mendenhall families in the county too, and one of their descendants would become President. But Richard Milhous Nixon was not a man toward whom Edward R. Murrow ever felt much neighborliness.[12]

The Civil War had been over for more than forty years when Egbert was born. But in Guilford County, the scars were still sensitive to the touch. The war had riven the county, with township pitted against township, sect against sect, and family against family. The county's Quakers had freed their slaves in 1774. The nation's first manumission society to abolish slavery was organized at the Centre Friends meeting where the Murrows worshipped. Before the war, Murrows had helped runaway slaves escape the South on the Underground Railroad. After the war, Joshua Murrow won his seat in the state legislature as a Republican Reconstructionist.

The Lambs, however, had been slaveholders and remained unreconstructed believers in the Lost Cause. Grandfather Lamb had enlisted in the Twenty-Second North Carolina in 1861 at the age of 24, mustered in as a sergeant. His company elected him a second lieutenant the following year. He was wounded at Mechanicsville, Chancellorsville, Gettysburg, and Jericho Mills. He was mustered out with the rank of captain and carried a minié ball in his leg to the grave.

Certain Lamb prejudices were also carried to the grave. A cousin of

Ed Murrow's, Louise Lamb Dennis, recalls hearing Grandmother Lamb "standing by our fireplace, her elbow propped on the mantle, talking about the 'nigger lovers' helping the slaves escape over the Underground Railroad. Grandpa fought the war with arms, but Grandma continued the war into the twentieth century with her tongue." Among the despised "nigger lovers" were the forebearers of the Murrow family into which Grandma Lamb's daughter, Ethel, had married.

A history of Guilford County, written about the time of Egbert's birth, reveals the attitudes surviving almost a half a century after emancipation. Slavery, the county historian wrote, had admittedly been a "doomed institution." But in its day it was "the greatest of blessings to the Negro." Thus, for young Egbert, as a Murrow and a Lamb, the lingering divisions, the resentments, the hatreds, the conflicting visions of the Civil War, lived on under the very roof where he spent his earliest years.[13]

Given Roscoe's meager earnings, was the Murrow family poor? By any standard in which money alone is the measure, the family lived humbly enough. Without unremitting labor, the family would go hungry. Lacey and Dewey, when they reached the age of 8, were put to work running a hay rake. Egbert at 4 drew water from the well, fed the chickens, weeded the garden, and slopped the pigs. The blessing for the Murrow children as they grew up was that everyone they knew lived much as they did. They were poor, but they did not know it.[14]

They were raised, nevertheless, in an emotionally penurious home. Ethel Murrow's love was expressed for her children more in constant worry than in affection. If Dewey and Egbert went into the woods to pick wild blackberries, Ethel started worrying as soon as they disappeared from her view. If they failed to return on time, she assumed that tragedy had struck. Every tardiness, every mishap, every irregularity, was instantly interpreted by Ethel in its direst possible outcome. Her constant refrain for an overdue child was, "I just know I'll never see Sonny again," Sonny being her all-purpose name for all three of her boys.

Ethel Murrow ruled by copy book maxims with a rule to fit every moral crossroads. She fretted more about her boys being poor in the sight of God than poor in wordly goods. Ed Murrow once told a friend about the first money he ever earned: "I hoed corn all day long in the hot sun as a little boy in North Carolina. At the end of the day, my father gave me a fifty-cent piece. My mother made me put it in the missionary box. That colored my feelings about missionaries for life."

Ethel Murrow's reason for being was her duty to her children and to her husband. Her Christian burden, she believed, was to raise her boys to be God-fearing and honest, generous to friends and helpful to each other. She also made clear that she expected them to amount to something. Roscoe, on the other hand, assumed that his sons would become what he had become, a working man who earned his bread with his hands.[15]

Roscoe was allowed to play, when he had time, only at the diversions

Ethel approved of in a Christian home. She forbade smoking, drinking, card playing, and dancing. On the Sabbath, she lengthened her list of proscribed activities to include fishing and ball playing. Her puritanism was hard on three high-spirited boys, full of energy and mischief. Ethel had to pry them from the woods or the creek where they would slip off on Sunday mornings to raid a bird's nest or to catch tadpoles in a bottle. She would scold Roscoe who happily let the boys lead him astray for a little pitch and catch. It was hard enough raising three boys, she complained, without raising four.

On Sundays Ethel would stand on the porch and call out "Laay-sih! ...Dyew-ih!...Aig-birrt!" And the boys would reluctantly abandon whatever sport they were pursuing and come home and get dressed for the Quaker meeting. They always obeyed because they had it ingrained in them early that, as Ed Murrow's wife, Janet, put it, "they had to please Mama to have peace in the family."[16]

The voice of Egbert Murrow was first heard publicly at the Centre Friends meeting. The meeting followed the Quaker custom of encouraging members to pray aloud, to exhort, to confess—whenever "moved by the spirit." The spirit moved Egbert at age 4. The boy had a booming voice, almost freakish coming from so small a body. Unprompted, he jumped to his feet and confessed that that morning he had trapped a rabbit and sold it for a dime, violating the Quaker commandment to rest on the Sabbath. The elders praised him for his forthrightness and addressed him for the first time as "Brother Egbert." Ethel, with her hopes that this boy would one day enter the ministry, told friends that she glowed at that moment.[17]

On Sunday afternoons, the Murrows usually visited Ethel's family. Captain Van was still an imposing figure, then in his mid-seventies, erect, his face lean and hard, his beard still almost black and full. He liked to sit in a rocker under a walnut tree and without much prompting would repeat for his grandchildren the old tales of facing starvation in The Wilderness, and how the Johny Rebs had to trap animals to stay alive. He described the sensation of gunsmoke searing his eyes and lungs on his first day under fire. In 1863, just after Chancellorsville, Stonewall Jackson was accidentally and fatally wounded by his own men. According to Grandpa Lamb, it was he who caught the stricken Jackson as he slipped from his saddle. That was the boys' favorite story.[18]

Captain Van told a story well. His daughter Ethel inherited the art from him. Roscoe was a good storyteller himself. Thus, all three Murrow boys grew up steeped and skilled in the raconteur's art.

It was Ethel's storytelling flair that largely saved her from becoming a tedious crepehanger. She was one of those people who are unconsciously amusing when they are most serious. Her family and friends found her descriptions of everyday tragedies more entertaining than depressing. When Dewey pulled a china closet down on top of him, getting a deep gash in his head, Ethel described the calamity to a neighbor: "I slapped my hand across the top of his head and just held it there. I knew if I took it away, his brains would fall out."

She was forgiven her fussing because it was always over someone else's well-being. Did her guest care for more biscuits? Were they warm enough? Did they need more butter? Could she bring some soup over to a sick friend? Could her neighbor use the clothes that Egbert had outgrown? She was much loved, particularly by her nieces and nephews. For Ethel, like many a firm-handed matriarch, was far more lenient with other people's children than she was with her own.

Just as it was accepted around the Creek that Ethel had poor lungs, it was accepted that Roscoe Murrow was henpecked. He never complained, but went on swapping stories with his cronies, teaching his boys to play ball, stealing a nip now and then, and continuing his vague daydreaming. Since his marriage, he had acquired another 120 acres from his father. With 240 acres, his spread was now over twice as large as most neighboring farms. He worked harder and longer than ever. Still, he did not prosper.[19]

Ethel had a cousin named Terry Eli Coble. Coble had left Polecat Creek and had gone to live in the state of Washington at a time when the Pacific Northwest represented the last frontier. It was an era when the federal government was still opening up hundreds of thousands of free acres of land to homesteaders in Washington, Idaho, and Montana.

In the summer of 1913, when Egbert was 5, Terry Coble and his family had come back to Polecat Creek for a visit. They had about them the air of those who have seen the promised land and have returned to share their knowledge with their benighted kinfolk. In the Cobles' case, their paradise was Blanchard, a sawmill town on Puget Sound.

To Terry Coble, Cousin Ethel was looking frailer and more peaked than ever. He raved to her about the bracing salt air and the temperate climate around Puget Sound. To Roscoe he described the fertile soil, an observation that Roscoe met with controlled enthusiasm, and the opportunities in logging, at which Roscoe's eyes brightened. Egbert and his brothers listened to these accounts of faraway places with the rapt wonder of children who have never been anywhere.

After the Cobles went back to Blanchard, they continued writing, and urging Roscoe and Ethel to come on out. Late at night as they lay huddled in their bed, the boys could hear Roscoe's voice, gentle and pleading, and Ethel's, emphatic, negative, and prevailing. Roscoe was the eldest son, and Ethel said that she would not be responsible for taking him away from his folks. On another occasion she objected that the long trip west would cost too much money. Roscoe responded: "Getting you well is the only thing that matters to me." Family legend has it that at this point young Egbert jumped out of bed and waved his piggy bank, saying that he was giving it all "to make Ma well."[20]

In the end, Ethel relented. Her motives are not entirely clear. It may have been the desire to regain her health. It may have been the strain of living so close to the bone on Roscoe's poor income. It may have been her awareness at how sick to death her husband was of farming. It may, contrary to her protestations, have revealed a desire to get away from the competing influences of her in-laws. If, however, her respiratory problems were a reason, the decision to move appears to have been poorly thought out. Blanchard lay in one of the dampest parts of the United States. Whatever the reason, in the summer of 1914, the Murrows decided to move west.

Ethel distributed her favorite pieces of furniture among the family. Roscoe arranged for the auctioneer to sell off the rest of their wordly possessions including all the farm implements. That fall, after the last harvest, Roscoe added the proceeds to the stake they had been accumulating for the move.[21]

Egbert at this time was 6 years old, Dewey 8, and Lacey 10. The clay of their character, particularly of the two older boys, was starting to assume its permanent form. Lacey was the leader, and not by seniority alone. He was born with the leader's touch. He was tall for his age, a strong, intelligent boy, looked up to by other children. He took his responsibility for and his primacy among his younger brothers seriously and entirely for granted, at which Egbert bridled more than Dewey. Dewey was less driven, more accommodating in his nature. From the beginning, he possessed more innate serenity than either his older or his younger brother.

Egbert was an unusual boy. He looked as though an adult's head had been planted on a child's shoulders. His serious expression and the loud voice reinforced the anomaly. He gazed up intently at grown-ups, his mouth pulled down, as though judging them with precocious severity. What kept the face childlike were his great round cheeks and a sudden, gleeful, devilish grin. He was moody, tempestuous, mischievous, curious, and outspoken.

As the baby, Egbert might have gone in one of two directions. He might have known the overprotection, the special privileges, the pampering, and protracted infancy that sap the growth of character. Or as the youngest and the smallest, he might have been bullied and ridiculed, forced to do the bidding of older and stronger siblings, the debasements that tend to destroy a child's sense of self-worth. He was neither coddled nor abused. Ethel treated all three of her boys with an evenhandedness that bordered on the mechanical.[22]

In the fall of 1914 the day arrived for the Murrows to depart for the West. What they were undertaking seemed a bold move. The state of Washington was virtually the farthest point from Guilford County in the United States. Ethel filled several shoe boxes with fried chicken and packed them into two wicker hampers so that they would not have to pay for food on the train. Grandpa Lamb was to take them to the Southern Railway

Station in Greensboro in his buggy, a fine rig, the seat and foot covered with white sheepskin. They left Polecat Creek moving up the dirt road past the Centre Friends meetinghouse and the cemetery where five generations of their forebearers lay buried. Their itinerary was to take them through New Orleans, Texas, and Oklahoma; through Chicago, Kansas City, and San Francisco; and finally north to Washington. Ethel had purchased coach tickets, which meant that they would be sitting up for six days and nights.

At the stop before Chicago, Ethel learned something from newly boarding passengers that confirmed her life-long pessimism. Chicago, they said, was in the grip of a diphtheria epidemic. By then, the hampers of food were running low. Still, the Murrows never entered the dining car. As the train approached Chicago, the boys became hungry and restless. They begged their mother to let them get off the train so that they could at least buy fruit from the vendors on the platform. A reluctant Ethel finally yielded to their pestering, but only on the condition that they keep their mouths closed against germs all the while they were outside of the train.

Lips pursed, the three young Murrows descended. They took their place in line and conducted their business, evidently in sign language. Then they reboarded. The instant the wheels began to turn, Dewey blurted out with a gasp, "Boy, I never wanted to spit so bad in all my life."

They broke their journey in San Francisco with a visit to Chinatown, and then proceeded north, watching the golden California hillsides turn green, then greener still, and more rugged as they penetrated Oregon. They crossed the border into Washington and were awed by the richness and density of the forest, the great hemlocks, tall firs, towering spruces, and giant cedars that all but obscured the towns and villages they passed. In the distance they glimpsed the Cascade Range and snowcapped peaks that made molehills of their native Blue Ridge Mountains.

They arrived at last in Blanchard to an inauspicious beginning. The Murrows' first home in Washington was a tent pitched in the Cobles' backyard. And Roscoe found his first job as a field hand on another man's farm.[23]

CHAPTER 3

A Northwest Passage

The new Edison High School bus driver was a six-footer, as lean and taut as a leather strop. The trim body was the product of a summer spent logging in the nearby forests. It was the fall of 1923, and the driver was 15 years old, in his junior year in the school, and still known at that point in his life as Egbert Murrow.

The Murrows had now been living in Washington for nine years. They had backtracked briefly once. After the first year, Roscoe Murrow had been unable to find anything better than work as a hired hand. Ethel's asthma had failed to improve. And so they went back to Polecat Creek. On their return, Roscoe learned that nostalgia is a sweet longing, but a poor practical guide. All that he had disliked in North Carolina was still there, waiting for him. After a few months, the family went back to Washington, this time for good.[1]

Ed Murrow was later to recall the early years, times when his mother ate nothing so that her children might eat a little more. Not until Egbert was 14 did he live in a house with indoor plumbing. The family never had a telephone while he was growing up.[2]

Eventually, Roscoe's fortunes changed. He had been working in a sawmill when a job came along that turned out to be the pivotal point of his life. The Samish Bay Logging Company ran a railroad hauling timber from the mountain slopes into town, where the Great Northern Railroad took over the job. Samish Bay hired Roscoe as a brakeman. He loved railroading from the first day he set foot in the yards. He moved up quickly to locomotive engineer. After that, Roscoe Murrow never cared to work at anything else.[3]

In Blanchard, Ethel had looked for a Quaker meeting, and finding none, reenlisted in the Methodist religion of her youth. Methodism was sterner stuff

26

than the gentle faith of the Quakers anyway, which suited Ethel fine. For with each passing year she became more fixed in her conviction that life was a trial to be endured, and not a journey to be enjoyed.

From the beginning, Ethel took on what she considered her Christian obligations. She agreed to be treasurer of the Blanchard missionary society. She developed a fairly wide circle of friends in Blanchard. Yet this straitlaced woman could not bring herself to adopt the easy familiarity of westerners. She addressed people, no matter how long she knew them, as mister or missus.[4]

Because of Roscoe's frequent absences from home, Ethel became the family disciplinarian. "Wait till your father gets home" was never a threat that passed Ethel Murrow's lips. When the boys misbehaved, she sent them out to cut a fresh switch for the whipping. She had a technique that was sufficiently painful without being harmful. She whipped them around the ankles.

Virtually the only corporal punishment that Roscoe delivered was in sport. As soon as he came in the door, the boys would pounce on him. He took them on, one by one, in wrestling matches of unfeigned ferocity. A terrified Ethel would circle the tumbling bodies, wringing her hands and begging Roscoe to stop. The bigger and stronger the boys grew, the harder Roscoe fought, and he took deep satisfaction in pinning them even when they were grown men.[5]

Just before bedtime, each member of the family had to take a turn reading aloud from the Bible. Ethel read just as she did everything else, with theatrical flair, pumping life into the scriptural characters. Dewey Murrow once remarked, "The world lost a great actress when my mother didn't go on the stage."[6]

Work was woven into their lives as deeply as religion. Indeed, among the Murrows, work was a form of secular religion. As soon as his sons reached 12, Roscoe hired them out to nearby farmers. Dewey Murrow operated the first mechanical milker used in Skagit County. Egbert drove a line horse on neighboring farms. Among the farmers around Blanchard, getting a Murrow was considered a bargain. They were serious and dependable, unlike some of the smart-aleck kids from town. Egbert performed his tasks with no particular pleasure, but without complaint either. One did what had to be done. There was no other way in the Murrow household. In later years, he would recall, "I can't remember a time in my life when I didn't work."[7]

Lacey and Dewey spent one summer working in a sawmill. When it came time to return to school, the mill owner offered them $5 a day to stay on piling lumber. Ethel held a family counsel. The money, they decided, was too much to pass up. Ethel, however, also arranged to have the high school principal tutor her sons at his home three nights a week. She paid the man in cash. Ethel Murrow always paid cash, and she counseled her boys. "If you can't pay for it, you can't afford it."[8]

One task was redeemed above the cheerless drudgery of the others. Roscoe had a 12-gauge shotgun, and he took turns teaching his sons how to use it. The hoeing, the hay raking, the weed pulling, and the milking were devoid of any shred of romance. But to boys of the Murrows' background the mastery of firearms was a rite of passage.

On the night before Egbert's turn to learn to shoot, a neighbor showed up at the house looking for someone to haul water for a crew that he had hired to fill his silo the next day. He was prepared to pay a dollar. Egbert waited for his father to explain about the shooting lesson. Instead, Ethel spoke up first. "Egbert will be there at six," she said. Roscoe said nothing. All Egbert's protests were in vain. Ethel was adamant. A Murrow did not turn down work for pleasure.

That Egbert ultimately became a crack shot had as much to do with economics as skill. It was pounded into his head that shotgun shells were expensive, 5 cents apiece, and that he could only get a dime for each bird he shot, leaving scant margin for poor marksmanship.

Egbert first learned to hunt to put food on the table. Men had done the same thing for thousands of years to survive. Thus the pleasure of hunting was interwoven, in his mind, with an atavistic utility. So natural was this enterprise in the Murrow family that Ethel, who could worry about sending her boys berrying, apparently thought nothing of allowing a 12-year-old to go out alone with a shotgun.[9]

Egbert Murrow's education began in 1914 in the Blanchard grammar school, little more than a two-room shack. Two teachers taught twenty-five students the first eight grades. Egbert attended the school from the time he was 6 until he was 14. From the beginning he demonstrated that dichotomy common to verbal children. He excelled in English, history, and geography, but arithmetic left him bewildered.

His brothers called him "Eber Blowhard" because he was loud and assertive. His spunk won him, or rather saddled him, with the lead in a grammar school play. It was hardly a coveted part for a boy. The play was an adaptation of the nursery rhyme about the old woman who lived in a shoe. The teacher decided that only Egbert had the stage presence to play the title role. The name Egbert was enough of a cross for a boy to carry into an American school yard without playing an old lady in a school play. But the more the children rode him, the more stubbornly determined he became to see the thing through. On the night of the performance, Egbert, stuffed with pillows under a long dress and with a rag tied around his head, dominated the stage.[10]

He had a hot temper and tended to lash out when he could not have his way. He displayed a fearlessness that verged on rashness. When he was 7, an older boy tried to scare him with a BB gun. Egbert taunted his tormentor to go ahead and shoot. The boy obliged, hitting him between the eyes, causing him to yelp in pain and giving him a scar that he carried for life.[11]

The neighbors thought that he would probably fulfill his mother's hope and become a preacher; others said a carnival barker. The Murrows had a neighbor named Breckel, a man with a penchant for sticking nicknames on people. When North Carolina-born Egbert passed by, Breckel would crack, "How you doing, Tarheel?" Egbert responded, without hesitation, "Doing fine, Clam Digger." Breckel complained to Ethel, "You'd better watch that boy of yours. He's either going to be a great man or a bad one. There ain't going to be any in between."[12]

When they reached 14, the Murrow boys followed their father into the logging camps. In the summer of 1922, Egbert's turn came. He began at the bottom. Roscoe arranged a summer job for him as a whistle punk in a camp near Blanchard. His job was to ride a steam-powered donkey engine and blow the whistle to signal to the men the next step in the timber-cutting process. A whistle punk's duties were light enough, but the boy was working on the periphery of danger. Logs broke loose from cars, crushing life and limb. Brakes gave way on mountain grades, sending the flat cars hurtling over embankments. Whole trains derailed. Dewey Murrow had narrowly escaped death when he was thrown from a runaway flat car and struck his head on a rail.[13]

Blanchard was too small to maintain a high school, and so the town's children attended the high school in Edison, five miles away. When Ethel felt that she could afford it, she gave Egbert money for the trolley. When she could not, he walked.

He was no scholar, but plunged into school activities as though discovering a buffet after the meager offerings of the Blanchard school. He was a good right-hander on the Edison pitching staff, made the starting five on the basketball team, and played the ukulele in the school orchestra. His voice deepened, and he sang baritone in the glee club. In his junior year he landed a solo lead as the Marquis de la Tour in the operetta *In Old Louisiana.*

At Edison High, he encountered the first of the mentors who were to influence his life. Her name was Ruth Lawson. She taught English and dramatics and coached the Edison debate team. Dewey Murrow had been captain of the team, and his class will bequeathed his "excellent speaking voice to his younger brother." Ruth Lawson persuaded Egbert to come out for the debate team.

But Egbert, so uninhibited as a child, now found himself sweating profusely whenever he had to speak before an audience. Ruth Lawson told him how to conquer his fear. People are seized by stage fright, she explained, because they are thinking about the impression that they are making on their audience. They see themselves as the target of a thousand critical eyes. The trick, she said, was to turn the dynamics around, to think, instead: "I'm doing something for these people. They are here because they are eager for knowledge, and I am giving them knowledge. Or, they are here to be entertained, and I am entertaining them." Egbert found that this psychological jujitsu worked. He learned to speak with force and conviction. He was chosen "best debater" in a state competition, but he still could not stop the sweating.[14]

During the time that Dewey Murrow attended Edison High, the school acquired a bus, a jerry-rigged affair with a wooden coach bolted to the chassis of a Model T Ford. Dewey was considered serious and responsible for his age, and became the school's first bus driver. When he graduated, Egbert was given the job. He had to start the bus with a crank. If the temperature looked as though it might drop below freezing, he had to drain the radiator, since the school could not afford antifreeze. On crisp mornings he also had to warm water on the stove to start the engine. Every day he drove a thirty-mile round-trip that included eight unguarded railroad crossings that were often obscured by fog. Recalling the day that Egbert got the bus-driving job, Ethel Murrow was later to remark: "I was done for then." Egbert, she said, was "no where as careful and deliberate as Dewey."

Driving in his first snowstorm, Egbert watched a car spin out of control in front of the bus and fishtail across the icy road. He slammed on his brakes and managed to bring the careening bus to a stop. The car that was out of control shot off the road. Egbert sprang from the bus and ran to the car where he found two injured men. He ordered two students from the bus to set out flares. He sent another boy to a nearby house to phone for a doctor and an ambulance. He found blankets on the bus and wrapped the two injured men in them. He then went back on the bus and comforted the younger children who were crying. Of this period Ethel later said, "Those were the worst two years of my life."[15]

He began to mute his explosions of ill temper. He learned to sublimate his anger and impatience, to rein them in and redirect the energy positively at best, or at worst to lock up his furies in long, brooding silences. The silent withdrawals into some secret place within himself became a fixed habit in his teens, and a bafflement to his friends. Egbert was among them, laughing, horsing around one minute and, without warning, depressed and impenetrable the next. The withdrawals could last for hours.

He was seen by his elders as serious beyond his years. He unabashedly entered into conversations with older people, indeed seemed to prefer their company. His relatives recalled him arguing with them late into the night, always holding his own, deliberately taking the opposite side of an issue just to prolong the debate.

An old farmer asked Ethel if Egbert could speak at his funeral. When, shortly afterward, the old man died, Egbert indeed delivered the eulogy. It seemed to Ethel, at that moment, that her dream might come true, that Egbert had taken his first step on the road to the ministry.[16]

The work never ceased, summer and winter, in school and out. Between baseball practice, debate, orchestra, and homework, he cut wood, mowed lawns, and was still hired out to farmers. Rest on Sundays, as imposed by his mother, was uncomfortably tolerated, rather than enjoyed, since ball playing, music, and virtually any other pleasures were prohibited. After the ceaseless activity of the week, the idleness in the silent house seemed unnatural. Egbert felt a nagging guilt that he was supposed to be doing something.[17]

He first heard a radio on an evening early in the twenties at his Uncle Terry Coble's home. Ed's Uncle Terry was the first person in Blanchard to buy a kit and assemble his own wireless receiver. The Murrows came over and took turns putting on the earphones and listening. Ed Murrow later recalled what he heard—an eerie, otherworldly whine and sputter as Coble adjusted large black knobs. And then, with incredible clarity, a man's voice came through. The voice was briefly obliterated by static, and then music poured out of the earphones. Uncle Terry confidently tossed off the call letters of stations they might have picked up—WWJ in Detroit; or KDKA in Pittsburgh; or most likely, KFI in Los Angeles.[18]

Egbert Murrow's last year at Edison High was a triumph. He had the lead in the operetta *The Belles of Beaujolais*. He made the ice-skating team and the baseball team. He helped the Edison Spark Plugs take the Skagit County basketball championship. He knew briefly a glory approaching that of a Spartan warrior. He was carried off the court not quite on his shield but over his coach's shoulder after being knocked unconscious in one game. He was elected senior class president, president of the student body, and "most popular" student. He did not, however, walk off with any particular scholastic honors in his graduating class of six boys and four girls. The caption under his photograph in the *Mazda*, the school yearbook, contained a rather prescient line from *Love's Labor Lost:* "A man in the world's new fashion planted, that hath a mint of phrases in his brain."

Egbert had grown to a spare 6 feet 1 inch. There was little of the boy left in his appearance, except for the jaunty, engaging grin. His face was too angular, the eyes too intense, the beard too dark and heavy. He was still wearing double hand-me-downs from Lacey and Dewey. But something in his bearing gave almost everything he wore a certain flair. He seemed older than his 17 years. "He couldn't wait to grow up," his mother recalled. And he was no longer Egbert. While working summers in the lumber camps, he had decided that the name "Ed" was safer than Egbert in the company of lumberjacks.

He had been voted "most popular" by his classmates. Yet he made no effort to court popularity. There was an effortless magnetism about him, abetted by his self-sufficiency and mysterious silences. He did not have to extend himself because others came to him. Friends liked to imagine they were close to him; but the truth was that not one of them became the inseparable companion of his youth. He was a loner masked by charm.[19]

The prestige campus in the state was the University of Washington in Seattle, much closer to Blanchard. It was attended by the children of better-off families. But both of Ed's brothers had gone on to Washington State College in Pullman, 250 miles away, a school referred to, even by its students, as a "cow college." Its curriculum was heavy with courses in animal husbandry, veterinary medicine, engineering, and mining. Lacey had gone there to study engineering. Dewey majored in agriculture.

Ed did not want to go to a cow college. He wanted to go to the University of Virginia to study law. But the family had no money for such fancy aspirations. And so he decided to work for a year in the logging camp where he had spent the past few summers until he had saved enough money to go east.[20]

At that point the Murrow family fortunes took an unexpected twist. Roscoe Murrow was a man of seemingly bottomless forbearance. He took his wife's nagging and her prohibitions against his little pleasures with good humor. He was known for his ability to get along. However, Roscoe had fallen into the clutches of a foreman named Albion, a small, mean-tempered man who liked to flaunt his authority over big, affable Roscoe Murrow. Roscoe now came home after every run complaining of the latest indignity suffered at the hands of his boss. Ethel grew to hate Mr. Albion for what he was doing to her husband, and to the Murrow family's standing in Blanchard.

One night after Roscoe had recounted a particularly galling abuse, Ethel exploded. "You shouldn't put up with that, Roscoe Murrow," she scolded him. "Where's your gumption?"

Deep in that phlegmatic soul, she had touched a raw nerve. The next day, Roscoe arrived at the yards, strode up to Albion, and without a word laid him out cold with a single punch. He then came home and announced to Ethel, "I've quit."

Whatever praise he might have expected from Ethel was not forthcoming. How could he have done such a fool thing, she wanted to know? How were they supposed to eat now? She was mortified that Roscoe had resorted to violence. For one of the consuming terrors in Ethel Murrow's life was what other people might say.[21]

Roscoe was saved from the consequences of his rashness by a boom in the lumber business. He easily got another job with Bloedell-Donovan, a big firm in Bellingham. The move meant another disruption for the family. Bloedell-Donovan had hacked a rail line from the forests of the Olympic Peninsula to Clallam Bay on the Pacific and needed engineers for the new line. Bloedell-Donovan also promised Roscoe a job for his son Ed.[22]

Thus, in 1925 the Murrows moved one hundred miles west across the Olympic Peninsula to the company town of Beaver, and rented a small, white, look-alike cottage in a row of company houses. Ethel shined the place like brass, kept it spotless, and sought to give her new home a desperate touch of individuality by planting boxes of petunias on the front porch.

The house was humble and the town crude. But the Murrows were nevertheless living amid stunning natural splendor. White-crowned Mount Olympus, like a monarch on a throne, dominated the peninsula, visible from virtually every direction. Along the lesser slopes, vast stands of Douglas fir rose, trees that took ninety years to reach their full height of

300 feet. Jewel-like lakes glittered amid the deep-green carpet of trees. One of the largest and the bluest of them, Lake Crescent, yielded, from its icy depths, trout weighing up to thirty pounds.

In the midst of this grandeur, the roughneck company town seemed like a setting for a poem by Robert Service. Twice a year, on Christmas and the Fourth of July, the loggers, a conglomeration of Scandinavians, Poles, and French Canadians, came pouring into Beaver. When they hit town, the whiskey flowed like water, in spite of Prohibition. Polish accordionists played polkas until the small hours for loud, sweating, stomping dancers. Then the lumberjacks took their monumental hangovers back into the forest, and Beaver quieted down until the next holiday.[23]

Ed started with Bloedell-Donovan near the bottom of the lumber-jacking hierarchy as an axman. But, early on, he caught the eye of a man named W. Kenneth Merredith. In the rank-ridden world of the loggers, Ken Merredith was a member of the elect, a timber cruiser. He worked ahead of the other logging operations, scouting virgin forests for the amount and grade of timber that could be harvested. His decisions were crucial to the profitability of the company. The timber cruiser worked alone, save for an assistant, his compassman. Merredith had found young Murrow eager and quick to learn. From the beginning Ed had loved the spectacle of a doomed hemlock falling in the forest, the sharp crack of branches breaking off as the stricken tree plummeted to earth, the cries of animals and birds scurrying from its path, the clouds of pine needles, dust, and twigs thrown up as it slammed to the ground; and the awesome silence that followed. Merredith chose Ed for his compassman. The experience was to mark the youth for life.

In the rough fraternity of lumberjacks, Ken Merredith was a gentleman, a humane, intelligent professional who was mastering the business from the ground up and clearly being groomed as a comer. He was, at the time, seven years older than Murrow, enough of a difference to exert a fatherly influence. The work required that the two of them travel alone deep into the forest for long periods. They worked the Sol Duc Valley where Ed's job was to help Merredith map new stands of timber. They surveyed visually for the most part, lining up reference points and pacing off mile-square parcels through trackless woods, across streams, and up mountainsides.

They worked long hours and slept under the stars. Ed was discovering an America as beautiful and untouched as Lewis and Clark had found. He was moved by the majesty of this natural world. The regal firs, the shimmering, cloud-haloed peaks, the infinite openness, dwarfed a man, yet, at the same time, ennobled and elevated him. He felt, at one moment, overpowered, a speck in the cosmic design, and, then, God-like, as he stood on a mountaintop and looked upon the untrammeled beauty spread at his feet. At times he experienced profound loneliness in this uncharted wild. Yet the very loneliness became for him a time of intense private communion with himself.

Accuracy was God in this work, and Murrow forever remembered the day that Merredith sent him out to map his first mile alone. Using his compass and a tree, a rock, a cleft on the landscape, he began pacing the mile, fording streams and clambering up rocky hillsides. He hit his mark within fifty feet. Twenty-five years later, he was still telling friends the story. It was, he said, the joy of discovery that he could do a manly task completely on his own and do it well.

Occasionally, he and Merredith came in and spent the night in the lumber camps. Ed liked the camaraderie. He found an elemental drama in the lumberjacks' lives, in the struggle of men pitted against nature, wresting their livelihood from an environment that punished them instantly and mercilessly for a careless step, an unsure grip, a miscalculation, a foolish risk. He admired the courage that their skills demanded, the grace of a logger balanced on a lone timber floating downstream.

He liked the way the men ribbed each other, the jokes they told in which the Swedes were usually the butt. He listened as they sat smoking around the camp fire, swapping stories of prodigious feats of woodcutting by some legendary lumberjack; reminiscences of olympian drinking bouts and accounts of horrible accidents. He loved the profane poetry they spoke, the tang and bite of their words. And so young Ed Murrow started to smoke, learned to take a drink, and acquired an "extensive vocabulary of profanity," what he called "the exquisite expressiveness," through which the lumberjacks communicated.

He worked in the Sol Duc Valley for a year. Often he had been cold and hungry. "I was always wet," he later recalled. Nevertheless, he toyed for a time with the notion of staying on, making an honest, useful living in the out-of-doors that he had come to love. The experience had given him a set of primal values about nature and men. But he knew that another side of him was withering in the forest. His body and soul were well fed in Bloedell-Donovan's employ, but his brain was undernourished. He told Ken Merredith that he wanted to go to college. Merredith told him that he had a job any summer that he wanted to come back. To Ed, the offer meant that he had successfully completed his first apprenticeship in manhood. He shelved the cigarettes, the drinking, and the profanity for the time being and went home.[24]

By the time each of the Murrow brothers was ready to leave home, their mother already had a permanent hold over them. As one of Ethel's future daughters-in-law later described it, "They were unconsciously seeking her approval. But she always held back. She could never bring herself to say 'that's wonderful' or 'you did a fine job.'"[25]

She placed her Christian duty ahead of her family. Lacey had been the first Murrow to graduate from college. Ethel was supposed to go to Pullman for the ceremony. She was just about to leave when she learned that a neighbor, a logger, had been badly injured in the woods and taken to the hospital at Port Angeles. "She's not capable of ordering her own groceries," Ethel said of the wife, and took over management of the family's household. When the man died, Ethel made all the arrangements to have the body sent back to his hometown in the East and put his wife and children on the train. As a result, she missed Lacey's graduation.[26]

Ethel's speech retained the old locutions that had survived in the Piedmont since before the Revolution—"ere" for "before"; to be "in good kelter" for "fit"; "commence" for "begin," as in "Egbert commenced to holler like a banshee," and "forth and back." She favored Quaker inversions, "This I believe," and said "t'was" and "t'would." Ed Murrow relished these forms and used them throughout his life.[27]

Ethel's legacy to her sons was the commandment to achieve, to subordinate pleasure to duty. Indeed, she bred in them a certain guilt over pleasure. Roscoe Murrow, on the other hand, taught his sons by his example how to get along with people, when to shut up and when to let things pass: in short, tolerance and affability. Roscoe and the boys rebuilt an old car motor, and when they started it, a rod went through the hood. Roscoe cursed softly and then burst out laughing. His sons laughed too. Ed Murrow loved his mother; he revered her. But he enjoyed his father.[28]

He had never gotten along well with Lacey. Lacey, with his quick mind, his rakish good looks, his charm and polish, his immense popularity with men and women, was considered the Murrow to watch. He had been a big man on campus, the ROTC cadet colonel. He graduated with honors and a degree in civil engineering. As soon as he graduated, the State Highway Department snapped him up. One of his classmates was later to describe Lacey Murrow as "one smooth article."

The antagonism between Ed and Lacey had less to do with differences between them than with similarities. Physically, they were the dark Murrows, dark-haired and dark-eyed. Dewey was shorter, blue-eyed, and blonde. The darkness of the other two suggested their natures. They both displayed quicksilver changes of mood. They were both driven and congenitally dissatisfied strivers. They both exhibited a wry pessimism. They both slipped into bouts of depression. At a particularly hard-pressed point in his college career, Lacey told his parents that he expected to have to sell pencils for a living after he graduated. Ed granted Lacey the respect due an older brother, but they were too much alike to be complementary and too competitive to be comfortable together for long.

Ed preferred Dewey. Dewey wore better. He was less self-absorbed, more even-keeled, and more giving. During the war, in a letter home, Ed wrote, "Of course, Dewey is the only one who has good sense....He doesn't want power...he has too good a sense of humor to desire it. But Lacey and I must try."[29]

The University of Virginia was out. The Murrow family fortunes had taken a bad turn. Ethel later made veiled references to the failure of a local bank. And so Ed lowered his sights and applied to the cow college, Washington State.

CHAPTER 4

The Undergraduate

The incoming freshmen of the Washington State class of 1930 were met at the railroad station by a welcoming committee of faculty and local luminaries. Pullman was essentially a one-industry town. The college was the industry and the students the product. Thus the townspeople's welcome was warm. Milling among the crowd were upperclassmen, scouts dispatched by the fraternities and sororities to reconnoiter the freshmen.[1]

Washington State occupied the high ground overlooking Pullman, in 1926 a city of some 3,000 inhabitants. What Ed and his classmates saw as they were driven in a motorcade up College Hill were redbrick buildings, the brick made from the native clay. One structure was Georgian, another Renaissance Italian, another Greek revival, another medieval with turrets and Romanesque arches. Van Doren Hall, which was to dominate Ed Murrow's college life, had a Flemish appearance. The total effect gave the hillsides of this small American town a jumbled, yet appealing, European aura.

The motorcade stopped at Bryan Hall, with its gothic clock tower dominating College Hill. There, the freshmen, necks craning, trooped into the auditorium to be greeted by Dr. E. O. Holland, the president of Washington State, a fussy, portly, middle-aged bachelor with the manner of a mother hen to whom the college was wife, mistress, and child.[2]

The new freshman class brought the student enrollment to just over 2,800. They were a homogeneous lot on the whole, predominately male, only a quarter of them women, almost all of northern European stock, and Protestant. Sprinkled among them were a handful of Orientals. A contemporary edition of the *Chinook*, the college yearbook, revealed one black student in a photograph of the track team.[3]

The freshmen passed their first week performing the traditional collegiate rites of initiation. The hazing period, Rough Week at Washington State, required, among its contrived indignities, that the freshmen eat their dinner while lying on the floor. There is no record of what Ed Murrow, after a year as a lumberjack, thought of all this. What was clearly on his mind immediately was money. Virtually his first act at college, before attending a class, was to get a job washing dishes in a sorority house for meals and a room in the basement.[4]

Ed made his first college friend on the job, Edward J. Lehan, who had transferred to Washington State from Gonzaga College. Lehan shared the kitchen chores and the basement cubicle with Murrow. They were, on the surface, cut from the same cloth, both tall, slender, good looking, and personable. Lehan's good nature, however, was far more reliable than the mercurial Murrow's. They were to be friendly rivals over the next four years.[5]

Both enrolled as business administration majors, neither knowing quite why. Lehan had confessed to Murrow that his heart was in the theater. As for Ed, he had little idea at this point of what he wanted out of life. The youth who had stepped off the train at Pullman, for all his small-town triumphs, was as green as the surrounding Palouse Hills. He had grown up among utterly unsophisticated people on America's last frontier. His father had once said, "I'm not sure how a man can earn an honest living without using his hands." He was the product of a provincial education acquired among youths as raw as himself. His knowledge of the working world was as a lumberjack. He had brought with him to college a piece of redwood from the Sol Duc Valley. He had sanded the edges, painted them, and attached a jacknife to the wood by a small chain. He kept this memento on his dresser, a link to a world in which he felt comfortable and had proved his mettle.[6]

If his enthusiasm for the business major was muted, he nevertheless plunged ahead, taking three economics courses in his first semester. And he enrolled in compulsory ROTC. The Regular Army officers who ran the military training eyed the latest Murrow with a certain expectation. Lacey had been the college cadet colonel.[7]

Ed, in flaring britches, chocolate-dark jacket crossed by a Sam Brown belt, cavalry boots, and gold-braided cap, seemed born to a uniform. He liked to hear the sharp commands echoing across the drill field on crisp November afternoons. He liked the spectacle of a hundred men, arms swinging, legs striding in unison, and the manly camaraderie. He was then and was always to be drawn to the military.[8]

Washington State had over twenty fraternities, among which Kappa Sigma stood near the pinnacle of prestige. Sigma Nu had its drinkers and good-time Charlies; Lambda Chi its solid student citizens; Phi Delta its athletes. Kappa Sigma also had its quota of jocks, including the football captain. The fraternity also boasted aspiring actors, singers, campus politicians, and even playboys, or what passed for them at Pullman. And Kappa Sigma threw memorable parties.

Lacey Murrow had pledged Kappa Sigma and used the fraternity network to become a campus hotshot, with a reputation as a formidable drinker and ladies' man. Dewey had by now dropped out of college to prospect for gold in Colombia. But he too had pledged Kappa Sigma. That fall, Ed joined the fraternity of his brothers.

What most distinguished Kappa Sigma from the other fraternities was a touch of class. Good manners and observance of the social niceties were instilled at the Kappa Sigma house. Kappa Sigs dressed for dinner. The fraternity gave teas. On Saturday nights, Ed and his fraternity brothers drank bootleg beer run over the border from Canada, 175 miles away. They mixed alcohol with juniper and orange juice in a laundry tub in the basement of the fraternity house and made their own gin. Ed, who had apprenticed in logging camps, displayed early that talent so admired by American males: he could hold his liquor. He was known among his Kappa Sig brothers as Tall Timber, and he liked the name.[9]

He became part of the fraternity system, but he did not like the incestuous social isolation that the system bred. He had met people he liked during those first weeks of college, people like Paul Coie, who had joined another fraternity. He had no intention of cutting himself off. Coie was the son of a professor on the Pullman faculty. Ed knew virtually no one from a professional background. To this son of a simple railroader, Coie's friendship was valued in its own right, and it was a step up too.[10]

Besides the dishwashing, he took another job tending the furnace in another sorority house. On light class days and Saturdays, this member of the gentlemen's fraternity put on his logger's boots, went down to the Pullman railroad yards, and wrestled sacks of wheat aboard freight cars. Then, exhausted, he would fall into his bed in the sorority house basement.[11]

With all the part-time work, his studies should have suffered. They did not. Ed Lehan later recalled, "Ed would sit through classes all week, and he'd never take a note. But come Friday night, he could spout back the professor's lecture almost verbatim." A near photographic memory enabled him to earn a string of B's in three economic courses virtually without studying. But the only A he received that first semester was in ROTC, in military science.[12]

Fundamentals of Freshman Speech was a required course, taught by one of two professors. One was Maynard Daggy, chairman of the department of speech and dramatics, a small, dapper man of enormous energy and self-assurance. The other teacher was a young woman of 26 named Ida Lou Anderson.

Ed's roommate, Ed Lehan, had taken freshman speech the first semester from Professor Anderson. Lehan was so affected by the experience that he promptly dropped his business major and switched to speech.[13]

Murrow, remembering his skill and pleasure in high school debate, thought about changing too. But was speech a serious academic pursuit? His brother Lacey was building highways with his degree. What could Ed do with speech? How could he justify the sacrifices his family was making to let him go to college? Nevertheless, he went to see Professor Anderson. There is no record of his immediate reaction to this woman. But we do have Paul Coie's recollection on first meeting Ida Lou Anderson. "She was repellent" he said, "until she opened her mouth." What repelled Coie was a double curvature of the woman's spine that had left her barely 5 feet tall and severely deformed.

Ida Lou Anderson had been born in Morgantown, Tennessee. The family had moved to Colfax, Washington, just outside Pullman, when Ida Lou was 3. Five years later, she was stricken with polio. Thereafter, her life became an unremitting struggle against sickness and pain, much of it spent in a succession of hospitals and sanatoriums.

Ida Lou Anderson loved to perform. She loved acting. She loved public speaking, and had no intention of letting her deformity stand in the way of her passions. She entered Washington State and majored in speech and dramatics. She won every college speaking competition in the state. She pocketed her pride and took the part of a cripple in a college play. Her performance was a triumph. She next auditioned for a straight dramatic role and got the part. She went on to star in several college productions. She shared that quality of all gifted actresses, the capacity to make the audience forget what she was and to see only the person she portrayed. It was as Paul Coie had said: she was repellent until she opened her mouth.

After graduation, Ida Lou was hired by the WSC speech faculty just two years before Ed's class arrived at Pullman. She was soon proving a rival to Chairman Daggy in attracting the best speech and drama students.[14]

Ed went to see Professor Anderson to enroll in her freshman speech course and to ask her permission to switch his major. He also had a fairly audacious request. He wanted to be allowed to enter advanced speech courses without having had any prerequisite work. The woman he met barely came up to his shoulder. Her face was plain. She wore her brown hair short and straight. Her eyes, however, were remarkable, large, luminous pools, and all-knowing, as though she had glimpsed truth through her suffering. As they talked, Ed was struck by her voice, which drew attention away from her misshapen body. The voice was cultivated, rich, and melodious, a voice that one would expect to emanate from a tall, stately, and beautiful woman.

She turned him down. She informed Ed that she did not accept freshman having no speech background in her advanced classes. Ed came back to her a few days later. "I pleaded for permission to enter her classes," he later recalled. Something in this earnest young man reached her, since on this second visit she yielded. If he could get Chairman Daggy's permission, she said, he could enter her Intermediate Public Speaking course.

Maynard Daggy was not as taken by the young man as was Ida Lou. Indeed he was to have no particularly favorable memory of Murrow until Ed returned to the WSC campus years later, a famous man. Daggy later recalled that Ed came to him "with the idea of ultimately training for the law," and told Daggy that he thought speech would provide a good foundation. Daggy, though unenthusiastic, chose not to overrule Ida Lou and allowed Ed to take the advanced course.[15]

Ed was soon to witness the two professional faces of Ida Lou Anderson. She was a snob for talent. If a student was gifted and committed, she gave of herself without stint. For the lumpen students, the ag and home ec majors, whom she had to get through freshman speech, she was direct to the point of rudeness, her instructions being "Stand up, speak up, shut up." She reserved her serious guidance for the chosen, her speech majors. "Avoid a style," she told them, "that belongs to only one place and time. Seek a style that is true and universal. Avoid becoming the sterile prisoner of someone else's style."[16]

Ida Lou quickly recognized the potential in her new student. The voice, the manner, the physical appearance—all were there, like high-grade ore, waiting only for her refining process. Soon after his first classes, she invited Ed to stop by her home. It was all eminently proper. The spinster teacher lived with a married sister. There, in her sister's parlor, Ida Lou Anderson began the private education of Edward R. Murrow.[17]

She started by assigning him poetry and passages of prose to read on his own. He would then come back, and they would sit and read aloud to each other. Ida Lou would interrogate him. What was the author's intent, directly or obliquely? What devices had been used to achieve the effect? Did they succeed?

Her own hero was Marcus Aurelius, the Roman philosopher-emperor. She set out to convert Ed to the Aurelian way. She had him memorize aphorisms from the *Meditations*. She urged him to make the Stoic philosophy his personal creed: "If thou workest at that which is before thee, following right reason seriously, vigorously, calmly, without allowing anything else to distract thee, but keeping thy divine part pure, as if thou shouldst be bound to give it back immediately, if thou holdest to this, expecting nothing, fearing nothing, but satisfied with thy present activity, according to nature, and with heroic truth in every word and sound which thou utterest, thou wilt live happy. And there is no man who is able to prevent this."

Ida Lou introduced Ed to her favorite poets. Her taste ran to the romantic, the wistful, and the ironic, but works which ultimately provided lessons for life. She loved John Masefield and Christina Rossetti. "George Gray" from Edgar Lee Masters' *Spoon River Anthology* was an Ida Lou favorite:

> For love was offered to me and I shrank from its disillusionment.
> Sorrow knocked at my door, but I was afraid.
> Ambition called to me but I dreaded the chances.
> Yet, all the while I hungered for meaning in my life.

She was, in effect, carrying out her own version of Dr. Eliot's "Five Foot Shelf" for Ed Murrow's private benefit.

She had found an apt pupil, and a thirsty mind. The young Murrow was like someone who had drunk only tap water and suddenly discovers wine. He found Ida Lou subtle, provocative, and clever. She would drop thoughts into her conversation that seemed terribly wise to him. "You might read all the books in the British Museum," she once said, "and remain an utterly illiterate, uneducated person. But if you read ten pages of a good book, thought by thought, that is to say for real comprehension, you are forever more, in some measure, an educated man."

She would suddenly say something with a mischievous grin that struck the erstwhile lumberjack as the height of sophistication, as when she said of someone, "Besides being a gentleman, he was also queer and original in other ways." She had one maxim that he never forgot. "God will not look you over for medals, degrees or diplomas, but for scars," a conviction obviously drawn from her own scarred survival. Ida Lou's wordly maxims quickly displaced his mother's tediously repeated homilies. And he adopted her moral mentor, Marcus Aurelius, as his own.

Ed looked forward to the visits to her home like a child greedily anticipating a new present. And Ida Lou awaited his arrival with the satisfaction of a teacher who knows that she is doing exactly what she was put on earth to do, to awaken a mind. But she also waited for him with an anticipation in her eyes that went well beyond the pleasure a teacher takes in a gifted pupil. He did not notice this look or chose not to notice.[18]

He smoked heavily she noticed, but she did not reproach him. It was a different age. The biggest advertisers in the college newspaper, *The Evergreen*, were the cigarette companies. Lucky Strike's campaign featured a series of suave-looking men who lived by their voices—actors, singers, and radio announcers. One Lucky Strike ad pictured the then dean of radio announcers over a caption reading: "Norman Brokenshire keeps the quality of his voice in perfect condition." In Brokenshire's hand was the evidently perfect voice conditioner, a Lucky Strike. In that age, Ed Murrow's major in speech and his smoking habit seemed as natural as breathing.[19]

He had little to do with girls that first year. He was taking himself terribly seriously. Girls were a distraction, a self-indulgence, an expense. When he was expected to bring a date to a fraternity function, he usually brought his brother Dewey's fiancée, Donna Jean Trumbull. She was an attractive, warm-hearted, unaffected young woman with whom he felt completely at ease.

Dewey was still away gold prospecting in South America. And so it was Ed who brought Donna Jean to Beaver to meet her future in-laws for the first time. The young woman proved to have a good eye for the idiosyncrasies of the Murrow clan, particularly those of Ethel, which she later recalled: "Mother Murrow never let you leave a hat on the bed, or open an umbrella in the house, or have thirteen people at the table. She believed that it meant bad luck. When she had company, she didn't sit at the table anyway. She'd poke at her food and hurry back to the kitchen. She had the idea that it was somehow unladylike to put food in your mouth." Donna Jean also detected a touch of martyrdom in Ethel's self-confinement to the kitchen, a need always to be doing for others while denying gratification to herself.

Donna Jean became aware of Ethel's near slavish concern over what others thought of her. The woman went to embarrassing lengths to ingratiate herself with people. At one point, Ethel told a neighbor, "Donna Jean has just been saying that your daughter has the most beautiful hair she's ever seen." Donna Jean was dumbfounded. She had said no such thing. But as a future member of the family, she had to make a good impression on the neighbors, even if Ethel had to make it for her.

Ed had pointed out to Donna Jean a bottle of whiskey that his mother kept high on a cupboard shelf for medical emergencies. But, she was later to observe, "No one was ever so near death's door that she ever brought the bottle down." As for Roscoe, Donna Jean found him as easygoing as his wife was high-strung. She noticed that Roscoe disappeared from time to time into a shed behind the house. Before one of these exits, he shocked her by asking with a whisper and a wink if she would care for "a little snort."

Something else struck the young visitor: "I never saw any affection between Mother Murrow and her son, never any hugging or kissing. When her husband would put his arm around her and go to give her a kiss, she would turn her head so that he just glanced off her cheek."[20]

At the end of his freshman year, Ed had received an A from Ida Lou in the undemanding freshman speech course. But in the course that mattered, his first advanced course in his new major, she surprised him. Private parlor sessions or not, she gave him a B in Intermediate Public Speaking. He was annoyed, but more respectful of her.[21]

He went back home to Beaver before going to work for the summer for Bloedell-Donovan. But he was no longer at ease in the little company house. His father remained irrepressibly good-natured, easy to take. But Ed now recognized that his relationship with this simple, contented man was never going to grow. It was never going to rise above the wrestling, the car-tinkering, the corny jokes, because these were Roscoe Murrow.

His mother's constant sermonizing, the repeated bromides, her nervous perpetual motion, her phobias that had to be walked around like land mines, became increasingly irksome. He was still young enough to bridle at the constant pressure she exerted and not yet old enough to observe her quirks with amused detachment. After a brief visit, he gladly went back to work in the woods.[22]

The Industrial Workers of the World, the Wobblies, were then at the tail end of their influence in the radical labor movement. Their small victories and grand failures lay behind them. Ed Murrow had met his first political radicals in the Wobbly lumberjacks working on the Olympic Peninsula.

Before, Ed had regarded the Wobblies as amusing eccentrics, men who spoke with rough passion about things that bored or confused a boy. But now he found himself curious about their message. They were not simply political freaks, but living witnesses to the historic conflicts that he had been studying in college, the timeless struggle of the weak against the strong, the poor against the rich, the dispossessed against the possessors.

The Wobblies argued not only for bread and butter benefits, but for a new social order, for the abolition of the "wage slave system." Outside the camps they might be scorned as traitors for pulling a strike during World War I and as Bolshies whose hearts belonged to Moscow. But in the camps they were respected if not blindly followed. Some loggers carried the Wobblies red membership card as a gesture of solidarity.

Ed Murrow heard the Wobblies' message with a mixture of sympathy and amusement. All their talk about the exploited masses did not square with what he had witnessed in his own life. His family lived in reasonable comfort, as long as Roscoe held his job. His brother Lacey had already escaped wage slavery and had become a professional man. Still, the spirit of these brawny ideologues appealed to him. He listened avidly to their tales of fights with company goons and of the martyrs of Bloody Sunday when five Wobblies had been killed by sheriff's deputies in nearby Everett. He joined in their songs celebrating Joe Hill and other heroes in the Wobbly pantheon. In the struggle between the haves and the have-nots, the Wobblies stood with the have-nots. And that, emotionally, was where he stood too. But he was later to claim that he never carried the Wobblies' red card. He was a college man now. The lumber camps with their proletarian radicals were only a way station on his road to something better.[23]

In September of 1927, he was back at Pullman. He had returned with certain objectives that would have given a Wobbly pause and that demonstrate the human capacity for embracing contradiction. He no longer felt quite the same gnawing financial insecurity that had plagued him his first year. His family was getting along reasonably well. Lacey, whose career with the state highway department was flourishing, was helping him. He moved out of the sorority house basement and into the Kappa Sigma house. Life at the fraternity house offered something beyond greater comfort. He had observed in his first year that the fraternities formed an interlocking directorate of power and influence on campus. Living outside of the Kappa Sig house had left him on the periphery of that world. The rambling old white Victorian mansion with a long veranda and gables poking from the slopes of the roof was to be Ed Murrow's home for the rest of his college career.[24]

He had girlfriends, but they were precisely that, friends who happened to be girls. He was 19 now, a young man of startling good looks and with a manner that was bound to intrigue women, outgoing and attentive one moment, moody and self-absorbed the next.

Most of the girls that he knew lived catty-corner from Kappa Sigma in the Kappa Alpha Theta sorority house. One of them, a dark-haired, dark-eyed young woman named Hermine Duthie, recalled Ed at this time: "Girls fell in love with him by the droves. But he didn't have time or money to pursue them." Nor apparently the inclination, according to his friend Paul Coie. "He didn't go out with many girls. He didn't like the small talk, the triviality. And he was very selective about women."

Another Kappa Alpha Theta friend, Helen Hazen, recalled going on rides with Ed over the border to Moscow, Idaho, where they drank bathtub gin and warm strawberry soda chasers. Ed occasionally took Helen to fraternity parties where she remembered, "He always seemed bored. I found him to be a loner. But he could get away with it because people were drawn to him anyway."

When he was expected to have a date for a dance, he continued to escort his brother Dewey's girl. He thoughtfully made sure that Donna Jean's dance card was filled, for this handsome, graceful young man would not dance himself. Helen Hazen recalled Ed and Donna Jean at dances: "You'd always see Ed busily talking to the older people, to our chaperones and the faculty, people he could learn something from." He had not yet known a serious romance.[25]

And then he met Willma Dudley.

She was the daughter of the mayor of Yakima, Washington, and she had just entered WSC that fall as a freshman. There was about Willma Dudley an elemental appeal. She was good-looking in a fresh, unselfconscious way, with honey-colored hair, warm eyes, and the full mouth and full figure of a budding earth mother. She had come from a strict home and had arrived at Pullman in a state of near total innocence. She had also come to college with no clear sense of why she was there. Her father wondered why a girl needed a college education. The best reason that Willma could summon up at the time was that "college ought to be fun." She had pledged Kappa Alpha Theta, where she went to live. There Ed Murrow spotted her sometime in the fall of 1927.

It had been a bright fall day when the sun threw its glow over bare trees and yellowing lawns. Willma was sitting in a basement study room at the sorority house when she heard a voice at the window. They had passed each other on the campus before and had looked with lingering gazes. Now, here he was crouched beside her window. As Willma recalled the moment nearly sixty years later: "He flashed that marvelous smile and he said 'It's too nice a day to study. Let's go for a walk and get something to eat.'" Willma abandoned her books on the spot.

They strolled through Tanglewood, a favorite trail for campus lovers. Afterward, they stopped by a hangout called Neal's where Ed bought her a lemonade and a sandwich. From the first day, the relationship was characterized by two qualities, easiness and long silences. Willma was surprised that the gifted speaker of Ida Lou Anderson's courses, the young man who liked to engage chaperones in serious conversation at college dances, was often mute when alone with a girl.

On Sundays they followed the local custom, parading down Maiden Lane in their Sunday best. Ed's wardrobe, she knew, was limited. Still, he managed to look good no matter what he wore. After the stroll, he would often take her to the Hotel Pullman for chili. He might be talking volubly, and then, without warning, withdraw into silence. Willma, unlike the other girls who were unsettled by this behavior, never complained. Her unquestioning acceptance of his idiosyncracies was part of her attractiveness to him. Another reason that Willma appealed to him, although she was unlikely to hear him say so, was that she was the daughter of a mayor, which impressed a young man from a company town who was nevertheless "very selective about women." As for Willma, with or without conversation, she was content simply to be with Ed, since she had fallen hopelessly in love.

He seemed happiest when they could get away from the campus for long walks in the woods. There he talked freely, telling her of his life on the Olympic Peninsula. His eyes danced when he spoke of pacing off a mile or of some legendary logger. On the way back they would stop at Neal's and again she would lose him. The more he unburdened himself when they were alone and out of doors, the deeper were his withdrawals when they came back, as though the living part of him was still in the woods. To Willma, he laughingly referred to himself as "old stone face."

As for the caressing words that a girl in love longs to hear, he was silent. The clues that he cared were infrequent and oblique. Once she received a bouquet of roses with no message. "It took me awhile to figure out who sent them," she later recalled, since Ed never mentioned them. They were both emotionally inarticulate and for the same reason. As Willma put it: "We were raised by families that gave love but not affection."

At the Christmas holiday, Ed explained to Willma that he would not be able to buy her a present. Instead, he gave her his favorite cuff links, a pair with the letter "M" engraved on them.

One person who viewed the romance with alarm was Ida Lou Anderson. Her unhappiness was always expressed on a high, selfless plane— that Ed had a boundless future before him, that he must not throw it all away on a fleeting college romance. All of which was doubtless sincere, along with an unspoken and utterly natural jealousy.[26]

Ed took every course that he could from Ida Lou. She was now concentrating on his delivery along with content and meaning. She taught him the power of silences. She showed him when to pause between words, thus quickening the listener's expectations and heightening the drama. She taught him tonal understatement, how to end a phrase on a falling inflection to give his words a quiet authority. She taught him economy, that less words carry more freight, that the right noun alone is better than one that has to be propped up by adjectives. In teaching economy of language she found an apt pupil in Ed Murrow, a young man already disposed to ration his sentiments.

And always, she returned to Marcus Aurelius, to the *Meditations*. His thoughts, she said, should be the foundation of Ed's character. She used the Roman's maxim on pain—"It is not fitting that I should give pain to myself, for I have never intentionally given pain even to another"—to counsel Ed about his drinking. She knew that he enjoyed a certain fame around campus for his capacity. She spared him the pleasure-is-sin hectoring of his mother. Ida Lou put it the way Marcus Aurelius had, that only a fool would drown his gift, in effect, give pain to himself. He did not abstain, but he did moderate his drinking.

Until now, he had only spent time with Ida Lou in classes or at her home. Then, one evening, during a lecture at Bryan Hall, tall, slim, smiling Ed Murrow came down the center aisle, and beside him, moving with slow, pain-wracked grace, was Ida Lou Anderson. He began escorting her to more lectures, to concerts, to speaking competitions. Now it was Willma's turn for hurt and confusion.[27]

He was juggling his activities, his studies, his jobs, and he was seeing Willma often enough so that in the parlance of that era they were "going steady." He had, however, still not committed himself to her. Willma was troubled by his unwillingness to express his feelings. Still, she said nothing. She knew that to pressure him was to risk losing him.

Willma loved dancing, and Ed took her to dances. But he still did not dance himself, and had no desire to learn. When she asked him why, he avoided a direct answer. Nevertheless, he seemed free of jealousy and had no objection if Willma danced with other men. He even encouraged her to go to the Green Lantern, another college hangout where students danced to the music of a victrola. He was, she said, "a trusting person and he expected you to trust him too."

The issue of trust was soon to come up in a context that she had not anticipated. He was a serious-minded and ambitious young man, and he was already starting to display some of the single-mindedness of young men on the move. Feminine wiles were usually lost on him. Open pursuit drove him away. But Willma held an attraction for him rather like the outdoors. Her beauty was unconscious, natural, and unspoiled, her impulses direct and uncalculating, her manner unaffected. Like the woods, she was simply there for him.

It happened after they had been dating for a few months. They found themselves alone in the woods, and Ed asked if she "trusted" him. As Willma recalled the moment, "I didn't know exactly what he meant, and so I said, 'Yes.' I was taken by surprise when I found out what he meant." He proved, she said, "as sexually naive as I was." Thereafter the intimacy continued to the extent that it could for two young people in a small college town with little money and less privacy.

To a girl of Willma's background who had now given herself to the man she loved, the only remaining question was how soon before they were married. She tried to ignore the fact that he never spoke about their future. She nonetheless assumed "an unspoken commitment" since he had finally told her that he loved her.[28]

The second semester of his sophomore year, he became involved in a new enterprise. One night after dinner at the Kappa Sigma house, one of Ed's fraternity brothers pulled him aside and said quietly that some of the fellows from different fraternities were getting together for a drink on the outskirts of town. They wanted Ed to join them.

In another part of the campus, Paul Coie was getting a similar invitation that night, and he later explained what lay behind it. "One of the upperclassmen, usually a fraternity brother, would bring you out someplace, maybe some farmer's barn. A lot of bootleg booze was consumed. Finally they'd get around to telling you that they'd chosen you to be a member of TNE. It was considered a great honor."

TNE stood for Tau Nu Epsilon, a secret society on the Pullman campus, its membership small, usually about twenty students, with two or three drawn from each of the leading fraternities. TNE was utterly undemocratic and self-perpetuating. New members were selected after long scrutiny and debate by the existing members.

The organization wielded considerable covert power. No major student office at WSC was won until TNE had cut its deals. TNE controlled the editorships of the school newspaper, *The Evergreen*, and the college yearbook, *The Chinook*. Major policies put before the student government had usually originated in secret sessions of TNE. The only office beyond its reach was cadet colonel of ROTC, which the Army controlled. As Paul Coie described TNE's machinations: "We'd decide who should get president of the student body or vice president of the junior class or editor of the newspaper." The members would then agree to throw the support of their fraternities behind the TNE slate. "We were," Coie said, "a college level Tammany Hall."

The school authorities, beginning with President E. O. Holland, were aware of the existence of TNE, and deplored it. They disapproved of its undemocratic nature, its elitism, and its conspiratorial aura. But since the membership was secret, they had been unable to rid the college of this invisible hand.

Ed, who had easily won the popularity contests of high school class elections, now learned more convoluted exercises in power and found the game much to his taste. What TNE counted on—and the lesson that it taught him—was a political truth applicable to a campus, a city hall, or a world capital. Where the mass of the electorate is apathetic, a tiny, energetic handful can exercise power by manipulating the very machinery that has been created to ensure democratic rule.[29]

In the spring, TNE met to apportion the spoils for the following academic year. Kappa Sigma was due for the junior class presidency. Ed became the TNE-annointed candidate. The hidden hand performed flawlessly. Ed defeated an opponent named Gus Ihler by 219 to 87 votes. The total turnout represented under 38 percent of the eligible voters.[30]

College politics began to crowd out some of his old interests. He had been a fair athlete in a small high school. But among the brawny ag majors and phys ed majors drawn from across the entire state, he quickly recognized that he was outclassed. And Ed Murrow did not do things that he did not do well. He took up a new game appropriate to the gentlemanly inclinations of Kappa Sigma. He learned to play golf. He had found a set of left-handed clubs cheap and learned to play left-handed. He also pitched for the fraternity in the intramural baseball league. Walter Wyrick, a classmate and fellow TNE member, recalled years later Ed's performance on the diamond: "He didn't have much stuff. He was no great hitter either. But, he was so damned serious when he played ball, like everything else he did." Then Wyrick added with a tinge of envy still audible in his voice, "He'd open his mouth and the words would just flow. Everything went his way. Everything fell in his lap."[31]

Ed auditioned for the lead in a play that sophomore year, George Kelley's Pulitzer Prize-winning *Craig's Wife,* a drama "illuminating the shifting patterns in American marriages in the twenties." Cynthia Lowry, a young, new arrival on the drama faculty, was to direct. Hermine Duthie, Ed's friend from the Kappa Alpha Theta house and a campus actress herself, remembered his maiden audition. The transformation in him as he waited his turn, she said, shocked her. He sat stiffly. He got up and paced awkwardly. He rubbed his hands continuously, which, as in his old high school debating days, were drenched with sweat. Then came his turn to read. He was instantly in control of himself, no trace of the recent stage fright visible. His nervous energy was invested in the part. Cynthia Lowry chose him for the lead. It was a merit selection; he had been better than the other candidates. But his prospects had not been harmed by the fact, as Hermine Duthie put it, that "Cynthia Lowry was crazy about him." He had also beat out his perennial rival, Ed Lehan, for the part. On the playbill, he was listed for the first time in print as "Edward R. Murrow."

Of his theatrical debut, *The Evergreen*'s drama critic wrote: "As Mr. Craig, Ed Murrow, playing his first lead in a college production did some of the best work seen in college plays. He was in no sense melodramatic, but gave just the right significance to his lines.... He spoke calmly and with wonderful control. But beneath the calmness there was a depth of emotion superbly expressed...."[32]

Toward the end of the school year, Willma took Ed home to meet her family. They borrowed a car and with another friend drove to Yakima. The day of the trip was sweltering, and as the car struggled up a steep hill, it developed a vapor lock. Ed and his friend got out and opened the hood. Willma, dewy with sweat, her hair in wisps, began to sing a ditty she had recently heard. It was a harmless bit of naughtiness that began, "The sun was hot on Molly's back," and ended, "Molly was some hot tamale." Ed turned on her in cold anger. He did not want her singing that kind of song, he said.

After they arrived in Yakima, they were in the driveway of her home washing the car. Willma bent over in what Ed regarded as an unladylike posture. Again he criticized her. She detected a pattern. When they were alone, he was easygoing and considerate. But when others were liable to be watching, he became, she said, "insensitively critical" toward her, rather like a sergeant major afraid of being embarrassed by an unpresentable recruit.

Her parents took Willma and Ed up to their summer place on the Naches River. There the young couple managed to get off by themselves, to ride horseback, hike, and fish. The somber, moody, self-absorbed, sometimes self-important, campus striver disappeared, as though he was sloughing off an alien skin. As they stretched beside a stream, he spoke freely, confessing to Willma his deepest fears and shames, along with his ambitions. Ed began singing at the top of his lungs ribald songs that he had learned in the lumber camps, teasing her, and chasing her. To Willma's near disbelief, her solemn suitor was frolicking!

He invited her and her parents to come to Beaver to meet his folks, since Willma's father had mentioned having some business up that way. This was clearly the seal of approval that she had been waiting for. But back in Yakima, while on a walk at night, Willma lit up a cigarette, and Ed observed cuttingly, "What do you suppose my mother would think if she saw that?"

The Dudleys did come to visit the Murrows at Beaver. Ed took Willma into the Sol Duc Valley. They lay beside a sylvan spring, and he became lyrical describing the trees and the sky overhead. Willma saw a serenity in his face that she never observed at school. He confided to her that college was becoming a financial ordeal. He might have to go to Lacey for more help, which he resisted and resented. There had to be another way, he said. She began to glimpse for the first time the disquieting undertows that pulled at this seeming golden boy. Here in the wilds, it all came out, the dissatisfaction, the indecision, the inner conflict over what he wanted of life.

And for the first time, he started to talk about their future together. "Where would you be happiest?" he asked her. Before she could answer, he began to tell her about a piece of land that he had his eye on here on the Peninsula. He was sure that there were mineral deposits on it. They could build a home on that spot, he said. Of course, college was supposed to lead to a better life, more money, higher status, elevated causes. But there were causes here too. He thought he might become a leader in the western conservation movement, he told Willma. Then, in almost the same breath, he started talking about how much he enjoyed the theater. He talked about becoming an actor. He speculated on his chances of landing a Rhodes scholarship.

The Dudleys went back to Yakima, and Willma came close to never seeing him again; for in that summer of 1928, Ed Murrow nearly died.[33]

CHAPTER 5

"We All Knew He'd Make a Name for Himself"

He was working that summer in the Sol Duc Valley when a fire broke out and consumed vast acres of Bloedell-Donovan's timberlands. Ed had been sent out to help survey the damage. He was working on the side of a stream that separated the untouched forest from the still-smoking corpses of charred trees on the other side. A sudden burst of wind carried the fire to the other bank. He fled, with flames licking at his back and suffocating waves of heat rolling over him. The air became so hot, he later remembered, that "I felt like I was inhaling the flames." He managed to save himself by diving into the stream at a point where it turned away from the pursuing inferno.

It looked for a time as though he might have suffered serious lung damage. But he was sent home without medical treatment. For a logger, it was all in a day's work. Only the Wobblies would have thought the company owed Ed Murrow more.[1]

This brush with mortality evidently taught him what mattered in his life, at least for a time. For, as Willma Dudley recalled: "I was already back at school that fall. Ed was supposed to arrive a few days later. It was a beautiful, sunny afternoon. I was in front of the sorority house. I looked up and there he was, running across the lawn toward me. He kissed me right there in front of the house." More startling than his unexpected appearance, she said, was the kiss. It was his first display of public affection toward her.

The closeness did not last. She waited in vain for him to say something about marriage. Underneath her pliant, eager-to-please, reluctant-to-offend pose she was miserable. Her mother was constantly pressuring her not to confine herself to this man who promised her nothing. Mayor Dudley still wondered what his daughter was doing in college anyway. Her life at Pullman was becoming unendurable.[2]

50

Ed was still involved in campus politics, though there is no evidence at this point that he was politically conscious beyond the campus. If he were, he would have been an exception in 1928. The mood of college students reflected the mood of the nation. The country was headed for an economic abyss, but thought it was on a permanent spree. Editorials in *The Evergreen* bristled with indignation at such injustices as the long waits in Pullman's barbershops now that all the women were having their hair bobbed. The college newspaper that year ran one editorial that dealt with anything beyond student gripes. A black baritone had given a concert in Bryan Hall, and *The Evergreen* observed loftily "talent has no color."[3]

World War I had been over for a decade. The swing of the pendulum was now to pacifism. Channing Pollock had written a play, *The Enemy,* about Carl Behrend, a gifted young Austrian playwright who goes off and is killed in the war. Ed Murrow and Ed Lehan both tried out for the part of Carl Behrend. Murrow got it. *The Evergreen*'s reviewer praised his growth over his performance in *Craig's Wife* and particularly cited "the emotional power of his departure for the front." College classmates who were asked about Ed Murrow decades later still mentioned his performance in *The Enemy.*

Cynthia Lowry next planned to give Ed the lead in Eugene O'Neill's *Beyond the Horizon,* the story of Robert Mayo who abandons his dream of seeing the world to marry a woman who loves him. He stays on the farm, and descends into ruin. The play provided an apt parallel to what was happening between Ed and Willma, except that he refused to play a real-life Robert Mayo.[4]

Willma could have tolerated a love affair leading to marriage. But a love affair leading nowhere left her sick with guilt. When she asked Ed why he wouldn't marry her, he became evasive. One reason was Ida Lou Anderson. Of course, Ida Lou said, she hoped, one day, that he would marry a fine woman, the right woman. But he must not betray his promise by a premature marriage to a pretty, pleasant, but perfectly ordinary, girl.

His ardor was cooling anyway. Willma had worked herself into a paradox. She had given herself to him, and thus she had passed the test of love. But in doing so she had failed the test of maidenly virtue. It all became too much for her. Three months into her sophomore year, she told Ed that she was going back to Yakima. He did not try to talk her out of it. On her last evening at Pullman, she slipped out of the sorority house and they spent most of the night together. The next day she was gone.[5]

He resumed his unentangling alliances with girls simply as friends. Kay Fulton, a sorority sister of Willma's, recalled Ed during this period: "He had a reputation as a playboy, but he was too serious for that. He wasn't about to be hooked. We all knew he'd make a name for himself."[6]

The girl he saw the most of now was Hermine Duthie. She was intrigued by a certain remoteness in Murrow. "He was very close-mouthed about himself, about his family, his past," she recalled. "Before he'd pick me up I'd say to myself this time I'm going to find out what he's all about. I'm going to learn about his personal life. But by the time he'd bring me home, I realized that he'd learned much more about me, and I had learned almost nothing about him."[7]

His charm, when he chose to use it, was considerable, and it cushioned him from the potential social damage of his withdrawals and black bouts of depression. Helen Hazen, now Helen Rymond, still glowed as she talked about Ed Murrow decades later. But in a final observation she found, "well, something of a selfishness about him." Not thoughtlessness toward others, she said, since he could be considerate, but rather an absorption in self. "Ed Murrow didn't do anything that he didn't want to do," was the way she put it. Professor Daggy was blunter. "I knew him to be introspective, ambitious and somewhat self-centered."[8]

Near Thanksgiving Willma wrote to Ed that she was pregnant. Soon afterward, she was packed off to relatives in Minneapolis.

She had made no demands of him, but merely let him know. But after she arrived in Minneapolis, she got word from Ed that he was coming to see her during the Christmas break. He said that he had to go to Washington, D.C., to testify about the forest fire that summer, and he was going to stop by to see her on the way. On Christmas morning, Ed showed up unannounced at the home of Willma's relatives, a childless aunt and uncle. They were shocked by his unexpected arrival, especially when they learned that he had not come, as the phrase had it, to make an honest woman of their niece. Ed stayed for two uncomfortable nights with Willma's relatives. Between Christmas and the New Year, he went to see a friend in neighboring St. Paul. Willma tells what followed next: "Ed called me to tell me to meet him at a certain hotel one morning. I told my uncle I was going to meet a sorority sister and spend the night as [Ed] instructed. I met him and we talked. We sat on the edge of the bed with him holding my hands and watching my face. Sometimes he'd put an arm around me. He talked about not being able to support a family and finishing college. He was sorry it happened."

And then Ed told her of Lacey's advice. Lacey Murrow was not an older brother whose counsel could be dismissed lightly. At 26, he was the youngest district engineer in the state. He had become a protégé of Governor Clarence Martin, and there were murmurs of a political career for Lacey too. He was helping to pay Ed's way through college. And he had had a great deal of experience with women.

Ed told Willma that Lacey had sent him the money and that he had made arrangements for an abortion. "He asked me if I'd feel better about it if we got married first. I said no. Even then something got through that it would spoil everything for him and any relationship we might have in the future.... So we went to the doctor and he waited for me. When I was called he leaned down to kiss me and I turned away.... The doctor had arranged a hotel we could go to [afterward] no questions asked. So that afternoon we went over to what turned out to be quite a nice place. Ed was very solicitous, helped me lay down and lay beside me just holding me in his arms, saying nothing....We stayed there that night and I can't remember what was said. All I really remember was the tenderness of being held all night."

The next morning, they took a trolley back to Minneapolis. A block before her relatives' house, they got off, he kissed her, and they said goodbye. It was the last time that Ed Murrow ever saw Willma Dudley.[9]

This time the journey back to Pullman, the bleakness of the winter landscape seen from the train window, the patches of hard earth swept clear of snow by the howling winds, the barrenness of the scene, matched his mood. The depth of his guilt and self-contempt at the time can be read in something that he was to write thirty-one years later when he was a famous and much esteemed man. Ed Sullivan, riding the crest of his phenomenally popular television variety show, was writing a book about how various celebrities recalled a particularly memorable Christmas. Sullivan had asked Ed Murrow to contribute. Murrow wrote back, "I try never to remember Christmas....I have no memories of any Christmas worth recounting and if I did try they would be of such a nature that no publisher would print them. Sorry."[10]

Back in Pullman, he plunged into a distracting whirl. But the periods of depression came more often and stayed longer. He was taking a debating course that year and decided to enter an extemporaneous speaking competition held by the Pacific Forensic League. The speakers were to argue the proposition: "That the modern diversion of women from the home to business and industrial occupations is detrimental to society." He was to argue the pro position.

He was accompanied to the competition by a young professor from the speech department, W. H. Veatch, who later described Ed's performance. "He started out with one of the most beautiful introductions that I had ever heard. And I settled down as only a coach will whose contestant sounds like the best speaker in a contest. Then he began to hesitate and feel around for words and limp to a very poor close. After the contest, I asked what had happened. He said that as he began to bring out the viewpoint he wanted to make, he realized it was totally unsound and false and that he did not want to stand up there in front of a couple hundred people and try to make a point that he did not believe and that he could not shift his ideas fast enough to make a good speech out of it."

It may well have been, with the Willma experience fresh in his mind, that he was much too aware of the injustices borne by women to argue the condescending proposition of the debate with any heart. Whatever the reason for his poor performance, the result was a devastating and rare taste of defeat. He placed fifth.[11]

Back at school, Ed went on the road with a play called *The Valiant*.

His friend Hermine Duthie described his strength as an actor: "He could find the character and then stay in the character." There was one role, however, that he would not perform. Ed Murrow refused to take comic parts. His life was a climb, an effort to rise above his origins, to project social assuredness, an objective, in his judgment, that would not be advanced by his playing the clown.[12]

That spring, Ed began to maneuver for a class office that would ultimately affect his life more than any course he took in college. He wanted to be president of the student body. Election to this office would automatically elevate him to membership in the Pacific Student Presidents Association. With TNE maneuvering behind him, Ed was easily elected.

One week later, he went to the annual conference of the Pacific Student Presidents Association at Berkeley in California. He came back with an unexpected honor for one from so modest a campus. He had been elected president of the association.[13]

He spent another summer logging, and in September of 1929, Ed was back in Pullman for his senior year. Willma Dudley had continued to write to him, and one of his answers, written late in October, provides insight into his frame of mind at the time. The stationery on which he wrote her was a heavy rag paper of high quality. The letterhead bore a coat-of-arms with "Ed. Murrow" printed beneath it, embossed in gold. It was hardly the stationery of an impecunious college student, or at least one who wanted to be thought an impecunious college student. He wrote using an Indian nickname that he favored for Willma:

Dear Hunka,

It seemed mighty good to hear from you again and your letter came just when I needed it most. I think you know why I have not written to you. I wanted to make things as easy as possible for you and I thought that was the way you wanted it. I am intensely interested in you and what you are doing. I have heard considerable, most of which I can't believe. If you feel like it, write and tell me about the man you are to marry, tell me anything you like. Perhaps you think it strange that I can write in this manner. Well perhaps it is. Time has not been much of a healer for me I can say that. I have been going night and day for the past two weeks, preparing for homecoming and then I had a lot of work to do with the Pacific Presidents Association yesterday. Your letter brought up a lot of memories and tonite I'm down in the depths but that's allrite. I'm getting used to it.... I haven't even had time to even find out about the speech department. I'm carrying 19 hours and I'm sure doing some work. I have been sick for a couple of weeks this fall as usual. The doctor claims my nerves are shot all to pieces. And advises me to quit school for a semester at least. Imagine my nerves gone. Can you? I can't.

Sometime this fall I'm supposed to go to Elleberg to speak to the high school, also in Yakima I believe. I'm going to Portland on PSPA business the second of November and to Los Angeles with the football team the thirtieth. I still have hopes of graduating in the spring. Have a couple of nice offers to go to work. But I don't think I'll want to settle down for a few years.

I'm disappointed that you could not come over this week-end, although I imagine you wouldn't have cared to see me. I was through Yakima this fall but didn't call for obvious reasons.

This letter hasn't been easy to write. I'm a pretty proud boy I reckon but if you say friends why friends it is and with all my heart. You have one friend who is wishing you all the happiness and sunshine that anyone may have. You deserve it. The outlook at present for me isn't too bright. It's plenty gloomy in fact. But I like wise deserve that. Write me when you care to. I'll always find time to answer and not as boring as this I hope. All the happiness in the world to you.

Ed

How he felt after this first disastrous liaison is fairly clear. He mildly encourages continued contact with her, at least through the mail, which allows him in some degree to salve his conscience. Her announcement to him that she was getting married even allows him to play the injured party, though he does not protest too much. He even manages to sound the good sport ("tell me about the man you are to marry"). But the unspoken, and perhaps unconscious, message of this letter is that he is relieved to be free. There is no attempt to dissuade her from the marriage. There has been no attempt to see her, even though he has been in her hometown recently and will be passing through it again shortly. In sum, the letter reveals a young man who has just had a close shave with his independence and is happily escaped. Within a month, Willma Dudley did marry.

The letter further reveals a usually well-concealed capacity for self-pity: ("Time has not been much of a healer for me." "The outlook at present for me isn't too bright."). This is not an Ed Murrow whom fellow Kappa Sigs, TNEs, or ROTC cadets were ever permitted to see. Indeed, throughout his life he would show this side of himself to only a tiny circle of women including his mother, certainly never to a male friend.

The letter also reveals the beginnings of a pattern of behavior that will become ingrained for life ("The doctor claims my nerves are shot all to pieces."), a compulsion to drive himself, to take on more and more work, to push himself to the edge of exhaustion.[14]

That fall, it was Ed Murrow, along with President Holland, who greeted the incoming freshmen in Bryan Hall. He stood before the class of 1934 in a dark-blue, three-piece suit that somehow looked tailor-made, though it was off the rack. He seemed too mature, too polished for a college senior, and could more easily have passed for a college administrator. He told the incoming class, "There are two types of men who enter Washington State, those who grow, and those who swell." In his own case, growth was clearly dominant, though some slight swelling could also be observed.[15]

Six years earlier, a new American student organization had been born on the Princeton campus, the National Student Federation of America, the American offshoot of a post-World War I European movement, the Confederation Internationale des Etudiants.[16]

In December of 1929, the NFSA was to hold its annual convention at Stanford University in Palo Alto, California. Ed was determined to go. The problem was money. And the solution was a man named Earl Foster. Earl Foster served as a member of the WSC administration, with the title "Student Manager." Ed and Earl got on much the way that Ed had with Ken Merredith. Foster was old enough to command a certain deference, yet young enough to be a friend. It would cost $200 for Ed to attend the NSFA conference at Stanford. He had thought through how to make sending him to the conference benefit the school as much as himself. He reminded Earl Foster that he had gone to the Pacific College Association meeting and had come home with the presidency, thus bringing honor to Washington State. Now they were dealing with a national student association. If Earl could see his way to tapping the student treasury for the $200, Ed might bring a more lustrous prize back to Pullman. Earl Foster, who could never say no to Ed Murrow, gave him the money.[17]

When Ed arrived at Stanford, the name on everybody's lips was "Mrs. Rieber." Winifred Rieber was the wife of the Dean of Letters and Science at UCLA. She had lost a son in World War I, and preventing another war had become the woman's consuming purpose. Mrs. Rieber was also a talented portrait painter. While painting Harry Chandler, the publisher of *The Los Angeles Times,* she had extracted a pledge from Chandler to donate $30,000 to NSFA if she could demonstrate that American college students were interested in something besides football, bootleg hooch, and campus hijinks. NSFA was surviving hand to mouth. Mrs. Rieber, the student delegates believed, was going to be NSFA's angel.

Ed began to employ the tactics he had absorbed from TNE, as he began to reach for a new prize. Votes are best wholesaled through deals that deliver whole blocs rather than retailed voter by voter. He already had a core of supporters from neighboring Pacific Coast colleges as president of that association. Building on that nucleus of delegates, he began to branch out, making new friends. Key among them were four influential student leaders, Martha Biehle from Wellesley in Massachusetts; Lewis Powell, the student body president of Washington and Lee in Virginia; Chester Williams, a senior from the University of California; and Deirdre

Mason, from Rollins College in Florida. They were all idealistic, imbued with the faith that they could change the world; and conveniently, for Ed's purposes, they represented a useful geographic spread.

At Stanford he displayed a talent maturing since boyhood. Ed Murrow had an innate capacity to make people feel that his relationship with them was unique, that they shared a special bond. With Deirdre Mason, it was that both she and he were theater people. With Martha Biehle it was their sophistication in campus politics. To Lewis Powell, Ed confided his true ambition, to be a lawyer, which happened to be Powell's intended career. With Chet Williams, along with a shared pleasure in philosophical bull sessions, Ed behaved as though he was utterly oblivious of Chet's lameness, which was all that Williams wanted of people, an insight that Ed had gained from associating with Ida Lou Anderson. He allowed each into a compartment of his life, which the less discerning mistook for the whole.

His behavior might be seen as opportunistic. It might just as well be judged as thoughtful. He took the pains to build a bridge to an individual. This quality lies at the heart of personal leadership. It is the gift of all successful politicians, those in politics itself or in the politics of business, academia, the Army, or the clergy for that matter. If Ed profited from this behavior, as indeed he was about to at Stanford, few friends ever complained of being used by Ed Murrow. If his choice of these four was calculated, it was hardly ephemeral. Ed was to remain a valued friend of all four for the rest of his life.

They talked late into the night, plotting a strategy to win Ed Murrow the NSFA presidency. The key, they knew, was to win Ed a key speech on the program where he could show his stuff. Getting him on the program was relatively straightforward. He was president of the Pacific Coast Student Association, the host group, and hence a logical choice to address the nationwide delegates.

The overriding issue at the conference was peace. As Deirdre Mason recalled, "We were all motivated by a will never to have another world war." One of the older invitees to the conference, she remembered, was George Creel, chief propagandist in the Wilson administration during World War I. "He told us 'we fooled you kids the last time with all that nonsense about German soldiers bayoneting Belgian babies. It wasn't true. Don't let it happen again.'" "I was," Deirdre Mason said, "converted to Pacifism on the spot."

When it was the turn of the Pacific Coast Student Association president to speak, Ed charged that American college students were too provincial, that they were preoccupied with "fraternities, football, and fun." He called on the delegates, as the next leadership generation, to raise the vision of their fellow students throughout America, to awaken a new generation to serious issues, above all, to the imperative of ending war forever.

He poured every device that Ida Lou had taught him into the speech.

The delegates were moved by both the message and the passion of the speaker. Lewis Powell, well over half a century later, when he had become a justice of the U.S. Supreme Court, recalled the effect of the moment: "Ed made the handsomest presence of anybody I'd ever seen. And the speech, it had such a polished quality, not a bit theatrical, but he was so poised. He was so confident and mature. I was just enormously impressed."

Ed had demonstrated Winifred Rieber's point that American students could make serious commitments. She now knew whom she wanted leading the American student movement, and she let her choice be known among the delegates. Ed Murrow was elected president of the National Student Federation of America.[18]

When he got back to Pullman, the front-page headline of *The Evergreen* trumpeted, "Ed Murrow Is Elected to Represent Nation." The student body passed a resolution extending "heartiest congratulations to Ed Murrow for bringing prestige" to Washington State. He had done the cow college proud.[19]

At the NSFA convention Ed had found himself lunching with anthropologists from a half a dozen countries. He debated the British class structure with English students. He met Americans from the East who challenged the innocent wisdom of heartland America. The experience was an intellectual jolt. He came to realize that much of what he accepted as objective truth was no better than opinion. But he happily discovered that he could shed old notions and embrace new ideas if he were persuaded by fact and logic. This was the opening of his intellectual pores that Ida Lou had prepared him for. When he got back to Pullman, he told some of his friends that he was considering a new career, the diplomatic service.[20]

One change, however, did not occur at Stanford. Unlike his new friend Deirdre Mason, Ed was not converted to pacifism on the spot. Before he went to Stanford, he had been named cadet colonel of the Washington State ROTC contingent. When a startled Mason learned that her candidate for NSFA president was the top military student at his college, she observed, forgivingly, "I'm still sure his skepticism of raw, unexamined patriotism must have been influenced by the speeches we heard at the conference. But I could see that he sure loved that ROTC."[21]

In his last semester at college, Ed spoke his first words over the radio on the campus station, KWSC. Maynard Daggy had become an early convert to radio. Daggy saw the new medium as a respectable academic discipline, a decidedly minority opinion in faculty rooms in 1930. And so when Daggy designed his college course in radio, the first in the country, in order to get it into the college catalogue, he masqueraded it as "Speech 40, Community Drama." Among the first twenty-four students was Ed Murrow. At the end of the semester, Maynard Daggy gave Edward R. Murrow a B in radio.[22]

His senior year was, nevertheless, to be Ed's finest hour as a scholar. *The Evergreen* reported him making the honor roll for the first time. He was listed as Egbert Roscoe Murrow, still his legal name.[23]

He felt certain that he would make Phi Beta Kappa. The scholarly society had just installed a chapter on the Pullman campus that year. Ed and his friend Paul Coie were both contenders. But when the eighteen members selected from the class of 1930 were announced, neither Murrow's nor Coie's name appeared.

Years later, in a statement he included in a CBS publicity biography, Ed's resentment still bristled. "I graduated with qualifications for a Phi Beta Kappa," he wrote, "but was not elected because of a thundering row with a faculty member on the selection committee." The cause of the row was Murrow's and Coie's membership in the cliquish TNE. The unidentified faculty member had found out that the two seniors were members and expressed the school's disapproval of the secret society by blocking their membership in Phi Beta Kappa.[24]

He never became serious with another girl while in college after the Willma Dudley affair. After he was elected president of the student body, he told his friend Kay Fulton, "I'm going to take this job very seriously. No more drinking and partying." She recalled wondering at the time, "How much more serious could Ed Murrow get?"[25]

Ed now escorted Ida Lou not only to lectures. He took her to plays. He took her to cast parties. Most eye-popping on the Pullman campus, he took her to dances, an unlikely pair, one of the handsomest men at school and the dwarfish, crippled spinster. But he did not dance with her or anyone else. For years girls had wondered why they could not drag him onto a dance floor. The too obvious answer was that he had been inhibited by his upbringing in a home where dancing was forbidden. Yet, one by one, he had shucked his mother's Puritan prohibitions. The difference with dancing was simply that his lack of early involvement left him afraid that he could not do it well. And Ed Murrow did not do things that he did not do well.[26]

What were his motives for squiring Ida Lou to concerts, to plays, to dances? Thoughtfulness? Gratitude? The pleasure of her company? Opportunism? He was an ambitious young man, and this behavior served his ambitions. But he was to acknowledge openly all his life his debt to this woman. She had not simply taught him to read words movingly. She had altered him. He had found a way, immensely pleasing and flattering to her, of repaying his infinite debt to her. His behavior also revealed a certain assertiveness of character. He did what he wanted without worrying too much about what others thought.

Willma Dudley may not have been good enough in Ida Lou's eyes for Ed Murrow. But the rejected girlfriend understood the symbiosis between Ed and Ida Lou with admirable clarity. As Willma later said: "Every time he started to take a side road from the one Ida Lou had charted for him, she pulled him back....Another thing she did was to give him social assurance. This was his vulnerable streak. Part of his appearing so serious was a cover-up for his insecurity. What made him a good actor was his ability to hide this vulnerability. He learned to cover it up very well indeed. Sometimes the people that seem most in charge have the most fragile egos....Ida Lou fed his ego and he fed hers."[27]

As Ed later described his relationship with Ida Lou, "She took a raw kid and gave him goals in life." He tried to explain years later in a letter to his future wife what Ida Lou had meant. "She taught me to love good books, good music, gave me the only sense of values I have....She also caused me to stop drinking myself to death," he added, with a touch of hyperbole. "She knows me better than any person in the world. The part of me that is decent, that wants to do something, be something, is the part she created. I owe the ability to live to her...," he concluded. It was high praise from a student to a teacher. It was high praise from one human being to another.

Ida Lou expressed her feelings more directly to Ed. "You are," she said, "my masterpiece."[28]

It had been a love affair, lopsided to be sure, but a love affair nonetheless. For Ed's part, it was a loving respect and a loving gratitude. For Ida Lou's part, it was simpler and purer, the love of a woman for a man, mixed admittedly with a teacher's pride, but a romantic attachment doomed for her by the deforming trick that nature had played on her years before.[29]

A front-page story in the last issue of *The Evergreen* that year announced: "Murrow to Leave for Summer Tour." The president of the NSFA was to make a swing through the organization's offices in Los Angeles, Dallas, and Atlanta, and then go to Washington where he would meet with the secretary of the interior, Ray Lyman Wilbur, an adviser to NSFA; then it was on to the NSFA national headquarters in New York and finally to Europe to represent the United States at the Confederation Internationale des Etudiants. And all expenses paid. To WSC students, most of whom had yet to leave the state, it was heady stuff.

He graduated on June 2, 1930. Alongside his photograph in *The Chinook* is a densely packed paragraph summarizing his accomplishments. Beneath the photo, a pedestrian, or perhaps exhausted, caption writer had written: "An A plus personality together with a level head and the ability to see clearly into the problems confronting the college students of the present day...."

He appears in several snapshots scattered throughout the yearbook. One shows him in a white suit looking debonair. He is holding a cigarette, by now a rooted habit. The caption reads: "Here's one prominent citizen the tobacco companies overlooked when they went to collect testimonials."[30]

Ethel made this graduation. Roscoe did not. She wore an orchid that

Ed had presented to her on her arrival, and she continually referred to the tall, grave-looking president of the student body as "Sonny."[31]

How transformed was the "raw kid" who had arrived at Pullman in the fall of 1926? Most significant in his own mind was the voyage of intellectual discovery. He had received a solid if not prestigious education from able, often dedicated, and occasionally brilliant teachers. His quick mind and retentive memory had served him well. Others might drink more deeply at the Pierian spring, but Ed Murrow remembered what he imbibed virtually for life. His furious outside activities had not meant that he disesteemed the history, the literature, and philosophy that he had been taught. Rather, he had been able to grasp the material with less investment of effort than most of his peers, which left him considerable time for other pursuits.

The Kappa Sigma house had marked him too. Once when a friend asked why he had joined a fraternity, Ed joked, "The Kappa Sigs taught me table manners." He had come to college with his mother's respect for the forms of polite society and as little actual knowledge of them as she possessed. Ethel had guessed at the rules or made them up as she went along to suit her sometimes askew notions of correct behavior. At Kappa Sigma her son learned the right rules. He also had natural gifts to build on. A roll of the genetic dice had blessed him with good looks, a strong physique, a proud bearing, a distinguished voice, and high intelligence. The acting, particularly, had provided the workshop where he could polish these high-grade raw materials to a convincingly well-bred gloss. He had become a gentleman.

He may have acquired the propriety that his mother prized. But he had shed her fundamentalist morality as easily as a snake does an outworn skin. He left college a drinker, a smoker, and an occasional card player. He had experienced a jarring introduction to sex, and he had abandoned formal religion.

The work ethos had become calcified in him. He habitually overextended himself to a degree that suggested a shame, even a fear, of inactivity, an inability to relax; and as an inevitable consequence, he suffered frequent bouts of physical and emotional exhaustion. Consciously or unconsciously, he was following Marcus Aurelius, "to live not one's life as though one had a thousand years, but to live each day as the last." He tried not only to do too much but to excel no matter how thinly he spread himself. Consequently, he was virtually always dissatisfied with the quality of his performance. By the time he graduated from Washington State, he had clearly eclipsed Lacey's college career. But, by now, the compulsion to compete was so ingrained that he was essentially running against himself.

And for reasons best explained by psychiatry or biochemistry, he developed an unshakable pessimism. What he turned his hand to usually turned out right. He was leaving college covered with laurels. As his classmate had said, "Everything went his way. Everything fell in his lap." Yet, behind the smile that tended to flash and fade rather too quickly, he was plagued by despair and periods of depression. He was a golden boy with the soul of a Cassandra. As he had written Willma, "The outlook at present for me isn't too bright. It's plenty gloomy in fact." It was nonsense. His outlook had never been brighter.

He had wavered between careers in business, in speech, in the law, and in diplomacy. He felt that his education was scattershot, that it had not pointed him in any clear direction. As he later described his years at Pullman, "I took a bastard course, everything from philosophy to animal husbandry."[32]

His friend Paul Coie recalled those waning days at Washington State: "Ed and I were just anxious to get as far as possible from Pullman." When pressed by a questioner about why, Coie replied, "Have you ever been to Pullman?"

Away from Pullman, yes. But where? He was later to tell his wife that his keenest ambition at this stage was still to become a lawyer. But the law was financially out of the question. The Depression was deepening. Job prospects for the class of 1930 were grim. But NSFA offered something intriguing. He had been elected for another term as president, and the association's executive committee, essentially his friends, had agreed to provide him not with a salary, but with $25 a week in living expenses to go to New York and run the national office.

Men his father's age were standing in bread lines. Women as proud as his mother were living on the dole. Banks were failing and factory gates were closing. And here was the NSFA offering him money to live, if modestly, in the greatest city in the country and to work at least on the periphery of another field that intrigued him, higher education. And so, days after graduation, with $40 in his pocket and several debts still hanging over his head, he boarded the train in Seattle for the swing through NSFA's regional offices, a trip to Europe, and eventual settlement in New York.

He had not yet found what he wanted to do with his life. Rather, something that he could do had found him. Among the few possessions in the cheap suitcases that he carried as he headed East was that link to the past, the slab of redwood that he had kept in his room at Pullman these past four years. It was a reminder of the world of his father in which men earned their livelihood with their hands, a world now ended for him.[33]

CHAPTER 6

A New York Apprenticeship

Late in June of 1930, Ed Murrow arrived in New York. He went directly to NSFA headquarters at 218 Madison Avenue and found a place utterly in keeping with the organization's pinched circumstances, one room in a basement. The walls were papered with travel posters; the office equipment consisted of a couple of battered typewriters and a mimeograph. The furniture was eclectic, some of it looking as if it had been scavenged from trash heaps, along with a few stylish cast-offs donated by the families of well-to-do members. There may have been, as well, a couch or a cot, since Ed, who would be leaving for Europe in a month, gave his home address at this time as the association's headquarters.

Two of his partisans from the Stanford convention were already at NSFA, Chet Williams, serving as acting secretary, and Martha Biehle, an unpaid staff volunteer. Biehle was a large young woman, rather more imposing than attractive and possessed of a dead seriousness that softened noticeably in the presence of Ed Murrow.[1]

NSFA was essentially a moderate and middle-class student organization, politically lightweight and following a scattershot agenda. It opposed subsidies for college athletes, wanted Prohibition repealed, and called for the withdrawal of American troops from China. But the posters on the wall signaled a more immediate interest. One attractive feature of NSFA membership was cut-rate trips abroad. Ed thus found himself much of the time on college campuses functioning as an international travel agent.[2]

Paul Coie had also come East and was working at the Library of Congress in Washington. Coie came to New York to visit Ed, and Ed told him that soon after his arrival in New York, he had auditioned as a radio announcer with the National Broadcasting Company and had been offered

63

a job. Radio failed to attract him. Rather, he was looking forward to the foreign travel that his NSFA presidency offered.[3]

He applied for a passport on July 10, 1930, to attend the congress of the Confederation Internationale des Etudiants in Brussels. He listed his occupation as "student." He had no birth certificate. In Polecat Creek, births were recorded in family Bibles. Thus, Ethel had to send a notarized affidavit giving the date and place of his birth. She did it in longhand and had started to write "Egbert," crossed that out, and wrote "Ed. R. Murrow." Since there was no other official document recording his birth, he was now legally Edward R. Murrow.

The passport put a $6 hole in his $25 dollar a week expense allowance. He sailed on the *SS Rotterdam* on July 26 with two NSFA allies from Stanford—Deirdre Mason, now an aspiring actress, and the Virginian, Lewis Powell.[4]

Ed and Powell shared a tiny stateroom. They easily picked up the friendship where it had left off at Stanford, "Because," Powell recalled, "we were both Southerners. Ed never seemed like a Yankee to me." In fact, Ed had not lived in the South since he was a child, but it was again part of the Murrow attraction, the ability to create a linkage that made a friendship special. Powell in the meantime had graduated from Washington and Lee University, magna cum laude, and, unlike Ed, had made Phi Beta Kappa.

Ed took to calling Powell "Judge," which proved to be prescient. It was another part of his style, this adoption of private nicknames, his way of signaling admission into the small circle of his affection. To all the world his sister-in-law Donna Jean was "Donnie." But to Ed alone she was always "Jean." Later, among the correspondents, Charles Collingwood was to be "Bonnie Prince Charlie"; Bill Downs, "Doctor"; Eric Sevareid, "The Gloomy Dane."[5]

As the *Rotterdam* docked in England, the former logger and cow college graduate made an unlikely entrance. He came down the gangplank wearing a striped blazer and a straw boater and twirling a cane, the appearance, evidently, that he thought befitted a young American abroad. He was disappointed with England, and was later to say, "I thought your streets narrow and mean; your tailors over-advertised; your climate unbearable; your class consciousness offensive. You couldn't cook. Your young men seemed without vigor or purpose. I…suspected that the historians had merely agreed on a myth."

It rained the whole two weeks that he was in England, ruining the boater, which he chucked into the English Channel, along with the cane, while crossing the Channel from Dover to Ostend. Still, a touch of the dandy was to stay with him for life, though muted over the years.[6]

The conference at Brussels was an eye opener, a continuation for Ed of the education in the world's layered complexity that had begun at Stanford. NSFA's agenda at home called for banning freshman hazing, protesting faculty interference in student government, and debating whether college credit should be given for the French club. The students he met at Brussels were older and more politically sophisticated than the Americans, many of them professional activists who had not set foot in a classroom in years. They had no interest in quelling campus teapot tempests, but rather in ending the ancient, blood-soaked conflicts among their countries.

The NSFA delegates had come to Brussels imbued with the simple notion that goodwill could remove age-old hatreds and save the world from war. Instead they found Italians and Austrians squabbling over Bolzano; Serb and Croatian delegates fighting over who should represent their new nation, Yugoslavia; Flemish students feeling bitter at being lumped with the Belgian delegation; and Germans and Poles at each other's throats over Danzig. Delegates from the countries allied in World War I did not think the Germans belonged at the conference at all. Thus, the German delegation was permitted only to attend sessions but denied membership in the CIE. In the evenings when the delegates gathered at student cafes to dance and listen to American jazz, the Germans were cold-shouldered.

Ed Murrow, with the message of Channing Pollock's *The Enemy* fresh in his memory, led a movement to remove the sins of the German fathers from their children. These young Germans, he argued, had not started the world war, had not fought the war, and ought not to be punished for losing the war. He favored full German membership in the CIE. The French, the Belgians, and the British were unyielding.

The congress failed, run aground on the reefs of ancient antagonisms. Next to nothing had been accomplished. But while the congress failed, Brussels was a personal triumph for Ed. There was something in his appearance and manner that caused him to be taken for the head of the British delegation. His passionate championing of the unloved Germans struck an appealing, if unavailing, chord. Naïveté had its charm and suggested fresh hope to the cynical Europeans. He was perceived as something of a student Woodrow Wilson. Ed was offered the presidency of the CIE. But he would not take the office, he said, while the Germans were excluded.[7]

Before heading home, Ed and Lewis Powell made a shoestring version of the Grand Tour. They spent a week in Paris and then took a boat trip down the Rhine. The Rhineland had been under Allied occupation since 1919, and only weeks before, occupation troops had finally been withdrawn. A young German woman serving as a tour guide on the boat announced gloatingly, "I want you all to know. This is our Rhine again." Suddenly, the wariness of the British, the French, and the Belgians seemed more understandable.

They did, Powell recalled, virtually no carousing, no chasing after women. Powell found Murrow terribly serious and inclined to internalize even the most public of issues. International squabbles became his personal anguish. He used the personal pronouns for countries—"we," "they," "our." And in one so clearly favored as Murrow, Powell was puzzled to discover Ed's deeply pessimistic streak. As he came to know him better through the years, witnessing Ed's dark moods whether in good fortune or bad, Powell concluded that the pessimism was "genetic."[8]

The money ran out, and early in September, Ed was on the *SS Vollendam* headed home. Back in New York, he pooled his resources with Chet Williams, and they rented a third-floor walk-up in an old brownstone on East 37th Street with the kitchenette in the bathroom. The rent was $45 a month.[9]

At night, before turning in, they would play poker. The loser had to bring up the milk in the morning. Chet Williams had spent much of his life in wheelchairs after a childhood attack of polio. He had undergone seventeen operations. He had eventually learned to walk without crutches or a cane, but at a painful cost. He was not much of a card player and usually wound up going down the three flights of stairs and back for the milk.

Years later, Williams spoke of the experience with great warmth. Ed Murrow, he said, had not eroded his dignity with misguided sympathy. "This was a surprise and a relief to me," Williams recalled. "I was accustomed to people concentrating on what I couldn't do. Ed never did anything for me until I asked him."

Williams regarded himself at the time as a socialist and a "practical pacifist." His hero was Norman Thomas. To Ed, it was too simple to think that there was a single magic bullet that could end all of mankind's pains and follies. It was that "genetic" pessimism again that Lewis Powell had detected. To Williams's flights of idealism, Ed would answer teasingly, "Yes, Chet, you're going to change human nature."

Often as they talked, Ed would say things that Chet found provocative, and he would ask, "Is that one of Ida Lou Anderson's ideas?" As often as not, Ed answered, "Yes." Years later, he was to confess to Williams, "Sure, I may borrow or appropriate ideas. But that's what ideas are for. And who knows who really originated an idea."[10]

The Depression was driving the country to its knees. Eight million unemployed, five times as many as two years before, mocked Herbert Hoover's faith in a self-correcting American economy. In the midst of this economic drought, Ed Murrow was trying to raise money for a student organization. He succeeded. He had hit upon an ingenious strategy. NSFA had one economic resource, its members from wealthy families. Among them were young women eager to become a part of the national headquarters under any terms, as unpaid volunteers, if necessary.

Ed told them that unless they were paid, no one would take them seriously. He and Williams would then approach their families for donations to NSFA, enough to cover the daughter's salary with something left over to nourish the treasury. When a pet program faced extinction, the young women would put the arm on their dads to save it. They hosted fund-raising teas at posh Upper East Side addresses. Thus, the near penniless Murrow and Williams found themselves gyrating from caviar to pork and beans, from drawing rooms to their kitchenette in the bathroom, from one day to the next.

Given the built-in opportunities of the situation, Ed made no effort to combine pleasure with business. He made no passes at the rich young ladies. He was polite, even courtly, and good company. His smile was quick and his conversation engaging, but his eye remained on the target, keeping the NSFA alive. He dated rarely, sometimes Lewis Powell's sister, Eleanor, who was bright and vivacious and lived in Manhattan. But he was serious with no one.[11]

Between Christmas and the New Year of 1930, NSFA planned to hold its annual convention in Atlanta. The descendant of the Murrows who helped black slaves escape through the Underground Railroad and the grandson of a Lamb who never forgave the "nigger lovers" had reached a moral divide. The NSFA constitution called for a racially integrated organization, and the convention was going to be held in a thoroughly segregated city. NSFA's position on integration was laudable, but largely academic. No blacks had attended the previous national convention in Stanford. When Ed took over the New York operation, one black school, Howard University in the District of Columbia, belonged to the association. Ed pondered NSFA's moral responsibility with Williams. They could allow the virtual snow-white composition of the organization to see them through a trouble-free convention in a Deep South city. Or they could dare strike a blow for racial justice where it most needed to be struck.

It was a time when *Brown v. Board of Education* ordering desegregated schools was still nearly a quarter of a century off. Martin Luther King, Jr., was an infant. The word "sit-in" had not yet entered the American vocabulary. It was a year in which twenty blacks were lynched, six of them in Georgia.

Murrow decided to integrate the Atlanta convention.

He began by persuading a half-dozen black colleges to join NSFA and to send delegates to Atlanta. He next visited white campuses in the South with the objective of signing up a particular kind of member, especially young women from places like Sweetbriar and Rollins, well-bred belles, liberal on race. His ulterior objective would unfold later.

He then went to Atlanta's Hotel Biltmore and asked the manager if he was interested in hosting a convention for over 400 delegates. Times were lean. The Biltmore was indeed interested. He and Williams drew up a contract that included a provision requiring the hotel to accommodate *all* NSFA members attending. Attached to the contract was a copy of the NSFA constitution and a list of member colleges. Ed gave the papers to the hotel manager, who glanced through the list and evidently failed to notice the black colleges listed, including local Atlanta University.

Ed next managed to wangle an appointment with Adolf Ochs, publisher of *The New York Times*. He explained to Ochs the potential explosiveness of what he intended in Atlanta. He did not plea for sympathetic treatment. All he asked of *The Times* was that the paper assign a southern reporter to cover the story. Ochs, who had started in journalism as a newsboy in Knoxville, Tennessee, discerned Murrow's train of thought and agreed.

The day before the convention, Ed sprang the integration issue to the NSFA executive committee. Since the conference was being held in the South, a preponderance of delegates were southerners. He started talking with traces of a southern accent which Williams had not remembered hearing before. According to their constitution, Ed said, they were required to integrate the dozen or so black delegates expected in Atlanta into the conference. Lodging was not an issue, since the blacks were staying in dormitories at local black colleges. But they had to be integrated into the hotel's meeting rooms and, more ticklish, into the final dinner in the Biltmore ballroom. "The question before us," Ed went on, "is whether the committee wants me to press the hotel for full execution of our contract or not?"

As casually as he had tossed out the question, it was nevertheless a hand grenade. The debate was hot and hard. Chet Williams later described how Murrow handled the situation. "Ed...did not argue a point of view. He just listened and waited. He had a marvelous gift for synthesis, for giving each viewpoint its due, and for waiting for the right moment." At a propitious point, he said simply that he would be happy to take up the integration problem himself with the hotel management. As Chet Williams recalled, "Everyone looked relieved to have this cup pass from their lips."

Ed adjourned the meeting and called together the southern women he had recently recruited. They were to serve as ushers during the conference, he told them. At the first sign of trouble, they were to form a "flying squadron" to isolate any troublemakers. He was hoping by using the young ladies that southern chivalry would prove stronger than bigotry.

The following morning, the delegates began to fill the ballroom for the plenary session. Ed delivered a brief welcome, covered some convention business, and introduced the morning's speaker, Mrs. Nellie Ross, the first woman Assistant Secretary of the U.S. Treasury. Mrs. Ross took note of her integrated audience and praised NSFA. But a palpable brittleness settled over the room. The instant Mrs. Ross finished, a delegate from Texas Christian College began to bolt for the door, crying, "Where's the telegraph office? I've got to wire my college I'm leaving this convention." The flying squadron moved in and quickly smothered him with soft appeals to calm himself. The reporter from *The New York Times* came over. As promised, he turned out to be a legitimate son of the South, a young man from Birmingham who spoke to the Texan in a reassuring accent.

"Do you really want to walk out of this convention," the reporter asked, "and force me to write a story for that Yankee newspaper I work for that will make your college and all of us southerners look like a bunch of bigots?" After ten minutes of careful stroking, the Texan agreed to return to his seat. The NSFA was integrated.

The manager of the Biltmore, however, flatly refused to serve blacks at the final banquet. If word got around, he said, it would give the Biltmore "a black eye." Ed pointed out to the manager that whites and blacks sat together peaceably throughout the convention. Then just let them sit together at the banquet and don't worry about the Biltmore staff having to serve them, he said.

That night, he scattered the dozen black delegates among the banquet tables and seated one of his female ushers next to each black. When the waiter served these white women, they simply passed their plates to the black students. The waiters, black themselves, found the white contortions amusing.[12]

Shortly before the Atlanta conference, Ed had met a man in New York named Fred Willis. Willis was a suave Englishman who had left advertising in Britain to pursue his fortune in America. He had found himself stranded and jobless in New York City in the midst of the Depression. Willis later liked to tell how he used his last nickel to make a phone call to CBS. The call led to an interview and a job. Willis, with no broadcasting credentials, managed to talk himself into the directorship of educational programming for the radio network. His job was to find speakers to lecture over CBS. Fred Willis had a touch of the showman. More than distinguished names, he wanted famous names.

Chet Williams had previously been working on an arrangement through which CBS would give NSFA an hour a month for educational programming over a hookup to a hundred colleges. He and Ed now went to Willis and persuaded him that they could produce the resonating names he wanted, and without a dime of expense to CBS. The program was to be called the *University of the Air*.

Albert Einstein was to arrive in New York on the *SS Bergenland* early in December en route to the California Institute of Technology. Murrow rashly assured Willis that he could deliver Einstein for an exclusive CBS interview.

Sailing with Einstein was the historian Hendrik Van Loon, whom Ed had come to know through his NSFA university visits. A distinguished jurist, John Basset Moore, had once told Ed, "When you meet men of great reputation, your judgment of them will be greatly improved if you view them as though they were in their underwear." Ed evidently now imagined Albert Einstein in his drawers. He tapped NSFA's slender resources to send Van Loon a cable at sea asking him to invite Einstein to speak to the students of America over CBS radio when the *Bergenland* arrived in New York. Einstein himself sent back a telegram accepting.

As the *Bergenland* picked its way through the harbor channel into New York, small boats laden with reporters began to swarm around the hull. Einstein was so unnerved that he hid in his stateroom. He was finally persuaded to come out long enough to talk with newspaper reporters for fifteen minutes. His wife translated. He was asked what he thought of a rising nationalist politician in Germany. "I do not enjoy Mr. Hitler's acquaintance," he answered, [but] "Hitler is living on the empty stomach of Germany. As soon as economic conditions in Germany improve, he will cease to be important."

An NBC correspondent managed to get his microphone before Einstein for a few questions, thus costing CBS an exclusive. But a half hour later, Einstein did speak from his stateroom over the CBS network, with Van Loon introducing him. The scientist disarmingly protested his innocence of the rivalries between American radio networks. He was not aware, he said, that there was more than one broadcast system in the country. "I had the same experience with the two companies that Jacob had with his wives Leah and Rachel," he said. "He did not know which of them he should marry."

Murrow had produced Einstein for CBS. Using international cable, he also helped arrange talks for the *University of the Air* by Rabindranath Tagore, Mohandas Gandhi, President von Hindenburg, and Prime Minister Ramsay MacDonald. Willis was suitably impressed.[13]

Early in 1931, Ed lost his roommate. Chet Williams married and left their walk-up apartment. Decades later, after Murrow's death, Williams wrote a memoir of their days together and gave it to Ed's son, Casey. Here, and in other accounts, Williams painted a picture of a young man still not sure who he was and what he really valued. "He liked to talk," Williams said, "about the north woods and the 'real guys' he had associated with there. He would make fun of city concerns as somehow less basic, less human.... He disliked posturing people. He was attracted to solid types cut out of old cloth and a yard wide.... He liked the language of down-to-earth people. When we'd discuss the potential of some project, he liked to say things like, 'Does this put any hay in the barn?'

"His idea of a good time was to go over to the shooting galleries that they used to have on Times Square. He never drank cocktails, like martinis. It was always scotch and soda. And he'd order a double. He could curse like a logger, and took some pride in it. But he never cussed in front of a woman.

"He would speak of his brothers often, apologetically, as though he had somehow overshot their goals. And he'd kid himself about their rural upbringing, comparing the way he lived then, with the life he led now."

That summer, Chet Williams, hard-pressed to support a wife on his NSFA allowance, went to work for the New York Life Insurance Company. Ed, as a young bachelor, was an unlikely life insurance prospect. Yet he let Williams sell him a $5,000 policy. Williams later wrote, "I suspect that he only bought the policy to encourage me."[14]

Ed was in Europe again that summer for two and a half months. The CIE was holding its annual congress in Bucharest, and Ed drove to Romania from Paris with two friends in an ancient Ford. During this trip he addressed the Deutsche Studentenschaft, the German student organization. Of this experience he wrote E.O. Holland, back at Pullman, "I received the distinct impression that the opposition to the Hitlerite movement is composed of the really first-class German students." But he held out scant hope for this opposition. "The general feeling in Germany seems not to be concerned with whether or not Hitler will come to power—it is believed that he will eventually, but the primary question is what will happen after he does assume the reins of government."[15]

The NSFA was politically centrist if not neutral. But as the Depression deepened, even the middle had moved left. Virtually all student organizations across the political spectrum, including NSFA, agreed on a core of beliefs—in government intervention to break the Depression, and in antimilitarism, antifascism, and stringent neutrality. Early in 1932, Ed Murrow, former ROTC cadet colonel, with a Reserve commission in the Army, reported to member colleges that "the seventh annual NSFA convention passed a resolution: Resolved that we go on record as opposed to compulsory military training." NSFA also belonged to the United Students Peace Committee, which stood for a total abolition of ROTC, opposition to all wars, and an end to foreign alliances. His personal feelings about these issues are nowhere recorded. As the organization's leader, he simply passed along the majority sentiments without comment.

NSFA had a handful of radicals, among them the Marxist Frederick Vanderbilt Field, who had served on the executive committee and on the advisory board, and Corliss Lamont, a Socialist. Martha Biehle's assistant was a Communist. Ed's secretary married a Communist. Field and his co-religionists wanted to use student organizations like the NSFA not to repair the old order, but to scrap it. Nevertheless, under Murrow's leadership, NSFA remained shades paler than even parlor pink. Ideology still did not move him. In fact, during his tenure the association lost members to the more radical American Student Union.[16]

James T. Shotwell was a distinguished Canadian-American historian, a Columbia University professor who had played a role in the 1919 Paris Peace Conference. He was also an outspoken anti-Communist. Ed had come to know Shotwell when he booked him for the CBS *University of the Air*. Shotwell was then 58, a stocky figure with a great shock of white hair and a deep, captivating voice. He had formed a study group that met weekly in his Manhattan apartment. Professor Shotwell deliberately brought together students from across the political range and liked to let them go at each other. Inevitably, these meetings turned into verbal brawls over communism. Ed Murrow was occasionally in attendance.

Shotwell himself took the position, even with the Depression growing worse, that the country could be saved without succumbing to the siren lure of Marxism. It was precisely what Murrow wanted to believe. Shotwell's stature gave him something to hang onto. Consequently, the younger and the older man hit it off from the start.

Frederick Vanderbilt Field decided to ambush Professor Shotwell at one of the weekly salons. He stacked the attendance so that the professor faced a room full of Marxists who ganged up on the older man. Some years later, in 1938, Field wrote a letter saying that everyone present that afternoon, except Shotwell, was a Communist. The letter came to light during the fifties when a U.S. Senate subcommittee was investigating subversion in the Institute of Pacific Relations with which Field was associated.

At that point, the right-wing columnist, Westbrook Pegler, cagily called Professor Shotwell to find out if Ed Murrow had been among those present that long-ago afternoon. Indeed, he had, said the professor, but Field had the lineup wrong. Yes, most of the students were Marxists, but one young man stood with Shotwell that day, and he was Ed Murrow. Still, Field's 1938 letter resting in the files of a Senate committee investigating subversion was scarcely a source of comfort to Murrow when the fifties witch hunts began.[17]

Murrow's resistance to the voguish radicalism of the time was of a piece with his resistance to Chet Williams's idealism. He innately distrusted one-word answers—communism, socialism. He had liked the hearts of the Wobblies, but distrusted their heads. He had been reared in an environment where the individual pitted himself against nature's or man's obstacles, and overcame them by individual struggle, he and Ken Merredith, for example, charting virgin forests. That is what he and his brothers were doing, pulling themselves up, from the humblest origins.

With Williams now married, Ed took a tiny apartment in Patchin Place in Greenwich Village to save money. He was often homesick for the openness of the West in this city of stone. His friend from Washington State, Hermine Duthie, had moved to upstate New York where she had taken a junior instructorship at Syracuse University, and she occasionally took the long New York Central train ride to Manhattan to visit Ed. Her companionship was a connection to a world not only that he missed, but in some strange way, she sensed, that he felt he had abandoned.[18]

He was still constantly traveling to colleges, ultimately 300 of them. On a swing through Virginia he visited Lewis Powell, now practicing law in Richmond. They went quail shooting at the Powell family place, and as Powell remembered, "This was a little fancier shooting than Ed was accustomed to." Before Ed headed back north, Powell had some advice for him: "I told Ed he was making a mistake staying with NSFA. It didn't hold out a future large enough for his talents. I told him it was a dead end."[19]

Whether he took Powell's advice to heart or whether the same suspicions had already dawned on him, at some point in 1932, Ed decided that he needed a real profession. He was planning to enroll in the elite "dean's course" at Columbia Teachers College, which would prepare him to be an educator and, presumably, one day, a college president.

He never made it to Columbia. He went to work instead for Dr. Stephen Duggan.

Stephen Duggan was a former professor at the City College of New York. During the World War I, he had become convinced that the United States was dangerously insular. Thus, he had founded the International Institute of Education to encourage student exchange among the countries of the world. When Duggan wanted to impress foreign students with the growing sophistication of the U.S. student movement, he took them to NSFA headquarters to meet Ed Murrow.

By 1932, Stephen Duggan, then in his mid-sixties, was looking for an assistant and presumptive heir at IIE. When Murrow learned of the new position, the prospect of several more years of student poverty at Columbia Teachers College palled. He applied for the Duggan post. He was 24 but was always taken for older. Consequently, he added two years to his age when he applied for the job.[20]

At about the same time, he received another job offer, which, if his hankering for the woods and "real guys" was more than sentimental, he might have accepted. Bloedell-Donovan, on the recommendation of Ken Merredith, offered him a job running the company's Shanghai office at a salary double what IIE could pay.[21]

But Stephen Duggan chose Ed Murrow, and Ed Murrow chose IIE. In the fall of 1932, he resigned from NSFA, but remained an honorary member of the board, and went to work in the IIE offices in a loft on New York's West Side.

As a board member, he still attended the NSFA convention in New Orleans during the college Christmas break that year. He had, by then, two trips to Europe under his belt. He had soberly lectured American students on campuses across the country about their "political apathy and complacency." He was now no longer an unsalaried student leader but a professional in international education. Friends at the convention recall him at this period as modest except as one friend put it that, "He knew all there was to know about international affairs."[22]

CHAPTER 7

Janet

He was standing on the platform of the Greensboro, North Carolina, railroad station in the gray dawn of winter waiting for a train to take him to the convention in New Orleans. He had stopped on his way down from New York to visit his kin in Polecat Creek, the first visit since he was a child. Ed stayed with his Aunt Grace, his father's sister. He breakfasted on hot biscuits, did some hunting, and found his speech slipping comfortably into the cadences of the Piedmont. It had been a happy reunion. Aunt Grace's daughter, Nell, remembered her cousin Ed at the time, as "so handsome, so outgoing and lively."[1]

The train pulled into the Greensboro station, and Ed boarded a coach car. As he afterward liked to tell the story, he was coming down the aisle when he was struck by "a damn good-looking leg."

The legs belonged to the leader of student government at Mount Holyoke College in Massachusetts who was also en route to the NSFA conference. She was a 21-year-old senior, Janet Huntington Brewster. It was the first time that Ed had noticed Janet Brewster. But it was not the first time that she had seen Ed Murrow. Two years before, Ed had attended an international student conference at Mount Holyoke. A frustrated Janet had watched the proceedings from an auditorium balcony, since she was suffering from poison ivy, her face smeared with a garish purple permanganate. From her aerie she had observed the president of the NSFA in action on the floor. And she claimed that she did not like what she saw. As she later described the scene: "He was always surrounded by women. He looked like a very spoiled young man to me. He was just *too* perfect." Now, two years later, as the train pulled into Greensboro at 6 a.m., a sleepy Janet Brewster had pushed up the shade, and there on the platform stood Ed Murrow.

74

She was sitting with friends from Wellesley, Smith, and Vassar. Ed, as the recent NSFA president, moved down the aisle exchanging pleasantries. He talked briefly with her group, and as Janet remembered, they exchanged glances charged with a certain electricity.

When the train arrived in New Orleans, he invited her to meet him for breakfast the next morning. She was flattered and a little stunned. As she was to say later, "When I was that age, I saw myself as very unsophisticated. I'm not able to fathom why Ed chose me. I've never really known."[2]

There was one obvious reason. Janet Brewster was a beautiful young woman. Her features fell somewhere between the classical and the sensual. She had a full, contoured mouth with a hint of a beguiling smile in the corner. Her nose was long, straight, and patrician, her eyes thoughtful and intelligent. She had a glow about her, a freshness in her coloration, hair tinted a coppery brown, fair skin that retained traces of childhood freckles. She had a fine figure and moved with a serene carriage. Her demeanor was cool and contained. She could look, by turns, reserved yet desirable, or desirable but unapproachable.

At breakfast, Ed insisted, though it was midwinter, that Janet have fresh strawberries. Janet disliked strawberries. The price was exorbitant. But she liked the grandness of the gesture, and so she ordered them. On this first encounter, his appearance, his manner, the way he spoke, everything about him, led her to assume that he was from one of the Ivy League campuses, where all the boys she knew went to school.

The conference was to last five days. When Ed was not occupied making speeches, attending meetings, or otherwise promoting the interests of his new employer, he was with Janet. "The chemistry," she said, "was immediate." Still, apart from the strawberries, ardent courtship was not his style. Of their time together, Janet recalled, "We didn't go night-clubbing, or dancing. Ed didn't dance. We'd meet to have something to eat, or just have a cup of coffee together." Her girlfriends did not like what was happening. They had talked about Ed Murrow before, about what a conceited coxcomb he was, with women falling all over him. And here was Janet breaking ranks, taken in by his slick airs. They behaved, she said, "as though I had somehow betrayed them."[3]

Though Ed was seemingly everywhere at once and spending every free minute with Janet, he found time in New Orleans for an audience with Huey Long. He was still lining up speakers for the CBS educational series, and he may have been trying to schedule Long, who had just given up the Louisiana governorship to take his U.S. Senate seat. Ed wrote later of the encounter with Long, "He told me there might be smarter men than he was, but not in Louisiana."[4]

After the conference, Ed and Janet rode the train back north together. Ed had to get off at Nashville on IIE business. As she continued the journey alone, Janet Brewster accepted that "I was smitten, and I sensed that my life was about to change."

Janet Huntington Brewster was born in a rambling Victorian house in Middletown, Connecticut, descended on her father's side from Elder William Brewster, the spiritual leader of the Pilgrims aboard the Mayflower. Her father, Charles Huntington Brewster, was a handsome and amiable man, who had been something of a pioneer himself on a new American frontier. When the motorcar was young, before Detroit and the assembly line, when automobiles were virtually handcrafted in small factories around the country, Charles Brewster left the family farm to go to work for the Knox Motor Company of Springfield, Massachusetts. There he learned everything about an automobile from the crank to the tail lamp.

Knox treated its best customers with a solicitousness matching their investment. The company would dispatch young, personable Charles Brewster to spend as much time with the buyer as necessary, as much as a week, during which time he might even move in with the family as he helped them make the transition from horse and carriage to the automobile age. In time, Charles Brewster moved to Middletown and set up his own business. At the time Janet met Ed Murrow, her father owned the local Studebaker dealership.

Charles was the first of the Brewster line to wed outside of New England Yankee stock. He had married Jennie Johnson, the daughter of a Swedish immigrant. With New England bred into his bones, Charles gave little thought to what he was or where he came from. He knew. Jennie, on the other hand, was acutely conscious of what she had been and what she wanted to be. Her father did not even bear his own name. He was August Swan when he arrived in this country at the age of 14. He identified himself to the immigration authorities as August, John's son. And so he became August Johnson. The boy began laboring in the brownstone quarries around Middletown. He later owned a saloon for a time and ultimately accumulated a considerable amount of farmland. He was hardworking and genial, an effusive man who spoke with a lilting accent all his life. Janet loved him.

Of her parents, her mother was the stronger influence. "I always felt myself more Brewster than Johnson," she recalled, "mostly because of my mother's attitudes. She did not encourage me to ask questions about Grandfather Johnson's side, about his life in Sweden." And Jennie Brewster preferred to forget that her father had been a saloon keeper. "My mother would probably not approve of my saying that our background was fairly middleclass," Janet would later say. "My brother Dart and I were always expected to do the proper thing. My mother placed great emphasis on respectability and acceptance by the community. It meant a great deal to her to have both. Still, we did not move in exalted circles."[5]

A lifelong friend of Janet's, Catherine Atwater, later the wife of the economist John Kenneth Galbraith, recalled Janet as a child, "with red curls, freckles, fresh looking and beautiful." Of their high school years together, Kitty Galbraith remembered, "Everything that Janet was president of, I was vice president of. Janet was head of the debating society, the editor of the school magazine, a class officer. She was extremely well organized, efficient and very, very popular."[6]

She had hoped, after finishing high school, to go to the New England Conservatory of Music and train for a career as a concert pianist. Mrs. Brewster, however, wanted her daughter to go to college. Janet had an Uncle George, the organist at St. George's church in New York City, and the family decided to abide by Uncle George's verdict. Janet later told the story with characteristic frankness. "Uncle George came up for the weekend and I played for him. He said I would never be more than a good accompanist." And so she had gone to Mount Holyoke College and majored in sociology and economics.

She followed a familiar political trajectory for the time. Coming from solid, conservative Republican stock, she had found her social conscience awakened by her professors and became a campus activist and a Democrat. She hoped, ultimately, to go to New York City and become a social worker in the Henry Street Settlement House.

After the NSFA convention in New Orleans, Janet returned to Mount Holyoke for her final semester. Ed began writing to her and coming up to the South Hadley campus. He was, in the beginning, a reserved suitor. "Ed was not especially expressive in words, in a romantic sense," she remembered. After a while he began to open his letters to her as "Dear Hunka." Janet thought the name probably had something to do with her Swedish origins. It was the same Indian expression he had used years before with Willma Dudley.[7]

The two historic tides of the thirties, the Depression and fascism, were about to engulf Ed. Letters began pouring into IIE from students, no longer looking for opportunities to study abroad, but pleading for help just to stay in college. Out-of-work college professors haunted his office begging for job leads. The situation was about to be exacerbated by events abroad.

On January 30, 1933, Adolf Hitler became chancellor of Germany. Soon after, Ed wrote Janet with certain prescience, "If interested in the springboard for the next European war, get out a map and find Danzig at the mouth of the corridor. Last summer I flew up there from Berlin and spent a couple of days. The Polish munitions dump on the Werterplatte is bound to cause trouble, and it represents one of the many mistakes of this League of Nations, that august body that turned out to be merely an instrument of thinly veiled imperialism. It is shot through with intrigue even in its cultural cooperation work." It was hardly a love letter. She had fallen in love, she accepted, with a deadly serious man.[8]

Three months after Hitler took power, he told two German Catholic prelates at a private audience that he considered the Jews "nothing but pernicious enemies of the State." He intended, Hitler said, to drive them out "especially from academic life and the public professions." Josef

Goebbels, the führer's minister of propaganda, immediately began to realize Hitler's wish, dismissing Jews and political unreliables from German universities.[9]

Ed's boss, Stephen Duggan, called together a half-dozen high-level people to consider what America should do for the victims of Nazi academic thuggery. They formed the "Emergency Committee in Aid of Displaced German Scholars." Duggan named Ed the committee's secretary. "I was the youngster who did the donkey work," he would later say of his role.

Unemployed college professors were almost as common as out-of-work hod carriers in 1933. Five thousand American Ph.D.s were hunting for jobs. American universities were retrenching, not expanding. Yet the Emergency Committee set out to place refugee German-Jewish and anti-Nazi professors on American faculties. The solution the committee fixed on was not unlike the one Ed and Chet Williams had used to put well-heeled young ladies on the NSFA payroll. On behalf of the Emergency Committee, Ed approached American universities with a tempting proposition, a chance to have world-renowned scholars on their faculties in "honorary lectureships" at virtually no cost. Next, the Emergency Committee sought out private sources of money, wealthy Jews and Jewish organizations for the most part, to finance the honorary lectureships. Thus, the problem of foreigners competing against Americans for scarce teaching positions was circumvented. Ed would shop the list of available scholars around to American campuses. When he found a home for a scholar, he would then go before the Emergency Committee's finance board, made up mostly of Jewish intellectuals, and argue the case for a stipend to support the lecturer.[10]

He found himself emotionally caught up in the plight of the refugees, living out their dramas as though they were his own. He told once of escorting a scholar to CBS where the man was to give a radio talk. The cab driver suddenly hit the brakes at an intersection, flinging his passengers against the front seat. The refugee professor instantly dropped to the floor of the cab, waved toward a black car behind them, and said in a voice quaking with fear, "Someone is trying to stop me from speaking on the radio." The later Murrow broadcast style, he said, was influenced by this early involvement with the refugees. He once said, "That's when I learned to talk slowly, too, because some of them couldn't speak English very well."[11]

He always kept a copy of the *Meditations* of Marcus Aurelius on his desk. A friend asked why, and he answered that as he faced the despair of his age, it reassured him to think of that wise man thousands of years before wrestling with no less daunting challenges. In January of 1934, Ed drafted the first annual report of the Emergency Committee. He recalled how Greek scholars had been expelled from Byzantium in 1453 and settled in Italy where they helped to inseminate the Renaissance. Huguenots were driven from France to England, to England's profit and France's loss. The Jews' current plight at the hands of the Nazis was not new. They had been thrown out of Spain in 1492, and, as a consequence, some of the finest scholars, scientists, and mathematicians of the fifteenth century were scattered. Now the United States was about to become the beneficiary of this latest exodus of talent.

He was proud of his first semipublished piece of writing. He sent a copy of the report to Ida Lou Anderson and wrote on the cover: "This little statement outlines only in part a piece of work—the credit goes to my partner who gave me the power to do it. These German scholars are grateful—their gratitude should be to you."

By the time the committee had run its course and disbanded a few years later, 288 refugee academics and scientists had been placed. As Murrow had said, the clear winner was the United States. Paul Tillich, Otto Nathan, Kurt Lewin, Martin Buber, Hans J. Morgenthau, Jacques Maritain, Herbert Marcuse—all came to America through the Emergency Committee's efforts. The beneficiaries were American physics, American chemistry, American mathematics, American nuclear science.[12]

And another beneficiary was Ed Murrow. At an early age, he was thrown into intimate contact with some of the great minds of the era. The upheaval that had cast them up on America's shores placed Ed in a curious role reversal. They may have been giants in their own field and their own country, while he was a young and lightly educated man. But now they were aliens in an alien land, often not knowing the language, ignorant of customs and frightened for their futures. They looked to him to save them. They needed him. In their vulnerability, they clung to him the way an aged parent does to a grown son.

As Ed later described the experience: "My greatest educational debt is to Hitler. . . . The best education I ever received came from German professors who were flung out of German universities by Hitler." He had been a private pupil in a "revolving seminar." He told an interviewer, "Most of my time was spent with people twenty to forty years older than I was. They took me seriously and I guess I took myself pretty seriously." This episode was, he said, "the most satisfying thing I ever did in my life."[13]

Janet Brewster had graduated from Mount Holyoke in June of 1933. During her last semester, Ed came up often to see her. Her friends disapproved of the romance. However serious the inner man, the outward appearance was of a peacock. One outfit he favored was beige gabardine slacks, a Norfolk-style jacket, a brown shirt, and a canary yellow tie. He was too handsome, too smooth, too clever by half, her friends said. They did not trust him. Kitty Galbraith met Ed at about this time and remembered thinking "He was a bit old for Janet." Actually, he was only two years older. Janet would later say of her friends, "They looked upon Ed as terribly worldly and sophisticated, which actually he was not. The dean of the college was worried that this was not a friendship that was going to last. She and my friends all thought that he was just playing around and that he was going to break my heart."[14]

They were alike in one respect. Janet had the New England Yankee's natural reserve, the tight rein over her emotions that some saw as aloofness. Actually, she masked her insecurities behind this shield, the same device, essentially, that Ed had adopted. Consequently, there was between them little outward display of passion. They were both moved by strong undercurrents not visible on the surface.

Janet still wanted to go to work in the Henry Street Settlement House after graduation. But her mother did not want her living in New York, "a den of iniquity" by Jennie Brewster's reckoning. "At this point in my life," Janet said, "I would not buck my parents."

But there was another obsession bedeviling her. "I was stage struck," she later said. "I had to get it out of my system." She successfully auditioned for a place in a summer stock company in New London, New Hampshire. She moved up to better parts until, by the end of the season, she had the lead in Sidney Howard's *The Late Christopher Bean*. To her delight, Ed came up to New London with her brother Charles "Dart" Brewster to see her. After the play, Janet was showered with praise, and deservedly, since she clearly had talent. Ed, with his own acting background, had to know this. She waited eagerly for his reaction. He said nothing. They spent the next day together, having an otherwise delightful time. Still, she waited for him to say something about her performance. He went back to New York without saying a word. She was terribly hurt.

Shortly afterward, Janet abandoned the idea of a life in the theater. She tried to find a job as a social worker without success. She did ultimately find a position teaching freshman English and commercial law at the high school in Middletown. It was not what she wanted, but as she later explained, "You did not turn down jobs in the heart of the Depression." And so Janet went back home to live with her parents and teach school.

She was not to learn until some thirty years later, when Ed was a sick and dying man, why he had remained so painfully silent about her performance that night in New London. "He told me that he was afraid that if he told me how good I was that I wouldn't want to marry him."

Ed Murrow had fallen in love. He was a young man who, for all his outward suavity and confidence, was still wracked by self-doubts and subject to unshakable fits of depression. Janet possessed strength in places where he did not feel strong. She had a sense of self to counter his confusion about what he was, a steadiness to balance his mood swings, and her religious faith to counter his skepticism and pessimism. He had found the right woman.

Janet was also an authentic heir to one of the purest American lines. Her position in the American social spectrum was unassailable. Yet her actual circumstances were not so elevated that she was beyond his reach. And the Swedish immigrant strain added a nice democratizing touch. It was as if with her Ed could have it both ways, the Mayflower and Ellis Island. She had all the graces and virtues of her class, without a trace of snobbery. She was beautiful. She was strong. She was good. And he loved her. He wanted her for his wife, and he had not wanted to lose her to a career in the theater.

In the fall of 1933, he went to Middletown to see Janet. They borrowed her father's car, drove into the country, and he proposed. They came back to the house, and Ed told the Brewsters that he wanted to marry their daughter.

"My mother," Janet recalled, "was taken aback." Jennie Brewster had never been comfortable with Ed Murrow. He was too smooth, too self-assured. And she knew nothing about him. He came from a remote part of the country. She had never met any of his family. Charles Brewster, however, was not at all unhappy with the match. "He was not a worrier," Janet would say of her father, "and he wasn't worried about Ed."

The member of the family whom Ed liked best was Janet's grandfather. Here was a known quantity, an East Coast counterpart of the Swedish lumberjacks he had known on the Olympic Peninsula. August Johnson, ex-saloon keeper, teller of funny stories, unselfconscious, exuberant, and unvarnished, was Ed Murrow's kind of guy. The old man possessed the quality that he and Janet both envied but had disciplined out of their own make-up, an unaffected, unintellectualized joy in living.[15]

The couple planned to marry within a year. Ed had already written to his family about Janet. He telegraphed Ethel and Roscoe, "Your son, Edward, joyfully announces the acceptance by Janet Huntington Brewster of a personal permanent fellowship, providing room and tuition, from next summer till death do us part."

Now that the decision had been made, he became almost effusive by Murrow standards. He began addressing his letters to Janet, "Hello, Mrs. Edward R. Murrow." He displayed uncharacteristic flashes of playfulness, signing his letters with nonsense names. He told her that he was "practicing to be a swell husband." He seemed happily resigned to a domesticity predestined for young Manhattanites on the move. They would get married and live in town, he wrote. Then "when little Edward comes along, we'll move out to Long Island and I'll commute."

For a time, he became positively lyrical as he spoke of their future together. "Marriage," he wrote, "has always been and still is an extremely serious business for me, but I have unlimited confidence in us. So many people stop growing and expanding when they are married. We shall be the kind of people whom people will look twice at when we are 50—of whom our children may be proud. We shall make of our lives a real work of art....Above all there must be nothing cheap and nothing small in our lives. They must burn with a clear bright light. No matter what happens we will, like Cyrano, keep our white plume." He gave up a trip to Europe that year rather than be separated from Janet. "The next time I go abroad," he wrote, "you will be with me." During this period, deeply in love with Janet Brewster, he came as close to being happy and free-spirited as Ed Murrow was capable of being.[16]

He wrote to Ida Lou of his pending marriage. Her response was what it had been six years before. Wasn't he acting too hastily, before he had a chance to establish himself?

For all Ed's protestations that Ida Lou was merely his mentor and teacher, that she was a poor, crippled creature, Janet felt a natural apprehension about a woman who predated her and who was so obviously significant in the life of the man she loved. In order to end any misunderstanding, Ed wrote Janet, explaining Ida Lou's role: "She is very much a part of my life and always will be, but in a way that is hard to understand....I talked over in letters [to her] every decision. She knows me better than any person in the world....I owe the ability to live to her. And to her you owe the things you like in me."

Janet began corresponding with her future in-laws. The replies both amused and instructed her in the Murrow maternal prejudices. "Ed," according to his mother, Janet remembered, "was always the best. The best basketball player, the best debater, the best ROTC officer."[17]

Ed was loving. He was thoughtful. He was attentive. It was not, however, a mood that he could sustain permanently. Slowly, he began to unveil to her the darker chambers of his soul. He warned her that he was subject to episodes of black despair. Sometimes the moods seized him for no apparent reason. But his present work provided ample cause. The director of IIE's Berlin office had been thrown into a concentration camp. Fritz Beck, a harmless old man who ran a student hostel in Munich and, to Ed, "the best friend I had in Germany," was shot by the Nazis. Herr Probst, head of the German Catholic Youth Organization and another "very good friend of mine," was shot "while trying to escape." Some fifty appeals a day now poured into the IIE office from banished German scholars. For every established figure for whom he found a place on an American faculty, hundreds of lesser known, but no less desperate, people had to be turned away.

His congenital pessimism surfaced. His letters to Janet careened between the optimistic and the lugubrious. "It's really a pretty rotten world, isn't it?" he wrote his bride-to-be. "No one can look at what is happening without realizing that civilization is disintegrating and there are no standards left. Every one is lost and wandering in a thick fog...." In another letter he wrote, "I have no confidence in the future, and little pride in the past, feel no responsibility for posterity."

What must have been the reaction of a young woman of 23, deeply in love, soon to be married, on receiving a letter from her intended that read: "I've been sitting here trying to figure out what the years may hold for us. We have no money, and I have no profession, and on top of that I'm at heart a bum and a vagabond and will always be that way. For a very few short years we should be happy and then would come bitterness and thoughts of what might have been." In this marriage, Janet Brewster was apparently going to need all the strength of character that he saw in her.[18]

"A bum and a vagabond." It was a curious sentimental conceit existing no where but in his head. He was, in truth, an obsessive, compulsive achiever, constitutionally incapable of indolence. As for his complaint that "we have no money," as of October 1, 1933, Stephen Duggan raised him to $5,000 a year—this for a 25-year-old in the midst of the Depression when the median income for an American *family* was $1,231 a year. He was able to abandon his hole-in-the-wall on Patchin Place and take a smart apartment uptown. He had apparently impressed somebody in the new Roosevelt administration through his refugee work because, he wrote Janet, his name was "under consideration" as commissioner of immigration for the Port of New York. This post would have paid $7,500 a year.

IIE continued to bring him into association with the Eastern Seaboard power structure, where he continued to impress his elders with his capacity and precocity. He was elected to that bastion of the establishment, the Council on Foreign Relations, at an age when most of the members were old enough to be his father. He worked hard. He had earned what he had achieved. It may well have been "a pretty rotten world." But it was doing well by Ed Murrow.

Stephen Duggan believed that Americans, particularly educators, ought not to quarantine themselves from any regime and that the great god Education could eventually overcome any evil. Even with the brutal character of the Nazi regime revealed, IIE was still arranging educational exchanges with Germany. The night before Ed had to welcome a party of German students to New York, he wrote Janet, "I hope the fools don't arrive in brown shirts."[19]

The more ugly the Nazi regime became, the more appealing the Soviet Union looked to certain American intellectual soul seekers. To them, American capitalism had obviously failed the test of the Depression. Nazi Germany had certainly chosen the wrong path. The light now seemed to shine from Moscow. There was strong interest on American campuses in visiting Russia to see if the "future" that Lincoln Steffens wrote of really did work.

Stephen Duggan had long wanted to involve the Soviet Union in educational exchange. As early as 1925, Duggan had gone to Moscow and talked to Commissar Lunacharsky, the Soviet education chief. But the Russians were then distrustful.

However, by 1932, a thaw had set in. By 1932 the United States was preparing to grant recognition to the government that had ruled Russia for nearly fourteen years. In December, with Stephen Duggan's blessing, Ed began dealing with Soviet authorities to arrange a summer seminar at Moscow University where American students and teachers could learn about the Soviet Union. An advisory council of prestigious Americans was created to oversee the program. In the beginning, Ed tried to control the curriculum, to keep it academic and not propagandistic. But the Soviets proved both truculent and obstinate, and control began to pass into their hands. In 1933, a small group of Americans attended the first Moscow University seminar. The next year, 22 teachers and 212 students went to Russia. A third seminar was scheduled for 1935. NSFA was still the sponsor, and Ed was among those serving on the advisory board. Long years afterward, in the age of McCarthy, the whole affair would come back to haunt him.[20]

Ed and Janet were married on a Saturday, October 27, 1934. Janet's mother wanted a church wedding. But the Depression had hurt Charles Brewster's Studebaker dealership badly. "Life" said Janet "was not easy for my parents after that." Ever the practical Yankee, she insisted on a small wedding at home.

Ed waited upstairs in the Brewster's guest room for the ceremony to start. The Episcopalian minister who was to marry them came up to bolster him. The tense, pacing groom blurted out, "I'd give anything for a drink right now." When Ed came down, he related the incident to Janet's parents with a nervous laugh. Mrs. Brewster was not amused. She and her husband were both teetotalers.

It was a small affair with no more than twenty-five guests present, mostly Brewsters. One of them was Janet's cousin, Kingman Brewster, later president of Yale University. No member of Ed's family attended. As it turned out, Ethel Murrow never went to the weddings of any of her children. She did not travel, she said.

For their honeymoon, Ed wanted to show Janet his world, his North Carolina roots and the West. He asked Stephen Duggan for two months off. He had worked himself into a state of near collapse with the refugee committee, and so Duggan agreed. The lengthy trip was to become something of a pattern with him, exhausting stretches of work broken by long vacations that were something akin to a convalescence.

As they drove through the South, Janet noticed the changes coming over Ed. He became more relaxed, more reflective. He occasionally parted the curtain on his past. He told her stories about his boyhood, about the primitiveness of life in Beaver. Just as quickly he would close the curtain. "Life is over too fast to look backward," he said. "We have to look forward." She also noticed, as he talked to gas station attendants, waitresses, and hotel clerks en route, that he started slipping into a southern accent. It was to happen every time they visited the South.

They were passing through a then largely rural and impoverished country, and he told Janet something that spoke volumes about his sense of self and place. "He said that he could understand a country like Poland because it had been overrun, conquered, and dominated, the way the South had been by 'northerners' like me," she recalled.

He began to bring up something else, sometimes good-humoredly and sometimes with a biting edge. He would describe Janet to his relatives and friends as "a descendant of old Elder Brewster who did the praying when

the Mayflower encountered rough weather." He said it in the manner of
a down-home boy showing an earthy lack of reverence for high-falutin'
folk. Nevertheless, he had managed to make known Janet's pedigree.

They made a sentimental journey to New Orleans and then dipped
into Mexico, where Ed was laid low by the flu. It was Janet's introduction
to the weak lungs, inherited from his mother, that were to plague him all
through his life. She was rather surprised that the champion of international understanding and amity refused to let a Mexican doctor treat him.
They arrived at last in the state of Washington, drove north into the
Olympic Peninsula, and went on to Beaver.[21]

Janet met her in-laws for the first time. She found in Roscoe Murrow
the seed of the charm in his son. She liked the direct, unaffected communication between Ed and his father, the way they picked up as though
Ed had never left home. Roscoe appeared all but oblivious to the changes
that had taken place in his son's life. Ed asked his father what he thought
of Janet. And Roscoe answered, "You got better than you deserved."

Ethel Murrow remained throughout the visit, Janet recalled, "very
much the Southern lady." She was cordial, but not instantly accepting of
her new daughter-in-law. "I gathered," Janet remembered of that day,
"that I would have to work harder to please Mother Murrow." There was
still one more formidable hurdle for the bride. Ed telephoned Ida Lou
Anderson to tell her he was coming to Pullman. He and Janet arrived at
night and checked into a hotel. Janet was uneasy: "I had heard all about
her, and I knew she was in love with Ed."

Her anxiety was scarcely eased the next morning. Ed left Janet alone
and went off to see Ida Lou. "I stayed in the hotel by myself until late in
the afternoon," she remembered. When Ed did come back, it was to tell
her that they were going to Ida Lou's for dinner.

Ida Lou was coolly polite. After Ed introduced his bride, Ida Lou
seemed to forget that Janet existed. Throughout dinner, she fixed an ador-
ing gaze on Ed and chatted gaily with that marvelous voice of hers and
with what Janet recognized as an accomplished storyteller's art, reliving
moments from her and Ed's private past. Ed finally began to steal guilty
glances at Janet, as Ida Lou relentlessly ignored her. "It was one of those
evenings that one has to get through" Janet would later say.[22]

Ed and Janet were back in New York toward the end of 1934 and
found an apartment on the corner of Third Avenue and 68th Street. As
Ed put it, "The Third Avenue El came in one window and went out the
other." The racket became unbearable to him, and they soon moved to
another apartment in the same building but facing an inner court.

The honeymoon was over. Ed was again swallowed up in the lives of
his refugees. And he was not one to leave the tensions and frustrations of
the job at the office. He brought them home. He had forewarned Janet
about his moodiness, his emotional tailspins. And he proved as good as
his word. "Sometimes he would come home exhausted," Janet recalled,

"and he'd be gloomy and he wouldn't want to talk." At other times, he would blow up at her, because Janet did not appear to understand the fine points of some problem he faced at IIE.

They proved to be opposites in handling the stresses of everyday life. When Ed was in a bad mood, Janet took it that he was angry at her, rather than that she was the handiest target. "He'd get mad," she recalled, "and then I'd sulk. Then he'd get madder because I was sulking. I'd say 'better one of us should sulk while you're mad.'" To Janet, what Ed called "sulking" was "simply holding my temper." To Ed, his outbursts were merely "a way of letting off steam."

Part of the problem during this period of adjustment was Ed's associates. Ed and Janet had some friends their own age. They occasionally went to a movie or played golf. But Ed's life had become the refugee scholars. He worked with them all day and brought them home at night and weekends. His social and personal worlds blurred. Janet was 23 years old. Her own social life until now had largely been lived among friends from college and from Middletown. Overnight, she was plunged into his world, and she confessed to feeling "terrified of these renowned people."[23]

One of the most formidable was Dr. Alfred Cohn of the Rockefeller Institute of Medical Education, and a member of the Emergency Committee. Alfred Cohn was a research scientist in cardiology. He was also a man of protean interests and deep learning, an author on philosophy and American political traditions. Bill Paley's wife, Dorothy, also knew Cohn. As she described him, "He was white-haired, with glasses and a pouty mouth. A fussy dresser. He had a good sense of humor, but what I remember most about Alfred Cohn was the force of his views. And he expressed them with great power. He was a dominating personality, an intellectual giant, a fascinating man."

The Murrows were invited to the Cohn's apartment on Central Park West. They spent weekends at Iron Hill Farm, the Cohn's country place in Connecticut. An evening with Alfred Cohn meant involved examinations of the nature of democracy and the heart of truth, the deep, unfrivolous subjects of conversation that Ed loved. At Iron Hill, Ed met Alfred Cohn's closest friend, Felix Frankfurter, then on the Harvard law faculty, before Roosevelt appointed him to the Supreme Court. Through Frankfurter, Ed met Harold Laski, while the English Socialist was lecturing in the United States.[24]

These were the kinds of friends who entertained the Murrows and whom Ed expected to entertain in his home. And Janet was to be the hostess. She was overwhelmed. But since she had sublimated her own dreams to become Ed's wife, she was determined to make a success of her part. They gave frequent small dinner parties for half a dozen people. Janet would begin days in advance to plan them, making meticulous preparations for the dinner and subsequently becoming an excellent chef. But Ed ate whatever was put in front of him, his attention all the while fixed on his guests, oblivious of the effort Janet had invested in the success of the event. "I sat quietly and listened for the most part," she said of those evenings, "while they talked."

Still, she felt a tremendous pride in Ed and savored the excitement that he had brought into her life. Causes that she had supported in the abstract as a student activist came alive in her own living room. She was impressed by the way these eminent people accepted her young husband as an equal. She was touched most by his evident sympathy for the refugees, his immersion in their struggles, not as clients, but as fellow human beings on the same sinking boat.

He was a loner, an emotional mustang who needed to be broken to marriage. The clashes, the silences, the moods at times, made Janet wonder if the marriage was working. As she later confessed, "I thought I was the cause of his depressions." In truth, a woman of less steely determination would not likely have made a go of it. Being Mrs. Edward R. Murrow was not an easy role.

That first year of the marriage, Ed received a heady offer. He was known, through his travels, to virtually hundreds of college officials. He was 26, with only a B.A. degree, and he was offered a college presidency. Granted, the school was small, Rockford College, a women's institution in Illinois. Still, the post would mark his arrival as a professional educator. He was about to accept when the offer was withdrawn. He again had tacked 2 years onto his age in applying for the job, and years later, he described what happened: "The ladies hadn't pursued their investigation far enough to learn how young I was, or to find out that I didn't have some of the qualifications they thought I had. When they did find out, the whole thing fell through."

The rejection marked a turning point. Until now, he had assumed that, one way or another, he would continue to be connected to education. With NSFA he had been a student politician and organizer. He had for a time considered becoming a proper educator at Columbia Teachers. At IIE he had plunged into the lives of other academics. But he was always on the margin, not really an educator or an academic himself any more than a concert hall manager is a musician. He had been rather successful without the scholar's union card. He had dealt on equal terms with people possessing far more scholarly baggage than himself. As he later reflected, after the Rockford offer fell through, "That got me thinking that there was no future for me in the world of scholarship because I didn't have the credentials." What he did not mention was another discovery, that while he had started as the heir presumptive at IIE, Stephen Duggan was proving to be an old man jealous of his prerogatives and possessed of great staying power. Ed was dead-ended again. The solution, he thought, might be a few blocks away from IIE, at 485 Madison Avenue. As he later put it, "I heard that CBS was looking for somebody to work on education and that seemed to be the answer."[25]

CHAPTER 8

An Empire Built on Air

When Ed Murrow first considered entering broadcasting, the medium was young. Only fifteen years had passed since the first serious commercial radio station had gone on the air. The concept had been divined centuries before, in a prophetic and intuitive leap, by Joseph Granvill, chaplain to Charles I of England. "The time will come," Granvill had written in 1661, "and that presently, when by making use of the magnetic waves which surround our world, we shall communicate with the Antipodes." The clergyman's timing was a few centuries off, but his physics were remarkably knowing.

Radio fever swept America. On the night that Ed Murrow was born, Professor W.C.A. Hammel was up in the county seat of Greensboro demonstrating the miracle of radio by sending a transmission right through the walls of the public library. All over the country, mechanically inclined kids were filing down nickels to make their own "coherers," winding wire around anything cylindrical, oatmeal boxes, tin cans, baseball bats, to make their own coils. They set up their equipment in attics, alleys, and woodsheds and talked to each other. Radio clubs sprang up in schools and colleges. The hobbyists spoke a private language of crystals, diodes, condensers, and wavelengths much the way a later generation would run on about computers. So profuse were these amateurs that the babel threatened to jam transmissions to ships at sea. In 1912, the federal government had to come in and regulate radio.

Harold Powers, a former Tufts College student and radio missionary, contrived to have himself hired as the wireless operator on J.P. Morgan's yacht, the *Corsair*. Young Powers so intrigued Morgan with his ideas for turning radio to profit that the financier gave him $25,000 to start his own business. Powers then talked Tufts into letting him put up a transmitter on land the college owned. He enlisted the Tufts radio club to run what he called "The American Radio and Research Corporation," and in 1915 he was broadcasting news and music from phonograph records. But World War I diverted Powers from commercial radio to the Army Signal Corps, and his transmitter went silent.

Harry P. Davis was neither scientist nor tinkerer but a Westinghouse Electric vice president. Davis saw in radio, not limited sales of elaborate equipment to ocean liners and the U.S. Army, but a potential mass market for a future Westinghouse product, a simple radio for everyone. As a lure, he decided to offer prospective customers something more attractive to listen to than radio amateurs relaying baseball scores from one backyard to another.

Davis built a 100-watt transmitter on the roof of a Westinghouse building in Pittsburgh. In 1920, the transmitter went on the air, licensed by the Department of Commerce as KDKA, Pittsburgh. KDKA's broadcast of the Harding-Cox election that year serves, as well as any other milestone, to mark the arrival of commercial broadcasting in America. Within a year, the federal government licensed seventy-six more stations. And Westinghouse offered an easy-to-assemble kit within almost everyone's financial reach, the kind that Ed Murrow's Uncle Terry Coble had put together in Blanchard. Radio hobbyists no longer needed to wrap wire around oatmeal cartons.

A rich vein had been opened. New entrepreneurs began to work it, and none more assiduously than an immigrant Russian Jew who had come to America at age 9 from a cluster of wooden huts in Russia called Uzlian. By the time David Sarnoff was 21, he had already earned a footnote in radio history. It was a day in April in 1912. Sarnoff was then the American-Marconi Company's best telegraph operator, with a famed and instantly recognized fist. Sarnoff was working in a wireless room on the roof of Wanamaker's Department Store in New York City, communicating with the company's Philadelphia operation. From somewhere over the North Atlantic, he picked a faint signal out of the ether, "*SS Titanic* ran into iceberg, sinking fast." Sarnoff became the sole link between the dying ship and the world. A nation hung on him as he spent seventy-two straight hours taking down the names of survivors transmitted from the rescuing *SS Carpathia*. Nine years later, Sarnoff was president of his own Radio Corporation of America, into which he had absorbed his former employer.

Like Harry Davis, Sarnoff saw radio as a market. But he went one step beyond Westinghouse and offered, not a kit, but an assembled, ready-to-play radio. He priced his first model at $75, and in 1922 sold over $10 million worth. The next year, sales more than doubled. The following year RCA sold almost five times as many radios as in the first year.

With no great interest in broadcasting itself, Sarnoff backed into the business as a way to generate demand for his product. He made deals with existing radio stations to provide them programming from a central source. He had created a radio network, the National Broadcasting Company.

Even the Depression could not kill radio. Indeed, radio thrived on hard times. Legions of the unemployed were at home with time heavy on their hands. Competition among new manufacturers continuously drove down the price of a radio. Installment buying made a receiver available virtually for pennies a week. Here was music, entertainment, sports, and news at one's fingertips, without the listener having to leave the house or spend a dime. A new piece of furniture, as ubiquitous as a Morris chair, appeared in American living rooms—big, handsome, wood-encased sets bearing company names like Philco, Atwater Kent, and Zenith.

Nothing before had knit America together as closely as network radio. The railroads, the automobile, and aircraft all shrank distance and time, and thus gave the country a physical unity. But radio gave America unprecedented cultural unity. Books, the theater, newspapers, and magazines had not been able to achieve such swift, all-encompassing homogenization. Only the movies came close, and yet ran a distant second as a social unifier. Films lacked the rapidity and reach of radio in stamping new features on the country's cultural landscape. Radio created fame with the speed of sound. A voice, a personality, could become as known, within weeks, as one's next-door neighbor. Instant heroes, idols, phrases, products, jokes, expressions, and slogans formed a pool of shared knowledge, a reflecting pool in which Americans saw a common identity. Before this phenomenon, communities were still somewhat culturally atomized. No such swift highway had ever linked them before. With network radio, the era of mass culture, of universal if passive experience, for good or ill, or rather for good and ill, had arrived.

On a March evening in 1933, Ed and Janet, along with millions of Americans, heard Franklin Delano Roosevelt, in the eighth day of his presidency, address the country over the radio. His remarks were not billed as a speech. The occasion was rather like Dad sitting down in the living room, assuring an anxious family that in spite of hard times, everything was going to be all right. Before this "fireside chat," White House mail had been handled by a single employee. After the broadcast, a half million pieces of mail piled up in the White House corridors, and shifts of employees had to be hired to process the deluge.

As the media historian, Eric Barnouw, put it, radio achieved "a loyalty that seemed almost irrational. According to social workers, destitute families that had to give up an icebox or furniture or bedding still clung to the radio as a last link with humanity. What did it all mean? Perhaps, as a later observer, Marshall McLuhan, put it, "a new 'tribal unity' was being forged by nationally distributed voices."[1]

William S. Paley had gone into radio seven years before Ed Murrow began thinking about going to work at CBS. Both men had been born around the aroma of tobacco, Murrow from the few acres of the leaf that his father planted on that unloved North Carolina farm, and Paley from his family's cigar business. There, all similarity in their origins ended.

Bill Paley was the son of a Russian immigrant father, Samuel Paley, who came to America at age 13 from Russia. Bill Paley's paternal grandfather, Issac Paley, had settled in Chicago early in the 1880s with his family. Issac Paley had imagined a life of leisure, of sipping coffee around the samovar and conversing with his friends. He soon lost his money in bad investments, and since he held labor beneath him, it fell to Sam and his brothers to pursue a life of work and self-denial while their father continued to enjoy his leisure.

In 1896, Sam Paley, then only eight years in the United States, turned 21, became an American citizen, and made his first million dollars in the cigar business. Soon after, he married 16-year-old Goldie Drell. Their first child, William, was born a year later, on September 28, 1901.

Sam Paley was a short, black-mustachioed dynamo with piercing eyes and boundless energy, a man so consumed by the pursuit of success that his son never felt close to him during the years in which the boy was growing up. Sam Paley remained a remote, idealized figure. "To me," Paley would later say, "my father was a genuine hero."

While the insecure Bill was growing up, Sam Paley joined forces with his brothers and formed the hugely successful Congress Cigar Company. In a play on the family name, their product was the "La Palina" cigar.

The Paleys were shrewd businessmen, but evidently not model employers. In 1919, when Bill Paley was 18, Samuel Gompers called a strike against Congress. The Paley brothers outflanked the strikers in a simple maneuver. They picked up and relocated their business in Philadelphia.

There, young Bill attended the University of Pennsylvania's Wharton School of Finance. By his own admission, Paley was half student and half playboy. He studied enough to get by, no more. He had matured into a polished, impeccably dressed young man, well-mannered and possessed of quiet charm.

Bill Paley learned that there were things his money could not buy, notably, an exemption from anti-Semitism. It was odd that he should have to pay a price for his Jewishness since he wore it so lightly. The Paleys did not deny that they were Jews. They barely noticed it. Young Paley experienced double discrimination on an Ivy League campus, from WASP patricians and the Jewish aristocracy, the *hochjuden*, German Jews who looked down on Jews whose roots were in the muddy shtetls of Russia and Poland. At Penn, Bill Paley settled for a Jewish fraternity, which a former college official rated socially as "B" grade. But he would be first, even if not of the best. Paley became his fraternity's president.

The young man who graduated from Wharton in 1922 was well liked but not taken seriously by his teachers or friends. He was a delightful enough companion, with a taste for pleasure, a way with women, and the money to indulge himself. He had quicksilver interests, as intense and brief as infatuation, but he had no particular direction. And so after college, he did what was expected of him; he went into his father's firm.

By that point, his unquestioning idolization of his father was no more. He had recognized the psychological loop in which Sam Paley was trapped. He had watched as Sam repeatedly put off pleasure and leisure until another deal was concluded, until another million was made, with the cross-bar raised higher every time Sam cleared it, in an endless, winless competition with himself.

When he was 18, Bill Paley had vowed that by the time he was 35 he was going to be independently rich, retire, and live what his grandfather had only half achieved, a life of leisure sustained by wealth. But for now he was working for Congress Cigar. Three years later, he was vice president, advertising manager, and secretary of the company, his salary approaching $20,000 a year. He appeared set on a course as inevitable as the rise of an elevator, a steady climb abetted by retirements and deaths, to the top of the company.

He worked hard and played hard. He was as much apprenticed to that anticipated life of pleasure as to the tobacco business. He liked to gamble, to drink in the poshest speakeasies, to make the nightclub circuit and date showgirls. He combined business trips to the international tobacco markets in Amsterdam with pleasure jaunts to Paris, where he frequented Bricktop's in Montmartre and envisioned himself as part of the twenties legend, an American in Paris.

He returned from one of these journeys with a $17,000 Hispano Suiza. Bill Paley felt oddly ambivalent about the stares that the car drew and wrote in his autobiography, "...one of the paradoxes of youth, at least mine, was that I wanted an attention getting object without the attention. It may be that I haven't changed much in that respect in the last fifty years." And indeed he would continue to be a collector of inanimate and animate objects all his life, following a pattern of early excitement, fading interest, and ultimate disposal.

In the mid-twenties, Sam Paley and his brother Jake went on a business trip to Europe, leaving Bill in charge of the company. Young Bill seized the chance to take a modest flier. Radio was in its emergence, and Bill had become entranced by the current fad. With the senior Paleys gone, he tells how "I bought an hour program to advertise La Palina cigars on the local station, WCAU. Cost? The munificent sum of $50 per broadcast. But when they returned, my uncle upon going over the books immediately spotted the new expenditure. 'What kind of foolishness is this?' he demanded. 'Cancel it right now.' Reluctantly, I followed instructions."

A few weeks later, Bill's father was puzzled. "Hundreds of thousands of dollars we've been spending on newspapers and magazines," he said, "and no one has ever said anything to me about those ads, but now people are asking me 'What happened to the La Palina Hour?'" The gimlet-eyed uncle sheepishly agreed that he too had faced the same question.

Paley's next venture in radio involved a family friend, a rich and successful Philadelphia building contractor, Jerome Loucheim. Loucheim, also a radio buff, had bought the controlling interest in a small, floundering radio network, United Independent Broadcasters (UIB). He asked Sam Paley to advertise La Palina cigars over the network.

This time Bill's judgment was accepted, and the family allowed him to invest a hefty $6,500 a week in the "La Palina Smoker," a fast-paced half hour of dance music, vocals by "Miss La Palina," and comic repartee between the singer and patrons of the imaginary "smoker." Producing this program was more pleasurable than anything Bill Paley had ever done in his life, certainly more satisfying than peddling cigars.

UIB had been started almost out of pique by Arthur Judson, a concert impresario who believed he had been shabbily treated by David Sarnoff at NBC. The small network had skirted the edge of disaster ever since its maiden broadcast in 1927. Among UIB's in and out backers was the Columbia Phonograph Company. Thus, UIB had first gone on the air as the Columbia Phonograph Broadcasting System. When the record company pulled out its investment, the UIB network became simply the Columbia Broadcasting System.

Two events were to transform Bill Paley from a cigar maker into a broadcaster. Within ten months of acquiring CBS, Jerome Loucheim was back to the Paleys, this time not looking for advertising, but trying to unload a loser. The sixteen-station network was at one point losing $20,000 a week. CBS owed over a million dollars to AT&T to rent the lines to transmit its programs to its affiliates. Loucheim admitted that he had bought a lemon. He asked his friend Sam Paley to take it off his hands. Loucheim, who had made his millions building bridges and subways, argued, "Sam, you at least have a cigar to advertise." Sam Paley had no interest in moving from cigars to lemons, but his son Bill was fascinated by the prospect.

The second event that was to transform Bill Paley's life also occurred in 1927. His family sold the controlling shares in Congress Cigar to the Porto Rican-American Tobacco Company. Under the deal, Paley's father and his uncle received five-year employment contracts to continue managing the company. Bill did not receive a contract. The sale, however, made him a rich man. When he had first gone to work for Congress, he had been given a block of stock, which meant little to him at the time. The sale of the stock to Porto Rican-American left him with over a million dollars and without a job.

It was just as well. By now Miss La Palina had utterly seduced Bill Paley. He loved radio. He far preferred associating with writers, artists, and musicians than tobacco barons. And so with his father's wary permission, he took his new-found freedom and his million dollars, and, "a bit in awe of him," went to see Jerome Loucheim about buying the Columbia Broadcasting System. He came away with a controlling 50.3 percent of stock costing him $503,000. In accepting Loucheim's price, which instantly cut his personal fortune by half, Paley remembered, "I did not blink an eye."

On September 25, 1928, three days before his twenty-seventh birthday, at a time when Ed Murrow was entering his junior year of college, Bill Paley was elected president of the CBS network. It was, in his own description, "a patchwork, money-losing little company." Nevertheless, he was as excited as a child with a scandalously expensive toy. The acquisition also included an intangible asset. It took Bill Paley out of Philadelphia, which now bored him, and to New York, which he had come to love.

He took over a network by now composed of twenty-two affiliates, sixteen employees, and a four-room suite of offices in the Paramount Tower in Manhattan. He was so youthful-looking that the first time he arrived at the company, the office boy would not let him in.[2]

What was this *thing*, a radio network, that he had bought? It was an abstraction, really. It was a sheaf of contracts with independent radio stations under which CBS agreed to provide them with programs over leased telephone lines. Between the cost of producing the programs and leasing the lines, the network Paley had acquired was awash in red ink.[3]

The staff soon saw a tough entrepreneur beneath the playboy sheath. NBC was then the Goliath of network broadcasting and CBS the David. NBC had over fifty affiliates, including the country's largest radio stations. CBS had less than half that number, mostly small stations. NBC had strong financing. CBS had debts. CBS stood alone. NBC was part of David Sarnoff's Radio Corporation of America, which in turn was linked to AT&T, the General Electric Company, and Westinghouse in a cartel-like behemoth that found CBS about as menacing as a flea. But Bill Paley studied the way NBC conducted the radio business and thought he spotted Sarnoff's Achilles' heel.

In those early days, local radio stations were usually on the air from eight in the morning until midnight. Most were lucky if they could sell three of those sixteen hours to advertisers. The rest of their programming was "sustaining," that is, unsponsored. And whatever the station put on the air during the unsponsored hours, music, entertainment, news, speakers, was at its own expense.

NBC's arrangement with its affiliates gave the local stations a certain independence. When NBC had a nationally sponsored program to transmit, an affiliate could take it and share the advertising income with the network, or leave it and stick with its own programming, if more lucrative. Thus, NBC could never guarantee that it could deliver the full network to an advertiser. As for the unsponsored programs that NBC provided, if the stations took them, they paid for them.

Paley saw his opening. He wired station owners all over the Eastern Seaboard and invited them to the Ambassador Hotel in New York to hear Bill Paley's deal. It sounded irresistible. CBS would provide its programs *free* to its affiliates. Instead of putting out their own money to hire local bands, singers, monologuists, and actors, the affiliates had only to throw a switch and receive, for nothing, talent of national stature from CBS. In return, Paley expected a guarantee. Whenever CBS had sponsored programming, the affiliates would have to take it. Advertising fees would be split, with the network getting about 70 percent and the affiliates the rest. Here was a clear difference between the fledgling and the giant. NBC could never assure its sponsors of a full network. Bill Paley could guarantee to prospective advertisers that *all* his stations would carry their commercials.

For local stations the Paley plan was virtually a no-lose proposition: free programming for their sponsorless hours and handsome fees for any sponsored network shows they carried. All they had to do to make money, virtually, was stay on the air.

But who was this boy singing this siren song? His aides quietly made known that Bill Paley came out of the Congress Cigar fortune. And they all knew about Congress Cigar.

They rushed to sign on. Before the day was over, the CBS network had grown from twenty-two affiliates to forty-seven. A cycle was set in motion. The expansion made CBS attractive to advertisers. And the more advertisers CBS obtained, the more affiliates wanted to join the network. Virtually overnight, Bill Paley turned the dying infant into a robust youth. In the first year of his stewardship, CBS's gross earnings grew from $1.4 million to $4.7 million. By 1935, the network had ninety-seven affiliates, more in fact than NBC, although they comprised less total wattage. But Paley had lured major stations out of NBC's orbit into his own—WJR Detroit, KBL Salt Lake City, WRVA Richmond.[4]

Paley moved from four rooms in the Paramount Towers to four floors in a new building rising at 485 Madison Avenue. He opened the new CBS headquarters on September 18, 1929, with President Herbert Hoover delivering a message of good wishes and with Miss Radio cutting the ribbon across the doorway.

Few men have been better mated to their time and place than Bill Paley. He lured to CBS Paul Whiteman's orchestra; Will Rogers, who said he would never work on radio; Kate Smith; and the Mills Brothers. He signed Bing Crosby, Fred Allen, and George Burns and Gracie Allen in those early years.

He was now hobnobbing with the haut monde, the very people who a few years before would have looked clear through this first-generation, new-moneyed cigar maker's son without even seeing him. Averell Harriman became his friend. In the early thirties they traveled together in Europe, duck hunting in Hungary, gallery hopping in Paris. Harriman took Bill around to the stylish Parisian art dealers. Paley bought his first Cezanne, and then began adding other Impressionists.[5]

When he was 31 and one of the most eligible bachelors in America,

Bill Paley fell in love. The woman was a dark-eyed, porcelain-skinned beauty, with quick intelligence, a lively curiosity, and a sharp eye for the world around her. And she came from the socialite background that Paley revered. The only problem—that she was a Christian was a plus, not a problem—was that she was married to Paley's friend John Randolph Hearst. Within a year, Dorothy divorced John Hearst and married Bill Paley.[6]

He had by now acquired a double persona. In his social circle, he was warm, affable, and witty, a good friend and a sought-after companion. In his professional life, he was charming and agreeable too, until crossed. And then his colleagues and competitors discovered the granite beneath the silk. The eyes twinkled warmly when he was pleased and glared icily when he was unhappy—the shift occurring with terrible swiftness. He kept his private and professional lives separate. As he described his philosophy, "I could see the dangers of socializing with my office associates... who were so important to me in the development of CBS. This separation was more or less understood and accepted at CBS and became a long-standing way of life for me." He went on to say, "I have had very few intimates.... I do not like the idea of depending on others. I don't feel safe. When I find myself becoming dependent on one particular person, I start to worry about what would happen if he or she were no longer there, about who would take his or her place." Here was self-centeredness on a stunningly honest plane.[7]

Bill Paley, by his thirty-fifth birthday, was the rich man he had sworn to be, indeed far richer than in his wildest imaginings. This was the age at which he promised himself that he would not become another Sam Paley, that he would live not for work but stop working and start living. But as his network grew, as he garnered one hit program after another, as he continued to close in on NBC, as his influence and wealth brought him into intimate association with the most powerful figures of his time, no life of leisure could begin to compete with the pleasure he took simply in going to work in the morning.

It was to this man's world that Ed Murrow was now drawn. Ed had learned about the CBS opening from Fred Willis, the man for whom he had secured Albert Einstein and other notables for the *University of the Air*.

Willis carried out a ragbag of public affairs jobs at the network—government relations, public relations, educational programming. The bands and singers, the radio dramas, and the comedy shows—the sponsored part of the schedule—paid the bills and made the profits. But most of the network's schedule was still unsponsored public affairs. The quality of this programming gave the network its tone, and Bill Paley savored tone along with profits. Testifying before the FCC in the early thirties, Paley proudly pointed out that CBS devoted "approximately seventy five-percent of our time on the air to public service as contrasted with sponsored programming."

The network thus had a voracious appetite for speakers to fill the hours devoted to public affairs. Willis had more or less carried out the speaker function with his left hand, helped by people like Ed Murrow. CBS now needed someone full-time to concentrate on educational programming, a "director of talks," a title borrowed from the BBC. Willis knew of Murrow's abilities and wanted him to take over the expanded talks program, so that he could get on with his own climb up the CBS ladder. Ed was interested, but did not immediately leap at the opportunity. He knew that he was dead-ended at IIE. But he was also secure. And his work with the refugees had become a personal matter. He had IIE business in Europe over the next few months, and the trip offered the opportunity to fulfill his promise to take Janet to the Continent. Though Willis was urging him to come to CBS, Ed postponed making a decision until after his return from Europe.[8]

He and Janet were still counting every penny. They found jobs as social directors on the Dutch liner *Statendam,* organizing Ping-Pong and bingo games and bridge tournaments. Thus the trip was to cost them nothing. They sailed on June 25, 1935.

Amidst the IIE work, the refugee work, and sightseeing with Janet, he found time to visit the CBS London office where he met an elfin, rather self-important man named Caesar Saerchinger. For someone with Murrow's taste, Saerchinger's job looked like the dream job at CBS. He was the network's representative for Europe.

Ed and Janet flew from London to Paris, her first airplane flight. They journeyed to Compeigne and saw the railroad car in which Germany had surrendered to the Allies. A plaque at the site read: "Here on the 11th of November 1918 succumbed the criminal pride of the German empire vanquished by the free nations which it tried to enslave." Janet wrote in her diary, "If I were a good German, a thing like that would whip up my fighting spirit."

They went to Germany next and found its fighting spirit indeed whipped up, which proved not a pleasant spectacle. Berlin was supposed to be the high point of the journey. To Ed, Europe's future would be determined by what was then happening in the German capital. Three years had passed since his last visit, and an era as well. Fast disappearing was the Berlin of high culture and low cabaret comedy. Gone was the city of tumult and energy, of alternating chaos and creativity. In its place he found a chilling order, a strutting, jut-jawed, self-satisfaction. Berlin was awash with uniforms, black for the SS, olive green for the Reichswehr, blue-gray for the Luftwaffe, brown for the crude proletarians of the SA. Berlin was a bully spoiling for a fight. Berlin was frightened professors sneaking up to the Murrows' hotel room late at night, begging Ed to help them get out of Germany and into America. "Berlin," Janet wrote in her diary, "was too many swords and daggers, too many Heil Hitlers." The visit was a disappointment and an omen. A few weeks after they left

Germany, the Nuremberg laws went into effect robbing German Jews of full citizenship.[9]

By September Ed was back in New York. The talks job was still open at CBS. Willis was still eager for Murrow to take it. But the man he had to see first was Ed Klauber.

Edward Klauber was the second most powerful man at CBS. Of him his colleagues would variously say, "Nobody dared look him straight in the eye." "I never felt comfortable using his first name." "Mr. Klauber was not given to smiling." "He was one of the three cruelest men I have ever known." "He would discipline a subordinate by putting him with ten other associates, then berate him in front of the others." "He liked to pull the wings off insects, metaphorically." "He enjoyed firing people."[10]

Ed Klauber had been a brilliant, prickly night city editor at *The New York Times* and later served briefly as an unlikely public relations man before coming to CBS in 1930. His sponsor, the public relations pioneer, Edward Bernays, had leveled with Paley. Here, in some ways, was a perfectly dreadful man, but a massively able man, capable of prodigies of effort. Of their first encounter, Paley later wrote: "I almost passed him by. When he first came to the office, I saw a short, heavy-set, taciturn man who walked with his hands behind his back, Napoleonic style, and who at 43, seemed to me an old man." Klauber was not the sort of person whom suave, social, Bill Paley wanted around him.

Yet Paley, no detail man, desperately needed someone to relieve him of the joyless administrative side of his business. He finally hired Ed Klauber as "Assistant to the President." A less flattering account of the hiring, whispered about the CBS corridors, had it that "Bill Paley's father picked Klauber to look after sonny boy when he came to New York."

Like lava swallowing up everything in its path, Klauber began relieving Paley of one thankless duty after another, enlarging his own domain along the way. "He was an indefatigable, day and night worker," Paley said of Klauber, "always keeping in touch with me, providing me with written reports and eventually becoming my adviser on everything."

It was, while it lasted, a useful union. The king required charisma. And Paley had it. His executioner did not have it and did not need it. Paley dispensed charm. Klauber dispensed fear and pink slips. Paley wooed sponsors. The abrasive Klauber was kept out of their sight. Klauber was exactly what Paley needed, yet did not care to play himself: the heavy in the corporate drama.

But the gritty chores Ed Klauber performed for Bill Paley were the least part of him. What he deserves to be remembered for was his seminal role in the maturation of broadcast journalism, a role that unfolded along with the Murrow story.

Klauber lacked the knee-jerk contempt for radio news exhibited by most journalists of the time, a disdain then largely deserved. Radio did not even pretend to serious news coverage. It was an era when announcers finished reading their news summaries with: "For further details read your daily newspaper." But Klauber sensed in this new medium not a lesser but a potentially different form of journalism. He believed that radio could be made something more than a music box and an aural billboard. And so among the CBS operations that he enfolded into his embrace was the network's public affairs broadcasting, which included the news.

When he interviewed Ed Murrow, Klauber was 48 years old. Everything about the man was heavy, his thick-waisted body, his bulging jowls and unsmiling lips, his manner, his speech. His words came in an intimidating growl, occasionally lowered to a hoarse whisper.[11]

Klauber's first choice for the talks job had been a much admired broadcaster, Raymond Swing. Swing had made one of the early conversions from print journalism to the air. But Klauber, for all his devotion to reporting, also recognized radio as a sound medium, and the voice that issued from Swing's lips displeased him. He could solve two problems at once by getting Swing off the air and into the talks job. But when Swing learned that the job involved no broadcasting, he turned Klauber down. Swing thereafter took his first-rate commentaries and second-class voice to the Mutual Network.

When Klauber interviewed Murrow, he took pains to explain that the job was not an on-the-air one. Murrow was not dissuaded. He still saw himself as essentially an educator.

There was a rare rapport between the two men. Klauber's baleful gaze, his gruff speech, his abruptness, did not intimidate Ed. Klauber had encountered what the bully instantly respects, someone who will not be bullied. They discovered common ground. Klauber, under his harsh exterior, was an idealistic New Deal Democrat. He worshipped President Roosevelt. So did Ed Murrow. The ogre that others described disappeared, and Klauber began speaking in a comfortable, conversational tone. Ed sensed in Klauber another older, able figure like those who had served him as friend, mentor, and teacher in the past, another Ken Merredith, Earl Foster, Stephen Duggan, Alfred Cohn. The two men liked each other.[12]

Murrow was 27 at the time he was interviewed by the Columbia Broadcasting System. When he had been under consideration for the Rockford College presidency, Ed had added two years to his age. This time he added not two years, but five years. He presented himself not as a speech major, but as a political science and international relations major in college. He claimed to have studied at the more impressive University of Washington, in addition to Washington State, though it is difficult to imagine that this fine distinction would have meant much in the East. And he claimed an M.A. from Stanford University. Searchers of the files of the University of Washington and Stanford reveal no evidence of his attendance at either institution.

Why? Ed Murrow would go on to carve a reputation as the premier broadcast journalist of his time. At the heart of his work was an indestructible integrity. A distaste for sham and pretense marked his entire life. The core of his character, attested to by virtually everyone who knew him, was incorruptibility, an honesty as reliable as true north on a compass. Why then these early exaggerations and inventions? Why did someone who almost invariably impressed people without trying try at this point to impress them?

Clearly, there was in him a lingering insecurity. He still harbored a suspicion that what he came from was not good enough for what he wanted. Both with NSFA and IIE, his college travels had sensitized him to the snob factor in education. He had learned from the Rockford experience, and from living in New York, that cauldron of ambition, that people indeed played the status game. He was thus unsure that his youth and cow college credentials qualified him for the league in which he wanted to play.

The second reason for hyping his résumé, a reason only superficially in conflict with the first, was his confidence in himself. He lacked faith in his background more than in Ed Murrow. He had succeeded in everything he had turned his hand to, even with his modest credentials. He had been entrusted with heavy responsibilities by men every bit as able to judge his mettle as Ed Klauber. And he had always performed superbly. He moved easily among older people, including figures of world reputation. He had made friends of them, as well as colleagues. And so he employed a self-serving rationale. He knew that he could do the job. And he would say whatever he had to say so that he would not lose this opportunity simply because he lacked on pieces of paper what he knew he possessed in his mind, his heart, and his spirit.

Ed Murrow was hired and, in late September of 1935, took up his duties at 485 Madison Avenue as the CBS director of talks.[13]

CHAPTER 9

A CBS Apprenticeship

Helen Sioussat went to work for Ed Murrow seven months after he became the CBS director of talks. Her perceptions of him remained, long afterward, vivid and acute.

At the time of their first encounter, Sioussat was 34 years old, a Baltimorean of genteel southern breeding from a family in which women simply did not work. Sioussat, however, also had an independent streak and had worked at everything from college president's assistant to Spanish adagio dancer with a touring band. She had also shed two husbands somewhere along the way. She was a head-turner, a sultry brunette beauty with a direct, self-possessed manner softened by southern charm.

Sioussat was working for the radio producer Seth Parker, creator of *Mr. District Attorney, Gang Busters,* and *We the People,* when she decided to try something new. She was on her way to NBC to scout the possibilities with a radio network when she happened to pass the CBS offices at 485 Madison Avenue. She stopped in on impulse and learned that the energetic new director of talks had worked himself into a desperate need for an assistant. She was sent upstairs for an on-the-spot interview. As she later described her first meeting with Ed Murrow: "I was struck dumb by one of the handsomest creatures my eyes had ever beheld. I'm usually glib, but this time my tongue felt thick. We started talking, but his secretary reminded him that he was already late for an awards luncheon at the Astor Hotel. I assumed that that was it for the day. Instead, he grabbed his hat and guided me firmly toward the elevator. 'Do you mind if we continue in the cab?' he said. On our way down in the elevator he said nothing and then he turned and suddenly asked, 'What do you do evenings?' My heart sank. Here's another one, I thought. I won't be able to take this job even if he does offer it to me. I pulled myself up straight and

101

said coolly, 'I go to the theater, I go dancing, I...' 'No,' he said, 'that's not what I mean. What about newspapers, magazines, books? Do you read? It's important for this job.' I breathed a sigh of relief. On the way over in the cab he kept firing questions at me. He was all business." At the end of the cab ride, he said a quick goodbye, dashed out, and loped into the hotel. Two days later, Ed called Helen Sioussat to tell her that she was hired.

He was, she quickly discovered, a driven man, yet he lacked the transparent ambition that disfigures many young men on the make. Instead, the word that kept coming back to her when Helen Sioussat spoke of the early Ed Murrow was "thoughtful." "He was thoughtful towards people, thoughtful about the way he did his work." She found him an exacting taskmaster, not because he was difficult or demanding, but, rather, because he maintained a furious pace, and his unspoken assumption was that she would keep up with him.[1]

Murrow was imaginative and resourceful in finding speakers. He had a knack for balancing viewpoints, or, rather, for striking sparks by pitting natural adversaries against each other. Working through Ceasar Saerchinger in Europe, he arranged a shortwave relay of a talk, in fitful English, by Benito Mussolini. Then he scheduled the crown prince of Ethiopia to describe Mussolini's aggression against the prince's defenseless country. During the 1936 presidential campaign, Murrow scheduled Earl Browder, the secretary-general of the Communist party U.S.A., along with other major- and minor-party candidates. Browder's appearance brought howls of protest from CBS affiliates and sponsors. Demonstrators picketed in front of 485 Madison Avenue. Ed could have explained that he was merely following the letter of the law, in effect since 1927, that required equal time for presidential candidates. But he felt that he was doing more than fulfilling legalities. He thought the American public ought to hear all points of view, to know what it feared before fearing it.

A CBS publicity release described his work in breathless, but essentially accurate, prose: "It is Murrow whose work has caused him to telephone Rome at 1 a.m. of a day early in December and arrange for a speaker to go on CBS at 9:15 the same morning with a report of ailing Pope Pius XI's condition. It was he who gave a Canadian newspaper writer six hours to interview representative Toronto subjects and report in a fifteen-minute broadcast their expressions on the Windsor-Simpson affair. He it is who watches as Congress goes into session, ready to place on the air speakers representing both sides of a legislative development as it comes out of committee."

He learned that radio departed from the classic rules of speech and rhetoric in which he had been trained. He wrote a guideline to help his prospective speakers recognize the difference: "The only recipe for making a speaker understand the demands and limitations of radio as a medium is to ask him to imagine himself standing before his own fireplace, perhaps leaning with one elbow on the mantel, talking to six or eight people in his own home. His visitors might include a business associate, a university professor, a couple of day laborers.... The speaker, as the host, must engage the interest of all.... He will engage the interest of millions if he can discover the essential intimacy of a medium which puts every listener within whispering distance of his lips."

He told a friend that he was appalled by the people who filled the CBS reception room, expecting him to put them on the air. It mystified him that someone who would not dare sing a note in public was only too willing to inflict untrained speech on a radio audience. But this was long before the era of the radio talk show when listeners proved that they indeed enjoyed hearing the untutored voices and unformed opinions of their neighbors. Ed told a friend that he regarded the eager faces in the reception room as "radio's real amateur hour."[2]

In the summer of 1936, Ed Klauber sent Murrow with the CBS news team to cover the Republican National Convention in Cleveland and the Democratic Convention in Philadelphia. Ed Murrow was supposed to arrange the broadcast of major speeches. But he himself would still not be on the air. Nevertheless, he appears at about this time to have felt the first stirrings of suppressed desire. Bob Trout, already a legend in radio for his unsurpassed ability to ad lib, was also on this trip. Trout had a marvelous radio voice, cultivated yet accessible, rather like the speech of a lord with democratic impulses. He was FDR's favorite broadcaster. Once, when the President was waiting to go on the air, he became so entranced listening to Trout's effortless extemporizing that he missed his cue to begin speaking.[3]

At the convention, Ed observed Trout's gift firsthand. He began asking him about his techniques, since Trout's work was far different from the formal rhetoric which Ed had been taught by Ida Lou. He was most intrigued by the conversational quality that Trout was able to bring to the microphone. What was it like, Ed wanted to know, talking to a piece of metal? "I don't think I could ever be a broadcaster," he told Trout. "I need to see their faces and feel their reactions." Trout, essentially echoing Ed's own advice to his speakers, said he should not look at the microphone as a megaphone for reaching crowds, but instead talk into it like a telephone reaching one person.[4]

Later, in Philadelphia, Ed tried to hire Raymond Swing to analyze the significance of each day's events at the Democratic Convention. He had met Swing, the reluctant favorite, while he had been under consideration for the talks job, and the older and younger man struck it off. Ed now experienced, firsthand, Klauber's autocratic rule. Raymond Swing's voice was not to be heard over CBS, Klauber informed him. And that was that.[5]

John Daley, who had been a CBS newsman, described another classic Klauber exchange. Daley had originally gone by the name "John Charles Daley." "One day, Klauber summoned me to his office," Daley recalled, "and I went in shaking:

'Daley?'

'Yes sir!'

'John Charles Daley is too cathedral in tone. Hereafter you'll be known only as John Daley.'

'Yes sir.' And out."[6]

Helen Sioussat once dared to answer the "executive phone" in Murrow's office, which was reserved for communication between department heads. "Is this a secretary?" Klauber bellowed. "No I'm not," she answered with as much composure as she could summon. "Don't you know you're not supposed to answer that phone? You're a woman," Klauber said, slamming the phone in her face. He would not permit a woman to set foot on the twentieth floor where he and Paley reigned. He hired male secretaries for himself and Paley.[7]

Murrow's reversal at Philadelphia over the Raymond Swing matter was, however, an exception. He was still largely exempt from Klauber's crotchets, foibles, whims, and cruelties. "Ed Murrow," Helen Sioussat observed, "didn't get terrified when Klauber called him, the way everyone else in the building did."

"Ed always spoke glowingly to me of Mr. Klauber," Janet recalled. "He was an idol to Ed. He told me that he considered Klauber the man with the greatest integrity in the news business. He didn't mind his toughness, because he saw it as a demand for high performance." The relationship that began with mutual professional respect grew into genuine affection, an emotion that neither man could express easily.

Still, their friendship remained the exception around CBS. At about the same time that Klauber was shaping Ed's broadcasting ethic, Ralph Colin, Paley's attorney, was telling Paley, "You've got to get rid of that guy. It doesn't matter how able he is. People can't stand him. Klauber's destroying your organization."[8]

Ed had conquered the second-in-command at CBS. But he had as yet had no impact on Bill Paley. Asked in later years his first recollection of the man who was to bring his network such luster, Paley recalled: "My first awareness of Ed Murrow was coming back from Washington by plane. We sat together and chatted. Talked generalities. I had no particular strong impression, other than that he was a sober, earnest young man." Paley was surrounded by bright young men in those days. And it was his style, indeed his policy, not to fraternize too closely with the help.[9]

Helen Sioussat became both an indispensable assistant to and a student of Ed Murrow. "All the women were crazy about Ed, married or single. It didn't make any difference," Sioussat recalled. "He did nothing to encourage it. Not only was he so very handsome, he had that reticent manner that women like. And men liked him as much as the women did. It seemed to me that he hated his good looks. Absolutely hated them. He was afraid that he would be judged on his appearance. On a couple of occasions I said, after some woman had met him, 'She certainly fell for you. She said you were terribly handsome.' He'd get angry. 'Don't say that,' he'd tell me. 'I hate that word.' There was a weight to Ed Murrow. He was a serious man." She was astonished long afterward when she eventually discovered that her mature, self-assured boss was still in his twenties when she worked for him, and six years younger than she was.

What Ed seemed to enjoy most about the job, she observed, was the intellectual byplay with the people he booked for talks. Norman Thomas was a great favorite. The pacifist-socialist was then 61 and planning his quadrennial presidential run when they first met. "Ed would sit for hours with Thomas," Sioussat remembered. "We'd put in a long day. But at the end, he'd be exhilarated if Norman Thomas stopped by." What stood out most in Helen Sioussat's mind, watching the two men argue, was "how easy they were with each other," the equal footing between the older, famous figure and the young network official.

The first time that Janet came to the office, Ed introduced her to Helen Sioussat as "my child bride." And indeed there was something in the way he treated her, at least in front of his assistant, along with his own mature aspect and Janet's fresh youthfulness, that suggested an exaggerated age gulf. Janet was not at all the wife that Helen Sioussat had expected. Sioussat thought that Janet seemed overpowered by her husband.

Since coming to CBS, Ed was no less easy at home than he had been during the stress-filled IIE days. Part of the reason was that he was again overprogramming himself. He had been emotionally unable to desert his work with the refugees for the Emergency Committee. Unknown to CBS, he had merely added the refugees to his new responsibilities. And so he came home tense and tired. Their apartment served as a safety valve where he could blow off the pressures that built up in him during the day. As Janet put it with New England economy of phrase, "Ed sputtered a lot."[10]

He was a success in the Talks Department. He gave the operation shape, direction, and dynamism. The people he scheduled did the network credit, and helped lift CBS to the premier position in network public affairs programming. Klauber was pleased. Paley was proud of the superior standing CBS enjoyed, for this was a time when he took as deep a pleasure in prestige as in profits.

But the satisfaction with Murrow was not universal. Paul White was not happy at all.

Paul White had been Klauber's first protégé at CBS. He had originally come from Pittsburg, Kansas, where his father was a stone contractor. He went to the Columbia School of Journalism and, like Murrow, was a debater, and possibly a better one. White had been chosen to go to England and debate against Oxford and Cambridge. Debating Oxonions illustrated one side of the split White character, which combined intellectual brilliance with a street-smart, tough-guy facade. White's appearance favored the latter. He was built like a bulldog, with a barrel chest, a round head, and, as one colleague described him, "a pugnacious face and a chip on his shoulder." He had an unnerving tic: his eyes were constantly blinking.

After college, White had gone to work for newspapers in the Midwest and then joined the United Press for six years. John Daley described the White reportorial style. "Paul came from the school of journalism where you worm your way into the house of the bereaved widow and while you're there, you steal a picture of the deceased for the paper. But, damn it, he was a great journalist."

Indeed, White was a wire service legend. Around the bars where reporters hung out, stories circulated of White pitted against eight reporters from the larger Associated Press and beating them to a story. White was brilliant, talented, ambitious, loud, flamboyant, and, by turns, amusing or obnoxious.

One of Ed Klauber's first moves after absorbing the news operation was to bring in Paul White to elevate radio reporting above its then low state. Indicative of that status, when White came aboard as "news editor" he was subordinated to the CBS Publicity Department.

A colleague in publicity, John G. Gude, later Ed Murrow's agent, recalled the circumstances of White's recruitment. "The news at the time was little more than press agentry. Paul moved in with a brisk, energetic, imaginative approach to make the news into news. Many people didn't like him. He was a 'hail-fellow-well-met' and it didn't take with everybody. But, everyone admitted that he was a gifted editor."

Where White had previously scooped rival reporters, he now set out to surpass NBC. He hired his own radio reporters, freeing CBS from the regurgitation of newspaper stories as the network's main news source. He had AP and UP Teletype printers installed in the CBS newsroom. He set up short-wave listening posts to pick up stories from abroad ahead of anybody else.

White fit nicely into the Klauber mold. His speech was gruff, his manner abrupt, his patience nil. "He did not suffer fools gladly," Ed Bliss, who wrote news for White, recalled. When a subordinate ran afoul of him, "Paul's face turned red, and he looked like he was going to explode," Helen Sioussat remembered. Watching White's behavior over the years, she summed him up in a phrase, "He had seen *The Front Page* too many times."

In part, the hard-driving, hard-boiled style was defensive posturing. For a small voice occasionally whispered in White's ear that he had left real journalism behind when he entered radio. Typewriter or microphone, he was going to show them: Paul White was still one hell of a newsman.

As his years and his successes mounted, White began nourishing a dream. He told Bob Trout, "I want to be a CBS vice president. But the people on the twentieth floor think I'm a roughneck." And, indeed, to the urbane Trout, White hardly seemed the sort whom Bill Paley would have to lunch in the board room.

One September morning in 1935, Trout recalled, he arrived at the office. "And I found someone new on the seventeenth floor. We now had a Talks Department which I hadn't heard of before. I knew that my boss, Paul White, was a great empire builder, so I went into his office and I said 'Is this bad for you?'" White's answer was immediate. "Absolutely not," he responded. "Talks are a bore and I want no part of it." Somehow, Trout felt, the response was too quick.

White and Ed Murrow were fated to collide in the then small CBS universe. Friction was virtually built into the new arrangement. White had by now become director of the Department of Public Events and Special Features. The line between Murrow's talks and White's special features was hazy. A talk by the secretary of state was clearly Murrow's province, and the Armistice Day Parade was one of White's special events. But if the secretary of state spoke at the Armistice Day ceremonies, whose show was it? And who should dominate at a national political convention, with its alternating faces of circus and substance? The answer often depended on who was the best in-fighter. And both White and Murrow were ambitious men. Bob Trout sometimes found himself working for one and then for the other, depending on who reached him first. Just as often, he was caught in a crossfire trying to serve two masters.

Sparks crackled almost constantly between Murrow's and White's offices. The friction was not generated wholly by their overlapping responsibilities. "Paul had expected Ed to fall on his face," Helen Sioussat recalled. "When he didn't, he became terribly jealous. He was jealous of Ed's looks, jealous of his closeness to Klauber. Jealous of his manners and poise."

On his arrival, White would greet Ed with a mocking smile and "Ah yes, the very dapper Edward R. Murrow!" Ed would stiffen visibly and try to ignore White. It was precisely the kind of gibe that rankled since it suggested what Murrow hated most of all, being considered a mere pretty boy.

White continually attempted to undercut him, to stretch the definition of special features to a point that would have left Murrow virtually unemployed. "They were," John Daley remembered, "at each other's throats most of the time," but they handled the antagonism differently. "I'd show Ed what Paul was up to and he'd just laugh it off," Helen Sioussat recalled. "Don't bother," he would say, "we can get by," as he evaded another of White's bureaucratic ambushes. "Ed refused to get down on White's level no matter how Paul provoked him," Sioussat observed. "He'd smile and walk away, which made Paul all the more furious. It was clear Paul had a grudging respect for Ed along with the jealousy. He was too able himself not to recognize ability, and that was what bothered him most about Ed Murrow."

Along with his passionate attachment to the news, Paul White had two other addictions. He perpetually badgered his staff to play cards with him. If White wanted to play during his lunch hour, they played then. If he wanted to play after work, they stayed late, no matter how much they wanted to go home. His treatment of those who did not indulge him was bad assignments, denial of raises, even the sack. And when they played, they always lost. "He had to win," said Bob Trout, "even if it meant he had to cheat." And there was little that his hapless subordinates could do but be cheated or punished professionally.

When White made one of his half-invitations–half-threats to Ed to play poker, Ed ignored him. But as for White's other passion, Ed took up the challenge.

White could go for weeks without a drink. Then he would disappear on monumental benders. Klauber would storm onto the seventeenth floor asking, "Where's White?" The news staff, fearing White's retribution, would cover up for their boss and start combing White's favorite haunts. The performance disgusted Murrow.

In the summer of 1936, White had headed the CBS team, including Ed, covering the two national conventions. The CBS staff stayed at the Bellevue Stratford in Philadelphia, and there, in the hotel bar, White challenged Murrow to a drinking match. The weapon was to be French .75s, a shot of cognac in a glass of champagne. Bob Trout, who witnessed this spectacle, remembered that "Ed drank White under the table." As Helen Sioussat put it, "Ed could hold his liquor beautifully."[11]

"Ed offered friendship very slowly," John Daley remembered. But with friendship finally won, and with alcohol dissolving his reserve, Murrow could become an unexpected hell-rake. "He came down to Washington once on business, and we went out on the town, and drank too much," Daley recalled. "I had a Buick convertible and Ed wanted to drive it. It was late at night, and we were riding past the east side of the Capitol. Ed whipped around and started driving the car up the Capitol steps. He thought it was amusing as hell."[12]

The courtly Trout was also surprised at this unsuspected side of Murrow. "I was in Washington covering the Roosevelt White House," Trout recalled. "Late one night, the people at the local CBS affiliate had thrown a party, and Ed had had a good deal to drink. I was practically a teetotaler. I was tired and all I wanted to do was go to bed. But well after midnight, he dragged me to a carnival. He immediately headed down the midway to the shooting gallery. He spent forever firing a .22 at metal ducks. I remember one of the shell casings popped up and stuck in his hair, and there it stayed." This was not the earnest director of talks whom Trout knew from the seventeenth floor.[13]

Rather like White and his binges, Ed Murrow would become saturated with the oversophistication of his present life. He was living in a socially complex, professionally exacting urban pressure cooker. Nothing seemed to him as direct, open, and natural as out West. And so, occasionally, he needed to break away, to plunge back, however briefly, into the simple, even mindless, pleasures of the life he had left behind.

At the Publicity Department Christmas party in 1936, he kept pressing the almost abstinent Trout to keep up with him. As Trout recalled: "I still didn't know anything about handling alcohol, and suddenly I remembered I had to do a five-minute newscast at ten o'clock."

Ed had continued to buttonhole Trout from time to time about the secrets of his seamless delivery, whether reading from a text or speaking without a note. This night, Ed followed Trout to the studio. Trout picked up the news summary that had been prepared for him. He was getting ready to go on the air when Murrow lifted the page from his hand and said, with the exaggerated gravity of the semi-intoxicated, "You can't go on the air. You've had too much to drink. I'll do it." Trout was too lightheaded to protest.

He later described Murrow's maiden broadcast: "He was overly careful, very, very precise. And he spoke in something of a monotone. But there was not the slightest hint that he had been drinking. He was word perfect."

Trout was standing by to give Murrow the cut sign one minute before he was to finish the broadcast. But between his own wooziness and his anxiety, he gave the sign too early. Thus, apart from a flawless reading, Murrow, in his news debut, committed one of broadcasting's mortal sins; he left forty-five seconds of dead air.[14]

During his first year at CBS, Ed's Grandmother Lamb died at age 88. He wrote to his mother, and the surviving letter provides a rare instance of Ed Murrow baring his soul on paper. He wrote late on a Saturday night, using a pencil and yellow-lined legal paper: "I am terribly grieved. They didn't let me know [in time] in order that your baby might have gone down to offer you his prayers in person to the gods who gave you such a mother." He went on describing the strength that he knew her religion had given Grandma Lamb and said, wistfully, "I've wished for a real and fundamental religion, something I could hold onto." But he had not found it. Throughout, he referred to Ethel as his "darling mother." Here, in a brief letter, was more unfettered sentiment, even sentimentality—the reference to himself as "your baby" is startling coming from Murrow—than his friends would hear in a lifetime of association with him. Outside the bosom of his family, and usually within it, he was a man who recoiled at expressing naked feeling.[15]

He continued to attract impressive figures to his talks schedule. He scheduled John Maynard Keynes, John Masefield, G.K. Chesterton, and Mohandas Gandhi. He carried the principle of presenting both sides of an argument to a point of acute discomfort for his network. At the time, Father Coughlin was inflaming the country with fascist and racist views from the right. Ed scheduled his one-time NSFA board members, the Marxist Frederick Vanderbilt Field and the socialist Corliss Lamont, to present the other end of the spectrum. President Roosevelt was building the New Deal, and Ed scheduled former President Hoover, who attacked Roosevelt bitterly. He managed to provoke both left and right—precisely what he intended.

In February of 1937, Ed went to New Orleans for the National Education Association Convention. Because of the special place the town held in their lives, he took Janet with him. He had been in the talks job at the time not quite a year and a half, and it was all about to end. For while in New Orleans, he was to receive a fateful phone call.[16]

CHAPTER 10

The Last Tranquil Year

Caesar Saerchinger had been living in Europe for nineteen years. It was, he felt, time to come home. And unknown to Saerchinger, CBS agreed.

He had gone to Germany as a newspaper correspondent in 1918, four months after the Armistice ended the Great War. By 1930, Saerchinger was working in England for *The Philadelphia Public Ledger* and *The New York Post* and covering the London Conference to limit the size of the great navies. CBS had sent a man named Frederick Wile to arrange talks from the conference, and Saerchinger had helped Wile find speakers. When the London assignment ended, Wile asked Saerchinger if he would like to work full-time as the CBS representative in Europe. Saerchinger accepted.

Thus Caesar Saerchinger came to do abroad what Ed Murrow did in New York, arranging talks and also, like Paul White, broadcasting special events. Much of the time he found himself producing audiotravelogues: Bastille Day from Paris, Guy Fawkes Day from England, *saengerfests* from Salzburg, and tulip festivals from Holland. In his second year with CBS, Saerchinger was honored by American radio for producing "the most interesting broadcast of 1932," the transmission live of a nightingale singing in Kent.

In all fairness, Saerchinger also broke new ground in serious radio journalism. Along with the Kent nightingale, he arranged the first broadcast by Leon Trotsky, after the father of the Red Army had been exiled by Stalin. Through Saerchinger's initiative, H. G. Wells and George Bernard Shaw made their first broadcasts to America. Shaw, then 81, mortified the prim Saerchinger with his greeting to his American listeners: "you dear old boobs." In 1932, Saerchinger persuaded the Nazi Party chief, Adolf Hitler, to speak over CBS. But first Hitler wanted a $1,500 fee. Saerchinger cabled New York for instructions and was told "Unwanted Hitler at any price."

In 1936, Britain's Edward VIII was forced to choose between his throne and "the woman I love," the Baltimore divorcee, Wallis Warfield Simpson. As the British constitutional crisis reached its climax, the prime minister was about to read a royal message to the House of Commons. Saerchinger was there and, before the prime minister could speak, the CBS representative announced, "The King has abdicated. Here is Sir Frederick Whyte to speak to you about this momentous event." Thus, Saerchinger scooped every other news medium in the world on the story. With the abdication scoop, Saerchinger reached his summit. He had been with CBS for almost seven years. He had been away from home nearly twenty years. He had taken the London assignment as far as he could stretch it, he believed. The wise career move now was to return to CBS in New York.[1]

In New York, Klauber, White, and Paley had come to the same conclusion, at least concerning Saerchinger's usefulness in Europe. Saerchinger was 46, an old man by CBS standards. His performance on the abdication story had been admirable, but in other respects they found his work sluggish. Klauber particularly had a sense, with Hitler's rise to power, that CBS needed somebody younger and more energetic in Europe. And he knew precisely whom he wanted.

Fred Willis was English, charming, and sophisticated on the one hand, able and ambitious on the other. Willis was perfect for the London post. Willis, however, knew all about England. There, he would be just another Englishman. It was in America that he was special, virtually CBS's house aristocrat. He turned Klauber down.

Klauber directed another of his subordinates, William B. Lewis, to canvass other candidates. Lewis's reaction was immediate. He had just the man, Ed Murrow. Klauber rejected the idea out of hand. Murrow, he said, was indispensable as director of talks.

But later, Fred Willis also urged Murrow on Klauber as someone possessing the requisite combination of urbanity and drive that the network wanted in Europe. Klauber began to reflect. He had two outstanding men in Murrow and Paul White. They also represented constant irritation for him with their feuding. The London opening afforded a chance to solve two problems with one assignment. A few weeks after the initial discussion with Lewis, Klauber told him, "I've thought of exactly the person we need for the European job." "Who?" Lewis asked. "Ed Murrow," Klauber replied. Lewis, a discerning student of Klauber's crotchets, complimented him on "a brilliant suggestion."[2]

As these discussions were going on in New York, Ed and Janet were in New Orleans for the annual convention of the National Education Association. Ed had just returned from an afternoon of golf. They were entertaining friends in their room at the Hotel Roosevelt when the phone rang. It was Klauber, who proceeded with his customary lack of ceremony. "How would you like to go to Europe?"

The offer caught Murrow completely unprepared. "Do you need the decision right now?" he asked.

"The sooner the better," Klauber told him.

"I'll have to discuss it with my wife, and get back to you," Ed answered.

In these moments the Murrow marriage was its best. Ed was impatient with Janet; he could inflict his moods on her and use her as the lightning rod for his frustrations. But he depended utterly on her steadiness and her judgment. As soon as they could be decently free of their guests, they began to struggle with Klauber's offer. As Janet later recalled, "We stayed up all night discussing the pros and cons."

The idea of going to England was no obstacle. That was the principal attraction of the offer. Janet's only reservation was in leaving her family to go so far away for so long. But Ed, by now, was sufficiently practiced in the labyrinthine ways of network politics not to judge Klauber's offer simply as a paid vacation abroad. The move had to be examined in terms of what it said about his future in the company. CBS was a hive of ambitious, talented strivers, and his absence from the center of power could leave him out of the competition. The thought, out of sight, out of mind, inevitably struck him.

He also had to consider the possibility that he was being sent abroad because he had lost the rivalry with White. As he was to write to his mother several years later in reflecting on this sea change in his life, "I was sent over here because I caused too much trouble at home or rather, in the New York office." There was another rub. Organizationally, the London post fell under White's domain. If Ed took it, he would no longer be White's rival; he would be his subordinate. He would report, not to Klauber, but to Paul White.

The discussion ended in the middle of the night. They would go to Europe. The opportunity was just too attractive to resist. And then they went to sleep.

On their return to New York, they faced one last hurdle. They were summoned to the Klaubers' for dinner, where, Janet observed, she "was looked over carefully." She had not yet met Ed Klauber, and she knew that this invitation was really her audition as the wife of the CBS European representative. The office monster that she had heard about was nowhere in evidence. Instead, she found Klauber at home a devoted husband to a charming wife, an attentive host, a stimulating conversationalist, and considerate, almost paternal, toward the young couple.[3]

As the time for their departure drew near, Ed made the rounds of CBS offices, saying his goodbyes. He poked his head into the office of James Morgan Seward, whom he and Janet had invited once for dinner. Seward knew that Ed's new job meant a salary increase to $8,000 a year, not all that much more than he had earned at IIE, but handsome enough in 1937. Seward reminded Ed that as CBS's man in Europe, some of his living expenses would now be picked up by the company. "Why don't you let me hold part of your salary back and save it for you?" Seward asked. He also suggested, with Ed going into an uncertain world, that he might want to review his life insurance coverage.

Explaining his action, Seward later said, he "wanted to be a part of this man's life," even if the way was to take over his financial chores. It was a common experience for Ed Murrow. People liked to "do" for him. For Murrow's part, there was something about Jim Seward, something in his spare, hawklike features, in his plain, sensible speech, that inspired trust.

"Fine," Ed said to Seward's suggestion. "Hold out the amount of the raise." He also went along with Seward's advice and bought more life insurance.

The matter of the insurance policy was to be a cause of some embarrassment. Ed's application for the policy exposed at least one of the misstatements he had made to CBS when he was hired. Seward looked at the age given on the insurance policy and asked Ed if the age given CBS was "a mistake." Ed grinned sheepishly and said yes.[4]

His colleagues threw a going-away party for him. Some of the network brass made graceful speeches suggesting the opportunity now open to Ed to use radio to forge a closer friendship between the two English-speaking democracies. The thought, however, did not sit well with everybody. "Broadcasting," another speaker said, "has no role in international politics." It was, after all, the CBS coup in airing the song of the Kent nightingale that had won the network laurels abroad, not sticking its nose into Europe's messes.

Publicity issued a press release announcing Ed's appointment as "Columbia's representative in Europe." In it, he was quoted as saying he intended to "reveal the inner and colloquial life of these nations." He had, by now, been to England three times. He had been appalled by its class structure, its system of unearned, hereditary privilege. He also knew that beneath the thirties film image Americans had of the country—a land apparently peopled by fops in monocles speaking in drawing-room accents— were the British equivalents of the Murrows of Beaver. And it was these people—their work, their pleasures, their customs, their beliefs—that he said he wanted CBS radio to capture.[5]

The Murrows sailed for England on the *SS Manhattan* on April 1, 1937. This time, instead of working for their passage running bridge tournaments and shuffleboard games, they traveled cabin class. Aboard ship, Ed ran into Harold Laski whom he had met through Alfred Cohn. Laski, at this point, was teaching at the London School of Economics, and was the dominant theorist in the British Labour Party. He was returning from a U.S. lecture tour. Janet recorded in her diary, "Ed and Harold Laski played Ping-Pong all day." And they talked all night. Or rather, Ed listened, since Laski was a mesmerizing monologuist. As soon as the Murrows were settled in England, Laski said, they must come visit him at his country place in Essex.[6]

They were up before dawn on April 27, peering out the porthole at an English coast shrouded in mist as in an Arthurian legend. After docking at Plymouth, they took the train to London. As the sun began to burn away the haze, England revealed herself to them in all her spring splendor. Azaleas were everywhere in bloom. Flower boxes were perched on virtually every window ledge. They approached London and gazed on endless rows of chimney pots atop ancient brick houses. Janet felt as though they had stepped back into the world of Dickens.

They were met at the Waterloo Station by Richard Marriott, foreign liaison officer for the British Broadcasting Corporation, whose duty it was to squire foreign broadcasters like Murrow. Marriott deposited them at the Langham Hotel, a nineteenth-century hostelry under whose high ceilings the "red-cheeked gentry," as Janet described them, eyed the American visitors with raised eyebrows.[7]

Later that day, they met Caesar Saerchinger and his wife for lunch. Saerchinger favored double-breasted suits, wore dark-rimmed glasses, and was handsome in a fussy sort of way. He had a self-important manner and at 5 foot 2 was self-conscious standing in the lee of his tall successor. But as for the job, he behaved toward Ed like an unctuous owner about to unload a ramshackle house on an unsuspecting buyer, while he himself prepares to flee to a posh apartment.

Ed's first day in England was not yet over. After lunch he had to go to a hospital to visit, of all people, his new chief, Paul White. White had wangled himself and his wife, Sue, passage to England, purportedly to make sure all arrangements for CBS's coverage of the upcoming coronation of George VI were in order. A miffed Saerchinger made clear to Ed that White's presence was totally unnecessary. He had already made all the arrangements. On the crossing, White's chronic arthritis had flared up, landing him in the hospital, where Murrow, resignedly, now went to comfort him.

Their stay at the Langham was brief. The Saerchingers had a country place where they intended to wait out their return to America, and they offered the Murrows their apartment in town on Queen Ann Street.[8]

At the coronation in mid-May there was little for Ed and Janet to do but enjoy it. Saerchinger had indeed made all the arrangements. He had lined up British journalists and writers to interpret the spectacle to America. There were no CBS broadcasters covering the event, apart from Robert Trout, who was there only to introduce the speakers. At that point there were no foreign correspondents in broadcasting.

Ed and Janet were seated with the VIP guests in front of Apsley House on the corner of Hyde Park. As they watched the ancient ritual unfold, they were surprised at the listlessness of the crowd and, for that matter, the lack of animation of the new king and his queen. The only ones who seemed genuinely thrilled at what was happening were the two young princesses, Elizabeth and Margaret Rose.[9]

The coronation over, Ed undertook the agreeable duty of seeing the

Paul Whites off on the train for the Channel ferry where White had next arranged to be in France for the marriage of the erstwhile Edward VIII, now the duke of Windsor, to Mrs. Simpson. White, Murrow noticed, was badly hung over.

White was soon back from France, feeling fit and in high spirits. With Murrow no longer a rival and instead a subordinate, White began to dispense his heavy-handed brand of bonhomie. He wanted Ed to play golf with him. Ed began to wonder if White was not more bearable as an antagonist than as a pal. Finally, on June 9, the Murrows, with the high spirits summonable at the departure of unwanted guests, put the Whites on a ship bound for home.[10]

A month later, Ed had more auspicious CBS visitors. The Paleys were coming to London. Their arrival coincided with the debut of a prestigious CBS Shakespeare series at home, and the New York office advised Ed that Mr. Paley would like to hear the premier broadcast while he was in England.

What Mr. Paley wanted was no small feat. Ed went to the BBC and drew on what little credit he had been able to build up in his short stay to plead for the BBC's representative in New York to relay the CBS broadcast across the Atlantic to England via shortwave. There, the engineers at the Broadcasting House, the headquarters of the BBC, would have to pick up the signal and pipe it to a speaker in a private room where the Paleys could listen. Ed worked feverishly, and by the time the Paleys arrived, all the arrangements were in place.

Because of the time zone difference, the New York broadcast would not be heard until 1 a.m. in London. Ed took meticulous pains to make sure that everything was in order that evening and then went home to catch a few hours of sleep. He then returned to Broadcasting House, where he and the BBC foreign representative, Richard Marriott, waited and waited. The Paleys never showed.

The next morning, Bill Paley, with a casual grin, said that he had forgotten all about the broadcast. "I fell asleep," he said.

Ed next invited the Paleys to join him and Janet at the theater. They declined. They were too busy. Janet, who had yet to meet her husband's employer, wrote home that Mrs. Paley "was interested only in so-called high society."

The Paley visit had been virtually Ed's first solo performance before the head of the network. He had done exactly what he should have done. But by no stretch of the imagination could the Paley visit, from Ed's standpoint, be scored as a professional or social triumph.[11]

The Murrows had come to live in England in a gray season, politically and economically. The terrible blood-lettings of the Somme, Mons, and Ypres were only twenty years behind, and the peace that this slaughter had won for Britain and her allies was already beginning to unravel. The economy was slack, and the pervasive mood was one of apathy and lethargy. The Germans, on the other hand, were experiencing unaccustomed euphoria, an excitement approaching mass eroticism. "The German form of life is definitely determined for the next thousand years!" Hitler was thundering to wildly cheering crowds. The *führer* was restoring pageantry and color and a touch of mysticism to the drab lives of Germans in the thirties. England remained dreary.

Briefly before Murrow's arrival, Hitler had broken the Treaty of Versailles by rearming the right bank of the Rhine. He enlarged the Reichswehr and created the Luftwaffe, ignoring the limits the Allies had imposed on German arms and armies at Versailles. This renascent German militarism had not stirred the British to vigilance. Rather, talk of war and preparedness fell on weary ears. England was spiritually exhausted. There was no will to fight again so soon. Britain's real battles, the socialists, the pacifists, and the young believed, were against poverty and lingering social injustice at home, not the Germans abroad. The Oxford Union debated the question "Resolved: This House will not fight for King or Country," and young Englishmen voted overwhelmingly in favor.

The energy now lay with Europe's dictatorships, with Nazi Germany and Fascist Italy. Britain, and France too, had sunk into a soul sickness and a blind hope that the ominous stirrings in Berlin and Rome would go away if only they looked away. And so when Italy invaded Ethiopia in 1935, Britain and France came up with a plan to dismember the primitive kingdom to placate Mussolini. The plan fell through, and Italy, instead, swallowed Ethiopia whole. When Francisco Franco rebelled against the legitimate government in Spain, Germany and Italy sent arms, aircraft, even troops to his aid. England and France practiced an exquisite noninterference throughout the Spanish civil war.

Britain's leaders could not turn a blind eye to the menace on the Continent indefinitely. In 1937, the Baldwin government made tentative efforts to rearm, but moved slowly in the face of a resistant public. Englishmen had already had their Great War.

Neville Chamberlain succeeded Stanley Baldwin as prime minister. Chamberlain was convinced that those who came to power in great nations were, after all, responsible people like himself. The prime minister was disposed to see the other fellow's side and, within reason, give him what he wanted. He announced his policy, appeasement, in his second week in office.

When Murrow and other foreigners talked of British politics, the question inevitably came up, had the British become soft? Had they lost their nerve? Murrow's response was interesting for seeing the British character through the lens of history. "You may be right," he answered. "There is evidence to support your view. But I have a suspicion that you are wrong. Perhaps you misjudge those young men who are rather languid and wear suede shoes, and resolve that they will fight not for King and Country."[12]

Soon after his arrival in England, Ed had arranged an appointment with the director general of the BBC. Broadcasting House, an art deco wedding cake, was built on the point where Regent Street meets Portland Place. Before Broadcasting House stood a statue of Prospero holding Ariel. Inside the lobby, a plaque read "Dominus Ioannes Reith," denoting the director, Sir John Reith, whom Murrow was about to see and who, in British broadcasting, was indeed Dominus.

Murrow met one of the more formidable figures in England, a giant Scot with a face like a craggy masiff, brows like brushes, and an outcropping jaw. One side of his face was scarred by war wounds. Sir John started off with a forehand compliment for Murrow and a backhand swipe at CBS. Taking note of Ed's background in education, Reith said, "I dare say your company's programs in the future will be a little more...intellectual."

Murrow answered, "On the contrary, Sir John, I want our programs to be anything but intellectual. I want them down-to-earth and comprehensible to the man in the street."

"Then," said Reith, "you will drag radio down to the level of the Hyde Park Speaker's Corner."

"Exactly," Ed replied. He was still determined to capture and transmit home the quality of everyday life among the British.[13]

The CBS London office was on Langham Place, virtually across the way from Broadcasting House. On Ed's arrival in London, Caesar Saerchinger had introduced him to "Miss Kathryn Campbell, that paragon of secretaries." Kay Campbell was then in her mid-twenties. She had left her family of Scottish hotel keepers at 17, had taken a typing course, and had gone to work for CBS five years before. She was a pale, plain, pleasant-looking woman with reddish blond hair, and even at this point had the aura of the spinster about her. She was also, Ed noted, crisp of speech and quick of mind. The woman exuded competence. Like Murrow, she was also a heavy smoker. He called her "Miss Campbell," having observed early that instant Yankee intimacy was poor form in English offices. And he asked her if she would stay on with him now that Mr. Saerchinger was leaving. She agreed instantly.

There was a protocol in the England of that era for communicating with the important people. If one wanted to see, say, a cabinet minister, one wrote asking for an appointment. The telephone was considered far too blunt an instrument for this level of contact. Miss Campbell was horrified at the ignorance, or was it the impudence, of her new boss when Mr. Murrow asked her to put him through to Winston Churchill. He compounded the offense by telling her that if she could not reach Churchill in his office in the House of Commons, she should ring him up at home.

She did as she was told, and her shock turned to astonishment to hear this young American chatting assuredly with Churchill. Churchill was then the member of Parliament for Epping, out of power and out of step with the pacifist mood in England. He was only too delighted to take a call from a man positioned to amplify his lonely voice and to carry his case for preparedness to America.[14]

Still, for the most part, Ed was functioning, like Saerchinger before him, as a light entertainment impresario. He traveled frequently, to the Netherlands to arrange a broadcast from an international boys' encampment, to France for a grape harvest festival, to St. Andrews in Scotland for the British Open. At the golf tournament, the press had been assigned working space in a small building near the eighteenth hole. There was a break before the players were to make their crucial putts. Meanwhile, a band of bagpipers entertained the spectators. Ed was working with Robert Dunnet, a BBC producer, and he said to Dunnet, "You know, if we open the window, we can get the sound of that pipe band into the broadcast." The idea had never occurred to Dunnet.

Ed was occasionally on the air himself, introducing speakers. At Wimbledon that year, rain suspended play on center court, and Ed attempted to fill in the time with the sort of impromptu commentary he admired so much in Bob Trout. He recognized Sir Samuel Hoare arriving with the duchess of Kent and reported, "Sir Samuel is wearing a saucy black straw hat with a white ribbon trailing down his back." Trout's position as the preeminent ad-libber was still safe.[15]

Ed found himself utterly dependent on the BBC in getting his broadcasts out. His BBC liaison, Dick Marriott, was his sole source of studios, land lines, transmitters, and frequencies. Marriott provided his services to all foreign broadcasters on a first-come–first-served basis. He was thus in a position to observe the rivalry between CBS and NBC. At that point, Marriott knew that it was no contest. NBC was miles ahead. The difference in England was a man named Fred Bate.

Bate was twenty years Murrow's senior and had been living in Europe for the last twenty-five years. He was a failed painter and a gentleman. He had worked for several American firms in Europe before joining NBC. Bate's greatest value to the network was his membership in the social circle that orbited around the prince of Wales, later Edward VIII, until the latter's abdication. The king had enjoyed the company of this charming American. Bate and his wife were frequent guests at the royal retreat, Fort Belvedere, where Edward was able to enjoy Mrs. Simpson's company in regal privacy before he elevated her to a duchess, and she reduced him to a duke. Bate's connections in England could scarcely have been improved upon. CBS's Caesar Saerchinger could not begin to compete.

Saerchinger was resentful and had poisoned Ed's attitude toward Bate with stories of the NBC man taking unfair advantage of CBS. Thus, when Saerchinger finally introduced Ed to Bate on a chance meeting in the lobby of Broadcasting House, Murrow was uncharacteristically belligerent. He warned Bate that he played hard and rough when he had to. Bate, making generous allowance for the excesses of youth, assured Ed that there were more than enough flower shows and members of Parliament to go around for everybody. Murrow was properly chagrined and quickly recognized in Bate, his NBC rival, a man far more to his taste than Saerchinger, his CBS colleague. From that point on, he and Bate became gentlemen competitors and friends.[16]

Max Jordan, NBC's man on the Continent, was even better deployed to compete against Ed. Jordan, a German, had spent years covering Washington as a newspaperman. He was now based in Berlin and had exclusive contracts with DRG, the official German broadcast agency, and Ravag, Austrian state radio. To the Germans, the "National" in NBC was taken almost literally, as though the network were the official American broadcast arm. CBS struggled along in Germany and Austria on any remaining crumbs left by Jordan. NBC's dominance rankled Murrow. He began to think about how to break Jordan's near monopolistic grip on the Continent.[17]

Any social discomfort that the Murrows had felt in those early days in the Langham Hotel passed quickly enough. They were that most desirable combination, attractive people who, by virtue of Ed's position, were also useful people. Ed's old associates from IIE days descended on him. The Murrows were soon swept up in a whirlwind of invitations. Their first English country weekend was spent not with the common people of England whom Ed had sworn to celebrate over American radio; rather, they were the guests in Gloucestershire of Sir Edward Grigg, KCMG, KVCO, DSO MC, and Lady Grigg.

The kid out of the company town of Beaver, Washington, somehow managed to appear immediately at home among British patricians. He behaved intuitively in the way Shaw had Henry Higgins counsel Eliza Doolittle. The great secret was "not having bad manners or good manners or any particular sort of manners, but having the same manner for all human souls: in short, behaving as if you were in Heaven, where there are no third class carriages, and one soul is as good as another." Murrow instinctively seemed to know this.

It was not quite the same for Janet at first. In those early days she found British upper-class women absorbed in men or themselves. "They had a quick way," she remembered, "of letting you feel that you weren't particularly useful to them."[18]

Harold Laski, as promised, invited the Murrows to come to his country place two hours northeast of London. The Laskis address charmed Ed, "The Manor Cottage, Little Bardfield, Near Braintree, Essex."

Harold Joseph Laski was then 43 a descendant of Polish Jews who had settled in Manchester. His father had made a fortune as a cotton merchant and became prominent in Liberal politics. When Harold was 15 Winston Churchill, then in his Liberal political incarnation, ran for Parliament and was a house guest of the Laskis' during the campaign. That night, he sat on Harold's bed and talked at length and without condescension to this precocious boy.

Harold was indeed mature for his years, and strong-willed to boot. He went to Oxford and promptly renounced Judaism. At 18 he married a 26-year-old gentile, Freda Kerry, a physiotherapist, a student of eugenics, and as fiercely independent as her young husband.

When the war began in 1914, Laski had tried to enlist but failed the medical examination. At the age of 22, he went to Canada and taught political science at McGill University. He became a close friend of Felix Frankfurter, then on the law faculty at Harvard. Frankfurter lured Laski to Harvard, where he stayed for the next four years. Laski thereafter spent a third of his professional life on American campuses.

At the time the Murrows visited him, Laski was teaching at the London School of Economics. He was the leading strategist of the British Labour Party, and, as much as any single individual, dominated the intellectual life of England in the 1930s. One colleague described Harold Laski as a Labourite politically, a Socialist economically, and a Marxist sentimentally, with a romantic attachment to the ideal of the brotherhood of the oppressed.

Laski pursued enough interests to occupy a dozen men. He was a scholar, a political philosopher, a teacher, an author, and a journalist. He had a mind like flypaper. Whatever he read, or heard, stuck to him, seemingly forever. He had the enviable capacity to summon up exactly the right fact, or apt quote or anecdote, to drive home his point at the right time. He was regarded by many as the most brilliant talker in England.

On an occasion in Washington, Laski addressed an audience of foreign policy specialists. When he finished, he took questions, twenty of them, before uttering a word. He then proceeded to answer them all, in order, without a note.

He was a legend at the London School of Economics, a brilliant teacher, but also a notorious name dropper whom his students loved to parody: "And then Stalin said to me, Laski...." But there was always a kernel of truth even in his most outlandish posturing. He was, in short, an egoist with much to be egoistic about.

Physically, Laski was a small man, quick and energetic, with a hawk nose, lively eyes, and hands that flew about as he spoke; usually clenched between his fingers was a perilously short cigarette from which he took frequent, deep drags between bursts of words.

During the Murrows' visit, he took Ed and Janet on hikes through the countryside. He played croquet and tennis with the same combativeness that he had displayed at Ping-Pong aboard the *Manhattan*. In the evening, surrounded by friends, Laski came into full flower. He particularly astonished Ed by his feel for America, studding his conversation with references to baseball players, blues singers, Abe Lincoln, even Mormon saints. He described to Murrow his vision of the current state of England: "hell for the poor, paradise for the rich and purgatory for the intellectuals." One visitor described a night with Harold Laski as "verbal fireworks."

As an Americanophile, Laski found something quintessentially American in Ed Murrow. He was delighted when Ed confided to him his intention of presenting the image of everyday Britons to Americans over the radio. Laski thereupon took Ed's arm and insisted on bringing him to the Spread Eagle, the local pub, explaining that pubs were "the only democratic institution left in England."

At the Spread Eagle, Laski pointed out the son of the local squire playing darts with a tenant farmer. Murrow listened avidly to the exotic accents around the bar. A village character, Uppy Andrews, burst into a song, "The Cat Came Back." Professor Laski followed with "My Old Kentucky Home," and Ed harmonized on the chorus. This, Murrow decided, was the England he wanted America to hear.[19]

He was back at the Spread Eagle the following month for a beat of sorts, the first overseas broadcast from England's last remaining democratic institution, capturing the conversation around the bar, Uppy Andrews' songs, right on down to the publican's closing "Time, gentlemen, please."

The attraction between Murrow and Laski was immediate. Ed liked the man's erudition and humanity, his formidable intellect enlisted in the service of ordinary people, his equal expertise in political systems and English music hall comedians. In the early years in England, the Laskis and Murrows became fast friends. In the course of their visits to Manor Cottage, Ed and Janet fell in love with the English countryside.

Janet's childhood friend, the former Catherine Atwood, arrived in England that year with her husband, John Kenneth Galbraith, who had just won a fellowship in economics at Cambridge. The two couples were also soon seeing a good deal of each other.

Kitty Galbraith came from a prominent New England family, and her father had been a famed yachtsman. Ken Galbraith's distinction was all in his six-foot, seven-inch height and in his head. He had left a farm in Ontario, Canada, to become a brilliant economist with that rarity in his profession, a prose style, not only comprehensible, but graceful and witty. But at this stage of his life, social aplomb was not Galbraith's forte. He had yet to develop the somewhat astringent charm that later characterized his manner and writing. In those days there was more astringency than charm. He could be difficult, Janet recalled, and "had a chip on his shoulder," a defensive posture growing out of a social unease he felt, aggravated by his being in class-ridden England.

But Ken Galbraith liked Ed Murrow. He liked his company very much indeed. Here was a man cut from his own cloth, the natural aristocracy of those who were rising, not through inherited privilege, but on the wings of their own talent and work. The difference was in the grace with which Murrow was managing his ascendency and the growing pains that the process was causing Galbraith.[20]

Murrow was always noticed. The pattern had held for the boy in Beaver, the student at Pullman, the young man in New York. Two months after his arrival in England, he met, in that stream of people who passed through Harold Laski's parlor, Ellen Wilkinson. Wilkinson had risen from working-class origins to become first a union organizer and, when Ed first met her, a Labour member of Parliament. An impassioned socialist, she was "Red Ellen" to her enemies.

After meeting Ed at the Laskis, Ellen Wilkinson wrote in an article for the influential weekly, *The Sunday Referee:* "Talking of clever people who carefully keep themselves out of the ordinary news, a recent acquisition to London is Edward Murrow who has taken over European control of the Columbia Broadcasting System. He just knows what is really happening in Washington, but so modest is he that no one would suspect him of having met most of the people who really matter anywhere."[21]

Six months after his arrival in England, Ed was invited by the Royal Institute of International Affairs to lecture on "The International Aspects of Broadcasting." He spoke at Chatham House, on St. James Square, once the home of Wiliam Pitt. He opened his remarks with the kind of irony savored by British audiences: "I have no desire to offend or to criticize, without intent." Again, his theme was the potential of radio to make life better by making the mass of mankind better informed, a goal which rejected the elitist Reith view of broadcasting.

The speech was well received, but not universally. Dick Marriott had become an avid Murrow booster and had expressed his high opinion to his chief, I.D. Benzie, the foreign director of the BBC. Miss Benzie heard the Murrow speech and was not persuaded. Her criticism is interesting in that it sounded a fairly common refrain among those who, through the years, resisted the Murrow spell. The lady found, she said, "a tinge of histrionics in his character."[22]

The Murrows were living comfortably in the Saerchingers' Queen Ann Street apartment, two floors in a good neighborhood in a building whose architecture shifted from traditional to modern, depending on the floor. They inherited, along with the apartment, the Saerchingers' maid-of-all-work, an apple-cheeked coal-miner's daughter from Wales named Betty Matthews. She had come to London to better her lot, and it is indicative of the life of a Welsh miner's family that the $5 a week she earned from the Murrows actually represented a step upward for her.[23]

His NBC friend-rival, Fred Bate, took Ed to his tailor on Savile Row, and for the rest of his life Murrow's clothes always displayed the English cut. Within weeks of his arrival, Ed also bought a car, a modest little British Ford four-door sedan. But almost immediately his eye began to rove over more rakish models.[24]

He had also found more agreeable golf partners than Paul White, and began to play often. His game was totally at odds with his appearance. He was entirely without finesse, an erratic, idiosyncratic, and obviously self-taught golfer. He had what one of his partners called a "Babe Ruth swing." He seized his woods like a baseball bat, and when he connected, made enormous drives. And he soon discovered the shooting galleries in the penny arcades on Leicester Square.[25]

In mid-October of that first year in England, the Murrows eagerly accepted an invitation to a cocktail party thrown by the Saerchingers to celebrate their return, at last, to America. Caeser Saerchinger had become a chore. He would drop into the CBS Langham Place office and think nothing of tying up Kay Campbell, dictating twenty letters to her at a time. She, in the meantime, had shifted her loyalty from her officious former boss to Ed and bridled at Saerchinger's presumptuous impositions. Ed told her to be patient.

His own patience, however, was wearing thin. Whenever he had important Americans to his office, Saerchinger contrived to be on hand. The man would flagrantly start promoting himself, since it was becoming evident that what CBS was offering him in New York did not square with Saerchinger's earlier lofty expectations.

He badgered Ed endlessly to write letters of recommendation for him. Ed was torn. His nature was to be generous to friends in need. But Saerchinger was not exactly a friend. He had no real knowledge of the man's capabilities. And from what others had told him, confirmed by his own experience, Saerchinger was a difficult personality. Within the bounds of conscience, he wrote as favorably as he could about Saerchinger. It suggests Murrow's delicacy in handling such a situation that through all the following years, Saerchinger looked upon Ed Murrow as his good friend.[26]

That fall, the Murrows gave several parties to show their latest acquisition. The BBC had recently inaugurated a television service, one hour every evening, Monday through Friday. The schedule included dramas, newsreels, sports, even calisthenics. At the time there were 1,500 receivers in use, and the signal was strong up to seventy miles from London. The BBC had given Ed a television set for his office that produced a small black and white picture of remarkable clarity.

Ed persuaded CBS to let him buy another set for his apartment, an HMV (His Master's Voice), a handsome floor model in polished wood with a six-inch screen. In the beginning, he and Janet watched television every night. But the novelty quickly palled. After a few weeks, Janet recalled, "Ed lost interest in television. He never looked at it."

But he did turn on the set for one visitor, a gangling 23-year-old named Eric Sevareid. Sevareid and his wife, Lois, were then touring England and planning a bicycling trip in Europe. Sevareid had gone to Murrow's office earlier with a letter of introduction from Jay Allen of *The Chicago Daily News*. He was a painfully shy young man and felt himself awkward and utterly lacking in the social graces. Of this first encounter with Murrow, Sevareid remembered, "I saw a young American in a beautifully fitting suit and hard collar chatting easily on the phone with Lady so-and-so." Sevareid was impressed by Murrow's aplomb: "His ease, the cultivation in his voice...coming from the far West, or wherever it was...was difficult for me to believe."

Sevareid had already met several famous Fleet Street people since his arrival in London. But none, he said, had impressed him as much as this "tall, thin man with a boyish grin, extraordinary dark eyes that were alight with intensity one moment and somber and lost the next. He seemed to possess that rare thing, an instinctive, intuitive recognition of truth."

Ed had subsequently invited Sevareid and his wife to his apartment for dinner. Afterward, he turned on the television set and they watched R.C. Sheriff's play, *Journey's End*, on "an enormous piece of furniture," Sevareid recalled. When the program ended, Ed turned off the set and announced, "That's television. That's the wave of the future right there." It was unclear whether he made the observation with enthusiasm, dismay, or resignation.

As Sevareid later described that evening in his own autobiography: "He [Murrow] talked about England through half the night, and, although he had been there only about a year, one went away with the impulse to write down what he had said, to recapture his phrases, so that one could recall them and think about them later. I knew I wanted to listen to this man again, and I had a strong feeling that many others ought to know him."

Ed and Janet spent their first Christmas in England with a couple they had grown close to, the Darvalls. Frank Darvall was then the number-two man in the American Division of the British Ministry of Information, a good and helpful friend. Ed had to break away late in the evening for Broadcasting House. He was putting on the BBC Singers in a concert of Christmas carols, and broadcasting a holiday greeting to America from the Ethiopian emperor, Haile Selassie, in exile in England after the Italians had seized his kingdom. There was a thirty-five-minute wait before the emperor spoke. His retinue remained standing, as did the BBC staff. But as the time dragged on, the ex-logger from Beaver grew tired and sat down, the only one seated in the emperor's presence.[27]

The time in England had been a renewed honeymoon. Ed had never seemed happier, more at peace with himself. Absent was the coiled tension of his refugee rescuing days, his wearying daily combat with Paul White. His wildly swinging moods, his black depressions, went into remission. During his trips to the Continent, he wrote Janet affectionate, even whimsical, letters. He opened with "Dear Guppy" or "Dear Bippo" and signed himself "Hyman Kaplan" or "John Hyman Calvin Murrow." He wrote her, "I hadn't needed people before, but I feel your absence when I'm away."[28]

His duties were not onerous, and he brought to them more talent and energy than they demanded. He and Janet had fallen in love with England. They had a wide circle of friends. They had their country weekends and time for golf. It was the most serene period of his life. And it was to be his last tranquil year.

CHAPTER 11

This Is London

Ed Murrow would begin 1938 a successful but obscure representative of a broadcast network. He would emerge from it a man just beginning to be illuminated by the dawning light of fame. The history of broadcast journalism can fairly be divided into before Murrow and after Murrow. And in this year, he was about to cross that bridge.

In 1929, when Bill Paley had been in charge of CBS for a little over a year, news at the radio network amounted to one five-minute summary during a half-hour morning variety show called *Something for Everyone*. CBS's news-gathering resources consisted of a United Press Teletype in a corner of the Publicity Department and whatever newspapers the mailroom delivered. The news function at rival NBC was scarcely more developed. It was a time when people turned on the radio to be entertained. They read the newspaper to be informed ("For further details, consult your local newspaper.")[1]

Yet radio could do something that no previous medium of communication could do. It could report not only what had happened, but what was happening. It could achieve immediacy and actuality. In the early days, radio exercised this power on the level of novelty. An enterprising station manager might dramatize a heat wave by letting listeners hear the sizzle of an egg frying on a sidewalk, or broadcast the sound of Niagara Falls, or cover a wedding performed in a balloon.

The first attempt to make the news come alive was more theater than journalism. In 1931, CBS began broadcasting a program produced by *Time* magazine, *The March of Time*. On it, current events were reenacted with radio actors taking the part of newsmakers; an actor, for example, playing President Roosevelt adding a new alphabet agency to the New Deal, or Joseph Stalin ordering the trial of old Bolsheviks. The portrayals were

125

often so convincing that it was difficult to distinguish the voice of the actor from the original. *The March of Time* was frequently well done, entertaining, even informative. But it had about the same historical integrity as a later generation's television docudramas. Whatever it was, *The March of Time* was not news.[2]

Radio's unique capacity to transport as well as report was demonstrated virtually by accident. On April 21, 1930, a CBS affiliate in Columbus, Ohio, WARU, was broadcasting a concert by the prison orchestra from the Ohio State Penitentiary. During the program, some disgruntled prisoners set a small fire to protest overcrowding in the prison. The fire flared out of control and was soon raging through the cell blocks.

A black inmate, a self-taught lay preacher known as the Deacon, convicted of hacking his mother-in-law to death, seized the microphone and began to describe the horror around him. WARU notified CBS, which threw a master switch, and the Deacon's voice was heard over the entire network. People listening in distant states heard the crackle of flames, the roar of the fire, the screams of the dying, as 335 men perished. Here was reporting of almost unbearable immediacy, a sensory experience that the most vivid newspaper account could not capture.[3]

Four months after the Ohio fire Ed Klauber came to CBS and soon brought Paul White over from UP to realize radio's news potential. In this, the two men had Bill Paley's enthusiastic support. "The prestige" of his network, Paley said, depended on CBS's treatment of the news. White increased the frequency, depth, and length of newscasts. CBS press releases carried a new masthead boldly proclaiming: "Columbia, the News Network." But White was soon to become the victim of his own success.[4]

This upstart, radio news, made newspaper owners nervous. If readers heard it first over radio, why should they buy newspapers? And falling circulation would mean falling advertising revenues. The publishers began to counterattack. They pressured the wire services, AP, UP, and the Hearst chain's International News Service, not to supply news to the radio networks. By the spring of 1933, the networks had been effectively boycotted. Two courses were left open. They could rehash newspaper stories as their newscasts. Or they could take a far bolder step. They could start gathering the news themselves.

That is what NBC and CBS did. An energetic NBC publicity writer, A. A. "Abe" Schecter, became, in effect, NBC news. Schecter asked other publicity people working for NBC affiliate stations to tip him off on breaking news in their areas. Schecter created a news network virtually overnight. He also read the newspaper and then placed calls to state governors, police chiefs, and district attorneys and interviewed them for more details. Schecter found the phrase, "NBC is calling," an open sesame. The amount of news that one man was able to generate using nothing more than a telephone astonished and alarmed the newspaper publishers.

Paul White decided to go Schecter one better. He hired his own radio reporters and opened CBS news bureaus in New York, Washington, Chicago, and Los Angeles. He contracted with stringers in smaller towns and paid them by the story. He called his operation the Columbia News Service.

Again the publishers struck back. They embargoed any newspaper stories on businesses that advertised over CBS. The American Newspaper Publishers Association adopted a more insidious strategy. ANPA pressured its member papers not to print CBS's daily program schedule, a strike at the jugular. CBS was paying a heavy price for becoming "the News Network."

Paley had loved the excitement of challenging the newspapers, and in the process, winning fresh plaudits for CBS. But he was a businessman first and a realist. The radio networks had no choice but to make peace with the press. In December of 1935, they all met at the Hotel Biltmore, the radio people on one side of the table, and AP, UP, INS, and ANPA on the other. Radio capitulated.

Under the terms of the peace pact, a devastated Paul White dismantled the Columbia News Service. NBC agreed not to build up a similar organization. Instead, the wire services agreed to set up a Press-Radio Bureau to supply news to radio stations. But no item was to be more than thirty words long, and only two five-minute newscasts per day were to be permitted. Radio news was also to be secondhand; it could only be broadcast in the morning, after the morning papers came out and in the evening after the afternoon papers hit the street. Network commentators were not to discuss any news item less than twelve hours old.

It was galling. It was enraging. More to the point, it was futile. News was not a commodity to be doled out like bread in a famine. It was not a franchise to be exercised only in allotted territories. News came out of every pore in the country. Local radio stations simply ignored the restrictions and broadcast local news at their pleasure.

Profit then reared its head. Major advertisers, like Standard Oil, knew that radio news drew huge audiences for their commercials. They offered enticing payments to the wire services to resume providing unrestricted news to the networks. UP and INS accepted, breaking ranks with the newspaper alliance. AP soon followed. The richer newspapers adopted a can't-lick-'em-them-join-'em policy and bought their own radio stations. Within a year, the Biltmore peace pact collapsed.[5]

Paul White quickly rebuilt the Columbia News Service. Klauber persuaded Paley to adopt an objective, nonpartisan news policy, one drawn from his own service at *The New York Times* but carried to a rarefied level of objectivity to serve the special character of radio. Paley thus announced his news credo in 1935:

> We declare CBS to be completely non-partisan on all public controversial questions including politics.... Broadcasting must for-

ever be wholly, honestly, and militantly non-partisan. This is true not only in politics, but in the whole realm of arguable ideas. To put it another way, it must never maintain an editorial page nor seek to maintain views of its own on any public question except broadcasting itself. Moreover, it must never try to further either side of any debatable question regardless of its own private and personal sympathies.... Why may the press be as editorially partisan as it pleases, while we may not: For the reason that there can be an unlimited number of publications devoted to countless purposes whereas the number of broadcasters is rigidly limited for physical reasons, and, therefore, an editorial attitude on the part of broadcasters would always carry with it the danger of one side of a vital argument being maintained preponderantly or exclusively.

Paley would allow analysis over CBS, but not opinion. In Paley's lexicon, an analyst analyzed a situation, but took no position. Opinion meant taking sides and had no place on CBS.[6]

The policy had a noble ring, and the distinction between radio and the press had a certain validity. But his position might be more convincingly explained by the fact that a radio network, unlike a newspaper, might risk its government license, and hence its life, by having a mind of its own. Thus Paley's policy served twin interests, objectivity and survival.

Objectivity was to become virtually Paley's avowed religion. He clung to it like the true cross. The policy would occasionally be violated by his broadcasters. But violators were like sinners, to be forgiven, never condoned. Disagreement over the hairline differences between analysis, opinion, commentary, and editorializing was eventually to hang like a black cloud over Ed Murrow and Bill Paley.

Ed Murrow was still essentially an overseas impresario scheduling broadcasts about dog shows and talks by members of Parliament. The CBS no-opinion policy pertained virtually to only two people at CBS. CBS had one regular commentator, Boake Carter, a gentleman with a British accent who regularly made hash of Paley's objectivity standard as Carter savaged the New Deal and labor unions, a sinner, but a profitably sponsored sinner. H.V. Kaltenborn, an ex-*Brooklyn Eagle* reporter, with an inimitable, and much parodied, delivery, also dispensed occasional analysis over CBS. But Kaltenborn was unsponsored and constantly being warned not to express a "point of view." Kaltenborn became so exasperated that he named his country house in New Jersey "Point of View," because, he said, it was the only place he could have one.[7]

That was where radio journalism stood at the time when Murrow began serving as CBS's European representative—the facts in five-minute news capsules, the drama of pseudo-news through *The March of Time*, and analysis by a handful of commentators.

International broadcast journalism was even more embryonic. The first worldwide broadcast ever made had taken place eight years before at the opening of the London Naval Conference, the event that had led Frederick Wile to hire Caeser Saerchinger for CBS. On January 21, 1930, a BBC announcer intoned, "We now take you to the House of Lords." There King George V was to welcome the delegates. CBS was transmitting the king's speech to its affiliates when a mechanic, Harold Vivian, tripped and broke the cable carrying the royal welcome. Vivian had the presence of mind to seize the two ends, one in each hand, and thus became a human conduit through which the king's English was transmitted to the CBS network.

Thereafter, formal talks were broadcast from abroad, not news really, but rather the speakers that a Saerchinger or a Murrow would arrange to put on the air, government officials, academics, journalists, authors, alternating with the church choirs and sporting events.[8]

There did occur in 1936 a brief suggestion of what foreign radio reportage could be. H.V. Kaltenborn had been traveling in Europe when the civil war broke out in Spain. Kaltenborn went to Hendaye, a sliver of France that protruded into Spain near Irun. Kaltenborn described live over a circuit to New York what he could see of the fighting on the other side of the border. His microphone caught the distant rattle of machine guns and the thud of artillery, the sounds of a war heard for the first time in American living rooms. But there were no radio correspondents in Spain reporting the war. The foreign correspondent was still a newspaperman. When the fighting had first broken out in Spain, Caeser Saerchinger was in Berlin making arrangements to broadcast the 1936 Olympics. And that was where he stayed because that was where CBS wanted him. Europe's struggles, H.V. Kaltenborn's initiative notwithstanding, were not radio's dish.[9]

Ed Murrow took up Saerchinger's duties, presenting bagpipers from St. Andrews, Christmas greetings from Haile Selassie, and the Grand National from Aintree, interspersed with guest lectures. The new journalism of the air was emerging at home, but abroad, it was yet to be born. In the summer of 1937, Murrow, in an attempt to overtake NBC's Max Jordan, sowed the seed that was to create modern broadcast journalism, at home and abroad.

William L. Shirer was living in Berlin, 33 years old, broke, out of work, with a pregnant wife, when he received a telegram from London. Shirer had been born in Chicago, the son of a lawyer, who died following an appendectomy when Bill was 10. The family then fell on hard times, and Bill went to live in Cedar Rapids, Iowa, raised on the wrong side of the tracks by his grandmother, a severe and sober-minded woman. The experience was to mark him for life. As someone who knew Shirer well later remarked, "He had this thing about people with money and privilege."

He was a precocious boy, burning with curiosity about the world be-

yond Cedar Rapids. He took to journalism like a bird to flight. When he
was 16 he became the high school correspondent for the Cedar Rapids
paper. He graduated from Coe College in Cedar Rapids, became a friend
of the artist Grant Wood, and knocked about with a tent crew on the
Chatauqua circuit.

When he was 21, Shirer took a cattle boat to Europe and subsequently
went to work on the Paris edition of *The Chicago Tribune*. He was part of
that surging mob on Le Bourget field on May 21, 1927, when Charles
Lindbergh landed in the *Spirit of Saint Louis*. Shirer later lost the sight in
one eye in a skiing accident, married an Austrian woman, and became
the Berlin-based correspondent for Universal Service, the overseas arm
of Hearst's International News Service.

One year into the Hitler regime, he wrote in his diary: "I'm in the
throes of depression. I miss the old Berlin of the Republic, the carefree,
emancipated civilized air, the snub-nosed women with the short-bobbed
hair....the constant Heil Hitlers, clicking of heels and brown-shirted storm
troopers, or black coated SS guards marching up and down the street grate
on me...." He would not have to tolerate Berlin much longer. Hearst was
losing money on its Universal Service and in the summer of 1937 shut
the operation down. Bill Shirer was given two weeks notice.

And then he received the telegram. "Will you have dinner with me at
the Adlon Friday night." It was signed, "Murrow, Columbia Broadcasting." Shirer wrote in his diary that day, "I dimly remembered the name,
but could not place it beyond his company." Nevertheless, he wired back,
"Delighted."

They met in the lobby of the Hotel Adlon. Shirer later recorded his
first impression of Murrow: "As I walked up to him, I was a little taken
aback by his handsome face. Just what you would expect from radio, I
thought. He had asked me for dinner, I considered, to pump me for dope
for a radio talk he must make from Berlin. We walked into the bar and
there was something in his talk that began disarming me. Something in
his eyes that was not Hollywood."

The man Murrow met was a stocky, balding, rumpled figure who wore
a beat-up fedora and who spoke with the flat, uninflected speech of the
prairie. There was nothing at all remarkable about Bill Shirer until seen
up close. Then his gaze was lively and curious, the expression on his face
animated, even roguish. What he said impressed Murrow and bore out
the good reports Ed had heard of Shirer from Raymond Swing and
Ferdinand Kuhn, of *The New York Times*.

They talked over drinks and dinner. Much to Shirer's surprise, Murrow had not come to pick his brains. Instead, he offered Shirer a job, but
on one condition. The condition was almost as unexpected to Shirer as
the job offer. Murrow said, apologetically, "...you see, in broadcasting it's
a factor. And our directors and numerous vice presidents will want to hear
your voice first." Shirer later wrote in his diary: "Who ever heard of an

adult with no pretensions to being a singer or any other kind of artist being dependent for a good, interesting job on his *voice?* And mine is terrible." Shirer's estimate was accurate. His voice was the sound of an overly bright Iowa adolescent undergoing a voice change, at a time when rich baritones were the standard in radio.

He was nearly paralyzed with fear when he made the test. The microphone stand jammed at maximum height and Shirer had to sit on piled-up crates, with his legs dangling like a child's, in order to reach the mike. He then waited three agonizing weeks for the result. On September 13, much to Shirer's surprise, Murrow phoned to say he was hired.[10]

At the end of the month, he went to London for a week of orientation and came to know his new chief better. Shirer was later to write a roman à clef in which the main character, Robert Fletcher, was patterned after Ed Murrow. As Shirer described Fletcher/Murrow, "There is something in Fletcher that always draws me out, making me more talkative than I ordinarily am. And apparently I have the same effect on him....He was modest about his own success, but not about his ambition, which was driving and passionate, to transform radio...into something far more imaginative and exciting and adult and honest...."

Later, as Fletcher/Murrow describes what the new man can expect of radio, he says, "It isn't complete freedom of speech....As you will find, there are a number of pressures at home, besides that of the sponsor.... But perhaps it's more freedom than you'll find anywhere else in the world. And if you don't take advantage of it, Raymond [Shirer], I'll fire you." Shirer has the Fletcher/Murrow character say of himself, "They call me an idealist and they mean no compliment."[11]

To his diary, Shirer confided: "Murrow will be a grand guy to work with...." Still he was perplexed. He had been twelve years in Europe, confident that he understood the politics of the Continent as well as any American there. But, Murrow explained, Shirer himself would not do any broadcasting. His job was to find qualified speakers, often journalists, to make the actual broadcast. This perverse prohibition, scheduling journalists no better qualified than himself, was frustrating enough to Shirer. But what had the voice test been all about? Murrow explained that he was under the same prohibition. Murrow, however, had never been a journalist.

He decided that Shirer should be based in Vienna, which pleased the newsman, since Berlin had become so oppressive to him. But the lengthening shadow of nazism followed Shirer. He and his wife, Tess, feeling uneasy about it, rented an apartment vacated by a Jewish family who had fled Austria because of growing Nazi sentiment in the country, and who had gone to live in Czechoslovakia.[12]

The Murrows were still living in the Saerchinger apartment on Queen Ann Street. Ed was in the bathroom, shaving. It was a day in February of 1938. The next morning, he would be leaving for a long trip to the Continent. Janet was in the bedroom at her dressing table. The room was chilly, and she noticed that the coil in the electric heater was not working. She grabbed the heater to jiggle it, and 220 volts of electricity shot through her body. She was flung around the room like a rag doll and later remembered thinking. "I'm never going to see Ed again. I don't want to die." She was thrown so violently that the heater smashed against the floor, breaking the circuit. Thus she was saved. But the palm of her right hand had been seared to the bone. Her fingers were fused together and her flesh hung in charred shreds.

Janet went to a doctor. The visit unnerved her. The man looked at her hand and then reached for one of his medical texts. He had never treated burns before, he said. The next doctor she saw was, if anything, more unsettling. He told her that if she did not have restorative surgery soon, the hand would contract into a claw. The cost of the operation alone was estimated at over $2,000. She left the doctor's office "in a state of shock." She told a friend, Charlotte Ramsay, that the price was "immoral." Ed, on hearing the figure, said quietly, "That's a quarter of my annual salary."

Delay only increased the risks. Thus that summer, Janet was operated on by Sir Harold Gillies, the leading British specialist on burns. The procedure was so difficult, Janet recalled, that "spectators came to watch Dr. Gillies operate."

When it was over, Ed wrote a letter to his family revealing his lingering economic insecurity. "Entirely between us," he wrote, "I've taken a terrible beating on Janet's hand but won't mind that if it turns out all right. I'm afraid it will always be crippled. Even if all goes well it will cost me five months salary—not what I can save in five months but every nickel I make in five months...as you know I hate being in debt. She's had literally the best doctors in the world in the best hospital in London....this is a strange town from a medical point of view. You are either a charity case and in a filthy old-fashioned hospital with butchers for doctors or you are in a palace and pay for it. The cost for the anaesthetic alone was $150. Please don't mention all this to Janet. She wept about the cost and wanted to leave the hand as it was. But I wouldn't have it."[13]

Just before the accident, Janet had finally found them a home of their own. She had located a flat within walking distance of CBS and the BBC. They moved that spring to Weymouth House 5, 84 Hallam Street, W.1. The rent was £280 a year, approximately $117 a month.[14]

Because of Janet's accident, Ed had postponed his trip to the Continent. But ten days later he went, feeling uneasy about leaving Janet alone for what was expected to be two months. He would instead be home in three weeks, a period after which neither his life nor the world would ever be the same.

During those weeks, he visited Rotterdam for a broadcast on the maiden voyage of the Dutch liner *Nieuw Amsterdam*. Then he was off to

Eindhoven for another feature story. His thoughts, however, were else-where. As he wrote Janet, "Things look bad in Austria. There's likely to be bloodshed."

The previous chancellor, Engelbert Dollfuss, had been murdered in the failed Nazi takeover attempt of 1934. His successor, Kurt Schuschnigg, hoping to defuse an incendiary condition, had thereafter jailed leading Nazis. Hitler summoned Schuschnigg to his Berchtesgaden retreat and ordered him to free all imprisoned Nazis, restore the Austrian Nazi party, and put the party's chief, Arthur von Seyss-Inquart, in his cabinet. If Schuschnigg refused, Hitler said, he would invade Austria. Schuschnigg caved in, aware that he had likely signed an independent Austria's death warrant.

Ed had been following these events intently and consequently was look-ing forward to the next stop on his itinerary, Berlin. There Shirer would join him and brief him on what was happening. He found Shirer also con-sumed by the Austrian crisis. And both men were furious over the attitude in the CBS home office. Europe faced its deadliest peril since 1914, and the network was insisting that Murrow go next to Warsaw and Shirer to Ljubljana, Yugoslavia, to arrange broadcasts of children's choruses.[15]

Paul White, a news bloodhound at home, kept investing CBS's lim-ited resources in Europe in frivolity. Murrow suspected that White was not about to add to Murrow's power in Europe by allowing a rival news center to flourish there.

With the children's broadcast completed, Murrow was still in Poland. But Shirer had taken the train from Ljubljana back to Vienna. He ar-rived on Friday, March 11, to find himself on the cutting edge of history.

Two days before, the beleaguered Schuschnigg had announced that he would put the question of annexation of Austria by Germany to a vote. On Sunday, March 13, Austria was to hold a plebiscite on the issue. But Hitler lowered another ultimatum on Schuschnigg. Hold the plebiscite and Germany would invade, he threatened. Schuschnigg called off the election.

That night, Shirer was home listening to Strauss waltzes on the radio when a voice interrupted the music and introduced Chancellor Schusch-nigg. Hitler, he said, had demanded that he name the Austrian Nazi, Seyss-Inquart, as chancellor. Schuschnigg was finished.

Seyss-Inquart then came on the air, and Shirer learned that though the Austrians had conceded to all of Hitler's demands, the German army was nevertheless on the march. Hitler was swallowing up Austria into the Third Reich. Annexation he called it, *Anschluss.*

Shirer had been scribbling down what he heard. As he later described the moment, "I had the most important story of my life and I had it to myself so far as reporting firsthand on American radio was concerned. My sole rival, Max Jordan of NBC, was not here." He dashed to Ravag, Austrian state radio. But Austrian storm troopers had taken over the build-ing and told him all lines were dead.[16]

In New York, Bill Paley was home in bed with the flu and a temperature of 102 degrees when the ever-faithful Ed Klauber called. Klauber had learned of Shirer's predicament. Paley's combative instincts were instantly aroused. He bridled at the idea of losing any opportunity to beat NBC. From his sickbed, he picked up the phone and had the overseas operator put him through to the director of Ravag. Paley knew the man from his European travels, and the two had maintained a cordial relationship. In the midst of chaos, the man took Bill Paley's call. Paley began explaining his unhappiness at being shut out of the *Anschluss* story. But before he could finish, the director broke in, and in a choking voice said, "I am sorry, Mr. Paley, I am no longer in charge here. I cannot do anything. I would if I could." Paley heard a sob and then a click. The line went dead.[17]

Shirer, in the meantime, had tried to call Murrow in Warsaw to alert him to what was happening in Vienna, but had not been able to reach him. He returned from the radio station to his apartment in the early hours of the morning of March 12 and the phone rang. Warsaw had Murrow on the line. Ed, in the meantime, had been in touch with Paul White, who had finally accepted that CBS ought to report a Europe in turmoil. They had agreed that Shirer should get out of Vienna to some place where he could escape Nazi censorship, lease a transmitter, and report the *Anschluss*. His would be the first unexpurgated eyewitness radio report to America. Murrow told Shirer to get himself to London as fast as possible. And then Murrow made a fateful decision. He himself would fly to Vienna. He would take over for Shirer while Shirer went to London.

By 6:30 that Saturday evening, Shirer was before a BBC microphone giving the first, uncensored eyewitness account of the death of independent Austria. He described crowds shouting themselves hoarse, parroting Hitler's rallying cry, "Ein Reich, Ein Volk, Ein Fuehrer!" (one state, one people, one leader). Shirer closed his broadcast with: "That's what they got, and as I said, very quickly, too."[18]

Meanwhile, Murrow was finding it difficult to get from Warsaw to Vienna. There were no flights to Vienna from the Polish capital. He boarded a plane to Berlin to see what he might manage from there. On his arrival he found that nothing was immediately available from Berlin to Vienna. He managed to raise $1,250 in Berlin on a Sunday and chartered a Lufthansa passenger plane. Shortly afterward, the only passenger aboard, he stepped off the plane at Aspern Airport in Vienna.[19]

Paley, in the meantime, still in bed, was racking his brain for an angle to outperform NBC on the *Anschluss* story. He had an idea, something that had not been attempted before. As he later wrote in his autobiography: "I thought about it for a while and realized that every capital in Europe must be seething in reaction to Hitler's takeover of Austria. I thought, suppose we had a report from most of the major European capitals to see what that reaction was."

Innocent of the technical obstacles, Paley told Klauber he wanted a roundup from all around Europe in one half-hour broadcast. Soon Klauber called him back. Ed Klauber did not like to fail Bill Paley. Indeed, he dreaded saying no to Bill Paley. But the CBS engineers had told him that what Paley wanted was impossible. As Paley later recalled their conversation, "I said, I will not accept that answer." Klauber called back again in an hour and said it would be tricky, but the engineers would try.

Klauber next had Paul White call Shirer in London. It was, by now, one o'clock on a Sunday afternoon New York time. By eight o'clock that evening, White said, Shirer and Murrow were to have commentators on the air from London, Paris, Berlin, Rome, and, if possible, Vienna. Shirer called Murrow in Vienna and explained what Paley wanted accomplished in the next seven hours.[20]

The obstacles were formidable, likely insuperable. In that time, they had to find a qualified journalist in each capital. They had to obtain permission from the employers of the correspondents allowing them to broadcast over a rival news medium. Then, Murrow and Shirer had to lease land lines and shortwave transmitters in each city. All this had to be accomplished on a Sunday evening, European time, when offices were closed and most employees were off for the day and their facilities were in the hands of weekend caretakers. Assuming the logistics could be worked out, each report had to be timed to the split second so that the commentators, who would not necessarily be able to hear each other, would come in at exactly the right time, without overlapping the previous report or leaving dead air before the next. And it all had to be done live, since, in that era, the networks did not permit recorded broadcasts.

Frank Gervasi, then heading the INS Bureau in Rome, described his experience. Gervasi happened to be in his office in the Galeria Colonna when somebody named Shirer called him from London, "just a stranger's voice on the end of the line," as Gervasi remembered. Shirer wanted him to do an analysis of what Italy, Germany's chief rival for influence over Austria, thought of Hitler's action. Gervasi immediately tried to locate the engineers at Italian state radio. The Italians told him there was not enough time to arrange a shortwave transmission to New York. He then phoned Switzerland to attempt an alternate land-line connection to Geneva, which had a shortwave transmitter that could reach New York. As the hour for the broadcast approached, Gervasi was still trying unsuccessfully to find a transmitter and banging out his comments at the same time.[21]

In the meantime, Murrow and Shirer were on the phone all over Europe. They managed to line up Gervasi's INS counterpart in Berlin, Pierre Huss, an aggressive reporter who some of his colleagues believed was somewhat too friendly with his Nazi news sources. In Paris they enlisted Edgar Ansel Mowrer of the *Chicago Daily News*. In London, Shirer tracked down Murrow's admirer, the Labour MP, Ellen Wilkinson, who raced in from a country weekend to Broadcasting House. The correspondent from Vienna was to be a rank amateur, someone with no journalism experience at all who was making his first appearance as a reporter, Edward R. Murrow.[22]

Whether Murrow attempted unsuccessfully to engage any other print journalists—Vienna was then full of them—or whether he deliberately seized the moment, to play out a secret and burning ambition, is unknowable, since he was operating alone. Nevertheless, the decision to go on the air himself was pivotal in his life. In between calls to Shirer, to the reporters, to transmitting facilities, and to Paul White in New York, he began to pick out his maiden report with two fingers on a typewriter.

Ever since the Austrian crisis had begun, the networks had been breaking into scheduled programs, peppering listeners with bulletins. Attention centered on the movements of Adolf Hitler at likely the sweetest moment of his life. He was returning to his native Austria and to the Vienna that had spurned him in his youth. Like an unexpectedly successful son taking a parent into his home, he would now officially enfold Austria into Germany.

The bulletins recorded his progress. Hitler had left Germany. Hitler had crossed the Austrian border near Braunau-am-Inn, his birthplace, as cheering Austrian border guards tore down the barrier. Hitler had entered Linz, where 100,000 people, in a city of 120,000, gave him an ear-splitting welcome. Hitler was on his way to Vienna, riding in an open Mercedes Benz.

At 8 p.m. that Sunday evening, from Studio 9 on the seventeenth floor of the CBS building, Bob Trout came on the air and announced, "The program, 'St. Louis Blues,' will not be heard tonight." Instead, CBS would present a special half-hour report of reactions from European capitals on the annexation of Austria.[23]

Judged as a technical feat alone, the first international news roundup was impressive. Every reporter came in like clockwork. Even Frank Gervasi, who in the end had not been able to broadcast, managed to phone his text to London in time for Shirer to read it over the air. But it was not the technical feat that lifted broadcast journalism to a new plateau that night. Rather, it was the listener's sensation of being on the scene, as though some knowledgeable friends had dropped by to explain exactly what had happened. It happens everyday now, and with pictures. And no one gives it a thought. But there is always that moment when something is done for the first time. This was such a night.

To Murrow, then approaching his thirtieth year, the moment marked a man finding himself. The Nazis had reopened the Vienna–to–New York circuit, and Murrow had begun his report: "This is Edward Murrow speaking from Vienna. I arrived here by air from Warsaw and Berlin only a few hours ago....From the air, Vienna didn't look much different than it has before, but, nevertheless, it's changed. The crowds are courteous as they've always been, but many people are in a holiday mood; they lift the right arm a little higher here than in Berlin and the 'Heil Hitler' is said a little more loudly. There isn't a great deal of hilarity but at the same time there doesn't seem to be much feeling of tension. Young storm troopers are riding about the streets, riding about in trucks and vehicles of all sorts, singing and tossing oranges out to the crowd. Nearly every principal building has its armed guard, including the one from which I am speaking. There are still huge crowds along the Ringstrasse and people still stand outside the principal hotels, just waiting and watching for some famous man to come in or out. As I said, everything is quiet in Vienna tonight. There's a certain air of expectancy about the city, everyone waiting and wondering where and at what time Herr Hitler will arrive."[24]

It was an embryonic effort, but like an embryo, the outlines of what was to be were already there. Evident was an eye for details that the listener could visualize ("young storm troopers...tossing oranges out to the crowd"). There was an ear for revealing sounds (in Vienna, "the 'Heil Hitler' is said a little more loudly" than in Berlin). He conjured up an ambivalent mood ("every principal building has its armed guard....huge crowds along the Ringstrasse...."). In whatever minutes he had on the air, Murrow sketched a portrait of Austria suggesting a bourgeois hausfrau who has been abducted, is waiting to be seduced, and is not particularly unhappy over this unexpected midlife adventure.

The roundup format was successfully repeated the following night. Murrow continued broadcasting from Vienna. Of the occupying German troops, he said: "They're sleeping on straw and there are stacked rifles and iron helmets arranged neatly along the wall....They don't talk a great deal with the Viennese, but they're always courteous and they certainly give the impression of iron discipline." The images were simple and unadorned, and they made the listener see what he saw.

Years later, Howard K. Smith, who would eventually work for Murrow, tried to explain the man's instant flowering as a broadcaster: "Ed didn't know how to write like a newsman, which freed him to write with his own fresh eye and ear. I went through the files of his first broadcasts and they were just notes on paper. The man was ad-libbing transatlantic broadcasts!"[25]

Lewis Powell, Murrow's lawyer friend with whom he had knocked around Europe in his student days, remembered his astonishment at suddenly hearing Ed Murrow on the radio, "so calm, so incisive, so at home in what he was doing," and so suddenly a public figure.[26]

When the crisis was over, Shirer returned to Vienna and Ed met him. They went out for a drink to try to digest what had happened to them and to radio in three epic days. Shirer headed for a favorite hangout, but Ed steered him away. He had been in the place the night before, he told Shirer, and had seen a man, a Jew he thought, take an old-fashioned razor from his pocket and slash his throat.

It would be excessive to suggest that a hastily assembled collection of one-shot radio commentators in a half-hour broadcast had matched the depth and quality of newspaper coverage of the *Anschluss*. Murrow and Shirer were fully aware of both how much and how little they had accomplished. Radio had contributed not better or even equal coverage, but rather a new kind of coverage that increased the perception and comprehension of a historic moment. What both men believed, above all, was that there was no turning back now. CBS must shift its priorities from covering featherweight "special events" to reporting the upheaval on the Continent. Furthermore, there must be no more farming out to newspaper correspondents what radio correspondents could do for themselves. They wanted an end to international broadcasting as some sort of travelogue-cum-circus-cum-folk-festival and to build instead a new journalism.[27]

The plane that flew Ed out of Vienna was filled with fleeing Jews, among them an old couple who took the seats in front of him. As the plane stopped at Prague, the copilot came out of the cockpit, stood grinning in the cabin doorway, and announced that they were outside of German territory. Ed watched the old man smile, reach over, and take his wife's hand.[28]

He came home a man obsessed, unable to let go of the story. On his arrival in London at 2:30 a.m., he went directly to the BBC facilities and made another broadcast. When he finished, he corralled Cecelia Reeves, a BBC staffer. "His text," she said, "was shattering and when he had finished, he asked me if I was tired, because he had not slept since he came back and would appreciate it if I would stay and have a drink and let him talk about it. I had many Austrian friends, all Jewish, and was hungry for news. We sat for about an hour while he told me the first of those stories of people beaten up in bars and so on which were to become all too familiar later."[29]

Janet was shaken by the transformation in him. She confided to her diary: "He is completely consumed with thoughts of intrigue, politics, and war." A few days later, she wrote: "Ed very curt and uninterested in seeing me....I must be patient. I do hope it's not true that love is purely a matter of habit. He has gotten out of the habit of seeing me. But it does hurt so much to call him up and have him say, 'Is it anything important? If not, hang up'....Treats me like a stranger whose bothering him....later [he] realized he was being nasty and made an effort to be nice."

They had lunch with the Galbraiths, and as Ken Galbraith remembered, "Ed seemed devastated by the *Anschluss* experience." What his wife and friends were witnessing was again the Murrow compulsion to make public events his own private travail. He acted as though he had experienced the *Anschluss*, not as a detached journalist, but as an Austrian patriot or a fleeing Jew. They were also witnessing a man who, after several agreeable but nevertheless false starts, had found his reason for being, a startling discovery that tended to crowd out other interests, even other people. His obsessive, compulsive nature, in remission during the previous year of calm, had found the perfect outlet.[30]

The lull after the *Anschluss* forced Ed back into the chafing routine of European scheduler of special events. He was like a decorated combat veteran returning to his job as a postal clerk in his hometown. He went to Geneva to attend a conference of the International Broadcasting Union. There he met Shirer again. Ed talked obsessively about the future of radio. Again they fed off of each other's excitement. They felt the exhilaration of men on the rim of an uncharted frontier, glimpsing a new world and marching into it ahead of all others.

There was little personal chitchat. Shirer found the private Murrow difficult to penetrate. Shirer enjoyed women, and the subject would have been common conversational ground for men in their position, swapping tales of conquests, reverses, and techniques of seduction. But Shirer found that Murrow did not share his amatory interest. Instead, Murrow cautioned Shirer to be careful about his roving eye. He did not speak, Shirer remembered, as a boss warning him, but as a friend concerned "on moral grounds, because, I imagined, of his strict upbringing." If anything, Murrow, in Shirer's judgment, seemed to have little interest in women.

Only when they talked about radio did Murrow become passionate. Shirer found Ed otherwise detached, elusive, devoid of small talk and mundane interests. "Ed Murrow did not seem to need people," as Shirer put it. He sensed this self-containment in the restraint between Ed and Janet. The Murrows were an enigma to Shirer. There was between them none of the tempestuousness of the Shirer ménage. He found Janet particularly remote. Her diary entries at the time, however, reveal a highly vulnerable young woman who had learned to mask her insecurities by keeping quiet when unsure of herself and by facing life with a determined composure that Shirer and others misread as coldness.[31]

Bill Paley was back in England that August. He was still the diffidently glamorous, rich overlord and Ed Murrow his subordinate. But there was an unmistakable shift since their last encounter. Paley was impressed by two things, talent and social position. The Murrow he met this season was able to deliver on both. As a broadcaster, Murrow had revealed an instant star quality that Paley admired as much as that of any entertainer he had lured to his network. Ed also had made impressive friends in British society, the kind of people Paley wanted to know, and Ed saw that Bill met them. When it was time for Paley to go home this time, Murrow went with him to Southampton to see him off on the ship. Just before Paley left, he told Murrow to send him a report every two weeks on the situation in Europe. Ed was to cable the report directly to Paley and no one else. It was still employer to employee. But the gulf was narrowing.[32]

In September, Janet's brother, Dart Brewster, came to England. By then, the reconstructive surgery on her hand had succeeded. She was in good spirits, and so she and Dart went off on a pilgrimage to trace the Brewster roots. At a placed called Scrooby, they found the trail of their famous ancestor, the Mayflower's Elder William Brewster. Janet wrote in her diary: "Tiny little house our William is supposed to have lived in. Plaque says 'William Brewster lived here 16– to 16– (dates partially undecipherable)."[33]

Ed had not joined the Brewster pilgrimage because the fragile calm on the Continent after the *Anschluss* was already falling apart. The Chamberlain policy had not appeased Hitler. It had only sharpened his appetite. He now reached out to Czechoslovakia.

Ed and several American journalists had had a chilling preview of what was about to happen. Virginia-born Lady Astor, the first woman ever to sit in Parliament, agreed wholeheartedly with Chamberlain's foreign policy. She had made Cliveden, her country place, the salon of the appeasement crowd. Two months after the *Anschluss*, she arranged for Chamberlain to explain to the American reporters the beauty of his scheme for preserving peace in Europe.

What the prime minister told Ed and the other Americans, off the record, astonished them. Before he had confided in his own ministers, before he had informed his own party, to a group of foreigners, Chamberlain explained how he expected to pacify Hitler. There were in Czechoslovakia's Sudetenland three and a half million ethnic Germans, Czech citizens technically, who spoke German and who chafed at their treatment as a minority. Hitler had seized on their discontent to demand that Czechoslovakia return the Sudetenland to Germany. "Return" was loosely employed, since Germany had never possessed the Sudetenland. The Soviet Union, on the other hand, had pledged to come to Czechoslovakia's aid if she were threatened.

Given this background, what Chamberlain proposed was breathtaking, whether for its audacity or its naïveté. His scheme, he told the Americans, was to have England, France, and Italy agree to cede the Sudetenland to Germany. That should satisfy Hitler's ambitions and preserve the peace. The dismemberment proposal was startling not only for leaving out the Russians, but, incredibly, for excluding the Czechs.

As September arrived, Hitler became bolder in his claims on the Sudetenland. Murrow, forewarned at Cliveden, proposed to New York that CBS broadcast every day, or at the very minimum, once a week, out of Prague. But the New York office had quickly resumed the entertainment-as-usual vision of its European operation. Paul White turned Murrow down.[34]

The decision was particularly exasperating to Murrow. He had come to feel close to the beleagured Czechs. He had become friends with the Czech ambassador to London, Jan Masaryk, son of Thomas Masaryk, the first president and virtual father of the Czech republic. Jan Masaryk, then 54, was an immensely appealing figure, a rotund, gregarious man with a zest for life, a man who loved to have his friends in while he prepared spicy Czech dishes, spun tales, and sang folk songs in a rollicking style. He could also be as American as Murrow when he chose. Masaryk's mother was American, he had been educated in the United States, and spoke American English. Ed had Masaryk on the air several times to explain Czechoslovakia's plight, which was rather like explaining fox hunting from the viewpoint of the fox.[35]

Throughout September, Hitler maintained his drumbeat against Czechoslovakia. On September 12, he addressed a Nazi party rally at Nuremberg and vowed to the Sudeten Germans that the fatherland would rescue them from Czech oppression. Radio caught the chilling roar of tens of thousands of German throats pouring forth on cue "Sieg Heil! Heil Hitler!"

A few days later, Chamberlain met with Hitler at the führer's alpine retreat above Berchtesgaden to determine Czechoslovakia's fate. Murrow called Shirer to tell him to go to Berchtesgaden, but the talks broke off before Shirer could get there.

Murrow prowled the streets of London the evening of Chamberlain's return. An air of foreboding hung over the city. In Hyde Park, he watched army lorries lined up with their headlights on, as soldiers dug trenches by the harsh light. Troops piled sandbags against government buildings and passed out gas masks. Major subway stops were suddenly closed "for urgent construction work."

In a broadcast from Ten Downing Street, Chamberlain lamented, "How horrible...incredible it is that we should be digging trenches and trying on gas masks because of a quarrel in a faraway country between people of whom we need know nothing."

Ed spent hours riding buses, talking to cab drivers, buttonholing hotel doormen, trying to catch the mood of ordinary Britons. That night, he forsook the studio to try to give his listeners the feel of London. He spoke from a balcony on the third floor of Gudley's Bank in Whitehall, and opened with the phrase he had adopted from Caeser Saerchinger's London broadcasts, "Hello, America. This is London calling." He reported the reactions of people in the street to that "quarrel in a faraway country." He recounted what a World War I veteran had told him: "Thirty or forty years ago, I was in your country, out in Colorado and I saw those big poker games going on in the gold mines. And the events here remind me of those games I saw out in Colorado many years ago." Czechoslovakia was a distant game, one in which the average Englishman felt no stake.

On September 22, Chamberlain was back in Germany, this time at Bad Godesberg, again discussing Czechoslovakia's fate with Hitler. The Bad Godesberg talks also broke off indecisively, with Hitler threatening immediate military occupation of the Sudetenland in the absence of an agreement.

Within hours, Ed had Jan Masaryk on the air, speaking to America. Masaryk summoned up the spirit of his father, "buried just a year ago." "My unified nation" he went on, "is assembled around his grave, firmly resolved to safeguard the principles he laid down for us and we are convinced that truth, decency, freedom and love will triumph in the end. We shall defend it to the last breath." Czechoslovakia, Masaryk said, would resist Hitler, "in full confidence that this time, France and England will not forsake us...." "I tell you America," he closed, "our powder is dry."

Masaryk's confidence in England and France proved misplaced. Chamberlain trotted off to Germany a third time—this time to Munich where he met with Hitler, French Premier Edouard Daladier, and Italy's Benito Mussolini. Russia was conspicuously excluded. The meeting followed the Cliveden script that Chamberlain had outlined four months before. The four leaders sat like men with a small fowl on a plate before them and proceeded to carve it up. At thirty minutes after midnight on September 30, they signed a pact that gave the Sudetenland to Germany.

NBC enjoyed its traditional advantage in covering the story. Max Jordan was allowed to broadcast directly from the Munich *führerhaus*. Shirer was left out. Jordan was given an advance text of the pact, which he discussed on the air an hour before anyone else. But Murrow, from London, scored the first beat of his broadcast career. He was following events over Munich radio with the help of an interpreter and instantly flashed the word to America the moment he heard that the pact had been signed.

It has since become fashionable to make of the slight, stooped figure of Neville Chamberlain, with his wan smile, drooping mustache, and folded umbrella, the metaphor for muddle-headed optimism. He is seen as the fool-leader who, virtually alone, believed that he had bought "peace in our time" by appeasing Adolf Hitler. But when Chamberlain returned from Munich and stepped from his car at Ten Downing Street with the peace pact clutched in his hand, Murrow was there; and he reported how crowds filled Downing Street and Whitehall and cheered the prime minister wildly. The British press speculated whether Chamberlain would be knighted while in office, an honor that had occurred only twice before in British history. Chamberlain was the favorite for the Nobel Peace Prize. *The Daily Mail* caught the feelings of Britons at large. The paper hailed the returning prime minister as "The Prince of Peace."[36]

Murrow was in the minority. Just days after the Munich Pact he wrote home, "It was gained at a terrible cost and many who cheer now will weep when they realize what has happened." The BBC's Cecelia Reeves recalled running into Murrow after Munich. He took it hard, she said. He felt "shame and misery."

He was also, Reeves remembered, the only correspondent who took the trouble to look up Jan Masaryk during his ordeal. As Murrow himself later reported, "I sat all night with him in his London embassy the night his country was sacrificed on the altar of appeasement." The following night he had Masaryk on the air. After the broadcast, they went back to the Czech Embassy and brooded. They agreed that the surrender to Hitler guaranteed war. Of Masaryk's behavior that night, Murrow later recalled, "There was no bitterness in the man, nor was there resignation or defeat.

We talked long of what must happen in Europe, of the young men that would die and cities that would be smashed to rubble....As I rose to leave, the gray dawn pressed against the windows. Jan Masaryk pointed to news photos of Hitler and Mussolini and said, 'Don't worry, Ed. There will be dark days, and many men will die, but there is a God and he will not let such men rule Europe.'" Murrow remembered thinking, "His belief at that time was greater than my own."

By the end of the Munich crisis, Murrow was thoroughly blooded as a broadcaster. Between September 10 and September 30, he had been on the air thirty-five times himself and arranged 116 other broadcasts. He went for three weeks without a full night's sleep. He became impossible to live with after the first five nights and then went numb. He sent Janet to the country when it looked as though "They might start dropping things on London."

He was exasperated by the indifference of the British. He had dashed home at one point for a fresh change of clothes in the midst of the crisis only to have the maid tell him, "The vegetables were delivered, Mr. Murrow, the tailor brought your suit and, oh, yes, here's your gas mask." An English friend had phoned him at the height of the tension to ask him to play golf![37]

He was like a deep-sea diver who had to be brought back to sea-level pressure gradually. He asked Shirer to meet him in Paris. He was depressed, he said, and wanted to drown his sorrows with a pal. They trod the streets, Shirer recalled, Ed gloomy, but immersed in "talk, talk, talk," hour after hour, downing champagne along the way. Paris appeared to breathe a collective sigh of relief that war had been averted and never mind the cost. Bankers and businessmen toasted peace. Waiters and taxi drivers shared a sense of deliverance. On the left, the socialists were shot through with pacifism, and on the right, Fascist sympathizers celebrated the pact with Hitler. Murrow was disgusted.

He and Shirer, two joyless revelers, speculated on what would happen next. They agreed that war would come the following fall, in 1939, as soon as the harvest was in. And they were convinced that Hitler would strike Poland next. Shirer recorded in his diary, "This crisis has done one thing for us. I think radio talks by Ed and me are now established. Birth of the 'radio foreign correspondent' so to speak."[38]

The *Anschluss* had indeed created an appetite for radio news, and Munich had confirmed the habit. During the latter crisis, the American networks, for the first time, provided news on a twenty-four-hour basis. CBS's analyst in New York, H.V. Kaltenborn, was on the air even more than Murrow. During the crisis, Kaltenborn had moved a cot into Studio Nine and over the next eighteen days delivered eighty-five broadcasts.

Kaltenborn was a newsman of towering ego who spoke in aristocratically accented staccato bursts. Didactic and pontificating, he had the announcer introduce him as "H.V. Kaltenborn, here with a keen analysis..."

of whatever issue confronted the world at that moment. As his colleague Bob Trout recalled, Kaltenborn's keen analyses were so relentlessly forthcoming that in time they became one word, as in asking a secretary, "Have you finished typing H.V.'s keenanalysis yet?"

Before the Murrows had gone abroad in 1937, they and the Trouts had been invited to Kaltenborn's Brooklyn Heights home for dinner. H.V. was conducting a marathon monologue during which Murrow turned to Kitty Trout and said, unfortunately, just as H.V. made a rare pause, "Are we really having a good time?"

During the Munich crisis, radio listeners had become accustomed to Kaltenborn in New York, "Calling Ed Murrow. Calling Ed Murrow." There was something querulous and commanding in his voice, as though Murrow was somehow responsible for the atmospheric disturbances that often delayed a "keenanalysis."[39]

They were all becoming familiar now, almost household voices, broadcasters like Murrow, Shirer, and Kaltenborn. The difference between the print journalists and broadcast journalists was nicely caught by a writer who interviewed Murrow not long after Munich.

Robert Landry, writing in *Scribner's Magazine*, had been intrigued by Murrow as the exemplar of the new breed. Landry wrote, "...he has more influence than a shipful of newspapermen. This influence has not been generally recognized for the reason that the newspaper correspondents have tradition on their side, and partly because the networks have played up their commentators (like Kaltenborn) rather than their correspondents (like Murrow). But the influence is there, great and growing—and obvious to anyone who knows both radio and the press. Murrow has three advantages over correspondents for the greatest American newspapers: 1. He beats the newspapers by hours [Indeed, during Munich, radio virtually killed off the romantic newspaper tradition of newsboys hawking special editions and shouting 'Extra! Extra!' The radio bulletin was now the Extra.]; 2. He reaches millions who otherwise have to depend on provincial newspapers for their foreign news; 3. He writes his own headlines. His, unlike a reporter's, are not strained through cablese, copy editor, or headline writer...people begin to feel that they know him."

Murrow, still insecure in his own finances, had no problem, Landry noted, spending CBS's money: "He lived in the air and in a suitcase and used the long distance telephone with the lavishness of a Hollywood film producer."

An interesting feature of the Landry profile is that the fictions in Ed's background persisted. The *Scribner's* article even has Murrow graduating from high school 1 year early and spending two years as a compassman in British Columbia and Alaska, all untrue and likely devised by Murrow to explain his whereabouts during those years that he had added to his age. Landry appears to have innocently picked up the misstatements from CBS publicity releases. Murrow either had not yet taken the time to correct the errors or was reluctant to call any further attention to them. By this point, he had no need to be anyone but himself. Landry quoted *Variety* on the man who had entered 1938 in obscurity: "His name was figuratively put up in lights for the first time."[40]

Ed and Janet were back in America in November for their first visit home in eighteen months. Ed had come back to talk to Klauber and White about the network's readiness for the war that he said was inevitable. He wanted to expand the European operation. He wanted, in Shirer's phrase, to hire more "radio foreign correspondents."

While Ed was home, a 23-year-old theatrical genius had scared hell out of a good share of the country with a radio adaptation of H. G. Wells's *War of the Worlds*. Orson Welles had achieved a frightening verisimilitude in this story of an invasion from another planet by using the break-in bulletin, the on-the-scene report, the man-in-the-street interview, even the static and hum of shortwave broadcasts, all of which had only recently entered the public's consciousness during radio's treatment of the *Anschluss* and Munich crises.[41]

Ed was back in London early in 1939, now using a new opening for his broadcast. Ida Lou Anderson wrote to him almost every week. "The letters," Janet remembered, "went to Ed's office. I didn't see them." The woman's health had failed badly. She was losing her eyesight. She had been forced to give up teaching at WSC. She had attached herself to the Murrow family and now referred to Ethel as "Mother Murrow." The high point of her now empty days was to hear her "masterpiece" on the air. Ed's growing fame, and the fact that he spoke to millions, did not, however, overawe the teacher in her. She told Ed that Saerchinger's opening—"Hello America. This is London calling"—was trite. She had a better idea, which she spelled out, down to the appropriate accent and stress. In the midst of the Czech crisis, in a broadcast on September 22, Murrow tried it for the first time. He began, "This is London." The phrase would become synonymous with the man, imitated endlessly, usually poorly. The mistake was to assume a pause "This...is London." Murrow made no pause, but accentuated the first word and understated the last two, which, spoken in his darkly arresting delivery, gave the simple phrase its surprising power and drama: "THIS is London."[42]

CHAPTER 12

"A State of War Exists"

In the summer of 1939, Murrow received word that the Paul Whites were again coming to London. Janet wrote in her diary, "It's so distasteful to do things for people when you don't like them—because you're expected to." White and his wife would reach London in July at the same time the Murrows planned a brief escape to the country. Janet was concerned that the bumptious White might invite himself along. As a diversionary tactic, the Murrows had the Whites over for dinner and took them to the theater, and then the two couples went dancing. Ed mentioned that he and Janet would be away for a few days and White immediately asked if he and Sue could use the Murrows' apartment. Ed gratefully seized on the lesser of two impositions.

Relations between the two men, even with an ocean between them, had deteriorated since Murrow's emergence as a newsman. Now they were in the same ring, with Murrow excelling at White's game. White's insecurity came out in bullyboy office tactics. Ed would suggest an idea for a broadcast. White would reject it. Then, when it was too late to arrange it, White would want the broadcast, thus virtually ensuring Murrow's failure to deliver.

The bad blood was unfortunate. For however much they differed as men, Murrow and White shared a common passion, their belief in the new journalism which they were both bringing into being. On another network Murrow would have been a respected rival. Within the same network, White saw him as a threat.

Whether Ed liked White or disliked him, whether he entertained him out of pleasure or duty, did not matter this time. Murrow was pleased with the reason that brought White to London. White was coming to see whether the threat of war did justify enlarging CBS's European staff.

146

Bill Shirer would be joining them too for the talks. Shirer was returning from leave in the States and stopping in London on his way to his new post, Geneva. Vienna was no longer a European capital. It had been relegated to a provincial seat in the Third Reich. Geneva possessed a convenient central location. It had a powerful shortwave transmitter. Most important, Switzerland was free.

A third correspondent would join them, Tom Grandin, whom Ed had hired for Paris. Grandin, then 30, was a Yale graduate, a gentle man with a precise radio delivery that White did not find manly enough. Tom Grandin was not White's sort at all, and White hinted to Murrow that he intended to get rid of him.

On this visit, fortunately, White's instincts as a journalist proved stronger than his emotional insecurities. Murrow convinced him that CBS should continue to hire its own correspondents, much as a newspaper. The decision represented a major Murrow victory, and a risk. NBC was going off in an entirely different direction, a clever stratagem too. Sarnoff's network was planning to sign up prestigious figures in every major European country, offering an exclusive contract, say, to Winston Churchill to report from England.

The matter settled, Ed went off on his vacation. When he returned, Kay Campbell told him that Paul White had cabled Klauber saying that Ed was "resting" in the country and that he, White, was running the London operation. Ed was furious. But Shirer advised him not to let White upset him. He had talked to Paley and Klauber while he was in New York, and final decisions regarding CBS news, Shirer said, still remained firmly in Ed Klauber's hands. And as far as Klauber was concerned, Murrow could do no wrong.[1]

But Shirer did tweak Ed on another matter. Murrow was an ex-lumberjack out of Beaver, Washington. Shirer was a kid raised on the wrong side of the tracks in Cedar Rapids, Iowa. Shirer retained the self-made man's contempt for the undeserving rich, and he twitted Murrow that he was becoming a snob.

Ed had indeed gained entry to a rarefied level of British society. In part, he had been admitted by virtue of his position. An influential American journalist was a prize sought after by both sides in the continuing British political debate between the appeasers and the preparedness faction. Both wanted American support and American understanding. American journalists in England were the most direct route to American public opinion. So much of politics in Britain was conducted socially that the American correspondents found themselves courted by government officials, members of Parliament, and politically ambitious hostesses. They were invited to lunch at the good clubs, to Mayfair dinner parties, and, if sufficiently presentable, to country weekends at the great houses. They were almost all sought after. Yet, British hostesses seemed to fight for Ed Murrow.

Through Fred Bate, the Murrows had come to know one of the greatest houses and fortunes of England. Ronald Tree was the son of Americans
and the scion of the Chicago Marshall Field fortune, but now an Englishman. When Ed first met him, Tree was a member of Parliament and married to Lady Astor's niece, Nancy. Dytchley, Tree's country home in
Oxfordshire, dated from the reign of Charles II. The main house was
surrounded by "the park," 4,000 acres that swallowed up several small
villages. After their first visit to Dytchley, Janet described it as falling somewhere between "a palace and a country club."

Life at Dytchley took on an opulent ease. The Trees might have a
dozen or more weekend guests, but servants outnumbered guests. Every
wish was anticipated. Fresh-cut flowers appeared in every room every day.
Clothes were laid out by a staff so unobtrusive as to appear invisible. Another guest wrote of a stay at Dytchley, "One was tempted on rising to
stop, half dressed, and gaze interminably onto the sunny terraces onto
which the windows gave a view and think of the dead generations of your
predecessors in that room."

Winston Churchill was a frequent guest at Dytchley. So were Anthony
Eden and the socially prized Duff Coopers. The Trees' stately home was
the political rival of the Astors' Cliveden. At Dytchley the anti-Fascist, anti-
Munich, anti-appeasement wing of the Conservative party gathered to deplore Neville Chamberlain.

Ed was instantly welcome at Dytchley. In part it was his own ill-
concealed disdain for appeasement. But he also enjoyed another entry,
though it certainly was not the right schools, clubs, or ancestors. The sharp
eye and quick reflexes that he had honed as a boy putting food on the
Murrow table with his father's shotgun had a social cachet among the
English gentry. Ronnie Tree's passion was shooting, and Ed was a crack
wing shot. At Dytchley, however, it was done rather differently than in
Beaver. Tree's gamekeeper and crew loaded the guns, and then Tree's
dogs beat the woods and meadows, flushing out pheasants that Tree and
his guests slaughtered en masse.

Entering British society was rather like climbing a rope, hand over
hand, the Murrows found. One handhold led to another higher still. In
their first year in England, they had come to know Victor Cazalet. Cazalet
had a sister, Thelma, married to David Keir. The Keirs had a great house
in Kent. The Murrows and Keirs became friends. And it was David Keir
who put Ed up for membership in the Savile Club, favored by prominent
actors, writers, and journalists.

Through Sir Edward Grigg, their host on their first English country
weekend, the Murrows came to know the Right Honorable the Viscountess Milner, widow of a former British foreign minister. Lady Milner had
an appropriately Wodehousian country address, Great Wigsell, Hawk-
hurst, Kent. The viscountess was something of an English eccentric. As a
girl in the 1890s, she had taken the then daring step of going off on her

own to study art in Paris. She later married, and lost a son in World War I.
As she grew older, she became more idiosyncratic and unrepressed in her
beliefs, which she was able to indulge as the editor of a monthly magazine, the *National Review.* The magazine also allowed her to surround herself with a coterie of young writers. Though then in her seventies, Lady
Milner still had an undiminished appreciation of handsome men. She
adored Ed Murrow.

Through Lady Milner, the Murrows came to know her nephew, Lord
Cranborne, a close confidante of Winston Churchill. Soon after the Murrows met him, Cranborne was elevated to the peerage and became the
marquess of Salisbury. But to their friends, including the Murrows, the
marquess and the marchioness remained Bobbety and Betty. They had a
country place, Hatfield House, in Hertfordshire, which to an American
eye looked more like a museum of medieval history than a home.

These were the friends who inspired Bill Shirer's taunts that Ed
Murrow was going high hat. At the same time, Ed continued his close
friendship with Harold Laski, socialist paragon and champion of the dispossessed. An American friend of the Murrows', Charlotte Ramsay, recalled that one of Ed's favored themes at the time was "railing against the
social inequality in England."

What did it mean, his split vision regarding class? Was it hypocrisy, a
covering of all bases? Was it a confusion of identity in his own mind
brought on by his dizzying climb from the lumber camps of the Far West
to the stately homes of England?

Murrow had another American friend in England, Vincent "Jimmy"
Sheean, from Illinois, a gifted reporter and writer. Sheean, if anything,
had more glittering friends than Murrow. He had also married a woman
who provided him entry into English society. Among the Americans who
constantly ribbed Sheean about his patrician chums was Ed Murrow.
Sheean claimed to be a socialist and had a rationale for his behavior, and
it is interesting to consider it in light of Murrow's own attitudes toward his
patrician friends. Sheean had written, "I have no patience with the feudal
system, for organized privilege...." Rather, he said, "he had a desire to
see poverty abolished and an honorable socialist equality insured...." He
might spend his leisure drinking champagne with a duke or telling jokes
with brainless British colonels. "But I know that my brothers are toiling
and dying....In my heart, I am with them." But his upper-class friends
were people, too, Sheean argued, which his socialist friends refused to
acknowledge. As Sheean saw himself, "Few proletarians have traveled the
social continuum of an age and come to speaking terms with all of it without foreswearing their own identity or faith."

Ed Murrow never claimed to be a socialist. Nor did he ever commit
such a self-serving apologia as Sheean's to paper. But there were parallels.
Murrow also saw his upper-class companions as people first. His friends
or enemies were not predetermined by class. As Charles Collingwood put

it, "Ed *was* impressed with his social and political betters. But he didn't truckle to them." But Murrow's response to Shirer's gibes was a somewhat defensive "These people are valuable to me."[2]

In April of 1939 he began a regular Sunday afternoon broadcast. His disdain for the Chamberlain government's policy filtered subtly through his texts. But he was blunt in letters home: "I'm getting pretty prejudiced as far as the British are concerned, and they have made it quite clear that they don't like some of the things I've said lately. It may be that I shall be thrown out of this country before the war starts. Several people in high places have been giving me fatherly advise about it being in my own interest to do talks favorable to this country." Later he wrote his mother, "This is from your sleepless baby....Don't worry about me. Janet will go to the country and I shall have the nicest and softest bombproof cellar that you can imagine. I have no thought of dying for Columbia Broadcasting, nor for anyone else, if it comes to that. This business is a strain on the nerves, but there will be little actual danger, probably no more than there used to be from 'widow makers' when I was in the woods." The BBC studios had, in fact, been located deep below ground in the bowels of Broadcasting House and made bombproof and gasproof.[3]

His favorite beat was the House of Commons. "I like to sit in that rather dingy little room," he wrote, "listen to speeches and debates, then jump in a cab, go to the studio and try to take Americans right through the window and into the room."

He particularly enjoyed the verbal cut and thrust of that feisty backbencher, Winston Churchill. During a debate over the state of readiness of the Royal Navy, an MP had risen in the House and cautioned, "We must not take too harsh a stand against the Admiralty. Let us remember the traditions of the Royal Navy." Afterward, as Murrow told the story, Churchill muttered, "The traditions of the Royal Navy be damned. The only traditions of the Royal Navy are rum, sodomy, and the lash."[4]

Murrow's disapproval of Chamberlain brought him into conflict with the Cliveden set, beginning with its favorite American. Joseph P. Kennedy had been appointed ambassador to Great Britain in 1937, the year that Ed arrived. What more savory plum for this son of impoverished Irish immigrants than the Court of Saint James? Joe Kennedy had pulled himself up from a Boston Irish ghetto, building a fortune en route. In 1932, his wealth helped elect Franklin Roosevelt President, as, years later, it would help elect his own son to the office. When the embassy in Great Britain became vacant, it was Kennedy's for the asking. And he asked.

Joe Kennedy was fundamentally a businessman. He soon learned what British business and banking interests wanted. War would jeopardize their investments on the Continent. Learn to live with the Nazis, they said; don't fight them. The alternative to the Nazis in Germany was the Communists. Joe Kennedy saw it that way too. Neville Chamberlain was bending over backward to avoid war. Kennedy supported him. And so, soon after presenting his credentials, Ambassador Joseph Kennedy had been rapidly and happily absorbed into the Cliveden circle.

During Munich, Kennedy had confidently assured Chamberlain that President Roosevelt backed his position, a distortion which won Kennedy a stiff reprimand from Roosevelt. Still, Joe Kennedy went home for several months during 1939, and he spent much of the time traveling around the country preaching neutrality and isolationism. Should war break out in Europe, England was not the horse to back, Kennedy said. He had it on the best authority. Charles Lindbergh had been to Germany, and Lindbergh told Joe Kennedy that the Luftwaffe was invincible. Whether Janet was expressing her own or Ed's opinion, she wrote home, "Beware Mr. C.A. Lindbergh. He's a good disciple of National Socialism."

Still, Joe Kennedy cloaked his opinions in enormous personal charm. He was a gregarious man, possessed of Irish wit, wealth, and an immensely attractive family. To the American press corps in England he was marvelous copy, and he played its members like a harp.

Ed Murrow, however, was not seduced by the Kennedy beguilements. He found the man's charm rather too calculated. He disapproved of his instant alliance with the moneyed people in England. He did not like what he heard of Mr. Kennedy's womanizing. But none of the personal behavior mattered alongside Murrow's distaste for Kennedy's defeatist-appeasement line.

Harold Nicolson, well-connected, and a member of Parliament, blistered Kennedy in a piece in *The Spectator.* Ambassador Kennedy was welcomed in England, Nicolson wrote, only by the bankers and "...the peace pledge union, the friends of Herr von Ribbentrop and members of former pro-Nazi organizations." Murrow could not himself directly criticize an American ambassador on the air. But he happily read Nicolson's piece during his broadcast.[5]

The summer of 1939, Hitler was pressing Poland for territory, the Polish Corridor, Danzig, Posen, and Silesia. Murrow seized the mood of renewed crisis to strengthen his staff. He remembered the brooding Nordic he had brought home to dinner two years before. What he had learned of Eric Sevareid since confirmed his initial good opinion. Sevareid was now working in Paris holding down two jobs, as city editor of the Paris *Herald Tribune* and as night editor for the United Press.

Sevareid had come out of an urban speck in the wheat plains of North Dakota, a town called Velva. His father was the lone banker and hence presumed to be the richest man in town, a modest feat in Velva. Young Eric was tall and rangy, but had little interest in the sports that consumed the leisure of his schoolmates. He was a dreamy, bookish youth who felt isolated from his contemporaries by his solitary passions and his family's position. He left Velva for the University of Minnesota in 1930 and was quickly caught up in the peace movement. Violence repelled him. He opposed ROTC. He took the American equivalent of the Oxford oath: "I will not bear arms for flag or country."

The competitive spirit that he never displayed in athletics found its outlet in journalism. After college, Sevareid went to work on *The Minneapolis Journal*. Katharine Hepburn came into town one day and promptly secluded herself in her hotel room, refusing to see any reporters. Sevareid dressed himself up as a waiter, a raw-boned figure in an unconvincing role. He, nevertheless, served her breakfast in bed, and came away with an exclusive.

In the summer of 1939, the president of UP, Hugh Baillie, was in Paris and offered Sevareid a promotion. But Sevareid was not comfortable with wire service reporting, with its frantic pace and fleeting nature. While he was mulling over Baillie's offer, as he later wrote in his autobiography, "The phone rang; it was a call from London with Edward Murrow at the other end, asking if I would like to try reporting by radio. 'I don't know very much about your experience,' he said. 'But I like the way you write and I like your ideas. There's only Shirer and Grandin and myself now. But I think this thing may develop into something. There won't be any pressure on you to provide scoops or anything sensational. Just provide the honest news, and when there isn't any news, why, just say so. I have an idea people might like that.'"

In later years, when those who knew Murrow reflected on what made him succeed, they invariably pointed out that he was an unerring judge of talent. He had a scent for it. He read people well. He had only known Sevareid briefly. Yet when he wanted to hire him, he knew intuitively what cards to play. A man who wrote and thought like Sevareid, Murrow judged, was likely uncomfortable with the breakneck world of wire service reporting. He struck precisely the right chord in suggesting that reflective reporting rather than speed or novelty was what he wanted, exactly what Sevareid wanted to hear. Sevareid went on the CBS payroll on August 22, 1939. He could scarcely believe his good fortune. CBS was going to pay him $75 a week.[6]

UP became Murrow's hunting preserve. Larry Le Sueur, also with the wire service, stopped in to see Paul White before going to Paris. Le Sueur had done some free-lance radio work for White, and White suggested that he ought to stop in on Murrow in London. Le Sueur did, and Murrow promptly hired him. The European staff now totaled five. It was a happy ship, but occasionally had to accommodate a difficult passenger. That August, with the Polish crisis at a fever pitch, H.V. Kaltenborn arrived in London.[7]

There was an imperiousness about Kaltenborn, visible in his stiff-necked appearance, audible in his exaggerated speech. (He pronounced words like "America" with a rolling "r"—*Amerrrrica*.) He had an odd background. His father was Baron Rudolph von Kaltenborn-Stachau, who emigrated to Milwaukee where his son, Hans, was born in 1878. Thus, when Murrow knew him, Kaltenborn was an ancient by broadcasting standards, already in his sixties.

The titled father apart, Kaltenborn had to leave school at 14 and thereafter held every sort of job, including, at one point, juggler. He entered Harvard College at the age of 24, graduated cum laude and, as a colleague noted, "Never let anyone forget it." He was Phi Beta Kappa and never let anyone forget that either. He eventually became an editor on *The Brooklyn Eagle*. With his distinctive and distinguished diction, he was fated for radio.

Kaltenborn became the stuff of legend at CBS. While he was broadcasting, H.V. would roll a small chunk of amber between his fingertips like a single worry bead, a mind control technique that he had picked up in his travels to the Orient. His passion for keen analysis was so uncontainable that after a broadcast of the Pope's prayer for peace, H.V. analyzed the prayer.[8]

The pomposity apart, Murrow admired H.V.'s industry and dedication to radio. He admired H.V.'s stubborn determination to think critically, to have a point of view, no matter how often he was muzzled by Klauber. But it was the Kaltenborn manner that grated on Ed.

H.V. advised Murrow that he would be arriving in London on Friday, August 11. He "instructed" Murrow to set up appointments for him over the weekend with Prime Minister Chamberlain, Winston Churchill, and Hore-Belisha, the minister of war. As Janet noted in a letter home, "The English see no one" over the weekend.

Eric Sevareid, when asked how Ed Murrow expressed anger, related a Kaltenborn incident. Sevareid's first broadcast after being hired by CBS was done with H.V. during this August London visit. H.V. finished his prepared text and proceeded to ad lib, cutting deeply into the time left to Sevareid. As Sevareid later described the moment: "It fouled me up, made me nervous. I had to cut as I read. Ed just darkened with rage. Maybe at me, but mostly at Kaltenborn." Immediately after the broadcast, a tight-lipped Murrow marched out of the studio clutching a pencil in his hand. He said not a word. He simply squeezed the pencil until it cracked.

Kaltenborn went back to New York and did another broadcast, with Murrow participating from London. Bob Trout and Paul White were in the New York studio. Murrow spoke first. H.V., in his turn, was not content to give his own report, but analyzed what Murrow had said before him. After the broadcast, Murrow called New York on the cue channel, the circuit reserved for staff communication. "Someone," he said, "has just been on the air explaining what I said.... I don't need anyone explaining what I say." The voice was cold as ice. As Murrow spoke, Trout recalled, "The redness started at H.V.'s forehead and moved visibly across that glistening dome. Paul White and I did not dare say a word."[9]

Murrow's anger reflected the tension he was under. With Europe teetering on the rim of war, he was making a supreme effort to give the greatest possible precision to his words, to avoid oversimplification or misunderstanding. Conditions were far more fraught with peril than in the Austrian and Munich crises of the year before. England and France had been bound to Czechoslovakia by bonds no stronger than simple justice and sympathy for the underdog. These bonds had failed. But the Allies were bound to Poland's defense by formal treaty obligations. If Hitler moved against Poland, he would force Chamberlain and Daladier to choose between going to war or reneging on solemn international agreements.

Murrow had long been convinced that war was inevitable. On August 24, an event occurred that removed any possible doubt from his mind. He called Shirer in Berlin to find out what he knew about a seemingly incredible story that he had heard over German radio. Hitler and Stalin, the cobra and the mongoose of European politics, had signed a nonaggression pact. Shirer was stunned and embarrassed. He had missed the report, and there had been no earlier public hint of this unholy alliance. Shirer later estimated that no more than a half-dozen leading Nazis were privy to the pact. Hitler had been elevated to power in no small measure to save Germany from the Bolsheviks. His rise had been accompanied by the sound of Nazi Brown Shirts cracking Communist skulls in Berlin streets. What the Berlin-Moscow pact told Murrow, and anyone else with eyes in his head, was that Stalin, in effect, had given Hitler carte blanche to attack Poland.

As Europe began to unravel, Murrow and Shirer were driven to exasperation by the orders they were getting from New York. What, Paul White wanted to know, were they doing about *Europe Dances?* As Shirer later explained, "Someone in the home office got the bright idea of doing a broadcast from a cabaret in London, another in Paris, another in Berlin. The show was scheduled for the last week in August. Neither of us wanted to do it. We were convinced war was practically here, and in the face of that, the whole idea seemed revolting. I found a place in Berlin and Ed found one in London. But we kept sending cables trying to get them to drop the idea. We couldn't convince them it shouldn't be done. So in the end we just refused to do it."

Kaltenborn had come home and told his radio audience and his CBS colleagues that there would be no war. People were weary of doomsayers, CBS executives believed. Listeners wanted the charm of the Old World. They ought to hear *Europe Dances.* But there was more to White's insistence. Murrow might have created his own news principality in Europe, but it was still part of White's kingdom. *Europe Dances* was a move in a power play, a way to remind Murrow that White was still boss. Of that period, Shirer remembered, "I got in trouble sometimes because I received one instruction from Murrow in London and another from White in New York."[10]

On the last day of the month, August 31, Murrow planned a joint broadcast with Shirer, who was in Berlin. Ominously, as Ed prepared for the broadcast, he learned that communications between Germany and other European cities had been suddenly cut off. The two men had to transmit separately to New York. At daybreak the following morning,

Hitler implemented Case White. German armies poured over the Polish border under a canopy of bombers and drove on Warsaw from the west, north, and south.

Now it was the Allies who were issuing ultimatums. England and France gave Hitler forty-eight hours to pull out of Poland, until 11 a.m. September 3, or they would come to Poland's defense. To Hitler, who had kicked these toothless lions around with impunity for four years, the challenge must have sounded like a tired and empty growl.

During those hours, Europe hung suspended. Would France and England actually go to war over a country more distant even than Czechoslovakia, or would they seek another Munich, expending face and honor to buy peace?

Ceceila Reeves was ideally placed to observe how American correspondents judged England's will. She was now working as a BBC censor in an office that sounded as though it had been christened by Dickens, the Scrutineer's Unit. Foreign correspondents had to clear their copy in advance with Reeves. With the past performances of the Chamberlain government as their guide, she recalled that one American after another came down on the side of surrender; England, they believed, would back down.

Murrow was the last to file his story with Reeves. He was terribly tense, she remembered. He handed his copy to her and said, "Am I right on this? I've got to be right!" He began by quoting *Macbeth:* "Stands England where she did?...Some people have told me tonight they believe a big deal is being cooked up which will make Munich and the betrayal of Czechoslovakia look like a pleasant tea party. I find it difficult to accept this thesis. I don't know what's in the mind of the government, but I do know that to Britishers their pledged word is important.... And that's why I believe that Britain in the end of the day will stand where she is pledged to stand, by the side of Poland in a war that is now in progress."[11]

Fifteen minutes after the September 3 deadline, Neville Chamberlain announced over the BBC from Ten Downing Street that a state of war existed between Britain and Germany.

Within the hour, Murrow was on the air again. He had not had time to get a script written and cleared, and so he ad-libbed his first broadcast of World War II from the bombproof subterranean depths of Broadcasting House. A censor stood at a switch ready to cut him off should he betray security. "Forty-five minutes ago," he began, "the prime minister stated that a state of war existed between Britain and Germany. Air-raid instructions were immediately broadcast, and almost directly following that broadcast the air-raid warning sirens screamed through the quiet calm of this Sabbath morning. There were planes in the sky, whose, we couldn't be sure. Now we're sitting quite comfortably underground. We're told that the all-clear signal has been sounded in the streets but it's not yet been heard in this building.

"In a few minutes we shall hope to go up in the sunlight and see what has happened. It may have been only a rehearsal. London may not have been the target—or may have been.

"I have just been informed that upstairs in the sunlight everything is normal; that cars are traveling through the streets, there are people walking in the streets, and taxis are cruising about as usual. The crowd outside Downing Street received the first news of war with a rousing cheer, and they heard that news through a radio in a car parked near Downing Street."

In his next broadcast, Murrow discussed a subject that held a fascination for him, the British class structure, viewed now through the prism of war. He handled the subject with the insight of a man who had hauled himself out of the working-class trenches: "This is a class conscious country. People live in the same small street or apartment building for years and never talk to each other. The man with a fine car, good clothes, and perhaps an unearned income doesn't generally fraternize with the tradesmen, day laborers, and truck drivers. His fences are always up. He doesn't meet them as equals. He's surrounded with certain evidences of worldly wealth calculated to keep others at a distance, but if he's caught in Piccadilly Circus when the sirens sound, he may have a waitress stepping on his heels and see before him the broad back of a day laborer as he goes underground. If the alarm sounds about four in the morning, as it did this morning, his dignity, reserve, and authority may suffer when he arrives half-dressed and sleepy, minus his usual defenses and possessed of no more courage than those others who have arrived in a similar state. Someone, I think it was Marcus Aurelius, said something to the effect that 'death put Alexander of Macedon and his stable boy on a par.' Repeated visits to public air raid shelters might have produced the same results." There was a hint in the tone of this friend of lords and ladies that this was rather what he hoped would happen.[12]

He had started out writing his broadcasts pecking away at a typewriter with two fingers. But he noticed that most BBC broadcasters dictated their commentaries to a secretary. He tried it and was hooked. All the long-ago training at Pullman, the declamation, the recitation, the acting and debating, began to flower in a faraway place and in an unanticipated profession. Dictation was not simply faster and cleaner than his typing. The sound of his voice proved a useful guide. It led him not only to the right word, but to the right-sounding word. He rediscovered that certain words worked in print but were ineffectual in speech. Other words were aural; they fell boldly or subtly but, nevertheless, effectively on the ear. His best work began to take on the quality of lean, oral poetry. And an image became fixed in the minds of all who worked with him—Murrow perched on the edge of his chair, a cigarette clenched between his fingers, dictating. And Kay Campbell, a cigarette dangling from her lips, typing his dictation.

The hallmark of a Murrow broadcast was a certain authority, the sound of a man utterly in command of his thoughts and himself. Yet the

BBC people were amused by the contrast between what the listeners heard and what they saw. The voice was indeed assured. But underneath the table, his foot bounced like a trip-hammer, and sweat poured down his face just as when he had been a schoolboy debater.[13]

The smoking increased after he became a broadcaster. Janet had been a moderate smoker, but gave it up the day the war began. "I did it," she later recalled, "as a patriotic gesture and because I was disgusted with the palls of smoke in our living room." But Ed was now up to three packs a day. He devoted part of one broadcast to a paean to smokers during the blackouts: "I don't know how you feel about the people who smoke cigarettes, but I like them, particularly at night in London. That small, dull red glow is a very welcome sight. It prevents collisions and makes it unnecessary to heave to until you locate the exact position of those vague voices in the darkness. One night, several years ago, I walked bang into a cow, and since then I've had a desire for man and beast to carry running lights on dark nights. They can't do that in London these nights, but cigarettes are a good substitute."

It was not, however, navigating through darkened streets that bound him to cigarettes. He was driving himself furiously. He felt crushing pressures. Cigarettes were his opiate, soothing him, helping to keep the lid on a potentially volcanic temper, his nicotine tranquilizer.[14]

The outbreak of the war produced a curious, almost perverse, reaction from American radio. President Roosevelt half-heartedly restated America's formal neutrality. Two networks, NBC and Mutual, took their cue from the President and ceased broadcasting news from Europe for a time. NBC also silenced its commentators at home, at least those who were not sponsored. The professed motive was to preserve the spirit of neutrality. War news, the reasoning went, must inevitably inflame Americans against one side or the other. That was the good excuse to abandon reporting the war. The unspoken reason was that broadcasts from abroad were expensive operations. Not only did they cost money to produce, but the special reports and the break-in bulletins cut into the sponsored schedule. Covering Europe raised the network's costs, while it reduced income. It is to Bill Paley's everlasting credit that he did not seize upon this handy rationale. Instead, Murrow received a cable from New York saying that CBS would go it alone and keep on covering the war.[15]

Ed continued to drive himself remorselessly. Since the Polish crisis, he had lived virtually between the CBS office and Broadcasting House, sleeping fitfully, eating poorly, going on the air at any hour, day or night. He became a familiar sight, hurrying along Langham Place, eyes usually riveted on some unseen point on the ground, lost in his thoughts and oblivious of the world. He had taken to wearing a shapeless, wrinkled raincoat over his well-tailored suits, and the suits began to sag as he lost weight. A friend described him during this period as "cadaverously handsome." On September 8, he reported the fall of Warsaw. The defeat was as much in his voice as in his message. Bill Shirer, listening to him in Berlin, thought Ed sounded "dead tired."[16]

His next addition to the staff was daring for the time. During the voyage to England on the *Manhattan* in 1937, Ed had run into Marvin Breckinridge, who had preceded him as a president of NSFA. She had been christened Mary Marvin Breckinridge. But there were already two Marys in the family and so she became Marvin. Her family was well connected, descended from Vice President John Breckinridge. When she and Ed met aboard ship, Breckinridge was traveling with her parents to attend the coronation of Edward VIII. She was later presented at court. She also was a professional photographer commissioned to take pictures for *Town and Country* and *Harper's Bazaar* while in England.

When she and Ed met again in London, Marvin Breckinridge was doing a different kind of photography. She came to dinner at Hallam Street and described to Ed and Janet a photo story she was preparing on British slum children being evacuated to the country and another on how a typical English village was preparing to face war.

Ed was fascinated and asked her to go on the air with her story. He was so pleased with the way she handled herself that he decided to break a barrier. A study of listener attitudes had revealed that most Americans preferred to hear their radio news from a man. Women were acceptable only in commercials and dramas. Murrow, nevertheless, hired Marvin Breckinridge, and told her, with a conspiratorial smile, to speak low and make sure that she stuck to the name Marvin. She became his correspondent in the Netherlands, the first woman to hold such a position at CBS.[17]

Poland surrendered, and the war slipped into an anomalous state, war without warfare. Senator Borah of Idaho coined a phrase to describe the condition, the "phony war." To the British it was the "bore war"; to the Germans, the *Sitzkrieg*, the sit-down war.

The stresses of even an unfought war were forcing to the surface certain qualities in the British character that intrigued Ed. He went to a local board set up to hear the cases of conscientious objectors. One, an Oxford student, particularly interested him, and Ed reported to his listeners: "He says that he is willing to defend Britain, but he does not believe that this is a defensive war. Rather than wreck the world, he would submit to German domination. He quotes Chamberlain as saying that the war is being fought in defense of small nations, and goes on to say that he is not interested in the small nations, and is prepared to go to jail rather than fight. His case takes twenty minutes before it is decided that he needn't fight."

Murrow later talked to the board members: "I asked them for a definition of conscience and they couldn't give me one. But they all agreed that a British subject should have the right to say what his conscience dictates before he is forced to fight."

He was impressed. It was as though he had pressed the limp-appearing outer surface of the English and found a steely character underneath. England was not going to fight despots by imitating despotism. Should that happen, then the whole point of the war was lost, even if the victory were won. He wondered how long the British could stick by this principled position as the days ahead darkened.[18]

As Murrow found himself in his new profession, Janet struggled to find her own identity. "Ed always encouraged me to do things," she later observed. "In part it was that he was so busy that he did not want to feel responsible for me all the time. I had had a good education and he felt I ought to use it. And we had no children at the time, though we wanted them very much."

On Thanksgiving Day, he let her take over his broadcast, to tell what the face of war looked like to the ordinary British family—what it felt like to be handed gas masks, to evacuate one's children to the country, even to far off Canada or America. Whatever inner terror she felt, her theater training saw her through. She was poised, had a warm voice, and projected an obvious caring. CBS executives wanted more. But what mattered most to Janet was that she had satisfied the one critic who counted. She wrote home proudly that she had written her own script, and "Ed never changed a word."[19]

On that same Thanksgiving Day, November 23, British and German arms clashed for the first time in the war. The Germans sank an armed British merchantman, the *Rawalpindi*, in a skirmish off Iceland. A British soldier was later shot in a random exchange of fire on the western front. And that was the extent of the war into December.

Ed was itching for action. The only action available in England at the moment were minesweeping operations to keep the ports open. Ed proposed to Paul White that he be allowed to go on one of the patrols. White turned him down. The next message White received informed him that Ed would be unavailable for a few days; he and Janet were taking a cottage in Berkshire.

Murrow had actually gone to an unidentified port town with Fred Bate of NBC. They followed an escort officer aboard one of the rusty trawlers jamming the harbor. The deck was wet and slippery. The hold still glistened with fish scales and stank of its recent cargo. The seamen wore no uniforms. They looked smaller to Ed than American sailors. Up forward he spotted a gun turret "shaped like a toadstool." The fantail was lined with depth charges "like squat milk cans."

As the trawler got under way and passed beyond the breakwater into the Channel, the crew struck the red duster of the merchant fleet and hoisted the white ensign of the Royal Navy. This foul-smelling hulk was now officially a man-of-war. The seamen lowered the mine-cutters into the sea and swept their assigned sector, back and forth, like a plow turning a watery field. They found no mines. As they returned late in the day, the White Cliffs of Dover loomed, Murrow said, "like a dirty white sheet hanging from a green roof." He struggled to invest the experience with drama. As he described the patrol over the air, "Minesweeping may not be magnificent, but it's war."[20]

Soon afterward, he made out his will. It read simply: "I leave all my wordly goods to Janet. She shall use her own judgment in providing funds for her immediate family and for my own mother and father." If Janet preceded him in death, his estate was to be equally divided between his parents and hers, an uncommonly generous attitude.[21]

Slow news days left him restless, and he would mine whatever material was at hand for broadcast ore. One afternoon Kay Campbell watched him seemingly gazing idly out of his office window. That night he reported the results of his window gazing. Two out of every three women on London's streets carried gas masks, but all of them carried umbrellas. Among men, half carried gas masks, and two out of three carried umbrellas. From which he concluded, "The British find the weather more menacing than German gas bombs."[22]

He and Janet passed the first Christmas of the war with an old friend from Ed's student leader days. Ivison Macadam was now deputy director of the Ministry of Information. It was a somber holiday. Macadam and his American-born wife sorely missed their two children, who had been evacuated to the United States. Ed excused himself to make some phone calls. When it was time for him to leave for his nightly broadcast, he invited the Macadams along to the underground studios of Broadcasting House. What he had earlier been secretly arranging on the telephone was for the Macadams to talk to their children in Portland, Oregon. To American listeners on a Christmas night, the war, for one brief moment, was not a distant quarrel between nations, but ordinary people like themselves whose lives had been torn apart.[23]

As the new year began, Ed felt a need to see Bill Shirer. Their close thinking on the war, their shared excitement over the profession they were building, had brought Shirer closer than Murrow ordinarily permitted anyone. Shirer, though still based in Geneva, was now spending most of his time in Berlin, and in January of 1940, Ed asked Shirer to meet him in neutral Holland.

Shirer took Murrow to the best restaurants, where Ed would order scrambled eggs. They both drank a good deal. Mostly they talked. They compared notes on the drabness that had begun to settle over London and Berlin with the nightly blackouts, the wartime controls, the first shortages. Murrow told Shirer, with unconcealed contempt, how the British expected to win the war. They intended simply to tighten the noose of their naval blockade until Germany starved, and expected thus to win a cheap, bloodless victory.

Marvin Breckinridge, Ed's new Netherlands correspondent, arranged meetings for them with Dutch officials. The Dutch were less concerned with defending themselves than with avoiding any act that might possibly provoke Hitler. The very thought of a joint defense with the British made them shudder. They were as blind as Chamberlain, Ed thought, and it depressed him.

Still, the two correspondents were reminded that peace could be sweet.

The shops of Amsterdam overflowed with the best meats, fowl, oysters, bananas, oranges, coffee—items already growing scarce in the countries at war. They were "intoxicated," Shirer wrote in his diary, by "the lights at night, fine food, like a couple of kids escaped from reform school."

They were returning to their hotel after dinner when snow began to fall "like confetti." They "fought a mighty snowball battle," during which Shirer lost his glasses and his hat. They limped back to the hotel exhausted and happy. The next day they went ice-skating with Marvin Breckinridge.[24]

Ed returned to London and immediately paid for the frolic. He came down with his now customary respiratory infection and was in bed for a week. Too soon, he was out of bed and off to Paris to work with Eric Sevareid. It was a damp, cold winter. Sevareid went to the Ritz to pick up Ed and found him, deathly pale, trying to shave. Ed lacked the strength to stand up and fell back onto his bed. He told Sevareid, "Don't tell Janet." His wife was in Switzerland visiting Tess Shirer and other friends, and he did not want to spoil her vacation. Fred Bate was also in Paris. He came to see Ed, took one look at him, and rushed him to a good hospital where Murrow was diagnosed as having pneumonia. The doctors were not sure that they could pull him through, so Sevareid notified Janet, who took the next train from Zurich to Paris. She wrote in her diary of "a very pale and thin and sick Eddie. Poor darling." The doctors told her to get him to the south of France until he recovered. Instead of the Riviera, he insisted on returning to London. The first night back, he went to the BBC, made a broadcast, and got to bed at 2 a.m.[25]

The phony war ended in April of 1940 with the German invasion of Norway. Britain sent an expeditionary force of 25,000 men to help the Norwegians. They were defeated in fierce fighting at Narvik and beat an ignominious retreat.

Ed had gone to the House of Commons to hear the debate over the debacle. Since the outbreak of the war, Winston Churchill had been taken into the government in his old World War I post as first lord of the Admiralty. Chamberlain had preferred Churchill inside the tent spitting out, rather than outside spitting in. The strategem failed to mute Churchill. For an hour and a half, he flayed Chamberlain for his conduct of the war. Murrow, watching from the press gallery, found him "magnificent." He had just witnessed, he said, "the best bit of acting I've ever seen." Chamberlain barely managed to survive a close vote of confidence.[26]

On May 10, German Stuka dive-bombers burst from the clouds and struck Belgium, Holland, and Luxembourg. Panzer units and infantry poured over the borders, and parachutists fell from the sky.

That evening Neville Chamberlain spoke to his countrymen from Ten Downing Street. A broken man bent under the burden of a discredited policy, he announced his resignation as prime minister. Winston Churchill succeeded him, a man for most of the previous ten years out of favor, out of power, and out of step with a pacifist public, a lonely, bitter, and at times tediously bellicose voice crying out in the wilderness. The new prime minister spoke on taking office and chiseled his phrases into the English language: "I have nothing to offer but blood, tears, toil, and sweat."

Murrow in his next broadcast compared the two prime ministers. Chamberlain, he said, "made the mistake of asking too little rather than too much of the people of this country." Of Churchill, he said, "He enters with the tremendous advantage of being the man who was right. He also has the advantage of being the best broadcaster in this country."[27]

By now, the best known American in London was Ed Murrow. Janet wrote a friend, "Our flat has become sort of a gathering place. Around our fireplace you'll find one to ten newspaper correspondents, broadcasters, members of Parliament, 'hush-hush' people.... I'm kept busy providing food and drink...and listening as hard as I can to their words of wisdom. You'd be surprised how screwy some of them are."

Ed ordinarily finished his broadcasts at one o'clock in the morning London time in order to make the evening news back home. Then, too excited to sleep, he would drag friends to the Hallam Street apartment where they would talk until dawn. A typical conscript was Alan Wells of the BBC home news service. Wells lived across the street, and he and his wife, Clare, exemplified to Murrow Londoners at war. They had evacuated their little girl to the country and were volunteer fire wardens in the neighborhood."[28]

His broadcasts were beginning to achieve the distinctive stamp that makes something unmistakably one's own. Winston Burdett, a later recruit to Murrow's circle, described a Murrow broadcast: "Accurate diction, economy, filed sentences, firm phrasing—these gave to his scripts a kind of magnificent clarity that bordered on the epigrammatic. Take the following two sentences, the opening sentences of a radio spot from London: 'The debates in the House of Lords are often more interesting than those in the House of Commons. The Lords have more leisure.' What could be plainer? But think of his voice and his phrasing as he reads the two lines. We are startled by his statement, charmed by its simplicity, and delighted by the juxtaposition of the two sentences; we smile at the irony and we are alert for what will come next."

He was performing two roles in the early theater of broadcast journalism, actor and producer. He had a talent for attracting talent. He infected his people with his religion; he brought them to the mountaintop to see what he saw as radio's future. NBC was still farming out broadcasts to "experts." But during that first year of the war, Murrow had his own correspondents in six European capitals. They thus achieved a continuity of coverage. They were acquiring an identity and a following at home. They had a recognizable style—understated, deliberate, measured, literate, wry—a style that avoided both pretension and ersatz folksiness. It was to become the sound of CBS news and mirrored the man who invented it.[29]

CHAPTER 13

The Blitz

If a man had to choose a year of his life on which to stand or fall, a year during which he was most fully alive and fulfilled, for Ed Murrow that year was about to begin.

During that spring of 1940, waves from the military debacle on the Continent began to lap against the English coast. Poland had fallen, then Denmark. Norway was soon to surrender. The Netherlands and Belgium were being overrun. France was fighting a poor and losing battle. By mid-May, German armored columns reached the English Channel, trapping the bulk of the British Expeditionary Force at Dunkirk.

Murrow saw his first victims of the war near Earls Court, civilian refugees straggling in from the Channel ports, hollow-eyed and numb, waiting to be processed through an emergency center. Their drab appearance was an anomaly among the explosion of azaleas, the tulips and lilacs, the English couples holding hands and kissing in the park.

He came home one evening in May, tired and in a foul mood. He had been up since 5 a.m. to beat the competition to the story of the surrender of Belgian's King Leopold. The game of scoops and beats bored him. That was artifice journalism, Paul White journalism, he felt. What difference did it make who reported a story five minutes before someone else? What mattered was how the story was told, and what it revealed; meaning not speed. He was also distressed that the Belgian king had given up so quickly in what Ed called Leopold's "early abdication." He told Janet that he would happily enlist as a tail gunner if he knew that "everyone would fight to the finish." Janet wrote in her diary that he had clung to her that night and told her no matter what this war did to them, their love must keep them together.[1]

At the end of May he went to Folkestone to cover the evacuation of

163

the British army from Dunkirk. Glazed-eyed, sunburnt Tommies clambered from every conceivable craft that could float, from barges, tugboats, rowboats, and yachts. As he watched them come ashore, he was touched by "the sound of a shell-shocked mongrel brought back from Dunkirk by a couple of British sergeants."

He went to a nearby RAF field used by fliers who were providing air cover for the men still trapped on the beaches. There was a jauntiness to the airmen, absent in the stunned and exhausted foot soldiers. He watched a pilot taxi his Spitfire for take off. As he throttled down, the flier waved and shouted, "Be back in time for tea."

A boy, no more than 20, weighing perhaps 115 pounds, jumped out of a station wagon and asked if anyone could give him a lift to his own airfield. His uniform was torn and damp. He was wearing oversize tennis shoes. And he spoke in a toneless shout. When he was gone, Ed asked an officer, "What's the matter with him?" The officer answered, "Oh, he was shot down over Dunkirk on the first patrol this morning, landed in the sea, swam back to the beach, was bombed for a couple of hours, came home in a paddle steamer. His voice sounds like that because he can't hear himself. You get that way after you've been bombed for a few hours."[2]

Ed saw ancient cannons being hauled out of British museums and dragged down to the beaches. The German army was twenty-one miles away, and England waited inevitably to be invaded. On June 10, with France on her knees, Mussolini brought Italy into the war on Germany's side. "Now," Ed said, "all the bastards are on one side."[3]

President Roosevelt went on the air. "The hand that held the dagger," he said, "has struck it into the back of its neighbor." Jimmy Sheean, Ed's reporter friend, came over to Hallam Street to ask Ed what he thought Roosevelt's speech meant. Janet suppressed her displeasure at Sheean's arrival.

Jimmy Sheean was an extravagant man. What he did, he did to excess: talk, write, drink, spend, womanize. He was big, handsome, witty, possessed of an overblown charm. He had made a brilliant marriage to the daughter of Sir Johnston Forbes-Robertson, one of Britain's most distinguished men of the theater. Sheean lived at Claridges, and was seen in the company of the Churchills, the Duff Coopers, George Bernard Shaw, Somerset Maugham, Noel Coward, but few of the socialist friends he was always talking about. As Eric Sevareid described Sheean, "All the great homes were open to Jimmy," until his drinking became intolerable. And then "the doors of all the great houses were closed to him."

Ed still found "a deadly fascination in an argument," Janet recalled, as when he had been a boy challenging his elders in Beaver. Sheean was brilliant and argumentative too, hence always welcome at Hallam Street, at least by Ed. "Ed loved Jimmy Sheean," Sevareid said. "They would argue hammer and tongs. They were drawn by each other's flames. They liked to argue for arguments' sake. Then they'd suddenly break out in a duet, sing some old labor song.... 'Last Night I Saw Joe Hill.' They both had wonderful voices." Murrow was taken with Sheean's wide-ranging knowledge, his manly vices. He liked to say, "Jimmy Sheean can swear fluently in five languages."

That night, at Ed's apartment, Sheean maintained that Roosevelt's speech signaled an imminent American declaration of war. Ed countered that Roosevelt was only paving the way to send aid to the Allies. They drank as they argued, and the more they drank, the louder they argued, until the debate degenerated into a shouting match. Janet woke up and tried to join the discussion, but by then it was all shouting and no listening. The two men went at it until six in the morning when Ed announced that he was going to bed and that he was too tired to take Janet to the country as he had promised. It was always like that when Jimmy Sheean called.[4]

Whatever Franklin Roosevelt's intentions, the advice that he was getting from his ambassador in Great Britain was to steer clear of a sinking ship. As for providing aid to the British, Joe Kennedy warned, there was not enough time. England could not hold out: "So if this is going to be a quick war all over in a few months, what could we do?"

Winston Churchill rolled out his best weapon, at this point virtually his only weapon, his words, to rally his countrymen's battered spirits and to dispute the Kennedy vision of an England doomed. "We shall go on to the end," Churchill told the House of Commons. "We shall fight in France, we shall fight on the seas and oceans, we shall fight on the beaches, in the fields, in the streets, in the hills. We shall never surrender."[5]

That night, Churchill's speech was repeated over the BBC. Supposedly, Churchill put his hand over the microphone afterward and added, "We'll hit them on the head with beer bottles which is all we have to fight with." Another account had it that an actor, Norman Shelley, impersonated Churchill for the BBC repeat.[6]

Ed and Fred Bate were at Hallam Street eating an impromptu dinner out of cans, listening to the prime minister. When Churchill finished, Ed said that England would last as long as Churchill led her; otherwise, "Disaster." He told his American audience that "I've heard Mr. Churchill in the House of Commons at intervals over the last ten years.... Today, he was different. There was little oratory. He wasn't interested in being a showman. He spoke the language of Shakespeare with a direct urgency such as I have never heard before."

On June 22, France fell, and England stood alone. Invasion was assumed to be only a matter of time. Ed watched Tommies rolling coils of barbed wire around the Houses of Parliament and the government buildings in Whitehall, erecting sandbag fortifications in Hyde Park among the laburnum and lilacs. He went home and found a circular in his mail entitled "If the Invader Comes." It listed the steps to take—"Don't give any German anything. Don't tell him anything. Hide your food, bicycles and maps. See that he gets no gasoline.... Think always of your country before you think of yourself." Janet bought a can of clear varnish mixed with liquid rubber. They were supposed to paint the windows with it to make the glass lightproof and shatterproof.

She also received a letter ordering her to register as an alien and informing her that she was not to drive a car or ride a bicycle. Ed, as an accredited journalist, was exempt from these restrictions. Fred Bate's wife, Jebbie, was leaving for home with the couple's two daughters. It was time for Janet to leave too. Ed booked passage for her to New York. She refused to go.

Friends pleaded with her to get out, telling her that London was going to be burned to the ground. "It won't be any worse for me than anybody else," she answered. If she had had children, she would have been compelled to leave, she said. She did not. She had been raised under a code that said a wife belonged with her husband, whether on a rocky New England farm or in a city at war. Ed later admitted that he was glad that she decided to stay. She was the steadier of the two, and he needed her steadiness.[7]

His moods continued to swing violently from manic excitement over what he was doing to self-flagellation that he was not doing enough. He found himself in a perpetual contest of wills with Paul White, even across the ocean. White had never liked Murrow's man in Paris, Tom Grandin. He thought that Grandin's broadcasts sounded "pansyish." He sent a cable, over Murrow's head, ordering Grandin to resign. Ed sent a cable back telling White it was unspeakable to fire a man without a hearing; and he told Grandin to hold fast. White backed down. Murrow knew that if he ever stopped standing up to White, he would be steam-rollered. But the constant internecine warfare wore him down.[8]

When he became tired, he would lash out, saying things designed for shock value. He wrote Ed Dakin, a friend and public relations man with whom he seemed able to lower his customary guard, "Long ago I came to the conclusion that my future is not to be found as a radio commentator. I...don't seem able to develop the necessary illusion of omnipotence. What I'll do when I come back doesn't cause me much worry or thought. But I think occasionally of a job teaching in a small far western university. One thing is certain. I have no intention of returning to 485 Madison Avenue...."

He wrote to a BBC friend, Charles Siepmann, who had gone to teach at Harvard, "haven't the guts to quit and go home, and I haven't even the energy to argue with myself about it any more. I have come to realize in the last few months just how few friends I have and how little it matters to me what happens to most of them. I hope that life goes well for you in America and that your nostrils are not assailed by the odour of death and decay that permeates the atmosphere. My own thoughts turn more to the Far West. If I ever escape from this treadmill, I hope to go back there."

The Far West, the little college campus, they were fantasies to which he had given sentimentalized perfection. His thoughts drifted into this harbor of daydreams whenever the pressures became too much and clouded his fatigued mind. But the next day he could write another friend, "Sometimes I wonder whether we shall ever get back to the States and sometimes I wonder if I ever want to come back." He would fire off memos to the BBC foreign office exploding with new story ideas—trips to Iceland, Gibraltar, and Egypt, a torpedo boat mission, a patrol between Scotland and Norway, a visit to an internment camp, a day at the Bow Street Police court to describe "British justice during war time." Professionally he had a sure compass, but emotionally he floundered.

Sheean found Murrow "dark and taciturn, beset by gloom," on the one hand, and "capable of sustained hilarity and high spirits" on the other. In the latter mood, Ed told friends that on his first meeting with Winston Churchill, the man had told him "Murrow, be droll. You are a witty man." When the mood was on him, he would regale visitors to Hallam Street with stories of lumberjacks, English lords, and cockneys told with the flair of a skilled mimic. Certain lines stuck in his mind, and he delighted in repeating them over and over. He particularly enjoyed something his CBS colleague in New York, Elmer Davis, had said: "A filthy mind is a great consolation."

Then, without warning, the black curtain would descend, and he would slip into depression. When he drank, he became particularly maudlin as on the day France fell. He came home and told Janet that "the Murrow luck" would not hold. He was not going to survive the war.[9]

England now waited for the dawn when German ships must materialize in the Channel. Yet daily life went on with an unnatural naturalness. Ed and Janet still went for country weekends. They attended a stag hunt where they watched pink-coated huntsmen lead a party over the moors in a scene that looked like an old English print. They continued to visit Dytchley where Ed and Ronnie Tree went shooting. Tree was now head of the American Section of the Ministry of Information, which made both friends valuable to each other. Lady Milner wrote that her house was now in a war zone, "So I can't say come down." But, she said, she must see Ed in London. She wanted an explanation from him of "how pro-German the Columbia Broadcasting System now is and how Commie we [English] are...."

Even in an England waiting to be invaded, he could play golf. Ed particularly enjoyed golfing with James Reston of *The New York Times*. He found Scotty Reston in the Murrow mold, of a breed with Shirer and Sevareid. He admired Reston's analytical powers and his lean, freighted prose. Reston had a fine radio voice to boot. He had already done a few anonymous broadcasts for Fred Bate on NBC. Murrow tried to lure Reston to his fold. But Scotty Reston had *The Times* in his bloodstream. "Ed," he said, "that's like asking me to leave my wife."[10]

The German invasion did not come by sea. It began by air. The Nazi amphibious assault, Operation Sea Lion, was scheduled for mid-September, after the Luftwaffe had knocked out the British coastal defenses and ports. German control of the skies had to precede the invasion. In August, waves of Heinkels, Dorniers, and Junkers battered gun emplacements and shipping along the English Channel. But the RAF struck back with unexpected fight, downing too many of Goering's bombers. The Germans decided to move the raids inland, to cut off the RAF at the root by destroying airfields and aircraft manufacturing plants. Between August 24 and September 6, the Luftwaffe flew over 1,000 sorties. Still, the Hurricanes and the Spitfires kept coming up, inflicting unacceptable losses, stunting the effect of the German attacks.

In the meantime, the RAF struck twice at Berlin, modest raids meant more for their psychological impact than anything else, since the German people had been told that the RAF had been destroyed.

By September, it became clear that the German air objective, to break the back of the RAF as the prelude to invasion, had failed. Operation Sea Lion, though the British did not then know it, was canceled. The Battle of Britain, as history would record those struggles in the air, had ended. The battle left no cratered landscape, no empty trenches, no rusting hulks of dead tanks or smashed artillery to mark the battlefield. All that remained was an empty sky.

The air war was not over. The British raids on Berlin had given the Germans justification for their next strategy. They would bring England to her knees by razing London and other major population centers from the air.

Murrow was to witness this inauguration of the Blitz from an unexpected vantage point. On September 6, he drove Jimmy Sheean and another reporter, Ben Robertson, down the Thames estuary looking for a fresh story on the coastal bombing. He had long since unloaded his plain Ford for a low-slung, modish, 10-horsepower Talbot Sunbeam.[11]

Ben Robertson was a round-faced, boyish-looking South Carolinian in his mid-thirties working for the innovative, ultraliberal New York tabloid, *PM*. He spoke with a liquid drawl, and his ambition was to go home and run for political office. The fields the trio drove by were freshly plowed by recent raids. They passed an old man, sucking on his pipe, sitting on a porch that teetered over a crater. A woman hung out her wash with the dust of the last raid still in the air. Children played with toys that they had improvised from chunks of spent shrapnel and antiaircraft shells. The reporters arrived at Gravesend, checked into an inn, and went to bed.

The next day they pushed on to Chapham, past antiaircraft batteries, past more destroyed buildings, and past villages untouched by the twentieth century, much less the war. They bought some apples and had stretched out on the side of the road to eat them when suddenly German planes appeared, thirty of them in the first wave. They watched British fighters streak up to meet the Germans. The raid was like the others thus far, striking at British coastal defenses and RAF installations. Late in the afternoon, the attack broke off and the Germans headed home. The devastation left behind was awesome. Greasy black columns of smoke coiled up into the sky from stricken oil tanks and blotted out the sun. The reflected orange-red flames from the fires danced on the waves of the Thames.

They drove back to the inn at Gravesend and had dinner, expecting that the Germans would probably return for a night raid. Ed called Janet and told her that if she went up on their roof and looked downriver, she would probably see some spectacular fireworks in the distance that night. As night fell, they drove up to a hilltop that afforded a clear view. Ed parked near a haystack. They could lay under the hay for warmth if the night turned cold.

Within ten minutes they heard the first wave of bombers. The planes flew directly over the haystack following the afternoon's course. But this time something was different. The Germans continued beyond the point at which the daylight raiders had done their work and turned back. "They're following the line of the river as easily as if it were Main Street," Ed remarked. It was clear where they were headed. "Are you glad you're not in London tonight?" he said, and then suddenly remembered that his wife was indeed there.

A few isolated bombers had flown over London before, but nothing remotely comparable to what they now witnessed. Shortly before, Hermann Goering had stood on a cliff at Cape Gris Nez and watched wave after wave, 300 bombers and 600 of his fighters, streak over the Channel headed for London. Murrow and his companions, stretched on their backs on the haystack, could see the metal bellies of the bombers reflected by the fires still raging along the Thames. Searchlights began to knife the night, impaling German planes on their beams. Antiaircraft batteries began their steady poom, poom, poom, followed by yellow-orange sunbursts among the bombers. The planes continued in twos and threes at three-minute intervals, forming an endless metal necklace across the throat of the sky. The three reporters could see fires starting as the bombs fell on London. Hour after hour it went on, a wave of planes, a silence, then the next wave. Murrow and the other two crawled under the haystack, trembling in the raw night. As they lay there, Sheean recounted with nervous amusement his adventures during the Spanish civil war. Robertson tried to talk about his political plans. Then he would look out at the glow over the city and drawl mournfully, "London is burnin', London is burnin'." At three o'clock in the morning, the raid showed no sign of letting up. Ed decided that the odds of being hit were no worse in a haystack than in bed. They piled into the Talbot, and he drove through the dark at breakneck speed, back to the inn. They went to bed and tried to sleep. But the floors of the inn heaved, the walls shook, and the windows cracked with each near burst.

In London, Janet had taken Ed's advice. She had gone to the roof of their apartment house to watch, she thought, a distant spectacle. Instead, she heard the alarm sounded for central London and found herself out in the open in the first full-scale raid of the war on the city. She started back downstairs. But the roof door had locked behind her. She looked down into the street and saw people scurrying into the shelters. She shouted for help, but the wail of the siren drowned out her cries. Bombs began to explode. The building shook. The report of the ack-ack guns deafened her. Shrapnel fell on the roof. She was starting to panic when she spotted a man coming out of a pub on the other side of the street. He heard her cries and came up and opened the door for her. They took the elevator down to her floor. On the way down her good breeding overcame her recent terror. She began to think, "I'm all alone in the apartment. This man has just done me a great service. Was it or was it not proper under the circumstances to invite him in for a drink?" By the time the elevator arrived, she had still not decided. She merely said, "Thank you," and closed her door.[12]

Back in Gravesend, Ed had given up all hope of sleep; the bursts of the bombs and the sun were competing in bringing on the light. He gathered his companions, and they began to drive back to London. It was Sunday morning. As they rode along, the last of the bombers disappeared from the sky. The raid had lasted over ten hours.

They arrived by a roundabout route through the East End, passing by the docks and working-class boroughs of Bermondsey, Stepney, West Ham, and Poplar. The poorest neighborhoods of London had taken the brunt of the raid. The destruction was indescribable, H. G. Wells's nightmare of annihilation from the skies come true. Whole city blocks had been reduced to rubble. Collapsing buildings and unexploded bombs had been roped off. First-aid teams were pulling the injured and dead from the wreckage and setting lifeless bodies to one side. Homeless people, blankfaced and strangely mute, stood in long queues waiting for buses to ferry them to emergency shelters in the West End. Cleanup crews shoveled glittering heaps of broken glass and burrowed paths through the debris. It was odd; the bombs had caused the glass to blow out into the street instead of into the buildings as they had expected. That night, over 400 Londoners died.

Murrow, in his broadcast, was moved to a poetry of havoc: "The fires up the river had turned the moon blood red. The smoke had drifted on till it formed a canopy over the Thames; the guns were working all around us, the bursts looking like fireflies in a southern summer night. The Germans were sending in two or three planes at a time, sometimes only one, in relays. They would pass overhead. The guns and lights would follow them and in about five minutes we could hear the hollow grunt of the bombs. Huge pear-shaped bursts of flame would rise up into the smoke and disappear. The world was upside down."

When Ed got back home, Janet told him what had happened to her during the raid and how she had resolved her quandary over the hospitality she owed her rescuer. "Only a Mount Holyoke girl," he answered, "would treat a man like that."[13]

The raid on the night of September 7–8 was followed by another the next night, and another the following night, on and on until a nightmare took on the unremarkability of persistent bad weather.

In another broadcast, Ed analyzed his emotions during an air raid: "...this business of being bombed and watching air fights is the sort of thing which fails to produce the anticipated reaction. The sense of danger, death and disaster comes only when the familiar incidents occur— the things that one has associated with tragedy since childhood. The sight of half a dozen ambulances weighted down with an unseen cargo of human wreckage has jarred me more than the war of dive bombers or the sound of bombs." The science of modern warfare took on a chilling horror as he explained its very ordinariness. "What had happened was that three or four high school boys with some special training had been flying around over London in about $100,000 worth of machinery. One of them had pressed a button—the fire and a number of casualties was the result. We could see the fire and hear the clanging of the fire-engine bells; but we hadn't seen the bomber—had barely heard him."

Murrow was widely praised for the harrowing immediacy of his broadcasts. Still, he was dissatisfied. He was not using the unique capacity of radio to let the listener share an experience as it happened. No matter what he himself had observed—the guttural hum of a bomber overhead, the whistle of a bomb sailing to earth, the shouts of a rescue squad pulling victims from wreckage—the listener still got it secondhand. The moment itself was lost.

Two obstacles stood in the way of his reporting an air raid live. For security reasons, the Air Ministry refused to let him report a raid in progress because German monitors might pick up the broadcast and guide their bombers depending on where the reporter said the bombs were falling. The bombardiers could then correct their aim. Murrow might find himself serving as an unwitting Luftwaffe spotter.

He could still capture the moment if he were allowed to record his report during an actual raid and then play the recording on the air. The recording equipment then available to CBS was clumsy, essentially unwieldy transcription disks. Nevertheless, it could be done. There would be no security risk in this approach. But the American networks forbade the use of recordings. The prohibition went to the heart of what a radio network was all about. A network was still only those leased lines feeding programs to affiliates. Once devices like recordings came into use, who could tell where it might end? Why would the affiliates need a network, the executives reasoned.

And so Murrow reported from a studio in the BBC's Broadcasting House. As Britain's voice, the BBC was a natural Luftwaffe target and was kept under tight security. Murrow entered the sandbagged building passing between sentries armed with rifles and fixed bayonets. He then went through a heavy screen doorway behind which more guards checked his credentials. He walked down a stairwell, with gasproof steel doors and more sentries at each landing, to the third below-ground level. There he walked along a corridor lined with cots and sleeping bodies, stepping over cables snaking along the floor to Studio B-4, which he shared with other American broadcasters. The studio was hardly more than an oversized closet and had recently been a storeroom for the BBC canteen. A curtain divided the room into a broadcast booth and a work area crowded with filing cabinets, a clothes tree, a desk, and a cot, usually occupied by a sleeping reporter. Engineers and censors, working around the clock in three shifts, were always present in Studio B-4. The air was stuffy and reeked of body odors and cooking smells from the canteen.

Reporting the war from this mole hole frustrated Murrow. Above ground, the greatest drama of the age was unfolding. He had the technological capacity to report it live, but he was being thwarted by military security and corporate rigamarole. He made a proposal to the Air Ministry. Let him go up on a rooftop and record a broadcast during a raid, not to use over the air—his own network would not permit that—but to prove that he could describe what was happening without giving away information of value to the enemy. The Air Ministry turned him down, but made a counterproposal. The Air Ministry would let him put a live mike on the roof of the BBC during a raid, while he broadcast from Studio B-4. It was an awkward arrangement, and he turned it down.

Finally, after repeated nudging, the Ministry relented. He would be allowed to make a test. He was not to do it from the roof of the BBC, but from a building a few blocks down the street on Portland Place. He was to make six sample recordings during actual raids, after which the Air Ministry would decide if he had violated security.

He was not bothered at being out of doors in the middle of an air raid. He had thought through that risk. He never had gone into an air-raid shelter, except to get a story. "Once you start going into shelters," he told Larry Le Sueur, "you lose your nerve." Following his example, Janet did not go into shelters either, though there was one in the mews behind their apartment building. They sat under an oaken table in Ed's study or stretched out on the floor. More often, as soon as he heard the siren, Ed would get into the car and start riding around blacked-out London looking for his story, leaving Janet alone.

For six nights, Ed stood on the rooftop. The German bombers never failed him. They came every night. He captured on recordings the unearthly howl of a bomb as its fins cut the air and the crumpling sound it made when it exploded. He caught the cursing of an antiaircraft battery as the crew worked its gun. He submitted his test records to the Air Ministry, which promptly lost them.

He went back up to the rooftop on Portland Place and started over. The Air Ministry heard this batch of recordings and concluded that he had not betrayed any useful information. But it turned him down anyway. Who could tell what a man might blurt out with a bomb falling on him? At this point Murrow abandoned bureaucratic channels and got word to the prime minister. The journalist in Winston Churchill understood instantly what Murrow was trying to achieve. Furthermore, Churchill wanted America to hear what London was going through. Pressure from the top down worked, as it usually does, and Murrow at last received permission to broadcast live during an actual raid.

The first attempt was a disaster.

He went up on the roof. Cables had been run from his vantage point to Broadcasting House. Almost on cue, the sirens wailed and the bombers followed. They came in low, in waves. The beams of the searchlights stitched a delicate, swaying latticework in the sky. Antiaircraft guns bellowed from Primrose Hill. Batteries in Hyde Park responded. Hot iron from spent shells clanked to the ground around him. Ed was enveloped in the sounds of war. In five seconds he would go on the air to New York. And then the focus of the raid moved to a far part of London. The rumble of the bomber engines faded. The antiaircraft batteries around him stopped firing. As he began to broadcast, all was utterly silent.

"I'm standing on a rooftop looking out over London," he said. "At the moment everything is quiet. For reasons of national as well as personal security, I'm unable to tell you the exact location from which I'm speaking. Off to my left, far away in the distance, I can see just that faint red angry snap of antiaircraft bursts against the steel-blue sky. But the guns are so far away that it's impossible to hear them from this location.

"About five minutes ago the guns in the immediate vicinity were working. I can look across just at a building not far away and see something that looks like a flash of white paint down the side, and I know from daylight observation that about a quarter of that building has disappeared, hit by a bomb the other night. [The searchlights went on again around him.] I think probably in a minute we shall have the sound of guns in the immediate vicinity. The lights are swinging over in this general direction now. You'll hear two explosions. There they are! That was the explosion overheard, not the guns themselves. I should think in a few minutes there may be a bit of shrapnel around here....The plane is still very high. Earlier this evening we could hear occasional—again, those were explosions overhead. Earlier this evening we heard a number of bombs go sliding and slithering across, to fall several blocks away. Just overhead now the burst of the antiaircraft fire. Still the nearby guns are not working. The searchlights now are feeling almost directly overhead. Now you'll hear two bursts a little nearer in a moment....There they are! That hard, stony sound."

On subsequent nights, the Germans were more accommodating. He was able to describe raids in their full fury and provide a graphic account to Americans sitting comfortably at home. Of an antiaircraft battery near him, he reported: "They're working in their shirtsleeves, laughing and cursing as they slam the shells into their guns. The spotters and detectors swing slowly around in their reclining carriage. The lens of the night glasses look like the eyes of an overgrown owl in the orange-blue light that belches from the muzzle of the gun. They're working without search-lights tonight. The moon is so bright that the beam of the light is lost a few hundred feet off the ground. Someone should paint the chimney pots and gables of London as they're silhouetted in the flashing flame of the guns, when the world seems upside down." One night, he was still in the street as a raid began. He crouched in the gutter and held his microphone to the ground so that his listeners could hear the sound a bomb made when it hit the ancient London pavement.

His word images were not all struck from his brow on the instant. As he watched the deadly pyrotechnics he would form phrases, work them over in his mind, store them, and use them at the proper moment: "It's a bomber's moon tonight."

He could be as clinical about the nut-and-bolt aspects of a raid as he could be imagistic about its effects, and with the same grim effect: "When you hear that London has been bombed and hammered for ten to twelve hours during the night, you should remember that this is a huge, sprawl-ing city, that there is nothing like a continuous rain of bombs. Often there is a period of ten or twenty minutes when no sound can be heard, no searchlights seen. Then a few bombs will come whistling down. Then si-lence again. A hundred planes over London doesn't mean that they were all here at the same time. They generally come singly or in pairs, circle around over the searchlights two or three times, and then you can hear them start their bombing runs, generally a shallow dive, and those bombs take a long time to fall."

He also reported from the underside of a raid: "No words of mine can describe the spectacle over London tonight, so I'll talk about the peo-ple underground. I visited eleven air raid shelters in the West End of London during this raid—the longest we've had so far....Over near Wimpole Street, two stories underground, a man was telling about the narrow escape he had when driving on the icy roads of the Midlands last winter....Each time I entered a new shelter people wanted to know if I'd seen any bombs and was it safe to go home. At one shelter there was a fine row going on. A man wanted to smoke his pipe in the shelter; the warden wouldn't allow it. The pipe smoker said he'd go out and smoke it in the street, where he'd undoubtedly be hit by a bomb and then the war-den would be sorry."[14]

He set down for the guidance of his staff the tone he wanted in broad-casts: "The reporter must never sound excited, even if bombs are falling outside. Rather, the reporter should imagine that he has just returned to his hometown and the local editor has asked him to dinner with a banker and a professor. After dinner your host asks you 'Well, what was it like?' As you talk, the maid is passing the coffee and her boy friend, a truck driver, is waiting for her in the kitchen and listening. You are supposed to describe things in terms that make sense to the truck driver without insulting the intelligence of the professor." It was the same cross-sectional cast and the same advice, updated for war, that he had given his speakers when he was director of talks.[15]

Murrow now had two other men, besides himself, in London, Larry Le Sueur and Eric Sevareid. Sevareid was mortified to find himself in London. He and Tom Grandin, the Grandin whom White had tried to fire, had been working out of Paris. Grandin had fallen in love with a Romanian woman. After a whirlwind courtship, they married, and he brought his bride back to Paris. When France began to collapse, Grandin took his wife to Bordeaux to put her on a ship bound for America. At the last minute, they could not bear to part. Grandin called Sevareid to say that he was sailing too. To Murrow, who had saved his career, he said nothing. Sevareid also managed to get his young wife and infant twin sons on a ship to the States. Without authorization from anyone at CBS, he too left a defeated France for Liverpool.

Murrow had given Eric Sevareid his great professional break. When CBS had refused to pay the passage to send Sevareid's dependents home, Ed had offered to guarantee the fare. After Grandin's departure, Sevareid felt that he was deserting his post. Still he did not know what else to do. On arriving in England, he uneasily telephoned Murrow—the man "who had put his trust in me." Murrow told him, "This is the best news I've had for a long time. We've been in a sweat about you people." He told Sevareid to get up to London right away, "There's work to be done."

Sevareid had won Murrow's professional respect. The two men had rich, satisfying conversations. But there was another Murrow whom the serious Sevareid could not reach. Ed, at times, needed pals, just as he needed to go off to a shooting gallery now and then. Sevareid recalled, years later, Ed "loved Larry Le Sueur....Larry was terribly easy going and relaxed and funny, and he was good for Ed, I thought. No, I was a much more uptight sort of fellow as they now say."[16]

Le Sueur later described their routine in the midst of the Blitz. "Ed and I would walk along the paths cleared between the debris. They called them 'rat runs.' We'd come back from dinner and the sirens would start and the guns went to work. One day you passed a building. The next day it was gone. There was a perverse exhilaration to it all."

Murrow had a favorite restaurant in Soho, L'Etoile, on Charlotte Street, and a favorite table in the restaurant under a skylight. There, he expected Le Sueur to dine with him, night after night, during the height of the bombing, under a canopy of glass. Then they would head for the office, Murrow with his tin helmet set at a rakish angle, often sporting gray flannel slacks and a hound's-tooth jacket. The helmet had a shrapnel dent, a badge of honor in London.[17]

NBC had, by now, followed CBS's lead and had its own correspondents. One of them, John McVane, told of a night he spent with Murrow. McVane had been drinking scotch at 84 Hallam Street when the bombs started dropping "with the shriek and roar" of an express train. Finally, Murrow could stand it no longer. He took McVane with him and started driving around the city, following the flames. They finally had to stop when the glass heaped up in the streets threatened to puncture the tires. They got out and stood by a giant jet of burning gas from a main that had caught fire. There they watched the rest of the raid. That night 200 bombers came over London and left 412 dead.

Sevareid recalled sitting with Murrow in the Hallam Street apartment, a dwindling bottle of scotch at their side. As the bombs fell, Ed spun tales of the Swedes he had known in the lumber camps. "In those moments," Sevareid recalled wistfully, "his laughter had the gaiety of boyhood." Ed wrote to his old boss, the timber cruiser, Ken Merredith, that bombs sounded "like stumps being blasted." He still boasted that he carried "a pretty good map of the Sol Duc Valley" in his head. He told Merredith that he believed he could pace a mile "and hit it within 150 feet. Maybe by fudging a little I could make it 100."

Sevareid found Murrow's sangfroid beyond him. He and Ed went to the office at Langham Place after a raid and found the place a shambles. "Bill Paley's picture hanging by one wire, plaster all over his [Ed's] desk. All the windows broken. We had to move out," Sevareid remembered. They moved to an office on Portland Place. It too was bombed out. Whenever the siren sounded, Sevareid felt his stomach twist into knots. Janet wrote in her diary, "He [Sevareid] had the kind of nervous tummy that doesn't stand up to air raids." Sevareid had been away from home for three years. He had a young wife and two babies in the States. "I was both ill and homesick," he said. He asked Ed for reassignment home. Ed saw him off toward the end of October at Waterloo Station.[18]

During one raid, Broadcasting House suffered a direct hit. A bomb sailed through an upper-story window, crashed through the floor, and came to rest on the floor below. It lay there for 45 minutes. While the bomb squad was roping it off, it exploded. Seven people were killed outright, and more were injured. Murrow was on the air as they brought the broken and lifeless bodies past Studio B-4 to the aid station. He described to his listeners in America the smell of iodine wafting into the studio. Most of the casualties were people who worked for Dick Marriott in the foreign liaison section. Ed knew them.

He faced danger with stoicism, avoiding shelters, standing on rooftops, sketching word pictures of a man-made hell as it happened. Some of his colleagues scoffed at his behavior. They found it a damn-fool pose, theatrical bravado. He himself regarded his behavior much the way a fireman looks at a fire. You go into it because that is the job. He never denied his fears. He particularly feared, he said, being blinded by flying glass. He deflected self-conscious discussions of bravery versus foolhardiness with an offhand, "I have a peasant's mind. I can't write about anything I haven't seen."[19]

The war began to strike close. Alan Campbell, his secretary Kay's youngest brother, just turned 21, had been a pilot instructor in the RAF and was chafing for a combat assignment. Campbell got his wish, and Janet spotted his name in the "Lost on Active Service" column of the newspaper.[20]

Yet life found a routine, even a life of ritualized destruction. In the heart of the Blitz, Murrow reported, "My own apartment is in one of the most heavily bombed areas of London. But the newspapers are on the door step each morning, so is the bottle of milk. When the light switch is pressed, there is light and the gas stove still works." On another night he said. "About an hour after the 'all clear' had sounded, people were sitting in deck chairs on their lawns, reading the Sunday papers. The girls in light, cheap dresses were strolling along the streets. There was no bravado, no loud voices, only a quiet acceptance of the situation."

On the eighteenth day of uninterrupted bombing, he had come home to find a letter from "The China Campaign Committee." He was being asked to sign a petition that read, "We demand the immediate and unconditional reopening of the Burma Road." The letter said that a quarter of a million signatures had thus far been collected in London in the previous fifteen days. Would he add his?[21]

At about the same time, Ambassador Joe Kennedy sent a telegram to the President that read, "I can not impress upon you strongly enough my complete lack of confidence in the entire conduct of this war....it breaks my heart to draw these conclusions about a people that I sincerely hoped to be victorious, but I cannot get myself to the point where I believe they can be of any assistance to the cause in which they are involved."[22]

Ed Murrow thought about people who collected a quarter of a million signatures during two weeks in which they had been bombed every day, signatures urging greater resolution in a military campaign halfway around the world, and he saw a different England than did Kennedy. "These people are stubborn," he told his listeners. "Often they are insular, but their determination must be recorded."

He went into Soho while a raid was still in progress where a bomb had removed one wall of a building, exposing the apartments on each floor like an architect's cross-sectional rendering. An old man was crawling around on the third floor on his hands and knees. An air-raid warden shouted at him above the din, "Get down, I say. Can't you hear? Get down." The old man moaned. "I can't find me teeth." The exasperated warden shouted back, "What the hell do you think they're dropping on us—sandwiches?"

Murrow watched a cockney street cleaner sweep up broken glass while people looked on. When the man realized he had an audience, he took a couple of soft-shoe steps, twirled his broom over his head, and sang out, "'itler's blinkin' 'ousemaid, that's me!'

Signs on bomb-blasted stores read, "Shattered but not shuttered," and "Knocked but not locked." Londoners developed a vocabulary of euphemisms for living with their lot. A particularly bloody raid was a "flap"; a direct hit on one's house "a bit of trouble." Ed cherished the words of a man he met who was tired of hearing how Londoners could take it. "Do you think we're really brave," the man said, "or just lacking in imagination?" The point was not to make too great a fuss. Murrow was by nature predisposed to the style. A friend recalled running into him after one of the worst raids of the Blitz. "A bit crisp, wasn't it?" Ed remarked, and went on.[23]

He went along with the tight-lipped insouciance. Still, the strain and overwork had become bone-deep. But he could not stop. When he could not find friends to bring home after a broadcast, he wandered the streets alone gazing at the fires until dawn. As he dictated his scripts, his colleagues learned to judge his exhaustion by the angle of the cigarette. At first it jutted straight out, then began to droop, and, finally, hung from his bottom lip. Eric Sevareid recalled Murrow broadcasting during the Blitz. "He looked like a ghost. Pale. Shaken. I thought he was going to keel over. But he'd sit down and the cue would come, and there was that voice, steady as a rock. I couldn't do that." He was living on coffee and cigarettes. During the Blitz, he lost thirty pounds.

Only when he wrote home did he drop the stoic mask. In the privacy of letters aimed primarily at his mother, he bared a romantic self-image: "...I am working hard...never harder...but then I was brought up on hard work....Frequently I am in trouble with the authorities but you taught me not to run away from trouble....Often when I sit here typing a broadcast...the guns and bombs shaking the window...I say to myself ...this night I shall do a piece of which two people out in Washington shall not be ashamed....If at times the stuff sounds cold and hard that's because I have seen my full share of human misery in this world and death and destruction don't hit me as hard as they once did....Too many good friends have been lost....This is the end of an age...the end of things I was taught to love and respect and I must stay here and report it if it kills me....one life more or less means nothing....you know that and so do I....you raised a boy with a big voice....he worked hard and was lucky and has not yet used that voice to mislead the people who trust it....Staying over here is hard...it means that we shall have no children...and we had hoped to present you with a grandson...but Janet agrees that there is nothing else to do. She was thirty the other day and I forgot."[24]

The sacrifice of postponing a baby was not quite accurate. Both he and Janet desperately wanted children, even with the war on. When Janet had written out her resolutions at the beginning of the new year, a baby was her first hope.

The normality within lunacy sometimes took on a surreal aspect. Ed still played golf with Larry Le Sueur, Scotty Reston, and other friends. They played a little nine-hole public course a subway ride away at Hampstead Heath. He and Larry usually broadcast late at night and did their legwork in the morning. And so they could occasionally slip in a round in the afternoon before the bombing began. The fairways were pocked with craters and roped-off, unexploded bombs. They played around them. If a ball rolled inside the ropes, Scotty Reston recalled, "That was judged an unplayable lay." They only gave up golf when the last scarred ball disappeared in the rough and no new ones were obtainable.[25]

Hallam Street continued as part club room, part office, part boardinghouse, part pub, part snack bar, and part refugee center. When the Portland Place office was bombed out, Ed brought Kay Campbell home to work until they found another office on Duchess Street. Betty, the Murrow maid, had married and had taken her own flat until she was bombed out. She and her husband, Reg, then took a back room in the Murrow flat. They all shared one bath. Larry Le Sueur had an opulent apartment on Portland Place, once reputedly the home of Somerset Maugham. He was bombed out and moved in with the Murrows for a time.

Ed liked shooting darts in the pubs so much that he put a dart board in the apartment. He continued to bring home friends after his broadcasts for poker, but mostly for talk. R.T. Clarke, a Scot and a senior editor at the BBC, was a Murrow favorite. Clarke was a student of German affairs and an American Civil War expert. He particularly endeared himself to Ed because he had managed to make the Nazi blacklist. Clarke had a cot in his BBC office and lived there. Consequently, Murrow was constantly dragging him home. Janet wrote in her diary, "Still a little furious today with Ed." He had brought R.T. and four other men home at two o'clock in the morning. She had been wakened by Ed shouting to Clarke, "Well R. T., what *should* Meade have done at Gettysburg?" The discussion broke up at 6 a.m.

In part, the chronic socializing was to enable him to uncoil. But he was rarely without motive, even in his leisure. Another Hallam Street regular from the BBC, Michael Balkwill, perceived a purpose behind the talking that went on into the small hours. Balkwill recalled how Ed would introduce a subject: "Well, Brother, for my money..." and then elicit the other person's opinion. Balkwill found, "He'd be interested in anything that interested anybody else. If you'd said, 'I always played chess during the Blitz,' then Ed would either say, 'Oh, you play chess too. Have you tried the opening gambit of...' Or 'I've never played chess. Why did you play chess during the Blitz? Do you find it soothing or stimulating?'" It was not small talk, Balkwill concluded. It was Murrow educating himself.[26]

He maintained a far-flung correspondence with friends and colleagues. He had a way of directing this correspondence toward useful ends. What a careful review of these letters reveals is that he had maneuvered his friends into an informal news network, his unwitting stringers, as it were. His files were full of single-spaced multiple-page letters giving him detailed accounts of conditions at home, in Egypt, in the aircraft industry. What he did not much like were people who used the mails "to leave their souls about." A reporter named Robert Reed remembered flying with Murrow. Ed steered the conversation to a recent military campaign that Reed had covered. Before the ride ended, Reed realized that Murrow had extracted "every single detail of where I was, what kind of microphone, how quickly had it taken to link up with the engineer and how it was flown back to England."

The home office informed Murrow that he was no longer merely a prestigious, but expensive, ornament to the network. He had become a source of income, a salable commodity. Janet noted in her diary, "Night show was being auditioned by General Motors." That year, Socony Vacuum and Sinclair Oil started to sponsor Murrow's regular broadcasts. Ed wrote his stateside correspondent, Ed Dakin, "Have now accumulated eight or nine offers from publishers to do a book." With his fame growing, he wrote to the CBS publicity office asking that the misstatements in his vitae be straightened out, particularly in well-known reference works like *Who's Who*.[27]

As 1940 ended, Murrow's circle began to take on the quality of that old gang breaking up. Sevareid had already gone back to America. In June, Ed had lost his only female correspondent, Marvin Breckinridge, to marriage. In October he and his other comrade of the haystack, Ben Robertson, went to Paddington Station to see Jimmy Sheean off. Sheean was going home, he said, to make some money on the American lecture circuit. As his train began to pull out of the station, the first bombs began to fall. Sheean told Ed that he felt like a deserter.

Joe Kennedy left England in October too, a changed man. Just before going, he said, "I did not know London could take it. I did not think that any city could take it. I am bowed in reverence." Murrow was happy with his departure. He had already made known to the Roosevelt administration his preference for the post, John Gilbert Winant. Early the following spring, Winant was named U.S. ambassador to the Court of St. James.

H. V. Kaltenborn was gone too, at least from CBS. He had been lured to NBC by a lucrative contract that April, where the keen analyst was now billed as a "star commentator." Kaltenborn, though a supreme egoist, nevertheless proved a generous colleague. After he left CBS, he wrote Murrow, "…each time I listen my admiration grows. During this past crucial week you have been a tower of strength to millions of Americans who share your belief and mine in the survival of democracy. I find it almost impossible to be as objective as you are, and yet I am three thousand miles away from the bombs that fall at your feet. Well, anyhow, you are doing the greatest job of radio reporting that has so far been performed by any one, anywhere."

In December, Bill Shirer planned to go back to the States. Since the outbreak of the war Shirer had been broadcasting from Berlin as a neutral correspondent and felt that he was suffocating under Nazi censorship. He had spent most of his adult life abroad. It was time to go home. He and Ed met early in December in Lisbon, for "a mighty reunion" before Shirer left.[28]

Ed got back to London to learn that on the day he had left for Lisbon, he had lost another friend. The Germans had captured a stockpile of British sea mines at Amiens during the French debacle. They had their own superior models, and so rather than waste the British mines, they parachuted them into London. These black oblongs, carrying a ton of dynamite each, settled to earth in utter silence, like a leaf in autumn, and went off without warning with a doomsday roar. One of them had exploded in front of Broadcasting House. Fred Bate was among the casualties. The blast severed the tendons in both his legs, almost tore off an ear, and riddled his head with bits of stone. Still, he tried to drag himself into the BBC to do his broadcast. Bate was evacuated home. The same blast also destroyed Murrow's latest office and the old Langham Hotel where he and Janet had felt the cold eyes of the English gentry on their arrival four years before.[29]

CBS had arranged a hard-to-come-by air reservation to New York via Portugal any time that Ed wanted to leave. He wrote Jimmy Sheean in December that most of their colleagues were indeed waiting around "for a plane to Lisbon." The word around the bars that the reporters frequented was that big money could be made cashing in on their war stories. Ed told Janet that this talk disgusted him.

Instead, with Shirer now gone, he asked CBS to find out from the Germans if he might broadcast from Berlin. The Germans replied that he could, provided he gave his word as a gentleman that afterward he would not return to England until the war ended. That price he found too high.[30]

Historians record the Blitz as the period from September 7 through November 3, fifty-seven days during which German bombers struck London and other British cities every night. Bill Shirer had obtained a perspective on the Blitz from the other side. While he was still working in Berlin, a German airman whom he knew had dropped in on him after flying several missions over London. He told Shirer that the Germans were overwhelmed by the vast expanse of the city and disappointed that so much of it survived the pounding. He also told Shirer that on one of the raids, Hermann Goering had flown over London. Winston Churchill told Murrow that it would take the Germans ten years to destroy half of the city. And after that, progress would be slower. The bombing had gone on long after Operation Sea Lion was abandoned. The raids had been transmuted from a prelude to invasion to a strategy of indiscriminate destruction, a strategy of terror, for which the Allied air forces would later repay Germany with usurious interest.

Hitler had made a psychological blunder. In the beginning, the bombs fell almost exclusively on the cockneys' London, and class bitterness began to surface. Had the Nazis confined themselves to the East End, they might have exploited a growing feeling among the British working class that this was a rich man's war, but a poor man's fight. But then the Luftwaffe started bombing all over the city, the West End and the East End, Mayfair along with Stepney. On September 15, the Germans made a deliberate, low-level bombing run on Buckingham Palace. Murrow loved the reaction he heard from a bus conductor: "Well, blimey. If I ever thought the Jerries would go for Buckingham Palace. I thought all those people were in it together."

After November 3, the nightly raids ended, though intermittent and often frightful air attacks went on. The score during the Blitz was over 2,300 German aircraft destroyed against 900 of the RAF. From June of 1940 to June of 1941, 43,381 British civilians lost their lives in air raids, a cold statistic that Murrow thought failed to capture the essence of the ordeal. During a raid, he had gone down into an underground control station that dispatched fire engines to burning buildings. That night he reported in spare prose, "I saw a man laboriously copying names in a ledger, the list of firemen killed in action during the last month. There were about one hundred names."

Over 120 American correspondents covered the Blitz. The words that best captured the feel and sense of it for America were Edward R. Murrow's. Hundreds of his countrymen wrote him to say that for them the war was his reporting. It had taken them from neutral detachment to support for the British in their struggle. A woman from Louisiana sent him a poem:

> With him I see a dark unpeopled street where old cathedral
> walls still brave the gloom.
> I hear the roar of guns instead of choirs, I smell charred
> wood instead of hawthorne's bloom.[31]

CHAPTER 14

America at War

Janet found them a place in the country at Bishop's Stortford; "a shapeless mass of red brick victorianism," she described it. The house was supposed to provide an occasional respite for them and the CBS staff from the stresses of life in London. She was often there alone waiting for him. Janet kept a diary during the war, and wrote in it at the time "...my darling Ed, you are the only thing that matters and in this funny life, it's hard to let you know."

It was a constant refrain, this deep love for her husband and her unhappiness over the separations and the intrusions that kept him away from her. She had built her life around him. She was never really content apart from him. Yet she competed with a jealous mistress, his career. And to that mistress he gave himself unreservedly.

She loved a book she had read, *The Voyage*, by Charles Morgan, the story of two people completely happy with each other. She wrote in her diary: "Sometimes I think Ed and I are—other times not. When we're not, it's mostly my fault. I guess I'm too possessive. I wish I weren't. I try not to be. I think it comes from my feeling of inferiority. I fear all the other gals too much. I'll make a note of that. I'm not inferior to them—most of them." Her vows to become a better person are a recurring refrain throughout the diaries, a reflection of the Puritan ethic of self-improvement through self-discipline in which she had been reared. She had started the diary with a new year's resolution: "I hope to be more temperate this year in eating, drinking, dreaming and generally wasting time."

After reading the Morgan book in the country, she was moved to call Ed at their London apartment. It was a short, unhappy conversation, their problem in microcosm. He had gone to bed late after another grueling fourteen-hour day, and she had wakened him out of a sound sleep. He was annoyed and in no mood to discuss a book.

The cycle that had emerged early in their marriage persisted, now under greater stresses. Ed would do or say something thoughtless that hurt her. Janet's hurt would put her in a peevish mood. And her moodiness would then annoy him. He promised her one afternoon that he would be home in time for tea. She made a sweet that he liked. He failed to show up. When he finally arrived, too late, she was crying and "looking a mess," which irritated him. He canceled movie dates with her three times in a row because he had found golf partners instead. She knew he needed the relaxation that he found in male companionship. She came from a hard-working family herself and expected her husband to work hard and, when he had the opportunity, to play hard. But, she felt, "Sometimes he seemed not to have any energy for me."

She had voluntarily risked her life to stay with him in England. Yet he could be intolerant of her slightest complaint. He wrote her while she was in the country, "...think of those English women who've been separated from children and husbands for years."

Was he totally insensitive to her needs and feelings? Apparently not. He wrote his parents that Janet "did not have much of a life. She doesn't complain although I can't see why she doesn't....She is the world's best and I love her deeply." He should have told it to her rather than to them. But he was completely swallowed up in his work and totally sure of her love for him. Her devotion was like a hardy plant that endured whether he watered it or not. And so he rarely did.

If she had a child, she knew that she would not be so dependent on him for attention. But they had been married for seven years and had virtually given up hope. They began talking about adopting children. That, however, would have to wait until after the war, when they thought they might adopt war orphans.[1]

Ed's secretary did not help matters. Janet yearned to look after her husband. But it seemed to her that Kay Campbell did more "taking care of Ed than I did." The other correspondents in the office detected "secretary love" in Kay's possessiveness toward Ed, the hopeless passion that some women feel for the men they work for, who make of their jobs a fantasy substitute for marriage, a marriage with no shared holidays or anniversaries or bed. There was no man in Kay's life other than Ed Murrow. Larry Le Sueur found her so slavishly devoted to Ed that he dreaded going to the office. Kay made him feel an intruder. Ed did nothing to encourage her romantically. From him she received respect, admiration, gratitude, and her salary. If anything, he was overly formal. She was "Kay" to everybody else. But to Ed she was always "Miss Campbell," and he was always "Mr. Murrow" to her.

That Kay resented his wife was predictable enough. Janet found that she could not discuss even so common a subject as the war without provoking Kay's sarcasm. Kay was particularly caustic with Janet about America leaving the fight against the Fascists to England alone, a criticism more fairly lodged with her boss than with his wife. "I know she resents me, my being able to broadcast," Janet wrote in her diary, "and is probably more fond of Ed than she should be."

Janet came back to the apartment one afternoon, excited because she and Ed were going out to the house in Bishop's Stortford together for the weekend. She found Kay working in the apartment. Ed not only insisted on taking both of them to lunch, he invited Kay to join them in the country. Janet told herself that he meant nothing more than kindness and sympathy. Kay was grieving deeply for her brother Alan. He was still missing in action. (It was later confirmed that Alan Campbell had been killed.) Janet wrote in her diary, "I hate only seeing Ed at parties and with other people."[2]

She was an unfairly harsh critic of herself. She was highly attractive. She was not idle. And she was not untalented. She was entrusted with international broadcasts made to millions of listeners over a major radio network on which her husband's reputation rested, as well as her own. She provided the "woman's angle" on the war, talking about food shortages and clothing rationing, and interviewing female members of Parliament. She had a nice eye for the telling detail. "There is nothing more forlorn than limp curtains dangling out of blown-out windows," she reported.

She worked with the American Committee for the Evacuation of Children, arranging to send children to the States. She worked hard but was clear-eyed enough to wonder if it was wise to part young children from their parents and "deprive them of their heritage." And, she asked herself, if overseas evacuation was such a good idea, why wasn't it good for all the children. Instead, she found that priority went to the children of families who had influence. She wrote her parents, "Here, as well as everywhere else, money counts."

Paul White's wife, Sue, had helped launch something in America that year called "Bundles for Britain" to collect food, clothing, and money to aid the British. The movement needed a director in England to distribute the American largess. Sue White asked Janet to take on the job. She plunged into it as director of Bundles for Britain. The work brought her into contact with the prime minister's wife. Clementine Churchill took a liking to this serious, quietly competent young American. Janet Murrow was invited to Ten Downing Street for lunch. The prime minister came in and expressed his delight at meeting Murrow's wife. She shook his hand and later recorded in her diary her surprise at the softness of the hand of the redoubtable war leader. She was invited to lunch again, and this time the prime minister sat her next to him.

Her causes filled her hours. But they did not fill her life. Janet Murrow, for all her outward appearance of composed self-sufficiency, was, as her diaries reveal, a sensitive, romantic, and vulnerable woman. The

fact that her husband loved her but rarely expressed it left her emotionally undernourished.

The Murrows and the Philip Jordans had been friends since 1938.
Philip was a journalist with the London *Evening Chronicle,* much admired
as both a reporter and a graceful writer. He was also a talented novelist.
Jordan was one of the journalists whom Ed had put on the air during the
Munich crisis. The two men were political soul mates, liberal but
nonideological. Something that Jordan wrote could have been written by
either one of them: "...one hates Fascism equally, whether it's German,
Italian or British, and...decent men and women are not interested in destroying one brand in order to put another brand in its place."[3]

In 1941, Philip Jordan was 39 years old, not a conventionally handsome man, but attractive in his own way, slight of build, with a sensitive
face and wide, sympathetic eyes. He had about him the touch of the poet.
He also possessed that quality that women find so appealing, and so rare,
in a man; he listened to them.

The Murrows and Jordan and his wife were together fairly often. Philip
was such good company, a good talker, well-read, witty, amusing. Eric
Sevareid described Jordan as "a superior guy. A lovely, suave, gentlemanly
man. A gallant, sensitive free spirit." When Lacey Murrow's wife, Marge, visited Ed and Janet in England, of all their friends, she liked Philip Jordan
best. After an evening in his company, Janet wrote in her diary, "I loved
seeing Philip again....He's a dear person. He has brains and is sensitive...."
She saw him occasionally for lunch. He was attentive and considerate. He
was easy to take, not moody, not compulsive, not given to long, inexplicable
silences. Philip Jordan made her feel attractive and desirable.[4]

It was a time of sudden separations and uncertain reunions, a time
when men boarded ships and planes and did not always return. It was a
time when one lunched with a friend one day and he was blown to bits in
the street the next. The war compressed and heightened feelings, fears,
loneliness, the sense of fleeting and unrecoverable time. People clung to
each other quickly and intensely and then let go. Tomorrow was a void;
only the present was certain.

Their friendship ripened into what they believed was love. Janet and
Philip talked about a future together. They were both married, and Janet
confided to a friend that the situation could become "messy." Of their romance, she wrote in her diary, "Perhaps it will enrich our lives; make us sensitive to the suffering and beauty of the world....one must take what comes."

What came along was the same force that had brought them together,
the war, which now parted them. On June 22, Hitler broke the nonaggression pact with Stalin and invaded the Soviet Union. Philip Jordan was
virtually the first British newspaper correspondent to go to Russia after
the invasion. A few months after his involvement with Janet had begun,
he was on a Catalina flying boat headed for Archangel. Janet wrote in her
diary, "cannot get used to the idea that I am alone once more." And on

another day: "I pray that he will be safe, that it will be a successful and exciting adventure; and that nothing will happen to break his spirit."

Philip Jordan was gone for fifteen months. By the time he came back, the flame had died for both of them. Janet recognized that Jordan had made her feel whole and alive and wanted. And she had loved that feeling more than she had loved the man. The man she continued to love all her life was her husband.[5]

German bombers no longer came every night; but still they came. On May 10, 1941, they unleashed the greatest raid of the war. Incendiaries set over 2,000 fires. The House of Commons, Westminister Abbey, Big Ben, the British Museum—all were hit. Over 2,000 people died in a single night. Ed had found Kay Campbell at their latest office streaked with plaster, looking as though she were wearing a fright wig. She said of this third experience in being bombed out that it grew "tiresome." One had to search the debris for petty cash, and clean the typewriters, and hunt up new quarters. "We were getting known and people didn't want to take us in." They found their fourth office at 49 Hallam Street just down from Ed's apartment.[6]

One evening, Ed and Janet had finished dinner at L'Etoile at about 10 p.m. and were walking home. A raid had already been in progress for a half hour. Shrapnel from the antiaircraft guns fell and clanged around them. They passed the Devonshire Arms, a BBC hangout. A thin crack of light showed along the bottom of the blackout curtain. Ed said that he wanted to drop in and shoot some darts and have a drink with the boys. "Would you mind much going home alone?" He asked Janet. "I certainly would," she answered. When they reached the apartment, they went to the roof to watch the hellishly beautiful spectacle of an air raid. Flames from incendiary bombs had set off raging fires. Flares hung like lanterns among the stars, and searchlights waved silver fingers through the darkness. They stood entranced. Then, a tearing, whooshing shriek seemed to be coming down on top of them. They wrapped their arms around their heads to protect their eyes and ears. The blast flung them against a wall. The building shuddered. A column of smoke, shot through with sparks, rose near them, close enough, it seemed, to touch.

"My God," Ed said. "It's the office!" Kay Campbell was there waiting for him to come in later and dictate that night's broadcast. He grabbed his tin hat and rushed out into the street. Janet watched him disappear toward the pillar of smoke and flames.

Ed found Kay blown under a rug, but unharmed. The bomb had fallen directly on the Devonshire Arms. Everyone in it was killed, along with several people outside. Allan Wells, Ed's friend from the BBC home service, had been on fire-watch near the pub with his wife, Clare, when the bomb fell. Clare was killed outright. Alan died a few days afterward. Their little girl was safe in the country. A few days later, Ed and Janet attended a cremation ceremony for the couple. On the way out, Ed said with a grim smile, "I could just see Alan sit up and say, 'Don't do this to me!'"

Jimmy Sheean returned to England that spring of 1941 with a lucrative contract to report the war for the *Saturday Evening Post.* Ed told Sheean that he had come back to a different England: "You won't find any of that high-spirited, we-can-take-it stuff of last year." The novelty of chipper heroism in the face of death and devastation had worn through.[7]

Sheehan told Ed that while home he had gone to interview President Roosevelt one day and was startled that the first thing the President asked him was, "Did you get to see Ed and how is he?" FDR, Sheean reported, was a regular listener to his broadcasts, along with most cabinet members.

Ed was back in America himself in July of 1941. He was completely run down and came back for a series of medical tests. The tests revealed only that he was overworked, eating too little and too poorly, and not resting enough. He made no attempt to slow down. Instead, when he returned to London, he had a special switch installed in his office so that when he was not there, his telephone would ring at home.[8]

About that time, he saw his brother Lacey for the first time in three years. Lacey had gone on active duty as a lieutenant colonel in the U.S. Army Air Corps. He was now 39. Too old to fly, he had been sent to learn about constructing airfields from the RAF. It was ironic in a way. Ed was the one preaching, obliquely on the air, and vehemently off it, that America belonged in this war. He wrote Chet Williams, "At the risk of being labelled a war monger, if this country goes down, we at home will tear ourselves apart in five years maybe less." Yet, it was the apolitical Lacey who had come closest to doing in fact what Ed was urging in principle.

They had never been close. Ed found Lacey too provincial, a typical engineer, impatient with social and political disorder and convinced that all problems could be solved by practical men with slide rules. Ed wrote his parents: "Lacey lacks experience and tolerance....I have both and can help him. [Still] You should be very proud of him. I am....Lacey has a brilliant career ahead of him."[9]

Ed had no trouble with the home office now in expanding his staff. Charles Cummings Collingwood was an American reporter in his midtwenties working in London for the United Press when he received a message to call a "Mr. Morrell" at CBS. He did, and was crisply corrected by Kay Campbell, "You mean Mr. Murrow."

Collingwood was almost too much of a good thing. He was handsome, charming, amusing, and articulate. He spoke in finished sentences and coherent paragraphs. He had originally come to Oxford as a Rhodes scholar to study medieval law. When the war broke out, he chose not to go home, nor did he want to stay at Oxford watching his classmates go off to war. He considered joining the British army but instead went to work for UP. Reports of his talent had filtered back to Murrow. Ed invited Collingwood to lunch at the Savoy. There was a touch of the dandy, almost too much ease and assurance in this young man on their first meeting. Murrow would later tell how he had glanced down at the wild expanse of Argyle socks that

Collingwood wore, all the rage then at Oxford, and wondered if this was someone he wanted at CBS. He had forgotten the dandy who had himself embarked in England at 21 with blazer, boater, and cane.

Ed told Collingwood that he was looking for someone with reporting experience, but "who had not been contaminated by print." Collingwood's stock rose as the conversation progressed. This young American with the blasé air of an English patrician had worked summers, of all things, as a timber cruiser. He had found the job through his father, a forester and a disciple of the fabled conservationist, Gifford Pinchot.

Days later, Ed and Collingwood went to a training exercise at an RAF airfield still under construction. Murrow spotted a surveyor's chain lying on the ground. He picked it up, coiled it, and with a quick movement of the wrist, heaved it expertly. He handed the chain to Collingwood without a word. Collingwood threw it just as expertly. Here was a Rhodes scholar, the role Ed had once coveted, one who could discuss medieval law, speak beautifully, and heave a surveyor's chain. Here was Murrow's kind of man. Charles Collingwood joined the CBS London staff.

Collingwood loved his new job. He wanted to be as good as Murrow. He wanted to *be* Murrow. He watched Ed dictate his scripts to Kay Campbell and thought, "If that's the way a great broadcaster does it, then I'll try it." It did not work. Ed Murrow wrote with his ear. Collingwood found that he could only write with his mind. He studied Murrow's texts and commented to Ed, "You use short, declarative sentences, don't you?" Ed had not been aware that he did. It was the way he talked, and hence the way he wrote. He found adjectives, he told Collingwood, "lurid." "The last thing I want you to do," Ed warned him, "is sound like me."[10]

Imitation of Murrow had become an occupational hazard at CBS news. After Eric Sevareid went back to work in America, Bill Paley told him, "You sound just like Murrow." Helen Sioussat, Ed's former assistant, remembered that "Eric dressed like Ed, talked like Ed, even pulled his fedora down like Ed. On the air, he had that same terse eloquence." Bob Trout, she said, "would tease Eric unmercifully. He'd see Eric come in and he'd say, 'Why, here's Ed Murrow in from London. Oh, excuse me. It's Eric. I thought it was Ed.'" Asked years afterward if he did indeed try to emulate Murrow, Sevareid grinned and said, "Yes, but not consciously. We all did." It was not that they were trying to imitate the man. They were trying to do it the way that seemed right, and it came out sounding like Murrow.[11]

He himself was still being tutored by a tiny, pain-wracked woman some 7,000 miles away now living in Corvallis, Washington. On his Christmas Eve broadcast in 1940, Ed chose not to say "Merry Christmas." The phrase had virtually disappeared that holiday season in England. Since the war, Londoners had started saying, "So long, and good luck." And so he closed his broadcast, "Good night, and good luck." Ida Lou Anderson wrote to him to stick with it, which he did for the rest of his broadcasting career.

Ida Lou wrote Ethel Murrow, "I get tired of hearing men from

Europe tell how many planes were shot down, how many tons of shipping were destroyed etc. etc....What pleases me about Ed is that he gives
us his personal observations from which he draws some bit of thought
that is bigger than the observation itself."

He had instructed his friend and money manager, Jim Seward, to
send Ida Lou a check for $75 that Christmas, and a new radio. Ida Lou
wrote to E.O. Holland, still Washington State's president, "I haven't said
very much about it to any one...for no reason except something inside
me can't talk about it very well." To Ed she wrote that receiving the radio
had her "feeling like Cinderella."

The gift was more appropriate than he knew. Along with her other
infirmities, Ida Lou Anderson was now almost completely blind. The radio took the place of her once voracious reading. When Ed came on the
air, everyone around her had to be quiet. Her body would stiffen in concentration, and her eyes remained shut tight, as if to drive out all distrac-
tions while he spoke.

In September of 1941, the telegraph office phoned the Murrow apartment. Janet took the message. Ida Lou Anderson was dead at the age of
41. When Janet gave Ed the news, she recalled, "He broke into tears and
went off by himself into another room." Later, President Holland wrote
asking him to contribute a message for a memorial service for Ida Lou at
Pullman. He had learned to capture in his phrases the death throes of a
nation or the agony of a city. But he still found it painful to reveal the
simple feeling of one human being for another. He wrote President
Holland, "I have tried four times to write the appreciation of Ida Lou
and have failed each time." At the last minute, he completed his contribution: "...Any adequate tribute to Ida Lou Anderson should employ the
eloquence of all the ancients, and it should be read aloud. I know of no
one who can command the language, and even if that were possible, there
is not one of her students who could read the words with a steady voice.
She 'believed nothing and reverenced all.' She was a tolerant skeptic with
all the tenacity of her Tennessee ancestors—a great teacher and a great
student of those she taught....for a few short hours, in the course of a
few classes, we had been in the presence of one who was, in the true sense
of the word, greater than anyone we had met or were ever likely to meet.
To every one who deals with words there comes a time when there are no
words to express what is felt, what is remembered, and what is owed. Miss
Anderson would understand that."

The words "believed nothing and reverenced all" and "tolerant skeptic" were revealing. He meant them for her. But they also were the qualities of character that he liked to believe that he possessed.[12]

Had Ida Lou lived just a few months longer, she would have seen Ed
Murrow again. In the fall of 1941, he went home for a speaking tour to
promote CBS news. Bob Trout was dispatched to England to relieve him.
Trout had heard that Ed was trying to give up smoking, and so he brought

him a handsome pipe. Ed tried weaning himself from cigarettes to the pipe. But pipe smoking, the bowl filling, the lighting and relighting, the cleaning, took too much time, he said. His cigarette habit was now creeping up to four packs a day.

He complained to Trout that he did not expect to be doing this work forever: "I don't fancy myself a broadcaster." Trout, ever the gentleman, neither scoffed nor protested, but accepted these now familiar gripes that Ed made around CBS staffers as something that he needed to voice, perhaps even believe, out of some unfathomable emotional need.

After Ed left, Trout and another CBS newsman, Wells "Ted" Church, had to go to the Murrow apartment to retrieve some equipment from a closet. There they saw his wardrobe from Anderson and Sheppard Ltd., 30 Savile Row, the somber pinstripes along with the bold hound's-tooth jacket, the dented helmet. "You know," Church observed, "there's a little Hollywood in Ed Murrow."

To his friends left behind, his departure seemed as though he had escaped from a penal colony and was bound for Canaan. He carried a list of what each wanted most, jams for Viscountess Milner; American cigarettes for the BBC gang; silk stockings for Kay Campbell; canned orange juice for Pamela Churchill, the prime minister's daughter-in-law, for her baby. He sailed on the *Excambion* out of Lisbon and arrived in New York on November 24. Janet had gone home a month before. His itinerary called for briefings in New York and Washington, a short vacation with Janet in Florida, and then three months on the lecture circuit in cities with CBS affiliates.[13]

He had been told that he was famous, but he did not believe it. The side he saw of fame was an airless, underground cubicle, reeking of cooked cabbage, where he sat alone and talked to an unresponding piece of metal. But he underwent the same experience that Eric Sevareid had described on coming home the year before. Sevareid had written, "...to stand on a street corner and hear Larry Le Sueur's words spoken that moment in the curtained underground studio blaring from the passing cars" was "thrilling beyond compare. I wanted to write to them that the whole thing was real after all, and not pantomime in an empty room." Ed heard Trout and Collingwood broadcasting from London and had the same reaction. It was indeed real.

He found himself, one week after his return, at the age of 33, honored as the foremost broadcast correspondent in America. He was seated on the dais in the grand ballroom of the Waldorf-Astoria for a testimonial dinner that *Variety* called, "The most celebrity-studded ever held for a radio employee." He sat between Bill Paley and the poet Archibald MacLeish, looking out over 1,000 guests in black tie and gowns. He heard MacLeish, the speaker that night, say of him, "...you destroyed in the minds of many men and women in this country the superstition that what is done beyond three thousand miles of water is not really done at all; the ignorant superstition that violence and lies and murder on another continent are not violence and lies and murder here....Sometimes you said you were speaking from a roof in London looking at the London sky. Sometimes you said you spoke from underground beneath that city. But it was not in London really that you spoke. It was in the back kitchens and the front living rooms and the moving automobiles and the hotdog stands and the observation cars of another country that your voice was truly speaking....You laid the dead of London at our doors and we knew the dead were our dead—were all men's dead—were mankind's dead—and ours. Without rhetoric, without dramatics, without more emotion than needed be, you destroyed the superstition of distance and of time."

When it was his turn, Murrow in white tie, looking worldly worn beyond his years, rose. He dismissed the Blitz and the rooftop reporting in a single sentence: "I know that the work of many other radio correspondents is being honored through me...." And then he launched into a subject that showed more Harold Laski than Winston Churchill. Should Britain win this war, he said, a major casualty was going to be a society falsely divided between those destined to be rich and privileged and those doomed to be poor and exploited: "The women of Britain are well on their way to winning economic equality as they won political equality in the last war. The class-conscious educational system, which has failed in its principle task of providing leaders, will not survive this war. It has been admitted that a boy who is good enough to fly a Spitfire may after the war be fit to represent his majesty's government abroad, even though he didn't go to Eton or Harrow....If Britain survives this war, it will be a simpler, more democratic place to live."

Something in him had crystallized in those four years abroad. Superficially, he was a new kind of star, the news celebrity. And he was a successful practitioner of social leapfrog, an ex-logger who now shot grouse with titled Englishmen on Sussex moors. But the Murrow that he chose to unveil publicly on this night was a far different man, a stinging critic of unearned privilege, a champion of the underdog, an advocate of a new social order. The war to Murrow was not solely against the Nazis, but against the stacked world that had prevailed before war broke out. He had not abandoned his proletarian roots for fortune and fame, he made clear. He was employing his new power in the service of his democratic convictions.

Bill Paley had arranged the testimonial dinner for his prize employee. He also demonstrated his admiration in more tangible coin. Ed had already received a raise and a bonus that year totaling over $5,000. Now Paley virtually directed the CBS board to vote him another $15,000 bonus and to provide another $25,000 to his family, should he be killed during the war, which, considering the way Ed was covering it, did not seem at all improbable.[14]

He and Janet were invited to supper with President and Mrs. Roosevelt a week after the Waldorf dinner, on December 7. They were staying in

Washington with friends from before the war, Louis and Eleanor Gimbel of the department store fortune. The Gimbels were the sort who put their wealth in the service of art and causes. Lou Gimbel had helped Ed place refugees in America during the Emergency Committee days. When it seemed that America might be drawn into the war, Gimbel asked Ed to see if Lacey could pull strings to get him an Air Corps commission. Lacey delivered. It was hardly a romantic billet, assistant materials officer in the Air Ferrying Command, but it put a happy Lou Gimbel in his country's uniform.

Though it was December, that Sunday was warm enough for Ed to play golf with a foursome of New Dealers at Burning Tree Country Club. On the fourth hole, a CBS messenger came trotting down the fairway after him. He had been sent to alert Ed to a news bulletin: the Japanese had attacked Pearl Harbor. Ed asked whose report it was. "Reuters," the messenger answered. "Pay no attention," Ed told his companions, and they went on to play the next hole. But the story continued sweeping over the golf course, and it was true.

Janet assumed that the supper invitation with the Roosevelts was off, but called Mrs. Roosevelt anyway to make sure. "We still have to eat," Eleanor Roosevelt told her. "We still want you to come." Ed came back to the Gimbels' home, changed, and shaved for the second time that day.

They arrived at the White House at eight o'clock to join a small group. The other guests were Trude and Joseph Lash, friends of Mrs. Roosevelt, and some of the Roosevelt children. FDR remained in the study adjoining his bedroom, seeing a parade of cabinet officials, congressional leaders, generals, and admirals.

Eleanor Roosevelt presided over the supper, serving the scrambled eggs, milk, and a pudding dessert to her guests herself. From time to time a staff member came and slipped her a note. Some of the information she passed on to her guests. Some she kept to herself. She had only recently been at the embassy of the Japanese while they were obviously planning to attack her country. Her mood throughout the meal was well-bred outrage. By 10:30, the Murrows were preparing to leave. But Mrs. Roosevelt told Ed that the President had sent word he wanted to see him. Janet left by herself.

Ed waited on a bench outside the President's study and watched a parade pass by of the people who ran the United States, among them the secretary of state, Cordell Hull; secretary of war, Henry Stimson; and secretary of the Navy, Frank Knox. He exchanged a few words with each. They seemed puzzled to find a newsman camped outside the President's inner sanctum.

Harry Hopkins, possibly the man closest to Roosevelt, emerged from the study and invited Ed to wait in the bedroom he occupied at the White House. Hopkins was frail, sick, a man crushed under the burdens he carried for the President. He resembled, Murrow thought, "a deathshead." Hopkins put on his pajamas, and, Ed later wrote, "flung himself on a large four-poster bed. He looked like a tired, broken child, too small for the bed. He murmured, to himself it seemed, 'Oh God, if I only had more strength.'"

It was nearly one o'clock in the morning. The ashen faces continued to file in and out of the study, and still Murrow was told to wait. Finally, the President summoned him. Roosevelt was wearing a gray, shapeless "sack jacket." His complexion matched the jacket. He looked physically drained, but, Murrow wrote, "Never have I seen one so calm and so steady." The President was having a beer and a sandwich and asked Ed to join him. He said nothing about the attack on Pearl Harbor. He asked about London. He wanted to know how the British were bearing up under their ordeal. He inquired after people he knew in London. He had already talked to Winston Churchill over the transatlantic telephone that day and had told him, "We're all in the same boat now."

Then, suddenly, he began speaking in cold, controlled anger, reeling off the losses that Admiral Stark, the chief of Naval Operations, had relayed to him from Pearl Harbor, the ships lost, the planes destroyed, estimates of the dead and wounded. He recited them in toneless disbelief. When he got to the planes destroyed, he pounded his fist on the table and said, "On the ground, by God, on the ground!"

Reports conflict as to whether Ed was alone with the President or whether General William J. Donovan, then building the country's first espionage system, the Office of Strategic Services, was present also. Whoever was there, the President's disclosures with a member of the working press present were extraordinary. Murrow was shocked and confused. The dimensions of the disaster were far greater than the American public suspected. The President said nothing about going off the record. He had spoken, it seemed, as he would to a trusted aide rather than to a reporter.

It may well have been that Roosevelt, a man who did little without calculation, had wanted to see Murrow to get an assessment of the British reaction to America's sudden involvement in the war, and then, in the course of a long, exhausting day, had let his guard down temporarily and made the astonishing revelations. Whatever the motive, after the President bade him good night, Murrow left wondering what he was supposed to do with what he now knew.

He went down to the White House Press Office in the West Wing. Eric Sevareid was there working late. Sevareid knew where Murrow had just been. He eyed him expectantly. Murrow said, "It's pretty bad," and added nothing more.

Later, back with Janet, he paced the bedroom, pounding his fist and sputtering, "I've got the greatest story of my life and I don't know if I should go with it or forget it." In the end he said nothing until the information he had heard from the President's lips was released by the White House.

Later, a conspiracy theory would grow up around the Pearl Harbor attack. Franklin Roosevelt, according to this thesis, was so eager to get the United States into the war that he contrived to have the U.S. Fleet in Pearl Harbor, supine and irresistible, virtually inviting the Japanese attack. Murrow had watched the men in whose hands the defense of the country rested that night. He had been with the President. He later did a broadcast on this conspiracy theory and said: "If they [Roosevelt, Stimson, Hull, Knox] were *not* surprised by the news from Pearl Harbor, then that group of elderly men were putting on a performance which would have excited the admiration of any experienced actor. I cannot believe that their expressions, bearing and conversation were designed merely to impress one correspondent who was sitting outside in the hallway...."

Murrow's reputation at the BBC was already legendary. When it was learned that he had been with Roosevelt on the night of Pearl Harbor, BBC staffers asked Bob Trout, "Is this why he went home? Did he know this was going to happen?"[15]

His lecture tour brought him to Seattle late in January of 1942 and to a reunion with his mother and father. Their circumstances had changed, but they had not. Roscoe's health had begun to fail, and so he had given up railroading. He and Ethel tried for a time to make a go of a clutch of tourist cabins on the Olympic Peninsula, a forerunner of the contemporary motel. The venture had not succeeded. They moved to Bellingham, north of Seattle. With the military buildup, the shipyards were booming and Roscoe Murrow got a job as a night watchman.

Ed took them to dinner at the best hotel in Seattle. He ordered champagne and insisted that his mother have the most expensive steak on the menu. Ed teased his father that he looked like Roosevelt. And, indeed, in a rough way he did. But Roscoe remained as ordinary as his overalls. He tried the champagne and said it tasted "like ginger ale." Ethel Murrow had changed little. She had long ago settled into her mannerisms and had chosen her face for life. She still worried. She still fluttered. She still nibbled at her food, except when she found out what the steak had cost—whereupon she proceeded to devour it.

Ed visited Lacey, and they went hunting, Ed said, "to shoot a duck before going back to be shot at myself." He visited his brother Dewey, his wife, Donnie, and their two little girls. Ed spoke to the grade school class of his niece Helen. Afterward, he observed that British schoolchildren were better mannered and more disciplined than Americans, but he was impressed at "how much more inquisitive our kids are."

He made a triumphal return to Washington State. Seven thousand people overflowed the gymnasium to hear him speak. The full faculty sat on the dais behind the guest of honor. The transformation in his life in those eleven years since leaving Pullman seemed like a voyage to another planet.

He had been alerted by his reporter friends that there was gold to be mined in America from their war experiences. He covered 17,000 miles and indeed earned a good deal of money lecturing. But, he wrote an old mentor at college, Earl Foster, "...one of my age cannot go about on a lecture tour making profits out of recounting the heroism of others, and then put the money in the bank." He wrote Air Chief Marshall Sir Phillip Joubert, "Lecturing is for anyone who has acquired a tinfoil reputation through broadcasting, a very lucrative business.... being afflicted with a Quaker conscience, I found it impossible to bank the lucre.... I decided to give it away." He donated virtually all of his lecture fees to an RAF benevolent fund and to Washington State College.

Eric Sevareid remembered of the Murrow visit home a ride they took in New York during a howling snowstorm. Ed rolled down the window, and the snow and cold came blowing in. "Don't you think that window ought to be closed?" a shivering Sevareid asked. "No," Ed answered. "I like the feel of it. It gives me a sense of confidence." He had, Sevareid thought, a need to touch nature, even if it was for a few minutes from a car window in the middle of Manhattan.

He saw Bill Shirer in New York too. Shirer had prospered since leaving Europe as a $150-a-week correspondent. He had a sponsored weekly commentary over CBS and a respectable Hooper rating. (Radio ratings were supplied by C.E. Hooper, Inc., which gauged listenership through phone calls to homes. Hooper was supplanted in 1949 by the A.C. Nielsen Company.) Shirer had written a book about his European experiences, *Berlin Diary*. While Ed was still in London, Shirer had been driving a country road with the car radio on and had heard Ed devote part of his broadcast to praise for Shirer's book. He remembered thinking what a generous friend Ed Murrow was. The book became a best-seller.

Ed had been urged to write himself. "But," he said, "to a broadcaster there is something rather frightening about being asked to write for print. It's such a cold, impersonal and permanent medium. I never read anything of my own in print without a rather hot, embarrassed feeling." The most a publisher had been able to talk him into was an anthology of his best broadcasts. It was called *This Is London*.

For all Shirer's prosperity, Ed still found the man a sartorial disaster. They had come out of Ed's favorite New York restaurant, Louis and Armands, after much drinking. As Ed later recalled their walk back to the office, "That old hat of Bill's got on my nerves. I told him that now, since he was in the money, he could afford a new one.... I grabbed his hat and shied it into the street. A couple of taxi cabs and a bus fixed it up so even Shirer wouldn't wear it any more. So then he let me buy him a new one. I felt my trip home was a great success."

The playful interludes were rare and more than offset by a sense of frustration that began to overtake him. He wrote Harold Laski, "I spend most of my time trying to keep my temper in check...." He felt no awareness among Americans that civilization was facing a test of survival. Even Laski's friends whom he met during the visit, like Felix Frankfurter, now a justice on the U.S. Supreme Court, could not understand why Harold would want to stay in England with a war on.

He took his former talks assistant, Helen Sioussat, to lunch. "He walked along Fifth Avenue and Madison and saw the stores stocked with beautiful things," she recalled, "and it positively made him angry. He'd see all the food in the restaurant and say 'I don't think I can eat, when I think of what's going on back there.'" He complained of "...wealthy friends moaning about ruinous inflation." He had become a stranger in his native land. By late April of 1942, he was happily back in London.

He sent President Roosevelt a gift. Ed had developed, as one of his few indulgences, a taste for antique silver and was building a modest collection, tea caddies and salvers, including a salver from "His Majesty's ship *Intrepid*," dated 1770. He sent Roosevelt an expensive silver cigarette box. FDR sent Ed a personal note:

Dear Murrow,

I am sorry for the long delay in writing to thank you for that lovely cigarette box which you sent to me. I am particularly glad to have it because the design of the sloop is more Dutch than English. I feel certain that the man at the tiller looks like a Roosevelt. With my grateful appreciation for your thought of me and with every best wish always.[16]

Pearl Harbor had shattered American isolationism in a single Sunday morning. Ed had long believed that America belonged in the war. Now his country was at war, which posed a dilemma for him. He was reared in a southern tradition that revered military gallantry. His brother Lacey, six years older than he, was already in uniform. His brother Dewey, 36, with two children and building airfields for the military, was under no obligation to serve. But Dewey was going to enlist.

Ed was reasonably healthy and young. He had held an ROTC commission in the Army until it lapsed in 1935. After Pearl Harbor, Janet recalled, "He felt uncomfortable" out of uniform. "I ought to be doing something besides sitting behind this microphone," he told her. During the months at home, he had twice gone to the War Department to discuss a commission, as he wrote his family, "not for reasons of bravery, but for reasons of escape, and twice I have been told that what I am doing now is more important." He asked Lacey to see what influence he could apply. Lacey wrote back that he could arrange a commission for Ed as a "specialist reservist" in the Air Corps, a public relations job, or as a major attached to the Highway Commissioner in the state of Washington. Lacey observed with dry precision, "I am not sure you would be interested in either of these."

Ed wrote back, a trace defensively, "Please don't think this outburst about what I'm to do with myself is dictated by any fear of what anyone else will say. After all, I was in and under this war three years before the brave boys who are now arriving over here. It's just the old Murrow conscience that's bothering me."[17]

Part of his uneasiness had to do with the contempt he felt for Britishers who left their country or failed to come home after the war broke out, people like W.H. Auden, Christopher Isherwood, and Aldous Huxley. He even had reservations about his friend Charles Siepmann, who had left the BBC to lecture at Harvard. And Siepmann was well over military age.

If he could not be in the military, he was nevertheless determined to be in the war in a tangible way. In April of 1942, the RAF began massive raids on German cities; 350 planes a night were hurled against Berlin and other population centers. On May 30, 1,000 RAF bombers struck Cologne. Murrow begged the Air Ministry to be allowed to go along. He was turned down. As a sop, he was allowed to fly a Liberator on a submarine-hunting patrol in the Bay of Biscay. No subs were sighted. It had been an airplane ride, not combat, too safe, too remote to stir the adrenalin. He wanted, he said, a raid over Berlin. He was still turned down.[18]

In the summer of 1942, the U.S. Army began to arrive in England in force. A 52-year-old general had been chosen over dozens of senior officers as U.S. Commander for the European Theater of Operations. Dwight Eisenhower was suddenly pushed onto a crowded British stage, uncertain about who were the serious leads and who the overly assertive bit players. He had with him a new aide, a freshly minted Navy captain named Harry Butcher. One month before, Butcher had been a vice president in the CBS Washington office. Of those early days, Butcher noted in his diary that Ike "was having difficulty in determining who was important and who was not, who should be seen and who could be put off....I got Ed Murrow to help us on this."

A mystique now surrounded Murrow. He was the man to see in England, the American believed closest both to the Conservative prime minister and the Labour Party leaders, Laski, Aneurin Bevan, and Ernest Bevin; the one to whom the Americans went to learn about the British, and to whom the British went to learn about the Americans. He was a two-way ambassador, far better known and more sought out than the actual American ambassador, John G. Winant, who was the first to admit it.

Thus Murrow came to know Eisenhower. He told his radio listeners, "I have seen him several times with high-ranking Allied officers, and he is just a combination of Kansas and Texas—an American who has been a cow puncher, ditch digger, professional ball player and agricultural laborer. ...he's just a normal, middle-class American soldier....he is quick and generous in his praise of subordinates. But, when things go wrong, the big grin disappears and he becomes as bleak as a Kansas cornfield in midwinter." But as for the man's military prowess, he withheld judgment: "I don't know whether Eisenhower is a good general or not."

Butcher and Murrow, as former CBS colleagues, used each other in a friendly, professional way. Butcher would bring his military comrades to lunch with Murrow, and Murrow would bring along his correspondents. Ed tended to treat the recent American arrivals the way a veteran in the trenches looks at green replacements, with tolerant misgivings, and suspicion of heroic posturing. He told Butcher that the bravest people in London were the hookers. "They stayed out on the streets in the heaviest raids."

During one lunch, a homesick Butcher ordered a hamburger. As he bit into it, he commented that it tasted sweet. Of course, Murrow answered, it was horsemeat. He had a way of saying these things, a faint smile playing across his lips, so that Butcher never was quite sure when he was serious.

Superficially, they were together for old times' sake. But Butcher detected a current running beneath the banter. What Murrow and Trout and Collingwood were trying to worm out of him was the very purpose of the American military presence in England. When would the second front open? And where?[19]

Eisenhower, practicing good public relations, allowed a committee of reporters to see him occasionally to thrash out press gripes. Ed served on the committee. In one discussion, the question of "colored troops" came up. Why were the soldiers of freedom and democracy segregated by color, the reporters wanted to know? Eisenhower said that his policy was absolute equality of treatment, separate yes, but equal. Military apartheid was not Eisenhower's doing. He was implementing national policy, not making it. President Roosevelt had to deal with a Congress dominated, through the seniority system, by entrenched white southern committee chairmen. He could rally them against Adolf Hitler, but not against Jim Crow; not yet, not in his lifetime.

How did Murrow, who had once integrated a student conference in the Deep South, explain to his listeners, to the British, to himself, the institutionalized American racism reflected in a segregated army? He occasionally was asked to speak on the BBC, and on one program, "Books That Made History," he discussed *Uncle Tom's Cabin*. "By the 1850s," he told his British listeners, "slavery was on the way out anyway. We needn't have fought a war over it....Slavery would have ended without the impetus of the Civil War had the Northerners not raised such a hue and cry about the immorality of the system. The Southerners, being mainly Anglo-Saxon stock, wouldn't stand for that, and they rose in defense of their system." As for the slaves, "They were well cared for generally. They lived under a feudal system...of course there were abuses." But *Uncle Tom's Cabin* was an "inflammatory document...not to be read as an accurate portrayal of slave life in the Southern states....Those who defended slavery with their lives and those who fought against it, now agree that American slavery was on the whole a humane and civilized institution compared with the present practices of the Germans."

His comfortable view of slavery is easy enough to ridicule today. But he was the child of poor southern whites speaking nearly a quarter of a century before the civil rights revolution. He was recalling a version of the Civil War learned at his Confederate grandfather's knee. He was also, obviously, propagandizing a British audience, explaining away a stain in America's past. He had shrewdly tailored his case to British prejudices. (White southerners being "mainly Anglo-Saxon stock.") Yet what he said was essentially what he believed.

The more important question, more revealing of his character than how he viewed the past, was how he dealt with race in his own world. He had acted on his convictions in Atlanta in 1930. The race issue now came up again in England in connection with a CBS series, *An American in England*. The network had sent Norman Corwin, one of the most gifted dramatists writing for radio, to England to do the series, in an effort to make the alliance with England more meaningful to Americans. Joe Julian, a popular radio actor, had gone to England to work on the series with Corwin. Julian had visited a segregated U.S. Army base and recorded a conversation with a black GI corporal:

JJ: How do most negro soldiers feel about the war?

GI: I think we feel it don' matter much what happens. We just know we have ta fight so we fight.

JJ: But you feel much more comfortable in the company of English soldiers.

GI: Sure, man, they drink with ya, they talk with ya. There ain't no difference with them. I'd like to stay here after the war, 'cept the United States is still your home an' ya have a feelin' ya wanna get back to your home no matter how bad things are.

JJ: Well, I hope it will work out. That's one thing this war is supposed to be about....

Julian wanted to include the conversation in the next episode of *An American in England*. Corwin agreed but said that it could stir up trouble at home and Murrow would have to make the final decision. To the contemporary ear it seems a harmless enough exchange. But it was recorded at a time when black GIs were being lynched by white American soldiers for dating English girls.

Joe Julian later described Murrow's reaction to the material: "The next morning Corwin and I met in Murrow's office. I showed him the dialogue with the corporal. His eyes gleamed, he banged a fist in his palm and said 'Let's do it! Let's raise a little hell back home!'... As he poured us each a whiskey, I had my first long look at this interesting man, with the inevitable cigarette dangling from his lips. I think my strongest impression was that of superbly controlled tension. In repose his face had a brooding, Lincolnesque sadness that would quickly dissolve in the sudden flash of his warm smile."

The program was broadcast with the black corporal's comments in 1942. Segregation in the U.S. military would not effectively end for another ten years.[20]

In November of 1942, the Allies opened a second front, not on the Continent, as the Russians were urging, but in North Africa. Murrow was outraged. To him North Africa spoke of European colonialism. He was angry that American blood should be shed to preserve the old order—for the very opposite reasons he had wanted his country in the war. He wrote Ed Dakin,

"Our policy…in North Africa looks like a sort of amateur imperialism which aims at making the continent safe for the National City Bank."

He also found the ally that the United States was courting in North Africa repugnant. Eisenhower had made a deal to win over the Vichy France commander-in-chief for North Africa, Admiral Jean François Darlan. Murrow was amazed at Eisenhower's naïveté, by his ignorance of the treacherous politics of the situation, by the fact that he would make common cause with the likes of Darlan. Murrow angered Washington and Whitehall by telling Americans over the air what kind of man Jean François Darlan was. When a German officer was killed in Nantes, Murrow reported, Darlan turned over thirty hostages—his own people—whom the Germans shot. One of the man's first acts on taking charge in North Africa was to send back to the Nazis refugees who had fled Europe to save their lives. Darlan implemented a policy of anti-Semitism in North Africa patterned after the German racial laws. This was to be our ally in the war against nazism? "Are we at some future time to occupy Norway and turn it over to a Quisling?" Murrow asked.

He had as yet never been a war correspondent in the pure sense. He had never moved up to the front with combat troops. He had given an eager Charles Collingwood the North African invasion assignment for CBS. The night before Collingwood's departure, they went out on the town. They got back to Hallam Street where a reeling Murrow kicked over a garbage can and stormed, "By God, I envy you for going off. I wish I could go along with you." Six months later he went.

The stark beauty of the North African battlescape moved him. He followed a GI column up a rugged Tunisian range and reported: "Off to the right, six hundred feet below, is the floor of the valley. At first there seems to be blue smoke floating knee-high in one of the little side valleys about three miles away. Finally, you realize that little valley is knee deep with morning glories, and the breeze makes them look like drifting blue smoke.…There is a cold, cutting wind. When the clouds hit the mountaintops you expect them to make a noise. There is dust and cactus and thorn bushes and bad roads. It is a cold country with a hot sun.…Where the road cuts down to meet the stream there is a knocked out tank, two men beside it and two men digging a grave. A little farther along a German soldier sits smiling against the bank. He is covered with dust, and he is dead."[21]

He came back to England unpersuaded by the underlying strategy of the North African campaign, but happily blooded as a combat correspondent. While there, he had also signed up a promising recruit, Winston Burdett, like H.V. Kaltenborn, an alumnus of *The Brooklyn Eagle*. Ed had found Burdett in Algiers, a reporter who wrote in hard, bright phrases that gleamed like light passing through a jewel. Burdett later described his audition for Murrow: "I took the microphone for a short news spot while he sat and listened, attentively, to me. He smiled in appreciation when I had done and later, only later, he said gently: 'sit down with your script more.…' The words were a revelation. They told me everything, how tight and formal and self-conscious my delivery was, and what I should do to mend it. Countless times in later years, inevitably tense before going on the air, I repeated Ed's advice....Sit down with your script more...."[22]

The diversion of Allied power to North Africa, the casualties suffered there, served only to confirm his fear that the right war was being fought for the wrong reasons. Ed was an admirer of Winston Churchill's leadership and his rallying rhetoric. But he was drawn to Harold Laski's political vision. In one of his broadcasts to the British over the BBC he said, "I would be willing to trade several squadrons of aircraft, a few hundred tanks if we might have Laski...in the States for a few years when this war is over."

What he was saying was that Laski wanted to right a social order that was wrong, not only in England, Murrow believed, but in America too. In a letter to his parents he delivered a harsh judgment that reflected his outlook: "There is no chance of going back to the old ways and the old life....an entire world is going down in ruins and I have no regrets.... maybe something better will be born of it all....It is unlikely that anything worse will emerge."

Late in 1943, with the Americans driving the Japanese back across the Pacific, with the epic Russian triumph at Stalingrad, with the Germans defeated in North Africa, in short, with the tide of battle turning toward an Allied victory, he managed to find a dark lining in the silver cloud. He wrote his old friend from the Emergency Committee, Alfred Cohn, "There was a time when I believed that out of this war there would come some sort of spiritual revival, some increase in dignity and decency, some refining of values; none of that has happened. One hears, here and at home, the rising chorus of the brittle voiced business men who have done very well out of this whole thing and who are at heart not in the least appalled at the prospect of a repetition in a few years' time." And on another occasion, to Cohn: "I fear that Allied policy may be no more than to achieve Fascism which will favour us instead of favouring Germany." He personally sat on top of the world; but it was a world which he found increasingly contemptible. This dichotomy—personal success within spiritual discontent—was becoming a permanent paradox in his character.

As for Harold Laski, he found him an admired, but difficult and possessive, friend. Laski's attachment to Murrow had become as fierce as a lover's. Laski published a book in 1942, *Reflections on the Revolution of Our Time*, and dedicated it to Ed. When Laski's father died, he wrote a long letter to Ed full of his feelings about the old man that he needed to share with his young friend. When Murrow let weeks go by without seeing him, Laski wrote:

> As I plow my lonely furrow
> I think oft of E.R. Murrow.
> Once I knew him very well.
> Once I thought he used to dwell

in a world in which I moved...
Now he lives in higher spheres...

Laski went on at length, reminding Ed that once they had been so close. They had been so much more than professional and mutually useful colleagues. They had been friends, and not merely Ping-Pong-playing and dart-throwing pals. They had been friends who shared the same political convictions; friends who agreed on who had mucked up the world; friends who knew which class was to blame and which class had to straighten out the mess. In Murrow, Laski believed he had made a friend of the political heart. And he had been sure that Murrow had done the same. But now, Ed seemed to be rising out of his reach. He chided Murrow for no longer visiting his "Fulham slum." Ed was now "that great West End resident," hobnobbing with presidents and prime ministers. His beloved Murrow had gone high-hat on him. Or so it looked to Harold Laski.

The mistake that Laski made was to think that Murrow shared his socialist politics and economics, when all that Murrow actually shared was a romantic vision of a world from which injustice and inequality would be banished. Murrow was an idealist, not an ideologue, and this explained in part his gloomy nature. The idealist longs for a better world and consequently is constantly being disappointed by mankind's repeated failures. In time, the idealism can sour into pessimism, but not necessarily into realism. He goes on being disappointed and becoming more pessimistic at each failure. The realist, on the other hand, accepts the world's imperfections and happily goes about trying to snag his share of its pleasures.

Since the idealist links his happiness to the happiness of mankind, his own good fortune is never enough. When he was sitting on top of the student world at Washington State, Ed had written his self-pitying letter to Willma Dudley. He now wrote home, "Several of my friends have gone down already....it doesn't hurt very much....they seem strangers to me. ...I'm not sure that one's sympathies should not be more for those who live than those who die...."

He complained in other letters that his nerves were shot and that he was going bald, with no supporting evidence at his hairline. "If I crack up," he told Janet, "Columbia will chuck me on the scrap heap. I've known that all along." This from the most famous correspondent of the war, a man who had picked up a lucrative sponsor for his weekly broadcasts that year and who could also announce to his parents, "I've been offered the editorship of the largest paper in Washington, D.C. Please say nothing about that. I may be crazy enough to take it if things crack up over here."[23]

He could rage at the "hypocrisy of the capitalist system." He could refer to a representative in England of an American philanthropy as "the one who distributes the Rockefellers' blood-stained money." He could invite the coal miner father and brother of his maid, Betty Matthews, into his living room for long talks on injustice in Britain. And then he would go off shooting with Ronnie Tree and his friends at Dytchley where fifty pheasants were bagged in an afternoon; or let few opportunities pass without mentioning that Janet was descended from the Pilgrim Brewsters; or even borrow her heritage when it suited him. On one of his BBC broadcasts, he told his British audience, "I am English, Irish, French and German—as American as ever was—with ancestors who went out to the new world in the overcrowded ship called the *Mayflower*."

It is the contradictions that give people their humanizing texture. Consistency of character is flat and soulless, the antithesis of being human. The Murrow character did not lack for humanizing contradiction. His moods and silences became part of CBS's folklore. Paul White put through a transatlantic call to Murrow at the BBC and was told by one of the staff, "He's about somewhere, wearing his customary crown of thorns." A woman named Ann Gillis, in the New York office, was a frequent correspondent of Murrow's and had the knack of pricking his balloon of inflated pessimism. "A nasty rumor is floating around that you were actually seen happy on two occasions," she wrote. "But your true friends know that is a rumor being spread by your enemies."[24]

Yet if a man chose pessimism, there was evidence for it to feed on in 1942. In one of his last broadcasts of the year, Murrow became one of the first to inform the world that something unthinkable was happening in Nazi-occupied Europe. "One is almost stunned into silence by some of the information reaching London," he reported. "Some of it is months old, but it's eye-witness stuff supported by a wealth of detail and vouched for by responsible governments. What is happening is this: millions of human beings, most of them Jews, are being gathered up with ruthless efficiency and murdered....And when you piece it all together—from Holland and Norway, from Poland—you have a picture of mass murder and moral depravity unequaled in the history of the world. It is a horror beyond what imagination can grasp....Let me tell you a little about what's happened in the Warsaw ghetto....The business started in the middle of July. Ten thousand people were rounded up and shipped off. After that, thousands more went each day. The infirm, the old and the crippled were killed in their homes. Some of them were driven to the Jewish cemetery, and they killed them there. The others were put in freight cars; the floors were covered with quick-lime and chlorine. Those who survived the journey were dumped out at one of three camps where they were killed. At a place called Treblinka a huge bulldozer is used to bury the bodies. Since the middle of July these deportations from the Warsaw ghetto have been going on. For the month of September 120,000 ration cards were printed for the ghetto; for October only 40,000. The Jews are being systematically exterminated throughout all Poland...."[25]

Thus ended Murrow's account of the first forty months of war.

CHAPTER 15

Unnecessary Risks

He had always had a talent to reassure, to make people feel that if Murrow worked for them, or if they worked for Murrow, they were all in good hands. Two such situations arose in 1943, one from a surprising source and the other from an astonishing one.

E.O. Holland was getting on. Ed had noticed it when he had made the sentimental journey back to Pullman. Washington State's president was nearly 70. He was still possessive about *his* school, but his leadership had slipped into an old-womanly fussiness. His earlier fresh enthusiasm had cemented into rote inspirationals. Earl Foster, the student manager, assured Murrow in a letter written in "strictest confidence" that he had the votes on the board of regents to have Ed appointed the next president of the college.

Ed had talked often to skeptical friends about chucking broadcasting, about going back to a college campus in the Far West. Now the opportunity had dropped into his lap. He neither accepted nor rejected the offer outright. But he kept it alive. He wrote Foster, "cannot face with equanimity the prospect of working in that treadmill in N.Y." He also felt compelled to let Foster know that this was not the first college presidency offered to him. He told Foster about the Rockford College offer a few years before. His pride would not allow him to let Foster know that Rockford had had second thoughts about his qualifications and had withdrawn the offer. Instead, he wrote, "having some awareness of my limitations, [I] had the good sense to turn it down." In any case, he told Foster that he could not consider any offer until the war was over.[1]

Murrow was so tempted, even stunned, by the next opportunity that he arranged a trip home to talk it over with people he trusted. Brendan Bracken, so close to Churchill that he encouraged rumors that he was the prime minister's bastard, had become Britain's minister of information. Bracken had flatly told Bill Paley, "I would give anything in the world if I could hire Ed Murrow. I'd put him in charge." He meant in charge of the British Broadcasting Corporation. Early in 1943, Bracken made his move. He went first to Churchill and asked what the prime minister thought of the idea of making Murrow the BBC director for programming. Churchill found it splendid. Bracken then offered Murrow the post.

Murrow had other business in New York as well, besides wanting to discuss the BBC post. He felt run-down again and needed another medical checkup. And he wanted to discuss expanding his staff further. He went first to Dr. Alfred Cohn, his older, much revered friend from the Emergency Committee. Cohn was still on the faculty of the Rockefeller Medical Institute, where he gave Murrow a thorough physical examination. He pronounced him healthy, but told him to stop driving himself so hard. Ed asked Cohn what he thought about the BBC offer, and Cohn urged him to discuss it with Justice Felix Frankfurter, a close friend of both Cohn and Harold Laski.

Frankfurter later described the meeting in his diary: "Murrow said this offer had its 'amusing' aspects. I said, 'How amusing?' He said, 'Well can you imagine an American broadcasting company asking an Englishman to take charge of it?" Murrow told Frankfurter that his more serious concern was that, "When peace comes there may be a real conflict of views between this country and Great Britain." Where would his loyalties then lie, with the land of his birth or the land of his employers? Frankfurter's advice was that he ought to take the job as a gesture of wartime solidarity between the two countries and not worry about the future until the war ended.

In the end Ed turned Bracken down. He did so out of old-fashioned patriotism. In all the years abroad, he had clung fiercely to his Americanism, albeit an international-minded version, but Americanism all the same. The BBC offer made him somehow uncomfortable. One did not pledge allegiance to another flag, even during the workday. All along, he had resisted something vaguely apostate in the expatriate life. Taking the BBC job, in his mind, would have crossed a line that he was not ready to cross.[2]

Under wartime regulations, he had been required to turn in his passport when he arrived in the United States. Now that he was leaving, he requested that the Passport Office send it back. Much to his annoyance the return of the passport was delayed. He asked the CBS Washington office to apply pressure on the State Department as the date for his departure neared. He was never to know the cause of the delay. Release of his file by the Passport Office over forty years later under the Freedom of Information Act revealed the reason. The State Department had been checking out a claim that at some unspecified point Murrow "attended meeting of Anti-Fascist Refugee Committee organization." Quite likely he had. During the time he had worked for the Emergency Committee, he had attended countless meetings of dozens of organizations involved in getting refugees out of Nazi Germany. Antifascism lay at the core of the refugee work. Further, at the time the passport was held up, a war was being fought against fascism. But in the lexicon of government security professionals, anti-Fascist translated into pro-Communist. In the end, the State Department, without explaining the holdup, gave him back his passport and he left for England on July 18.[3]

He saw another opportunity to experience another face of warfare and chose to return on a troopship through the submarine-infested Atlantic. He later did a broadcast on the crossing. He could not identify the vessel, he said. Actually it was the *Queen Elizabeth,* built to carry some 3,000 passengers and crew in her earlier incarnation as a luxury liner, now transporting 15,000 GIs.[4]

While he had been in New York, Ed had talked to Ed Klauber and Paul White about increasing his staff. He bluntly told White which people he did not want sent over. The days of turning the other cheek were over. He took White head-on now. But what he did not know was that the seemingly invincible Klauber, his staunchest champion, was on borrowed time. A few months after Ed returned to England, Klauber was out of CBS. Klauber told friends that he had left because his wife was dying of cancer and that he wanted to be with her. Paley's official version was that Klauber had suffered a heart attack. But it was neither heart nor wife that had cost him his job. Paley's wheel of fortune had simply turned. Klauber had passed from indispensable to disposable. As Paley later put it more candidly, Ed Klauber had "developed a strong sense of possessiveness toward me which in later years caused management problems."

Paley also dropped Klauber because he himself was going off to war, and the headsman makes an uninspiring regent for the king to leave in charge of the kingdom. Robert Sherwood, the playwright and overseas director of the Office of War Information, wanted Paley to spend six months setting up Allied radio stations in North Africa and Italy. Paley, then 42, leaped at the opportunity to be part of the great adventure. In the meantime, he wanted to leave the management of his company in the hands of someone closer to his own image than Edward Klauber. He chose splendidly. Paul Kesten was a graceful and gracious man, well-bred, well-dressed, equally at home with well-turned phrases and well-reasoned budgets. Kesten also had exciting ideas for the future of broadcasting. He had started out, years before, in the CBS promotion department, hired by the man he now displaced, Ed Klauber. In late 1943, Kesten became president of CBS.

Klauber had also brought Murrow to CBS, had made the fateful decision to send him to Europe, had imbued him with the ethic of a new journalism before he was a journalist, and had made of Murrow a rare friend. During the visit home, Klauber had asked Ed a personal favor, something exceedingly difficult for him to do. "When I'm finished," he said, "I want you to do something for me—just say a few words." Murrow, equally ill at ease in soul-baring moments, asked what Klauber would like him to say.

Klauber instantly donned his mask of protective rudeness. "That's your problem," he snapped back. "You'll be at least brief, though not brilliant, and this may give some pleasure to those friends who may be there."[5]

Paley, after his consultant hitch in North Africa, was offered an enticing opportunity to stay in the war. He went to London as chief of radio broadcasting in the Psychological Warfare Division on General Eisenhower's staff, with a direct commission as a colonel. His presence in London at this period was to have probably more impact on Ed Murrow's future than on his own.

"In England, you didn't go to our embassy first, you went to Ed Murrow first," Paley liked to boast. "I admired him. I liked the way he handled himself, his mind, his principles, his ideas." Paley's wife, Dorothy, caught the relationship perfectly. "Ed was a hero, and he was Bill's hero." The thought could be read both admiringly and possessively.

Paley liked Murrow's connections too, much enhanced since Paley's 1937 visit to London. He was, however, not without his own well-placed friends in England. He had been hosted on earlier occasions by the prime minister's son, Randolph Churchill, and Randolph's wife, Pamela. Paley was a friend of Brendan Bracken and the Duff Coopers. The Coopers' child was safe from the war on Kiluna, Paley's estate on Long Island.

Still, Murrow could open even more doors, to cabinet ministers and air marshalls, as well as the doors of stately homes. The Ronnie Trees, as close Murrow friends, were a particularly prized catch. Paley adored the English upper-class style, the casual manner in which those people lived amid splendid furnishings and art, a manner that bespoke wealth without ostentation, a style, Paley admitted, that he had made his own.

There was an element of awe in Paley's attitude toward Murrow in those days. Here was a genuine hero who had sprung from Paley's creation, his network. Not only was the man an extraordinary broadcaster, but he had all the charm and grace of any of Paley's society friends. And so Bill Paley lowered that barrier between employer and employee and made a rare exception. He admitted Murrow to his circle of friends.

Ed, for his part, behaved differently toward Paley than toward most men. If Paley looked up to him for his courage and dash, Ed looked up to Paley for the vision he had shown in building a great communications enterprise from a near shambles. He admired Paley's confidence and his swift, intuitive, usually correct, broadcasting judgments. For the self-sufficient Murrow, Bill Paley was to become one of the few people in his life whose approval he craved.

Murrow could also expose Paley vicariously to the thrill of the war. "He took me to an airfield where a squadron was going out to bomb Germany," Paley recalled in a mood of wistful reminiscence years later. "I was actually allowed into the briefing. I watched one fellow going out on his first mission. He looked terrified. I stayed until the last plane came back. Exciting night."

Murrow flattered Paley, but not through sycophancy, which to a man of Paley's power had about as much kick as drinking tap water. He did it subtly. In one broadcast, Ed told America about a network executive who had given up a beautiful paneled office with a fireplace, antique furnishings, and deep carpets back home to go to work for his country "in a cold, dark, rugless, space in London." The patriot went unnamed. The compliment was in the English style, rich but not ostentatious, exactly what Paley had come to value.

With both men now in London, they talked for hours about Murrow's obsession, the future of broadcast journalism. Paley told Ed that the future belonged to television. Murrow seemed not to want to hear it.

They were close but only at certain interstices, for they were far different men. Theirs was a mutual affection born of admiration between two accomplished yet noncompeting stars. They were not soul mates. Paley could never decipher the Murrow persona. "He was prone to see the worst side of things, a true pessimist," Paley said. "...one could never be sure of his mood from that somber and sad visage of his. He reported on the world, but he also carried the weight of the world on his shoulders." The latter comment implied that the figure bent under this load had an exaggerated sense of his responsibility for the world. Paley played his life rather as a game, a high-stakes game, and one he was determined to win. But he never confused himself with Atlas.[6]

Not long after Paley's arrival in London, Ed began to press harder for something that was not to increase Paley's admiration, but rather to make him wonder about Murrow's emotional health.

The bombing of Germany had become remorseless, with the British, in more vulnerable aircraft, going out every night, and heavily armed American bombers flying daylight missions. No correspondent had yet been allowed on these raids. The risks were certain, almost mathematically calculable. A typical strike, say 500 bombers, would likely sustain 5 percent losses or worse over heavily protected targets like Berlin, Schweinfurt, or Düsseldorf. And that 5 percent worked out to 25 planes, up to ten crewmen each, depending on the plane; or 250 men, killed, wounded, or taken prisoner in a night's work. From the time the raids began, Murrow had hounded the Air Ministry and later the American Eighth Air Force to be allowed to go.

In part, it was still the nagging sense that no matter what he did, he was not really in the fight. Dick Marriott, his liaison at the BBC from the time he had arrived in England, was no longer mothering foreign broadcasters. Marriott was now a fighter pilot in the RAF. Murrow admired that.

Ed pleaded with Paul White, who still had the right of refusal over projected stories, "Let me ride in a bomber and I can know a little better how the pilot feels when the tail is shot off." He might know how the pilot felt. But communicating the experience to American listeners after riding a tailless aircraft seemed problematical. White refused. First, there was the risk to what had become a valuable CBS property. But White also said that no good news story could come out of so foolhardy a venture anyway.

In January of 1943, the RAF agreed to let a correspondent fly on a raid over Berlin. A flip of a coin was to decide who would go. The winner was a new NBC man who had barely filed a story yet. Murrow was furious. He wrote Ted Church at CBS news, "All the screaming and crying I could do would not persuade them to take me along. Having worked on the thing for years, I was like a small boy whose promised bicycle doesn't arrive."

He did fly two uneventful missions over enemy-occupied territory. And then eleven months after he had missed the first opportunity, he won the coin toss. He was to fly on a strike against Berlin set for the night of December 2–3.

He was assigned to "D for Dog," a Lancaster of the 619th Bomber Squadron out of Huntington. Four other reporters were also chosen. Two of them Ed knew—Norman Stockton, an Australian, and Lowell Bennett, an American with the International News Service. Bennett had been assigned to a plane named "B for Betty."

Ed went out to the airfield and spent several days in orientation. He met D for Dog's pilot, Jock Abercrombie, a quiet young Scot of serious, reassuring aspect. The Air Ministry required the reporters to sign a waiver of all claims by them or their heirs against the British government should anything happen to them on the mission. Later, Murrow watched Bennett type out a news story entitled, "If I Don't Come Back."

They took off with the late afternoon sun dying behind them in the west, a flotilla of 660 Lancasters, each crammed with incendiaries and a two-ton blockbuster. On his return, Murrow broadcast this report:

Last night some of the young gentlemen of the RAF took me to Berlin. The pilot was called Jock. One day while we were waiting for the weather he drove me across a bit of England, through small villages with grey stone houses marching straight on each side of a small common. We passed innumerable airfields, and at about the fourth he remarked: "It's a pity; not one but would make two good farms." He explained that night bombing was really rather simple—there wasn't much real danger. And then we passed a field, and Jock remarked: "Last winter one of our crews bailed out just over there, in a snow storm. When their parachutes opened it jerked off their boots, and they had to walk home in the snow." And he added, by way of reassurance: "Now each time I fly I tie on my boots; for a man would have no chance of walking home from Germany without his boots."

Yesterday afternoon, the waiting was over. The weather was right; the target was to be the big city. The crew captains walked into the briefing room, looked at the maps and charts and sat down with their big celluloid pads on their knees. The atmosphere was that of a school and a church. The weatherman gave us the weather. The pilots were reminded that Berlin is Germany's greatest center of war production. The intelligence officer told us how many heavy and light ack-ack guns, how many searchlights we might expect to encounter. Then Jock, the wing commander, explained the system of markings, the kind of flare that would be used by the Pathfinders. He said that concentration was the secret of success in these raids, that as long as the aircraft stayed well-bunched, they would protect each other. The captains of the aircraft walked out.

I noticed that the big Canadian with the slow, easy grin had printed "Berlin" at the top of his pad and then embellished it with a scroll. The red-headed English boy with the two weeks' old moustache was the last to leave the room. Late in the afternoon we went to the locker room to draw parachutes, Mae Wests and all the rest. As we dressed, a couple of the Australians were whistling. Walking out to the bus that was to take us to the aircraft, I heard the station loud-speakers announcing that that evening all personnel would be able to see a film, *Star Spangled Rhythm*, free.

We went out and stood around a big, black, four-motored Lancaster *D for Dog*. A small station wagon delivered a thermos bottle of coffee, chewing gum, an orange and a bit of chocolate for each man. Up in that part of England the air hums and throbs with the sound of aircraft motors all day. But for half an hour before takeoff, the skies are dead, silent and expectant. A lone hawk hovered over the airfield, absolutely still as he faced into the wind. Jack, the tail gunner, said, "It would be nice if *we* could fly like that."

D for Dog eased around the perimeter track to the end of the runway. We sat there for a moment. The green light flashed and we were rolling—ten seconds ahead of schedule! The take-off was smooth as silk. The wheels came up, and D-Dog started the long climb. As we came up through the clouds, I looked right and left and counted fourteen black Lancasters climbing for the place where men must burn oxygen to live. The sun was going down, and its red glow made rivers and lakes of fire on tops of the clouds. Down to the southward, the clouds piled up to form castles, battlements and whole cities, all tinged with red.

Soon we were out over the North Sea. Dave, the navigator, asked Jock if he couldn't make a little more speed. We were nearly two minutes late. By this time we were all using oxygen. The talk on the intercom was brief and crisp. Everyone sounded relaxed. For a while the eight of us in our little world in exile moved over the sea. There was a quarter moon on the starboard beam. Jock's quiet voice came through the intercom. "That'll be flak ahead." We were approaching the enemy coast. The flak looked like a cigarette lighter in a dark room—one that won't light. Sparks but no flame. The sparks crackling just above the level of the cloud tops. We flew steady and straight, and soon the flak was directly below us.

D-Dog rocked a little from right to left, but that wasn't caused by the flak. We were in the slip stream of other Lancasters ahead, and we were over the enemy coast. And then a strange thing happened. The aircraft seemed to grow smaller. Jack in the rear turret, Wally the mid-upper gunner; Titch, the wireless operator—all seemed somehow to draw closer to Jock in the cockpit. It was as though each man's shoulder was against the other's. The understanding was complete. The intercom came to life, and Jock said, "Two aircraft on the port beam." Jack in the tail said, "Okay, sir, they're Lancs." The whole crew was a unit and wasn't wasting words.

The cloud below was ten tenths. The blue-green jet of the exhausts licked back along the leading edge, and there were other aircraft all around us. The whole great aerial armada was hurtling towards Berlin. We flew so for twenty minutes, when Jock looked up at a vapor trail curling across above us, remarking in a conversational tone that from the look of it he thought there was a fighter up there. Occasionally the angry red of ack-ack burst through the clouds, but it was far away, and we took only an academic interest. We were flying in the third wave. Jock asked Wally in the mid-upper turret and Jack in the rear turret if they were cold. They said they were all right, and thanked him for asking. Even asked how I was, and I said, "All right so far." The cloud was beginning to thin out. Up to the north we could see light, and the flak began to liven up ahead of it.

Boz, the bomb aimer, crackled through on the intercom, "There's a battle going on on the starboard beam." We couldn't see the aircraft, but we could see the jets of red tracer being exchanged. Suddenly there was a burst of yellow flame, and Jock remarked, "That's a fighter going down. Note the position." The whole thing was interesting, but remote. Dave, the navigator, who was sitting back with his maps, charts and compasses, said, "The attack ought to begin in exactly two minutes." We were still over the clouds. But suddenly those dirty gray clouds turned white. We were over the outer searchlight defenses. The clouds below us were white, and we were black. D-Dog seemed like a black bug on a white sheet. The flak began coming up, but none of it close. We were still a long way from Berlin. I didn't realize just how far.

Jock observed, "There's a kite on fire dead ahead." It was a great golden, slow-moving meteor slanting toward the earth. By this time we were about thirty miles from our target area in Berlin. That thirty miles was the longest flight I have ever made. Dead on time, Boz, the bomb aimer, reported, "Target indicators going down." The same moment the sky ahead was lit up by bright yellow flares. Off to starboard, another kite went down in flames. The flares were sprouting all over the sky—reds and greens and yellows—and we were flying straight for the center of the fireworks. D-Dog seemed to be standing still, the four propellers thrashing the air. But we didn't seem to be closing in. The clouds had cleared, and off to the starboard a Lanc was caught by at least fourteen searchlight beams. We could see him twist and turn and finally break out. But still the whole thing had a quality of unreality about it. No one seemed to be shooting at us, but it was getting lighter all the time. Suddenly a tremendous big blob of yellow light appeared dead ahead, another to the right and another to the left. We were flying straight for them.

Jock pointed out to me the dummy fires and flares to right and left. But we kept going in. Dead ahead there was a whole chain of red flares looking like stop lights. Another Lanc was coned on our starboard beam. The lights seemed to be supporting it. Again we could see those little bubbles of colored lead driving at it from two sides. The German fighters were at him. And then, with no warning at all, D-Dog was filled with an unhealthy white light. I was standing just behind Jock and could see all the seams on the wings. His quiet Scots voice beat into my ears, "Steady, lads, we've been coned." His slender body lifted half out of his seat as he jammed the control column forward and to the left. We were going down.

Jock was wearing woolen gloves with the fingers cut off. I could see his fingernails turn white as he gripped the wheel. And then I was on my knees, flat on the deck, for he had whipped the Dog back into a climbing turn. The knees should have been strong enough to support me, but they weren't, and the stomach seemed in some danger of letting me down, too. I picked myself up and looked out again. It seemed that one big searchlight, instead of being twenty thousand feet below, was mounted right on our wing tip. D-Dog was corkscrewing. As we rolled down on the other side, I began to see what was happening to Berlin.

The clouds were gone, and the sticks of incendiaries from the preceding waves made the place look like a badly laid out city with the street lights on. The small incendiaries were going down like a fistful of white rice thrown on a piece of black velvet. As Jock hauled the Dog up again, I was thrown to the other side of the cockpit, and there below were more incendiaries, flowing white and then turning red. The cookies—the four-thousand-pound high explosives—were bursting below like great sunflowers gone mad. And then, as we started down again, still held in the lights, I remembered that the Dog still had one of those cookies and a whole basket of incendiaries in his belly, and the lights still held us. And I was very frightened.

While Jock was flinging him about in the air, he suddenly flung over the intercom, "Two aircraft on the port beam." I looked astern and saw Wally, the mid-upper, whip his turret around to port and then look up to see a single-engined fighter slide just above us. The other aircraft was one of ours. Finally, we were out of the cone, flying level. I looked down, and the white fires had turned red. They were beginning to merge and spread, just like butter does on a hot plate. Jock and Boz, the bomb aimer, began to discuss the target. The smoke was getting thick down below. Boz said he liked the two green flares on the ground almost dead ahead. He began calling his directions. And just then a new bunch of big flares went down on the far side of the sea of flame and flare that seemed to be directly below us. He thought that would be a better aiming point. Jock agreed, and we flew on. The bomb doors were open. Boz called his directions, "Five left, five left." And then there was a gentle, confident, upward thrust under my feet, and Boz said, "Cookie gone." A few seconds later, the incendiaries went, and D-Dog seemed lighter and easier to handle.

I thought I could make out the outline of streets below. But the bomb aimer didn't agree, and he ought to know. By this time all those patches of white on black had turned yellow and started to flow together. Another searchlight caught us but didn't hold us. Then through the intercom came the word, "One can of incendiaries didn't clear. We're still carrying it." And Jock replied, "Is it a big one or a little one?" The word came back, "Little one, I think, but I'm not sure. I'll check." More of those yellow flares came down and hung about us. I haven't seen so much light since the war began. Finally the intercom announced that it was only a small container of incendiaries left, and Jock remarked, "Well, it's hardly worth going back and doing another run-up for that." If there had been a good fat bundle left, he would have gone back through that stuff and done it all over again. I began to breathe and to reflect again—that all men would be brave if only they could leave their stomachs at home. Then there was a tremendous whoomp, an unintelligible shout from the tail gunner, and D-Dog shivered and lost altitude. I looked at the port side, and there was a Lancaster that seemed close enough to touch. He had whipped straight under us, missed us by twenty-five, fifty feet, no one knew how much. The navigator sang out the new course, and we were heading for home. Jock was doing what I had heard him tell his pilots to do so often—flying dead on course. He flew straight into a huge green searchlight and, as he rammed the throttles home, remarked, "We'll have a little trouble getting away from this one."

And again D-Dog dove, climbed and twisted and was finally free. We flew level then. I looked on the port beam at the target area. There was a sullen, obscene glare. The fires seemed to have found each other—and we were heading home.

For a little while it was smooth sailing. We saw more battles. Then another plane in flames, but no one could tell whether it was ours or theirs. We were still near the target. Dave, the navigator, said, "Hold her steady, skipper. I want to get an astral site." And Jock held her steady. And the flak began coming up at us. It seemed to be very close. It was winking off both wings. But the Dog was steady. Finally Dave said, "Okay, skipper, thank you very much." And a great orange blob of flak smacked up straight in front of us. And Jock said, "I think they're shooting at us." I'd thought so for some time. And he began to throw D for Dog up, around and about again. And when we were clear of the barrage, I asked him how close the bursts were and he said, "Not very close. When they're really near, you can smell 'em." That proved nothing, for I'd been holding my breath. Jack sang out from the rear turret, said his oxygen was getting low, thought maybe the lead had frozen. Titch, the wireless operator, went scrambling back with a new mask and a bottle of oxygen. Dave, the navigator, said, "We're crossing the coast." My mind went back to the time I had crossed that coast in 1938, in a plane that had taken off from Prague. Just ahead of me sat two refugees from Vienna—an old man and his wife. The co-pilot came back and told them that we were outside German territory. The old man reached out and grasped his wife's hand. The work that was done last night was a massive blow of retribution for all those who have fled from the sound of shots and blows on the stricken Continent.

We began to lose height over the North Sea. We were over England's shore. The land was dark beneath us. Somewhere down there below American boys were probably bombing-up Fortresses and Liberators, getting ready for the day's work. We were over the home field. We called the control tower, and the calm, clear voice of an English girl replied, "Greetings D-Dog. You are diverted to Mule Bag." [Code for an airfield.] We swung around, contacted Mule Bag, came in on the flare path, touched down very gently, ran along to the end of the runway and turned left. And Jock, the finest pilot in Bomber Command, said to the control tower, "D-Dog clear of runway."

When we went in for interrogation, I looked on the board and saw that the big, slow-smiling Canadian and the red-headed English boy with the two weeks' old moustache hadn't made it. They were missing. There were four reporters on this operation—two of them didn't come back. Two friends of mine—Norman

Stockton, of Australian Associated Newspapers, and Lowell
Bennett, an American representing International News Service.
There is something of a tradition amongst reporters that those
who are prevented by circumstances from filing their stories will
be covered by their colleagues. This has been my effort to do so.

In the aircraft in which I flew, the men who flew and fought
poured into my ears their comments on fighters, flak and flares in
the same tones they would have used in reporting a host of daffo-
dils. I have no doubt that Bennett and Stockton would have given
you a better report of last night's activities.

Berlin was a kind of orchestrated hell, a terrible symphony of
light and flame. It isn't a pleasant kind of warfare—the men doing
it speak of it as a job. Yesterday afternoon, when the tapes were
stretched out on the big map all the way to Berlin and back again,
a young pilot with old eyes said to me, "I see we're working again
tonight." That's the frame of mind in which the job is being done.
The job isn't pleasant; it's terribly tiring. Men die in the sky while
others are roasted alive in their cellars. Berlin last night wasn't a
pretty sight. In about thirty-five minutes it was hit with about
three times the amount of stuff that ever came down on London
in a night-long blitz. This is a calculated, remorseless campaign of
destruction. Right now the mechanics are probably working on
D-Dog, getting him ready to fly again.

Murrow had run heavier than usual risks that night. Fifty bombers
were lost. And, as he reported, half the correspondents had not made it
back. He called Janet from the air base at four o'clock in the morning to
tell her that he was all right. "He sounded shaken," she remembered.

The broadcast became known as "Orchestrated Hell." The BBC asked
Ed to rebroadcast the story for British listeners. It was printed in newspapers across America and England. It was the only nonpress report to
win an award that season from the National Headliners Club. And in the
year of "Orchestrated Hell," Ed won his first Peabody Award, broadcast
journalism's highest honor. (The Peabody Awards honor the financier
George Foster Peabody. They were initiated by him in 1940 "to recognize
the most distinguished and meritorious service rendered each year" in
broadcasting.) Ed claimed that the praise he prized most came from one
of the men he flew with: "You got the crew chit-chat about right."

One month to the day after the Berlin raid, Jock Abercrombie and
his crew were shot down.

Paley was horrified by what Murrow had done. He told him, "All right,
now you know what it's like. You're not going to get anything more out of
it." He virtually ordered Murrow not to fly any more missions. Murrow
was almost contrite, and he agreed, "It's silly. I won't do it anymore."[7]

As close as he was to Paley, he did not confide to him, nor to anyone, something much on his mind during these months. It was a matter only indirectly related to the war, something in that prohibited zone, his interior life. From the time he had married, nine years before, there had never been the slightest suggestion that Ed Murrow was anything but a faithful, if somewhat neglectful, husband. Indeed, since the college affair with Willma Dudley, there was scant suggestion of passion ruling his behavior. His friends accepted that his ardor was reserved for the microphone. Bill Shirer found Ed chivalrous, even charming around attractive women, "but he never flirted, never seriously." Sevareid recalled, "I sometimes had the feeling that most women bored him.... He was totally at ease with Winston Churchill, but let a beautiful showgirl or actress come up to him and he'd be inarticulate." The wife of one of his correspondents, a highly attractive woman herself, concluded, "I don't think he had very strong sexual drives." Paley's wife, Dorothy, while a great admirer of Ed, found him "a kind of male chauvinist. I don't think women counted for very much with him."

Then Pamela Churchill, daughter-in-law of the prime minister and estranged wife of Churchill's son, Randolph, came into his life. Her marriage had not been happy. One friend described it as "Edwardian. Pamela produced a son and thereafter could do as she pleased." She moved at the summit of power. She presided over a salon that drew the principal actors in wartime England, from politics, from diplomacy, from the military. To be admitted to her circle was a boon to a foreign correspondent. Thus Ed Murrow was drawn into Pamela's orbit.

She was only in her mid-twenties, but possessed of the easy sophistication of her class. As Charles Collingwood described her, "Pamela had the most beautiful of the famous English complexions that you'll ever see in your life. Absolutely strawberries and cream. Blue eyes. A glint of red in her hair. Figure magnificent. Wildly attractive. Ed was knocked off his feet by this absolutely glorious and desirable young woman. Her connections impressed him. It was part of a journalist's job to cultivate such people. But it wasn't for any of these self-seeking reasons that he was attracted. She just bowled him over."

Janet could not ignore what was happening. In the beginning, she too had been invited to Pamela's salon. Later, Ed went alone. At one point, he had come home after a bad air raid, during which a terrified Janet had been left by herself. He said guiltily, "I should have been here with you, not where I was."

Janet did not know how to react. She did not want to provoke a break by confronting him directly. She was also enough of a student of her sex to recognize a remarkable woman in Pamela. And with her habitual candor, Janet could admit that her rival was able to give her husband something that she was unable to give. Janet was reserved and practical. Pamela was an unfettered spirit. "She was heady wine for Ed," another friend observed. All that Janet could hope for was that the wine would run out.

Friends who saw Ed and Pamela together saw an unrecognizable

Murrow. In her world, conversation was sparkling, cuttingly witty. Murrow had his humor, but it was more suited to newsrooms than drawing rooms. During a visit to England, Shirer had gone out for drinks with Ed and Pamela, and he found Ed acting out of character, trying to behave like one of Pamela's set. He had been immune, or resistant, for so long, that when finally he fell, it was a hard tumble.

The romance, however, did not distract him from his work. It was merely added to it. The fifth year of the war was to be pivotal. As 1944 opened, southern England virtually sagged under the weight of men and arms. The most casual student of the war knew that this was the year; at some point on some unknown shore, the Allies would invade the Continent.[8]

Murrow was building his staff for the day. He had lured Bill Downs from his favorite hunting grounds, UP. Downs was a rough gem, a florid, boisterous shouter who shouted exactly what he thought, and one of those who would later goad Murrow to take on Joe McCarthy. "No great intellect," Eric Sevareid said of him, "but no fool." Downs's father had been a Kansas railroad engineer, which to Ed was the equivalent of two easterners discovering their dads had been together at Groton. Downs won the final Murrow mark of acceptance, a nickname. For no apparent reason, he was "Doctor." Downs had first been sent to cover the Russian front and was brought back for the invasion.

Richard Hottelet, also with the UP, had covered Munich, the defeat of Poland, and the retreat from Dunkirk before the Gestapo put him in solitary confinement on trumped-up espionage charges. Hottelet was later exchanged for interned German journalists and subsequently joined the Office of War Information in London. He found the bureaucracy asphyxiating and went to Murrow pleading for a job. His credits were familiar to Murrow, virtually his own reporters' apprenticeship, and he liked Hottelet's terse, graphic handling of a story. Hottelet became a CBS correspondent in January of 1944.

Howard K. Smith had been a Rhodes scholar with Collingwood at Oxford where he was happily swept up in radical politics. Smith had picketed Ten Downing Street wearing a sandwich board to protest the Chamberlain policies. He was the first American to head the Labour Club of Oxford. Smith was not a direct Murrow recruit; he had actually been hired out of New York to replace Shirer in Berlin. When America came into the war, Smith managed to get out of Germany one hour before the border was sealed. Smith eventually made it to London and fit perfectly into the mold, one of Murrow's Boys by temperament and intellect, if not by actual selection.

He was looking, Ed said, "for people who were young and knew what they were talking about—without bothering too much about diction, phrasing and manner of speaking." He also valued erudition. The director of an American journalism college wrote asking him what aspiring reporters should be taught. "I am impressed," Ed responded, "that the best writing and on the whole the best interpretive comment appearing in British newspapers comes from men who spent most of their university career studying the classics." Hardly the answer a journalism professor was looking for.[9]

There was another UP reporter in London whom he also coveted, named Walter Cronkite. Murrow and Cronkite ran into each other occasionally at Air Ministry briefings, and Murrow had been much impressed. Collingwood was also high on Cronkite, a persuasive endorsement in Murrow's eyes. Ed invited Cronkite to join him for lunch at the Savile Club, and asked if Cronkite knew where it was. "Of course," Cronkite replied, not wanting to admit that he had not yet mastered the social topography of London. He thought Murrow had said the "Saddle Club," and spent much of the lunch hour in a fruitless search for a nonexistent club.

He found Murrow admirably to the point. Ed offered Cronkite a job and told him that he would be sent to replace Bill Downs in Russia when Downs returned to England, a choice assignment. "You'll get $125 a week and so much for every sponsored broadcast," Murrow told him. "I don't know the scale. But it adds up."

Walter Cronkite loved the UP. He had done a little radio broadcasting in the States and, by comparison, "I always thought it was a schlock kind of business, to tell you the truth," he was to say later. "I'd never been particularly happy doing radio. It was run by former program department people who didn't have much respect for the news." But he recognized that Murrow was lifting broadcast journalism to a new respectability. And he was only earning $57.50 a week at UP. The money from sponsors, he thought, "sounded too grand to count on. But the $125 a week sounded very good, indeed." Cronkite accepted.

When he got back to his office, he found that his bureau chief, Harrison Salisbury, had left a message for him: "I didn't have a chance to tell you, but I've been authorized by New York to give you a $12.50 raise." Then, to Cronkite's astonishment, he received a rare personal transatlantic telephone call in the middle of the war. Hugh Baillie, the UP president, was calling to ask if Cronkite realized that the company was grooming him to be the youngest chief in UP's history. On top of the $12.50 that Salisbury had already mentioned, Baillie was ready to add another $12.50.

A $25 a week raise to escape the silken trap of broadcast journalism. Walter Cronkite could not resist. He decided to stay with his beloved wire service. He went back to Murrow's office and told Ed that he had changed his mind. An instant chill settled over the conversation. No one so far had resisted Murrow's siren song. "Ed didn't take it too kindly," Cronkite remembered of that conversation. He would indeed eventually join CBS. But, he recalled, "After that incident, I always felt that Murrow had a question mark in his mind concerning me."[10]

As Murrow contemplated how best to cover the invasion, he was exasperated by what he considered a ridiculous constraint. The network would still not permit the use of recordings. Countless live broadcasts had been lost because of this maddening prohibition. Every shortwave transmission from Europe had to clear an obstacle course of natural phenomena. A broadcast originating from England departed under nighttime atmospherics and arrived in America under daytime atmospherics. Electrical storms and sunspots could completely blot out a broadcast. When this happened, the reporter, no matter what wisdom he had to impart, spoke into a void. The BBC permitted recordings. German radio used recordings. Only the American networks required their newscasters to broadcast live, with the resultant risks and lost transmissions. The stated reason was that anything less than a live broadcast detracted from radio's fidelity. The truth was that the networks still feared that recorded material would begin to loosen their hold over their affiliates. Songs could be recorded and played over the air, but not history in the making. "Maybe," Murrow said, "we need Bing Crosby over here."

He had occasionally violated the ban. He had once persuaded a BBC engineer to drive around London in a sound truck recording another raid in progress. He had used the recording on the air surreptitiously. On another occasion, he admitted to CBS, after the fact, that he had used a recording. He was warned not to do it again. One executive who heard the broadcast sniffed, "They could do better in the sound effects studio." But he broke the ban rarely and reluctantly, hoping only to shock the network into realizing what it was missing.

On his last trip home, Ed had gone to the Pentagon to see the latest in military recorders, a machine that used a spool of magnetized wire. The wire broke frequently and was almost impossible to edit. After deleting something, the two loose strands of wire had to be tied in a knot and then fused with a lighted cigarette. The equipment was primitive, and it was forbidden anyway.[11]

Ed next persuaded the commander of the U.S. Strategic Air Force, General Carl "Tooey" Spaatz, to let him report directly from a bomber by using a rudimentary portable transmitter.

He was flying over occupied France, and as he started to speak into the transmitter, his body inside the flight suit became soaked with sweat. His goggles began to steam. Fear, at last, he thought, had caught up with him. He was losing his nerve. Nothing quite so dramatic had occurred. After the plane landed, he discovered that he had accidentally plugged in his flight suit heater instead of the transmitter. The first live broadcast from a bomber was lost forever.[12]

Paley pleaded with him not to fly anymore. He agreed, but then continued to go his own way. He particularly liked flying with an ebullient 36-year-old Irishman named Joe Kelly who piloted a B-26. He flew ten missions with Kelly. He continued to fly with the RAF, and a second British crew was shot down over Schweinfurt soon after he had flown with them. "There was no way to make him stop," Paul White observed, "short of firing him."

Brendan Bracken wrote Ed, "I am told you are planning another flight over Germany. Your attempts to corner trouble are altogether deplorable. The value of your war work can not be overestimated and no one can take your place."

The repeated, unrequired risk taking was, Bob Trout recalled, the subject of endless and not always flattering speculation about Ed by the CBS staff. Another colleague observed, "Ed labors under a general compulsion to hit a home run every time at bat. In this case, I think he had to keep proving he was at least as rugged and as much of a reporter as anyone over there by doing roughly twice as much as anyone else."

Eric Sevareid had found himself unnerved by the Blitz of 1940. Thereafter, he had had his mettle tested more harrowingly. In 1943, Sevareid had flown a C-46 over the Himalayas. The plane lost an engine and started to go down. Sevareid parachuted just before the transport exploded against the side of a mountain. He found little glamour in airplanes plummeting to earth. After he was reassigned to London, he too pondered Murrow's strange compulsion. "I knew Medal of Honor winners in the war," Sevareid later observed. "One or two, Army psychiatrists would explain to you, simply had no sense of fear. They were not brave men; they were not normal men. Ed was perfectly normal in this. He could be plenty scared, but he wouldn't show it. What he was afraid of was being afraid....He did things that I thought foolish. But somehow they gave him confidence." Bill Paley said, "I used to think he was afraid he was a coward. But on reflection," Paley thought, "it's more complicated than that."

What did Murrow himself say? How did he explain repeatedly and needlessly gambling with his life? He later told a writer for *The New Yorker,* "Partly it was being a boy scout, I guess. Partly, I like fliers. Partly it was a dromomania I have. I even have it when I drive a car. Partly it was vanity. Three or four times in London, when I'd be sitting in the office, we'd hear the BBC playing back things I'd said and nothing has ever made me feel as good as that...I can't be logical about it."

He wrote a friend from his NSFA days: "In order to write or talk about danger, you must experience it. The experience teaches you something about what happens to fighting men and perhaps more important, it teaches you something about yourself." Here he was coming closer. How can we know what we are until the fabric of our character has been stretched to its limit? Until then, until we have stared into the black pit of our own nonexistence, everything we think we are is guesswork and likely judged in the guesser's favor.

Paley had said, yes, fly a combat mission once. But why over and over? Once one has known pure terror, what cubit of self-knowledge is gained by repetition? And, by the end of the war, Murrow would have flown twenty-four combat missions. He was driven by a compulsion to penetrate to the core of human experience. And the core reality of war in the sky was that airmen faced hell, and if lucky, survived, only to face it again and again. This was the psychological context of aerial combat, and it could not be captured in a single mission. And so he went back, again and again.

His most curious rationale was revealed in a letter Ed wrote to his sister-in-law, Dewey's wife, Donnie. He told her that he lived in an almost chronic state of "fatigue and frustration." He could not escape a nagging sense, in spite of all the plaudits, that he was failing, that he was not fully exploiting radio's potential to interpret the war. He was worn down by long, erratic hours, by lack of sleep, by pressures from disgruntled subordinates, suspicious censors, and company executives trying to second-guess him from New York. His affair had created a tense, unhappy situation at home that plagued him with guilt. "When I fly," he wrote Donnie of his depressed state, "it seems to go away. But it always returns." The raids were a pure, all-absorbing experience that left no room for any other emotion. To Murrow, flying bombers was a form of escape from pressures of a different kind.

This seemingly bizarre reason for risking his life appears to be borne out by the observations of others. Herbert Agar was a former correspondent himself who worked during the war as special assistant to the American ambassador in London. Agar bet other members of the Savile Club that he could always tell when Murrow went on another raid because, afterward, he would be so much more amiable, "so much less a denigrator of all men's hopes," as Agar put it.

Looking at death from a B-26 also helped clarify what he valued in his life, at least while he was airborne. He wrote Donnie of Janet: "I love her deeply and have discovered that danger shared is affection deepened." Still, on the ground, the relationship with Pamela Churchill continued and grew more involved. Rumors circulated of divorces and remarriages.

What of Janet? How did she bear up under the double jeopardy of losing her husband to another woman or to a German antiaircraft battery? Ed's lawyer friend, Lewis Powell, was, at the time, assigned to England as an Air Corps intelligence officer, and was a frequent guest at Hallam Street. He was with Janet one evening while Ed was on a mission. He was "amazed at her composure." Ken Galbraith was also then in London as director of the U.S. Strategic Bombing Survey and saw the Murrows occasionally. Of Janet, Galbraith said, "Even in the midst of war, she seemed to have an air of serenity about her. She was a collected person." Charlotte Ramsay, an American friend in London, observed, "She never complained when Ed went on those missions. She never complained about being left alone. Janet was not a complainer, period."[13]

On a June evening in 1944, a CBS monitor in New York picked up a BBC shortwave transmission beamed to continental Europe. The monitor had heard a BBC announcer repeat a message, first in English, then in several other languages. All persons living within eighteen miles of Europe's Atlantic coast were being warned to stay off the roads, to avoid bridges and railways. It was fifteen minutes past midnight in Europe, June 6, 1944. The invasion was at hand.

This time, CBS had been adamant. Murrow was not to go in with the invading force. It was not simply a question of his personal safety. Correspondents covering the epic event of the war required a supreme commander as well as the armies. For CBS the commander was Murrow. This time he did not quarrel.

He had had to make a fundamental decision. Did he want his correspondents with him so that he could deploy them quickly to the right place as the invasion unfolded and thus beat the competition to the story? Or should he assign them to combat units and have them go in with the troops? The latter option posed a risk. A week might pass before any of them would be in a position to transmit a word. Again he was ready to forgo the doubtful rewards of scoop journalism. He opted for depth of experience over speed. He assigned his people to combat units. Collingwood, Le Sueur, and Downs wanted to go in with the landing craft. Hottelet chose to fly. Murrow told them they were the "lucky ones." Of 500 American correspondents in England, only 28 were going in on D-Day.

Janet also had a D-Day assignment. They were living together, but virtually on separate paths now, the paths intersecting awkwardly and uncomfortably. Janet was an accredited CBS correspondent, and she continued to broadcast for Ed. She had done a splendid report on the treatment of GIs in military hospitals in England. And so she was asked to cover D-Day from a hospital ship attached to the invading force. Ed had left the decision up to her.

At about this time, Ambassador Winant also asked Janet to help him on a sensitive matter. Winant was flooded by complaints from Britons about the behavior of American GIs. Instances of drunkenness, reckless driving, rape, and a general contempt for the English way of life were poisoning Anglo-American relations. Ed had observed of these GIs: "They model their attitude after that of the Germans in Italy." Winant asked Janet to travel around England, to hear complaints and help him adjudicate disputes. She had already seen the young, broken bodies, the pitiable burn cases in military hospitals. She was a poor sailor, sick almost as soon as the lines were taken in. She was uneasy about taking part in the invasion. She told Ed that she thought she preferred to help Winant. Only then did he tell her that he was much relieved by her decision.

Early in June, the correspondents were instructed to report to their staging areas. Collingwood recalled, "We were put under lock and key and armed guards." Collingwood lugged a clumsy new Navy recorder aboard an LST. The contraption required a sound man to operate it. But it worked with gelatinous tape, an improvement over wire. He recorded: "Now we're up here, on the deck, on the main deck of the LST which is crowded and packed with vehicles of every sort. The trucks are full....just reading the names on the boxes on some of them....here's one that says 'cartridges' and another one says 'Hand Grenades'....I wonder what the soldiers feel like?...They're just as sealed here as though they had severed every connection with the outside world....I wonder what they feel about everything that's going to come. Let's ask one of them. Hey, soldier, come over here, will you...."

He recorded the awkward responses of ordinary men caught up in an extraordinary moment. He gave the tape to an Army public relations officer to get back to Murrow as soon as the LST was under way. He hoped Murrow would use it in spite of the recording ban. The soundman who went in with Collingwood, lugging the clumsy recorder, was later killed. And the ban on recordings was to remain in force until the final months of the war.

A half hour after midnight on June 6, a five-bell warning clanged on the AP ticker in the CBS news room in New York. AP London was reporting a German Transocean News Service story that the invasion of Europe had begun. Paul White was summoned from home. He called Murrow on the cue channel. Ed could only tell him, "No confirmation yet."

It was not until noon in New York that an announcer broke into the soap opera *The Romance of Helen Trent* and Murrow made his first D-Day report. It was sketchy, a recapitulation of what Churchill had just told Parliament. German shore batteries facing the armada had been knocked out. Underwater obstructions were fewer than expected. The Luftwaffe was strangely absent from the skies.

Not for another three hours did the Allies make it official. A U.S. Army public information officer announced, "Under the command of General Eisenhower, Allied naval forces supported by strong air forces began landing Allied armies this morning on the northern coast of France." About 4,000 troop-carrying vessels, 800 more warships, 11,000 planes, and 176,000 men had been committed on the first day.

Later, in his first detailed commentary, Murrow reported, "Early this morning we heard the bombers going out. It was the sound of a giant factory in the sky. It seemed to shake the old gray stone buildings in this bruised and battered city beside the Thames....Those who knew what was coming could imagine that they heard great guns and strains of the Battle Hymn of the Republic well above the roar of motors...."

The first CBS eyewitness account was made by Hottelet, back from riding a Marauder bomber that had flown in with the first wave over France. None of the correspondents who had gone in with the landing craft onto the beaches had yet been heard from. Murrow remained at the studio for fifty-six straight hours. And then the gruff, calm voice of Bill Downs, speaking over a mobile Army transmitter, came in reporting from an unidentified beach in Normandy.[14]

Six days after D-Day, an alien buzzing sounded over the working-class borough of Stepney. The buzzing was followed by a high-pitched whine and then silence. Ten seconds later a blast shuddered the earth, and 200 houses in Stepney were instantly flattened. The first V-1, a pilotless flying bomb, had struck London. Three months later, the first V-2 rockets, launched from pads 200 miles away in Holland, hit the city. The V-2s arrived in total silence, without even the courtesy of a buzz. The two weapons killed over 8,700 people and seriously injured 25,000 more before their launch sites on the Continent were overrun by Allied ground troops.

Murrow pondered the meaning of this dawning of a new age of destruction: "The significance of this demonstration of German skill and ingenuity lies in the fact that it makes complete nonsense out of strategic frontiers, mountain and river barriers....it means that within a few years, present methods of aerial bombardment will be as obsolete as the Gatling gun. It serves to make more appalling the prospect of another war."[15]

In the fall of 1944, he was elected president of the Association of American Correspondents in London. It was a moment filled with irony and sweet satisfaction. In his first years in England, radio broadcasters were not taken seriously enough to be admitted into the press association.[16]

He was physically and emotionally drained. He had driven his career and his personal life to a precipice. He had told Shirer when they met in Paris after the liberation that he was afraid he was growing away from America, from his roots. He still talked of abandoning broadcasting, of taking the Washington State presidency. "Each time a university letterhead hits my desk," he wrote a friend, "it gives me a small thrill of satisfaction." E.O. Holland put him up for an honorary Phi Beta Kappa key toward the end of the year and he was accepted. Ed responded, "I am tremendously pleased and flattered....I can now confess to you that I was slightly disappointed at not being elected in my last year [in college]...."[17]

His personal life was a confusion of forbidden happiness, guilt, self-reproach, and indecision. He was torn between a wife he loved and a woman with whom he was wildly in love. Of the relationship with Pamela Churchill, Bill Paley recalled, "I knew exactly what was happening, I felt bad about it. I thought it was a big mistake. But Ed never came to me." Nor did he confide his dilemma to anyone.

Janet had already gone home in September, to visit her parents. Several weeks later, Ed decided to join her. He was weary in body and in conscience and needed to sort out his marriage and his life. He arrived in New York toward the end of November and waded through unavoidable meetings with CBS executives. He went to Washington and had another dinner at the White House, after which he commented, "It did not serve to improve my spirits very much." His complaint reflected an idea now firmly rooted in his mind, that the war was being won, but the moral crusade was being lost. The Allied victory was making the world safe for the status quo ante.

In mid-December, he and Janet virtually fled to Gallaghers, a 10,000-acre dude ranch, thirty miles from San Antonio. He refused to tell CBS where he could be reached. He simply dropped out of sight. He wrote his parents, "The financial sacrifice is considerable, but I felt I had to do it. These last eight years have not been easy."

The ranch was full of game—deer, rabbits, wild turkey. But he wrote, "...for the first time in my life I am not much interested in shooting anything....maybe I've seen too much shooting." What they did was sleep late, eat huge breakfasts, go fishing and horseback riding, and sleep some more.

While they were at Gallaghers, the Germans made their last death rattle of the war in the Ardennes; the Battle of the Bulge ensued. Ed reared briefly, like a fire horse hearing the bell, uneasy at being away from a big story. Then he slumped back and went on enjoying the vacation. Early in March of 1945 he was back in England. Janet followed a month later.[18]

She sailed on the *Queen Mary*, now converted to a troopship. She rated passage only because she was an accredited correspondent. Nevertheless, she was traveling in violation of military regulations, since Janet was pregnant. She had told no one, not even Ed. The vacation, the relaxation, the absence of cares during the preceding weeks, had achieved what all her prayers and medical consultations had failed to accomplish after almost eleven years of marriage. Her condition seemed to her a miracle.

The new development brought the matter of Ed's romantic involvement to a head. As Dorothy Paley put it, Pamela "was the great passion of his life." Another Murrow friend, Mary Warburg, said that Ed once confided to her that he was "more in love with her than anybody in his life." Mary Warburg asked Janet, if that was the way he felt, why didn't she give him a divorce. Janet replied, according to Warburg, "I didn't think she would be a good enough wife to him."

With Janet expecting a baby, Ed was now pulled in three directions, by his wife, the other woman, and his conscience. In effect, the unborn child won. An Ed Murrow contemplating leaving his wife for another woman was essentially an aberrant Ed Murrow. The fundamental Murrow, in his inescapable skin, was the boy raised in a world where marriage, duty, and children were bedrock. Family responsibility came before individual happiness. He might scale the cool heights of English upper-class society, but he had been Ethel Murrow's boy first. Prophetically, he had written home earlier, "...small boys don't really ever grow up....they never escape from their early training...and when the going is tough, they return to a few fundamentals, drilled into them between the ages of six and ten."

There was no more talk of divorce. He told his wife that she was never to mention the matter, never throw it in his face, no recriminations, ever. The book was closed, the case sealed. He became excited, positively giddy, at the prospect of at last becoming a father. He felt renewed tenderness toward Janet. It was he who made the announcement to his in-laws: "For some time I have felt as though a bomb had fallen near me....we are going to have a baby....[Janet] is more beautiful than ever....right now we sit around the fire and debate names.... and when I can take him fishing...." He was, at bottom, a very old fashioned man.[19]

CHAPTER 16

Goodbye to All That

On an April night in 1945, Murrow was at a command post of General George Patton's Third Army, inside Germany, playing poker with the other correspondents. Charles Collingwood recalled the night: "Ed was a terrible player. He always felt a compulsion to stay in every hand, draw to inside straights, stay with a bad hand. But this night, everything went right. He was wearing his correspondent's uniform with lots of pockets. By the end of the game, he had money stuffed into every pocket. Over two thousand dollars, as I remember." They turned in. The next day, they were to move with the troops toward a place called Buchenwald.

Ten years before, he had been helping refugees from nazism rebuild their lives in the United States. Two years before, he had broadcast one of the first fragmentary reports of what had befallen Jews in Poland who did not escape the Nazis. Now he had arrived at the end point of the Nazi racial philosophy. He went in with the troops who liberated the Buchenwald concentration camp.

They were instantly engulfed by living skeletons, haunted men with slack mouths and eyes like dull glass. Desperate to do something, anything to overcome his confusion, Murrow began emptying his pockets, pressing his poker winnings into the prisoners' bony hands. He completed the tour of this charnel house and went back to headquarters to write his story.

It had been a day combining unimaginable horror and conventional grief, since, at Buchenwald, Murrow learned of the death of President Roosevelt. The President's passing was a shock, but a comprehensible loss. Seeing the slaughter at Buchenwald, the pallid, naked corpses heaped up like refuse, was an experience for which nothing had prepared him.

A new correspondent on the staff, Douglas Edwards, recalled Murrow on his return to London: "Ed was pale, unsmiling and chain smoking. The smell of death was still on his uniform." Other correspondents who had been with him at Buchenwald filed their stories immediately. For three days Ed did nothing. He needed time, he said, to "acquire detachment."

D.G. Bridson of the BBC was in Studio B-4 the Sunday when Murrow finally delivered his account of Buchenwald. Bridson later remembered, "I never saw him so cut up by anything; he was really sort of trembling. Yes, literally.... He was shaking with rage by the time he finished it."

Murrow reported:

...Permit me to tell you what you would have seen, and heard, had you been with me on Thursday. It will not be pleasant listening. If you are at lunch, or if you have no appetite to hear what Germans have done, now is a good time to switch off the radio, for I propose to tell you of Buchenwald. It is on a small hill about four miles outside Weimar, and it was one of the largest concentration camps in Germany, and it was built to last....

There surged around me an evil-smelling horde. Men and boys reached out to touch me; and they were in rags and the remnants of uniform. Death had already marked many of them, but they were smiling with their eyes. I looked out over that mass of men to the green fields beyond where well-fed Germans were ploughing.

A German, Fritz Kersheimer, came up and said, "May I show you around the camp I've been here ten years."...I asked to see one of the barracks....I was told that this building had once stabled eighty horses. There were twelve hundred men in it, five to a bunk. The stink was beyond all description.

When I reached the center of the barracks, a man came up and said, "Remember me? I'm Peter Zenkl, one-time mayor of Prague." I remember him, but did not recognize him. He asked about Beneš and Jan Masaryk. I asked how many men had died in that building during the last month. They called the doctor; we inspected his records. There were only names in the little blackbook, nothing more—nothing of who these men were, what they had done, or hoped. Behind the names of those who had died there was a cross. I counted them. They totalled 242. Two hundred and forty two out of twelve hundred in one month....

As we walked out in the courtyard, a man fell dead. Two others—they must have been over sixty—were crawling toward the latrine. I saw it but will not describe it.

In another part of the camp they showed me the children, hundreds of them. Some were only six. One rolled up his sleeve, showed me his number. It was tattooed on his arm. D-6030, it

was. The others showed me their numbers; they will carry them
till they die.

An elderly man standing beside me said, "The children, enemies of the state." I could see their ribs through their thin shirts.
The old man said, "I am professor Charles Richer of the
Sorbonne." The children clung to my hands and stared. We
crossed to the courtyard. Men kept coming up to speak to me and
to touch me, professors from Poland, doctors from Vienna, men
from all Europe. Men from the countries that made America.

We went to the hospital; it was full. The doctor told me that
two hundred had died the day before. I asked the cause of death;
he shrugged and said, "Tuberculosis, starvation, fatigue, and there
are many who have no desire to live. It is very difficult...."

We went again into the courtyard, and as we walked we talked.
The two doctors, the Frenchman and the Czech, agreed that
about six thousand had died during March. Kersheimer, the
German, added that back in the winter of 1939, when the Poles
began to arrive without winter clothing, they died at the rate of
approximately nine hundred a day. Five different men asserted
that Buchenwald was the best concentration camp in Germany;
they had had some experience of the others....

There were two rows of bodies stacked up like cordwood.
They were thin and very white. Some of the bodies were terribly
bruised, though there seemed to be little flesh to bruise. Some had
been shot through the head, but they bled but little. All except
two were naked. I tried to count them as best I could and arrived
at the conclusion that all that was mortal of more than five hundred men and boys lay there in two neat piles....

I pray you to believe what I have said about Buchenwald. I
have reported what I saw and heard, but only part of it. For most
of it I have no words. Dead men are plentiful in war, but the living dead, more than twenty thousand of them in one camp. And
the country round about was pleasing to the eye, and the
Germans were well fed and well dressed. American trucks were
rolling toward the rear filled with prisoners. Soon they would be
eating American rations, as much for a meal as the men at
Buchenwald received in four days.

If I've offended you by this rather mild account of
Buchenwald, I'm not in the least sorry....

Though he had lagged behind the other reporters with the Buchenwald story, even newspapers carried his full text. *The London Express* gave
it the front page. The BBC asked him to repeat the broadcast for its domestic service. Britain had been criticized during World War I for circu-

lating false atrocity stories. An account of mass murder reported by Murrow, the BBC reasoned, would be believed.

He himself felt that the broadcast failed. Years later, Ed told Ben Gross, the radio columnist of *The New York Daily News,* that the children's shoes in that heap had unnerved him. "I could have described three pairs of those shoes...but hundreds of them. Well, I just couldn't. The tragedy of it simply overwhelmed me." Critics, nevertheless, rated the "Liberation of Buchenwald," along with "Orchestrated Hell," as a classic of radio reporting.[1]

The war in Europe ended less than a month later. On May 8, 1945, Murrow was reporting the celebration of V-E day in London: "As you walk down the streets you hear singing that comes from open windows; sometimes it's a chorus, and sometimes it's just a single voice raised in song. 'Roll Out the Barrel' seems to be the favorite...." Much of the gaiety seemed contrived, almost obligatory, as though people felt required to revel. And he noticed, "Some people appear not to be part of the celebration. Their minds must be filled with memories of friends who died in the streets where they now walk....Tonight, walking through familiar side streets in London, trying to realize what has happened, one's mind takes refuge in the past. The war that was seems more real than the peace that has come."

It was after two o'clock in the morning when he finished his broadcast. He locked arms with Kay Campbell, Douglas Edwards, and some rival NBC correspondents and marched down the center of Regent Street, joining the brittle merrymaking, singing "Roll Out the Barrel."

At dawn, he walked home alone past block after shattered block where spirits of the dead lingered: Alan and Clare Wells, the neighborhood air-raid wardens; Alan Campbell, Kay's flyer brother; Ben Robertson of the haystack broadcast, killed in an air crash; Edward Cazelet, a friend lost escorting a refugee Polish general; John Rathbone, member of Parliament, husband of one of Janet's closest friends, killed on duty with the RAF; a dozen more friends lost in two direct hits on Broadcasting House. Yet life proved as stubborn as death. The first michaelmas daisies were sprouting in the damp earth of the bombed-out buildings he passed by.[2]

He was soon back on the Continent and traveled 2,000 miles throughout a now prostrate Germany. As a young man he had been offended by the idea that a whole people should carry the blame for a war. He had then believed that war was indeed hell for ordinary people on all sides. The villains were ambitious politicians, vainglorious generals, venal industrialists. He had argued against French, Belgian, and English students who wanted to keep the Germans out of the Confederation Internationale des Etudiants. He had rejected the notion of collective guilt. But that had been before Buchenwald and Dachau; he had also visited the latter with the "smell of death seeping through the disinfectant." He saw cities in Germany whose total devastation made London seem lucky. He watched German children scavenging in GI garbage cans. Along the cratered autobahn, he eyed endless files of German refugees. And he wrote Janet, "The casual observer might be inclined to feel sorry for these poverty-stricken and homeless people who never smile." Instead, he said, "The blame rests...on the shoulders of the German people. They permitted the Nazi regime to rise to power. They supported it to the end...denouncing it only after its downfall...and then only to save their own skins."

When he got back to London from Germany, he told Howard K. Smith, "I was impressed with the absence of any feeling of guilt. There didn't seem to be any remorse or sorrow for what Germany did to other nations." He observed in a broadcast: "No one has yet produced a formula for ridding the German people of their appetite for war, their recurring desire to shoot people and to take their land and their homes." His bitterness toward the Germans was to be long-lasting, his one discernible ethnic prejudice. They had, he felt, worked hard to earn it.[3]

Sick of the sight of war, he also wrote Janet, "Don't see how I'll stomach the Pacific." But that was precisely what he intended with the fighting over in Europe, to cover the war still being fought. He was stopped only by the atomic bombs dropped on Hiroshima and Nagasaki in August, which put Japan out of the war in eight days.

In a broadcast six days after Hiroshima, he glimpsed the coming nuclear arms race: "President Truman's declaration that Britain and America will not reveal the secret of the bomb until means have been found for controlling it brought no great reassurance. It does for the moment alter the balance of power, but such a solution is only temporary. Other nations, by research and espionage, are likely to solve the problem before we have mastered the countermeasures....Science has presented statesmanship with a problem, and its successful solution implies a revolution in the relations between nations."[4]

But he had begun to lose hope in such a revolution. "When we entered Buchenwald," he reported, "...I discovered that the hatred of Czech for Czech, Pole for Pole was much greater than their hatred for their German captors and butchers...that is Communist versus non-Communist. For they believed, these miserable, emaciated Czechs and Poles in different things...."

He predicted the state that would eventually be called the cold war. "Communism is an item for export," he commented. "So is democracy. The two are bound to compete." Instead of postwar harmony, the triumph of Allied arms "will not bring peace, but revolutions. And the course of these revolutions will be determined by whose armies are where....In most liberated countries there will be two or more competing factions. The governments-in-exile may seek to ride back into power on Allied food trains." The Soviets would create an overnight empire by dominating the nations they had presumably liberated, he observed, which is precisely what did happen in Poland, Czechoslovakia, Bulgaria, Romania, Hungary, and East Germany.[5]

He wanted the United States to grow up, to come out of the war as a mature leader rather than a big kid whose brawn had won out in a worldwide brawl: "Our industrial plant will be undamaged, our people will not be so fatigued as those of Europe. If we choose to return to reaction and economic isolation, we can do that but...if we do...we shall within a measurable time, find ourselves a long, straggling island off the coast of Kamchatka, with the rest of the world allied against us." He had picked up the Kamchatka metaphor from the historian R.H. Tawney.

He had said all along that he wanted the war to overturn the old social order. He had broadcast in a burst of proletarian romanticism, "The aristocrats in this country [England] are the people who work with their hands, who have grease under their fingernails." The war had, in fact, put officer's pips on the shoulders of schoolteachers and bank clerks. Warfare had demanded critical skills rather than perfect manners. The war forced the British government to nationalize and socialize; it had made government the engine of change, just as Laski and the Labourites had long preached. And the result had been victory. Still, Murrow, ever the pessimist, was worried that the common man would be cheated of that victory. He wrote his friend Elmer Davis, "I am more than half persuaded that the pigs are going to inherit the Earth."

That summer, Britain held the first general election since 1939, pitting the Conservatives led by Churchill against Labour, led by Clement Attlee. Ed completely misjudged the mood of the masses. He looked at the election more as an American hero-worshiper than as the student of British political and social currents. He had been caught up in the Churchillian mystique, captivated by a man who, in language, presence, and esprit, seemed John Bull incarnate. He failed to grasp that those proletarian aristocrats with the grease under their fingernails had borne the burdens of war, perhaps for king and country, but not for Winston Churchill. Churchill, as a politician without a war, represented "them," the privileged beneficiaries of the old order. Murrow had predicted "a small but workable majority" for the Conservatives. Labour won by the greatest landslide in the history of British socialism. Churchill was out. Attlee was in.[6]

Murrow freely confessed that Churchill had been his hero. His own language was influenced by Churchill, not so much the rolling and grandiloquent sonorities, but the other Churchill, the one who spoke in a simple, powerful Anglo Saxon imagery that sounded like the Bible in modern dress. He saw Churchill as "a gallant gambler, an aristocrat, an historian, an eighteenth-century cavalry officer...and an indestructible juvenile.... He is, I think, the most considerable man to walk the stage of world history in fifty years." Murrow was alternately admiring, amused, or shocked by this magnificent anachronism. He told a magazine interviewer, with a dash of hyperbole, "Here is this man, an early eighteenth-century character who has never dialed a telephone in his life, never turned on a radio, never traveled in the subway—and his wife was the one who provided the ground on which he stood."

He had seen more of the prime minister professionally and socially than other members of the American press corps. Churchill, who kept highly individualistic hours, thought nothing of summoning Murrow at 2 a.m., after a broadcast, for "several whiskies." Out of this exposure, Murrow absorbed an anthology of the quotable Churchill, parables for every occasion, which he cited with convincing Churchillian style all his life. When faced with obtuse arrogance in military men, Murrow would tell of the time General Mark Clark opened a conversation with, "Of course, you civilians...." " Churchill cut him short with, "Young man, I was killing people when you were puling and puking in your blanket."[7]

His personal hero had lost, but his philosophical hero had won. Harold Laski served as chairman of the Labour party during Labour's victory. Still, he had become a heavy cross for Murrow. When Ed visited the United States, Laski loaded him with requests for messages to deliver and books to bring back. He continued to berate Murrow for inattention. Two years before, Laski had overworked himself into a nervous breakdown. He became confused, delivering the same lecture to the same classes at the London School of Economics. Soon after the 1945 campaign, he lost a libel suit against a British newspaper, and the cost practically bankrupted him.

Eric Sevareid saw Laski as a tragic figure. "By the end of the war, Laski was bonkers," Sevareid said, "a pathological liar, a sick man." Still, Murrow tried to remain a faithful friend, making occasional, painful visits to the man to whom he owed a debt for a major part of his adult education, and giving Laski money to help ease the disastrous effects of the lawsuit.[8]

Murrow's appreciation of two men as unalike as Churchill and Laski seems odd at first, almost suspect. But Ed's colleague in New York, Ted Church, captured the irony perfectly. "Ed," Church said, "is a conservative American who is tinged with world reform." As Sevareid put it, "Ed was not a class man, but rather a moralistic man."

And he remained a dark-spirited man. "He was always a pessimist," Richard Hottelet recalled. "He expected things to turn out badly, that the curve of history was down. His camaraderie was superficial. He was always his own person. You never had a road map of the mind of Murrow."[9]

The single, pure unintellectualized joy in Ed Murrow's life was the birth of his son, Charles Casey Murrow, on November 6, 1945. Ed wrote his in-laws, the Brewsters, that he was so excited that he gave the obstetrician "my last two remaining golf balls...." " A few days later, Ed again wrote the Brewsters about the baby's birth, "There are two ways of doing something in England, cheap or very expensive....this was done in the proper style....I rather expect we are in for some hard days," an exaggeration intended, no doubt, to elicit appropriate appreciation for their son-in-law.

The name Charles was quickly discarded, and the boy would always be Casey. The origins of the name were clouded, mostly by the father. In one explanation, Ed said that the name honored his railroading father, by referring to the Casey "found in the wreck of old 97." In another explanation, Ed said that the name derived from "Casey at the Bat." In still another, the name was chosen because it rhymed with Lacey. One colleague guessed that the name was intended as a tribute to Ed's secretary by sounding her initials, K.C. Ed had simply come home one night and announced to Janet, "I've got just the name for the baby. We'll call her Casey." From that moment, the name was fixed regardless of the baby's sex.

"And he ain't going to grow up in a city…even if I have to edit a weekly paper in the midwest," he also informed the Brewsters. That declaration was soon to be tested. A month after the child's birth, Ed returned to New York alone to decide his future. He closed his last letter to his in-laws before leaving with "…think it may end with my quitting Columbia."[10]

Almost as soon as he checked into his hotel in New York, he began dispatching a flurry of letters to Janet. The first letter made clear that their marriage had entered a new era of trust "…dined with Paley and some woman last night….ONE woman, please note…."

Paley was now out of the Army and back as CBS chairman of the board. He had been nourishing an idea for well over a year, and now he sprang it. He wanted Murrow to give up broadcasting and become the network's vice president for public affairs. The job meant running the entire news operation along with education, politics, religion, virtually all nonentertainment programming.

The offer to Murrow devastated Paul White. White had been sustained by the dream of becoming a CBS vice president for virtually fifteen years. He was next in line for the top news position. He was, ostensibly, Murrow's superior. But the bond that had grown between Paley and Murrow in the London years doomed White. As Paley later explained his choice, "Ed was the better man. I reached that conclusion in Europe." White knew that he had behaved badly toward Murrow. Now he faced the prospect that Murrow would shift from being his subordinate to being his boss. Like a bully in full retreat, he started putting out the word that if Murrow took the job, he would be proud to work under him. "Nobody believed Paul," Helen Sioussat recalled of White's new pose. White also began drinking more heavily.[11]

The presidency of Washington State was still available to Ed. The Carnegie Corporation wanted him to run its philanthropies. Bill Benton, who had gone to the State Department from the *Encyclopaedia Britannica*, wanted him. "Benton has offered me a job," Ed wrote Janet, "…really trying to sell State Department policy to this country…t'would involve seeing [Secretary of State] Byrnes every a.m.…seeing all top secret stuff…."

He would be appointed assistant secretary of state, Benton told him. Paley was offering him $35,000 a year to take the vice presidency, with a bonus that would bring his total earnings to $50,000. Paley also suggested that the Murrows live in a comfortable house at Kiluna, his Long Island estate.[12]

But the most seductive offer was one that, if taken, would keep him on the air as a correspondent. While still abroad, Ed had become a client of Stix and Gude, an agency representing reporters, writers, and editors in their contract negotiations with the networks. John "Jap" Gude (the nickname derived from a boyhood case of jaundice that had temporarily turned his skin yellow) was a CBS alumnus, much liked and trusted by Murrow. The Campbell's Soup Company was eager to sponsor Ed in a fifteen-minute nightly newscast. Gude had worked out with Campbell the most coveted and lucrative news contract in radio.[13]

Murrow began an agony that a less tortured spirit might consider an embarrassment of riches. He wrote Janet once, sometimes twice, a day, pouring out his love for her, his longing to be with the baby, and his indecision. The one offer that he did not want to succumb to, he said, was Paley's. He loathed the idea of becoming an administrator. "Let's hope I have some courage during the next few days," he wrote.

"They are putting on the pressure," he wrote her later. "...Bill is going to be sore if I don't take it....I haven't had a drink for two days....this business calls for a clear head."

Jap Gude and Tom Stix listened to him think aloud for two hours over dinner at Louis and Armand's restaurant. Then they retired to Stix's apartment, where the soul searching continued. As Gude recalled that night, "He kept pacing the floor, chain smoking, muttering to himself, 'I don't want to be a god damned paper shuffler.'"

William S. Paley had not built CBS from a near bankrupt little company to a communications colossus without understanding human nature. He argued to Murrow that whatever he had accomplished for broadcast journalism in London, dividing his time between broadcasting and managing his staff, could be infinitely multiplied if he were running CBS news worldwide. He would have a substantial budget. He would report directly to Paley. How better to preserve what he had created thus far, to hold his team together, to bring in new blood, to push back the frontiers of radio journalism, than through the power Paley was offering him? Great conductors built great orchestras, not violin soloists.

He was invited out to Kiluna. Ronnie Tree was there in the midst of a divorce. Tree was with the woman with whom he had fallen in love and would eventually marry, Marietta Peabody Fitzgerald. The rarefied atmosphere of Kiluna, the kind of people with whom Paley surrounded himself, the aura of power in the very air, began to mock his daydream of a life on some bucolic campus. Ed wrote Janet, "The fact is I don't have the courage to tell them I'm going to a university."

On his fourth day back in New York, he wrote her, "am starting to lean toward the executive job." He allowed Jim Seward, who was still looking after his personal finances, to persuade him that he could save as much money on the CBS payroll as with Campbell's Soup's lucrative offer. The next day he wrote Janet, "Maybe at bottom I am intrigued with stopping broadcasting while I am at the top....Maybe I am afraid of the competition here."

On December 21, the man who was not going to raise his boy in the big city, who would run a college or small-town paper first, who was going to New York with the expectation "of quitting Columbia," cabled Janet, "Have taken executive job. Wish me luck." He spelled out his reasoning in a letter the next day. "In part it was to see how vain I am and how much I will miss the cheap glory....in part it was that for the time being I have reached the top....There won't be any more stories like the ones we covered and more broadcasting would have been anti-climactic....in part it was fear of becoming like most of the commentators over here. ...but at bottom it was because in this job I have at least a chance to do more than I could as a broadcaster." Paley's case had carried the day. But that night, Ed telephoned Janet in London and he cried. He missed her and Casey terribly, he said. Christmas came, and he spent it alone in the hotel, turning down all invitations.

What he had omitted was the emotional rationale for taking a job he did not want. Murrow, usually so much his own man, felt a bond to Bill Paley, a kinship that went beyond the simple hold of employer over employee. Few are so self-sufficient that they do not need someone else, someone whose approval represents a deep, psychological validation of self. For Murrow, Paley occupied that place. At bottom, Ed had simply been unable to say no to Bill Paley. He may have fumed in front of Stix and Gude and poured out his confusion to Janet. But to Paley, "He seemed very happy to take the job, enthusiastic, flattered."[14]

He had to make clear to himself and to the rest of the corporation that the link was indeed him to Paley. He had demanded in his contract an unusual clause. The contract no longer remained in force if and when Bill Paley was gone from the company. He did not work for CBS; he worked for Bill Paley.

Ed had told Eric Sevareid that if he did take the vice presidency, "I'm not going to get into that life of the townhouse on the East Side and the place in the country and going back and forth chasing money. I'm not going to do it."

But soon after the decision was made, he asked Jim Seward to find him a townhouse. "Brother Seward is beating the bushes and something will turn up," he wrote Janet. Why did he state his distaste for the rat race with such force—then reverse himself so quickly? When he used to wake up in the morning in his Hallam Street flat, he knew who he was and what he was. Now he was not so sure. And so he both loathed and embraced the accoutrements of his new life simultaneously, trying to convince himself that he was happy with the decision he had made.

But one thing he did now recognize—he was no longer, by any standard, a poor boy. He was slowly overcoming the childhood fear that poverty lurked around every corner waiting to reclaim him. With his new salary it was foolish to pretend that he was, if not rich, at least certainly well off. He bought a townhouse on the Upper East Side.[15]

It fell to the bypassed Paul White to put out the word to the affiliates on closed-circuit radio that CBS had a new vice president for public affairs, Edward R. Murrow.

A few days later, Ed was wakened from a sound sleep in his hotel by the house detective. A "Mr. White" was downstairs, the detective told him, demanding a key to Ed's room. Ed dressed and went down to the lobby. There he found Paul White drunk, ranting, with a bad cut over his eye. As Ed described the night in a letter to Janet, "tried to get him home....he was a mess....finally got him up to my room....he was crying....he loved me....finally went to sleep...after falling over the furniture....four-thirty he was up and rambling again....finally left about five....don't know what happened to him....but I know now what's going to happen to him....it's just a matter of the timing....I hate this part of the job...but its got to be done."[16]

By February of 1946, Ed was back in England temporarily preparing to turn over the office to his successor, Howard K. Smith. The difference between the land of plenty that he had just left and the land of want that he had returned to was evident in Smith's plight. "I don't have any clothes," Smith told him. "All my civilian clothes are from Oxford and they're at least six years old. And the British won't give me a clothing ration until I've been here a year." Ed unhesitatingly turned over his wardrobe to Smith, who later said of his windfall, "Great quality in those suits of Ed's."[17]

Now that he had taken the new post, Ed assumed the zeal of a missionary. David Schoenbrun, a former high school French teacher who had learned his journalism as an Army correspondent, came to see Ed at Hallam Street. Murrow had met Schoenbrun during the North African campaign and had been impressed by his deep knowledge of France. He asked Schoenbrun, with the war over, what he expected to do. Schoenbrun replied that teaching was still his first love. Murrow fixed him with his over-the-eyebrow gaze and said, "Well, one day I could give you the biggest classroom in the world....we are going to make CBS the greatest network in the world. We are going to inform and educate the people of America. They have lived almost all our history in isolation...but now America is the world's greatest power....that's why I see CBS as an international classroom." The implication was clear. He too was an educator who had never deserted. He went on, "I've been recruiting men with university backgrounds. Howard Smith was a Rhodes Scholar at Oxford. So was Collingwood. That's the kind of man I want....you know, you can't teach a pear-shaped tone or a pretty face to think. But you can teach a brain to broadcast."[18]

He was leaving the field, the acknowledged master of the craft he had virtually created. Elmer Davis expressed almost disbelief that such reporting was done "by a man who never worked on a newspaper in his life." Murrow, he said, "had an ability to compress and condense without distorting that I've never heard by anyone in radio, by anyone anywhere."

His lack of a newspaper background had been no liability. It had been his emancipation. It had freed him from the shackled style of one who writes to be read instead of heard. Daniel Schorr, who would ultimately go to work for Murrow, described the difference. Too often the convert from print to broadcasting, Schorr said, "might try to pack more information into his mere ninety seconds on the air by reading faster. The effect was to overload and confuse the listener. Murrow, not coming out of that world, never made that mistake. His cadence was unhurried. He matched the message to the time, and not the other way around. He dealt with a new medium on its own terms rather than imposing those brought over from another medium."

After hearing Murrow's D for Dog broadcast, Collie Knox wrote in *The Daily Mail,* "He made me want to hurl my typewriter into the Thames and never write another word." He was, Jimmy Sheean concluded, "the finest thing the new instrument of communication has given us." Possibly the most generous tribute came from his old NBC rival. Fred Bate, reflecting on the networks' battle of Britain, conceded victory to the opposition because, Bate said, "CBS had something we didn't have, Ed Murrow."

He scoffed at pear-shaped tones and hired his correspondents for their intellect and analytic power. In this, he was like a rich man who can afford to disparage wealth. The effect of his voice could not be separated from what he said. Scotty Reston once observed, "It was that voice that was arresting the country, not what we were writing. There was something about that voice....the voice and history happened to coincide. We couldn't do that even if we wrote in iambic pentameter...." Bill Leonard, a later colleague, commented, "Murrow had the best voice ever heard on the news. It sent a shiver through you."

It was a voice that fixed itself in the listener's memory and, decades later, could still be plucked from the blurred recollection of a thousand other voices. The tone was resonant, a continuous, barely perceptible vibrato that gave his speech the vitality of a current humming on a power line. The rolled final consonants—"Endeddd," "Foolll"—powered his words. His diction was perfect but not obtrusively so. He managed to achieve precision without affected preciseness.

He had learned to use pauses as masterfully as words. In Neville

Chamberlain's final discredited hours as prime minister, Murrow reported, "When Mr. Chamberlain concluded his speech, there was a dead...flat ...silence." The pauses after "dead" and "flat" said all that needed be said of Chamberlain's vanished authority. Like a camera panning for audience reaction, Murrow described Winston Churchill at that moment: "All during the prime minister's speech [here, Murrow let his voice sink] Mr. Winston...Churchill...slumped...in his seat." The listener could visualize Churchill sagging at his predecessor's ineptitude.

He kept his own speech lean by seeking the perfect noun rather than one less perfect that leaned on adjectives. He was not afraid to use an obscure word if the sound worked. He described the American spirit to a BBC audience as "rumbustious." The meaning was unmistakable. His Quaker roots and his boyhood Bible reading lent color to his speech. He talked about blackouts during the air raids where they "dasen't show any kind of light." He used old-fashioned forms like "amongst." But they were employed sparingly, enough to season without distracting.

His everyday conversation was jocularly peppered with Quakerisms— t'was, t'will, t'is, t'would. He would say, "It pleasures me to see you," or "What persuades you to believe that." He occasionally gave a Gaelic trill to a word—"wherrre" for "where." He savored boyhood colloquialisms. When he thought it best to leave well enough alone, he would say, "I'd just as soon leave it where Jesus flang it."

"Sometimes his words and phrases didn't look right to me in the script," Eric Sevareid once said. "I always discovered as I listened that they were right for the medium and that my changes would have been ruinous." A Murrow-dictated text might say, "I reported to you yesterday the increase in get on with the war sentiment...." It read awkwardly, almost syntactically wrong. But when he read it, he lingered slightly over "in" and ran "getonwiththewar" together like one word. The phrasing made the country's impatient mood unmistakable.

Once, when Murrow was not able to deliver his own script, he gave it to Douglas Edwards. Edwards felt that he handled the job poorly. Murrow's texts were like parts in a play written with a particular actor in mind. The lines did not work for someone else. And Murrow was both the playwright and the actor.

He had been raised in a world of concrete experience—feeding pigs, driving plow horses, firing shotguns, cleaning game, cutting timber. He had grown up on farms and in forests. And he tended to see things in concrete images. In his broadcasts, small incendiary bombs fell "like a fistful of white rice thrown on a piece of black velvet." Blockbusters went off "like great sunflowers gone mad." Seen from a bomber, fires spread in Berlin "like butter on a hot plate."

He kept a nice editorial distance by eschewing the repeated "I" in his broadcasts and originated instead the much copied "this reporter." If he believed a thought was best expressed through a classical allusion, a quote from Shakespeare or Marcus Aurelius, he used it. He did not, as he was told, assume that the audience was a collective 12-year-old. He was willing to let the listener work a little, to exercise the mind.

The voice was appropriate to the man. He had a dark magnetism. A BBC colleague, Godfrey Talbot, said of Murrow, "Ed had an intensity even before he opened his mouth that made you look twice. You know, the sort of man who saw through a brick wall.... He was a piercing man, piercing in the eye, in the inner calmness...." Winston Burdett said of Murrow entering a crowded room, "There was a shock of recognition, and what they instantly recognized was a man of stature. There was something sovereign about him."[19]

In his work, he was more than a virtuoso. He was the actor-manager, the player-coach, the talent and the talent scout. The people he enlisted shared a rugged intellectuality. They burned with his belief in the new medium. They shared his inquiring turn of mind. The hallmark of a Murrow broadcast by him or one of "Murrow's Boys," as they came to be called, was the determination to find the significance flowing beneath the cold facts.

A few of Murrow's Boys were, like Howard K. Smith, inherited. Most were his discoveries, an astonishing concentration of talent, most of whom had previously never touched a microphone. The people he hired in the London period alone included Winston Burdett, Charles Collingwood, Bill Downs, Richard Hottelet, Larry Le Sueur, Paul Manning, Eric Sevareid, Bill Shadel, Charles Shaw, and William L. Shirer. They created the standards for radio and later television journalism which were to give CBS news its durable supremacy. His stamp was unmistakably on them. They were indeed Murrow's Boys.

They were not, however, a selfless band of brothers. With success came friction. Ed complained to Janet that some of them "were getting swelled heads." He wanted to assign Howard K. Smith and Richard Hottelet to Germany. Sevareid said, "It will be a disaster. They don't speak to each other. When they do, they fight." Ed wrote home, "It's interesting to see these boys I helped develop....some get money mad, others want fame and some, like Downs, just go on doing an honest job...."

Whatever they felt toward each other, their unanimous adoration of Murrow was remarkable for such individualistic, often vain, personalities. As Collingwood put it, "...the people who worked for him had the most unstinting loyalty to him. The thing they most wanted to avoid was to make him unhappy, to feel they had let Ed down."

Theodore White, a later friend of Murrow's, observed, "Ed held to a certain standard of integrity. He had a remarkable sense of human pitch." White found Murrow and Henry Luce "the two best choosers of men I ever knew."

Still, Ed was dissatisfied with the product they produced. He wrote a colleague, "I gnash my teeth at this business of doing four or five minute spots from here which means one must deal really with headline stuff. There's no opportunity to talk about the fundamental things that are happening which cast a shadow over future happenings...." It was a complaint that could virtually be carved in granite to serve journalists in commercial broadcasting for all time.[20]

He was leaving England and, he assumed, his career behind a microphone. He would never leave this country entirely. England was in his bloodstream. Here, in a real sense, his life had begun. He had woven his reputation out of the stuff of England's contemporary history. The British spirit and style fitted him like his own skin. It was apparent in his dress, in his pleasures, in the understated speech he favored, in the values he emulated. Lady Reading said of him, "Ed possessed the three qualities every Englishman treasures above all others and wants for his son. He was absolutely fearless, had some ethical values and was very generous." John Daley worked with Ed at home before the war and later in England. The Murrow he found in London, he said, "aspired to be an English gentleman. I thought of him as Sir Edward."

When he had first come to England as a college student, his attitude had bordered on bemused contempt. He had found the country a "relatively unimportant island off the coast of Europe." He had found the people "slow, indifferent, complacent." He had been converted to love and admiration. What he said he admired most was that England had won the war without losing her soul. Two weeks before war had been declared, he had heard someone say over the BBC, "The greatest threat of the totalitarianism concept is that it forces those who fear it to imitate it." He had thereafter used these words to measure England's behavior as she shook off the successive blows. He had been astonished in the early days of the Blitz to watch the House of Commons spend two days debating the rights of enemy aliens held on the Isle of Man. He had been moved by the regard shown for the beliefs of conscientious objectors in a country expecting to be invaded any day.

On March 10, 1946, he made his last broadcast from London. He spent the previous hours wandering the city alone. A three-day blizzard had left five-foot-high drifts in the streets and in the ruins of bombed-out buildings. The first winter of peace had been brutal. A few days before, the government minister handling food supplies had flown to Washington to plead for aid to head off famine. Murrow, as he prepared to leave, felt like a deserter. He came back to the office and dictated his text to Kay Campbell. Howard K. Smith watched him and thought Ed looked tense and remote. Ed took his script to the BBC where the recently removed sandbags had left a damp-looking stain around the building. He went down the now unguarded stairwell to Studio B-4.

That night, he talked about a moment in D for Dog during the raid over Berlin. The plane had been corkscrewing madly. The crew was hurling boxes of tinfoil strips, called "window," out of the hatch to confuse

German radar. He recalled how "One of the crew said to me over the intercom, 'Mr. Murrow, would you please pass me another package of window.' That is what he said—please—and it seemed so natural that I forgot about it till we returned to base.

"I am persuaded," he went on, "that the most important thing that has happened in Britain was that this nation chose to win or lose this war under the established rules of parliamentary procedure." He ended the broadcast, "and now, for the last time, this is Edward R. Murrow in London."

When he finished, an engineer went into Studio B-4 and cut the cable to the big, old-fashioned microphone he had used. The BBC news staff had prepared a plaque and had it affixed to the base of the microphone. The words read, "This microphone, taken from Studio B-4 of Broadcasting House, London, is presented to Edward R. Murrow who used it there with such distinction for so many broadcasts to CBS New York during the war years, 1939–1945."

He accepted the tribute and could not hide his tears. He later observed, "This is the only trophy I have ever kept and I have received many...the most touching thing that ever happened to me....This I value above anything I have."

Days later, Ed, Janet, and the baby left 84 Hallam Street, the charmed address that had survived the war without a scratch, and they flew home to America.[21]

CHAPTER 17

The Reluctant Executive

The CBS that Murrow returned to in the spring of 1946 was vastly changed from what he had left in 1937. It was a far larger, more complex, richer enterprise. But the deeper difference was in the spirit of the corporation; and that had come about because of changes in the heart of Bill Paley.

In the thirties, Paley had boasted to a congressional committee that CBS devoted three-quarters of its time on the air to unsponsored public-service programming. In a 1934 statement, he rejected the pandering motive of simply giving the public what it wanted. Radio had too much power for good to set its sights so low. Radio, he said, ought "to reserve some program space to offer what the program director believes people would like if they had an opportunity to know about it. In these periods for instance, go cultural programs supported in the beginning by minorities—with a view to educating majorities to wider appreciation of their excellence...." Paley and Paul Kesten, the man he chose to replace Ed Klauber, carried on long discussions about the uplifting force that radio could be and that CBS would be.

When Paley came home from the war in 1945, Kesten excitedly presented him with his plan to realize their dream. Paley described Kesten's proposal in his autobiography: "In essence, he proposed turning CBS from a mass medium into an elite network, beamed at ten or perhaps 15 million homes rather than 30 million. He wanted CBS to become 'the one network that never offends with over-commercialism, in content, in quantity, or in tone....that presents superb and sparkling entertainment...an important forum for great public figures and great public issues, for education, for thoughtful and challenging presentation of the news and the issues growing out of it.... To be the network that is never corny, blatant,

243

common, coarse or careless, that is always bright, stimulating....' He wanted to find new affiliates which would agree to give CBS a solid block of ten hours of network broadcasting a day and then to find advertisers who would sponsor these nationwide programs. 'Perhaps it will strike you, Bill, that I've merely expressed briefly the things we've told ourselves we've been—or wanted to be—these many years....'"

It was a beautiful idea, what discriminating people had believed all along that radio should be, a miracle that would use its magic to raise rather than flatten public taste.

But either Kesten's or Paley's memory of the dream was flawed. Or Bill Paley had changed. Kesten, he said, had it all wrong: "What his plan amounted to was giving up the fight against NBC and giving up a national, cross sectional radio network, for a narrower, specialized network of dubious potential." Paley's goal was just the opposite. As he put it, "I was determined that CBS would overtake NBC as the number one radio network. I was not satisfied with second place." In Paley's reckoning, number one had a simple, unmistakable definition, the biggest audiences. And the route to mass audiences, to the highest ratings, was popular entertainment, pleasing the crowds, even if it meant displeasing the critics.[1]

Yet Paley was far too complex a man to be satisfied by profits alone. He believed that he could have it all, that he could overtake NBC in terms of sheer audience size, number of affiliates, and earnings on the one hand and still win the Peabodys with people like Ed Murrow on the other. He wanted both. And he was willing, if need be, to use some of the profits from one kind of programming to subsidize the other. He could surpass his commercial rivals *and* hold his head high among his more cerebral friends.

He was still number two, but steadily closing on NBC. He had pulled off coup after coup, luring top shows, the vastly popular *Major Bowes Amateur Hour,* and top entertainers Al Jolson and Eddie Cantor, away from NBC. He possessed an unerring divining rod for talent. Early in the war, he had gone to see a movie, *Ship Ahoy,* featuring the Tommy Dorsey band. He thought the vocalist was marvelous, though he had no billing. Paley had his people track the singer down and signed Frank Sinatra to a CBS contract. At the time that the public-service Paley was persuading Murrow to take over the news operations, the showman Paley was angling for the hottest comedian in radio, Jack Benny. It took Paley two years of courtship and contractual legerdemain, but in the end he eventually wooed Benny from NBC to CBS.

To Paley, building the profit-making side of the network was not an onerous, unavoidable chore. This was his talent, and he loved using it. He took enormous pride in his skill. Like the Hollywood moguls he admired, he delighted in playing the unseen force who controlled the famous faces and voices who were demigods to the public, but simply properties to a media baron.

He made an art, even a science, of scheduling, juxtapositioning programs like pieces on a chessboard to outwit and outflank the competition. He developed strategies, "defensive scheduling," for example, which meant pitting his strongest shows directly against the competition's best; and "offensive scheduling," grouping his best shows together on an evening when the opposition's schedule was weak. The objective in either case was the same, to capture the largest audiences. Numbers provided a hard-to-contest answer to the question, who was number one? Quality was an elusive, subjective measure, dictated by a handful of media critics. And try selling that to sponsors and stockholders.[2]

Stockholders were people whom Paley now had to consider. While Murrow had been away, CBS had passed from a privately held company to a corporation whose shares traded on the New York Stock Exchange. The change was significant far beyond the fact of dispersed ownership. It dictated the objective of the corporation. To Murrow, even to Paley in the beginning, what mattered most was what came out of the speaker. But to stockholders, what mattered was what came out in the profit and loss statement. Profits were earned through advertising, and advertising revenues depended on audience size, not Peabodys won. Public stock ownership made absolutely clear that CBS was, above all, a business. Stockholders could be perfectly happy with the company without ever listening to what it broadcast—if it earned profits. Thus, Paley, the man who had created the network from virtually nothing, was no longer fully its—or his own—master.

Not long after Paley had returned from the war, Norman Corwin remembered riding the *Chief* from Hollywood to New York and running into the chairman on the train. They talked about the dramas that Corwin had written for radio, and Paley said, "...you've done epic things that are appreciated by us and by a special audience. But couldn't you write for a broader public? That's what we're going to need, more and more. We've simply got to face up to the fact that we're in a commercial business." Culture did not uplift audiences; it lost them.[3]

Paley's new vice president for public affairs took up his duties at 485 Madison Avenue in the spring of 1946. Murrow was determined to succeed in the job, even like it. He lifted his standard before the public: "That radio in a democracy must be more than an industry, more than a medium of entertainment, more than a source of revenue for those who own the facilities. Radio, if it was to serve and survive, must hold a mirror behind the nation and the world. If the reflection shows racial intolerance, economic inequality, bigotry, unemployment or anything else, let the people see it—or rather hear it. The mirror must have no curves, and must be held with a steady hand." It hardly sounded like the "commercial business" that Paley had described.

Still, Paley was as good as his word. He gave Murrow a free hand to make his standard real. Ed immediately began experimenting with new possibilities for radio. He launched *As Others See Us,* an examination of what the foreign media were saying about America. He began a series eventually entitled *You Are There,* great moments in history recreated as breaking news stories, complete with interviews of Napoleon or Lincoln. He created a CBS documentary unit. He was attempting to provide, over commercial radio, programs of a substance and depth that would, a generation later, be aired almost exclusively on public broadcasting. Bill Paley continued to support him. Paley might be out snaring the singers and the comedians all day long, but he listened to and he liked what Murrow was producing in the public affairs schedule. And he beamed at what his intellectual friends said about CBS's superiority.

Ed's favorite among his early creations was *CBS Reviews the Press.* It was, in a sense, an enlightened form of revenge. He had seen radio kicked around as a stepchild by the newspaper critics as long as he had been in the medium. He was aware that to the press, radio was merely a gadget providing free entertainment, and a legitimate target for critical barbs when it pretended to be a fount of serious journalism. But if newspaper critics could pass judgment on broadcasting, why should radio not do the same with the press if, as Murrow wanted to believe, they were coequal forms of journalism? Thus was born *CBS Reviews the Press,* as Murrow described it, "an objective examination of the press. . . . we firmly believe that freedom of the press and freedom of radio are inseparable and that mutual criticism will benefit both." Unspoken was the message that if radio could constructively criticize the press, it had at last come of age.

Murrow admired a brilliant if erratic broadcaster and writer named Don Hollenbeck. Hollenbeck had a checkered past. He had worked for AP and quit. He had written for the innovative *PM,* and the newspaper folded. He had worked for NBC and been fired. He had worked for ABC twice and had been fired twice. But Murrow saw in Hollenbeck an original mind, deeply held convictions, and an arresting radio style. He hired Hollenbeck to do *CBS Reviews the Press* over the network's flagship station in New York City, WCBS.

Hollenbeck analyzed racism in a *Daily News* story that described an alleged assailant, not by name, but only as "a negro." He exposed exaggerated newspaper stories of welfare clients being booked into luxury hotels. He made enemies, particularly in the Hearst newspaper empire, but Murrow backed him.[4]

Ed remembered the GI journalist and ex-high school French teacher whom he talked to at Hallam Street just before leaving London. The man had a remarkable grasp of the national French character. David Schoenbrun had stayed on in Europe after his Army discharge and had done a few broadcasts as a CBS stringer. Murrow had him tracked down in an unheated apartment in Prague in the middle of a blizzard. Schoenbrun read Murrow's wire to his wife in disbelief: "If you are interested in being CBS News' Paris correspondent, please call me collect soonest." Schoenbrun telephoned Murrow in New York and said, "I don't know why CBS is paying me. I ought to pay to be your Paris correspondent." Murrow told him, "Don't worry, Buster. You'll pay plenty. We intend for you to earn your keep."

Later, Murrow explained to Schoenbrun his approach to reporting: "Dig down deep into your story; get fully into it and let it get fully into you. When you know what you want to say, say it as clearly and briefly as you can. When you reach a conclusion, put it forward, even if it runs counter to the prevailing wisdom. Do not seek to be different or contentious, but do not shrink from it."[5]

Schoenbrun became another of his boys. They were bound to him, if not to each other, by bonds that went beyond superior and subordinate. Ed was godfather to the Sevareids' twin sons, Michael and Peter. Larry Le Sueur was godfather to Casey Murrow. Janet Murrow was godmother to Bill Shirer's daughter, Linda. Some CBS staffers complained that they were a closed corporation. There were mutterings along the seventeenth floor that a reporter had scant hope if he were not part of Murrow's circle. One outsider complained, "He couldn't get it into his head that some of the others were just as good."

His good days on the new job involved bringing fresh program ideas to life and hiring gifted reporters. But the good days were few. The greater part of his time was spent in an unending succession of meetings, of immersion in matters that bored him stiff. He told Janet, "[I] never take the right papers...never know what the Hooper rating is on any show....still can't speak the language of these executives." He was besieged by people with the slimmest claims on his friendships and even slimmer talent, begging him for jobs.

He had to mediate fights. Douglas Edwards found it impossible to please his immediate superior and took his troubles to Murrow. Murrow spoke to the man and thereafter Edwards found that all was well. He asked Murrow how he had solved the problem. "I suggested," Murrow said, "that he be more gentle with those of us who have been out in the heat of the day."

He was not an incapable administrator; he was an unhappy administrator. He had the touch, but he lacked a taste for the work. While he did it, he exercised his authority with force and authority. Howard K. Smith recalled a time when Murrow came to London on a film negotiation. "CBS had a deal with Alexander Korda on a film and as the man in London, I had carried out the negotiations. We met with Korda, and I said, 'Sir Alexander, let me explain our viewpoint to you.' I saw the first cold flash of anger I'd ever had from Ed. He just stepped in and said, 'I'll talk about that.' And he took over the meeting. Ed didn't like anybody to displace him as number one."

Ed wrote E.O. Holland, by now retired from Washington State and elevated to president emeritus, "It's true that I am having some small difficulty in returning to the obscurity from which I emerged. But, in due course, I suppose the fact that I was once a broadcaster will be forgotten. So I am enjoying the anonymity of the job very much indeed, although some of the administrative details, I find less than interesting." His distaste was sharper in another letter: "The administrative end has ridden me like a piano on my back."[6]

He had plunged so quickly into the executive maelstrom on his return from England that he felt he had still not come home spiritually. That spring, he and Janet left eight-month-old Casey with an English nanny at Janet's parents' home and set out for a two-month journey of rediscovery of their native land in a huge black Lincoln equipped with an early portable telephone.

After living so many years in a war-worn island kingdom, the vastness and wealth of America staggered him. He remembered a sign he had seen in Texas, "El Paso 986 miles." He calculated that this distance within a single American state equaled the distance from England to Yugoslavia. He recalled a train where he had seen forty war brides in a dining car, their plates heaped with more meat than they would see in a week in their native lands.

He saw no old men pulling wooden plows through the fields, no old women bent under burdens of firewood, no one wearing shoes cut from old tires. As he and Janet crossed Indiana and Ohio, they looked out on well-fed farmers, and their wives and children in brightly colored clothes, and tractors silhouetted against the horizon. He wondered, did his countrymen envision all this as their good fortune or simply their due?

They drove to the state of Washington, where Ed was to give the commencement address and receive an honorary doctorate in law at his alma mater and visit his parents in Bellingham. While he was at Pullman, preparing to deliver the speech, his mother called with a message in the Ethel Murrow mode: "If you wish to see your father alive you'll have to come right away." This time her alarm was not exaggerated. Roscoe had suffered a stroke. Ed asked the college president to read the speech for him, and he and Janet drove immediately to Bellingham in heavy rain. They spent the next three weeks helping his mother look after Roscoe after he was released from the hospital. The stroke had left him completely paralyzed on his right side. His speech was impaired. He was supposed to carry out a regimen of physical therapy, but he gave it up after a few weeks. Roscoe Murrow was to spend the rest of his life in a wheelchair, tended by his wife.

Ed arranged to pay for Roscoe's nursing. But there was nothing more to be done. He and Janet returned to New York to what was becoming his own bureaucratic purgatory.[7]

Bill Paley was not unaware of Ed's growing discomfort. But while Paley respected a talent for journalism, far more significant in his scale of values was the exercise of executive power. That was what a first-class man did. That was where an Edward R. Murrow belonged. Still, Paley genuinely wanted Ed to be happy. They were friends. They were seeing a good deal of each other socially. The Murrows often went out to Kiluna, where, Janet recalled, the Paleys' guests "took their croquet very seriously." In the evenings, the men played poker. There was good talk. They saw movies provided by Paley's Hollywood producer friends, movies not yet released to the public. Bill kept urging Ed to take one of the houses on the estate as a weekend retreat. But Ed was working with Paley every day. He did not want to be at his beck and call on weekends too. And, Dorothy Paley detected, Ed did not like all the people he met at Kiluna. If the other Paley guests were people of accomplishment in their own right, Ed mixed well with them. But toward Paley's purely socialite friends, those whose sole distinction was to live in wealth and ease, Dorothy recalled, "You could sense a certain disdain, that he looked down on them."

Dorothy liked having the Murrows out. She found Janet a good, decent, intelligent woman who rationed her conversation and uncomplainingly "took a back seat to her husband." Bill Paley was also more of a listener. Thus, when the two couples were together, much of the conversation was between two more expressive personalities, Dorothy and Ed. Ed, she thought, seemed to find an assertive woman an unexpected phenomenon, something that he did not know quite how to handle, rather like a beautiful portrait that suddenly started talking.

Dorothy Paley was a keen observer, sensitive to the nuances in Ed's treatment of men and women. "One night," she recalled, "we had gone out to dinner. Bill was driving. Most of the conversation was again between Ed and me. Bill missed our driveway and I said something like 'You don't know your own way home.' I didn't say it with any malice, just made a remark. Ed lit into me. I had stepped out of place. I wasn't supposed to criticize Bill." Ed was not subservient toward Bill, she said, "but he did not set out to displease him. When Ed and I were talking, he would disagree vigorously. With Bill he was never confrontational. He was more tactful."

From time to time, Paley would ask Ed if he really wanted to stay on in administration. He told Ed that whenever he wanted to go back on the air, the door was open. Ed would answer, "No, Bill. It's fine. I'm perfectly happy."[8]

He was not. He brought his bad moods home at the end of the day, muttering that he wanted out. Janet would say, "Then why don't we go back to the West." He would then shift the burden to her back. "You couldn't be happy in a tar paper shack," he would say. She suspected by now that she would be far more adaptable to a tar paper shack than he would.

What he hated most about the job was having to fire people. "It seems," he commented to a friend, "whenever a guy is being considered for dismissal, he has a sick wife in the hospital or he's just started to make payments on a new car. I'm just not built for that sort of thing...." When he had to fire someone, he said, "I couldn't sleep for days afterwards."

Yet he carried out the task with surgical swiftness. Dallying over an execution, trying to prettify the ugly, only added a layer of hypocrisy to his discomfort. He simply laid out the employee's deficiencies in plain speech and said it was over.[9]

The Paul White situation had become intolerable. In the past, Klauber had tolerated White's bouts of drunkenness because White, when sober, had done a remarkable job in building CBS news. But now Murrow was CBS news, and Klauber was gone. White dissipated whatever sympathy his position might have won him by outrageous behavior. "Paul started drinking more after Ed became his boss," Bill Shirer recalled. Howard K. Smith came home briefly from London, and the Smiths, the Le Sueurs, and the Whites went to dinner at the Ambassador Hotel. As Smith described the evening: "White was knocking things over. He fell on the floor. The waiter wouldn't serve him. I took him up to my hotel room. He started opening Coke bottles on the door, chipping away the woodwork....It was terrible." White claimed that he drank to ease the pain of chronic arthritis. Jim Seward thought White was easing the pain in his heart.

The debut of the evening news sponsored by Campbell's Soup was an auspicious moment for CBS. After turning the program down himself, Ed had tried to persuade Campbell to accept Joseph C. Harsch, a distinguished journalist, if not a particularly radiogenic personality, who had come off the *Christian Science Monitor*. Campbell had balked. Bob Trout, elegant of voice and an able newscaster, was Ed's next candidate. Trout was more to Campbell's liking and a happy compromise.

Robert Trout with the News Till Now, as the program was called, was to be the centerpiece of CBS news coverage, much heralded in the industry press and boasting a $1.5 million annual budget, the most expensive such program in radio. The staff was deep in talent and resources, with thirty-five reporters, four wire services, and a five-person research team. *Newsweek* magazine hailed *The News Till Now* as "one of the most carefully prepared news programs ever to hit the air. The first brainchild Edward R. Murrow has put on the air since he became CBS News' head."

Murrow nervously awaited the opening of the program in his office. He watched the sweep hand on his wall clock touch 6:45 p.m. Paul White came on the air introducing *The News Till Now*. White was audibly drunk. Murrow was horrified. As soon as the program ended, Murrow, in hoary CBS legend, is said to have gone down to White's office and fired the man on the spot. However the execution was performed, ten years of undeclared war, uneasy truces, and false camaraderie were at last over.

Out from under Murrow's shadow, White appeared to regain control over his life. He went to work in broadcast management on the West Coast. He wrote an excellent text on radio journalism, *News on the Air*. In it he paid Murrow tribute: "...it seems fantastic to recall such jobs as those turned in by Murrow during the Blitz and after his bomber flight over Berlin [a broadcast White had initially opposed]....his decision to aban-

don the microphone for executive work was a distinct loss to spoken radio."
White and Murrow thereafter exchanged friendly letters. White opened
his to "Muggsie Murrow" and signed himself "Butch White." White died
in 1955 of emphysema and heart disease at the age of 52. The following
year, the Radio and Television News Directors Association created the Paul
White Award for persons distinguished in broadcast journalism.[10]

But at the time, Murrow had fired White for sufficient good cause.
He had warned the man repeatedly about his drinking. Still, the experience left Ed with a bad taste. As Janet remembered the moment, "Firing
Paul White literally made Ed sick." White was a frontiersman of early
broadcast journalism, as significant in his way as Murrow. The year before, when he was on top and Murrow was his subordinate, White had
won his own Peabody for the CBS news operation. That White had destroyed himself, through drink, through insecurity and envy, was small
consolation to Murrow. It was he who had to deliver the coup de grace.
He did not shrink from it. But he hated that part of his job.[11]

The White discharge was merely painful to Murrow. The next major
departure from CBS was to be a trauma.

If Ed had a true friend, and he allowed for few, it was Bill Shirer. In
their professional dreams and goals they were soul mates. Together they
had virtually invented the radio foreign correspondent. They were politically compatible, men of liberal bent who hated the fascistic streak in men
and nations.

Since coming home from Europe seven years before, Shirer had done
well. He had authored a best-seller in *Berlin Diary*. He had his own Sunday
afternoon program of news analysis sponsored by the J.B. Williams Company, well-heeled makers of shaving soap. He had a prestige address on
Beekman Place in Manhattan and a farm in Connecticut where the Murrows were frequent guests.

But by the spring of 1947, the J.B. Williams Company had grown
dissatisfied with Shirer. Shirer's strength was the intelligence he brought
to his commentaries, the cogency of his analysis, his lucid writing. He was
hardly a charismatic radio personality. And his ratings had fallen off in
recent years. Williams wanted a change. And it fell to Ed Murrow to break
the news to Shirer. Ed approached the matter with the masculine bonhomie that was the social currency in their circle. He told Shirer that he was
recommending to Williams that it take Joe Harsch, whom Ed now had
working in the CBS Washington Bureau. Murrow joshed Shirer, "I'm sure
you'll agree your replacement is no worse than you are." He would find
another time slot for Shirer, he said.

Shirer took it in good part. "It's no problem," he told Ed. "Call my
agent, Herb Rosenthal, at Artists, Ltd. There are two or three sponsors
who are dying to get the program."

But CBS did not immediately find another sponsor. Since Shirer's
contract with CBS still had eighteen months to run, Murrow sought to

assign Shirer another, but unsponsored, time. The loss of a sponsor meant a huge drop in Shirer's income. And so, in his next Sunday broadcast, Shirer announced that he was resigning from CBS. "This issue," he said "in a sense is much more important than I am, especially in these times. The important thing is that a soap company can decide who cannot be heard on the air." To Shirer the root of his problem was not ratings or an uninspiring voice. It was political. He was being "gagged" for his liberal views. Shirer's was in fact one of the few voices swimming against a growing conservative tide in those early postwar years. He said unflattering things about the exquisitely corrupt regime of Chiang Kai-shek in China. He questioned the Truman Doctrine of containment to combat communism in Greece and Turkey. These were views outside the conventional wisdom, and to Shirer, CBS was obviously truckling to a soap merchant out of political cowardice.

Shirer's charges stung Murrow. The idea that a sponsor could have a commentator thrown off CBS for his political philosophy was a damaging blow to the network and to Murrow's own sense of journalistic integrity. What Shirer had described amounted to censorship by economic pressure, a strangulation of free speech as reprehensible as repression by a dictatorship. The charge could not go unchallenged. Murrow issued a statement to the press denying that either the J.B. Williams Company or the sponsor's advertising agency, J. Walter Thompson, could order a change of commentators. Instead, Murrow announced that CBS was replacing Shirer with another commentator of the network's choosing, the distinguished Joseph C. Harsch. "We believe that Mr. Harsch, with his long experience in Washington and abroad, will improve Columbia's news analysis in this period." "Improve" his program? Murrow's words were like being stabbed through the heart to Shirer. He took them as a public insult, all the more painful because they had been uttered by his friend.

Murrow had, in fact, touched on the crux of the issue, the quality of Shirer's Sunday program. The soap maker's decision to replace Shirer had, in Murrow's view, merely forced the issue to a head. For some time, the word among CBS insiders had been that Shirer was coasting on his reputation, ignoring the legwork that must undergird solid news analysis. Howard K. Smith, who had an affection for Shirer as a charming rogue, had nevertheless written Murrow that while he and Shirer had been covering the war crimes trials at Nuremberg the year before, Shirer had behaved like a prima donna. Shirer had demanded special transportation. He grumbled about the meals and rooms. And when Smith needed help, "Bill didn't feel well."

Ed too had revealed an earlier urge to cut Shirer down to size. Eric Sevareid remembered Shirer coming to London toward the end of the war and attending a dinner that Murrow gave at the Connaught for Harold Nicolson and Brendan Bracken, both then members of Parliament and close to Churchill. As Sevareid recalled the evening, "Bill's book had been a big success in the States, while Ed was getting thinner and more exhausted in London. Bill had been holding forth at some length when Ed interrupted him brusquely. He turned to Nicolson and Bracken and said, 'Now let's hear from someone who knows something about Germany.' You could watch Shirer's face turning red."

Of Shirer's weekly program, Sevareid recalled, "The show had been getting weaker and weaker until it was embarrassing. He'd go through the week's news a bit, quote Walter Lippmann. That was it. The program had no bite." Charles Collingwood thought Shirer had become "a stuck whistle. He wasn't analyzing the news. He just kept preaching his beliefs over and over." Murrow was later to describe his own conclusions in a letter to Harold Laski: "For your own private information, Bill had become lazy. Nearly twenty percent of his copy consisted of readings from newspapers and magazines. The size of his audience had decreased steadily in the past three years. He spent seven consecutive weekends at Lake Placid last summer, and whatever the benefits of Lake Placid might be, it is not considered the ideal place from which to report and interpret world affairs." Murrow also included a check for £50 in the letter for the hard-pressed Laski.

Murrow told Collingwood, "The trouble with Bill is that he thinks because a million people hear what he says, that he's therefore a million times smarter than he is talking to us." But from another quarter, Shirer heard himself described, not as a lazy reporter, but as a martyr for free speech, a hero who was being hounded out of broadcasting for his outspoken liberalism. And the sound was sweet to a proud man whose work had been maligned. The Voice of Freedom, a group devoted to defending liberal commentators, threw a picket line around 485 Madison Avenue to protest Shirer's resignation. Jack Kroll, the feisty director of the CIO's Political Action Committee, threatened to file a formal protest against CBS with the Federal Communications Commission over the Shirer affair. A delegation of clergymen, Protestant, Catholic, and Jewish, called on Bill Paley to complain about the treatment of Shirer. A telegram studded with celebrity names attacked Murrow. Even Jimmy Sheean had signed it. Most mortifying to Ed, Archibald MacLeish, the poet who had sung his praises at the Waldorf testimonial dinner five years before, now wrote of his sadness that Edward R. Murrow was on the wrong side of an issue involving freedom of speech.

Shirer welcomed the support, though some of his supporters left him distinctly uncomfortable. He was aware that among those pickets marching around 485 Madison Avenue were likely members of Communist-front organizations exploiting him for their own ends. Still, in his position it was far easier to be persuaded that one was a hero rather than a slouch.

As for Ed, as Janet recalled, "I had never seen him so overwrought." "What should I do?" Ed asked Bill Downs, whose blunt judgments he so valued. "Bill Shirer's my friend." Downs was of the view that Shirer had dug his own grave.

What Murrow did was to propose a peace pact. He and Shirer met in the bar of the Hotel Berkshire. They were two old comrades with too much time spent together in the trenches to let it end this way. They agreed that both of them had been pressured into foolish postures. They managed to work out an accommodation whereby Shirer would stay with CBS and harassment of the network by Shirer's strange bedfellows would cease. They returned to Ed's office and drafted a statement to issue to the press putting an end to an ugly affair. When they finished, they took the statement to Bill Paley for his approval. Murrow handed Paley the draft and said with a relieved smile, "Bill, we have an agreement."

There were in that room three proud men, not the least proud being William S. Paley. Bill Paley did not like having to cross picket lines to get to his own network. He did not like being thought a Fascist by clergymen who knew nothing about broadcasting. He did not like being threatened with government investigations by rabble-rousing labor leaders. Above all, he did not like, indeed he could not fathom, disloyalty in an employee.

The year before, while in Chicago, Bill Shirer had met William Wrigley, the chewing gum magnate. Wrigley was an admirer of Shirer's and a friend of Bill Paley's. Wrigley wanted Shirer to do a news program sponsored by his company. It would require, however, Shirer's moving to Chicago. Shirer turned Wrigley down. He had refused Paley's friend for a reason beyond Paley's comprehension. He had refused for *personal* reasons. Bill Shirer simply preferred to live in New York. Until that moment, Shirer had known only the charming Paley, the admirer and rewarder of his talents. But that day, for the first time, he had witnessed the cold fire of Paley's displeasure. He described the experience in the thinly disguised character of "Robson" in his later novel, *Stranger Come Home:* "The grin would melt away, his face would harden, and the warm laughing eyes grew cold." After the Wrigley incident, things had never been quite the same between him and Paley. And now, with the latest discomfiture that he had caused CBS, Shirer came to Paley's office bearing a peace pact, but with his bank account of goodwill virtually depleted.

Paley brushed the statement aside. He told Shirer, "As far as I'm concerned, your usefulness to CBS has ended. You're out."

Stunned, Shirer looked expectantly to Murrow. As he later recalled the moment, Murrow's voice was subdued, and Ed said to Paley, "We had an agreement. But if you don't like it, Bill, you're the boss." That was all.

Shirer listened in disbelief. His friend had gone over to the despised side? To the side of money and power? In his view, Murrow had put ambition above loyalty to a friend. Shirer saw his whole future collapsing before him. All that he had constructed over the past ten years was falling apart in this room. He saw a life of comfort slipping away from him. As he was later to remark, "I was making a lot of easy money."

On the last day of March 1947, Bill Shirer made his final broadcast for CBS. In Shirer's recollection, the control room was jammed with CBS executives nervous over what he might say, presumably ready to pull the switch if he went too far. But he went quietly into the night. Of his troubles with the network, he commented only, "This is not the time or place to discuss them."

The final break between the two men was to occur in public. The Overseas Press Club invited both Murrow and Shirer to speak at a luncheon in mid-April, two weeks after Shirer's departure from the network. Murrow had prepared a text that eschewed personalities. But his objective was clear, to repair the damage done to CBS's image by the Shirer episode. "It will be a dangerous day for American broadcasting," his text read, "if we ever reach the point where they who have the most money are allowed to dominate the discussion in the market place of ideas."

Richard C. Hottelet was present at the press club and recalled hearing Shirer speak first, repeating the argument that he had been sacrificed by CBS for his politics. Shirer pointed to his recently won Peabody and numerous other broadcast awards to prove that he was no laggard. "Ed threw away his prepared text," Hottelet recalled, "and he said, 'Yes, prizes. I did my best work long before I won any prizes,' and then went on to make the case that Shirer had forced him to, that it was not Shirer's politics but his work that he had called into question. I never heard Ed more forceful or eloquent than on that day."

Whether or not Shirer had indeed grown lazy and let his program slide was almost beside the point. A larger issue had been at stake. Three months before the Shirer affair, the television critic for *The New York Times*, Jack Gould, had criticized the networks on the very question of sponsor influence over the choice of newscasters. Gould deplored the kind of people the networks put on, the "soap opera journalism of a Gabriel Heatter and patented emotionalism of a Walter Winchell, Drew Pearson, or Bill Stern." Gould decried the disappearance of analysts of depth and seriousness, particularly those of liberal bent. Gould was repelled by the idea that a sponsor should determine who was to report the news over radio. He likened the situation to advertisers in a newspaper picking the reporters. Murrow, in his position as the head of news for CBS, had felt at the time that he must come to the network's defense. *The Times* agreed to give him a full column to rebut its television critic. Murrow wrote, "Under no circumstances will we sell time for news and permit the sponsors to select a broadcaster who is not wholly acceptable to us."

It was a good half answer. But it conceded that sponsors could indeed pick newsmen. The network exercised only the right of veto. Gould was saying that the news should be totally divorced from sponsor influence. Murrow the broadcast journalist would have agreed. But Murrow the corporate executive was not free to say so.

Then, the Shirer incident had exploded, seeming to confirm specifically what Gould had deplored in general. It was indeed true, after dropping Shirer, that the J.B. Williams Company also turned down Murrow's choice of Joseph C. Harsch as a replacement. The company decided to get out of the glamourless sponsorship of news commentators entirely and seek more popular attractants for its shaving soap.

Most of Murrow's colleagues had understood what he had done in the Shirer case and why; but this was small solace to Murrow. On the night that his agreement with Shirer had fallen apart, he had gone out to dinner with an advertising friend, Joe Katz, Katz's son, and Katz's daughter-in-law, Edith. Edith Katz was awed to be in the company of the famous man. But she was astonished to see someone who had heretofore been a public icon to her so nakedly emotional. "He had much too much to drink," she remembered of the night. "And he just kept talking to my father-in-law, hardly noticing us, pouring out his feelings over this terrible thing that had happened to him and Bill Shirer. I remember there were tears in his eyes."

He had lost a valued, quite possibly his closest, friend. Shirer thereafter had been heard to refer to Murrow as "Paley's toady." Shirer was later to tell a magazine reporter, "Murrow destroyed my career for a while, but he got me writing books which was a blessing in disguise." Shirer was also convinced that Bill Paley had blackballed him so that he could not get work on another network. Of the years that followed, Shirer's wife said, "Times were very tough for us after Bill left CBS."[12]

The Shirer episode had been the sorriest chapter in the unhappy history of Murrow the executive. He was willing to fly bombers into hell for what he believed. But the battles in the executive suite left him spiritually drained, limp with the fatigue that comes from fighting unfelt causes.

Not long after Shirer's departure, Paley said to Murrow, "I really have the feeling that you're not happy as an executive. I think you should go back on the air." Murrow still protested that he was fine. But Paley pressed him: "You're either kidding me or you're kidding yourself. You know there's nothing between us that says you can't change your mind and go back to broadcasting." Murrow was quiet for a moment and then said, "Bill, if you order me to go back on the air, I will." Paley answered: "Then I'm ordering you." Murrow's face slowly broke into a smile and then a grin such as Paley had not seen in the eighteen months since Ed had taken on the vice presidency.

Looking back over his tenure as an administrator, Ed later pronounced a harsh judgment on himself. It was not the ordeal of firing people, the corporate compromising, the piano on his back of administrative chores, that had defeated him. He said: "It was my major objective to establish a clear cut and overt editorial policy. I failed." Hard-news reporting was simple enough. But what he believed that he had failed to find was that elusive boundary separating legitimate news analysis from bias. In truth, he had been an innovative news executive, a good manager of people, a capable administrator. Even the wrong man in a job can do it well with enough intelligence and energy. But he had indeed been the wrong man, and now the ordeal was over.[13]

CHAPTER 18

Listen to Murrow Tomorrow

For Bob Trout, landing *The News Till Now* represented the peak of his long career. He had spent seventeen years in commercial radio, virtually two-thirds of the medium's life. He was widely admired both as a man and as a broadcaster. Like Murrow, his voice and style lent weight to what he said. Trout was a gentleman, urbane and witty, without a trace of malice in his wit. With his tailored tweeds and good manners, someone had described him as "looking like a British colonel in mufti."

Murrow's first choice for the coveted news program had been Joseph C. Harsch. But Campbell's Soup did not want Harsch. When Ed proposed Trout, company executives first wanted to know if he was Jewish. Murrow later said of this question, "I replied that if they refused him on those grounds, they would have to put it in writing...and I would make such use of it as I saw fit....This is a very nasty world."

Trout then fell into the curious embrace of Ward Wheelock, who owned the advertising agency that handled Campbell's Soup. Wheelock was known around CBS as "the poor man's George Washington Hill," a reference to the advertising man of flamboyant legend. Wheelock was obsessive and theatrical, and he was a social climber. Murrow first met him in England during the war, where Wheelock had served as a lieutenant colonel in the Army. Back home after the war, he badgered Ed to use his influence with Ellen Wilkinson, then heading the Ministry of Education in the Labour government, to get his two young sons into Eton. That, to Ward Wheelock, was social arrival.

Campbell had been one of Ed's sponsors during the war, and Wheelock was disappointed when Murrow turned down the nightly news program for the executive job. Before Wheelock would accept Bob Trout, he dragged him to Philadelphia to the dean of the University of Pennsylvania Medical School for exhaustive medical tests. Trout was negotiating a ten-year contract, and Wheelock wanted to make sure that the 37-year-old Trout would last.

After he was hired, Bob Trout was no longer one reporter in the pack. He had the highest-budgeted news program in radio. He had that ten-year contract. He had his own office, his own writers and researchers, and a private secretary. A decorator named Wally was engaged to do his office. CBS and the sponsor spared no effort to put Trout in the strongest possible position to go up against formidable competition, NBC's enormously popular Lowell Thomas.

Wheelock led Trout to a new standard of living. Wheelock had a 60-foot schooner. He knew that Trout loved sailing. So he tracked down the sister vessel of his boat and persuaded Trout that he too could now afford such a craft. Trout went into debt to buy the schooner.

Trout went on the air with *The News Till Now* in April of 1946. Less than a year and a half later, in the fall of 1947, the bottom fell out. Murrow informed him that he was going back on the air, and Ward Wheelock wanted him to take over the Campbell nightly news.

Trout, with over eight years left on a ten-year contract and financially overextended, was stunned. What the contract meant, he later observed drily, was that, "Once a year for ten years, they had the right to fire me."[1]

Eric Sevareid learned that Murrow was coming back on the air from a story in *Variety*. Sevareid felt betrayed. At about the time that Trout had taken over *The News Till Now*, Murrow had asked Sevareid to go to Washington as CBS bureau chief. He had balked. He hated administration and was terrible at it, he told Murrow. Murrow understood. He was not happy with office drudgery himself. But, he argued, he would be "up there in New York backstopping everybody." Sevareid yielded. He became the Washington bureau chief, "only because Ed asked me to take it."

When Murrow resigned as vice president, Sevareid felt that he had been lured out on a limb and then had watched helplessly as it was sawed off. Years later, lingering traces of resentment filtered through his recital of the episode: "I was broken up. Almost sat there and wept. He hadn't told me! There was no warning of this. He didn't tell anybody." That was what hurt most, the assumption that he and Murrow had been close, and then finding out that the closeness was one-sided. Sevareid went up to New York to see Ed. As he described the meeting, "We sat around, sort of looking at one another, not saying much. Having a drink. And, finally, he said something like, 'Well, sorry you had to read about it in the papers. I should have told you.' You could always tell when he felt guilty about something. He wouldn't bull it through, but he'd make it up some way."

As he recounted these long-ago events, Sevareid gazed off as though still trying to pierce that opaque personality: "He was a difficult man, a strange man in many ways. But, he was the most extraordinary, exciting man I ever worked with or knew.... He just made our whole professional lives for us." To have been let down by Murrow had been a source not so much of anger, but of disillusionment.[2]

For Trout, his world changed overnight. The royal treatment was yanked from under him like a rug, leaving him on a bare floor. He no longer had his own writers, his researchers, his private secretary. Wally, the office decorator, disappeared. Trout had a meeting with Ed and Jap Gude, the agent for both of them, to discuss Trout's future. As Trout later described the occasion, "Ed didn't say to me, 'Bob, you're a big star, don't worry.' Instead he said, 'From time to time, you can do this or that for me.' He spoke to me as though I was just one of the pool reporters." Trout was not being fired. He had merely lost his stripes. Still, he felt that he had no choice but to leave CBS, his home for so long, and take an offer to join NBC. (Trout later returned to CBS and later still went to ABC, where, as of this writing, he is still an active correspondent.)

Murrow displayed, Trout said, neither regret nor apology for having bumped him off the air. That was his approach to the unpleasant, just the way he had fired people when he had to, a swift, surgical incision, and be done with it. He was not one to bare his uncertainties or inner turmoil. Thus, his behavior could appear cold and manipulative. The self-flagellation and agonizing were reserved for his private hours, for sleepless nights.[3]

By the time Murrow took over *The News Till Now* (now called *Edward R. Murrow with the News*), Lowell Thomas was no longer the opposition. Paley had lured Thomas to CBS. The major competition now, indeed the highest-rated newscaster on radio, was Murrow's cross of old, H.V. Kaltenborn, since 1940 with NBC. When Murrow came back on the air, H.V. had a Hooper rating of 10.9, virtually double Trout's last rating. The Murrow program was shifted to 7:45 p.m., pitting Ed directly against Kaltenborn, defensive scheduling in Paley's parlance.[4]

Ed was virtually oblivious of the financial provisions of the Campbell contract. He left the negotiating in the hands of Jim Seward, who still looked after his personal financing. Jap Gude, of Stix and Gude, was Murrow's agent, but now handling Ed's interests outside of CBS. To have Seward bargaining for Murrow was a peculiar arrangement. Seward by now had risen to become CBS's vice president for business affairs. He negotiated contracts on behalf of the company with the other correspondents and their agents and with labor unions. But in Murrow's case alone, Seward represented Murrow *and* the company. In effect, Seward was negotiating with himself. He would come up with a salary figure, and Murrow would say, "That's fine, Jim, if you say so."

The arrangement was as much a tribute to the relationship between Paley and Murrow as between Seward and Murrow. Paley was satisfied to let the man whom he paid to negotiate on his company's behalf simultaneously represent Murrow's interests. The issue of conflict of interest was never raised. In any case, Murrow had scant reason to dislike the terms of his employment. In leaving administration to go back on the air, he virtually tripled his salary. He was to be paid $2,500 a week and given another $20,000 a year for travel expenses.

What he did concern himself with was the broadcasting features of his contract, and here he was a hard-nosed bargainer. He would not tolerate, he told Wheelock and Campbell, any commercials in the middle of his program. He was not going to have his reporting of world events interrupted by a paean to the virtues of cream of mushroom. He would allow commercials only at the beginning and end of the news. Campbell was buying Ed Murrow to sell soup; the middle commercial was customary and important. But Wheelock had been angling for Murrow for nearly two years, and Murrow was adamant about the middle commercial. Campbell grudgingly yielded.[5]

Ed happily abandoned the executive suite for the grittier habitat of a reporter. His new office on the seventeenth floor was small and was sparsely furnished. He worked at a metal desk with chrome legs and a veneer wood top, standard issue from CBS office services. On the desk were two photos, one of Janet and one of Casey. The walls were virtually bare, save for two framed homilies by the nineteenth-century folk philosopher, Josh Billings. One read, "It is better to know less than to know so much that ain't so." The other read, "Silence is a hard argument to beat," a thought that Murrow's colleagues believed he had imbibed at his mother's breast. The only other nonfunctional item in the room was his old Broadcasting House mike that the BBC staff had given him. If Murrow's office could be said to be furnished, it was with reading material. Books were heaped on his desk, the most recent titles in history, biography, and the political and social sciences. A table was piled high with magazines skewing across the political spectrum. He had a stand-up desk installed where he preferred to read. Winston Churchill had a stand-up desk at Chartwell and had persuaded Ed of the merits of this reading posture. He had become accustomed in England to buildings with no central heating and kept the thermostat at a temperature his visitors considered Arctic.[6]

He set forth a credo on his first broadcast: "This program is not a place where personal opinion should be mixed up with ascertainable facts. We shall do our best to resist the temptation to use this microphone as a privileged platform from which to advocate action." And he warned off sensation seekers: "I think it is safe to say that no considerable amount of time will be devoted to news originating in divorce courts and maternity wards."

That he intended to avoid personal journalism was not quite so. He would call it analysis, bowing to Paley's prohibition on editorial opinion. The absorbing news question is not who, what, where, or when, but why. And Murrow intended to allow himself ample room to explore the why.

Edward R. Murrow with the News opened with Murrow delivering the day's hard-news items. He saved the end of the broadcast for a six-minute commentary. He called it his "tailpiece," a term borrowed from the BBC. Sometimes he called it "my pulpit." Or he used that segment to interview government officials, educators, politicians, and scientists to add understanding to a story's bare bones. At the end of the tailpiece, the announcer returned with, "Mr. Murrow will be back in a moment with his word-for-the-day." The word for the day was a device to hold the listener through the final commercial, an apt quote, an epigram, a witticism that brought the gist of the tailpiece to a sharp point. The word might be from Socrates or Josh Billings, Marcus Aurelius, or Will Rogers. In closing, Murrow resurrected his old London sign-off, "Good night and good luck." Finally, the announcer would invite the audience to "Listen to Murrow tomorrow."

When he had taken over the program, Bob Trout had urged him to retain two of his staff, Jesse Zousmer and John Aarons. Ed did, and eventually they would lead him into one of the most controversial enterprises in his career. But that was several years off and in another medium.

Jesse Zousmer was a tall, silver-haired, handsome, hard-driving man, an amalgam of suavity and toughness. One colleague described Zousmer as an "elegant ass kicker." He had come to CBS during the war from the Scripps-Howard newspaper chain and liked to boast that he was the first radio newswriter in the country to earn a five-figure salary. He was a phenomenal newswriter whose prose was like a closely woven fabric. He "defied anybody to take a word out of it" without diminishing the content.

Zousmer's sidekick, Johnny Aarons, resembled Zousmer only in energy and ambition. A short, balding, cigar-chomping barrel of a man, he hid his sensitivities behind a wise-guy facade. He had come to CBS after writing news at *The New York Times* station, WQXR. Aarons was the researcher on the evening news. Finding the word for the day was among his responsibilities, and he might spend up to six hours a day ransacking *Bartlett's* and a shelf of reference works before finding a phrase that satisfied Murrow.

Ed wrote the tailpiece. He dictated it, as he had in London, and to the same person. Howard K. Smith had inherited Kay Campbell and two other secretaries on taking over the London office. "They soon let me know," Smith recalled of the succession, "that I was trash after the great man." Smith wrote Ed, "I've got a Rebecca complex. We've got to do something about these three girls." Murrow proposed a solution that, to Kay Campbell, was an answered prayer. He asked her to come to America and work for him again. Smith wiped the slate clean by firing and replacing the other two Murrow-era secretaries.

Kay Campbell hung a large, framed picture of Ed on her new office wall. It embarrassed Ed, but it would have been more embarrassing for him to say anything to her about it. And he continued to maintain his professional distance. She was still Miss Campbell, except at parties, where his formality toward her would have been awkward. Only then was she Kay.[7]

Murrow made one genuine friend on his news program; and the manner of the making revealed his wary movement toward another human being. Bob Dixon was a lean, rangy, easy-talking, easy-moving man without, it seemed, a reflective bone in his body. He had the air of a cowpoke, and he wore cufflinks with pistols engraved on them. Actually, Dixon had been raised on a farm in the East. He was no fool, but intellectual was the last word on earth that anyone would apply to Bob Dixon. His pleasures were hunting, fishing, and amusing the staff with a bottomless fund of jokes. Dixon's personality was summed up in the expression "a waitress kidder."

He had started his professional life as an actor with touring companies and in summer stock and radio. By the time Dixon met Ed Murrow, he was earning a comfortable living as a free-lance announcer. He came to know Ed while working, in the parlance of the trade, as a "hitchhiker." Dixon delivered commercials between programs to which he otherwise had no connection. One of his spots came just after *Edward R. Murrow and the News.* And so he would arrive in the studio toward the end of the newscast. He found himself drawn to what Murrow had to say, and as one who made his own living by his voice, recognized that he was in the presence of a master. He started coming in earlier, sitting quietly in the corner of the studio to catch the entire broadcast. After delivering the word for the day, Murrow would often glance in Dixon's direction for a reaction. He found Dixon a good gauge, grinning broadly when the word struck home. Then Murrow would get up and leave with no more than a nod.

One evening, Ed was leaving the studio after Dixon had delivered his commercial and remarked on his way out, "Not bad for a guy with a speech impediment." Dixon instinctively knew enough to respond in kind and kidded Murrow back. The locker-room exchanges became a habit, with Dixon giving as good as he got—"You made sense tonight, Murrow, nonsense." The familiarity astonished the studio crew, which tended to treat Murrow with awe.

In time, Dixon came to understand that Murrow's gibes were a way of reaching out. "He didn't know how to show affection," Dixon said, "so he behaved like Charlie Brown in *Peanuts.* When he saw a girl he liked, he didn't know what else to do, so he hit her."

After a while, Dixon recalled, "He started inviting me back to his office for a scotch after the show. He'd start talking about horse harnesses, bridles, traces, whiffle trees, bits, circingles. We'd both come off the farm and I was the only one who knew what he was talking about. He'd say, 'Bob, do you know what the eveners are supposed to be hitched up to?' Partly it was a put-on, just to annoy the city boys like Zousmer and Aarons.

That's how he and I talked together. But other times, people like Sir Stafford Cripps from England would show up in his office, and I'd just sit there and watch an entirely different Ed Murrow."

Murrow's announcer on the news was Ernest Chappel. Of that relationship, Dixon observed, "Chappel came on strong with Ed. He had a big farm over in New Jersey and he was always pestering Ed to spend weekends at his place. He also had a habit of greeting Ed when Ed got to the studio with 'Hello, boy.' Ed did not particularly like that." After a year with Murrow, Ernest Chappel left the news. His replacement was Bob Dixon.

Ed liked to take Dixon hunting and fishing with him. Once in the out-of-doors, they never spoke of the office. CBS personalities were never mentioned. No serious issue ever intruded. Should something of moment accidentally slip into the conversation, Dixon would say, "Don't discuss that profound stuff with me, cause I'm iggerent." And Murrow would respond, "Damned if you ain't."

Arriving at his office in a black mood, Murrow would say "Ah, Deexohn [the French twist had become Dixon's nickname]. Have you any funny stories for me today?" And Dixon would oblige. After a broadcast in which Murrow stumbled over a phrase, Dixon ended the program with his standard closing, "Listen to Murrow tomorrow." After the slightest pause, he added, "He wasn't so hot tonight." Murrow looked up, horror-stricken. His eye went instantly to the red on-the-air light. The light was off. Dixon's timing had been exquisite. A slow grin broke over Murrow's face; then he howled with laughter.

He occasionally needed playmates, men with whom he could share intellectually uncontaminated pleasures. Dixon served perfectly. As Ed Bliss, a staff writer, put it, "Bob Dixon was Ed's relief from the Chancellor of the Exchequer." The Dixon friendship reflected the perennial wavering in his scale of values. What was real and what tinsel? Who was honest and who false? What really mattered? Power? Fame? Ambition? And in moods when he suspected that the answer was none of these, he sought out the escapist companionship of a Bob Dixon.[8]

Soon after he returned to the air, Ed arranged a broadcast from London. He had once asked Bob Trout, "Tell me, how long before you're no longer homesick for England?" The country held an almost visceral attachment for him. He seized the chance to go back to cover a foreign ministers' conference and Princess Elizabeth's marriage to her cousin Philip Mountbatten, duke of Edinburgh. Ed brought Janet with him. They saw Lady Milner and the Laskis. They visited Ronnie Tree and his new wife at Dytchley. Tree had just that summer married Marietta Peabody Fitzgerald. Ed sought out R.T. Clarke, and Clarke told him what peace had meant for his old associates at the BBC. With the continued rationing and food shortages, a healthy diet was hard to maintain. They were often sick, R.T. told him. He had lost 23 pounds since Ed had last seen him.

Ed met with officials of the Labour government, Ernest Bevin, and Herbert Morrison. They looked shabbier, grayer, wearier than he remembered them, a reflection of England eighteen months after winning a war. Ed and Janet called on the Churchills. After the war, Janet had been awarded the King's Medal for Service in the Cause of Freedom for her work with Bundles for Britain. In a sense, she was still carrying on Bundles. In the England of 1947, little luxuries were hard to come by, even for an ex-prime minister, and Janet had been sending occasional food parcels to the Churchills ever since the war. On this visit, they came bearing canned hams, and to Winston's rapture, Havana cigars.

Ed tried to bring to his coverage of the royal wedding at Westminster Abbey the same mood-stirring touches that he had given his wartime dispatches: "Through the entrance of this chapel, I can see Elizabeth adjusting her gown. The duke of Edinburgh is glancing back nervously to see how his wife's train is making out. It had caught earlier and caused some confusion. But the two pages seem to have things well in hand." It was not "Orchestrated Hell." And the broadcast almost seemed Murrow in parody. But people were tired of the war. Real-life fairy tales of princesses and Prince Charming were exactly what they wanted.

Back home, Ed broadcast a dialogue that he had overheard at the London airport.

CUSTOMS OFFICER TO YOUNG, RED-HEADED YORKSHIREMAN: Are you emigrating?

YORKSHIREMAN: Yes.

CUSTOMS OFFICER: Your ration books, please.

YORKSHIREMAN: You're welcome to 'em, chum.

Of the flight back, Ed remembered, "...seventeen hours is a long time to sit here and listen to the motors. You can't read all the time and you can't sleep, and so you just sit there and look out at that flat, gray motionless night....your thoughts go back to other nights watching the exhaust flames on a bomber in German skies....you remember the close companionship, the finger tip team work of the young men who fought in the air, the feeling that there was no distance separating the tail-gunner from the bombardier, or the navigator from the pilot. It was always and invariably as though each man's shoulder was touching the others. And then, a good-looking stewardess comes along and asks if you'd like a cup of coffee or a magazine."

The war years had become the permanent backdrop against which the rest of his life would be acted out. If he witnessed something powerful and dramatic, he would compare it to a similar sensation during the war. If a moment was serene—a stewardess offering coffee on a routine commercial flight—he was struck by the contrast with the terse repartee of tail gunners and pilots flying a sky red with flak.[9]

The Murrows were living on East 74th Street now in the house that Jim Seward had helped them find, four bedrooms and quarters for a domestic staff. They needed the help. Ed's hours had regularized only slightly since England. He started out broadcasting the evening news twice, at 7:45 p.m. and again at 10:45 p.m. for the West Coast. His position also required a good deal of entertaining. In order to meet the social demands and Ed's odd hours, they had help working in shifts, a day cook, a second cook for dinner, a waitress for evenings, a chambermaid, and a laundress. He was a long way from Beaver.

Norman Corwin, the radio dramatist, described an evening at the Murrows: "Most parties are fragmented clusters of small talk. That was not a Murrow party. Ed did not dominate, but he had a way of centering the talk on some serious issue and drawing everybody in."

Ed's home life took on a pattern, urban, sophisticated, privileged. Branch Rickey became a friend, and so when Ed watched the Dodgers, it was from the club president's box. He was there at Ebbets Field on a spring afternoon in 1947 watching Jackie Robinson dismantle the race barrier with sheer talent and courage. Robinson stole home, and Ed found himself on his feet cheering wildly. He later confessed that not until that moment did he feel that he had finally come home.

He became a fan and tried to explain the Dodger mystique to his listeners: "When the Dodgers lose, there is sadness in my heart. Ask not the reason for this devotion to the Dodgers. Brooklyn is no Grecian glade, Rickey no major prophet. A Dodger fan is first and foremost an unreasonable man, and it would be indelicate if not hazardous to ask him why he is what he is. There are times when I think my affection for the Dodgers stems more from their fans than from the ball club itself. There is that delicate blending of assorted prejudices, combined with fervent faith, that utter lack of reason, contempt for logic, the juvenile ability to be hurt or made happy by the outcome of a mere ball game, that makes the Dodger fan a noble and noisy citizen."

He joined the Century Club. His old friend, Professor Shotwell from Columbia, and Elmer Davis put him up. Before the war, Ed had not felt that he could afford the Century. Now, the club became his favorite haunt for mixing business and pleasure, much as the Savile had been abroad. A lunch date with Murrow usually meant lunch at the Century Club.[10]

Because he was late in becoming a father, he became a doting father. Not immediately, however. Mewling infants did not interest him. In the early months, he would hold Casey gingerly and surrender him at the first squall. But as the child began to grow, to take on individuality, Ed became entranced. He had Casey, at age 2, burble a greeting during his Christmas Day broadcast.[11]

Now that they were CBS colleagues, Lowell Thomas kept inviting Ed to bring his family out to a cottage on Thomas's country place. As long as Ed had been vice president for news, he was Thomas's boss, and felt uncomfortable about socializing with the man. Only among Murrow's Boys did the social and professional lines blur. But Lowell Thomas was not one of Murrow's Boys. Thomas was an established figure in his own right, and Ed felt that maintaining his authority required some distance.

Frank Stanton had another explanation for Murrow's reluctance to mix with Thomas. While Ed had still been vice president, he had resisted Paley and Stanton when they tried to lure Thomas from NBC to CBS. "Lowell wasn't a real journalist to Ed," Stanton said. "He was just a story teller. He had his scripts written in New York and transmitted up to his country place where he read them. I argued with Ed that we needed Thomas's kind of reporting too at CBS." Stanton regretted that Ed did not try to conceal his disdain for Thomas's work, "And the rest of CBS News took their cue from Murrow."

After he went back on the air, Ed felt comfortable about accepting Thomas's standing invitation. Hierarchy was erased; they were just fellow broadcasters now. The Murrows took a month's vacation at Thomas's place. Thus, Ed discovered Quaker Hill near the little town of Pawling, New York.

Quaker Hill lay sixty-four miles north of New York City, a promontory nine miles long and seven miles wide forced up out of the earth and affording sixty-mile vistas in every direction on a clear day. There, Lowell Thomas, a man of affable arrogance, was virtual lord of the manor. Thomas had come upon Quaker Hill in 1926 and bought an old house and 350 acres there. By the time Ed became his guest, Thomas owned over a thousand acres, a thirty-five-room Georgian mansion, guest houses, and two lakes. Thomas encouraged his friends to buy on Quaker Hill. Often he sold them the land. He liked a certain kind of neighbor. Solid, successful folks. Not the socialite crowd, the patrician rich, the society column headliners. Most of the Quaker Hill people turned out to be midwesterners and westerners, like Thomas and Murrow, people uncomfortable with ostentation or glitter, yet people who could afford their comforts. As one resident described his neighbors, "We wanted to get away from the inbred, country club life. We're not a very social neighborhood here. We're kind of square. The Southampton people would be bored to death with us." Quaker Hill was not as horsey as Tuxedo Park, Bedford, or Greenwich. Not as posh as the North Shore. Its pastimes were skiing, golf, hiking, shooting, fishing. The men did some gentleman farming. Their wives gardened and planned small dinner parties. "Quaker Hill is sedate and subdued," a resident put it. "It's like country houses in England where they wear black tie to dinner, but the tie is thirty years old and so are the dresses." The whole idea was that no one need ever shout, or push, or boast, or display, because to be there, living on Quaker Hill, was proof enough of what one was. Living there said, "I am a success, but I am unpretentious, level-headed, feet-on-the ground about it."

Some 100 families lived on Quaker Hill. A few were year-round residents. Most were people from New York who came up on weekends. They were partners in Wall Street law firms, bankers, and a few famous names like Thomas, who shrank from showy celebrity. Quaker Hill was Protestant and Republican. It went for Herbert Hoover in 1932, Alf Landon in 1936, Wendell Willkie in 1940, and Thomas E. Dewey in 1944, who had a farm there. The neighbors were a little uneasy about what was going to happen in 1948 when Tom Dewey would inevitably beat Harry Truman and become President and their Eden would become the Summer White House, with tourists and media hordes descending on them.

Ed Murrow loved Quaker Hill, loved everything about it from the first, its greenness so reminiscent of Washington State, its glens and gorges, its generous views, the fishing streams and good hunting only minutes away. But he did not care for the smug conservatism of the Quaker Hill crowd. When they first started visiting, he warned Janet, "I have only one bit of advice to give you. Don't get into any political discussion with the people there." Janet was still the unreconstructed liberal Democrat she had been in her college days. Ed told her she would find few soul mates at Quaker Hill. But at least they were people who had earned their reputations and money, who did something with their lives, unlike some of Paley's Long Island set.

Ed played golf with Lowell Thomas, and off the third tee they would pass a house that Ed always stopped and looked at longingly, a rustic lodge of log construction commanding a view across the Hudson River deep into the Catskill Mountains.

In the summer of 1948, Ed and Janet were on a train from New York City bound for Washington, D.C., where Ed was to talk to the British ambassador to the United States. By sheer coincidence, they ran into Thomas Murphy, a judge from New York City, and the judge's wife. The Murphys owned the lodge that Ed so admired. As Janet later recalled this encounter, "By the time we reached Washington, I knew we had bought the house." Neither she nor Ed had ever set foot inside it.

Property was not sold casually on Quaker Hill. Real estate agents knew enough, before closing a deal, to clear the prospective buyer with Lowell Thomas. Thomas was, in the Murrow's case, delighted to give his approving nod.

Ed liked to refer to the place as a "log cabin." It was indeed made of logs, solid cedar. The house had been built by Finnish carpenters brought to the United States expressly to build the Finnish Pavilion at the 1939 World's Fair. The Murrows paid $47,500 for the home and fourteen acres, rather on the high side the neighbors thought. The lodge had four bedrooms and two maid's rooms. When the Murrows came up for the weekend, they brought along Anna Marie, the upstairs maid from 74th Street, to look after Casey. When Casey Murrow grew a little older, he said that the wind rustling through the eaves of the house said to him, "rumblewood, rumblewood." And so the house became Rumblewood. And the Murrows became part of the world that Lowell Thomas built.

Quaker Hill boasted a nine-hole golf course, designed by Robert Trent Jones, the land and a barn for a clubhouse provided by Lowell Thomas. The fireplace in the clubhouse was built of stones that Thomas had brought back from his world travels. Most Quaker Hill families belonged to a boat and bathing club that Lowell Thomas had started, which gave them the right to use Lake Hammersley, his lake. Thomas also operated a ski lift and rented saddle horses. The center of community life was the Akin Hall Association, Lowell Thomas president. On Sundays, Dr. Lankler came over from the Presbyterian church in Cortland, New York, and preached a nondenominational service in Akin Hall. Afterward, the minister played golf with Lowell Thomas.

The Murrows settled into the pattern of weekend country living. They joined Thomas's golf club, annual dues $250. They joined the Akin Hall Association. They bought their groceries at Bartholomew Valenti's in nearby Pawling. They stopped for gardening supplies at Gordon Van Dyke's. On Sunday, they joined the station wagons parked outside of Abe Ginsburg's to pick up the Sunday *Times*. Janet went to church in Quaker Hill. Ed did not.

Ed played on the Quaker Hill softball team, the Nine Old Men. Thomas had chosen the name back in 1938 as a gibe at Roosevelt's Supreme Court packing plan that year. Eddie Rickenbacker, the fabled aviator, pitched. Robert Montgomery, the actor, played first base. Gene Tunney and Westbrook Pegler were also on the roster. One of their regular opponents was James Melton's Spark Pluggers. The metropolitan opera star's team arrived at the Quaker Hill diamond in Melton's collection of Stanley Steamers, Locomobiles, and Pierce Arrows.

Ed's favorite refuge was the nearby Dutchess Valley Rod and Gun Club. Bob Dixon remembered going one Sunday to the club with Ed for some pheasant hunting and duck shooting. They had come back to Rumblewood while Janet was away. The two men sat in front of the fireplace drinking scotch. Numerous scotches as it turned out. Ed had retreated into one of his silences. Dixon never questioned these withdrawals, never broke the silence. He simply waited uncomplainingly for Ed to come back. "We didn't need to talk," he said. Suddenly, Murrow snapped out of his reverie. He remembered that he had been invited to a neighbor's to hear Tom Dewey make a presidential campaign speech over the radio. Murrow ordered Dixon to go with him. Dixon protested that he had no clothes other than the slacks and sport shirt he had just changed into. Murrow loaned Dixon a sport jacket and dressed similarly himself.

When they arrived at the host's home, Dixon was chagrined to find all the men in black tie. Murrow, however, seemed to delight in his conspicuous nonconformity. Everyone was huddled around the radio. Lowell Thomas had recently been coaching Tom Dewey on his radio delivery. As they listened, Dixon heard a gentle snoring. He turned to see Murrow, hands folded across his chest, stretched out on the floor, sound asleep. A little low-grade iconoclasm now and then, tweaking his smug Quaker Hill neighbors, exercised his conscience and amused the rebel in him. Then, on another weekend, he would have *his* guests, Lord and Lady Salisbury, Bobbety and Betty, the Paleys, or the Trees, up to Rumblewood.

If he did not love his neighbors, he loved the sanctuary that Quaker Hill provided. Of his weekend drives from the city to Rumblewood, he said, "When I get as far as Brewster, I start to breath again." Janet recalled, "You could see him start to unwind." Friends from the city who visited him at Quaker Hill met an undiscovered Murrow. He may have been born to the flannel shirts, the Levis, and clodhoppers that he favored on weekends. Still, on this congenitally elegant man they somehow seemed an affectation. But as soon as he began showing the Collingwoods, the Sevareids, and the Le Sueurs around his property, a rare serenity came over his furrowed face. It seemed, for the first time, that they were seeing the man in his natural habitat.[12]

CHAPTER 19

Enter Stanton

The outcome of the 1948 presidential election was preordained. Harry Truman must lose and Tom Dewey must win. The public opinion polls made this conclusion inescapable, and Frank Stanton, now the president of CBS, believed in polls. A month before Election Day, Stanton had gone to lunch with the pollster Elmo Roper, and Roper showed him his latest figures. Stanton could read a poll as well as anyone in the business and told Roper, "I think you ought to forget about any more polling. This election is all over."

At Quaker Hill, Janet Murrow went to a neighbor's for lunch. All the talk was about what dresses the women were going to wear to Tom Dewey's inaugural ball. Some of the Quaker Hill crowd had already made reservations in Washington hotels for the inaugural festivities. Janet, the only Democrat present, felt like an impostor.

Election Day fell on November 2. At midnight, early returns gave Truman a slight lead. At four o'clock in the morning, Truman was 2 million votes ahead. But on NBC, H.V. Kaltenborn saw through the purely technical nature of Truman's edge and explained why he was still fated to lose. At 10:30 in the morning, Tom Dewey conceded the election to Harry Truman. For millions of Americans, the Depression was still too fresh a scar on the memory. And so they had voted not so much for Truman and against Dewey, but they chose between specters who haunted the recent past; they voted for FDR and against Herbert Hoover.

Ed Murrow had been no more prescient than H.V. Kaltenborn. Earlier in the year, he had told Howard K. Smith, "I think I'll vote for Norman Thomas." Smith told him it was terrible to throw a vote away in a sentimental gesture. "But," Murrow answered, "I can't vote for Truman, and I can't vote for Dewey. He had described Truman in a broadcast as

270

"dressed in the ill-fitting cape of Franklin Roosevelt." To Murrow and other Roosevelt worshipers, that was Truman's great sin. He was not Franklin Roosevelt. In the end, Ed had not voted at all.

One aspect of the Truman upset delighted him. On his broadcast the following night he said, "This election has freed us to a certain extent from the tyranny of those who tell us what we think, believe and will do without consulting us...." Two days later, he was again hammering away at the bloodless mechanics of public opinion measurement: "We know now that during recent months, many of us were taken in by something that wasn't true. We had almost come to believe that the hopes, the fears, the prejudices, the aspirations of the people who live on this great continent could be neatly measured and pigeon-holed, figured out with a slide rule....The experts and pollsters have, in fact, restored to us an appreciation of the importance, and the purely personal character of our own opinions."[1]

He scorned the market researching, nose counting, audience rating, mechanistic prodding of man's one divine aspect, his individuality. At CBS, the pollster mentality, in Murrow's vision, was embodied in Frank Stanton.

While Ed was still vice president for public affairs, CBS had carried a program called *The People's Platform.* On it, Lyman Bryson, from Columbia Teachers College, led a panel discussion on issues of the day. Stanton proposed including on the panel an Elmo Roper, a George Gallup, a polling professional who could say, as Stanton put it, "Now let me tell you how the people in this country feel about that issue."

Murrow's reaction was allergic. "Ed thought it was the worst thing anybody had ever proposed," Stanton remembered. "I had an uncle out West who was a journalist of the same ilk as Ed Murrow. Journalists knew what people were thinking. And they didn't need any goddamned social scientist to sit around and tell them." Frank Stanton had been a social scientist.[2]

He had started life with a far different aspiration. When he was a boy growing up in Dayton, Ohio, Frank Stanton dreamed that he would become an architect. The profession suited his natural bent, for he was a young man of both imagination and discipline, intrigued by new ideas, yet driven to impose a rational structure on them. His natural gifts surfaced early. While still in high school, he was hired by a downtown department store as a window dresser. His conceptions were so striking that he was soon earning $90 a week, a phenomenal paycheck for a boy in his teens in the 1920s.

He was admitted to Cornell to study architecture, but youthful passion overcame his ambition. He did not want to be so far from his girlfriend, and so he entered Ohio Wesleyan. He abandoned the profession, but he never abandoned his love of architecture.

He graduated from college in 1931 in the heart of the Depression.

"Things were so bad," he remembered, "I thought I'd go to graduate school and put in my time there instead of eking out an existence in menial jobs. I wrote to every school I could get an address for and offered myself for a fellowship." Ohio State University gave him a teaching instructorship in industrial psychology at $83 a month. While there, he earned a Ph.D. in the field.

Stanton had been one of those boys who tinkered with coils, oatmeal boxes, and cats' whiskers to build their own radios. As a young social scientist, he became more absorbed in why radio worked than how. "I was interested," he later said, "in how broadcasters decided what to broadcast, how they knew who was listening, who wasn't and why." Broadcasters did not know. The field was virtually wide open. And so young Dr. Stanton began filling the vacuum. His research led him to one conclusion, he believed, that was certain to excite broadcasters: people were more influenced by spoken advertising than by written advertising. He wrote to NBC and CBS, sharing his discovery. The response from NBC was immediate, a neatly typed letter from a network executive saying, as Stanton saw it, "Thanks for your interest, little boy. Now go on about your work." From CBS he heard nothing.

Then, after he had given up all hope, he received a long letter riddled with typing errors and corrections, obviously typed by no secretary. The writer was Paul Kesten, then in the CBS promotion department. Stanton's findings fascinated Kesten. He offered Stanton $55 a week to come to New York to work as a CBS research specialist. The Ph.D. was still not making what the high school boy had earned. Nevertheless, to Stanton, Kesten's offer "was like throwing raw meat to a lion." He went to CBS in September of 1935, virtually days after the arrival of another young man, Edward R. Murrow. Murrow was then director of talks. Stanton rose swiftly to become director of research.[3]

"I was a nosey kind of guy," Stanton said of himself during that period. "I sought out people who were interesting, and I found Ed Murrow interesting, though I thought he was a bit of a knock-it-off intellectual. We were not close, although we got along well enough. But, even then, he was skeptical about the audience measurement work I was doing. He wanted no truck with anybody who talked about anything as vulgar as a program's ratings."

Murrow went off to Europe and achieved a great public success. Frank Stanton stayed home and achieved a quieter if no less spectacular ascent in the network. He was the perfect corporate man, high intelligence fueled by high energy and run by steely self-discipline. He was a workhorse, the kind of employee who is already at his desk when everyone else arrives, including his secretary. He worked Saturdays, often on Sundays. To Stanton, a vacation was not an escape from work but an intrusion.

He had chosen well in his mentor. Kesten rose in power at CBS until, in 1943, Paley made him president, and Frank Stanton was at Kesten's side. By age 33, Stanton was Kesten's chief lieutenant and a CBS vice president. By 1945, he was named general manager and elected to the board of directors. While Paley was away during the war, Kesten and Stanton ran CBS.

Looking back on his life years later, Stanton mused, "I never had any idea I'd wind up in management. What I really wanted was my own research company, political polling, consumer preferences, audience measurement. I had been doing some of this work on the side for Elmo Roper even after I went to CBS. In fact, Roper offered me a partnership." Crawling into the mind of mass man, finding what went on there, was as compelling to Stanton as wanting to know how it felt to fly a bomber through flak over Berlin was to Murrow. Both situations dealt with probing human responses, although Murrow was retailing in human emotions while Stanton was wholesaling. In Stanton's case, the fascination lay in knowing that a million individuals did not represent a million fragmented tastes or opinions, but perhaps at most a dozen clusters that a scientific sampling and the right questions could divine. He had abandoned the idea of having his own public opinion research organization quite simply because he was rising too fast at CBS. But he never abandoned his faith in the tools of the trade. He merely employed them in the service of CBS.

Soon after Bill Paley returned from the war, after he had rejected Kesten's blueprint for an "elitist" network, he lost Paul Kesten. Paley had not appreciated Kesten's lofty vision of broadcasting, but he valued the man; and he was shocked to find that the 47-year-old Kesten was so pain-wracked with untreatable arthritis that he could no longer carry the burdens of a network chief executive. But, Kesten assured Paley, he had someone who could step into his shoes at any time, Frank Stanton.

Stanton represented not simply a first-rank broadcast executive already in place, but he had another unspoken appeal. Ed Murrow may have had the same attraction when Paley lured him on to the executive floor. "I'll say this and deny I ever said it," one CBS executive has said. "But, both Stanton and Murrow were gentiles. All Jews who make it the hard way, who have to deal with Washington and public relations, like to have some Christian ornaments around them." Possibly because he had the right ethno-religious credentials, but certainly because of sheer capacity, Frank Stanton, at age 37, in his eleventh year with the company, became president of CBS on January 9, 1946.

The new chief executive officer combined shyness and toughness, personal privacy with a chilly managerial style. He was also totally self-aware: "I came into the presidency barely ten years after I had left a college campus," he later reflected. "Just about all the officers under me were twelve to fifteen years older than I was. I was a bit of a pain in the ass to them. I didn't come up through the production side. I certainly didn't come through the show business side. They were uncertain about me. I was a slide rule manager to them, in today's words, a computer freak. I had brought the first tabulating machines and Hollerith machines into CBS. I had developed the 'K factor,' a short-cut way of projecting numbers. I did it because I was too impatient to wait for the accounting department to come up with figures. I was a month ahead of everybody by using the K factor. And so top management had started to turn to me for answers that should have come from accounting. So, you see, there were things about my make up that didn't endear me to many people.

"Also, I decided I wasn't going to be palsy walsy: My dealings with the rest of the staff were going to have to be on an arm's length basis, up and down. I'd seen one man go out of that company with a broken heart because, as he told me one day, he'd never crossed Mr. Paley's threshold. I made up my mind then that I was not going to let that matter to me. I wasn't going to break down in front of anybody."

He might maintain that he intended to hold himself at arm's length from the people he worked with, "up and down." But the only person above him was Bill Paley, and the tone in which he would later describe his relations with Paley suggests that he hoped for more than an employee-employer arrangement, for more than he offered his own subordinates.

On a Saturday morning toward the end of the war, he had gone to the office where he received a phone call from Paley. Paley invited Stanton out to Kiluna for lunch. It was short notice, but Stanton's first invitation to the chairman's country seat. Only after he had hung up, did he ask himself how he expected to get out to Long Island. He did not have a car. Gas was still rationed anyway. "I hadn't said to him, 'Where is Kiluna? How do I get there?' I just said yes." He managed to get his hands on a car and find his way out to the estate. There he discovered, to his disappointment, that he was one of a crowd of guests.[4]

In the summer of 1947, Bill Paley divorced Dorothy, his wife of fifteen years. The break had been long in coming. As early as 1943, Paley had asked Ralph Colin, his lawyer, to go to Dorothy and tell her he wanted a divorce. Colin, who by then had performed every imaginable disagreeable errand for Paley, drew the line at telling his wife that she was through. The marriage had dragged on, through Paley's absence during the war years and after. And then Bill met Barbara "Babe" Cushing Mortimer, one of three daughters of the eminent Boston brain surgeon, Dr. Harvey Cushing. She and her sisters had been bred like rare roses in preparation for brilliant marriages. One sister married Vincent Astor, another, John Hay Whitney. Babe's first husband was Stanley G. Mortimer, Jr.

Babe was beautiful, an exquisite woman. She had been chosen by the New York Dress Institute in 1945 as the best-dressed woman in the world. She worked for a time at *Vogue* as an editorial assistant. But Babe Mortimer did not so much report as embody fashion. What she wore, what she did, where she was seen, set the society standard. She was fashion. She also had the allure to Paley of being a Wasp.

The parents of Ed Murrow, Ethel and Roscoe. (*Janet Murrow*)

Egbert Roscoe Murrow (*left*) at Edison High School, at the time he started calling himself "Ed." (*Janet Murrow*)

Ed, age 14, atop the outhouse in back of the family home in Blanchard. The Murrows obtained indoor plumbing after Ed went off to college. (*Donna Jean Murrow*)

Ida Lou Anderson, Ed's speech teacher at Washington State College. This severely crippled young woman was to exercise a pervasive influence on his life. (*Washington State University*)

Ed with Willma Dudley, his first serious romance, at Washington State College. (*Willma Dudley Hill*)

Ed, a senior at Washington State College in 1930 and president of the National Student Federation of America. (*Eleanor D. Williams*)

Janet Brewster, who became Mrs. Edward R. Murrow in 1934. (*Janet Murrow*)

Janet and Ed (*third and fourth from left*) aboard ship on their first trip to Europe, 1935. (*Janet Murrow*)

Ed in London about 1940, at the dawning of his fame as a radio foreign correspondent. (*CBS Photography*)

Ed with two of his earliest recruits to radio journalism, Thomas Grandin (*top*) and William L. Shirer (*bottom*). (*CBS Photography*)

"This is London." Murrow, always a two-finger typist, prepares for a broadcast. (*CBS Photography*)

The war over, Ed and Janet return after nine years in London with their son, Casey. (*Donna Jean Murrow*)

Ed, in the inevitable suspenders and Savile Row cut, in his CBS office working at the stand-up desk he preferred. (*Washington State University*)

William S. Paley, CBS founder and chairman, with Ed at Quaker Hill in the palmiest days of their friendship. (*CBS Photography*)

Ed with brothers Lacey (*left*) and Dewey (*right*) at Quaker Hill in 1949. (*Janet Murrow*)

Ed with Fred W. Friendly (*right*), his most important collaborator and co-creator of *See It Now*. (*Irv Haberman, CBS Photography*)

Ed with colleagues Charles Collingwood (*center*) and Eric Sevareid (*right*), covering Senate campaign races in the waning days of radio journalism. (*CBS Photography*)

Senator Joseph R. McCarthy in his heyday, interrogating a witness in televised Communist-hunting investigations. (*CBS Photography*)

Murrow with his "Boys" at the annual year-end roundup. *Left to right:* Bill Downs, Daniel Schorr, Eric Sevareid, Richard Hottelet, Murrow, Bob Pierpoint, David Schoenbrun, Howard K. Smith, and Alex Kendrick. (*Bob Stahman, CBS Photography*)

The siren song of war. Ed in Korea with American GIs. (*CBS Photography*)

The "other Murrow." Ed prepares to interview Marilyn Monroe on *Person to Person*. (*CBS Photography*)

Murrow with the creators of *Person to Person*, Jesse Zousmer (*center*) and John Aarons (*right*). (*Irv Haberman, CBS Photography*)

Murrow at the opening of the classic documentary on American migrant workers, "Harvest of Shame." (*CBS Photography*)

Murrow, now director of the U.S. Information Agency, as President John F. Kennedy marks the agency's twentieth anniversary. To Murrow's left, Dean Rusk, secretary of state, and Donald Wilson, deputy USIA director. (*USIA/Donald Wilson*)

Ed and Casey frolicking at Quaker Hill. (*Washington State University*)

Ed at Quaker Hill instructing Casey in pistol practice. (*Washington State University*)

Murrow, after his cancer operation and near the end of his professional career, with top USIA deputies, Donald Wilson (*left*) and Thomas Sorensen (*right*). (*Donald Wilson*)

Ed Murrow at his
ease. (*Edward M. M.
Warburg*)

Murrow at the peak of his broadcast career, in a CBS publicity
still. (*Irv Haberman, CBS Photography*)

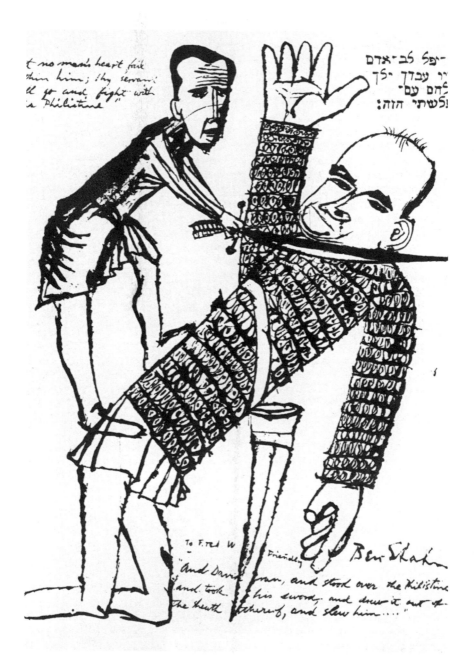

Drawing by Ben Shahn marking the moment when Murrow took on Senator McCarthy on *See It Now*. (*Bernarda B. Shahn*)

Bill Paley was mad about Babe. He courted her with all the ardor he could afford, which was considerable. When she had to spend a month in the hospital, Paley went to a different one of his favorite restaurants every night. He worked with the chef planning a special menu. The dinner was then placed in warming containers and delivered by Paley's chauffeur to the hospital, where Bill personally served Babe.

As soon as he had his divorce, Paley directed Ralph Colin to find a judge to marry him and Babe. Paley informed Colin that the wedding would be a small family affair. "Bill had always made clear that he did not want business associates as friends," Colin recalled of his association with Paley. "He said it right out." Still Colin had been Paley's lawyer since they were both young men. They had grown up together in the company. He was disappointed, he confessed, that he was not invited to the wedding.

Paley next went to Stanton. Stanton was a photography buff and Paley wanted to borrow a movie camera to film the wedding. Stanton was flattered that Bill had come to him. He loaned Paley a camera and gave him plenty of film. Paley did not extend an invitation to the wedding. Stanton too was aware that it was strictly a family affair. And so, on the wedding day, Stanton and Colin sat in Stanton's office alone toasting the bride and groom with champagne.

A few days after the wedding, Paley stopped by to return the camera and to ask Stanton to have the film developed and edited. Later, as Stanton ran the film through a projector, he discovered, yes, it had been primarily a family affair. There were no guests from the company, save Mr. and Mrs. Edward R. Murrow. Stanton told this story to Fred Friendly long afterward, and Friendly recalled, "There was still an expression of hurt disbelief on his face."

Ralph Colin softened the blow to his pride by his analysis of the Paley-Murrow friendship: "Bill liked to have Ed at parties. He liked to be seen with him. Ed was a celebrity, and much respected. But, it wasn't what I would call friendship. Ed was an ornament. But friends? Bill Paley knew everybody. But he didn't have the capacity for friendship."[5]

Frank Stanton was Bill Paley's closest associate in the company. But, Colin's view apart, Ed Murrow was Bill Paley's one genuine friend in CBS. Therein lay the rub. Yes, there was also a difference of temperament between Murrow and Stanton. Stanton, with his belief in audience research and statistical measurement, was to Murrow a "soulless mechanic." And to Stanton, there was in Murrow something of the peacock romantic. But their failure to relate well had a more visceral basis. Both men operated at the apex of the network pyramid, just under Paley. They were virtually fated to crowd each other. Paley had made Frank Stanton the president of CBS. Stanton was a vigorous and forceful executive, and all the company's lines of authority ran through him, except one. Ed Murrow walked right past Stanton's door and into Paley's office whenever he wanted something. And every time he did so, it was an affront to Stanton professionally, and a reminder of what he would never have with Paley, close personal rapport.

To Murrow, corporate decisions that placed profits and numbers ahead of quality and principles were Stanton's doing, never Paley's. Ralph Colin had observed Paley's near immunity from blame and recalled, "When Ed expressed his frustration to me, he usually blamed others, though it may have been Paley at fault. He couldn't bring himself to blame Paley." Murrow would resort to the vassal's refrain, "If only the king knew."

Paley himself later observed years after, "There's a school that thought there was a rivalry between Murrow and Stanton on account of me. I've heard that." He made the observation with a coy smile and an expression that suggested an aging beauty who enjoyed recalling two long-ago suitors who had dueled for her favor.

The rivalry between Ed and Frank Stanton expressed itself in odd alliances. In the midst of Bill Shirer's troubles with Ed and the network, Shirer had received support from an unexpected source. Stanton called him and said, "I'm all for you, Bill. I think you're absolutely right."

When Murrow left administration to return to broadcasting, he was not the only one to rejoice. Stanton was delighted. When Murrow had first taken over the news and public affairs division, it had represented to Stanton, "taking a good broadcaster off the air and making him into a poor executive." The judgment was harsh and inaccurate—but understandable. Murrow had shown disdain for Stanton in his sphere. Why should Stanton grant Murrow any competence in his?[6]

Still, Frank Stanton was not a small man. When Paley wanted Ed Murrow, his crown jewel, sitting on the CBS board of directors, Stanton thought it a fine idea, and worked out a sensible rationale: the board was supposed to represent a range of interests, yet the editorial side of the company had never before been represented. Thus, on April 20, 1949, Murrow was elected to the board.

Murrow's membership on the CBS board of directors must be seen again as a desire not to displease Paley, for the board was an unlikely perch for a working journalist. As Ed wrote Joe Harsch at the time, "A guy named Murrow—much to his surprise—was elected a member of the Board of Directors at Columbia where his counsel won't be listened to." Of Murrow's service on the board, Ralph Colin remarked, "Ed was a fish out of water. He didn't have the slightest interest in what was going on unless it directly affected his programs." It did not matter much what the board said anyway, according to Colin: "The Board was run like Paley's corner cigar store. The board never voted him down. The board was never given enough information to know if it should vote him down." As Richard Salant, another member, described the meetings: "Paley would raise an issue, then give us the correct answer. We'd all say, 'Aye.' And that was that. Ed Murrow never said a word."

Murrow's silent service was understandable given the stupefying inconsequence of much of the board's agenda. Virtually an entire meeting one day was devoted to deciding the pension the company ought to pay to Louis, the boardroom chef and waiter. Another member, Isaac Levy, teased the mute Murrow that he was getting $100 for every meeting and ought, at least, to say something. Thereafter, when Murrow spoke, Levy would appraise the Murrow contribution on a tally sheet, "$5," "$25," "2 cents."

To Murrow there was no point in pursuing his objectives through the papier-mâché power of the CBS board. When he really cared about something, he took his case directly and privately to Bill Paley. That was part of their understanding.[7]

Murrow's first full year back on the air, 1948, was a harsh year, well suited to a man of foreboding. It may be seen as the year the cold war—the term Bernard Baruch had coined in 1946 when the wartime alliance began to sunder—moved from expression to fact.

Murrow had shown a certain foresight over the ideological clash. Even before the hot war had ended, he had broadcast from Europe: "Communism is an item for export, so is democracy. The two are bound to compete." He had not, however, anticipated so belligerent a competition. Or, as he put it later, "Both the East and the West are doing what they can to bunch themselves into a fist."

He was haunted now by what he perceived as neo-isolationism in America, an insular complacency. In 1947, he gave the commencement address at Smith College and had this cheery message for young Americans about to enter the world, "We are in some considerable danger of becoming the best hated nation on Earth. We don't deserve to be. But remember that grievances are no less real because they are imagined." He repeated his pet geopolitical refrain: "We are in danger of becoming a great straggling island off the coast of Kamchatka." And in a later speech that year: "The dominant political fact of our time is that we are moving to the right while the rest of the world is moving to the left."[8]

In truth, by 1947, the United States was neither practicing blind isolationism nor taking an international hard right. It was embarked on the Marshall Plan, surely the antithesis of isolationism and quite likely the greatest enterprise in enlightened self-interest in history. The plan represented an economic strategy to innoculate the prostrate, war-ravaged countries of Europe against communism through capitalist-style recovery. The Marshall Plan also drove the wedge deeper between East and West. The Soviet Union warned the countries of Eastern Europe that if they took Marshall Plan aid, they would earn the Kremlin's displeasure. Thus, among the countries scared off was Czechoslovakia.

Shortly after the war, Murrow was reunited with his Czech friend Jan Masaryk in New York. Masaryk was no Communist, but he was taking the post of foreign minister in a coalition government with the Czech Communists. During dinner, Murrow asked Masaryk if such an arrangement with the Communists could ever hope to succeed. Masaryk said that he was optimistic. Ed was less sanguine. He told Masaryk that he doubted that any democracy could survive an embrace with Communists.

By early 1948, the Czech Communists had gained total control of the country. And one morning Jan Masaryk was found dead in the street, having reportedly "fallen out" of the window of a government building.

"They say he committed suicide," Murrow said in his newscast. "I don't know....For more than two years, he had hidden a heavy heart behind that big smile and his casual, sometimes irreverent, often caustic comment on world affairs." Ed recalled the night he had spent with Masaryk in 1938 when "his country was sacrificed on the altar of appeasement at Munich. ...When the war was over, he went home. Certain that his country had to get along with the Russians or as he used to say, 'they will eat us up,' his faith in democracy was no way diminished....I asked him why he didn't get out, come to this country where he had so many friends. He replied, 'Do you think I enjoy what I am doing? But my heart is with my people. I must do what I can. Maybe a corpse, but not a refugee.'" He was now a corpse, and the death of Jan Masaryk plunged Ed into despair. He remembered the enmities, Czech against Czech, Pole against Pole, that he had observed in the concentration camp inmates, hatreds exceeding their hate for their Nazi tormentors. Was this what all the bloodletting in Europe had been for? The destruction of patriots and democrats like Masaryk?[9]

Italy became another cold war battlefield in 1948, and Murrow went there. The country was holding elections that year, and the Communists, with a huge following among the masses and intellectuals, were conceded a chance for victory. Ed covered the campaign. The mood, he said, had a depressing resemblance to Munich in 1938. He had dinner in Rome with Howard K. Smith and Smith's wife. Ed told them that he had recently talked to General Omar Bradley in Washington and "The question is not if there will be nuclear war, but when we decide to begin it." Benedicte Smith burst into tears and fled toward the ladies' room. Howard caught up with her and said, "Don't take it too seriously. He always talks that way."[10]

In the summer of 1948, the Soviets blockaded the land and water approaches to Berlin to drive the Western Allies out of West Berlin. The United States responded with an airlift, an endless shuttle of transports flying into the city, one every three minutes, month after month, to provision the isolated outpost. Murrow went to West Germany to fly the airlift, his first flight in a military aircraft since the war. He boarded a C-54 at Rhine-Mainz and clambered over the payload of 13 tons of coal to the pilot's cabin. He was back in his element, visibly delighted, poised once again to transport his listeners to history as it happened. He later reported the moment: "You get the feeling you used to get when crossing the enemy coast with a bellyful of bombs, and then you remember you've got only coal on board....a cross wind hits you and you remember a night back in 1944. You're over Berlin in an RAF Lancaster when it was whipped around by a flak burst and the city below was a symphony of flame and smoke." He had the year wrong, but "Orchestrated Hell" was seared into his memory. For Murrow, the war would never really end.

He came back from Europe, and when he stepped off the plane in New York, he was again the foreign correspondent, trench coat appropriately rumpled, hat brim pulled low, the knowing expression on his face of one who has experienced what others only read and hear about. He was one year out of the executive suite, a happy man, or as close to that state as Ed Murrow ever came.[11]

His work routine acquired a certain rhythm. He got up late in the morning because he went to bed late. He liked to cite a character in a detective story that he had enjoyed: "He always made a point to do two things which he did not want to do as a matter of discipline. One was to get up and the other was to go to bed. I'm like that guy." He arrived at his small corner office usually after ten and spent most of the morning at his stand-up desk. There he went through *The New York Times, The Washington Post, The Times* of London, *The Manchester Guardian,* and the international edition of *The Herald Tribune.* He read leaning on one elbow, his chin cupped in his hand, a cigarette dangling from his mouth, flipping the pages with an insouciant snap.

He lunched usually at the Century Club with a guest. Lunch was rarely purely social, even if it began that way. Mary Warburg recalled a lunch for Clementine Churchill and the Murrows. With Lady Churchill was an Englishwoman, Pauline Rothschild, whom Warburg described as "an authority on fleas." As she recalled the luncheon conversation, "Ed fixed that woman with those eyes of his and proceeded to ask her one question after another until he had exhausted her rather detailed knowledge of her subject. You would have thought that the things that interested him most in life were fleas."

After lunch, Ed spent the early afternoon making phone calls, seeing visitors, and dictating correspondence. He carried on a merry exchange of memos with CBS's arbiter of pronunciation, Dr. Cabell Greet. On one occasion Greet twitted Murrow for pandering to the mob when he used a popular but incorrect pronunciation of a word. Murrow quoted Ben Franklin in defense: "Write with the learned; pronounce with the vulgar."

He created an ambiance of deceptive ease during the day. William Gehron, a young official with the Carnegie Endowment for International Peace, recalled being sent to ask Murrow's advice on a public relations problem, namely, how to deal with the fact that Alger Hiss, formerly with the Endowment, had been accused of being a Soviet spy. "I was amazed by the cubicle that Edward R. Murrow had for an office," Gehron later recalled. "But what I never forgot is that he had his jacket off and he was wearing these red suspenders—with pictures of nudes on them." Here was Murrow thumbing his nose at the pin-striped world he inhabited. It was also Murrow thumbing his nose at a side of himself. As though the raw-boned kid from Beaver, still in him, was mocking the kind of man he had become.

His visitors were surprised at the time he gave them. Here was an obviously busy man who sat with his feet propped on the desk quite prepared to indulge in what seemed a rambling discussion of whatever interested them. Only later, hearing him broadcast on matters in their field, did they realize that they had served as unwitting sources and had been wrung dry.

The serious work began at five in the afternoon. Kay Campbell would wheel her typewriter into his office where Ed dictated his tailpiece. He would already have jotted down his theme in a few key words scrawled in pencil on a yellow legal pad. He swung his swivel chair sideways, away from his desk, propped his elbows on his knees, lowered his head, and stared at the floor. In his right hand he held a cigarette that he used as a pointer to signal that he was about to begin. The words came slowly, as though they were being quarried from marble. The sentences were separated by periods of concentration so intense that the air around him seemed to crackle.

Dorothy McDonough, another secretary who occasionally took his dictation, described the experience: "He bends over in the attitude of the thinker and mumbles to the rug. Half the time he talks with a cigarette in his mouth. And if you miss something, he looks at you as though you were deaf. Then, he puts on his professional broadcasting voice, and you feel like an idiot."

The tailpiece complete, he would wander into the next-door office where Jesse Zousmer would discuss with him stories to go into the hard-news portion of the broadcast. Johnny Aarons would show him what he had harvested so far for the word for the day. Usually, by about 6:30 p.m., with one hour and fifteen minutes remaining before air time, he would return to his office for what he called "visiting hours." Correspondents would stop by for a chat, usually Murrow's Boys or others who had earned associate member status. He would pull out a bottle of Ballantine's scotch from his bottom desk drawer and pour himself and his visitors a drink, his with a splash of water from a silver carafe. He seemed, at this point, the most relaxed man on earth.

As the hour of the broadcast approached, his mood began to shift. By 7:15, he was restless, hopping up frequently to go to the water cooler. The furrows in his face deepened; his conversation trailed off in unfinished thoughts; his eyes drifted to some private place. Zousmer would pop in from time to time to discuss a change in the script required by a late-breaking news development. Aarons brought in more possibilities for the word for the day, and Murrow made a final selection. Kay Campbell showed him a final draft of the tailpiece. He changed a word or two. But usually he produced a near final draft with his first effort.

By 7:30, he was visibly tense. He locked his arms behind his head in a pose of determined nonchalance and swung his chair around so that he was facing the window, in effect, cutting himself off from the world while he disappeared into his private thoughts. Zousmer and Aarons, when they had to come in, would occasionally try to break the tension, Aarons with a bagful of wisecracks and outrageous parodies of the word for the day. Since Murrow insisted on a high tone in the news, Zousmer would amuse him by reciting the wire service stories he had left out, the trunk murders, titillating society divorces, the two-headed dog stories. Ed's amusement was brief, and he slipped back quickly into his solitude.

With three minutes left, he crushed out his cigarette and headed down the corridor. He walked with a rapid stride, his head bent and his eyes fixed at some point just ahead of his feet. His sleeves were rolled up, his collar unbuttoned, and his tie pulled down. The expression on his face suggested, as one colleague put it, "a man mounting the gallows." He entered Studio Nine, a 15- by 20-foot capsule of silence, with a glass wall front and back, one side looking out over the newsroom and the other the office of the news director, Ted Church. Inside the studio, Ed sat at a table facing the control room. Bob Dixon, the announcer, was to his left, the program director to his right. Watching through the window in Church's office were Zousmer, Aarons, Kay Campbell, and occasional visitors.

He shifted around in the chair seeking a comfortable position, partially unzipped his fly to give his diaphragm complete freedom, blew his nose, took a glass of water, and said a few words to test his voice. He sat directly in front of the microphone but avoided looking at it. His face looked stricken as Dixon delivered the commercial and intoned, "Now here is Edward R. Murrow." At the director's downbeat, Ed came in: "THIS is the news." The right leg began to bounce, discharging excess nervous energy into the carpet like an electrical ground. The sweat still poured down his cheeks, though he was doing something that he had done a thousand times before. He held the copy in his left hand, while with his right index finger he jabbed the air for emphasis.

Marvin Kalb remembered standing behind the glass in Ted Church's office and listening to the voice that he had grown up with during the war years: "When you closed your eyes, it was all so magnificently controlled. And then, when you opened your eyes, there was the sweat, the unbuttoned shirt, the unzipped fly, the bouncing leg. You were just amazed."

The program over, Ed went to the men's room and washed his face. He put on his jacket, lit his first cigarette since the broadcast, and took the elevator to the main floor of the building. A few stairs off the lobby led down to Colbee's Bar and Grill. There the Filipino bartender began to pour his scotch as Ed came through the door. Three barstools were informally reserved for Murrow and his friends. If they were occupied,

Ed Bliss recalled, "People would move aside, as though he created a proprietary right by his arrival."

Often he was joined by Zousmer, Aarons, Bliss, and others. He was silent for an unnerving period. "We knew he had begun to unwind," Bliss said, "when he would finally stop staring into his glass." Often they played liar's poker, using the serial numbers on dollar bills as the hand, with the loser paying for the drinks. If the mood struck him, Ed would tell stories. Churchilliana, real or apocryphal, were stock pieces in his repertoire. A favorite tale had the minister of trade coming to see Churchill about a request from the Russian army for condoms. "They're fighting in the Pripet Marshes," the minister explained, "and need them to keep the gun barrels dry. "Send them, by all means," Churchill said. "But make sure they're the largest we've got. And mark them all 'Size Small.'" Murrow's audience noticed that the stories were beginning to repeat themselves.[12]

He attempted to erase any traces of rank and celebrity and to melt into the crowd. He was not, except with his few intimates, particularly successful. He remained, to those who had not entered his circle, an inaccessible, even intimidating, figure. Some of those on the outside at CBS found him a shade pompous, a man of theatrical solemnity who took himself much too seriously. And they resented the exclusivity of Murrow's annointed few. Ted Church, as director of news broadcasts, was technically Murrow's boss, an authority he accepted as fictional. Church rejected an attitude around the seventeenth floor that all talent orbited around Murrow's sun. "Ed has collected the goddamnedest bunch of camp followers," he complained privately, "and not one of them is worth a damn."

Bill Slocum, a CBS staffer, was the reputed organizer of a waggish reaction to the cult of Murrow, the "Murrow Ain't God Club." All club members were automatically vice presidents, a gibe at the proliferation of this title at the network. The presidency was held open for Janet Murrow, who, the members said, had suffered longest from Murrow intimations of divinity. When Ed learned of the existence of the Murrow Ain't God Club, he applied for membership.

He customarily rationed himself to two drinks at Colbee's and then announced, "Now, I'll go home." John Daley recalled one evening when a fellow broadcaster joined the group uninvited. The man took a bottle of scotch, filled a water glass, and proceeded to drink it down in one draft. He looked to Murrow and said, "Well?" Murrow wordlessly filled another glass, emptied it to no visible effect, said his good-byes, and went home. In Murrow's world, men drank; they did not get drunk.[13]

The first year back on the air was a triumph. His evening news ratings took a sharp jump over the Bob Trout era. Murrow won three major awards in his first eight months on the air: the Alfred I. Dupont award for aggressive, independent, and meritorious news gathering; his second Overseas Press Club award for best interpretation of foreign affairs by radio; and his third National Headliners Award for coverage of the royal wedding in England. He was also earning, by the end of 1948, $112,000 a year.

The year had not been kind to him alone. It had been a triumph for CBS. Bill Paley had continued to snare NBC's hit shows, including now *Amos n' Andy.* For the first time in its history, measured by both ratings and advertising revenues, CBS pulled ahead of NBC. CBS radio was at last number one. Along with the public affairs prizes, CBS radio won the critics' plaudits for Ibsen's *Peer Gynt* and Shakespeare's *Richard III*, productions of the Columbia Workshop. Paley had believed all along that he could have it all, the ratings, the profits, the acclaim. Now he had done it.

Radio was first in broadcasting, and CBS was first in radio. But the medium was approaching the beginning of the end of its supremacy. Television cameras had been present at the political conventions as early as 1940, though most Americans were unaware of their existence. But by 1948, there were sets in some 400,000 American homes, which meant, for the first time, that a mass audience watched the spectacle of democracy from the living room. Jack Gould, *The New York Times* broadcasting critic, looked at the snowy images and saw the future. "Video's influence on politics," he said, "is going to be great indeed."

Murrow made his television debut that year. Franklin Schaffner, who would later make movies, including *Patton,* was then a young CBS television director assigned to the conventions. Schaffner put Murrow on camera and sensed something instantly: "He was right for the medium. Ed Murrow had on a television screen what Gary Cooper and Spencer Tracy had on a movie screen, the same virility, the same cinematic eyes. And he had that voice, that pure voice."

Murrow too had watched the flickering images on monitors at the conventions. And he was filled with unease. Cinematic eyes or not, radio was still his medium. Radio demanded more. It demanded a greater intellectual investment from its audience than television. It went to the brain, rather than to the eye. Serious treatment of vital issues belonged either in the newspapers or on the radio, not on a mesmerizing screen. Ed told a magazine interviewer not long after the conventions, "Is it not possible that an unruly head of hair, an infectious smile, eyes that seem remarkable for the depth of their sincerity, a cultivated air of authority may attract huge television audiences regardless of the violence that may be done to truth or objectivity?" As a vision of televangelism he had only the hairstyle wrong.[14]

CHAPTER 20

Enter Friendly

Ed Bliss tells the story of Fred Friendly working day and night on a television documentary on water. Friendly had a devil of a time finding the right opening, the thematic door that would get him into the story, after which all else would follow naturally. His wife had managed to drag him to the theater for a few hours of diversion for himself and at least one evening of respite from her de facto widowhood. They met friends in the lobby of the theater and took their seats. Just as the curtain went up, Friendly slammed his fist into the palm of his other hand and cried, "I've got it!" He bounded out of the theater without so much as a goodbye and rushed back to the CBS studios with an opening for the documentary that had suddenly struck him.[1]

This was the man who was to become Ed Murrow's closest professional associate, the man who would propel a wary and resistant Murrow into the television age.

He was born Ferdinand Wachenheimer in New York City in 1915. He was an unruly child. Looking back on those early tempestuous years, he later believed he may have suffered from the reading impairment, dyslexia, a condition not even diagnosed at the time. Rebellious and restless, he had difficulty learning, particularly learning to read. He would later look back on his life and say, "I was an underachiever—and I've come a long way from my frustrating beginnings."

His father was Samuel Wachenheimer, a moderately successful manufacturer of jewelry. Sam Wachenheimer moved his family from New York to Providence, Rhode Island, where he died a few years later. Thus, young Ferdinand was raised by his mother, Theresa, a tiny woman, 4 feet 10 inches, devoted to her difficult only child and to good causes. She was known around Providence as "Peace Wachenheimer" for her pacifist activities.

Much to Theresa's relief, young Ferdinand began to find himself in his teens. He at last became an avid reader. He was addicted to the thirties radio commentators, Boake Carter, Edwin C. Hill, and Raymond Swing. As he listened to their voices in the Wachenheimer living room, he became convinced that "I can do that."

He was, however, detoured. After finishing Nichols Business College, he went to work for the Outlet Store in Providence as an assistant rug buyer. But radio remained his passion. In 1937, at the age of 22, he managed to wangle auditions with two Providence radio stations. He prepared himself by renting a microphone and an amplifier and reading newspapers out loud. "The neighbors laughed," he recalled. "They all thought I was crazy."

He was not hired. "I was told I wasn't ready for Providence yet." But James Jennison, then managing WEAN, asked him if he had any ideas for programs. He did. He proposed a series of five-minute radio biographies. Jennison found a certain drama, a sense of suspense in Friendly's brief lives. Friendly opened with tantalizing facts about the undisclosed subject, and then, with the listener securely hooked, he would say, "His name? George Gershwin." Jennison asked when he was ready to start. Friendly wanted to know how much he would be paid. Nothing, Jennison told him, at least until he found a sponsor. And there was one other thing. The name Ferdinand Wachenheimer did not fall pleasantly upon the ear. And so he adopted his mother's maiden name and became Fred W. Friendly. He found a title for his program in Longfellow's *Psalm of Life:*

> Lives of great men all remind us
> We can make our lives sublime,
> And, departing, leave behind us
> Footprints on the sands of time.

Friendly gave himself six months to make *Footprints on the Sands of Time* pay off. The program was into its fifth month before a local laundry bought it. He did *Footprints* until 1941, when he was drafted into the Army.

Friendly had, as the British say, "a good war," and he would later refer to his military service as "my Rhodes scholarship." He was still recording and shipping aluminum transcriptions of *Footprints* back to Providence even after he went into the Army. Ultimately, he sold the backlog of 1,000 transcriptions to a Decca Records executive.

Friendly went overseas as a correspondent for the *CBI Roundup,* the China-Burma-India version of the *Stars and Stripes.* He worked mostly out of New Delhi and eventually made master sergeant. Toward the end of the war, he talked himself into a three-month film assignment about GIs in Europe. Out of this experience came a priceless self-revelation. He, a mere sergeant, had a knack for talking the highest-ranking officers into doing what he wanted them to do before his cameras. It was a lesson that he was not to forget and a talent that he was to elevate to an art.

Friendly came out of the Army with money in the bank from the sale of *Footprints* and a well-nourished ego from his wartime triumphs. If Fred Friendly had once not been good enough for Providence, he now decided that Providence was not good enough for Fred Friendly. He headed instead for New York. He was quickly brought to earth by the queen bitch of cities. He made the rounds of the advertising agencies, the radio stations, and the networks. Of that period, he recalled, "I free-lanced a few scripts here and there. But I went for two years without any real work."

In the meantime his savings were dwindling, but not his greatest capital, the ideas, good, bad, and impossible, that flowed from Fred Friendly like oil from a gusher. In 1948, he sold a quiz program to NBC radio, on which popular personalities tried to guess the source of quotations taken from the week's news. The program was called, *Who Said That?* The critics liked it, found the program "refreshing," "one of the happier recent inspirations on radio." However, *Who Said That?* did not win a sponsor, and NBC eventually dropped it.

He was no longer responsible only for himself. The year before, Fred had married Dorothy Greene, a researcher at *Time* magazine. His savings had run out. He had borrowed from friends. And time was running out too.

In his ceaseless quest for a job in broadcasting, he found himself one day in 1948 at CBS watching an editor at a machine cutting plastic tape with a razor and splicing it with scotch tape. It was his first exposure to tape recordings on plastic. GIs had stumbled onto the technology at the end of the war as they overran deserted German radio stations and found the stations still on the air broadcasting from great reels of magnetized plastic.

A creative pop went off in Friendly's head. The era of clumsy electrical transcriptions, bulky aluminum disks, and all but uneditable wire recorders was obviously over. Sounds, voices, music, could now be easily juxtaposed, and with astonishing acoustic fidelity. He could splice together the voices of the famous speaking at historic moments, Roosevelt on Pearl Harbor, Edward VIII on his abdication, and have it all pressed onto a salable phonograph record. He could create a "talking book."

Friendly was exclaiming over his idea to a talent agent who had taken an interest in this effusive but obscure producer. The agent was Jap Gude. To Gude, Friendly's scheme sounded like the aural equivalent of Frederick Lewis Allen's immensely popular history of the twenties, *Only Yesterday.* He took Friendly to see Allen to try to interest the writer in a collaboration, but Allen was too busy to take on another project.

"What I need," Friendly thereafter told Gude, "is the best voice in broadcasting. I need Ed Murrow." That was a possibility, Gude told an astonished Friendly. Murrow, he explained, was his client. Gude arranged a meeting of the two men.

"The first time I ever saw Ed Murrow," Friendly later recalled, "was in the lobby at 485 Madison Avenue. Jap and I had gone to CBS to get tapes so that I could show Murrow how the dubbing worked. He suddenly came through the door, his hair windblown from driving in his convertible down from the country. He was the most handsome and magnetic human being I had ever seen, in the prime of life." Gude introduced them.

What Murrow saw was a mastodon of a man. Friendly was roughly Murrow's height, 6 feet 2 inches. But where Murrow was trim and suave, Friendly was simply huge. His head was huge. His feet and hands were huge. His features were thick, the nose, mouth, and chin. His physical mass and furious energies suggested an elephant on pep pills. His voice had a strangely contrasting, purring quality, when he chose to control it, which he did with Murrow.

Over dinner at Louis and Armand's, Friendly described his idea for the talking book. Two men could hardly have been less alike, Friendly explosive and Murrow contained; Friendly ebullient, yet insecure, and Murrow intense, yet poised; Friendly all surface electricity and Murrow all surface calm; Friendly uneasy with his petit bourgeois background and Murrow patrician in spite of his background.

Friendly came away from the encounter floating on air. "Ed Murrow didn't ask me a lot of questions about myself," Friendly later remembered. "He listened to me and all he said was, 'Let's do it.'" Years later, he would exclaim in tones of disbelief, "This urbane, sophisticated man saw in *me* a colleague! Me, rough on the edges, effusive, exuberant." He spoke the words with a hushed awe suggesting that a princess had kissed a frog.

Gude managed a $1,000 advance for Friendly from the CBS records division. The money represented the difference between his sticking it out in New York or going back to Providence. The contract amazed Friendly: "Another man with Murrow's reputation would have said, 'Friendly, this deal is going to make you. So you take forty percent and I'll take sixty percent. Did he say that? No. He knew I was broke, and so he gave himself the smaller slice."

Friendly did the bulk of the work, wading through 500 hours of "recorded noise" taken mostly from old radio broadcasts. The final product was a 45-minute record entitled *I Can Hear It Now: 1933–1945,* narrated by Murrow. The jacket copy read: "...It has been said that colonial troops one hundred feet away from Washington at Yorktown missed Cornwallis's surrender because the wind was blowing the wrong way. Yet, GIs on KP at Camp Edwards, Massachusetts, heard MacArthur [on radio] accept the Japanese surrender faster and clearer than sailors on the superstructure of the battleship Missouri.... The voices of Neville Chamberlain at Munich, Hitler at the Sportspalast, Harry Truman addressing

Congress for the first time....all were part of a mosaic of voices and sounds which was part of the greatest mass adventure man has yet taken....This is a collection of some of those sounds."

The novice producers enjoyed a run of luck. The musicians' union had struck the major recording studios. Goddard Lieberson, the chief of Columbia's Masterworks records division, was eager to put his idled presses to work and to see how well a talking record might do. Friendly promoted the record aggressively, sending hundreds of complimentary copies to government leaders, newspaper and magazine editors, labor leaders, opinion molders, broadcasting figures, even entertainers.

I Can Hear It Now was released on Thanksgiving Day of 1948. By Christmas, Friendly was depositing a $24,000 royalty check in the bank. Within a year, the record sold a quarter of a million copies, the first nonmusical record in history to turn a big profit. Murrow and Friendly followed *I Can Hear It Now* with a second volume covering voices and events from 1945 to 1949 and a third covering 1919 to 1932.[2]

After the success of the first record, it was not for CBS, however, that Friendly went to work, but NBC. And it was not Murrow who eventually brought him to CBS, but a man named Sigfried "Sig" Mickelson.

Sig Mickelson had been the news director for CBS's Minneapolis affiliate, WCCO. He was brought to CBS at the end of 1949 to drag a resistant CBS news operation into the television age. Ted Church, the news director, a radio man of the old school, scorned television news, and Frank Stanton wanted somebody who saw the future more clearly. Mickelson was thus in the delicate position of being another of Murrow's putative bosses on the organization chart.

The man looked, and to a degree behaved, like a university academic. His manner was aloof, professorial, colorless. Opinion on Mickelson at CBS was divided depending on whether one was in or outside the Murrow camp. To one of Murrow's faction, Mickelson was "a faceless news bureaucrat with no real power base, the butt of jokes." To someone outside the Murrow fold, Mickelson was "very bright, like an inspirational professor. A great news executive who picked bad subordinates."

Like many men who lack fire themselves, Mickelson could feel it in others. Fred Friendly had been working on a documentary series at NBC on the atom bomb, called *The Quick and the Dead*. The CBS radio documentary unit that Murrow had originated was now in Mickelson's province, and Mickelson wanted Friendly making documentaries for CBS. He discussed the idea with Frank Stanton.

Mickelson knew what Murrow thought of Stanton: "Ed looked on Stanton as a mechanical man, a guy without any depth, warmth or understanding of the news business." The judgment was unfair, distorted by Murrow's personal antipathy. In truth, while Stanton had his finger in every pie at CBS, what he cared about most, what he respected most, indeed, what he listened to most himself, even more than Paley, was the network's news and public affairs programming. Stanton approved of bringing an obvious comer like Friendly into the organization.[3]

Thus it was that the team of Murrow and Friendly, which was to make television history, was brought into being by a team that Murrow disdained, Stanton and Mickelson. In fact, while Friendly was being courted, Murrow was not even in the country, but off in Korea.

He had been unable to resist the lure of battle. Eric Sevareid remembered sitting with Ed in his office reminiscing about the last war. "Suppose there is another war," Sevareid had said. "What do we do?" "We go off and get killed," Ed answered with a wry smile. "That's what we do."

In the summer of 1950 he seized the opportunity to exercise his cheerily macabre fatalism. After World War II, Korea had been divided along the 38th parallel into Soviet and American occupation zones. In 1948 the occupation ended and the zones emerged as two nations, North Korea and South Korea. On June 25, the north invaded the south. The United Nations branded North Korea an aggressor and called on member nations to come to the aid of South Korea. President Truman instantly committed the United States to the struggle. General Douglas MacArthur became the supreme commander of UN forces in South Korea. But it was largely an American fight.

Days after the war broke out, Ed was driving with Larry Le Sueur up to Rumblewood to join his family for the weekend. On the way up he rehearsed, in effect, what amounted to his reenlistment speech. They arrived at the lodge, and as soon as Janet had their drinks ready, Ed launched into his explanation, but she cut him short. "I already sent your uniforms to the cleaners," she said. "They came back yesterday."

Eleven days after the war broke out, Ed was on a plane headed for Korea, via Tokyo. A reporter saw him at the airport carrying an old German army rucksack with a pair of paratrooper boots strapped to the back. He also carried a red leather case with photographs of his son. "My heart is not in this one, believe me," he told the reporter. "I had nine years in Europe and thought I'd seen enough of dead men and beat-up towns." But his mood suggested Teddy Roosevelt's when the former President was asked why, in his mid-fifties, he was going off to explore the Amazon. TR had replied that it was his last chance "to be a boy."

Ed flew from Tokyo into Pusan aboard a battered military aircraft loaded with canisters of blood for the wounded. As the plane taxied to a stop, there on the runway was Bill Downs, in olive drab, a grin stretched across his face, waving Murrow off, shouting, "Go back! Go back! It ain't our kind of war!"

Korea was his first exposure to Asia. This thoroughgoing man of the West gave his impressions over the radio that night: "On the ground, this country seems only a few years ahead of the invention of the wheel. And the odors! The stench is as old as the world. Aside from the American military transports, the oxcart seems the modern means of transportation. Humans are pack animals, and even the packs are made of forked sticks tied together with hand-made ropes. The big bulldozers, tankers, even the little jeeps and especially the aircraft, blasting great dust storms off the field, appear to have been sent down here from another planet"[4]

He started out supporting the war. He saw Korea as a flash point that had ignited along the ideological front where the West and communism rubbed against each other. "We have drawn a line, not across the peninsula but across the world," he said. "We have concluded that communism has passed beyond the use of subversion to conquer independent nations, and will now use armed invasion and war. And we, for our part, have demonstrated that we are prepared to calculate the risks and face the prospect of war rather than let that happen."

He was the first radio correspondent to fly a bombing mission in Korea. Afterward, he went to an improvised press center set up in an abandoned school in Taegu to get out his story. He huddled under a blanket to cut off the roar of the guns outside. He read the script by the light of a candle. Sweat poured off his face. His heart might not have been in this one, but his colleagues noticed an expression of transport on his face when he emerged from under the blanket.

He wanted to get closer. He and three other correspondents boarded a C-54 transport and flew to the front. The hulking craft tried to land on a strip barely capable of accommodating a Piper Cub. The plane spun out of control and slithered into a paddy. James Hicks, a reporter with the *Afro-American,* recalled, "We were all scared, but Murrow was laughing out loud."

They trudged down a dark road in the fast-falling dusk headed toward a position manned by American Marines. Out of the darkness, a voice cried out, "Halt! Who's there?" Murrow said, "This is Edward R. Murrow of the Columbia Broadcasting System. We're correspondents."

MARINE: I don't have any orders to let any correspondents through.

MURROW: Look here...

MARINE: Shut up! One more peep out of you and I'll let you have it. [Sound of bolt on M-1 rifle shoving round into chamber.]

The Marine ordered them to put their hands over their heads and singled out Murrow to march ahead, alone into the darkness. He walked into the arms of a Marine lieutenant, who recognized his voice. The captain apologized for the rough treatment, but explained that his men had been alerted to expect to be attacked imminently and had been ordered to shoot anything that moved. The captain told the correspondents to take cover in a 105-millimeter howitzer gun emplacement and to try to get some sleep.

They were awakened in the middle of the night by the ringing of a field telephone. A sentry was reporting that he had heard cricket-like clickings, and he thought enemy troops might be signaling each other nearby. It was utterly still in the American position. And then an astonished Hicks heard a voice: "This is Edward R. Murrow. I am now located in Korea in a gun battery of the U.S. Marines who are expecting an attack any minute. I just heard a sentry report...." As Hicks's eyes became accustomed to the dark, he saw Murrow hunched over a tape recorder.

Ed was later to say of Korea, "I was more frightened than at any time during the European War. Maybe it was because I was older. In Europe, I felt the same age as those fighting, even if I wasn't. In Korea, I didn't feel that way. A B-26 gunner asked me if I had to fly combat to hold my job. I said, no, and he looked as if he thought I was daft. 'You're getting a little old for this nonsense,' he said."[5]

He could separate the terror-adventure, which satisfied an adrenal urge, from the politics of the war, which was beginning to raise doubts in his mind. At the end of six weeks in Korea, he flew into Tokyo on the first leg of his journey home. From there, he transmitted a commentary that was recorded in New York to be used on that evening's news. It began: "This is a most difficult broadcast to do. I have never believed that correspondents who move in and out of the battle area, engage in privileged conversations with commanders and with troops, and who have access to a public platform should engage in criticism of command decisions or of commanders while the battle is in progress. However, it is now time to cast up an account of the past ten days. For the question now arises whether serious mistakes have been made." He went on to describe an operation launched solely, according to one officer he had talked to, because "We decided we needed a victory."

"You will find battle-wise men out in Korea—some with stars and others with sergeant's stripes—who have fought Germans, Japanese, Italians, and North Koreans, who maintain that we gained nothing by this southern offensive.... I met no officer in South Korea who believes we can mount an effective offensive with our present strength.... And yet correspondents here have received cables from their home offices indicating that air-conditioned sources in Washington think the thing can be wound up this fall. To paraphrase the GIs in Korea—that ain't the way it looks from here.

"...I am aware that some of the things I have said may have violated directives from general headquarters, particularly in quoting officers who believe that we paid too high a price for that southern offensive. I have not identified them because no reporter knowingly embarrasses generals or sergeants with their superiors...."

He had indeed violated the spirit and probably the letter of an order promulgated by MacArthur forbidding reporters to criticize command decisions. During World War II, he had written home that he witnessed actions that even his ROTC training told him were military blunders. Now, watching kids die for older men's "victories," he felt that he had to speak out. He closed the broadcast with thoughts harrowingly true of America's fumbling search for a justification in another Asian war fifteen years later: "...when we start moving up through dead valleys, through villages to which we have put the torch by retreating, what then of the people who live there? They have lived on the knife edge of despair and disaster for centuries. Their pitiful possessions have been consumed in the flames of war. Will our re-occupation of that flea-bitten land lessen or increase the attraction of communism?"[6]

The arrival of the report in New York had scattered CBS officials like a falling high-voltage wire. Ted Church had watched the story come in over the Teletype and immediately took it to Edmund Chester, his superior. Chester took the story to Joseph Ream, a CBS attorney. Ream took it to Stanton and Paley. And there the story was killed. The reasons in management's eyes were manifest: the story violated MacArthur's directive; it would give aid and comfort to the North Koreans; it could be quoted as propaganda over Radio Moscow; use of the phrase "air-conditioned sources in Washington" was demagogic. Murrow, they said, was obviously exhausted, not thinking straight when he wrote the piece, or he never would have done it.

Ed was furious, and Stanton was the first to catch his fury. Ed called him on his way back from a stopover in Minneapolis and said, approved or not, he was going on the air with the story. Stanton was equally firm. If Murrow wanted to broadcast his piece, said Stanton, "I told him he'd have to do it as a private citizen."

Back in New York, Ed went immediately to Bill Paley's office. This time the king had to know. He had to be told of the suppression of free speech by his underlings.

The king knew full well. Paley accepted complete responsibility. Years afterwards, asked about this confrontation, he said, "Ed came to my office, very angry. I told him that we had agreed to a policy and I thought we were duty bound to live up to it and I told him he hadn't. He said, 'I think I did.' I told him, 'I'm sorry, but I have to make the final decisions. And I thought there was enough to the complaint to scrub the broadcast. I knew it was going to make you angry and I don't enjoy making you angry.' Ed said, 'How could you ever suspect me of doing something contrary to what I agreed.' I told him, 'You're not being accused of cheating or dishonesty. But it was up to us to decide if you were in the right or wrong.'"

After eight years of virtually unquestioned mutual trust, it was the first break. What Paley sensed was not so much that Murrow was angry, but that "he was hurt. Very hurt. He, Ed Murrow, the great man, the man who could never do anything unfair or unjust, was being made out to look like a guy who didn't live up to his word. The hurt just stood out on his face."

Ed Murrow could gladly contest Frank Stanton. He could brush aside the Mickelsons, the Churches, the Chesters. But Bill Paley came as close to being an idol as Murrow's nature permitted. And Paley had doubted him. That discovery, far more than whether or not he had violated a military regulation, cut him deeply. Paley had not stood by him. Or, just as painful to him, he had let Paley down.[7]

Ed also returned from Korea to the tag ends of another problem that had started before his departure. Campbell's Soup, sponsor of *Edward R. Murrow with the News,* had become dissatisfied with the drawing power of a news program. The Campbell people wanted to drop their sponsorship of the news but keep the prime 7:45 p.m. time slot and replace Murrow with a musical program. Campbell was putting pressure on Bill Paley, threatening that if the company could not keep the 7:45 time, it would also take another Campbell-sponsored program, *Club 15,* away from CBS too.

It was the Shirer case all over again. Who was to control the scheduling of news over radio, the network or the sponsors? And now it was Murrow in Shirer's shoes.

To understand the enduring loyalty that Ed Murrow felt toward Bill Paley, the contretemps with Campbell's Soup provides the text. No trace of resentment over the Korea broadcast was to influence Paley's behavior in the Campbell affair. Paley held firm. He told Ed that he could keep the 7:45 p.m. time even if he went unsponsored, even if it did cost CBS not one, but two profitable sponsorships from Campbell. Within weeks, he sold Murrow's newscast to five separate sponsors in five regions of the country, and thus no longer had to grant the customary fifteen percent rate discount that he had given Campbell for sponsoring a coast-to-coast program. This was the kind of man Ed Murrow admired, a loyal friend, a man of principle and courage, and a shrewd operator to boot.[8]

Ed was delighted not only to have his news program saved, but, with Friendly's arrival, to have a whole new vista opened to him. He and Friendly became coproducers of a weekly radio documentary series, something of a magazine on the air, covering a half-dozen "articles" every week. They called the program, exploiting the identity of their successful record, *Hear It Now.* When they first proposed the concept to Paley as a half-hour program, Paley said no; *Hear It Now* deserved a full hour.

Friendly would have preferred doing *Hear It Now* over television rather than radio. Had Murrow wanted it, doubtless, then and there, the new medium would have been theirs. But Murrow distrusted a medium that depended more on pictures than words. The kind of magazine of the air that he wanted to do was *Harpers* or the *Atlantic Monthly,* not *Life.*

CBS by then had been broadcasting television news since 1946, when there were 6,000 sets in the country. The network originally produced ten hours of television a week, and the news portion consisted of one Saturday night report delivered by Douglas Edwards. CBS television then emanated, almost furtively it seemed, from studios deep in the bowels of the Grand Central Terminal Building. The earliest transmissions were seen only in the New York area. So marginal was the enterprise that CBS virtually gave away its television time to anybody who would take it.

The infant, however, thrived, particularly as its vascular system developed. By 1947, coaxial cables linked New York, Philadelphia, and Washington, and over a quarter of a million sets were in use; by 1949 there were 1.6 million sets, and new sets were being installed at a rate of 100,000 a month. Television was then largely a visual spectacle, boxing, horse racing, baseball. And television was a money loser.

Sig Mickelson went to Ted Church, who was then running radio news, to try to bring the luster and drawing power of the celebrated names in CBS radio news into television news. Mickelson wanted a Murrow, a Sevareid, a Collingwood. But in the late 1940s, as inconceivable as it may seem to a generation virtually suckled on television, established radio correspondents snubbed television. Television was news as novelty, not the place for a serious reporter with a national following. Television existed on the margin; television was for novices breaking in. It was not for Murrow or his Boys.

In part Ed's resistance was explained by the rudimentary technology of the medium in the early years. With radio, words could be winged around the world in an instant. Not so then with pictures. Early television news was as time-bound as the newsreels, chained to film that had to be shipped, developed, and edited before it could be put on the air. The capture of immediacy, one of radio's triumphs, was still beyond television. Either television news was filmed and late, or it was static and dull, with a reporter reading wire service copy.

Murrow's distaste went deeper. He had always objected to things being judged by surface appearances, and people too, beginning with himself. Issues, and people, should be judged deeply, by their substance. He did not want to be part of a medium that treated news superficially, with images instead of intellectual effort. That was too much like judging a man by his profile rather than by what went on in his head.

Murrow rarely wrote at length for publication. But he took the time to spell out his feelings about television in an article for *The New York Times* that he wrote in February of 1949: "...The interesting area of speculation is not whether TV news is here to stay, but rather what form is it likely to take after the shakedown cruise....Is it to be a medium of entertainment or education? Do bathing girls on surf boards get preference over a first class but simple chart of the Middle East?...So far...there has been a tendency to tailor the news to fit the pictorial and animation possibilities rather than to give the news, as such, priority and try to tailor up such pictorial support as may be possible....If the editorial selection is based upon largely visual values, TV news will become an animated picture magazine or a newsreel....For example, at the Democratic convention in Philadelphia, a reporter spent a great deal of time learning just what the Alabama delegation was going to do when they walked out—who would ask the chair for recognition, what he would say, what other delegations would go with them. At the appropriate moment, the camera came down on a closeup of the Alabama delegation. The reporter started telling his story which was news. While he was talking—while the.issue was still in doubt—the camera panned up to the balcony for a closeup of a woman wearing an exotic and ridiculous hat. That was the end of the story about the Alabama delegation; you can't talk politics while the camera gives you a closeup shot of a funny hat. The pictorial judgment may have been impeccable, but it wasn't news judgment....if the top story of the day has to do with high echelon changes in the Soviet government, the TV newsroom had little pictorial or animation support for such a story. But, if it takes two minutes to tell that story, then it must be told, even if the audience has to look at a picture of Stalin, or even the reporter for that length of time. The alternative is to try to tell the story in thirty seconds and fill the other minute and a half with bathing beauties; or film of a recent acquisition at the zoo....I cannot see that television news will become more than a supplement to the daily newspaper...."

It is difficult to imagine that anyone connected with the good gray and linear *New York Times* would quarrel with Murrow's vision of television. Nevertheless, the article was never printed. Without giving any reason, Jack Gould wrote Murrow that the paper could not use the piece. Printed or not, writing the article no doubt had an agreeable cathartic affect on the author. When Murrow had first gone into broadcasting, he had had to endure the smug superiority of newspapermen. Now his generation had something to look down on, television journalism.[9]

Instead of television, he took on another radio program of curious origins. Murrow was having lunch in Bill Paley's private dining room one day with Paley; Ward Wheelock, the advertising man; and Donald W. Thornburgh, manager of the CBS Philadelphia affiliate, WCAU. The conversation drifted, as it can in sumptuous seats of power when important men have a good lunch inside them, to the deplorable emphasis on materialism in the modern world at the expense of spiritual values. The messianic Wheelock thought that they, as the privileged few, had a responsibility to redress the imbalance.

Soon after, Wheelock came up with an idea. He wanted Murrow to host a program on which successful people would describe their personal philosophies. He had the perfect name for the show, echoing the phrase that now virtually belonged to Murrow. It would be called *This I Believe.*

At that time, Edward P. Morgan came to Murrow looking for a job. Ed Morgan had worked as a CBS reporter in Berlin after the war. He had then free-lanced magazine articles out of Paris. By the summer of 1950, Morgan was back in the States looking for a more dependable paycheck.

Ed Morgan was a handsome, even distinguished-looking, man of sharp, piercing features, an aggressive reporter, and a crustaceous human being. He hardly seemed the sort to enlist in an exercise in mass spiritual renewal. Nevertheless, Murrow hired Morgan for $200 a week to line up guests for *This I Believe*, to tape their personal philosophies, and to write Murrow's introduction and close. "I took the job reluctantly," Morgan would say later, "for lack of anything better."

Morgan found that on the strength of Murrow's name he was able to land virtually any guest he wanted. Among the hundreds of contributors and their philosophies were Justice William O. Douglas, "My Father's Evening Star"; Dame Edith Evans, "What Does God Say to Me"; Aldous Huxley, "Learning to Get out of the Way"; Margaret Mead, "A New Control of Destiny; and Rebecca West, "Goodness Doesn't Just Happen." Even Bill Shirer took part. Shirer was then making a precarious living as an author. One of his books, *Mid-Century Journey,* had just been published in 1950. He was virtually unhirable on the air, and his appearance on the program appears to have resulted from Murrow's trying to make amends.

This I Believe opened over WCAU in Philadelphia. Eventually, it was carried on 192 stations, was syndicated in 85 newspapers, and was broadcast over the *Voice of America* in six languages. An anthology of the best philosophies was published in 1952. Ed Murrow wrote the introduction, and the book sold an impressive 300,000 copies. The series was offered to stations as a public service. Thus, neither Murrow nor anyone else, except Ed Morgan with his salary, made any money from *This I Believe*.

Murrow's introduction to the book version of the program is revealing for what it said about his fundamental convictions. "I would suppose," he wrote, "that men believe what they believe as a result of inheritance, indoctrination, the number of calories they are able to consume, the climate in which they live, and the ideas they acquire from others." It was a highly secular statement. Nowhere did he suggest that what people believe stemmed from any mystical, eternal, infinite, or supernatural force, from a religion, from God.

Ed Morgan had a sense that Murrow was not particularly interested in *This I Believe*. But the program required little effort, a recording session once a week at most, during which they taped a half-dozen shows. The two men worked quickly and spoke little. For in Ed Morgan, Murrow of the protracted silences met his match. "We would go to Louis and Armand's," Morgan recalled, "have a couple of belts at the bar and sit down to dinner in total silence. We must have looked like a couple of bumps on a log."

Morgan occasionally wanted to put somebody on *This I Believe* from outside the pale of conventional religion, even an atheist. He expressed his view at a lunch with Murrow and Wheelock. Wheelock was apoplectic. "No one," Ward Wheelock believed, "can live a complete and happy life without a deep belief in a supreme being." The discussion became contentious, and Morgan looked to Murrow for an ally. All he saw on Murrow's face was "a bemused detachment."

Morgan managed to obtain Eleanor Roosevelt for *This I Believe*. She delivered, without a note, one of the most compelling personal philosophies that Morgan had ever heard. She talked of her own beliefs and her doubts about rigid systems of religion. She said that she believed in a creator, but she did not employ the word "God," which upset Wheelock. Wheelock wanted the Eleanor Roosevelt program killed. This time Murrow was not neutral. He told Morgan to use the Eleanor Roosevelt broadcast no matter what Wheelock said.

As for Edward P. Morgan, he was just as happy to leave *This I Believe* when the chance came to return to radio reporting. He handed over his duties to Murrow's old friend, Raymond Swing, who now needed a regular paycheck himself. Swing had been the chief commentator for the *Voice of America*, but Joe McCarthy's anti-Communist bullyragging of the Voice had driven Swing to a resignation on principle. By January of 1955, *This I Believe* had run out of money. There were, however, so many unused scripts on hand that Murrow was embarrassed to disappoint the contributors by not using them. He paid $7,000 out of his own pocket to continue the broadcasts until the scripts ran out, when *This I Believe* died a natural death.[10]

Soon after Ed had returned from Korea in August of 1950, he and Janet sold the townhouse at East 74th Street and bought an eleven-room apartment at 580 Park Avenue. The owner had convinced herself that the outbreak of the war in Korea foretold the eventual destruction of New York City, and so the Murrows picked up a choice Manhattan property for a distress sale price of $30,000.

A visiting BBC chum, Robert Reid, recalled going with Ed to the Park Avenue apartment. As they rode the express elevator, Ed said, "It's a poor place, but it's home." The remark struck Reid as precisely the sort of thing a British aristocrat would make on bringing a visitor to his stately home.

Other visitors had a sense that the Murrows never struck their roots very deeply at 580 Park Avenue, that it was a way station until they could get up to Quaker Hill on weekends. The apartment was furnished, mostly in good English antiques, but sparsely. A CBS publicity woman once took a magazine writer who was doing an article on celebrity homes to the apartment. She remembered a coffee table spilling over with the newly published books that always surrounded Ed Murrow, a desk in a corner heaped with correspondence, and Casey's toys piled atop the grand piano and spilling onto the floor, making for treacherous walking. The writer, the publicist said, "fled."

Casey Murrow was 5 when the family moved into the apartment. He had become an appealing child with masses of golden curls and wide eyes that stared curiously about the world. When Casey was 2 and 3, Ed put him on his radio program to wish the audience a Merry Christmas. When he was 4, Ed took Casey through the toy stores with a tape recorder and used the child's comments for a radio report on the new toys. When Casey was 5, he interviewed Santa Claus over the air. It all seemed unlike Ed Murrow, more the behavior of a pushy stage mother. When Casey reached school age, "I discontinued it," Ed said. "I think that anything that sets a kid apart is no service to the kid."

Ed was proud of Casey's facility with words, naming the country house "Rumblewood," for example. Thus, when Ed bought his first fancy pointer, he told the boy that he could name the dog. Casey immediately picked the name "Spot." Ed gamely stuck by his word. As he told his friends later, "Can't you see me at the Hudson Valley Fish and Game Club hollering, 'Spot! Spot!'"

Actually, he saw little of his son except on weekends. Casey was already off to school by the time Ed got up in the morning, and usually asleep before Ed came home at night. The parent of daily and immediate influence was Janet. Still, Ed had strong ideas of what his son was to be, a little man. His conception of fatherhood had been shaped by his observations of child rearing among the British upper classes. "All I can hope to do is to teach him to tell the truth and fear no man," he said more than once.

On one point, Murrow was a stickler. Manners were drilled into the boy—how to behave at the table, how to conduct himself when adults entered the room, how to respond to introductions. Norman Corwin remembered dinner parties at the Murrows where "after dinner, little Casey would go around with a tray offering cigarettes to the guests." Corwin observed that the child, then no more than 4, behaved with total aplomb.

Marietta Tree thought that Ed appeared to be playing a role called fatherhood, a slightly self-conscious performance. "He said all the right words," she remembered of her visits with the Murrows, "but he really didn't have the time to be all that close to the boy. He'd say things like, 'Casey and I are going out and play some pitch and catch.' And the child was only three."

Yet Johnny Aarons, listening to Ed spin Casey stories around the office and Colbee's Bar, told his wife, "The kid's the most important person in Ed's life." The observation would have pleased Ed Murrow, and he probably would have agreed.[11]

CHAPTER 21

"The Most Important Program on Television"

In the fall of 1951, Archibald MacLeish sent his verse play, *The Trojan Horse,* to Ed Murrow to see if CBS radio was interested in producing it. MacLeish was a Pulitzer Prize-winning poet. His dramas had been successfully produced over radio before. Murrow passed the script along to the radio programming people, who rejected it. Months later, MacLeish wrote Murrow that the BBC had produced *The Trojan Horse,* and he said of the CBS rejection, "...I am afraid it means something not about my play, but the direction in which radio is going, and that saddens me."[1]

Where radio was going was into eclipse. Within three months of MacLeish's writing Murrow, a survey by the A.C. Nielsen Company revealed that for the first time, between the hours of 9 p.m. and midnight, more television sets than radios were turned on in America.

The only superiority that Murrow was willing to grant television over radio was in covering spectacle. Television was for coronations and conventions, ball games and circuses. Ed told Ben Gross, the *Daily News* radio columnist, "The people who say TV will destroy radio are as wrong as those who, twenty-five years ago, said that radio would kill the newspapers. I sincerely believe that radio news will become more and more important. Its listeners will be made up of the kind of audiences who tune in the philharmonic symphony concerts on Sundays." He proved more loyal than perceptive. The symphony lover turning on commercial radio over the next generation was doomed to raucous disappointment. Television would not kill radio as Murrow had helped create it, just render it unrecognizable.[2]

CBS responded to the new order in the summer of 1951. Previously, the network's radio and television operations were combined. Now they were split, each with its own president. Each had to make its own profit. CBS news operations were also divided into radio and television divisions.

Sig Mickelson was named head of television news. In his dogged way, Mickelson set himself an admirable objective, to achieve for television news the respectability that radio journalism had won. Mickelson would later deny it, but around CBS it was accepted fact that he wanted Murrow to take over the infant CBS evening television news. "Ed could have had it," Harry Reasoner remembered, "any time he wanted it." Murrow did not want it. He now regarded Douglas Edwards, who then did the television news, not as a journalist, but as a radio announcer with pictures. Murrow made occasional appearances on Edwards's program, but only as a pundit, delivering semieditorial tailpieces. The people Ed Murrow associated with scarcely acknowledged the existence of television, except to disparage it. When Ken Galbraith made his first appearance on television as an editor at *Fortune,* Catherine Galbraith had to go to the Murrows' to watch her husband. The Galbraiths did not own a television set.[3]

Murrow's attitude had a certain irony. As much as any single individual, he had glimpsed and fulfilled radio's capacity to enlarge human communication. He had created powerful pictures in sound—Berlin from a bomber, the Buchenwald death factory, London during the Blitz. Yet he acted toward television the way print reporters had toward radio. He thought it insufficiently cerebral.

Then, in March of 1951, a television image transfixed the nation. Estes Kefauver had taken his Senate investigation of organized crime to the Foley Square courthouse in New York and allowed live television coverage. Kefauver's star witness was one of the mobs *prominenti,* Frank Costello. But Costello's lawyers objected to having his client televised. Kefauver accepted a compromise. The cameras would be allowed to focus only on Costello's hands. They became the most famous hands in America—clenching, fumbling with documents, shredding bits of paper, reaching for a glass of water, sweating—as Costello described the netherworld he inhabited.

Among the 30 million people watching the Kefauver investigations was Ed Murrow. He recognized that the picture had not substituted for thought, had not trivialized the issue of organized crime. The picture had added another dimension. The brain, ear, and eye had been simultaneously stimulated, creating a fuller experience. After the Kefauver hearings, Murrow said, "The television performance has been fascinating." The magic of the new medium had happened, he said, when people realized "the midgets in the box have been real."[4]

Yet he wanted no part of television. He was again in one of those moods in which he managed to persuade himself that he wanted no part of broadcasting at all. Washington State was again looking for a new president in the summer of 1951. A man named Charles McAllister, on the search committee, called Ed and asked if he would allow his name to be submitted as a candidate. McAllister regarded the call as a long shot, and he was astonished by Murrow's reaction. "Here I am," he remembered Ed telling him, "living in a flat on Park Avenue. My son has to play on the roof, or he has to play in Central Park, assuming there's somebody to look after him. I'm making over $100,000 a year. I'm also getting up at three o'clock in the morning, working all day long and, frankly, breaking my back. I begin to ask myself, what is it all about? So when you talk to me about a $20,000 a year job as president of my old school, living in the president's mansion free, having a house maid and a company car, it sounds like a pretty good deal."

He made discreet inquiries about breaking his contract with CBS, which still had five years to run. He took advantage of a business trip to Spokane in July to meet quietly with members of the search committee. The matter progressed to a point where he was to provide six references by a certain date.

And then, as before, he pulled back from the brink. In August, he cabled the committee, "After prolonged consideration, I must with the utmost regret request that my name be withdrawn." The fantasy had again served its purpose, a temporary retreat from his now chronic dissatisfaction. In truth, he was not about to leave broadcasting. He was about to plunge in more deeply than ever.[5]

He and Friendly had been doing their radio magazine, *Hear It Now,* for less than a year. The show was carried by 173 radio stations. And had already won Murrow another Peabody. Yet, creating *Hear It Now* for radio in 1950 had been rather like building the best gas lamp at the turn of the century when most people were rewiring their homes for electricity. Friendly had been eager all along to get into television. In June of 1951, Murrow and Friendly made the decision. They would end *Hear It Now,* and instead coproduce a new weekly half-hour television documentary series. It was to be called *See It Now.*

See It Now was not to be the television equivalent of movie newsreels. It was not to be a passive recorder of events, be they political campaigns, baseball games, or beauty pageants. *See It Now* was not to follow headlines. *See It Now* was to be a news source itself, much the way an enterprising magazine or crusading newspaper could force an issue to public consciousness.

But neither Murrow or Friendly knew anything about television.

Palmer Williams was a veteran documentary filmmaker. Williams had gone into the profession in 1939 and spent the war making films for the Army signal corps. In 1951, while working for an independent filmmaker, Williams went one day to lunch at Barbetta's Restaurant in Greenwich Village, something of an unofficial employment bureau for the filmmaking crowd. There, he ran into a friend who told him that Fred Friendly was looking for somebody who knew how to make television documentaries. Williams went to see Friendly and told him, "I am a production manager, which is a good thing to be in this business." He knew how to put together camera crews, how to deal with the unions, how to work with film archives and optical houses.

"How much money do you want?" Friendly asked. "I told him $200 a week," Palmer recalled. "Friendly groaned and he said, 'I'll tell you what. I'll give you $175 and you can make another $25 on the expense account.'" He was hired, and thereafter, Williams said, he stretched his imagination to embarrassing lengths inventing fictional cab rides.[6]

Friendly, Williams quickly discovered, might be disposed to cut a corner on salaries, but he wanted the best people in filmmaking. Charlie Mack and Leo Rossi, then working for Hearst-MGM newsreels, were legends in the newsreel trade. Mack was a big, handsome, white-haired Irishman, bluff and voluble, a street-taught, savvy observer of the political scene. Rossi, "who dressed like an Italian count," had "never turned out a bad piece of film." The work of these men displayed an artistry closer to cinema than to newsreels. An arrangement was worked out whereby they stayed with Hearst-MGM, their regular employer, but also worked for *See It Now*. Norman Alley, another gifted cameraman, filmed for *See It Now* on the West Coast, Marty Bennet in Chicago, and Bill McClure in Europe.

See It Now could call on CBS's correspondents worldwide. But Murrow and Friendly wanted their own staff reporters as well. An early choice raised eyebrows at CBS. Edmund Scott had worked for the left-leaning *PM,* which, to certain eyes, left an ineradicable taint on the man. Murrow said that he preferred a potentially troublesome talent to a safe mediocrity, and Scott was hired. He and Friendly also hired Joe Wershba. The big, shambling Wershba was a nonstop talker of sprawling interests, steeped in the politics and history of his time. When he was not talking, he was a tenacious reporter and facile writer.

It was toward the end of the war, while Wershba was working as a CBS radio newswriter, that he had first encountered Ed Murrow. He later described the occasion: "Murrow came in, sat down in the chair behind the control panel for a 'talk-up' to London.... [he] sat slouched in the chair, a brooding, Lincolnesque figure, hollow of eye, gaunt of cheek, unshaven, hair unkempt, disdainful of other staff members, granting them nary a word of greeting." Of that first encounter, Wershba remembered, "I resented him bitterly." In no small measure, Wershba's resentment rose out of the fact that Murrow had the aura of a war hero without having been in uniform. Later on, Wershba worked on the *I Can Hear It Now* albums and the *Hear It Now* radio series. He discovered a Murrow who stood up for probing reporters against corporate nervous nellies. He found a Murrow willing, indeed eager, to court controversy. His earlier resentment of Murrow metamorphosed into hero worship.[7]

The division of labor between Murrow and Friendly in producing *See It Now* was never entirely clear. Program topics generated with either man or with the reporters. Friendly, in Charles Collingwood's phrase, "exploded with a hundred ideas, of which ten might be good." But, in general, Friendly had day-to-day supervision over the visual side, the deployment of reporters and camera crews, the editing of film. Script writing was a joint effort, with Friendly often doing a rough first draft since he first saw the film that had been shot. Murrow oversaw the final film editing and wrote the final script, in effect, controlled the final cut. Murrow also narrated *See It Now* and conducted its live interviews. As Friendly saw the division, "Ed was the publisher, the editor in chief. I was the managing editor. It was his paper." In another variation: "Ed was the company commander. I was the first sergeant."

To the cameramen, *See It Now* represented liberation. Unlike newsreel teams, chained to a predestined script, the *See It Now* camera crew and reporters went into the field to find the heart of the story. Also, unlike the newsreels which preached economy of film, Murrow's crews were to keep shooting until they had the best possible footage. They were to achieve spontaneity by shooting interviews unrehearsed. They were to shoot both image and sound. There was to be no dubbing of sound effects in a film laboratory afterward. While television news was using 16-millimeter film, which meant lighter equipment and more maneuverability, *See It Now* used bulky 35-millimeter cameras. They simply produced better pictures.[8]

On Sunday November 18, 1951, viewers watching CBS television heard Murrow say, "Good evening. This is an old team trying to learn a new trade." The voice and the hint of a smile on his face suggested a test pilot, grave and jaunty at the same time, readying an experimental aircraft for takeoff. *See It Now* was making its debut. Its late Sunday afternoon slot was, in that era, hardly prime time. Murrow described it as "the intellectual ghetto."

Coaxial television cables and microwave relays had just knit the country together the month before. The program opened with an inspired gimmick, the far ends of the continent were seen on a split screen simultaneously, for the first time over the Atlantic and Pacific shorelines, then the skylines of New York and San Francisco, the Statue of Liberty and Telegraph Hill.

Murrow had made occasional appearances on the television news. He had been seen briefly on television at the 1948 political conventions. But with *See It Now*, millions of Americans were seeing, for the first time, the man behind the voice. He was now 43. As he had grown older, his shoulders had narrowed, accentuating the large, well-shaped head. His pal Bob Dixon liked to say, "When Ed tried on a hat, they suggested he ought to wear the box it came in." The beard was black and heavy and had to be lightened with powder. Natalie Foster (later Natalie Paine), Friendly's secretary, had occasionally gone to the Murrow apartment to take dictation. She remembered, "It took him forty-five minutes to shave, because of what he called 'my crevices, glaciers, and warts.'"

The boy reared on hand-me-downs now wore shirts by "Bertollini, Chamisier," of Rome, shoes handmade in Scotland for his narrow feet, and suits still made by Anderson and Sheppard Ltd., 30 Savile Row, "Court, Civil and Military Tailors." The audience would not see the red suspenders, although they were there, one pair adorned with the naked women, another with "Mr. Plus," the logo of the rival Mutual Broadcasting System, Murrow's small, unseen sartorial gesture of defiance.

Howard K. Smith once said of Ed Murrow, "When he walked into a room, even if your back was turned, you knew a commanding presence had come in." The quality came through the television screen. Ed's occasional director, Don Hewitt, remarked, "If I had never seen him and only heard his voice, I would have hired him from a group of a hundred actors auditioning to play Edward R. Murrow." Hewitt found it "difficult to shoot Murrow from an angle where he didn't look good."[9]

Each half hour of *See It Now* offered from three to a half-dozen stories, a balance of issues and sensory encounters—a pint of blood traced from a donor in America into the veins of a wounded GI in Korea, an Oriental unsuccessfully trying to buy a house in San Francisco during Brotherhood Week, the first live broadcast from a submerged submarine.

The tone sought and largely achieved was a gritty integrity. Friendly rejected the use of a TelePrompTer. Murrow read from a visible script. What was lost in artificial conversationality was compensated for by a heightened sense of reality. At Hewitt's suggestion, Murrow operated from no set, but from the control room with the monitors, microphones, and control panel in full view.

Shooting both pictures and sound meant that the camera crew following an infantry company in Korea on that first broadcast had to bring along a sound man and lug heavy batteries, microphones, and other cumbersome equipment over rugged terrain. Palmer Williams, who had always dubbed the sound in his World War II filmmaking, said to Friendly, "Dear God, Why?" Because, Friendly said, "I want to hear that gun going off in that place at that time, and I don't want you putting in the sound of a sixteen-inch naval gun when they're shooting a howitzer."

When the film came back from Korea, Williams was amazed by the effects achieved: "You heard the sound of the GIs slogging through the mud, wise-cracking as they hauled the piece into position. The film was much richer."

The Korean segment on that first broadcast was a marked departure from World War II newsreels with their air armadas blackening the sky, landing craft disgorging divisions onto beaches and cities in flames. In effect, *See It Now* said come with us to Korea. We are going to walk invisibly alongside some GIs, Fox Company, Second Platoon, Nineteenth Infantry Regiment. We will follow these men out of the bunkers where they sleep, watch them horsing around in the mess line, see them writing letters home, share with them the alternating tedium and terror of the ordinary combat infantryman. At the end of the segment, each member of the Second Platoon stepped before the camera and gave his name and hometown. During the actual broadcast, Murrow reported that since the filming, half of the young men we had come to know were killed, wounded, or missing in action. The war in Korea became terribly real, as if the viewer had been able to wander among Lee's troops before they charged Cemetery Ridge at Gettysburg, and learned of their individual fate afterward.

Behind the film, no matter how visually compelling, Murrow wanted a point, a "therefore what?" Palmer Williams had learned that the Navy was about to take a newly launched ship on a shakedown cruise. Williams saw the visual possibilities of a segment on a ship being put through her paces. He went to Murrow with his idea and found him in his office having a scotch with Zousmer and Aarons before doing the radio news. Williams began explaining his scheme, when "Murrow cut me off at the knees." "What the hell kind of idea is that?" Murrow told him. "I'm not wasting my film doing that kind of thing." Action without a larger lesson, a context, was simply stunt filming. After the encounter, Williams recalled, "I stumbled out of his office and told Friendly what happened. He gave me a welcome-to-the-club look."[10]

Acclaim for *See It Now* was immediate, as though the critics had been waiting for the content of television at last to catch up to the technical miracle. In its first season, the program took the Peabody Award for television news and interpretation. *Variety* said of *See It Now:* "At a time when not only viewers, but most industry toppers had started to believe that video had exhausted all possible facets of programming, Murrow and his co-producer, Fred W. Friendly, jolted them into discarding that cliché with this entirely new approach to news reporting, an approach which uncovered a power in TV's ability to report the news which most of them had never even suspected. Where it had been generally accepted that video could never equal radio's job of reporting, Murrow and Friendly exploited to the full...the drama and excitement inherent in the news."

The success of *See It Now* inspired healthy competition. Within CBS itself, documentaries took on a new fashionability. A CBS television documentary unit began producing work, independent of Murrow, by gifted young producers like Irving Gitlin who had apprenticed on *Hear It Now.* The year after *See It Now* began, another oasis appeared on the Sunday afternoon desert. CBS produced, with Ford Foundation money, *Omnibus,* hosted by Alistair Cooke, with Leonard Bernstein on one week explaining music, Helen Hayes on another describing the art of the fairy tale, and E. Power Biggs on another demonstrating the glories of the organ. (*Omnibus* was offered to sponsors, but the program never drew high ratings. CBS produced it for four years, then NBC for two years, and finally ABC for its final year.) NBC launched *Project 20,* which produced, among other excellent work, the epic television naval history of World War II, naval war, *Victory at Sea.* Still, the question at NBC was, "Who is going to be *our* Murrow?"[11]

See It Now won another badge of respectability, one understood in board rooms and at stockholder meetings. By its third week, the program had a sponsor.

ALCOA, the Aluminum Company of America, had been embroiled in an antitrust suit since 1937, one of the few situations in which this near anonymous giant came to public attention. Sometime around 1950, the company commissioned a confidential public opinion survey which revealed that most people, if they were at all conscious of ALCOA, regarded the company as a faceless, corporate brute. In 1951, ALCOA hired Arthur Hall as vice president for public relations to give the company a more human face. Hall's solution was to have ALCOA sponsor a prestigious television program.

At that time, ALCOA manufactured few consumer products. It made its money selling aluminum to manufacturers, not kettles to housewives. What Hall wanted was a program that would deliver "thought leaders." *See It Now* was tailor-made. And so the company's executives and its advertising agency met with Murrow and Friendly.

Murrow's concern remained what it had been with Campbell's Soup. The sponsor could buy space during the half hour, but he wanted no interference in the programming, no more than a billboard should determine the direction of a highway. Irving "Chief" Wilson, then heading ALCOA, told Murrow, "You do the program and we'll make the aluminum. Don't try to tell us how to make aluminum and we won't tell you how to make television programs." Wilson proved as good as his word.[12]

Friendly had described the relationship between him and Murrow as managing editor to publisher, first sergeant to company commander. He had a telephone installed between his office and Murrow's. When the phone rang, Palmer Williams remembered, "Friendly would scoop it up with that big hand of his and say, 'Engine room!' Murrow was the captain on the bridge, and Friendly was down there stoking the furnace, keeping the whole thing going."

Years later, long after Fred Friendly had become a television legend himself, he looked back on that era with a self-effacement, even a self-abnegation, that seemed incongruous and unconvincing in so overpowering an ego. "I was," Friendly said, "a self-made clone of Ed Murrow. I absorbed all Ed's values. Every scrap of film I edited, I edited with his eyes. Everything I wrote, I wrote with his fingers." In Friendly, Murrow had found a sturdy mount to ride into his battles. In Murrow, Friendly had found his electronic knight whom he happily bore into the fray on his broad back.

"Fred just missed being obsequious with Ed," Palmer Williams recalled. "But he certainly was deferential. He was like the English peasant who comes to the squire with cap in hand. Later he gained confidence and he'd defend his position. But in the beginning, if Fred proposed something and Ed said 'No, I don't want to do it,' Fred would pull back as though he'd touched a hot stove."

In the early years, a doctoral candidate named Murray Russell Yaeger was allowed to observe the *See It Now* operation, rather like a fly on the wall. Yaeger has left an interesting study in contrasts in what he observed of the two men: "Murrow is famous for his understatement, and Friendly follows the same pattern. He even bows his head slightly and fingers his chin when he is in thought much the same way that Murrow does. However, in many ways these men are not at all alike. Murrow is calm and outwardly appears easy going, seldom revealing his inner emotions and conflicts. Friendly, on the other hand, is excitable, dynamic and obviously effervescent and depressed as his moods dictate. Murrow's reserve keeps him from displaying his warmth except to his intimates. Friendly too has a cold exterior which seems impenetrable at times, and then suddenly disappears to reveal a most ingratiating side."

They were sitting around a conference table, a half dozen of the *See It Now* staff discussing a script. A cellophane cigar wrapper caught fire in an ashtray. Friendly leaned forward and blew out the flame, sending a cloud of ashes over Murrow. Murrow shot back, as Friendly remembered the scene, with, "Why don't you just mind your own business." The only importance of this utterly trivial incident is that Friendly still remembered it in excruciating detail thirty years later. To be made to feel clumsy, to be put down in front of the staff by the man he worshiped, was a scalding and unforgettable humiliation.

The more they differed, the more they complemented each other, like pieces in a jigsaw puzzle. Jim Seward was a man in whom Murrow confided. And he confided to Seward that he had occasional questions about Friendly's taste. "Taste, that's the word he used," Steward emphasized. Friendly's taste might produce nine bad ideas for every good one. But Murrow knew enough about creativeness to accept this as a respectable average. He once described Friendly as "The only man I know who can take off without warming his motors." And so he accepted the excesses as a price worth paying and acted as the guidance system on an occasionally unguided but powerful missile. Murrow's timing and story sense were almost unerring, and once he felt right about a story, there was no one like Friendly to realize it, to deploy the crews, to pore over the miles of film that came back, to edit, to cut and juxtapose with a cumulative story-telling power that amounted to filmmaking genius.

They socialized. The Friendlys were occasionally invited to Quaker Hill. It meant a great deal to Fred. To be accepted into Murrow's professional circle had affirmed his professional worth. To be Ed Murrow's friend fed another part of his soul.

Janet, reserved and understated, found Friendly overbearing. When Friendly did something that outraged her, Ed would laugh it off with "Oh well. That's just Fred." Janet's sympathies were with Dorothy Friendly, a woman of a sensitive and artistic nature. As eventually the mother of three children and wife of a man whose irresistible mistress was his work, her life cannot have been smooth. "Dorothy was under great pressure," Janet said. "She suffered breakdowns. She wanted to leave Fred. But he wouldn't let her."[13]

Ed Murrow's relationship with the *See It Now* staff had something of a practiced bonhomie about it. He knew everyone by their first names. He knew what they did and was generous in his praise. Indeed, there was great skill in the timing and content of his compliments. Daniel Schorr remembered an early broadcast appearance with Murrow and Murrow's introduction: "Now here's Dan Schorr who goes out into the field really covering the news while I sit here mouthing it. Dan I cannot tell you what it means to have the freshness of your perceptions...." The sensation, said Schorr, was euphoria: "All of a sudden, you were being called a hero by your hero, by everyone else's hero in the business." Schorr was experiencing the knack that Murrow had possessed all his life for turning his total attention to a person and making that person feel that he or she was the most important figure in his life, when all their intelligence argued against the logic of such a pleasant conclusion.

He had an innate talent for directness that much impresses other men. He told one of his staff, with a withering glower, "You are a pompous ass!" And after a perfectly timed pause, added, "but you're one hell of a reporter." Then he walked away. His displeasure in a staff member was rarely articulated, but it was unmistakable. He usually said nothing. Those subordinates who experienced them describe Murrow's silences as more daunting than taking another boss's heat.

Those with whom he worked closely, like Palmer Williams, found him utterly without pretense. "When I'd put him on a plane to join one of the camera crews in the field, I'd ask if he minded lugging along mikes, and cameras. He'd just take the stuff and say, 'Point the body in the right direction.'" Yet his accessibility had a fleeting quality that kept even close associates off balance. "I never knew," Don Hewitt remembered, "if Ed Murrow was going to throw his arm around me or snub me."

He possessed that quality of all charismatic leaders for forging an us-against-them solidarity among his followers. "Them" meant the CBS news executives and financial people, the "bean-counters," in Murrow's view, who dared to exert influence over him. A frequent target was Sig Mickelson, putatively, as head of CBS television news and public affairs, responsible for *See It Now*. As Mickelson described the Murrow intramural style: "At meetings Ed did not indulge in give and take. He would hold back, on the fringe, and wait for his opening. Then he'd make a verbal lunge and grab center stage. You could feel the vanity, the need to dominate. You could see his impatience, sitting in on any meeting where he wasn't the center of attention. If his correspondents or his staff were there, you could just see them fall in line behind him as soon as he took a position."

It was as if two halves of different personalities had been welded together. He was magnetic at one moment and remote the next, effusive and reticent, approachable and inaccessible. He developed the same after-hours camaraderie with his *See It Now* people as he had with his radio news staff at Colbee's. After *See It Now* was over, the crew repaired to the Pentagon Bar on the corner of 43rd Street and Vanderbilt Avenue, across from the Grand Central Terminal Building. "If Ed invited you to sit with him," Hewitt recalled, "it meant you'd received his blessing for that day."[14]

The stokers in the engine room adored the captain. But day to day, they labored under Friendly, the chief engineer. To understand the man, to pardon or at least put into perspective his excesses, requires that one understand a simple premise: Fred Friendly existed for one purpose, *See It Now*. Friendly told Joe Wershba, when the series began, "They are going to end up calling me the worst son of a bitch in the business. But we're going to turn out the greatest show this business has ever known." That was it, the alpha and omega of Fred W. Friendly.

Palmer Williams came home at an ungodly hour after completing work on the first broadcast and told his wife, "I've got to find another job. These people will never be able to keep up this pace." They were working seventy and eighty hours a week under Friendly's unremitting pressure. Williams came back another day with the opticals for the first program's title. The word "See" was to flash on the screen, then "It," and then "Now," in quick, bold succession. Before anyone had a chance to edit the film properly, Friendly insisted on running it. Consequently, there was too much lag between the unedited words. "Friendly grabbed me by the throat," Williams recalled of the moment, "and screamed, 'You son of a bitch! If you're trying to screw this operation up, I'll kill you!'"

Another producer, Gene de Poris, came home well after midnight only to have the telephone wake him at 2 a.m. Friendly was on the line. After de Poris had hung up, his wife asked, "What can be left to say that didn't get said in twelve hours at the office?"

Every morning, Ed Bliss commuted from his home in Dobbs Ferry to CBS in Manhattan. On the way in, he would stop to pick up Fred Friendly at his apartment in Riverdale. "I'd go up to the apartment," Bliss recalled, "and Fred would be completely relaxed. 'Pour yourself a cup of coffee, Ed,' he'd say, 'the milk's in the refrigerator.' He was relaxed and affable. Then we'd start driving into town down the West Side Highway. Fred would be reading the paper. I could literally feel the tension build up. The big body would start to get tense. The pages would begin to snap. By the time we got to the office, the transmogrification was complete. The terror, the beast, the ogre, had taken over for the day." At night, they would get into the car, and the process was reversed. As they headed for Riverdale, Bliss said, "I watched the tension drain out of him and I'd leave off an affable Fred Friendly."

Virtually everyone at CBS who ever crossed his path had a Fred Friendly story. Johnny Aarons's wife Betsy, an able reporter herself, remembered her husband telling her of the Lakehurst incident. Aarons, she said, occasionally performed chores for *See It Now* while still working on the nightly radio news. He had been dispatched by Friendly to Lakehurst, New Jersey, scene of the Hindenburg disaster, to do a latter-day story about Navy dirigibles. Aarons drove out in a blinding snowstorm. The naval commander told him that the weather was too dangerous to put up an airship. Aarons called Friendly and explained the problem, whereupon

Friendly insisted on speaking to the officer himself. "Who's you're boss," Friendly reportedly demanded, and getting the name, called the admiral in Washington. The admiral backed his subordinate. To Aarons, Friendly behaved as though God had set out to thwart Fred Friendly with his snowstorm, and God was going to have to be overruled.

"Fred Friendly never had a nervous breakdown," Dick Salant observed of the man's behavior. "But, he sure was a carrier." The Lakehurst episode was the beginning of an unhappy relationship between Aarons and Friendly. Aarons's partner, Jesse Zousmer, also clashed with Friendly. There was an element of possessiveness involved. Ed Murrow had been theirs first, on the evening news. But Aarons and Zousmer were tough, resourceful men in their own right and would, in time, concoct a plan to win Ed back.

Friendly used Murrow's name shamelessly. When he was on the phone it was always, "Ed wants..., Ed thinks..., Ed says..., Ed expects...." Few at CBS, Friendly knew, were going to run the risk of challenging these proxy requests and possibly failing Ed Murrow.

Friendly adopted a stance of technical ignorance that served him well. He did not know what could not be done. He simply wanted it done. By insisting on the impossible, he managed to achieve a high rate of the improbable. He had hanging on his office wall a saying attributed to Murrow that read: "Difficulty is one excuse that history never accepts." Murrow may have said it; Friendly lived by it. He was congenitally incapable of settling for second best.

In later years, after Fred Friendly's self-esteem had been bolstered by success, he was able to judge his earlier self with surprising candor. As he once told an interviewer, "I had a paper to get out, a terrifying assignment. I was young, apprehensive. I was insecure. Getting out *See It Now* was my job. I did it the only way I knew how to do it. I was in the position of playing the heavy, the nasty guy. It was part of my job. Others might do it by being more tranquil. I was not programmed for tranquillity. My excesses have never been secret to anybody. I couldn't change if I wanted to. Your temper is your safety valve and I've got a big safety valve. But, don't forget, those people prospered under me. Short term? Embarrassment. Long term? When you've been part of something like the McCarthy show, nobody remembers the heartache. I screamed at people and out of it came magnificent television."

Ed Bliss remembered driving back with Fred from a memorial service for a friend. An uncharacteristically subdued Friendly said, "I didn't grow up with the social advantages you had." Bliss, son of a missionary and Yale-educated, who had himself felt Friendly's blowtorch, was "touched by what he told me."

The doctoral candidate Murray Yaeger painted this portrait of Friendly in his habitat: "Always in a rush, his primary concern is the program, and Friendly knows every notch in the film, every splice in the sound track, every word, authentic or dubbed. His mind is constantly working, and with seeming disorganization. He shouts an order to a reporter, asks a question of a cameraman, questions a sound engineer about the quality of someone's voice in a filmed interview for the next program, challenges the staff with suggestions for future possibilities of *See It Now* shows, cracks wise about not being asked to join the staff members who went downstairs to Colbee's for lunch and then dashes off to consider policy with Murrow."

As his self-confidence grew, he was able to get outside of his own insecurities and display an empathy to others. "Friendly was ruthless and brutal," Joe Wershba observed, "and yet could be tender and deeply sensitive to the needs of people around him." He would urge someone who had a sick child at home to take the day off. He could laugh at himself once a crisis passed. Asked once if it were true that he had thrown a chair at an assistant, he answered, "Not true. It was a table."

His fury was not always authentic. He and Williams had gone to screen a film, and the editor, who had labored half the night, was explaining the trouble the footage had given him. Friendly interrupted: "There's nothing wrong with that film, that a little hard work and imagination on your part couldn't cure," and stalked out. Outside in the corridor, waiting for the elevator, he turned to Williams and said, "I must be getting old. There was a time when I would have had him in tears with that line."

He learned in time what Murrow knew instinctively, that praise can inspire as well as fear. He took to calling the crew, "We band of brothers." He drove people, but he let the film editors, the reporters, and the writers have their say. He created an atmosphere of give and take that made his people feel part of the great enterprise for which he was working them to the bone. Stephen Fleischman worked for Friendly before moving to ABC and remembered of his CBS experience, "Friendly had the ability to make you feel as though you were the most talented guy in the world." And Friendly could be generous in his praise of others. He paid a touching tribute to his early recruit, Palmer Williams: "He was my teacher as much as Murrow."

He behaved like a pushy mother who drives her brood mercilessly, but let someone else threaten them, and she becomes a protective lioness. "He did something terribly important for reporters," Howard K. Smith said of Friendly. "Because they are looked on with distrust by executives, they must have a producer who will fight for them. Fred Friendly would fight for us."

Even David Schoenbrun, who thought that one of Murrow's few failings was that he did not hold Fred Friendly in check, who had "titanic battles with Friendly," and who found Friendly "an amoral journalist," said, "He and his staff gave an extra dimension to my work that was simply wonderful."

What no one ever accused Friendly of was demanding more of anyone else than he demanded of himself. His rages often felled innocent bystanders; but often as not they were really directed at Friendly himself out of frustration that he could not reach the impossible goals he set.

As Bill Leonard described the difference between Murrow and Friendly: "Murrow could be abashed. Fred could not be abashed by anything. He didn't care what you thought about him." Leonard had a peculiar word of praise for Friendly: "In the highest sense of the word, he was shameless.... You could tour the broadcast world," Leonard believed, "collecting horror stories about Fred Friendly without hearing a single lie. But, on the scales, none of it would outweigh his contribution to the art of documentary filmmaking."

Or as Friendly himself put it: "Regardless of what mayhem may have been committed during the day, at the end of the day, we did the impossible. I am what I am, a great overachiever."

Hearing the gripes of the staff about Friendly and shown their occasional wounds, Murrow once said to Bob Dixon, "Deex-ohn, I have created a Frankenstein. I don't know what to do." What the captain on the bridge was going to do was keep on making great documentaries and expect the broad-backed, sweat-streaked chief in the engine room to make it all possible by whatever means.[15]

Within CBS television news, *See It Now* was an independent and somewhat aggrandizing duchy. After the show had been on the air a little over a year, Howard K. Smith sent Murrow a five-page, single-spaced letter from London that read, "Where once we worked for one boss and one organization, we now work for three bosses and three organizations.... each behaves as though it had no idea the other existed." Smith was getting simultaneous orders from CBS radio news to cover a visit by the U.S. secretary of state in England, a CBS television news request to interview Marshall Tito in Yugoslavia, and a call from Friendly, on Murrow's orders of course, to drop everything else for a crucial *See It Now* assignment. Could the heads of the three divisions, Smith asked, occasionally talk to each other? Smith closed his letter explaining that he was sending it to Murrow: "Because I am persuaded by experience that Fred—a well-loved friend, but most inconsiderate manager—won't read a letter unless Murrow asks him to."

Other correspondents echoed Smith's confusion, and in time a central assignment desk was created. But the truth was that the correspondents preferred to work for *See It Now*. Murrow was a visible star. Murrow's programs reverberated. Unlike assignments from Sig Mickelson or Ted Church, which lived for one news cycle, *See It Now* was commented on in newspapers, reviewed in magazines, and talked about by literate people. A snob appeal rose around the program. *See It Now* was the creative edge of television news and public affairs. CBS radio was mere reporting and television news then the featherweight division of journalism. Around Colbee's and the Pentagon Bar, those outside the pale referred acidly to Murrow, Friendly, and their band of brothers as CBS's "third news division."[16]

Apart from the success of *See It Now*, Murrow still had trouble taking news on television seriously. In April of 1952, with a presidential election approaching, Sig Mickelson sent Ed a memo asking if he might use Joe Wershba and Ed Scott as television reporters at the nominating conventions that summer, after, of course, *See It Now* concluded its season. Murrow turned Mickelson down. He might need the two men on his nightly radio news, he said. So much for the authority of Mickelson and television. As the 1952 election approached, Mickelson was determined to field a strong television team. The 1948 campaign, with less than half a million television sets in the country, had been a dress rehearsal. Within four years, there were eighteen million television sets in the United States and a coaxial system connecting sixty-seven major population centers across the country. The presidential campaign in 1952 would be the first in which television would be not simply a witness, but a force. And Mickelson wanted a CBS correspondent who would be on camera virtually throughout the convention, someone to anchor the CBS coverage; "anchorman" was the term Sig Mickelson coined. He wanted a reporter who could comment knowledgeably, extemporaneously, and wittily; who could coordinate the coverage of reporters on the floor and in the candidate's suites; and who could do it all with staying power, hour after hour. He wanted Ed Murrow.

Murrow had earlier turned Mickelson down on the CBS evening television news. He turned Mickelson down again as anchorman for the conventions. Thereafter, with dogged perseverance, Mickelson went down the list of CBS luminaries, asking Collingwood and Sevareid, who followed Murrow's lead and said no. Finally, recognizing that he faced a closed shop among Murrow's Boys, Mickelson threw his net wider.[17]

During the war, Walter Cronkite had chosen the United Press over Ed Murrow. Cronkite thereafter remained with the wire service until his salary plateaued. In 1948, Cronkite reluctantly left his first love and took a job as the Washington radio reporter for a group of Midwest stations, learned the trade he had happily avoided for years, and instantly doubled his salary.

Cronkite's pivotal experience in life, as with Murrow, had been the war. And so when the fighting broke out in Korea, he too heard the fire bell ringing in the night. Most of the stations he worked for were affiliated with CBS, and so he used this angle to send Murrow a telegram saying that if the network needed correspondents to go to Korea, Walter Cronkite was ready. Talent superseded pride, and Murrow was willing to forget that Cronkite had once jilted him for a wire service. He urged CBS news executives to hire Cronkite. But instead of Korea, Cronkite went to CBS's Washington, D.C., station, WTOP. Within weeks of his arrival, Cronkite was asked to fill in temporarily on the CBS network's late evening radio news for an ailing Eric Sevareid. Cronkite sent Murrow a telegram, playing with the standard sign-off on Murrow's nightly news: "Now they can say listen to Murrow tomorrow. Listen to Cronkite tonight!" Murrow, Cronkite concluded, was not amused, since he received no reply. On later reflection, he thought that his telegram must have provided additional proof to Murrow that "this Cronkite was a brash young man."

After he joined CBS, Cronkite had a sense that reporters who were not one of Murrow's Boys were not quite among the anointed. Later, when there could be little doubt of his own stature, he would say that he understood the clannishness: "They were the cream of the crop." And maybe he was of a different stripe. Walter Cronkite was, indisputably, a superb reporter. But he was not the kind of journalist-intellectual who appealed most to Murrow. There was not about him or his work the cerebral aura of a Raymond Swing, an Eric Sevareid, a Bill Shirer, a fact that Cronkite was cheerily the first to admit: "I'm a newsman first, a get the facts, get your lead, old-fashioned reporter."

He also turned out to be very effective on television. He started out at WTOP doing reports on Korea, and eventually became the station's prime-time television newscaster. His reporting had the ring of reliability and authority. There was about Walter Cronkite, if not screen star magnetism, the appeal of a favorite uncle who wore nicely night after night in one's living room.

When Sig Mickelson failed to enlist any of Murrow's Boys for his convention anchorman, CBS executives urged him to consider Bob Trout, tested, dependable, and safe. But Mickelson had his eye on somebody else. And so he reached down into the CBS farm system for Walter Cronkite. It would be Walter Cronkite's last appearance on anybody's second string.[18]

He was superb at the nominating conventions that summer, endlessly knowledgeable, making sense of the exotica of the American quadrennial political circus, skillfully interweaving reports from his correspondents; and indefatigable. Cronkite indeed wore exceedingly well. The CBS reporters at the conventions, who had earlier disdained television, were not blind to success, both Cronkite's and the medium's. They began to mill around Mickelson letting him know that they would not mind at all helping Walter.

They should have been friends, Murrow and Cronkite. Bill Downs was no more "intellectual" than Cronkite, and he and Murrow were pals. But Downs was one of Murrow's Boys, a satellite and not a potential rival sun, which television was making of Walter Cronkite.

They had started out on the wrong foot after London, and the relationship remained out of step. They would cross paths at parties where, in Cronkite's phrase, "Murrow held court. He would sit there, sometimes with his coat off, tie undone, puffing on his cigarette, his elbows on his knees, staring at the floor making pronunciamentos of gloom and doom, while people gathered around him in hushed attention." Cronkite found it "hard to swallow." He also confessed that Murrow "intimidated" him.

Bill Downs and Cronkite had been friends at the UP. And so Cronkite and Murrow were both guests at a party the Downs gave at their home in

Washington early in Cronkite's television career. It was a heavy-drinking, broadcasting crowd. Downs began noisily berating Cronkite, telling him, "You're coming on too hard, trying to be a success, trying to push other people out of the way." Then, according to Downs's wife, Rosalind, Cronkite said a sympathetic word about sponsors. Sponsors, after all, paid the rent, Cronkite pointed out. It was the sort of statement designed to catch the attention of and to provoke Murrow, the news freedom purist against an apologist for commercialism in broadcasting. However, the purist was handsomely sponsored and the apologist, at this point, barely had his foot in television's door. As Roz Downs remembered the night, "They kept snapping at each other all evening. They were practically chin to chin. It was dreadful. After the party, my husband said, 'That was a small disaster. I didn't know they disliked each other that much.'"

Allowing for the inflammatory effect of the alcohol, the clash revealed a lurking trait in Ed Murrow. He was more magnanimous as a superior than as a rival. His dispute with Cronkite had less to do with commercialism in broadcasting than with the age-old wariness of the old stag toward a young buck.[19]

Murrow may have turned down the television role that Cronkite accepted, but with the coming of the 1952 campaign he accepted the medium as a resistless tide in American politics. He had interviewed General Eisenhower early in 1952 for *See It Now*, when it became increasingly likely that Ike would run for the presidency. He told Eisenhower that he was terrible on television and that he had better get some coaching. Eisenhower's dislike for television ranked, he said, with General de Gaulle's refusal to use the telephone. Like it or not, he warned the nascent politician, television was going to be the dominant medium.[20]

His involvement with another Republican candidate was to drive home the point.

In 1952, Robert Taft surely deserved the nomination of his party. Taft was the Republican senator son of a Republican President father, a Republican nonpareil out of the Republican heartland, "Mr. Republican" to the press and his party. Robert Taft was not, however, the sort of politician to appeal to Edward R. Murrow. Taft opposed the formation of NATO and had reversed his earlier support of the United Nations. Here was an insular figure who could fulfill Murrow's dread of America becoming a straggling island off the Kamchatka coast. Virtually a year before the election, *See It Now*'s cameras began to follow the senator from Ohio along the campaign trail, on the stump, even into his home.

Bob Taft trudged through the Christmas-card towns of New Hampshire, hoping to score well in the state's influential early primary. The *See It Now* cameras were there as Taft's colleague from neighboring Massachusetts, Senator Leverett Saltonstall, introduced the candidate. The cameras lingered ever so briefly over Taft's speech, then followed him as he left the platform. At the bottom of the steps, a cluster of children thrust their autograph books at him. The cameras caught Robert Taft brushing them aside with a dismissing wave of the hand as he kept on walking. Senator Saltonstall came down, saw the children, stopped to chat with them, and signed their books. No narration accompanied this portion of the broadcast. None was required. Television had said something about Bob Taft that no prepared speech would ever reveal.

When Murrow had broadcast from London during the war, he liked to describe speech reactions over the air, Churchill's slumping despair at the anemia of Neville Chamberlain's policies. *See It Now*'s cameramen adopted the technique. In Springfield, Illinois, Senator Everett Dirksen was introducing Taft with the oleaginous praise that had caused Dirksen to be called "The Wizard of Ooze." As Dirksen spoke, the camera shifted from the speaker to a close-up of Robert Taft, eyes closed, face wreathed in an expression of ecstasy. It was only four years since Murrow had publicly criticized television at the Democratic Convention for slighting a complex delegate fight and fixing its cameras on a funny hat. Now, Murrow's camera was killing Bob Taft over a foolish smile.[21]

The man who appealed to Murrow's intellectual prejudices became the Democrats' choice that year, Adlai Stevenson. In a speech he was to give later at the Guildhall in London on television and American politics, Murrow described what he liked about Stevenson: "...his gifts of oratory and political analysis, his ability to improvise sentences that would parse, his mastery of debate and the wealth of his ideas."

But he found Stevenson no better prepared for the television age than Dwight Eisenhower. "Stevenson just plain didn't like television," Murrow observed. "He resented the tyranny of the clock, the bright lights, the make-up, everything about it." Murrow was sympathetic. He felt the same way. Unfortunately, Stevenson communicated his distaste to the cameras.

Since becoming a broadcaster, Ed Murrow had never voted. He did not make a point of it. Virtually only his wife knew. Voting, in some way, he told Janet, might impair his professional objectivity. Yet, known to only a small circle, he did something in 1952 that could scarcely be considered nonpartisan. He coached Adlai Stevenson on the use of television. George Ball, then a key figure in the Stevenson camp, recounted in his memoirs how Murrow "arranged for a studio...and after a hassle, I persuaded Stevenson to cooperate. Murrow spent a long afternoon of patient coaching, but it did no good....In spite of his friendship and admiration for Murrow, Stevenson hated the whole exercise and did not conceal his distaste. He even chided me about the expense of the studio."[22]

All the people Murrow associated with, all his friends, with few exceptions, supported Stevenson. One exception was Bill Paley. Paley in his autobiography spoke of being raised as a Republican who crossed party lines often. Paley of the small, feisty, growing radio network supported Roosevelt, while Paley of the media giant and Paley, infiltrator of the eastern social establishment, supported Eisenhower. But for Murrow and most of his circle, Stevenson was their man. They were captivated by the idea that an intellectual, a man of erudition and wit, a "word" person like themselves, could become President.[23]

In 1952, Howard K. Smith wanted to come home from Europe to cover an American election. His first stop in New York was to Murrow's office. "Ed told me," he recalled of the visit, "'that this man Stevenson is something new. We've finally discovered somebody with greatness. He's going to win.' I said, 'I'm glad to hear that. He's impressed me from the little I've heard on the radio.'" Thereafter, Smith was assigned to cover the Stevenson campaign for two weeks and then the Eisenhower campaign for the next two weeks. After two days with Eisenhower, he cabled Murrow, "Hedge your bets. Eisenhower is going to win."

"Ed was not politically sophisticated," Smith said. "He didn't care much about politics. He became attached to personalities, to causes. He was more a crusader than a reporter. In Britain during the war, he came alive. He found a cause that brought out his intelligent intuition."

Churchill had led Britain from her darkest to her finest hour, and Murrow thought that Churchill would be elected prime minister in 1945. He was wrong. Stevenson stood for rationality in the face of rigid cold war postures and for democratic dissent in the face of McCarthyism. Murrow thought that Stevenson would be elected President. And Stevenson lost too. Smith was right. For all his professed journalistic objectivity, Murrow was a subjective reporter, and it was this very subjectivity that lent his reporting its heart and its fire. But subjectivity makes for a poor political handicapper.

Eric Sevareid and Ed joked about Ed's powers as a political analyst. "I would be on the heels of a campaign," Sevareid remembered, "but Ed had to be thrown into it. We used to have to backstop him on politics." He was uncomfortable working the midway of a political convention. He disliked functioning with 5,000 people milling around him and having to press himself on politicians in public. He was a famous man and felt conspicuous on the convention floor with the clumsy portable paraphernalia of early television strapped to his back. "He was," in Bill Leonard's phrase, "not at his ease in mad houses."[24]

Politics may not have been his strength, but communication was, and he later described what happened when American politics began to be played out on a small screen in the living room. "He [the politician] must have a quality not considered essential in the past, that is simplicity. A politician to be popular must not be too complicated. He must not appear to be too subtle....Eisenhower was simple, while Stevenson was considerably less so. Stevenson was more deft, had greater command of language and overtone and had much more humor....[Ike] could be trusted because he was not complicated....Stevenson on the other hand gave the impression that things are pretty complicated and would require some hard thinking and difficult decisions....Simplicity communicates itself more easily than complexity in persons and it also does when it comes to issues and this is part of the exchange brought about by television. This is by no means a boon....the art of self government is not going to be perfected by the process of simplification alone."[25]

He and other practitioners in this new craft were also beginning to sense in it a disturbing power absent in the press and radio. Newspapers reported the past. Radio could report the past and the present, by reporting an event in progress. Television could do both and, by influencing the behavior of those in camera range, could influence the future as well. A what-came-first riddle emerged, the television cameras covering an act or the presence of cameras generating the act? Murrow was of the generation that released this genie from the bottle.

The case of Robert Pierpoint is a small, but instructive, early example of the dilemma. In 1951, CBS radio hired the 25-year-old Pierpoint to cover the war in Korea. Pierpoint underwent his baptism of fire with Fox Company, Nineteenth Regiment, at a position less than 100 yards from the Chinese Communist lines. It was night. The American company commander had called in close artillery support. Pierpoint was cranking up a bulky Japanese tape recorder when a short round went shrieking overhead and sent him and other troops hurtling into a trench. The tape recorder caught it all and produced a stunning piece of radio verité.

At that time, Murrow and Friendly were still producing *Hear It Now*. Pierpoint knew that they were eager for fresh material, and so he sent his tape to Murrow. He not only received a warm cable of congratulations, but was told about the upcoming venture, *See It Now*, and that Murrow and Friendly wanted him to duplicate the same raw realism for their television cameras.

Pierpoint was shocked. As he later recounted his quandary, "There was no way I could take a television crew on that line at night. We'd need lights, and the minute we turned those lights on, I didn't know who would shoot me first, our GIs or the Chinese."

Pierpoint faced another problem in capturing the reality of combat. Since the earlier story, Fox Company had taken heavy casualties and had been sent to the rear. Pierpoint cabled back that the story requested was "Impossible." He received a reply, "Work it out somehow." And soon thereafter, a *See It Now* camera crew arrived in Korea.

Pierpoint took the crew to Fox Company's rest area, where "we shot hundreds of feet of film of GIs digging trenches, building bunkers, answering mail call, eating, singing, griping." Since the virus of television had also begun to infect the GIs, they happily fired off their weapons for the *See It Now* cameras.

In his communications to the home office, Pierpoint emphasized that Fox Company had not been near the actual fighting. And when the Korea segment appeared on the first broadcast of *See It Now*, Murrow did not say specifically that it was shot at the front. On the other hand he did not say that it was not. Pierpoint felt that the point had been "blurred." "I became a temporary hero to Murrow and Friendly," he recalled. But his fellow war correspondents were filled with scorn.

Pierpoint's initial reaction was to blame Friendly for his predicament. It was Friendly, he assumed, who had insisted on going through with the story. It was Friendly who would have edited the film. But, on fuller reflection, he knew that Murrow had seen the film, had worked on the script, and had final control over the program. Pierpoint, as a young, idealistic journalist to whom Murrow was a demigod, was disappointed.[26]

Television, they were all learning, was a far more viscous substance than print or radio. They were discovering that the television camera was not neutral, that it did not simply record, but intruded on, even provoked, behavior. And they were finding out that television, because of its great plasticity, tested the willpower and the judgment of its users. The mild ambiguity of the report on Fox Company in Korea merely presaged a perpetual quandary. Where is the line to be drawn between television journalism that observes and television journalism that incites? Can such a line even be discerned? Even when television journalists discipline themselves not to manipulate the subjects before their cameras, how do they prevent the subjects from manipulating them? As the sixties radicals raised on the medium were later to express it, unless something happened on television, it didn't happen. Does television record terrorism, or does it deliver the stage, lights, and sound recording for terrorist dramas that would otherwise wither for lack of an audience? There was no answer in Murrow's first broadcast of *See It Now,* when television was young. There is none yet.

Murrow had not been in Korea himself since the early weeks of the war. Two and half years had passed, and the conflict had dragged on longer and bloodier than anticipated. Since his trip to the front in 1950, the Chinese Communists had come in on the side of the North Koreans and President Truman had relieved General MacArthur of command in the boldest exercise of civilian over military authority since Lincoln. Truman's act made Murrow proud of his country. The supremacy of civilian over military power, he said in his nightly commentary, "may appear to some to be an academic point, but not to people who have witnessed what happens when the civilian authority abdicates to the military." He also found Truman's action emotionally satisfying, the little guy triumphing over an imperious centurion. He gave a speech before an audience of businessmen, and one of them asked what he thought of Truman's decision. MacArthur had been removed, Murrow said, "for what could properly be termed insubordination," and added that the general had subsequently retreated to New York, "thwarted in his political ambitions, sulking in his Waldorf tent."

Something in the conduct of the war in Korea offended Murrow's native egalitarianism. The Selective Service System had set up a program for deferring college students from the draft, provided they passed a standard examination. To Murrow the device smacked more of the hiring of substitutes in the Civil War than the democratic distribution of risk that had characterized World War II. He was incensed enough to make one of his rare appearances in print. In an article in the *Saturday Review*, he asked, "Is deferment going to be possible only for those whose parents happen to have been intelligent or wealthy?...If this rule had been applied in earlier days, people like the Wright brothers, Mark Twain, Phil Murray, Andrew Carnegie, Henry Ford, Thomas Edison and Harry S. Truman among others wouldn't have had a chance of being deferred, because none of them went to college....We have never proceeded in this country on the basis of giving preference to an intellectual elite....we have never, I think, decided who should carry a musket on the basis of his intellectual horsepower."

As for the war itself, he had lost confidence in it. Shortly after the Chinese entered the war, he made a speech in Birmingham and said, "We should set up lines at the narrow waist of Korea....and then call for the Navy to come and get [the troops].... We should concentrate on saving Western Europe, because the U.S. is in no position to fight for the European continent at the same time we are fighting in the East....for this country to become involved in a land war in Asia is unthinkable. If we decide, as we did three years ago, that Europe is our primary interest, and that militarily, Korea is of no strategic importance, then there is no reason why we should not pull out of Korea lock, stock and barrel."

It was a bold stand, and one that few Americans, particularly in his highly visible position, were taking at the time. He never uttered so clear a disapproval of the war over the air, either in his tailpieces on the evening news or on *See It Now*. In his radio commentaries, he limited himself to making clear his bias favoring Europe as the amphitheater of interest to America. Korea and mainland Asia were a bog into which American blood and treasure would sink without a trace.

The speech seems not to have reverberated beyond the circulation of the *Birmingham News*. Why he would speak out so bluntly against the war in a speech but not on the air has several explanations. Even with his special relationship to Paley, even with his sponsor's tolerance, a call for pulling out of a war, in effect conceding America's first military defeat, was more editorialization than the network or the sponsor could swallow. It went even well beyond what Murrow himself believed was appropriate for a figure who was above all a reporter and presumably not a polemicist or advocate. Platforms like that in Birmingham offered an opportunity for him to get off his chest—as an individual—what he did not feel was appropriate for a CBS correspondent.

His lack of enthusiasm for the war in Asia was hardly prompted by a tolerance of communism. It was a matter of where to apply the pressure. He was a man of Europe. If the Soviet Union was dealt with effectively in

Europe, there was no need for America to sink into the swamp of Asia, he believed. As he said over the radio, "The Russians are directing this whole global conflict, including Korea."[27]

Korea repelled him politically; but the dark charm of war still drew him emotionally. After the presidential election, in December of 1952, he informed Janet that he would not be spending Christmas with the family. He was taking *See It Now* to Korea.

He sent a memo in advance to his staff:

> Although this is to be a maximum effort, it is not to be a tour de force or an efficient flexing of our muscles or razzle dazzle or fancy gadgets and exciting switches. We are simply going to try to portray the face of war and the faces of the men now fighting it. It's our attempt to narrow the distance between the doughfoot out there and the people at home who may watch the show....the best picture we could get would be a single GI hacking away at a single foxhole in the ice of a Korean winter or a guy on an icy road trying to change a flat tire in zero temperature. We're anxious to know how you change a spark plug when your hands are too numb to coordinate. Or a close-up of what frost bite looks like, or a doughfoot explaining the science of how to keep your feet dry.

He took with him a fifteen-man camera crew and used six reporters, including Bill Downs, Larry Le Sueur, Bob Pierpoint, Ed Scott, Joe Wershba, and Lou Cioffi, who years before had served Murrow as a CBS copyboy. The size and aura of the entourage were such that the word around CBS, Bob Trout remembered, was that "If you didn't go to Korea with Ed, you were finished."

Pierpoint was on hand when Murrow arrived. Ed's first question, Pierpoint recalled, was, "Where's most of the action? I want to go up to the line and do something with the infantry."

He was 44 now, but uncomplainingly slept in a tent, ate a soldier's rations, and went out of his way to court danger. Pierpoint told him, "You know, you don't have to die to experience fear." To Lou Cioffi, "Murrow seemed a happier man in Korea than the man I remembered behind a desk in New York." Again, it was the attraction of pure physical and emotional experience luring a man who had a nagging feeling that what he did in an oversophisticated metropolis, juggling words all day, was not quite real. Like the bomber over Berlin, the front in Korea was for Ed Murrow an escape.

He also did radio broadcasts while in Korea, and they suggest a man half in love with war and death. "The trouble with middle-aged correspondents, he said, is that they know too much about what they are getting into. But there is a terrible fascination about danger, even that part of it that tells your stomach and your liver that they are not so steady as they once were. And there is something about trying to report a war that humbles a man, and at the same time makes him proud; proud to try to translate into words the things that no man has ever put into words and no man ever will."

"Christmas in Korea" was broadcast on December 28, 1952. Nearly twenty miles of film had been shipped back to Friendly in New York. What he carved from that mass was a prodigy of editing. The broadcast began with the scrape of an infantryman's shovel against the frozen Korean earth.

As John Crosby, writing for *The New York Herald Tribune*, described the broadcast: "There wasn't a single shot of a soldier yanking a lanyard on a 105 mm cannon, no shots of bombers tearing great holes in the Korean real estate. Instead, the cameras focussed on the soldiers of Fox Company of an infantry regiment, catching them as they ate and slept and gambled and groaned and joked, catching the tedium of warfare, the waiting, the humor of an essentially unhumorous occupation, the humanity of an essentially inhuman profession."

Harriet Van Horne wrote of "Christmas in Korea" that it "had the impact of a jagged rock under your bare feet....no matter where the cameras turned yesterday, one felt the aching sensation of cold." To Jack Gould in *The New York Times*, "Christmas in Korea" was "a visual poem, one of the finest programs ever seen on television."

In work like "Christmas in Korea," television attained an experiential power worthy of its technical genius. In the enlargement of human understanding, it mattered little that television could bring a comedian's routine to five million instead of 500 people. It mattered a great deal that, virtually for the first time, millions saw, unadorned, the naked face of war. In "Christmas in Korea," all the resources of *See It Now*—Murrow's will to penetrate to the heart of reality and transport it back to the viewer in as pure a form as possible, cameramen with the eyes of poets, several of the finest reporters in broadcasting, Palmer Williams's mastery of the technology of television, and finally Friendly's capacity to transform great masses of celluloid into a seamless whole—converged in a new art form.

Murrow intended, on the way back from Korea, to stop off in the state of Washington to visit his mother and father. But the exposure to cold, the lack of sleep, the punishing pace he had been maintaining, felled him. He wound up instead with influenza in a hospital near Seattle. He eventually returned to New York but could not shake off the fever and weakness. He checked into another hospital for a week of tests. Nothing specific was found beyond the fact that his lungs had again failed him.[28]

Murrow had taken on *See It Now* while also continuing the nightly news and *This I Believe*. After working all week, he and Friendly would disappear into the cutting room on a Saturday afternoon, not emerging often until two or three o'clock in the morning. They would be back in the studio by 11 a.m. Sunday to record the transitions between the segments. The program was a hybrid, part filmed, part live, which meant that Murrow had to be back in the studio in the afternoon for the actual broadcast.

The early technology was maddeningly complicated. The best effects were obtained by having the picture and sound on separate tracks. Thus, the film was projected from a production facility at 550 Fifth Avenue, the sound came in from CBS studios at 485 Madison Avenue, and the live portion originated at Studio 41 in the Grand Central Terminal Building where the three strands were braided. Often the mixing for a later segment in the program was still going on while an earlier segment played over the air.

Murrow invited David Lilienthal, who had headed the U.S. Atomic Energy Commission, to come on *See It Now* and describe research in the use of atomic isotopes to treat cancer. The projector failed, and the filmed portion ground down like an unwound Victrola and Murrow's voice along with it. The camera switched to Murrow live in the studio. He seized the "lifeboat" microphone and, with determined casualness, said, "We admit we don't know much about atomic energy. After this, we don't seem to know much about television either." He then proceeded to ad-lib a tour of the control room gadgetry. Afterward, Murrow shrugged off the incident as an inevitable part of the new medium's growing pains, and he left the studio to have a drink with Lilienthal.

But Friendly suffered. He stayed behind and had the technicians run the offending projector endlessly. He reported to Murrow later that the machine had run for six hours without a hitch.

Murrow regarded the hardware of television—the hundreds of pounds of equipment required, the cameras, tripods, film magazines, lights, and batteries, as so many millstones around his neck. The days of a single microphone in a cubicle in the BBC basement began to take on a pastoral quality in his memory. He told Bill Leonard, "I wish goddamned television had never been invented. It's tough enough to have to write. Then you have to report. Then you bring in the microphones. I can just about handle that much complication, when you add the camera and the lights. It's more than anyone should have to bear."

He told a reporter: "I wanted to do a piece on the inherent powers of the President when Mr. Truman seized the steel mills, but how do you show that on television? When the French cabinet fell, the last time, I couldn't find a way to contribute to the television viewer's understanding of complicated French politics....In radio at least you can deal with ideas and issues....I am in control in radio. I can always wrestle with a microphone. But, in television it has control of me. I am a prisoner of cameras, lights and newsclips."

He was having an after-work drink with Ed Bliss one evening, and Bliss mentioned the new programs coming up on television, including NBC's most recent entry, *The Today Show*. Murrow told Bliss that the idea of anyone looking at television while getting up in the morning struck him as "obscene."

"The sad part of television," he said, "is that I have lost my anonymity. I have my fair share of vanity, of course, but in traveling around the country, I would prefer to be unrecognized rather than be suddenly engaged in conversation by people I don't know. They're well meaning and polite, but I'd rather be left alone."[29]

He was, however, well paid for his loss of privacy. By the end of 1952, his annual earnings totaled $211,000, making Murrow the highest-paid person at CBS, outside of the entertainment field.

"Christmas in Korea" was the last in the *See It Now* series for 1952. Behind lay successes, failures, frustration, and a new form of communication. The series covered presidential candidates and the simple majesty of democracy in a West Virginia sheriff's race. It caught the plucky mood of isolated West Berlin, and what went on behind the black-robed formidability of the Supreme Court. Murrow's objective was always to penetrate reality, even to anticipate it. The Air Force staged a mock atomic attack on New York City to test the necessity for an air warning system. Three bombers were to make the imaginary attack accompanied by three jet fighters. Murrow flew in one of the jets. The plane suffered a flameout. He nearly blacked out in a steep dive. As the aircraft began to run out of fuel, the pilot began an emergency landing on Mitchell Field on Long Island. The landing gear jammed, and he had to use the auxiliary gear. As the plane screeched to a stop, Murrow staggered from the cockpit. "I'm getting too goddamn old for this," he said. But Palmer Williams noticed, "After the fear wore off, he seemed exhilarated." He had penetrated another layer of reality and revealed it to his audience.

In the fall of 1951, he took a crew to England to cover the British elections. Winston Churchill had already seemed an old man when he took power in 1940 at age 66. He was now campaigning again for prime minister at 77. The Murrows had continued to send little gifts to the Churchills through Britain's lean postwar years. In one thank-you note, Lady Churchill reported, "a parcel full of delicious and nourishing foods came here from you about ten days ago." Another note thanked Janet "for that luscious ham." Another thanked the Murrows for "your wonderful gift of eggs."

On this latest visit, Ed had a private conversation with Churchill the night of the old man's last campaign appearance in Plymouth. The humpty-dumpty torso sagged rather more than before, the back was hunched, the words did not flow quite so quickly; but they had the old bite. Churchill told Murrow that he was astonished that the incumbent Clement Attlee had allowed the Americans to place nuclear weapons bases in East Anglia free of British control. "It may well be true, as I read in the public print," Churchill told Murrow, "that your great nation has scores of atom bombs while the Russians have but a dozen.

However, if as a result of your policies, they should choose to cast down upon us a dozen, we shall be considerably inconvenienced."

Praise for *See It Now* poured in, but not profits. CBS's financial people were horrified at the spending. The show's cameramen had by now been cured of their old newsreel frugality. As a general rule, they shot twenty feet of film for every foot used. Stock footage from film archives was disdained. Friendly had a camera crew and reporters spend a month on the Orient Express for a story that ran for nine minutes and thirty-four seconds on the air.

Murrow took a perverse pleasure in his obliviousness to costs. "I'm the only one sitting on the [CBS] Board," he once remarked, "who knows where the bodies are buried." For producing "Christmas in Korea," he pulled an estimate of $10,000 out of thin air, but overlooked $20,000 in travel expenses alone. For each weekly edition of *See It Now*, ALCOA paid $34,000 for the air time and another $23,000 to cover production costs. Any additional costs, and a single program easily surpassed $100,000, came out of CBS's pocket. By the time the bills came in, Friendly said, "The show's a hit, and it's hard to squawk about a hit, even if it's a money-losing hit."

It fell to the hapless Sig Mickelson, as the television news chief, to try to discipline *See It Now*'s costs. Mickelson arranged meetings of Murrow, Friendly, and the businesspeople to see what was to be done about what Mickelson considered "outrageous" cost overruns. Of these sessions, Mickelson would later say, "I never felt that I was sitting talking with Ed on a man-to-man basis. I always had the feeling he was putting on some kind of an act, that he was holding back. It was hard to read his motives. I'd explain the problem, and he'd walk away. Or, he would say, 'If that's the way you want it, get yourself another boy.'" Of course, there was no other boy.

Later, Mickelson would learn what Murrow had been holding back. "I'd find out that he had gone to see Bill Paley and had settled everything upstairs and that my authority had been undercut again."

Murrow's quicksilver role changes rattled Mickelson. He had gone to Baltimore for an award ceremony and came back on the train with Murrow. Mickelson remembered of the journey, "He told me great stories all the way. We got along like we were old pals. He was warm. But as soon as we got to New York, it was back to famous correspondent versus pain-in-the-ass executive, especially if there were his other correspondents around to enjoy watching him take on the brass."

Reflecting years later on these exchanges, Mickelson spoke of Murrow with traces of ancient resentment and grudging admiration: "He was a man of colossal ego and vanity. He had a sense of theater about him. But, that's the quality that made him a success."

Bill Paley was content to absorb the losses from *See It Now* and bask in its accolades. For, as 1952 ended, and after accumulated losses of $63 million, CBS television operations finally went into the black.[30]

See It Now indeed gave luster to the network. After five weeks on the air, *Variety* awarded the program a special citation as "The most original, informative and entertaining type of journalism now riding the video waves." Gilbert Seldes had pioneered as a television director with CBS as early as 1942. Seldes later turned to cultural criticism and found in television much to criticize. But of *See It Now*, he declared it "the most important show on the air—not only for the solutions that it found to some problems, but also for the problems it tackles without finding the right answers."

In Don Hewitt's experience, "Television was never the same after the first *See It Now*. Ed Murrow made television respectable. All the big names in radio, Sevareid and Howard Smith and Collingwood, could stop looking down their noses at television. Ed was a hero of the intellectual establishment. So now it was respectable for them to own a television set—or admit they owned one."[31]

The sponsor was happy too. ALCOA's executives left Murrow and Friendly alone and rarely knew what they were sponsoring until they saw *See It Now* on the air. Arthur Hall, ALCOA's vice president for public relations, ran a survey and learned that a gratifying percentage of congressmen and government officials watched *See It Now*. Eighty-seven percent of its viewers could identify the program's sponsor. Popularity surveys revealed that the number of people who "liked" ALCOA was steadily increasing. ALCOA salesmen found that the program was one of the first things customers mentioned. The company's rank-and-file employees liked being identified with so prestigious a program. ALCOA might not sell a pot or a pan over *See It Now*, but the company felt that it was getting its money's worth.

See It Now had originally gone on the air at 3:30 on Sunday afternoon, the "intellectual ghetto." After the first successful six months, Murrow won a better slot, 6:30 p.m. The audience rose steadily from 1.4 million to 2.5 million homes by the end of the second season and continued to grow.

And yet that burr of discontent under Murrow's soul did not fail him even in this hour of triumph. He felt compelled to express his immunity to the siren lure of success on television. "I never see the ratings," he maintained. "I refuse to ask or be told....it's a mystery to me why a person, any civilized person, would be sitting at home on a Sunday afternoon watching television....a lot of people are deluding themselves that this instrument is supposed to be a weapon of intelligence and sophistication. I find too many people to whom this is a miracle instrument that will make people wiser, more discerning. It takes more than a camera, as it takes more than presses and newsprint to make a newspaper." These were the thoughts he expressed to a reporter interviewing him about winning his fourth Peabody Award with *See It Now*.[32]

CHAPTER 22

The Age of Suspicion

Deirdre Mason occasionally ran across Ed in the lobby of the CBS Building at 485 Madison Avenue. They had been good friends during his NSFA presidency, when she was a pacifist, bemused by Ed's pleasure in the ROTC. They had sailed to Europe together in 1930 for the Conference of the Confederation Internationale des Etudiants. She fondly remembered thereafter the earnest young man who preferred talking philosophy with her at the ship's rail to dancing in the ship's lounge. Mason had settled in New York and become an actress, working occasionally on CBS dramas. When their paths crossed, they exchanged warm greetings, but saw little else of each other.

One day in the mid-fifties, Deirdre Mason called to ask if she could see him. Something was troubling her, she said. Ed invited her to meet him for lunch.

At this stage in her life, Mason no longer considered herself particularly political. She was simply an actress. The extent of her activism was membership in Americans for Democratic Action. One day, without explanation, she was dropped from the Kraft Theater on NBC. Now CBS had sent her some sort of loyalty oath that she was to sign, along with her contract for a part in a play. She considered the oath a slur against her patriotism. Harking back to their NSFA days, she told Ed, "This is what we fought against. This is where we came in. What are we going to do about it?"[1]

Everyone employed by or under contract to CBS had received the same oath. "We were," Eric Sevareid said, "hurt by it." David Schoenbrun called the oath a "disgrace." Bill Downs said that he was damned if he would sign it. Don Hollenbeck asked Ed if they should not organize to fight the oath. Morris Ernst, the liberal lawyer, urged Ed not to sign it as an example to the rest of the industry.

In 1950, some months before the loyalty oath surfaced, Fred Friendly had gone to see one of the network's administrative vice presidents for approval to commission original theme music for *Hear It Now*. He gave the man a list of three distinguished American composers in order of preference. As Friendly later wrote of the meeting, "He glanced at the top name and asked, 'Is he in the book?'

"'I don't know,' I said, 'but I'm sure Music Clearance has his number.'

"'I know,' said the vice president, 'but is he in the book?'

"I started to ask a secretary for a telephone directory when the vice president pulled open a drawer of his desk and said, 'This is the book we live by.' It was a little paperback called *Red Channels*." The age of suspicion had arrived at CBS.

It is a mark of either Murrow's congenital pessimism or his foresight that he was not taken entirely by surprise. As he had told Janet when they flew home from England for good in 1946, they had witnessed perfectly civilized European countries behave barbarously, and Ed had said, "There's no reason to suppose it can't happen here."[2]

Within a year after his return, the House Un-American Activities Committee was subpoenaing film actors, producers, directors, and writers, investigating Communist infiltration of Hollywood. Murrow was at the time still a CBS vice president and fretted privately in a letter to Harold Laski, "Our 'red scare' continues and will, I think, increase in intensity and irresponsibility." By the fall of 1947, he was back on the air and in one of his earliest tailpieces sent a raking fire across the House Un-American Activities Committee: "A certain number of people have been accused either of being Communists or of following the Communist line. Their accusers are safe from the laws of slander and libel. Subsequent denials are unlikely to ever catch up with the original allegation.... Considerable mention was made at the hearings of two films, *Mission to Moscow* and *Song of Russia*. I am no movie critic, but I remember what was happening in the war when those films were released.... During all this time, there were people in high places in London and Washington who feared lest the Russians might make a separate peace with Germany. If these pictures, at that time and in that climate, were subversive, then what comes next under the scrutiny of a congressional committee? Correspondents who wrote and broadcast that the Russians were fighting well and suffering appalling losses?...either we believe in the intelligence, good judgment, balance and native shrewdness of the American people, or we believe that government should investigate, intimidate and finally legislate....The right of dissent—or if you prefer, the right to be wrong—is surely fundamental to the existence of a democratic society. That's the right that went first in every nation that stumbled down the trail of totalitarianism.... We might remember a little-known quotation from Adolf Hitler, spoken in Königsberg before he achieved power. He said, 'The great strength of the totalitarian state is that it will force those who fear it to imitate it.'"

He despised behavior that made America look foolish or frightened. Leo Isaacson had been elected to Congress from the Bronx on the left-wing American Labor Party ticket. In 1948, Isaacson applied for a passport to attend a conference in Paris on the civil war then raging in Greece. The State Department denied him a passport on grounds that his presence abroad "would not be in the best interest of this country." *The New York Times* adopted the same editorial position, declaring that "No citizen is entitled to go abroad to oppose the policies and the interests of his country."

Murrow had more faith that the Republic could survive one left-wing congressman than did the government or *The Times*. He said in a radio tailpiece "...In terms of the impact upon foreign opinion, it is doubtful whether any oratory or intrigue in which Mr. Isaacson might have been engaged would have been more damaging to the interest of this country than the fact that he has been denied permission to leave."[3]

In the thirties, he had worked with the Emergency Committee to find a place for gifted people in this country. Now, fear was locking them out. "If that intrepid navigator and national hero [Columbus] should arrive upon our shores today," Murrow broadcast, "he couldn't get in. He couldn't get a visa...." He was embarrassed that "Dr. E.B. Chain who won the Nobel prize [with Fleming] for the discovery of penicillin, was refused admittance to this country twice...."[4]

In December of 1948, the witch hunting struck close to home, and tragically.

Whittaker Chambers, former Communist, former Soviet agent, later *Time* magazine writer, while denouncing Alger Hiss as a fellow Communist and spy, aroused suspicion over several other present and former State Department officials. One was Laurence Duggan. Larry Duggan was the son of Dr. Stephen Duggan, director of the Institute of International Education, for whom Ed worked before joining CBS. The younger Duggan, after a fourteen-year State Department career as a Latin American specialist, had succeeded his father as director of IIE. Murrow served on the board of trustees that approved the appointment. He had known and admired Larry Duggan for eighteen years.

On the morning of December 21, 1948, he learned that Larry Duggan was dead. All that the police could say was that the evening before, Duggan had either jumped or fallen from IIE's sixteenth-floor offices at 45th Street and Fifth Avenue.

Murrow further learned that twelve days before, a man named Isaac Don Levine, publisher of an obscure right-wing magazine, had told the House Un-American Activities Committee that Whittaker Chambers revealed to him that nine years before, Duggan had passed confidential information to Chambers. In short, Laurence Duggan had allegedly been a Communist spy. Two days later, agents of the FBI questioned Duggan. Ten days later, the man was found dead in the street, leaving a wife and four children.

On the very night that Duggan died, Congressman Karl Mundt, acting chairman of a subcommittee of the House Un-American Activities Committee, called a peculiar midnight meeting of his subcommittee to share with reporters the secret testimony that had implicated Duggan in espionage. The "meeting" consisted of just two committee members, Mundt and a young California congressman, Richard Nixon. There was an aura about these midnight disclosures of now-you-know-why-he-did-it.

The following night, Murrow went on the air and spoke of the Duggan case, his self-control purchased at great cost: "Sumner Welles, who was Duggan's chief during most of his time in the [State] Department, said 'Laurence Duggan was one of the most brilliant, most devoted and most patriotic public servants I have ever known.'" Then Murrow added, "And when he dictated that sentence over the phone, he put the emphasis on 'patriotic.'"

Murrow went on: "Mr. Levine testified that...Chambers named Duggan as one of six State Department officials from whom he had received papers and confidential information....Today Whittaker Chambers says, to his knowledge, he never met Mr. Duggan. Asked if he ever named Mr. Duggan as having passed papers over to him, Chambers replied: 'I did not name Duggan as having passed papers over to me. To my knowledge, he was not a Communist.'" Later Richard Nixon was to say that Duggan had been "cleared" and the Justice Department found him a loyal American. But it was too late for Larry Duggan. He was dead. From that point on, Ed Murrow had little use for Karl Mundt or Richard Nixon.

Almost as soon as Ed was off the air, a distraught Ward Wheelock, who had Campbell's Soup's advertising account, was on the phone. The president of the company had called Wheelock to say that he was enraged by Murrow's use of a news program to defend Duggan. He was not paying for "editorializing." Wheelock told Ed that he was going to have to attend a meeting with him and the Campbell people. Murrow afterward recorded his reply to Wheelock in a memorandum for his files: "I did not propose to discuss with him or the client my news judgment...that if the client was sufficiently dissatisfied, he could, I assume, fail to pick up the option."[5]

Barely a year after the Duggan affair, Joe McCarthy, in that seedy ballroom in a hotel in Wheeling, West Virginia, opened the era that was to bear his name. The press was dazzled by his ever-shifting charges of the number of Communists in the State Department. But as one accusation after another collapsed for lack of evidence, McCarthy began to lose face. A month after his original charge, he announced to the press, "I am willing to stand or fall on this one. McCarthy said that he was about to expose "the top Russian agent in the U.S," indeed, "Alger Hiss's boss in the espionage ring at the State Department." McCarthy told reporters that four Russian spies had landed on the Atlantic Coast by submarine and had reported directly to this man. He was Owen Lattimore, director of the School of International Relations at Johns Hopkins University.

The subsequent questioning of Owen Lattimore by a Senate subcommittee epitomized all that Murrow despised in McCarthy and his *ism*. An individual was being compelled to defend his honor and his patriotism against charges which appeared to have popped into his accuser's head almost out of whimsical malice—baggy-suited Soviets, feet no doubt still wet, high-tailing it from a submarine to faculty row at Johns Hopkins to Owen Lattimore's house. Murrow came to the defense, not so much of Lattimore, but of fundamental rights. "Having listened to the charges against Lattimore and his reply," Murrow said in his radio commentary, "one conclusion is inescapable. If there exists hard factual information or evidence in support of the charges against Owen Lattimore, such evidence has not been reported to the subcommittee." He went a step further, recognizing that little of what Lattimore said in his defense could compete with McCarthy's dominance of the headlines. As Lattimore later described Murrow's role, "Even when the hysteria was at its height, before I could speak for myself he [Murrow] kept the record straight by repeatedly drawing attention to the fact that nothing had been proved against me. Later, by his program technique of using recordings, he gave me a national forum of my own, so that millions of people could hear me speaking for myself in excerpts of my testimony."

Owen Lattimore was a professor of frankly leftist views. He was not, however, as McCarthy charged, a State Department official, not a Communist, and certainly not a spy. Murrow did not share Lattimore's political ideas. But he was not aware that to hold them was a crime in a democracy.[6]

Lattimore was later indicted on seven counts of perjury for allegedly telling a Senate internal security subcommittee that he had not promoted Communist interests. In 1955, a federal court threw out the charges against him. Shortly afterward, the Justice Department dropped its case against Lattimore.

In 1948, Harold Laski had written Murrow that he was coming to America. Ed wrote back facetiously suggesting that Laski stay at his home so that the FBI could keep its eye on both of them at once, adding, "I suspect they are currently informed of my own activities and particularly the guests who stop with us."

Murrow had in fact entered the FBI's security files for the first time in December of 1942. At that time the Bureau received information that he had become a sponsor of an organization called "The Committee for the Care of Children in Wartime." The committee's purpose was to establish day-care centers for children whose fathers had gone off to war and whose mothers were working in defense plants. The Congress eventually enacted legislation providing federal funds to help support the committee's centers.

At the time this committee was being formed, Murrow was gaining fame for his broadcasts out of London. He was besieged by people wanting him to lend his name to their causes. Almost without exception, he turned them down. He regarded himself as an observer, not a missionary. Some appeals, however, could not be so easily ignored. Eleanor and Lou Gimbel had been good friends. They had been enormously helpful to Ed in placing Nazi refugees when he had worked with the Emergency Committee. Ed and Janet had been the Gimbels' house guests in Washington that fateful December 7. Eleanor Gimbel was a director of the Committee for the Care of Children in Wartime. It was Eleanor Gimbel who apparently contacted Ed, sometime in 1942, asking him to be listed as a sponsor of the organization, and he did not see how he could turn the request down. The FBI report thus listed "one Edward Murrow as a sponsor" along with several other individuals, labor unions, and children's organizations. It is also unlikely that he gave much thought to the matter. No mention of the committee exists anywhere in the extensive Murrow papers.

Eleanor Gimbel was a supporter of numerous left-wing causes which Murrow probably knew of and which, in the context of the thirties, was hardly unusual in a woman of wealth and social convictions. The Bureau described Eleanor Gimbel's Committee for the Care of Children in Wartime as controlled by persons "alleged to be active Communist leaders in New York City." It did so at the time when Congress was voting funds for the organization's work, which did not spare Murrow a black mark and an FBI dossier. Another submission to his file involved the matter of his alleged attendance at the "anti-Facist meeting" that had held up his passport during his trip home to discuss the Brendan Bracken BBC job offer in 1943.[7]

In 1949, a magazine writer, Wesley Price, did a profile on Murrow for the *Saturday Evening Post.* The article was worshipful, and in his eagerness for vivid touches, Price wrote that while Murrow was a lumberjack in the Pacific Northwest, he carried an IWW card for protective coloration, which technically made Ed Murrow a Wobbly. The FBI special agent in charge of the New York City office promptly alerted Washington that Murrow had "been reported to be a member of the Industrial Workers of the World." The IWW had been declared a subversive organization by the attorney general of the United States. Questioned on his claim, Wesley Price later admitted that Murrow had only talked about the Wobblies in the logging camps, and that he himself had invented the line about Murrow being a member. Ten years later, however, the information that Murrow was "reportedly a member of the IWW" continued to appear in FBI reports.[8]

Murrow's relationship to the Bureau and to J. Edgar Hoover had actually started off amicably. In the 1949 espionage trial of Judith Coplon, Murrow praised the FBI in his radio commentary for resisting the introduction of its raw, unevaluated data as evidence in the case. Hoover immediately sent Murrow a letter praising him for being "objective."

In June of 1951, Fred Friendly went to Washington and met with the Bureau's deputy FBI director, L.B. "Lou" Nichols, to discuss doing a story on the Bureau for *Hear It Now*. In correspondence preceding this meeting, Hoover had written in his small, cramped hand, "What do we know about Murrow?" In response, the staff came back with a memo containing one particularly striking paragraph: "Our files contain no information to the effect that Edward R. Murrow is a member of the group in CBS believed to be communistically inclined or fellow travelers....Murrow was in fact instrumental in firing (name blanked out) because of the latter's failure to obtain good news coverage." Based on internal clues in the report, the person whose firing confirms Murrow's Americanism according to the FBI appears to be William L. Shirer, certainly no Communist.

There was a reason why CBS was singled out by the FBI for presumably containing a "communistically inclined" element. Shortly after the war, Bill Paley had made a major sea change. Previously, most of CBS's entertainment programs had been produced and thus controlled by advertising agencies. CBS merely sold the air time. This arrangement, however, meant that the sponsors and their ad agencies could take a successful show away from CBS, should they get a better offer from NBC. Paley's response was to have CBS produce its own programs and sell them to sponsors directly. This change meant building up the network's own production department, hiring writers, directors, producers, actors, performers. Creative people, in their politics, are traditionally unconventional, often cause-oriented and, traditionally, on the left-hand side of the political spectrum. Thus, around the FBI, CBS was the "Red Network."

Nevertheless, Friendly evidently did a strong selling job at the FBI. He persuaded Lou Nichols, according to a memorandum that Nichols wrote after their meeting, that "the real philosophy of the Bureau as the guardian of civil rights and the like has never been really told and they would like to do it....[Friendly] wants to tell the real story of the philosophy behind the FBI, who its agents are, the extensive training they receive and why the FBI is not a Gestapo." Hoover gave his permission to proceed with the project. Nevertheless, the Bureau's New York office was directed "to make a discreet check" of Fred Friendly.

A month passed and the FBI heard nothing more about *Hear It Now*. Lou Nichols wrote Friendly asking if he and Murrow were still interested. What had happened in the meantime was that *Hear It Now* had been shelved in favor of *See It Now*. Murrow and Friendly were so consumed by the new project that the FBI project was forgotten.

Two years passed and Friendly again approached the FBI, this time proposing a number of story lines about the Bureau for *See It Now*. He was so consistently turned down that Friendly finally told Lou Nichols that he hoped he would "live long enough" to hear Nichols say "yes" to something. But Nichols had a long memory. He reminded Friendly that the Bureau had been left standing at the altar two years before.

In the interim, Murrow made a costly reference to the Bureau and Hoover in one of his evening newscasts. The matter involved whether or not Harry S. Truman, while President, had kept, even allowed to be promoted to higher office in the Treasury Department, Harry Dexter White, after the FBI informed the then President that White was allegedly a Soviet agent. J. Edgar Hoover testified before the Jenner Committee on this point early in November of 1953. Murrow discussed this testimony in a November 9 broadcast, noting that the FBI "does not evaluate material. It reports fact, rumor, gossip and attempts to give some indication of the credibility or reliability of witnesses." Murrow's implication was that Hoover was not supposed to be speculating in public as to who was or was not a spy.

Nichols, in an interoffice memo describing why he turned down Friendly's requests, mentioned the above Murrow broadcast and said, "We did not want to be kissed off as Murrow had kissed off the Director's presentation with a mere statement that the Director stated that the FBI did not evaluate things but that the Director had told the Attorney General that Harry Dexter White was unfit to serve." At the bottom of this memorandum, Hoover wrote, "Well handled...." From this point on, Hoover's attitude toward Murrow hardened into unremitting hatred.

Hoover's state of mind is suggested a year later when Walter Winchell, in his *Daily Mirror* column, wrote, "Will yez look who's after Edward R. Murrow on CBS (at 7:45) Wedzdee eves?" Alongside a clipping of the column, Hoover wrote, "What's this?" The faithful Nichols had to point out to Hoover, who was apparently immune to the wit of Walter Winchell, that the item referred to the fact that a program about the FBI was scheduled on CBS at 8 p.m., *after* Murrow's nightly news.

The FBI began compiling a file of columns by right-wing columnists impugning Murrow's loyalty, integrity, or intelligence regarding the Communist threat, columns by Westbrook Pegler, Victor Lasky, George Sokolsky. The file grew thick.

Hate mail and crank mail to the FBI attacking Murrow were treated with astonishing respect. A constituent wrote Senator John Bricker of Ohio that during the war the BBC used seemingly innocuous phrases to send coded messages to occupied Europe and that on one of Murrow's recent broadcasts, the listener had heard Murrow say, "the brown birds are flying." The letter went on, "I for one would not like having someone relay coded messages to the Communists in this country...." Senator Bricker forwarded the letter to the FBI, and it entered Murrow's file.

In another letter to the FBI, the writer wrote, "I know you men know your job, but why are men like Ed Murrow on TV? I am sure you have your eye on his '*Person to Person* contacts.' But why wait for a 'Pearl Harbor?'" Hoover wrote back, "It was indeed thoughtful of you to bring your observations and comments to my attention. In the event you acquire further data which you believe to be of interest to the FBI, feel free to contact the representatives in our office...." FBI informants were not to be discouraged simply for being paranoid.

Hoover told his deputies that he was concerned about "articles in publications which are severely and unfairly discrediting our American way of life and praising directly or indirectly the Soviet system." The director feared that there might be "factors in the backgrounds of prominent columnists, editors, commentators, authors etc. which could be influencing such slanted views."

The staff went to work drawing up a list of 100 "prominent molders of opinion." Twelve were immediately eliminated as having "no known subversive connections." Forty-eight more were cleared on subsequent investigation. But forty were found to have "pertinent factors in their backgrounds which could have a bearing on their reporting...." Edward R. Murrow made this final cut. The Bureau staff prepared for the director a booklet with brief profiles of the forty. Murrow had been included for supposedly being a member of the Industrial Workers of the World, for serving on an advisory council for an organization that was to send students to a summer session at Moscow University in 1935, and for narrating the English-language version of a Russian film, *The Siege of Leningrad,* made during World War II. Franklin D. Roosevelt may as well have been cited for sending arms to relieve Leningrad. The booklet was prepared for Hoover in "blind memorandum form to conceal the Bureau as the source...in the event the Director should desire to make available to appropriate persons some of the information on an informal and confidential basis."

The complete decay of the Murrow-Hoover relationship was revealed when Jesse Zousmer innocently invited Hoover to appear on the celebrity interview show, *Person to Person,* that Ed began hosting in 1953. At the bottom of the page of a memorandum forwarding this request to him, Hoover wrote, "I will never have anything to do with anything with which Murrow is connected." That the invitation was sent to Hoover in the first place makes clear that Murrow had no idea of the extent of his pariah status within the FBI. (As of this writing, the FBI file on Edward R. Murrow, obtained through the Freedom of Information Act, totaled over 1,000 pages.)[9]

The irony in the attempts by the far right to paint Murrow as a tool or dupe of the Communists is that he was a conventional anti-Communist. There was no love for him or his work in the Soviet Union. In 1946, the Russian government attacked the International Institute of Education and particularly criticized two of its trustees, Edward R. Murrow and John Foster Dulles. Murrow was described as "the reactionary radio commentator." Murrow saw the Soviet Union as the hand behind the Korean war and most international mischief. The *Voice of Freedom,* the left-wing monitor of American broadcasting, described Murrow's commentaries as "a mouldy dish of red-baiting rhetoric."[10]

He followed a near iron-clad rule in his later years of not involving himself in any organizations whose policies might impair his professional detachment. But he broke the rule to become a member of the Committee on the Present Danger, which, with some fairness, might be called the establishment wing of American anti-Communism. The committee stood squarely for the doctrine of Communist containment. It distinguished itself by its Europe-first bias—by a belief that Soviet expansionism in the Old World represented the greatest global threat, a view with which Murrow was perfectly comfortable. He supported the committee's call for more American troops in Europe, universal military training, and an expanded ROTC. He was at home with the kind of people on the Committee on the Present Danger, James B. Conant, president of Harvard; Leonard Firestone, the industrialist; David Dubinsky, from organized labor; Arthur Goldberg; Robert Sherwood; and Sam Rosenman. And for ballast at either end, the committee could point to General William J. Donovan, father of the wartime Office of Strategic Services, and J. Robert Oppenheimer, father of the atom bomb, who was now having his own security problems.[11]

Murrow defended the death sentences against Julius and Ethel Rosenberg for passing atomic secrets to the Soviet Union while other liberals deplored both the handling of the case and the severity of the sentences. From the propaganda standpoint, he recognized that the Rosenbergs were of more value to the Russians dead than alive. But, he said in his radio commentary, "There is here involved something more important than a small skirmish in propaganda warfare.... There was a trial, complete and open, conducted under the law. A verdict was reached by a jury. A sentence was imposed. And, as President Eisenhower concluded in one of the best written statements to come from the White House in a long time, he feels it his duty in the interests of the people of the United States not to set aside the verdict of their representatives. The case will—already has—damaged us abroad. But a departure from that principle might damage us fatally."[12]

His position on the Rosenberg case is a near perfect illustration of the Murrow public philosophy. He was not really political. He was not ideological. But he was viscerally attached to certain fundamental principles which were not necessarily owned by the left or right. In his belief in the immutability of these fundamentals, he was, if anything, a conservative in the classic sense. He believed in the rule of law. In the Rosenberg case, due process had been followed; a fair trial, he thought, had been conducted. He did not judge the outcome ideologically, but with constitutional neutrality. The rule of law had prevailed. And he was prepared to accept the verdict whether it meant the exoneration or the death of the defendants. What disturbed him about the far-right hysterics, the professional anti-Communists, the McCarthyites, was that they turned their hatreds inward upon any fellow Americans who differed from their notions of patriotic purity. He hated their shrill, self-righteous posture that anyone who questioned a picture-book America was somehow disloyal. He hated a mean streak that the far right aroused in the American character. He found dangerous and stupid the idea that genuine failings in the country could be dismissed simply by tarring those who spoke out against them as un-American. Patriotism, to Murrow, was not a blind defense of things as they are, but the Greek ideal of an honorable competition with one's ancestors. What bothered him most about the witch hunting and Red baiting was the disregard for the individual's right to a fair hearing, the denial of the right to differ, the presumed guilt by accusation, in brief, the real un-American activity, unfairness.

On the day in January of 1950 that Sig Mickelson took over news and public affairs for CBS, Frank Stanton handed him an onionskin sheet of paper with a list of names on it. "Stanton told me," Mickelson recalled, that day, "under no circumstances was I to use any of those people. No questions asked. Just don't use them." It was at this time that Friendly had run into the puzzling objections to the composers he wanted to write the theme music for *Hear It Now*.[13]

The blacklist had come to CBS.

It had all begun in 1946 with a young man named Theodore C. Kirkpatrick. Kirkpatrick had been a temporary FBI employee during the war and afterward went to work in the security department at Bloomingdale's in New York. He became restless as a department store detective. "It seemed to me small, petty," Kirkpatrick later said. "It was concerned with shoplifting when the Communists were taking over the country." Ted Kirkpatrick discussed his concern with two like-minded friends, Kenneth M. Bierly and John G. Keenan, fellow former employees at the FBI. In April of 1947, the three men formed American Business Consultants, Inc. What they consulted businessmen on was communism.

Staked by Alfred Kohlberg, a wealthy supporter of anti-Communist causes, American Business Consultants launched in May of 1947 *Counterattack: The Newsletter of Facts on Communism*. The yearly subscription was $24. Most subscribers were business firms and some government offices. Soon, American Business Consultants claimed to be grossing $100,000 a year from the newsletter. The most popular articles, the partners found, were about Communists in broadcasting. The subject had celebrity appeal and raised the specter of enemy tentacles penetrating into every home in America.

Occasionally, American Business Consultants also published special reports. In June of 1951, it dropped a bombshell, a 215-page paperback entitled *Red Channels: The Report of Communist Influence in Radio and Television*. *Red Channels* contained the names of 151 persons ostensibly linked to Communist and Communist-front organizations.

Eric Barnouw, in *The Golden Web*, the second volume of his epic broadcasting history, wrote of *Red Channels*, it "was a list of 151 of the most talented and admired people in the industry—mostly writers, directors, performers. They were people who had helped to make radio an honored medium." The "evidence" of presumed disloyalty "gave a summary of what these men and women—with countless others—had been concerned with over the years. They had opposed Franco, Hitler, and Mussolini, tried to help war refugees, combatted race discrimination...."

Among those cited in *Red Channels* were Leonard Bernstein, Lee J. Cobb, Aaron Copland, Ruth Gordon, Morton Gould, Langston Hughes, Garson Kanin, Burgess Meredith, Arthur Miller, Zero Mostel, Dorothy Parker, Irwin Shaw, and Orson Welles. Among Ed Murrow's broadcast colleagues cited were Norman Corwin, Joseph Julian, Alexander Kendrick, and Bill Shirer. The list comprised, Eric Barnouw said, "a roll of honor."[14]

Many of those who found their names in this obscure publication assumed it must be some sort of preposterous joke. They soon learned otherwise.

Lawrence A. Johnson was an elderly businessman of tall, dignified bearing, the owner of four supermarkets around Syracuse, New York. When Johnson's son-in-law was recalled into the Marines to fight communism in Korea, Johnson launched a crusade to fight Communists at home. Among his sources were *Counterattack* and *Red Channels*.

At this time, the energetic Johnson was elected to office in the National Association of Supermarkets. He shrewdly recognized the leverage that his new position gave him. He organized a campaign threatening to boycott food companies who sold to supermarkets if they sponsored programs that used Communists or their sympathizers. Typical of Johnson's tactics, a group representing supermarkets in Syracuse wrote to Frank Stanton saying they were going to set up ballot boxes in their stores allowing their customers to vote "yes" or "no" on the following proposition: "Do you want any part of your purchase price of any products advertised on the Columbia Broadcasting System to be used to hire Communist fronters?"

Johnson traded on his national office to appear to represent not just his stores, but thousands of supermarkets throughout the country in his Red hunting. Companies that lived by selling their soups, processed cheese, and toothpaste to supermarkets took Lawrence Johnson's threats very seriously. So did broadcast executives who feared losing the advertising of these firms. Thus it was that the networks and advertising agencies, before hiring anyone, began to check them out in *Red Channels* for possible Communist connections. *Red Channels* became the standard reference work on Communists, their sympathizers, and their dupes. The little book was the blacklist.

At first, the list was informally employed at CBS, a surreptitious glance through a copy of *Red Channels* kept discreetly out of sight in an executive's desk drawer. But by 1952, the process had become institutionalized. Daniel O'Shea, former chief counsel for RKO motion pictures, was hired as CBS vice president for security and given broad powers. CBS producers were required to submit the names of writers, directors, actors, and other professionals whom they proposed to use to O'Shea's office for political clearance. O'Shea would then inform the producer if the candidate could be hired. There was no appeal from O'Shea's decisions, nor was any explanation given or required when he turned anyone down.[15]

The case of Joseph Julian was typical. During the war, Julian had worked with Norman Corwin and Murrow on the series *An American in England.* After the war, Julian was an extraordinarily busy radio actor, until his name appeared in *Red Channels.* He had been listed because in 1942 he was invited to read a poem at Carnegie Hall by a group called Artists Front to Win the War. The poem celebrates artists who died fighting fascism. This reading was Julian's sole contact with the organization. *Red Channels* also mentioned that in 1949 Julian attended a rally of the National Committee of Arts, Sciences and Professions to abolish the House Un-American Activities Committee. After Julian was listed in *Red Channels,* his previously substantial earnings dwindled until in 1953 he earned $1,630.

Julian sued *Red Channels* for $150,000. He also complained to Bill Paley, who sent him to see Dan O'Shea. The encounter had about it the quality of *Darkness at Noon.* Julian told O'Shea that he had never been a Communist and had never supported communism. Of course, a smiling O'Shea agreed. But what had Julian done to fight communism, O'Shea wanted to know? O'Shea suggested that Julian do himself some good by attending American Legion rallies, perhaps joining General Lucius Clay's Crusade for Freedom. And it would be wise to drop the lawsuit against *Red Channels.*

Julian found himself agreeing that he could arrange to appear at a Times Square rally of Crusade for Freedom and make an appeal for contributions. But he began gagging on his own words as he spoke. Why was he doing penance for sins he had not committed, he asked himself? He left O'Shea's office determined to continue his suit against *Red Channels.*

Julian haunted CBS hangouts asking fellow writers and actors to testify on his behalf. He found much sympathy but no one who was willing to risk tainting his own career. Then, one day he spotted Murrow having a drink at Colbee's, went to him, and said, "Ed, I'm suing *Red Channels* for libel. Will you be a witness for me?" As Julian later described the moment, "Without asking a question, without the slightest hesitation, Murrow said, 'Tell me where and when, Joe.'" Once he had Murrow on his side, Julian found it easier to recruit other witnesses, among them Charles Collingwood. The trial opened and Murrow appeared. But the judge granted the defendants, American Business Consultants, Inc., a motion to dismiss Julian's suit.[16]

Ed Murrow was not listed in *Red Channels.* But *Counterattack* devoted an entire issue to him in which the self-appointed police of patriotism found Murrow more fool than traitor. "Though not pro-Communist" *Counterattack* claimed, "he [Murrow] is confused on communist issues and defends those involved in communist causes."[17]

In 1951, David Schoenbrun learned that a Pentagon security officer had denied his request for press credentials to cover NATO headquarters. The decision, if unreversed, represented a deathblow to Schoenbrun's broadcast career. Schoenbrun went to Murrow, who told him that he would have to clear himself. "Clear myself of what, Ed?" Schoenbrun asked. "How does a man go about proving he's innocent? Aren't they supposed to prove me guilty? What is the evidence? Who is my accuser? What are the specific accusations?" Murrow, Schoenbrun said, merely looked gloomy but had no answers. After a nightmarish struggle within the Pentagon bureaucracy, Schoenbrun finally managed to obtain his credentials. He bore Murrow no ill for not doing more for him: "He didn't know how to deal with something like this any more than we did."[18]

The case of Winston Burdett was especially thorny. Murrow had hired Burdett in 1943 in Algiers during the North African campaign. Burdett was then 30 years old, a magna cum laude graduate of Harvard who had broken into journalism as film and book critic on the old *Brooklyn Eagle*. He was a sensitive man, an idealist, and a writer of luminosity and perception. Burdett also proved a born broadcaster.

In 1955, Murrow heard a disturbing report from Burdett. Burdett confessed to him that during the thirties, while working for the *Brooklyn Eagle,* he had become a Communist. His wife had also been a Communist. Furthermore, he had been a courier for the party; in effect, he had served as a Soviet spy in Finland, Romania, and Yugoslavia. Burdett had not broken with the party until he had been hired by CBS. He was letting Murrow know all this because he was under enormous pressure to go before a Senate Internal Security subcommittee and testify in public about his past sins and to identify his Communist associates.

Burdett had already testified in secret to the subcommittee four years before and had cooperated with the FBI. Consequently, he explained to Murrow, he would not be revealing any information or names that were not already known by the government. What the committee wanted of Burdett was a performance, a ritual conversion, a formal recantation. They wanted the words out of Burdett's mouth to be heard by the world. Then he would be considered cleansed.

Burdett was suffering from ulcers. He had family responsibilities. If he resisted, he knew that his career was finished, that he would be unemployable in broadcasting. On the advice of his counsel, he intended to do what the subcommittee wanted.

He made his public penance. He gave the subcommittee the names of twelve *Brooklyn Eagle* colleagues and ten other newspaper people who he said had also been Communists. Senator James Eastland, the subcommittee chairman, wrote Dan O'Shea at CBS, "Winston Burdett has rendered a real service by his testimony....I know that he has some tough times ahead of him and I earnestly hope that CBS will stand by him." But with the word out about his past, a hue and cry rose from the right.

Burdett had to be kicked out of broadcasting. Sponsors pressured Paley to get rid of him. Some of Burdett's liberal CBS colleagues turned against him too. Bill Downs, whose opinion Murrow so valued, believed that Burdett had deceived them all and did not deserve to be saved.

Murrow thought differently. Burdett, as a young man, had made a mistake. He had subsequently renounced communism. He had made a clean breast of his past. What mattered now was the present man, a superior journalist with a valuable contribution to make to broadcasting. Should his professional life end for a past error? What end would be served but network cowardice?

Murrow worked out an arrangement to remove Burdett from the white glare of publicity. He had him assigned to Rome, where Burdett thereafter managed to live out a useful career. Murrow's action was not universally applauded, however. Many could not forgive Burdett for naming names. But to Charles Collingwood, who knew that the network executives would happily have fed Burdett to the wolves, "Ed had made CBS courageous."[19]

The loyalty oath that Deirdre Mason had complained about to Ed first surfaced at CBS in December of 1950, after blacklisting began. The oath had been sent to some 2,500 employees, accompanied by a memo signed by a CBS executive named Joseph Ream.

Joe Ream was a lawyer by training but functioned as Frank Stanton's troubleshooter. As Ream explained his work, "I tried to keep the drains unclogged." He was good at it, especially in handling situations that required a sure touch with people. For Joe Ream was an ingratiating man, a lean and ruggedly handsome southerner, with a ready smile and soft drawl, an easy man to like. He thought, however, much faster than he talked, for Joe Ream was of that breed best described as country slickers.

The oath was Ream's solution to a problem haunting CBS. Lawrence Johnson, the supermarket owner, and his anti-Communist tactics had thrown the fear of God, and of lost profits, into Madison Avenue. CBS was a favorite target, the Red Network to its enemies. How, Ream had wondered, could CBS "reassure the advertisers we weren't a nest of Commies." Ream later took sole responsibility for what happened next. There is, however, in his telling, something of the good soldier, uncomplainingly taking a rap best shared with others.

Ream knew that the federal government under the Truman loyalty program required federal employees to sign an oath. Ream merely adapted the federal oath to CBS. On the front of the oath were questions, the first being, "Are you now or have you ever been a member of the Communist Party, USA or any Communist organization?" On the back was a listing of organizations that the attorney general of the United States declared to be subversive.

Ream took his CBS version of the federal oath to his superiors. Stanton approved it. Paley was later to say, "I didn't like it. But, I knew we had to do something and I approved it. I wished to hell we didn't have to do anything." Paley bridled at the word "oath." "It was not an oath of any kind," Paley insisted. "It was just a questionnaire."

Throughout this period, Ream had been consulting with Ted Kirkpatrick, of *Counterattack* and *Red Channels,* about what he was doing with the oath. Kirkpatrick, Ream said, "Thought it was a fine idea." To Ream, the import of the loyalty oath was unambiguous. "If you didn't sign, you'd lose your job."[20]

Morris Ernst had gone to CBS with his publisher son-in-law, Michael Bessie, to urge Murrow to make himself the symbol of resistance to McCarthyism by refusing to sign the loyalty oath. "How," Ernst asked, "could people in a weaker position stand up to this threat if a man of your stature did not?" Bill Downs told Ed that he was not going to sign. David Schoenbrun told Murrow, "I love my country. I don't see why I have to prove my loyalty by signing an oath." Sevareid, Collingwood, Howard K. Smith, Alex Kendrick, Don Hollenbeck, all expressed their repugnance at being forced to certify their patriotism on a piece of paper.

Murrow had known about the loyalty oath before any of them. Joe Ream had gone to Ed for his reaction before the policy was adopted. Ream had explained the network's dilemma, the threatened losses of sponsors unless CBS, in effect, cleared itself of the taint of suspicion. As Ream later described this meeting, Murrow said very little. His attitude was a resigned well-if-there-is-no-other-way.

Murrow told the balky Bill Downs, "If you don't want to sign the oath, there is no way I can protect you." He told Schoenbrun, "If you don't sign it, suspicion will hover over you." He also added, "I'm signing. Do you have more integrity than I do, David?" Schoenbrun signed, as did Smith, Sevareid, Hollenbeck, Collingwood, and Kendrick. Murrow told Morris Ernst, "I have too many other fights on my hands and I'll weaken my position on them if I fail to sign." Sevareid never faulted Murrow for not leading a fight against the oath. "Nobody, including Murrow," said Sevareid, "can spend every day of his life slaying dragons."

It would be satisfying to say of Murrow that he stood up to the blacklist and fought the loyalty oath, thus causing the entire profession of broadcast journalism to rally behind him and thus bringing about the defeat of these odious instruments. He did not. He accepted them and was indeed a member of the CBS board of directors when these policies were adopted.

Yet to see the past through the eyes of the present is to judge from a safe remove. The hysteria of the fifties was real. Paranoia and suspicion were in the air. Murrow told Ed Bliss, "You have to choose your battles." He demonstrated his priorities after Deirdre Mason consulted him over what to do about the loyalty oath. He told her to go ahead and sign it. "I have. Everybody has. It's not that important." That was in February of 1954. His answer, she said, "upset me at the time, but the next month Ed Murrow took on Joe McCarthy."[21]

CHAPTER 23

Person to Person:
Another Murrow

It was on a night when Ed had retreated to Colbee's with Johnny Aarons and Jesse Zousmer after doing the evening news. The talk had drifted, as it often does in barroom colloquies, to the nature of man. The specific topic: What is the most universal human urge? Sex, Aarons said. Murrow remarked that he doubted if television was ready for it yet. They narrowed the list down to curiosity. And they agreed that a rampant form of curiosity was ordinary people's fascination with the private lives of famous people.

Soon afterward, in February of 1952, Johnny Aarons was dispatched to Tennessee to produce an interview for *See It Now* with Senator Estes Kefauver, who had catapulted himself into the Democratic presidential campaign by his investigation of organized crime. Kefauver was to be interviewed remote at his home by Murrow, who would remain in New York.

Thus, the seed was sown. It began to take root four months later when *See It Now* did another interview live from the home of Senator Robert A. Taft in Ohio. Aarons and Zousmer began thinking seriously about an idea that tantalized them. Here was the very phenomenon that they had talked about over drinks with Murrow, a way to part the curtain and let people peer into the lives and homes of the famous. Television made it possible.[1]

Since Friendly, in effect, was Murrow's chief of staff for television, Aarons and Zousmer went to him with an idea. Why not have Ed do a weekly series of visits to the homes of celebrities? Friendly was appalled. Ed Murrow was the leading broadcast journalist in America. It was beneath him to play Peeping Tom to satisfy the voyeurism of the masses. Murrow was already stretched too thin anyway, Friendly said. What they wanted him to do "would dilute the product."

There had been little love lost between the two men and Friendly

343

even before this moment. Aarons and Zousmer had resented Friendly's rough handling of them when they occasionally worked on *See It Now*. There had always been an unspoken rivalry between them for Murrow's attention since they had worked with Ed well before Friendly. And they sensed it again in Friendly's out-of-hand rejection of their idea. They were not so easily dissuaded. They decided to take the scheme directly to Ed.

Murrow liked Johnny and Jesse, liked them very much. They had been with him for six years, his earliest collaborators after he had gone back on the air. Jesse Zousmer was a tough-minded and sharp-witted man, the "house intellectual" around the CBS news room and a spirited after-hours sparring partner for Murrow.

The roly-poly Johnny Aarons was a fast-talking New York prototype, described by one colleague as a "round-eyed hustler." Beneath the protective cocoon of urban wiseacre, Aarons was a vulnerable man only playing the hand that nature had dealt him. Aarons had grown up in a world where a man was what he earned. He and Zousmer saw in their plan a chance to earn well indeed. Ed Murrow may have made television intellectually respectable, but they also saw in him a star brightness of mass appeal. As Scotty Reston once put it, "Ed Murrow was a very decorative man, a theatrical man." Aarons and Zousmer agreed.

Ed did not reject the idea. He was receptive. One reason was his habit of loyalty. Johnny and Jesse had been loyal and had worked hard for him. Consequently, when they asked something of him, he was inclined to say yes. He asked Friendly what he thought about their proposal. It was one of the few times when Friendly did not bow to Murrow. They had a heated argument. What Aarons and Zousmer were proposing was not worthy of Ed Murrow, Friendly insisted. Friendly felt that he had to save Murrow from himself, from his exaggerated notion of obligation toward these two men. He was already overworked. Where would he possibly find time to take on another program?

Aarons and Zousmer had anticipated the demands on Murrow's time. The cameras would be in the guests' homes and Murrow would remain in New York, just as in the visits to the homes of Kefauver and Taft. Remotes and split screens made it all simple and undemanding. At least for the host.

To Friendly's bitter disappointment, Murrow decided to go ahead with Aarons and Zousmer. Thereafter, the latter three men spent long hours at Quaker Hill brainstorming the new series. They called it *Person to Person*.[2]

Soon, famous figures all over the country were receiving a letter from Ed Murrow: "I have an old-fashioned belief that all of us are curious to see how others live—particularly those we've read about or heard about but seldom, if ever, had an opportunity to meet.

"What we hope to do is ask our guests to show us about the house and then sit down for a little informal talking. Who knows, in spite of television, it may still be possible to revive the art of conversation."

In the beginning, however, Murrow, resisted the idea of visiting only the homes of the celebrated. He saw in *Person to Person* an opportunity to pursue one of his abiding passions, to show Americans each other in the way, years before, he had shown America everyday England through the habitués of the Spread Eagle Pub. He wanted the rancher in Montana to understand how the railroad porter in Harlem lived. Aarons and Zousmer were uneasy. They wanted Names.

Person to Person was a half-hour program and involved two fifteen-minute visits to two homes each week. Aarons booked the guests, and he deliberately sought contrasts, the screen goddess and the atomic physicist, the college president and the jazz musician. The program debuted at 10:30 p.m. on Friday, October 2, 1953. Roy Campanella was the first guest, who, with Murrow's luck in timing, had hit the winning home run that day in the Dodgers' World Series game with the Yankees. The visit to Campanella's home was paired with a visit to the conductor Leopold Stokowski and his wife, Gloria Vanderbilt.

From the outset, *Person to Person*, unlike *See It Now*, was scheduled in prime time. It also benefited from the guidance of an outstanding authority on popular taste. After the maiden broadcast, Bill Paley sent Murrow a memo: "...you've got a sure winner in this show."[3]

In the weeks that followed, Murrow visited West Point's football coach, Earl "Red" Blaik; the Russian-born fashion designer, Valentina; then James Caesar Petrillo, head of the musicians' union; Arthur Godfrey; and a newly elected senator from Massachusetts, John F. Kennedy.

Theodore White was an early guest. White had first appeared on television five years before in a panel discussion on the effect that television was having on writing. On that occasion, White expressed his opinion that "television was a gadget. It would make no perceptible change." At the time he went on *Person to Person*, White had just published *Fire in the Ashes*, an account essentially of the success of the Marshall Plan in saving Western Europe from communism. He had stopped by Murrow's office, and Ed had said, "Teddy, you've just come back from Europe and I'd love to have you on a new program." White accepted, "thinking I was doing a friend a favor." The appearance, he said, "had a blast effect on my book. It shot from number nine to number four on the *Times* best-seller list in two weeks." Mary Martin reported that she received more mail after a single fifteen-minute appearance on *Person to Person* than she had during the entire run of *South Pacific*.[4]

In the early years, Aarons and Zousmer yielded to Ed's wishes and arranged visits to the homes of ordinary people too—a mailman, a clerk at Macy's, a redcap working in Grand Central Station. The redcap lived with his wife in a three-room apartment in Harlem. What did they do for entertainment? Murrow asked. The porter said that after he came home from work, "We look at TV....we look out of the window."

As Murrow later told a reporter, "The tone of the letters we got after that gave us pause. 'If I want to see how the average guy lives,' some of the letters said, 'I can visit my relatives.'" The little people disappeared from *Person to Person*.[5]

Paley on public taste proved unerring again. *Person to Person* was an instant success, its audience far larger than that of *See It Now*. On a week in 1956 when *See It Now*'s Nielsen rating was 11.3, *Person to Person*'s was 23.4. The show broke into television's top-ten most popular programs. Its audience grew, attaining in 1957 a 45 percent share of all homes with television sets. And *Person to Person* never lacked for eager sponsors.[6]

The critics, however, were not amused. They felt betrayed. *Time* magazine said of the first *Person to Person* broadcast, "...it is substandard Murrow" marked by "aimlessness and a degree of silliness, e.g. Murrow's asking Stokowski whether his piano was in tune." Harriet Van Horne wrote of *Person to Person*, "Midway through Friday's premiere, it became apparent that Mr. Murrow should hang up and dial again." Philip Mintoff wrote in *Cue*, "Some of the colloquies arising out of this desperation are pretty bad. Sample:

> MURROW: Valentina, what was the biggest thrill of your career?
>
> VALENTINA: Well, once I designed an eyelash that Alfred Lunt needed for one of his roles. I was very pleased to do that.
>
> MURROW: You certainly should have been."

Gilbert Seldes virtually held his breath, hoping that what he saw in those early weeks could not be the whole of *Person to Person*. Murrow, Seldes wrote, "has shown what radio and television can do; he has pushed the mechanisms to their limits; and he has always been a remarkably intelligent man with an abiding respect for the intelligence of his listeners. ...Mr. Murrow is too good to evade the obligations of his own instruments; he is too good to use them for purposes that go against their nature...."

The technical achievements of *Person to Person* represented a first-rate performance in a second-rate cause. This presumably casual fifteen-minute drop-in on the famous required bringing into the guest's home forty technicians and five tons of equipment. When *Person to Person* visited sports columnist Red Smith in Stamford, Connecticut, the crew erected, on the spot, a 140-foot portable transmitter. For the visit to heavyweight champion Rocky Marciano, the producer had a bulldozer lop forty feet off a hill that interfered with the transmission.[7]

Singer Georgia Gibbs recalled when *Person to Person* visited her Manhattan apartment. "There was nothing particularly marvelous about the show itself," Gibbs said. "It was Murrow's stature that gave it its cachet. Being on *Person to Person* meant that Edward R. Murrow had anointed you."

Before the program, Murrow invited Miss Gibbs to the Berkshire Hotel for a drink, an occasion that she recognized as an audition. She found Murrow more uneasy than she was. "He was terribly reserved," she remembered. "He did not look directly at you. He tended to talk around you." He did tell her, "I hope you're not going to do what everybody else does, show me paintings." Guests showing off their paintings had already become a cliché on *Person to Person.* People scheduled to appear on the program found that art galleries were eager to loan them valuable paintings just for the exposure. Detractors around the CBS newsroom liked to mimic the deep Murrow voice, asking, "Is that a picture on the wall?"

Technicians hauled thick cables to the eighteenth-floor roof of Gibbs's building and then snaked them down to her apartment. Inside the apartment, the crush of people and the lights drove the temperature to 95 degrees. Gibbs had to be fitted with a battery pack concealed under her dress. She stuffed a tiny microphone down her bra. Male guests had an easier time. They could put the batteries in their back pants pockets and hide the microphone in their jackets. When John Mason Brown appeared on *Person to Person,* an engineer said, "Mr. Brown, I'd like to charge your batteries." Brown responded, "Young man, not even God can do that."

Murrow, from the studio at Grand Central Terminal, could see Georgia Gibbs on a monitor. She heard only his voice over a concealed squawk box. No monitor was provided for the guests because Murrow did not want them gazing at themselves. What viewers saw at home was the guest alone, or Murrow from his studio, or both on a split screen.

Murrow always maintained that, in order to retain spontaneity, *Person to Person* was not rehearsed. But Aarons and Zousmer would at least have discussed with Gibbs fruitful lines of questioning and have fed Ed Murrow the questions.

Before air time, Murrow chatted with Gibbs for about fifteen minutes both to relax her and to allow the technicians to check out camera angles, lighting, voice levels, and mike positions.

During the actual broadcast, Georgia Gibbs had a sense that she enjoyed doing the program more than Murrow: "I had a feeling that he was uncomfortable, that the program was, well, show biz, that it was beneath him."

When *Person to Person* was over, the original placement of furniture, rugs, and paintings was meticulously restored. The maid was tipped for any added work the visit may have caused. And the next day, Georgia Gibbs received flowers and a kinescope of the program.[8]

Among the earliest guests on *Person to Person* were the newly elected U.S. senator from Massachusetts, John F. Kennedy, and his recent bride, Jacqueline Bouvier Kennedy. As the program opened, Murrow was seen in the studio, legs crossed, smoke swirling upward from his cigarette, apparently gazing out a window. "Good Evening, I'm Ed Murrow," he began and proceeded to greet his guests who joined him on a split screen. The camera switched to the Kennedys alone. They were seated on a couch in an apartment in Boston. Jack Kennedy was 36, terribly thin and boyish, resembling a high school valedictorian and basketball forward seen twenty years later. Jackie wore a dark dress and sat in a finishing-school pose, back straight, hands folded, legs crossed at the ankles. She looked quite beautiful.

The opening questions had a numbing triviality: "Have you opened all your wedding gifts?" Murrow asked. The pace picked up as Kennedy displayed a model of PT 109 and started to tell of his war experiences. He held up the coconut on which he had carved an SOS message after a Japanese destroyer sliced through his boat. He read a letter that the skipper of the Japanese ship sent to him after the war. Murrow finally asked a question of substance. Was America ready for another all-out war? Kennedy had a little speech prepared.

Murrow asked the senator about his reading habits and said, "Have you found anything inspirational?" On cue, Kennedy reached behind him for a book and said, "I do have something here written by Alan Seeger who wrote that famous poem, 'I Have a Rendezvous with Death.'" Kennedy proceeded to read the poem that Seeger wrote his mother just before he died in World War I. He read it well and movingly. The camera caught Murrow's face genuinely alight for the first time in the broadcast.

Jackie had drifted off screen, and the senator was now by himself describing what was wrong with the Taft-Hartley law. Out of nowhere, a dark shape loomed up on one side of the screen. It was Jackie shot ungallantly from behind at close-up buttock height as she moved toward her husband. She was carrying a football. She said with a breathless smile that the ball was a wedding gift from the Harvard locker-room manager. It was, the senator smiled, his favorite present of all.

Thus far, Jackie had been given little to do except carry the ball. Ed finally addressed her, harking back to Jackie's days as an inquiring photographer for a Washington newspaper. "Did it require more diplomacy," Ed asked her, "to interview a senator or a husband?" Before she could answer, Jack cut in and answered for her. He also conducted the tour of the apartment.

Jacqueline Kennedy, a woman of intelligence and some substance, had virtually no purpose on *Person to Person* except to play a stylized fifties wife—to be there, a worshiping smile fixed on her face, an attractive ornament. Should a future sociologist seek to understand what an American woman was supposed to be in the days before the women's liberation movement, Jacqueline Kennedy in this broadcast of *Person to Person* provides a museum piece.[9]

It would be unfair to say that every broadcast of *Person to Person* was insipid froth. The list of people who appeared on it is so long and so diverse that some of the visits had inevitably to excite interest, even good conversation. Sir Thomas Beecham told stories with an ease, wit, and flair that gave the viewer the sensation of eavesdropping on a brilliant Mayfair dinner party. Adlai Stevenson managed to forget the lights and cameras long enough to demonstrate a puckish charm. David Sarnoff's appearance on *Person to Person* was a tribute to Murrow's stature in broadcasting. Sarnoff had created CBS's chief rival, NBC. Sarnoff had tried for years to lure Murrow from CBS with no success. What Murrow appreciated most was that Sarnoff appeared on *Person to Person* at a time when many thought Murrow virtually radioactive, three nights after the *See It Now* broadcast on Joe McCarthy.[10]

The *Person to Person* staff unsuccessfully pursued the duke and duchess of Windsor for three years. Then Murrow read in the duchess's autobiography that as a child she had been the best jacks player in Baltimore. He sent a messenger to her hotel in New York with a gaily wrapped five-and-dime set of jacks and a rubber ball. The duchess played with them until three o'clock in the morning, and she and the duke finally consented to appear on *Person to Person*.

There was one other categorical rejection, from J. Edgar Hoover. But few other guests had to be persuaded.

The attraction of the program was elemental. "It had a *Vogue* and *House Beautiful* appeal," Eric Barnouw found, "along with a voyeuristic element." *Time* magazine's television critic came around to granting the program at least "an idiot fascination."[11]

Person to Person was frequently stiff, awkward, even fatuous. Murrow often resembled the opera star who turns up on a variety show and sings a pop tune to show what a good sport he is, the heavy voice overpowering a simple melody. But to its millions of addicted viewers, the program did create the illusion, however contrivedly, that they were stealing a glimpse into private life at the top, seeing their icons at their ease, and confirming what they needed to know all along, that the celebrated were just like them and nothing like them.

Janet took over *Person to Person* twice when Ed was tied up with *See It Now*. She interviewed Don Ameche and his family and the model Suzy Parker, whom she found semimute. Of Janet's performance, *Variety* said, "At the risk of starting a quarrel, she may be more effective as an interviewer than Ed. She is a good conversationalist, has poise, charm and warmth."[12]

Since the program was live and technically complicated, the list of gaffes became long. Sid Caesar, so inspired behind a comic mask, became petrified when he had to play himself in his own home. He forgot his wife's name. He started showing Murrow around the house and struck a mounted deer's head that started to fall off the wall. Caesar struggled to hold it up with his back while sustaining a determinedly nonchalant conversation. It was life imitating art, a spontaneous Sid Caesar sketch.

A.C. Nielsen demonstrated his audimeter on *Person to Person*, the gadget attached to television sets in a sampling of homes to record what people were watching and thus produce the omnipotent ratings. The audimeter failed to work.

It suggests the tone of *Person to Person* that Murrow, a congenital critic of polls and ratings, had the premier practitioner in his lair and never asked, for example, "What effect do you think your little gadget has had on the quality of television programming in America?" But *Person to Person* was not journalism; it was an animated fan magazine.

Ed struck a dry patch in an interview with Shelley Winters and fell back on one of his standby questions: "What kind of world do you hope your little girl will grow up into?" Winters answered, "I hope she grows up in a world dedicated to the principles of Franklin Delano Roosevelt." It seemed a harmless enough aspiration and one with which Murrow was sympathetic. But it was 1956, a presidential election year. Ed warned her that her remark was "out of place in a program like mine," and added, "If you say a thing like that, I must give someone else equal time to answer you." Which he did, forty-five seconds the following week to Jinx Falkenberg who sang the praises of Republicanism.

No hard questions, no hard answers for *Person to Person*. He was a guest in someone's home. Good manners must prevail. But at times the veneer almost wore through. During a visit with Liberace, Murrow asked the pianist if he ever intended to marry. "I want to someday find the perfect mate and settle down," Liberace said. "In fact, I was reading about lovely young Princess Margaret and she's looking for her dream man too." Murrow looked faintly nauseous but plowed on. He asked Liberace if he had met the princess. Liberace responded in his precious way, "Not as yet, but I have great hopes of meeting her when I go to England next season.... I think we have a lot in common. We have the same taste in theater and music. And besides, she's pretty and she's single!"

When it was over, Murrow appeared to flee from the studio. He was storming down the corridor, with Bob Dixon trotting behind. Murrow stopped so abruptly that Dixon slammed into him. Murrow turned and said in a cold rage, "In your whole life did you ever see anyone so obnoxious!" He continued stalking out of the building on over to the Pentagon Bar, where, Dixon recalled, "He had three scotches before he was able to utter another word."[13]

Still, *Person to Person* prospered. Its audience grew from an initial 1.8 million households to 8.3 million by 1958. But the critics remained unforgiving. Early on, Gilbert Seldes had virtually prayed that there had to be more than met the eye in what Murrow was doing. In 1956, after *Person to Person* had been on the air for three years, he was still so admiring of Murrow that he dedicated his book, *The Public Arts,* to him. But by 1957, Seldes could contain his disillusionment no longer. After dredging up possibly the tritest exchange in the history of the program (His guest is standing on her penthouse terrace. She says, "That's a plane up there." Murrow responds, "I can hear it."), Seldes wrote in the *Saturday Review,* "...the Edward R. Murrow mentioned above is not to be confused with the man of the same name who is the star and co-producer of *See It Now.* One of them is an imposter."

Seldes soon after ran into Murrow at the Century Club. He had asked Ed earlier to record a promotional announcement for a cause dear to Seldes, The Fund for Adult Education. He asked about the message. Ed answered testily, "I can't be sure what use you'd make of it." At first, Seldes thought that he must be joking. Later, he learned that Murrow was deadly serious. Seldes's criticism of *Person to Person* had struck a raw nerve.[14]

The most acid critic of all was John Lardner in *The New Yorker*, not a magazine in which Murrow would have chosen to be ridiculed. Ed had recently made his electronic visit to the home of the actor Robert Cummings, father of an apparently sizable brood. Lardner wrote: "By the time [Murrow] reached the lower echelon, his chuckles had begun to sound like the clanking of chains....a man who obliges himself to chuckle like an uncle at each child, in series, in the Cummings nursery may well become uncertain in time whether it is Moscow that has designs on Damascus or vice versa....Mr. Murrow does not wallow in *Person to Person*. You have the impression that he allows himself to be dipped into it at 10:30 after leaving careful orders to be hauled out again at eleven....I begin to wonder if the man really understands himself."[15]

Did it bother Murrow? Before he ever embarked on *Person to Person*, he was quoted in an interview saying, "Taste, that is where I am most tender. Criticism doesn't bother so much. If reviewers say 'he's pompous' or 'he has a voice like an unfrocked bishop' or even if they say 'he is wrong.' I can accept that easily enough. But when I am accused of bad taste. That bothers me." He was being accused of bad taste.

He had gone to lunch one day with Friendly at Louis and Armand's, and Senator Margaret Chase Smith walked in. As Friendly remembered the moment, she stopped by their table. "Ed," she said, "why do you do *that* program?" Murrow was taken aback and mumbled, "Yes, that's a good question....Someday...sometime I'll tell you."[16]

During this period, Don Hewitt and Murrow found themselves on the same flight returning from Paris to New York. They sat together. Murrow had been filming *See It Now* in the Middle East. Hewitt was returning from covering Grace Kelly's marriage to Prince Ranier. After a couple of drinks, Murrow said, "What the hell are you doing wasting your time at Grace Kelly's wedding?" Hewitt recalled that he hesitated, then blurted out what he was dying to say: "The same thing you were doing looking in Marilyn Monroe's closet on *Person to Person*." Murrow, head bent, stared over the tops of his eyes at Hewitt. He then let his hand rest on Hewitt's arm and said, "Kid, you got me."[17]

The most breathlessly awaited *Person to Person* broadcast had indeed been with Marilyn Monroe in April of 1955. She was, at the time, a house guest of the photographer Milton Green and his wife at the Greens' home in Westport, Connecticut. Marilyn had spent five hours putting on her makeup before the show. She wore a simple, tight-fitting jersey with a boyish collar. Her breasts appeared perilously cantilevered. Murrow's questions were dreadful: "I saw some pictures of you the other day at the circus riding an elephant. Did you have fun?" "Do you like New York?" "Do you like Connecticut?" And to Mrs. Green, "Does she make her own bed?" And puzzlingly: "Do you play a part to impress [directors] or please them?"

When given half a chance, Monroe answered with comedic flair. Murrow asked, "Your picture has been on the cover of almost all popular magazines, hasn't it?" Marilyn answered with a batting of eyelashes, "Not the *Ladies' Home Journal.*" In her shy, tentative answers, she seemed a vulnerable little girl, with 100,000 miles not showing on the odometer. Murrow throughout displayed his customary unease in the presence of a glamorous woman. His questions were often directed to Milton Green as though he were clinging to another male like a life raft.[18]

The people he respected did not respect what he was doing. Bill Paley's first wife, Dorothy, said of *Person to Person,* "I hated it. I didn't like that Ed allowed himself to be in that position." His old talks assistant, Helen Sioussat, found the program "beneath Ed." The very mention of *Person to Person* rendered Friendly apoplectic. "I was very public about how I felt," he said. *Person to Person* became such a sore point that he and Murrow simply stopped mentioning it. Around CBS, *See It Now* became the "high Murrow" and *Person to Person* the "low Murrow."

Friendly had feared from the beginning that the show would stretch Murrow too thin. He was doing the news nightly, *See It Now* and *This I Believe* weekly, and now *Person to Person* weekly. Murrow finally had to hire Raymond Swing to help write his tailpieces for the news. He had involved himself in collective and collaborative journalism in the past. But until now he had always acknowledged these as joint efforts. Swing, quite frankly, was now simply ghostwriting many of the commentaries which were presented as Murrow's work. The practice was not unheard of in broadcasting. But in Murrow, the change represented a disillusioning retreat.

In time, he developed presentable, even persuasive, reasons for doing *Person to Person.* When Bill Downs asked, "Why do you go on doing that lousy show?" Murrow replied, "To help Johnny and Jesse pick up a little change." Downs was a friend too. He could surely understand friends helping friends. Ed had a more elevated explanation for those who knew that there had to be a high motive for the low Murrow. Dan Schorr remembered being invited to Quaker Hill for a weekend, and at a point when the mood was right, Schorr dared express a thought long on his mind. "Ed," he said, "you don't look as though you enjoy doing that show." Murrow was quiet for a moment. Then he said, "You have a point." Another long pause, and he added, "I do *Person to Person* because that way I buy the right to do what I do on *See It Now.*" Or, as the explanation was ultimately refined, he did the program he hated in order to do the program he loved.

It was a good answer. It may have been the real answer. Frank Stanton had another explanation. When asked about Murrow and *Person to Person* years later, he answered like a man grown weary of hearing about a saint, a saint who considered Stanton a soulless mechanic. "That program showed Ed was not as hard-nosed a journalist as he liked to think he was. It also indicated he wasn't averse to a substantial amount of money."[19]

Person to Person indeed represented big money. The program was not owned by CBS. Murrow, Zousmer, and Aarons had formed the Person to Person Corporation to produce it, with Murrow as the major shareholder. CBS paid the corporation to create the show and made its money selling the advertising time. Later, Murrow gave 5 percent of the ownership to the two children of Jim Seward and two children of his tax consultant, Leo D'Orsey. They were astonished by his generosity.

Subsequently, Murrow bought out Aarons and Zousmer, and four months later, in 1956, CBS bought the program from him outright. As an independently owned package, Murrow could theoretically have taken *Person to Person* at some point to another network. Bill Paley wanted to make sure that it stayed on CBS.

Recalling the transaction years later, Paley said, "Ed didn't have any money sense. But, I had sense for him. I had no special desire to make him rich just for the sake of making him rich. What I bought had real value." Still, the deal was typical of Paley. The practical Paley locked up a valuable property, while Paley, the friend, helped Murrow "pick up a little change." *Person to Person* was sold for $1 million and made Ed Murrow a moderately rich man.[20]

Person to Person also lifted him to true celebrity, in the peculiarly American definition of the word. He crossed over the line separating those who are well known for doing something to those who have attained the semimystical state of being famous for simply being. So familiar had the distinctive voice become that Civil Defense officials chose Murrow as the voice they wanted informing the public in the event of a nuclear attack, someone instantly recognized and who would be believed and heeded.[21]

On *See It Now*, he was a dark avenger, an occasional scourge, a frequent public scold, a brooding conscience whom people respected but could only take in limited doses. *Person to Person* had a leavening effect on his public image. It made Ed Murrow a lighter, more comfortable figure. *Person to Person* also took some of the partisan edge off of his scarcely concealed liberal biases, since millions saw him week after week talking to all kinds of people about almost anything but politics or serious affairs. *Person to Person* broadened his popular base. By doing the program that he purportedly hated he was indeed forgiven much of what he did on the program he loved. CBS was still losing money on *See It Now*, and it was making money on *Person to Person*. One program made him a hero to thinking people. The other made him palatable to the bean counters.

The evidence suggests that he did not find *Person to Person* all that odious and that he took a close interest in its fortunes. "He came to me once," Paley said, "and asked why we couldn't move the show to a better time for a larger audience." Ed sent Jim Seward a memo asking, "Did anything ever happen about the idea of using the soundtrack of *Person to Person* for a fifteen-minute weekly radio show?"

He claimed that he never looked at ratings. But as Stanton remembered it, "Ed was very interested in the ratings before and after the Marilyn Monroe broadcast. He went out of his way to ask me."

Did Murrow do *Person to Person* for the money? Money as a motive is never a satisfying answer to hero-worshipers. But heros are not immune from economic insecurity, from even a normal quotient of greed. Ed's friend from Washington State, Paul Coie, had noticed a change over the years in Murrow. "In the beginning," Coie remembered, "Ed would say 'I don't mind paying taxes. That's the price of civilization.' But as the years went by and he had his own family, Janet and Casey, and his parents got older, he began to worry about what would become of them if anything happened to him."

Murrow did *Person to Person* in part because it gave him the first real economic security he had known in his life. To once poor boys, this is no small consideration. Ed Murrow was no materialist. There was nothing in him of the man who measures his human worth by his net worth. But the money that *Person to Person* brought him meant freedom; freedom from the old specter of poverty; freedom to do the other kind of television he wanted; freedom to live the way he wanted. He also did the program because few people, however outwardly oblivious to it, can resist the narcotic of fame, the phenomenon that tells a person he has been lifted above ordinary mortals to bring pleasure, or solace, or excitement, or inspiration, or wisdom, to millions of people; that he is loved en masse. It is an agreeable state of being. It is an explanation for *Person to Person* that the rational side of Murrow's brain would have spurned, but a part of his life which he obviously did not reject. He thus had his reasons, good reasons, rationalizations, and possibly unconscious reasons, for doing a second-class piece of work.[22]

But one corner of his soul was never persuaded. It was after a tough, controversial broadcast of *See It Now*. Ed was passing through the terminal at Washington's National Airport with Ed Bliss. A distinguished-looking man came up, seized Ed's hand, and said smiling, "Mr. Murrow, I never miss your program." Murrow's face lit up. The man went on, "My wife and I think *Person to Person* is the most entertaining thing on television."

"A mask fell over Ed's face," Bliss remembered. "It was as though the fellow had thrown cold water at him."[23]

CHAPTER 24

At His Ease

Jim Seward warned Ed that he ought to start thinking about sheltering some of his income. Since Ed loved Quaker Hill, Seward suggested that he buy a working farm there.

A property was available, Glen Arden Farm, 281 acres, with fifty head of cattle and fields sown in corn, wheat, and hay. But tax dodges and investment strategies left Ed Murrow cold. As Janet recalled, "He thought about the Glen Arden property for a long time. He would sit on our terrace and ask himself, 'Do I want to take on that kind of responsibility?'" The man who had watched his father flee from farming had few illusions about the life. "To Ed," Janet said, "a farm meant work." It also meant a heavy investment in 1954. Mrs. William Hamlett, the owner of Glen Arden Farm, was asking $150,000.

In the end, he bought Glen Arden, trading Rumblewood as part payment.

The main house was approached by a long drive lined with century-old maples. The road passed over an arched stone bridge, and there in the center of a sward of green stood a gleaming-white colonial. The house had been built in the year of Independence. It was commodious, with seven bedrooms, and had wide-planked floors. The farm had a guest cottage, barns, a silo, and a house for the farmer who worked the property. A trout stream meandered through lawns and fields, eventually plunging into a rocky glen under a canopy of tall hemlocks. The main house had served briefly as General Washington's headquarters during the Revolution. In the guest house, General Philip Schuyler had been court-martialed and acquitted.[1]

Ed bought Glen Arden because he had been told it was a smart investment. He came to love it more than any other spot on earth. He left the drudgery to the resident farmer. He had milked his last cow and cleaned his last barn long ago. He reserved for himself what he regarded as the pleasures of the land, turning the earth with his tractor, cutting trees, clearing brush from the glen with Casey's help, all tasks which he performed expertly. "You could tell he was at home working in the woods," Bob Dixon remembered of the Glen Arden Murrow. "He had an eye for spotting widow-makers. He could tell by a tree's position in the soil, or how it canted toward the sky. He was surprisingly strong. The kind of guy made of 'bone and wang leather' is the way we used to put it. They're stringy but muscular. It's not wise to tangle with them."

On Christmas of 1954, Ed and an excited 8-year-old Casey called Janet outdoors to give her her Christmas present. They led her to a 20-ton Caterpillar bulldozer that cost $10,000. They enjoyed their joke and then presented her with her real presents.

The following summer, Ed took two months off to play with the bulldozer. The major project was a dam and a pond that he scooped out of the earth. Dixon recalled, "I'd go over there and there'd be Ed with Casey on that dozer with a beaming smile on his face."

He finished the pond, stocked it, and he and Casey began to fish in it. But the dam broke. Ed had to call in a professional contractor to redo the job. Eric Sevareid came up for a visit and remembered Murrow's discomfort. "He was embarrassed," Sevareid said. "Ed Murrow could not laugh at his own humiliations. He looked on that dam as a personal failure. Ed derived a sense of power, of strength, of security over the way he did things. And if he did not do them well, it damaged his internal sources of support."

Ed once told an interviewer, "I get more satisfaction out of understanding the nomenclature of logging operations than writing a piece on European defense." He felt the same about what he did on the farm. Why was knowing how to bale hay more satisfying than understanding NATO? Either he believed that it actually was more important, or he needed to have people believe that he thought so. Either explanation suggested that all the years of city living and intellectual toil still did not satisfy his sentimental notions of true manliness.

Pete Martin came up to Quaker Hill to do a magazine photo story on Murrow at his ease. Martin found him the most difficult subject he had ever handled. "He simply refused to be manipulated...to pose, to appear as a glamour boy....he had a deep sense of the dichotomy between the intellectual and physical man. He had grown up on a farm, yet had become a man of the mind, a thinker and writer, Pawling...gave him a chance to return to his roots." Ed always made the point to a Sevareid or a Howard K. Smith or whoever visited Glen Arden, "This is a working farm. No swimming pool. No tennis court. Two hundred and eighty one acres."[2]

Dixon was the ideal pal for the Glen Arden Murrow. They would drive up together on a Friday after finishing the news and having a drink at Colbee's. Ed's bar-side conversation tended increasingly to involve his life in the country. He liked to tell about his car sliding into a ditch during a blizzard: "I got my tractor to pull it out and the tractor went into the ditch. Afterwards, I borrowed a jeep to pull them both out, and it landed in the ditch. It was great."

When Ford started sponsoring the evening news, the company gave him a price break on a black Thunderbird with red leather seats and a hardtop that retracted at the touch of a button. Friendly remembered once riding in the car in the Great Smokies with Murrow at the wheel taking hairpin curves at seventy miles an hour. Ed grew tired and asked Fred to drive. Friendly found himself, out of a fear of seeming a lesser man than his hero, careening along the mountain roads at the same speed, until suddenly he asked himself, "Why the hell am I driving like a maniac?"[3]

Dixon was a better companion on the road, speaking only when spoken to, unbothered by Murrow's tomb-like silences. An entire drive might pass without a word exchanged; or Murrow might initiate one of their routines:

MURROW: How many whiffle trees on a double horse harness?

DIXON: Two.

MURROW: Anything else?

DIXON: Yes, an evener.

MURROW: Yeh? What about the pole?

During a winter ride up to Quaker Hill with Dixon, the headlights on the car went out and they had to pull into an empty railroad station late at night to call a garage. They waited inside the cold, deserted station, two men huddled on a bench shivering in silence. Suddenly, Murrow jumped up and began singing, in a baritone that reverberated amid the rafters, verse after verse of *The Bastard King of England*, a rarely glimpsed Murrow, Dixon thought.

Ed and Dixon went hunting and target shooting. "He was too good for me," Dixon remembered. "We went trap shooting one time and Ed was so far ahead of me he was getting bored. He finally said, 'I'll tell you what. You shoot first. If you powder it, you win. If you don't I'll take the biggest piece left and if I hit it, I win.' He still beat me. He was a great wing shot, too. He could take doubles. He had a Winchester 21 gauge he'd bought at Abercrombie and Fitch. The ducks would be overhead doing fifty-five miles an hour. He'd take one with one barrel and hit another bird with the second."[4]

Ed's nearest Quaker Hill neighbor was ideal for a man of Murrow's pleasures. Robert Ducas was described around Quaker Hill as "the American counterpart of the English country squire." Ducas was either a financier or an antique dealer, depending on whom one asked. But he was a passionate sportsman. He imported his hunting dogs from Scotland. He raised his own ducks, quail, and pheasants. He accustomed the birds to eating from a pond on his property. Then, he would have them trucked out to a distant point and released, while he and his guests positioned themselves by the pond with their guns, waiting for the birds to come to feed.

Like delivering a broadcast or gouging out a pond, Murrow hunted in deadly earnest. Eric Sevareid remembered going pheasant hunting with Ducas and Murrow. Ed bagged a bird and his dog scampered off, presumably to retrieve it. The dog, instead, started digging a hole and burying the pheasant. "Ed was furious," Sevareid recalled. "He whacked that poor animal." Nothing must be awkward or foolish in his life, even the performance of his dog.[5]

Palmer Williams had often been to the apartment at 580 Park Avenue and was always surprised at its sparseness. It had, he said, "the atmosphere of a hotel suite." When he went to Glen Arden, he understood why. He was delighted by the warmth of the place, the hominess of Janet's kitchen, the lived-in feeling of Glen Arden. This, to the Murrows, was clearly home.[6]

"We were rather antisocial there," Janet recalled, a shade hyperbolically. They might attend three or four parties at the country club during the summer. They had dinner with the Tom Deweys about once a year. They gave a few dinner parties themselves, but less than the Quaker Hill norm. Ed's broadcast friends had a hard time envisioning Ed Murrow with the well-heeled, self-satisfied gentry among whom he passed his leisure hours. "Ed should have bought somewhere else," Bill Downs thought. "That place is too conservative for him." Ed told another friend, "While Tom Dewey and I are neighbors and friends, we have a sort of arm's length relationship when it comes to politics." He was disgusted by Dewey's behavior during the furor over Nixon's Checkers speech in the 1952 campaign. "Dewey," he wrote a friend, "practically held Nixon's hand by the telephone during the crisis...."

At times the fabric of decorum between him and Dewey failed to hold. Ed had brought Bob Pierpoint to the country club buffet where they saw Dewey. As Pierpoint remembered the moment, "Murrow said, 'Come with me, I want you to meet him.'" As they approached, Dewey held out his hand and said, "Ed, wasn't that great about Eisenhower?" Dewey was referring to a wrist slap that the President had given Joe McCarthy after a particularly gross McCarthy outrage. Murrow stiffened. "Tom," he said, "you know that was bullshit!" The two men glared at each other and then Murrow turned and marched off. Pierpoint was left standing alone with Dewey, saying, sheepishly, "Nice to meet you, Governor."[7]

Ralph Hetzel was a Quaker Hill neighbor, a cultivated man who directed the Motion Picture Association of America, a man rather more to the Murrows' liberal taste. Hetzel was also a keen observer of the Murrow menage. At dinner parties, Hetzel recalled, "Ed was quite capable of withdrawing in the middle of conversation as completely as if he had left the room. Janet was very skillful at taking up the conversational slack when Ed drifted away. She had a sharp sense of responsibility as a hostess. She was warm, but rather formal. Ed was a good ranconteur when his mind would return. He'd talk about his boyhood in the wild Northwest or the woman, Ida Lou, who taught him how to use the English language." The Murrows' entertaining, Hetzel remembered, "was structured like an English country weekend."

Glen Arden permitted Ed and Janet to return the hospitality in the form if not quite the majesty of Dytchley. Ronnie Tree and his American wife, Marietta, had become close friends of Ed and Janet. Tree had left a stagnating political career in England and moved to America to manage his inheritance, Marshall Field's in Chicago. When the Trees visited Glen Arden, with the ducks honking above the green fields, the blasts of the guns, and the barking of dogs, a patch of upstate New York seemed fleetingly not all that different from a corner of Oxfordshire.[8]

There was a touch of the Old World too in the Murrows' servants. The full-time staff at Glen Arden consisted of a Polish couple in reduced circumstances. Tadeusz Kaczorowski, the husband, had been a lawyer in Warsaw before the war. He hinted that his wife was a countess from a great landholding family. After the war broke out, Tadeusz had been a prisoner of the Russians for a time. He and his countess eventually managed to flee Poland, with all their worldly possessions left behind. After the war, they made their way to America and took whatever work they could find. Janet thought that the wife took her fate in good part. Not so, Tadeusz. He felt, she said, that "he had to show the Murrows how to live. He perpetually second-guessed the wine choice, the table settings, the right dishes for the side board." The refugee in Tadeusz was never entirely erased either. Janet had bought a huge rug that she wanted for Glen Arden. Tadeusz resisted laying it. "Madam," he said, "I speak from experience. If you ever had to escape, you couldn't take that rug with you." She found him quarrelsome and intimidating.

When Tadeusz needed money for a trip to London, Ed gave him a letter which stated that the man was supposedly traveling to gather "material for my radio and TV programs" on Czech and Polish refugees. He then paid him $800 "in advance." However pompously he dealt with Janet, Tadeusz was cringingly deferential around Ed.[9]

Ed Murrow was indeed a dominating, though not a domineering, figure in his home as much as in his work. Asked by a reporter about her home life, Janet answered: "Ed has very high standards of personal conduct. And he expects this kind of conduct from people he's fond of.... with me it means a quick rebuke if I say something catty or start to tell a juicy bit of gossip. Ed is the master of our house. He doesn't always ask my opinion on big decisions. He says, 'this is the way it is going to be....' He is the kind of a man a wife can be proud of."

By the time they bought Glen Arden, they had been married twenty years. Of the marriage, Howard K. Smith commented, "Janet was kind, compatible with everybody, while Ed was very much wrapped up in Ed and the empire of men he had hired. He was too dominant for Janet. They made you wonder how certain types ever got together. Ed became frightfully famous. And that's dangerous in a marriage."

His attitude toward his wife was of a piece with his attitude toward women generally. As Mary Warburg put it, "Ed did not treat women as equals. The woman he had been involved with in England, for example, it was purely a physical thing in my opinion. I don't believe he ever gave a thought to her mind."

"The word that comes to my mind is 'proper,'" Fred Friendly recalled of the Murrows. "Not much affection. On the other hand, Ed was always quoting Janet's judgment of our programs. He trusted her judgment. He considered her very intelligent, in a way, more intelligent than himself. In what she gave him, in what she contributed to his success, she did more than people recognized."

She had his admiration, his respect, his understated brand of love. But Janet did not always have his attention. Ed took her with him to West Berlin to film a segment of *See It Now*. When the work was done, Janet threw a party for the staff. The staff, in turn, surprised her with a gift of a silver platter. "How did you know," she said, with a gracious smile and a glance at her husband, "that today was my birthday." He had forgotten, and not for the first time.

Their lives, in a sense, were like railroad tracks. They ran alongside each other, close together year after year, carrying the same freight of life in the same direction, but slightly apart.

Marietta Tree thought that Janet was the only kind of wife who could have worked for an Ed Murrow. "If Janet had been more dynamic and emotional," she thought, "they would have been a hopeless couple. Janet complemented Ed. She provided the essential counterweight in their lives."

After a day's shooting, Ed and Bob Dixon would sit around the kitchen and drink. "After a few belts," Dixon recalled, "Ed would begin to nag Janet. He could get a little rough. She was a very serious lady. Janet didn't tease easily." A recurring theme was his "peasant" background contrasted with her *Mayflower* roots. "He would go on and on," Dixon remembered, about his bumpkin background and Janet's pedigree. Janet would say only, "Oh, Ed, please!" Actually, she would admit later that this routine of his did not bother her all that much: "In a way I liked it. It was the one way that I was more established than he was. I had to fight hard to find ways to hold my own with him."[10]

The one unambiguous emotional tie in his life remained his love for his son. Ed Murrow was virtually an absentee father Monday through

Saturday morning. He bridled at the thought of his boy growing up in the city. And so he tried to make it up to him at Quaker Hill. The move to Glen Arden farm provided a place where he and Casey could reconstruct the happy parts of his own boyhood and leave out the poverty.

Ed started pistol practice for Casey at age 5. Bob Dixon watched. "It was important to Ed," Dixon remembered. "He leaned fairly hard on Casey. But you could tell the way the kid handled a gun, he didn't much care for it. He had the best equipment. But he did not have the inclination. Ed never said anything. But I could see he was disappointed." As Janet remembered it, "Casey didn't like hurting animals, shooting birds."

Ed bought Casey a pony. One of his own pleasures in Manhattan, akin to his earlier disappearances to Times Square shooting galleries, was to go to Madison Square Garden when the rodeo was in town. Ed had made friends with the trail boss and saddle boss of the show. When Casey was 10, Ed enlisted them to find a pony for his son. He settled on a little, buck-skinned quarter horse called Pigeon. The pony was spirited, rodeo-trained with hair-trigger responses to the lightest touch on the reins.

Janet remembered Casey's excitement when Pigeon was delivered to Glen Arden. The first few weeks, Casey was allowed only to walk Pigeon around the paddock. Then, he mounted it and finally rode the pony. As Casey later described the experience, "Pigeon was too spirited for a first rider. I should have had an old nag. I had a hell of a time making the horse do anything." Pigeon threw Casey, but without serious damage. Then, Bob Ducas's son, William, a few years older than Casey, took the horse on a more daring gallop and was thrown in what could have been a serious accident. The boy escaped with only a broken arm. Pigeon was sold. Janet was surprised that Ed had not shown more sense about horses than he had in the Pigeon episode.

Ed was more successful in teaching Casey to work the land. He was a quick-minded, serious, responsible little boy. He drove the tractor. He learned to handle the bulldozer like an operating engineer. His father paid him and Ralph Hetzel's son, Dorn, $2 an hour to clear underbrush from the glen. Effort and reward, sweat and satisfaction, had been so much a part of his own growing up that he wanted his son to understand the link.

In part, Ed Murrow wanted to raise a little man. But another side of him wanted to extend the childhood that he felt he himself had been partly cheated of. When Casey was 10, he brought home a report card on which the teacher had remarked that he was "immature." Ed was furious. "By God," he said, "I should hope so."[11]

The man whom even his closest friends found remote and undecipherable had quite another effect on children. Dixon remembered Ed's treatment of his sons. "He'd always take time to answer the kids' questions, and some of those questions made you wince. But Ed would respond in a patient way that wound up giving them some insight, some

learning. He'd started out in education years before and I always found
something of the teacher in him."

Ed encouraged his guests to Glen Arden to bring their children. Jesse
Zousmer's son, Steven, remembered going to Glen Arden with his parents and the Aarons and their daughter. "I expected," Steven recalled,
"to be left in a corner." Ed instead happily abandoned the adults for the
children. He showed them how to shoot a pistol, to their city-bred parents' horror. He let them drive the tractor. He played baseball with them.
"One of my first adult perceptions," Steven Zousmer remembered, "was
to notice as a boy of ten or eleven that Ed Murrow was not patronizing to
me. We would have conversations. Adult conversations. He'd sit there with
his scotch. I'd sit there with my Coca-Cola and we'd talk. I never had any
feeling that this was an adult making strained conversation with a kid. It
was not in him to patronize. In the meantime, I knew all of the other CBS
giants. They were intimidating and imposing. They were courteous—
'Hello' and a little goo-goo talk for a kid—but Ed struck me as my friend.
I knew he was famous and that he was a giant. But he was not intimidating, just tremendously likeable."[12]

The man with the chain saw slung over his shoulder, disappearing
into the glen, his son tagging behind him, was a happy man, a man connected to a world of simple, enduring values. But five days out of seven
Ed Murrow's life was in the city. Descriptions of him in the city are ka-
leidoscopic, often contradictory, but they lean to dark hues and somber
tones.

At lunch he could usually be found at the Century Club, "holding
court," in Teddy White's phrase. "He'd be in an armchair having a drink
with half a dozen people forming a circle around him as if he were the most
eminent man alive. He'd spot someone on the outer perimeter and grandly
wave him in closer."

He would complete an interview with Sir Stafford Cripps on the de-
valuation of the pound and then drag Bob Dixon to Madison Square Garden for the rodeo. They went every year to watch the calf roping and
steer wrestling. After the show, they would go below to the stables and
mix with the broncobusters. Dixon was astonished at the ease with which
Ed slipped into the idiom of the range. The trail boss loaned him and
Dixon horses. Murrow would borrow boots, peel off his jacket, pull down
his tie, and begin riding around the aisles of the stables. Dixon recalled
him throwing back his head, breathing deeply, and exclaiming, "Deex-
ohn, this pleasures me!"[13]

He was either a brilliant conversationalist or a wretched conversationalist. "Ed Murrow could be as garrulous as an Irishman in a pub, or as
silent as the tomb," one friend said. "Ed was a marvelous companion,"
Ken Galbraith recalled. "You never spent time with Ed Murrow without
coming away with something over which to be amused or without a good
deal of information." To Eric Sevareid, "Ed was not really a conversa-

tionalist. If you asked him something, he'd stare at the floor forever, then deliver an utterance. There was no real give and take. He was a man who could go twenty-four hours without speaking. It was unnerving. I think it was a form of depression. The heavy smoking, the coffee, the drinking—he also told me he took sleeping pills—I think they had a cumulative depressing effect on his nervous system."

He hated large parties—"pig stickings," he called them. Charles Wertenbaker in a profile in *The New Yorker* gives a picture of Murrow as guest: "Large dinner parties have been riled by his between courses predictions of national and international misfortune at the hands of dictators, demagogues or plain politicians. After dinner talk dies when it seems that Murrow is no longer taking part or even listening, but is leaning far forward in his chair staring at the rug, his knees on his elbows and his fists slowly beating each other, smoke enveloping his face.... He crushes [his cigarette] out and picks up the conversation where it was dropped several minutes earlier."

After hearing his bleak visions one time too often, Mary Warburg asked Ed, "Since you're so gloomy about the deplorable state of this world of ours, do you mean people shouldn't have children?" "Oh no, Mary," he said looking stunned, even hurt at this logical extension of his pessimism. "I didn't mean that at all."[14]

He had a sense of humor, but not of the belly-laugh school. His ripostes were swift and steel-tipped. He once came out of Studio 41 and stood combing his hair in front of a mirror in the corridor. Out of another studio came an actor playing the role of a British army officer. He stepped in front of the mirror as though Murrow did not exist. Murrow tapped the man on the shoulder and said, "You know, you couldn't be ruder if you were a real British Colonel."

His *See It Now* reporter, Ed Scott, had bought a $5 raincoat while covering a flood in Arkansas. With the job done, Scott left the raincoat behind but included it in his expense account. The accounting office disallowed reimbursement because Scott had not turned the raincoat in to the wardrobe department. Murrow wrote a memo to accounting: "During Mr. Scott's stay in Judsonia," it began, "he came upon an orphan child whose mother and father had been killed by the tornado and who was crying in the street. It was raining and Scott being a gentleman and true representative of CBS-TV took off the raincoat and immediately gave it to the little boy, who stopped crying.... we have been able to trace the young man who is now living with an aunt in Searcy, Arkansas...." On and on, page after page, went the saga of the $5 raincoat.

Mary Warburg observed his features closely, even in moments of humor, and found, "He smiled without laughing. There was no mirth in the smile. He showed his teeth without humor showing in his eyes. They were always questioning."

The same man could slip into an uncontrollable fit of laughter on the air. He was quoting Mark Twain in his tailpiece one night, an account of a city boy trying to hitch a horse. Dixon, as his announcer, started to laugh and hid his head under the table to avoid distracting Murrow. The sight set Murrow laughing uncontrollably. He barely made it through the tailpiece, tears of laughter all the while streaming down his face. The outburst triggered a flood of mail, most of it in the vein, "I never suspected Edward R. Murrow of a sense of humor."[15]

Marietta Tree watched a change come over him through the years. She had first met Ed Murrow at Paley's place, Kiluna, during one of Ed's returns from England. She had been impressed by the intensity of his emotions. But, in later years, it struck her that he was "like an old actor, going through his lines with great skill, but not much heart." After he had been drinking, "He would get a baleful, outraged look in his eyes," she remembered, and begin the familiar litany of disaster lurking around the corner. She had a sense that "life became flat for him after the war. He'd see my husband, Ronnie, and that would trigger all his old war stories."

He had another pet theme. The more fashionable the company, the more predictably would he raise it. Year by year, the farm at Polecat Creek grew smaller, the soil stonier, the chores harder, and the Murrows poorer. The farm shrank to "forty acres of poor cotton land, watermelons and tobacco." He had "one pair of shoes a year." "Chickens wandered around the house." He told Mary Warburg, "I was the son of a sharecropper, what education I've had I've gotten myself." He told Dick Hottelet, "I never learned to play. There were no tennis weekends and sailing weekends. Who would you sail with in a logging camp?"

"He drove that one into the ground," Dorothy Paley remembered. "You'd never quite know why he dragged it in at some unlikely point in the conversation." "It became something of a bore," Marietta Tree thought. "I'd say, 'Ed, after all, we've all come up to something more than where we started.'"[16]

Why did a man whose very bearing, whose speech, mind, and spirit bespoke a natural nobility, need to make himself out to be a sharecropper's son? In part, it was a social preemptive strike. There could be no surprised glances down long noses when ancestors and schools came up in East Side salons. He had already admitted to Polecat Creek and a cow college. His success also allowed him to put behind him the days of the doctored résumé. He no longer needed to impress, exaggerate, or conceal. "Take me as I am," he was saying in effect. "Every bit your equal, and more." Indeed, by waving his work shirt in his rich friends' faces, he made clear the distinction between the natural aristocracy of talent and the accidental aristocracy of birth. There could be no question about where Ed Murrow belonged. But how could they know how high he had climbed until they knew how far down he had started? And so he told them.

Mary Warburg had been right about one thing. Whether in the country or in town, whether in drawing rooms or in barrooms, he was happiest in the company of men. "Ed admired the kind of men who went out and did physical things," Ed Bliss, his newswriter, had observed. "Guys who cut down trees, drove fast cars, flew planes, the essentially masculine world."

His pleasure in masculine camaraderie was evident in the year-end roundup. Beginning in 1950, the fertile mind of Don Hewitt had conceived the idea of bringing home CBS correspondents from around the world for a state-of-the-world report. That first year, Howard K. Smith came in from London, David Schoenbrun from Paris, Winston Burdett from Rome, Bill Costello from Tokyo, Eric Sevareid from Washington, and Larry Le Sueur from the United Nations, with Murrow presiding, quite possibly the highest concentration of talent in broadcast journalism ever assembled in one studio.

The year-end roundup took place during Christmas and New Years. The correspondents arrived two and three days in advance. They held strategy sessions and what amounted to dress rehearsals. They went out to dinner afterward and continued talking long and provocatively. The ambience was pure Murrow. Marvin Kalb describes Murrow preparing for the roundup: "When Ed spoke, everyone else went silent. If someone came up with an idea and Ed said, 'Yes, let's go in that direction' or 'No, I think we'll do something else,' no one ever stood up and said, 'That's a terrible idea.' They all bowed to his leadership." They were like ordinarily independent sons, home from college for Christmas, submitting again to a strong father's domination.

Murrow began a tradition of bringing the correspondents up to his Park Avenue apartment for a buffet and poker after the broadcast. To sit at that card table was to have penetrated to the innermost sanctum of CBS news. The host, however, proved a poor player. Murrow had a natural poker face, but he was an incautious plunger. "The sharks always took Ed," Sevareid said.[17]

He drank heavily during the poker games. He drank when he went out with the boys at Colbee's, the Pentagon, or Louis and Armand's. He drank sitting around the fireplace at Glen Arden. "He could put away a third of a bottle of scotch while we sat and talked," Bob Pierpoint recalled. Yet no one reported seeing Ed Murrow drunk—not in the falling-down sense. His speech was almost the only clue that he had been drinking heavily. The words came slower, the voice became louder. His chin sank into his chest. Ten seconds of silence might precede an oracular pronouncement. Murrow, the good listener, listened less and pontificated more when he drank. The alcohol seemed to dissolve his facade of modesty.

The night that President Eisenhower was inaugurated in 1953, Ed made a round of parties after work with Joe Wershba and Johnny Aarons. They returned to their hotel in the small hours, and Murrow said to the night clerk, "I want a bottle of scotch sent to my room for my friends." "I'm sorry, Mr. Murrow," the clerk answered, "we can't do that at this hour." As Wershba recalled the scene, "Ed adopted his most imperious British pose and said, 'You *will* send up a bottle of scotch!'" Still the clerk refused. Ed demanded to speak to the manager, who also turned him down. He stormed into his suite, slamming doors and fuming, "Did you hear that fool? Would you believe we can't get a bottle of scotch?" But he appears to have remained a social drinker. There were no morning eye-openers, no quick nips during the day, no solitary trips into Colbee's. However, he was a social drinker of the first rank.[18]

He wore his celebrity as a burden. On planes, he always insisted on a window seat and placed his traveling companion next to him as a buffer against the curious. When strangers did approach him, he was polite, but rarely said a word that might prolong the encounter.

He occasionally took Ed Bliss on trips with him because Bliss wore well. He was a shy man, short and balding, with glasses, who seemed more suited to the world of his missionary father than to electronic journalism. Bliss had become chief writer for the evening news when Jesse Zousmer became completely caught up in *Person to Person*.

On their travels, Bliss too sensed that the war was never quite over in Murrow's imaginings. They were flying a prop plane to a speaking engagement one night, and as Murrow gazed out at the blue-tipped flame of the engines' exhaust, he began reminiscing about a mission in a plodding bomber toward the end of the war. The Germans had just introduced their first jet fighters, and Ed recalled, "Our fiery engine exhaust was like a beacon that said, 'Here I am. Come and get me.' It made me very nervous."

Ed was invited to receive an honorary degree and to speak at Colby College in Portland, Maine. He took Bliss with him. Bliss's account of the trip offers revealing glimpses of the private Murrow. Ed chose to drive his Thunderbird. They traveled the newly built interstates, and Bliss remembered, "Ed drove ninety miles an hour with one finger on the wheel." When he grew tired, he asked Bliss to take over and disappeared into one of his silences, the kind of withdrawal that made friends wonder what they had done to offend him.

When Murrow finally spoke, he told Bliss, "You did well, Eddie Boy. You drove the car. The car didn't drive you. There's a way to do it, a right way and a wrong way. You should pass somebody like a train effortlessly switching from one track to another, no jerky movements, no abrupt speed changes." Driving, Bliss realized, was to Murrow no casual matter.

Jesse Zousmer had warned Bliss in advance, "When you travel with Murrow, make sure you know the territory." After an overnight in Boston, Bliss became lost trying to pick up the interstate again. "Where are you going?" Murrow demanded. Bliss answered with a nervous laugh, "Colby College." Murrow shot back, "Don't get smart with me, Buster." For the first time in five years of happy association with Murrow, Bliss had been rebuked. Whatever illusion of closeness he had felt on this trip instantly vanished. They were officer and enlisted man.

They checked into a hotel in Portland. It was the traveling companion's responsibility to wake Murrow up. Bliss went to Murrow's room the next morning. He was shocked. "Ed looked ghastly," Bliss remembered. "His skin was like bread dough." He told Bliss, "I didn't sleep a wink last night." It was Bliss's introduction to the tortured Murrow nights. Larry Le Sueur had once spent a night in a hotel room with Murrow and was awakened by what he thought was "somebody tearing the sheets." He was awakened a second time by what sounded like "the air conditioner breaking down." Both sounds had been Murrow grinding his teeth.

That morning at Colby College, Murrow asked Bliss if he wanted to come in to watch the ceremony and hear the speech. Bliss said that he thought he would wait outside and take a walk around the campus.

When Murrow emerged afterward, it was with the architect, Edward Durrell Stone, and Stone's son. Murrow told Bliss that they were going first to take the Stones to the Portland airport to catch a flight. Murrow drove. They came to an intersection and Murrow asked Bliss, who had feverishly studied the map, "Which way do I turn?" Bliss told him, "To the right." Murrow said in an accusing tone, "Are you sure?" "I am," Bliss replied. "If you're right," Murrow said, "it will be the first time this trip." Bliss was being made a fool in front of strangers. He felt a burning humiliation. "I wanted to tell him to stop the car right there," he recalled. "I'd get out and hitchhike."

Later, when they were alone again, Murrow's foul mood lifted, and from half-expressed clues, Bliss pieced together that part of the problem was that he had offended Murrow by showing no interest in hearing his speech.

They thereafter rode along in an aura of quiet good feeling that tempted Bliss to want to know better this man whom he idolized. He asked Murrow, "When you were a kid, did you ever feel that you had been placed on Earth for a special purpose?" Murrow went into one of his thought funks and after an eternity answered, "No. Only that whatever I did, I had to do it at the very peak of my ability." It was the closest to penetrating the Murrow persona that Ed Bliss ever came.

Murrow was niggardly in revealing himself, but otherwise he was the most generous of men. During the Colby trip, Bliss confessed to him a long-nourished dream. For years, Ed Bliss had wanted to write the life story of his missionary father. He had calculated that it would take him six months. But Bliss had a demanding job, a wife to support, and two children in college. He saw no way that he could manage a six-month leave without pay.

Murrow heard Bliss out and at first tweaked him. He had lost all use for missionaries, he said, and recalled the time his mother took the first 50 cents he ever earned, for hoeing all day long, and put it in the missionary box at the Quaker meetinghouse. More seriously, he said that he found something arrogant about missionaries going to a place like China, "The whole idea of foisting your truth on an ancient civilization."

But suddenly, Murrow said, "You have to write that book, Eddie Boy. You have to tell how a kid from a small New England industrial town winds up running a dairy in Fukien province in China. That's a compelling story." He eventually granted Bliss the leave and loaned him $4,000. He removed any sense of embarrassing charity from the gesture by telling Bliss that he also wanted to buy a 15 percent interest in the project for another $4,000. He was not doing an employee a kindness, he told Bliss. He was becoming a partner in a business. In the end, Murrow advanced nearly $10,000 to Bliss.[19]

Murrow had not seen Jimmy Sheean for years, barely at all since their drinking and shouting matches at Hallam Street during the war. Unfortunately, the drinking had undone Sheean. He wound up living in a decayed lodging house in London. His carefully cultivated upper-class friends turned their backs on him as he dissipated a formidable talent and a large income "through sheer incompetence," as Sheean himself admitted. In 1953, he wrote to Murrow about creditors in hot pursuit, and Murrow cabled him $1,000. The following year, Sheean asked Murrow to pay for his daughter's tuition at a fashionable American private school. He included a statement from the school that the girl was psychologically unsuited for the rigors of a public school. It was not the sort of argument to touch the heart of a graduate of a two-room school in Blanchard. Murrow, nevertheless, paid the girl's tuition. He continued loaning money to Sheean, though the loans were never repaid, and Murrow refused to allow Jim Seward to try to collect them.

Raymond Swing had been something of an intellectual father to Ed. Swing had resigned as the *Voice of America*'s chief commentator during the McCarthy inquisition. He fell on hard times. Ed learned of Swing's troubles through a mutual friend. He directed Jim Seward to get money to Swing, but to do it anonymously because Ray Swing was a proud man. And eventually, he had put Swing to work on his payroll.

Bob Dixon needed another partner to buy a ranch in Arizona. Dixon telephoned Murrow, who said yes over the phone without asking a question and without consulting Jim Seward, much to Seward's dismay. Earl Foster, Ed's old Washington State mentor, bought a sawmill and immediately ran into a cash flow problem. Foster called Ed and asked if he would like to come in as a part owner. Murrow sent Foster a check for $5,000 that day. Janet's brother, Dart, did not want to take a job transfer with his company to another city. He started his own label-printing business instead. He needed capital and went to Ed, who said yes. Ed also sent money to help educate Dart's children.

Murrow paid a substantial part of the astronomical medical bills of a CBS public relations man who was dying of cancer, a man he barely knew. He did it anonymously. He arranged for Dr. Paul Heller, one of the survivors whom he had met at Buchenwald, to come to America and practice medicine. When Heller fell ill, Ed loaned him money. As he explained the loan, "...I owe him a great debt. He demonstrated that a man can live for six years under conditions that are indescribable and emerge with his faith and hope intact."

He was virtually incapable of saying no. Eric Sevareid may have found the root of his behavior: "When anybody was in trouble, Ed would go out of his way to help. It was as though he were trying to get rid of the money, almost as though he felt guilty for having it."

He gave generously, but he received awkwardly. After they had been friends for years, Bob Dixon went to a gun shop on Center Street in New York and bought Ed an expensive .45-caliber pistol. He then ordered a custom-made belt and holster and had the letters "ERM" hand-tooled on the holster pouch. When the gun came back, Dixon took it in the box it came in and virtually dumped it on Ed's desk. "I hope you'll have some use for it," he said and walked out. It was the only way with Murrow, he had learned. Expressions of sentiment had to be handled with cowboy taciturnity.

Some months later, Murrow brought Dixon to his office and pointed to something wrapped in old newspapers leaning against the wall. "Take that home," Murrow said, "you might like it." It was a painting of horses by an artist, Dunton of Taos, a work Dixon knew that Murrow treasured. He remembered what Murrow once told him about gift giving: "Never give anything to anybody that you wouldn't rather keep for yourself."[20]

In 1954, Ed Klauber died, and Murrow kept the promise he had made a decade before to deliver the eulogy. This was a difficult gesture for him, to expose his emotions, to express personal sentiment in public. Yet his tribute struck to the essence of the man. "Ed Klauber," Murrow said, "was an intolerant man—intolerant of deceit, deception, distortion and double talk.... He was sparing with his praise and penetrating with his criticism, sometimes satisfied with the best a reporter could do, but always expecting improvement....It is easy to be tolerant, if you don't care. He cared to the last...."

Men loved Ed Murrow. Collingwood, Sevareid, Dixon, Seward, and others all confessed it freely. They were drawn to him because he combined so many of the qualities that men wish for in themselves, manliness, certainty, strength, courage, intelligence, humor, generosity, and an aura of mystery. David Schoenbrun used the word "homophile" to describe the love, in the Greek sense, that this man inspired in other men.

Yet the man to whom so many turned, turned virtually to no one but himself. Perhaps the one condition precluded the other. The oak is leaned on. It does not lean. The self-containment of his boyhood annealed with the passing years. He told a correspondent who had considered himself a friend, "I've never had any intimate friends. Only colleagues and acquaintances." To be needed by so many and to need, or to appear to need, so few seemed a peculiar curse.[21]

CHAPTER 25

The Broadcaster and the Demagogue

Years later, Fred Friendly would identify it as their moment of truth, a sudden flash of insight into the power they possessed. "The Case against Milo Radulovich, A0589839" was perhaps a modest canvas for so bold a claim. It dealt with an unknown figure in a small town caught up in a scarcely noticed controversy. But that was just the point.

Murrow made a deliberate attempt to avoid becoming a prisoner of the eastern establishment vision of the world. He liked to dip into newspapers from all around the country. Thus, he had come across, in *The Detroit News*, the plight of a 26-year-old senior at the University of Michigan, Milo Radulovich. Radulovich had previously served nearly eight years as an Air Force meteorologist and held a commission as a lieutenant in the Reserves. He was about to lose his commission.

Under Air Force Regulation 36-52, Milo Radulovich had been declared a "security risk" for having close associations with "Communists or Communist sympathizers." The Air Force had subsequently demanded his resignation. The close associations were with his father and sister. The senior Radulovich was an old man who had come to this country over forty years before, served in World War I, and thereafter spent his life in coal mines and automobile plants. His crime was that he read a Serbian-language newspaper said to support Marshall Tito of Yugoslavia. At the time that the Air Force was using this information to question the old man's loyalty—and by extension, his son's—Tito had broken with the Soviet bloc and was being wooed by the West, indeed was receiving loans from the same United States government that was persecuting Milo Radulovich. The sister was alleged by the Air Force to be a Communist, but no proof had been shown to the lieutenant.

Radulovich refused to resign his commission. Subsequently, the Air

Force had convened a three-officer board to review the case. The board recommended Radulovich's severance from the service. Again, at this hearing, no witnesses were produced and whatever evidence the Air Force had against his father or his sister remained unopened in a manila envelope.

This was the story that Ed had found in *The Detroit News*. The case reeked of McCarthyism. It was important because of its seeming unimportance. The plight of this obscure Air Force Reserve lieutenant revealed to Ed how deeply the cancer of fear and suspicion had eaten into the marrow of everyday life in America. Paranoia was becoming institutionalized. Due process, the rights of the accused, the presumption of innocence, could be denied without explanation. Murrow told Friendly to look into the potential of the Radulovich case for a segment on *See It Now*.[1]

A few months before, Murrow had paid tribute to the journalist's code of objectivity. "I favor" he said, "some such device as radio and TV stations ringing a bell every time a newscaster is about to inject his own view." If his suggestion had been adopted, the bells should have been clanging at CBS on the night of October 20, 1953.[2]

"The Case against Milo Radulovich, A0589839" was broadcast at 10:30 p.m., since *See It Now* had by now won a regular weekly slot on the outer rim of prime time. The case was a modern morality tale. An appealing young man appeared on the screen. "...Anybody that is labeled with a security risk in these days, especially in physics or meteorology," he said, "simply won't be able to find employment in this field of work. In other words, I believe that if I am labeled a security risk—if the Air Force won't have me, I ask the question, who will?...If I'm being judged by my relatives, are my children going to be asked to denounce me? Are they going to be asked what their father was labeled? Are they going to be asked why their father is a security risk?...I see a chain reaction that has no end."

Then an old man in halting English explained how he had written to President Eisenhower asking for justice for his son. Milo Radulovich's sister was also interviewed. She refused to discuss her own politics, but expressed anger that her brother's loyalty should be measured by her beliefs. Neighbors in Radulovich's town of Dexter, Michigan, spoke up for him, including the former commander of the local American Legion post and a union official.

Murrow had told Friendly to leave him time for a strong finish, "because we are going to live or die by our ending. Management is going to howl, and we may blow ourselves right out of the water, but we simply can't do an 'on the one hand on the other hand' ending for this one." The network had already shown its uneasiness by refusing to promote the program. Murrow and Friendly had thereupon dipped into their own pockets for $1,500 for an ad in *The New York Times*.

They were deliberately flying in the face of the CBS policy that forbade taking sides in political controversy. Ed himself, imagining that he worshiped at the shrine of reportorial detachment, had voluntarily included in his contract a clause pledging himself to scrupulous neutrality. But in his tailpiece, he threw his and the network's objectivity rule out the window. "We are unable to judge the claims against the lieutenant's father or sister," he said, "because neither we, nor you, nor they, nor the lieutenant, nor the lawyers know precisely what was contained in that manila envelope. Was it hearsay, rumor, gossip, slander, or was it hard ascertainable fact that could be backed by creditable witnesses? We do not know....no evidence was adduced to prove that Radulovich's sister is a member of the party and the case against his father was certainly not made....We believe that the son shall not bear the iniquity of the father, even though that iniquity be proved; and in this case it was not....Whatever happens in the whole area of the relationship between the individual and the state, we do it ourselves...it seems to Fred Friendly and myself... that this is a subject that should be argued about endlessly."[3]

Jack Gould, writing in *The New York Times,* understood instantly what happened on television that night: "The program marked perhaps the first time that a major network, the Columbia Broadcasting System, and one of the country's most important industrial sponsors, the Aluminum Company of America, consented to a program taking a vigorous editorial stand in a matter of national importance and controversy."

Harriet Van Horne, television critic for *The New York World Telegram & Sun,* sent Ed a personal note: "...You are his [Radulovich's] Zola." *Variety* declared the Radulovich story the most important television broadcast of the year.

ALCOA proved a sponsor of near saintly tolerance. The company was in the business of selling aluminum, not curing injustices. The Air Force was a major customer for its product. But all that Chief Wilson, ALCOA's president, said was that he hoped "civil liberty broadcasts" were not to become the sole topic of interest on *See It Now.*[4]

What Murrow and Friendly had done for Milo Radulovich was to give the man what his government had denied him, the right to defend himself. What they had done for television was revealed in a telephone call Friendly received a month later.

Friendly was at home taking a shower when his wife told him that Ed insisted he come to the phone right away. Ed told him to see that a camera crew was to be sent to the Pentagon within an hour. That night, *See It Now* did, in fact, involve another civil rights story, the attempt of Indianapolis American Legionnaires to deny the use of a hall to the American Civil Liberties Union. But first Murrow introduced the Secretary of the Air Force, Harold E. Talbott. "I have decided," Talbott said, "that it is consistent with the interests of national security to retain Lieutenant Radulovich in the United States Air Force. He is not, in my opinion, a security risk...."

Television had crossed a line. Its untested power for moral suasion had been used on an issue in which virtually the entire country had been cowed into submission. As Friendly put it, "Television journalism had achieved influence, like a great newspaper, like *The New York Times*. We found that night that we could make a difference."[5]

The Radulovich broadcast had another outcome. It put Ed Murrow and Joe McCarthy on a collision course. For it was this broadcast, the "Radwich junk," as McCarthy's agent, Don Surine, had called it, that led Surine to say that McCarthy had "proof" that "Murrow was on the Soviet payroll in 1934." And it was at this point that Murrow made the decision to use this new-found power of television to go after McCarthy, before McCarthy went after him.

To suggest that Ed Murrow was the first of his profession to dare confront McCarthy would be an injustice to a dozen brave journalists. Walter Lippmann did it. So did Drew Pearson, the Alsop brothers, and Herblock in his cartoons. Murrow's broadcast colleagues, Quincy Howe, Elmer Davis, and H.V. Kaltenborn, even Murrow's Boys, Sevareid, Smith, and Ed Morgan, along with Murrow himself, publicly exposed McCarthy's tactics and his menace over radio. Radio, however, even as early as 1953, was slipping into its eventual state as the medium that was overheard rather than listened to. It lacked force. Ed had even done a television segment on McCarthy on *See It Now,* in December of 1951, a montage of McCarthy's tirades against Owen Lattimore, Dean Acheson, and General Marshall. But it had lasted only four minutes, and Murrow had pretty much let the film clips speak for themselves. No one as yet had used the persuasive power of television in a direct confrontation with McCarthy.[6]

What McCarthy had on Murrow was circumstantial evidence. But it was the kind of innuendo that, in McCarthy's hands, had proved more than adequate to destroy other men. All that Murrow knew for certain that McCarthy knew was contained in the photostated newspaper clipping Donald Surine had given to Joe Wershba. There were two pages to it, a front-page story, continued on page six of *The Pittsburgh Sun Telegraph* for February 18, 1935. The headline read, "American Professors Trained by Soviet, Teach in U.S. Schools." *The Sun Telegraph* was part of the Hearst chain, thus the same story had been carried in Hearst papers throughout the country. The assertion of the article was that American educators were sending teachers to a summer school at Moscow University to be trained as "adept Communist propagandists." The chief target of this exposé was George S. Counts, a Columbia University professor. Counts was actually a midstream opponent of all forms of totalitarianism. But he had angered Hearst editors by calling an earlier Hearst series on education "fascistic."

The Hearst story "proved" that Dr. Counts was part of a conspiracy to teach communism because he served on a National Advisory Committee for the summer session in Moscow. The story also contained a box, listing Counts's twenty-four fellow members of the advisory committee, presumably equally disloyal. Among them was Edward R. Murrow.

When Surine had first shown Joe Wershba the clipping, Wershba asked how it justified Surine's charge that Murrow had been on the Soviet payroll. Surine told him that these seminars were conducted by VOKS, a Soviet cultural agency, which was part of the Soviet espionage apparatus. Ergo, Murrow had been working for Soviet espionage. To the dispassionate observer, the connection required a long leap of logic. But Joe McCarthy had done serious mischief with far less to work with.

It all went back to Murrow's job at the Institute of International Education nearly twenty-two years before when he had indeed worked with Soviet officials setting up summer seminars at Moscow University for Americans interested in Russian studies. He had also worked on nearly a hundred other study programs in dozens of other foreign countries while at IIE.

Some students had indeed attended the Moscow seminar in 1933, and more in 1934. But the 1935 session, on which the Hearst story was based, had been canceled by the Russians without explanation. Murrow had never accompanied the earlier groups. He had never been in the Soviet Union. As for the Advisory Committee to the study program, Ed had found himself serving with Harry Woodburn Chase, chancellor of New York University; Frank P. Graham, president of the University of North Carolina; Robert Hutchins, president of the University of Chicago; and John Dewey, the foremost American educator of the age, heady company for a 27-year-old with a bachelor's degree.

Immediately after Wershba passed along *The Pittsburgh Sun Telegraph* photostat to him, Ed directed the *See It Now* staff to start collecting any existing footage on McCarthy and to start filming his public appearances.[7]

On March 2, 1954, on the theory that no one can indeed slay dragons every day, *See It Now* presented what the crew called a "let-up," a relief from controversy, a profile of the New York Philharmonic and its director, Dimitri Mitropoulos. In his closing commentary, Murrow described the program as a break with "the cold war, with current crises, or with the retreat into unreasoning fear that seems to be part of the climate in which we live." And then he added, "We shall try to deal with one aspect of that fear next week." Not a single columnist, critic, or even CBS executive caught the hint and called to ask what he was talking about.

A few day's later, Janet was due to fly to Jamaica to meet old friends from England, the Cazalet-Griers. Ed came home late, exhausted, but, she recalled, he was strangely afire. "We're going with it," he told her. "I didn't have to ask what he meant," Janet said. She told him she would cancel the trip. But Ed said that there was no reason to do so; he asked only that she have her parents come down from Connecticut to look after Casey while she was gone.[8]

A tentative date for the McCarthy broadcast was set, the following Tuesday, March 9. The film editors had already started work on the

McCarthy footage the morning after the broadcast on the Philharmonic. They worked around the clock in a loft on Fifth Avenue, taking turns to slip home for a few hours' sleep. Two days later, on Thursday, March 4, Friendly and Murrow gave perfunctory notice to Sig Mickelson that the subject of the next *See It Now* would likely be Senator Joseph R. McCarthy. They decided that Sunday night would mark their point of no return. If they felt then that their material was strong enough, they would go on Tuesday. Otherwise, they had two other completed *See It Now* broadcasts available.

Promoting the program was something of a tightrope act. Too much early drumbeating might alert McCarthy partisans to a point where they could cow the network into canceling the program. Yet Murrow did not want this broadcast to sink like a pebble into the ocean. Minimally, he and Friendly wanted an ad in *The New York Times* the day of the broadcast. Friendly went to Bill Golden, the network's advertising chief, an intelligent, thoughtful man, much in sympathy with their work. Golden agreed to buy the ad. But later, he came back and reported that "management" had said no.

Murrow and Friendly said that they would pay, but asked Golden at least to place the ad for them. Again, Golden returned with a negative response. The ad was not to be billed to the CBS account even temporarily. He needed cash up front. Furthermore, no mention of CBS was to be made in the ad, not even use of the network logo. There were to be no company fingerprints on this piece of work.[9]

Then occurred one of those coincidences that tend to muddy the waters of a limpid historical narrative. On Saturday, March 6, three days before the planned broadcast, Adlai Stevenson made a speech critical of the Republican party, particularly for harboring the likes of Joe McCarthy. CBS television carried the speech. Thereupon, McCarthy stormed ashore from a fishing trip and demanded equal time. CBS resisted. Stevenson, as the previous presidential candidate, had spoken as head of the Democratic party. Joe McCarthy was not the head of the Republican party, not yet. CBS agreed only to allow Richard Nixon, as Vice President, to reply to Stevenson. Nevertheless, with the Stevenson attack broadcast over the network on Saturday and with Murrow planning to deal with McCarthy on Tuesday, the appearance was inevitable that CBS was ganging up on McCarthy. There was only Murrow's cryptic announcement after the Philharmonic program to prove that the timing of the Stevenson broadcast and his Tuesday program on McCarthy were pure coincidence.

On Sunday, March 7, Ed came in from the country in a flannel shirt, suspenders, and baggy slacks and went into the cutting room with Friendly. Originally, they had begun with three hours of film for a thirty-minute program. Still, they were dissatisfied. They did not have McCarthy at his most flagrant, at Wheeling, waving the list of 205 alleged Communists in the State Department. No television cameras had been present. They did not have McCarthy bullying General Zwicker over "who promoted Peress?" That event occurred at a closed hearing. But they worked with what they had, winnowing, paring, cutting, until the three hours had been shrunk to thirty-seven minutes by late Sunday afternoon, still far too long. They argued hotly over what precious seconds of film were to be saved, what sacrificed. By late Sunday night, they had made the final, painful cuts, leaving enough time for Ed's tailpiece. They turned the surviving footage over to the film cutters and sent out for coffee. Ed slumped exhaustedly into a chair in the projection room.

Friendly could not relax. As he later described his anxiety. "I had sensed a certain uneasiness on the part of some members in the unit. I was not sure whether this was timidity over our confrontation with the senator or whether there was something in their background which might make us vulnerable." Fred made a suggestion and Ed agreed. Late as it was, they called the *See It Now* crew back to the projection room to ask about "anything in their own backgrounds that would give the senator a club to beat us with." The staff trooped in and sat down, forming a semi-circle around Murrow. He went around the room asking what they thought of the program so far and asking about their backgrounds. The latter was distasteful business, proof, if any were needed, of how deep the fear sickness had penetrated. No one admitted to harboring any skeletons. Palmer Williams said that his first wife had been a Communist, but they had been divorced for years.

There was more concern about the quality of the program. In a sense, the footage, McCarthy making speeches, McCarthy holding hearings, McCarthy questioning witnesses, by itself, might merely provide the man with more television exposure. The net effect of the program would be shaped by what Murrow said at the close.

After the critique and the confessionals, Murrow assumed his classic posture, elbows on his knees, head bent, eyes riveted to the rug, cigarette dangling from his mouth. "We, like everyone in this business," he said, "are going to be judged by what we put on the air; but we shall also be judged by what we don't broadcast. If we pull back on this, we'll have it with us always." He crushed out his cigarette, rose, and said, "Ladies and gentlemen, thank you. We go with this Tuesday."[10]

ALCOA's indulgence as a sponsor was being tested to the outermost. Ed did not want the dramatic tension of the half hour snapped by a mid-point commercial on the romance of making aluminum. But rather than ask the company for permission to omit the middle commercial, he and Friendly simply decided to drop it on their own. They could make it up to the company some other time. Indeed, ALCOA received only the most perfunctory warning that it was about to sponsor a program about the most controversial figure in America. "I may have called John Fleming [an ALCOA public relations man]," Friendly said, "the day before the broadcast. I don't remember."[11]

The tireless Friendly did make other calls. He called CBS correspondents to try to line up support for the broadcast. Howard K. Smith, in London, remembered Friendly phoning to tell him, "We're taking on McCarthy. For God's sake get some testimonials from Churchill and others that Ed's a patriotic American." Churchill's reaction, as Smith recalled, was "I don't know what Mr. Murrow is going to say. I can't do anything about this." McCarthy was strictly a home-grown hot potato.[12]

The Monday before the broadcast, Murrow spent writing his tailpiece. This time the customary deliberate, phrase-by-phrase, one-take dictation failed him.

Fred Friendly describes what happened the night of the broadcast: "It was almost nine o'clock before Murrow and I and all the film and tape were in the studio....I asked the security department of CBS to furnish uniformed guards at the Grand Central elevator and just outside the studio. By this time Murrow was getting crank telephone calls, and emotions on the senator ran so high that conceivably some fanatic would try to crash the studio while we were on the air. Fifteen minutes before broadcast time, we finished the final run-through. Don Hewitt, our control-room director, told us that it was thirty seconds long, and we decided to kill the closing credits if we needed the time. The test pattern easel was pulled away from camera #1 as Ed settled into his chair. At 10:28 the assistant director whispered that we had one minute. Hewitt picked up the private line to Master Control and asked them not to cut us off if we ran long; there might not be time for credits and we needed every second we could squeeze....One of the outside lines rang and Don smothered it. 'No, this is not the eleven o'clock news. Try Forty-four. Operator, I tell you every week to shut off these phones. Now, *please,* no calls until eleven o'clock.'"[13]

In the meantime, phone calls had been winging between the radio people at 485 Madison and the television staff at Grand Central: "Ed's pacing in the corridor." "Ed's smoking furiously." "Ed's in with Friendly now." "The make-up girl is swabbing Ed's face."[14]

He was seated before the microphone, Friendly out of camera range at his feet. They watched the monitor as the preceding program faded from the screen. They waited through a thirty-second eternity of commercials and station identification. Fred leaned to Murrow and whispered, "This is going to be a tough one." Murrow answered, "After this, they're all going to be tough." The red light came on.[15]

"Good Evening," Murrow began. "Tonight, *See It Now* devotes its entire half hour to a report on Senator Joseph R. McCarthy told mainly in his own words and pictures." Then, with jarring incongruity, he said, "But first, ALCOA would like you to meet a man who has been with them for fifty years."

After the commercial, he reappeared on the screen seated in the control room. To Murrow's left were turntables and stacks of newspapers. His script was plainly visible in his hand. He began, "If the senator believes we have done violence to his words or pictures and desires to speak— to answer himself—an opportunity will be afforded him on this program." He had met Paley's requirement for equal time. But he had not been able to resist a twist of the knife. McCarthy, if he rebutted, would be debating with himself.

The first film clip showed Dwight Eisenhower as a presidential candidate after a meeting with McCarthy. Ike was explaining how he would deal with subversives: "This is America's principle; trial by jury of the innocent, until proved guilty, and I expect to stand to do it." The benign Eisenhower face was replaced by McCarthy's broad, scowling countenance, which seemed to blot out the screen. He was making a speech in Milwaukee responding to Eisenhower: "I spent about a half hour with the general last night, while I can't [he giggles in a high-pitched voice] while I can't report that we agreed on everything [he giggles again], I can report that when I left that meeting with the general [he giggles a third time], I had the same feeling as when I went in, and that is that he is a great American and will make a great President." The nervous giggles, unrelated to anything he was saying, were chilling, emanating from this menacing, bullnecked figure.

Then Murrow was on camera again, live, describing McCarthy, "often operating as a one-man committee, he has traveled far, interviewed many, terrorized some, accused civilian and military leaders of the past administration of a great conspiracy to turn the country over to Communism, investigated and substantially demoralized the present State Department, made varying charges of espionage at Fort Monmouth. The Army says it has been unable to find anything relating to espionage there."

Murrow continued this litany of McCarthy's excesses, while the viewer saw close-ups of the senator conducting hearings, interrogating witnesses. His paunch loomed as he took his seat in the Senate Caucus Room. His collar was too large even for his thick neck. The camera played over the thin mouth, the heavy brow, the small chin.

McCarthy was seen delivering another speech, this time in Philadelphia shortly after he had questioned General Zwicker. The speech had proved a windfall for Murrow. There were no cameras present to record McCarthy at the actual hearing when he first browbeat the general. But so pleased was McCarthy with this performance that he took advantage of the later speech to quote himself from the transcript of the hearing. This time, *See It Now*'s cameras were there. "I said," McCarthy began, "'then, General, you should be removed from any command. Any man who has been given the honor of being promoted to general, and who says, "I will protect another general who protects Communists," is not fit to wear that uniform, General.'" McCarthy stopped, grinned, and asked his audience, "Are you enjoying this abuse of the general?" Again there was the high-pitched giggle, ridiculous yet frightening, even a little mad.

Later, the cameras fixed on the turntables in the control room, as

Murrow played a tape of McCarthy speaking out against those who criticized him: "...the American people and the President will realize that this unprecedented mud-slinging against the committee by the extreme left wing elements of press and radio...." The flat, nasal voice rising from the slow-turning metallic disk had an almost hypnotic power.

Murrow turned to the two stacks of newspapers. One pile was roughly three times higher than the other. "Senator McCarthy claims that only the left wing press criticized him on the Zwicker case," Murrow began, gesturing toward the taller pile of newspapers. "These are the 'left wing' papers that criticized." He pointed to the smaller pile. "These are the ones that supported him. Now let us look at some of these left-wing papers that criticized the senator." He proceeded to read from editorials opposing McCarthy in *The Chicago Tribune, The New York Times, The New York Herald Tribune, The Milwaukee Journal, The New York World Telegram & Sun,* and *The St. Louis Post-Dispatch.* The condemning words, from paper after paper, achieved a powerful cumulative effect.

McCarthy was next seen describing Adlai Stevenson as a tool of the Communist conspiracy. A film clip showed McCarthy standing alongside a photographic blow-up of a barn in Lee, Massachusetts. "The American people" he began, "are entitled to have this coldly documented history of this man who says he wants to be your President. But, strangely, Alger... I mean Adlai...." McCarthy went on to explain that this picture-postcard New England barn housed "all the missing documents from the Communist front IPR [Institute of Pacific Relations]" and that one such document reveals that Stevenson was the choice of Alger Hiss and other alleged Communists to attend a conference on Post-war American Policy in Asia."

Murrow reappeared on the screen. As for Stevenson's name appearing on that document, Murrow pointed out that McCarthy failed to mention that other persons also suggested to attend the conference were, like Stevenson at the time, on the staffs of Frank Knox and Henry Stimson, both distinguished Republican members of the Roosevelt wartime cabinet. Murrow went on to point out that past members of the Institute of Pacific Relations included Senator Homer Ferguson, Paul Hoffman, Henry Luce, and Eisenhower's own secretary of state, John Foster Dulles. McCarthy's little red barn began to collapse.

Next, McCarthy was seen interrogating Reed Harris, a *Voice of America* official. To McCarthy, Harris was part of the Communist apparatus because he had once canceled a Hebrew-language broadcast over the *Voice of America.* McCarthy drove home his argument by establishing that Reed, as a Columbia University student, had once been suspended and that the American Civil Liberties Union had thereafter defended him. McCarthy described the ACLU as "a front for doing the work of the Communist Party."

Murrow came back on camera and said: "Twice, McCarthy said the American Civil Liberties Union was listed as a subversive front. The Attorney General's list does not and has never listed the ACLU as subversive nor does the FBI or any other government agency. And the American Civil Liberties Union holds in its files letters of commendation from President Eisenhower, President Truman and General MacArthur." No matter, Murrow pointed out, a month after this McCarthy charade, Reed Harris had been forced to resign from the State Department.

As the program closed, Murrow concluded, "No one familiar with the history of this country can deny that Congressional committees are useful....but the line between investigation and persecuting is a very fine one and the junior senator from Wisconsin has stepped over it repeatedly. His primary achievement has been in confusing the public mind as between the internal and the external threat of Communism. We must not confuse dissent with disloyalty. We must remember always that accusation is not proof and that conviction depends upon evidence and due process of law....We will not walk in fear, one of another. We will not be driven by fear into an age of unreason if we dig deep in our history and our doctrine, and remember that we are not descended from fearful men, not from men who feared to write, to speak, to associate and to defend causes which were for the moment unpopular.... we cannot defend freedom abroad by deserting it at home. The actions of the junior senator from Wisconsin have caused alarm and dismay amongst our allies abroad and given considerable comfort to our enemies, and whose fault is that? Not really his, he didn't create this situation of fear, he merely exploited it and rather successfully. Cassius was right, 'The fault, dear Brutus, is not in our stars, but in ourselves.'... Good night, and good luck."[16]

Friendly described the control room during those thirty minutes as "like a submarine during an emergency dive...." When the submarine surfaced, it was to an eerie silence. Banks of extra telephone operators had been set up to take the expected flood of calls. There were none. Murrow slumped back in his chair looking as though not another syllable could be wrung from him. He watched the local eleven o'clock news come up on the monitor. The announcer, Don Hollenbeck, was saying, "I don't know whether all of you have seen what I just saw. But I want to associate myself and this program with what Ed Murrow has just said, and say I have never been prouder of CBS."

Still, the phones were silent. A messenger poked his head into Studio 41 and asked if Mr. Hewitt still wanted the calls held back. The switchboard was flooded, he said. The staff broke out in relieved laughter.[17]

Ed later took the crew to the Pentagon Bar as the calls continued pouring in, calls of praise, calls of criticism, obscene calls. But they were running ten to one in favor of the broadcast. By noon of the following day, CBS and its affiliates had received over 10,000 phone calls and telegrams. Within days, hallways were piled high with boxes of letters. The letters, telegrams, and calls eventually totaled over 75,000, the greatest reaction to any single program in the network's history. The count continued ten to one in favor of Murrow.[18]

The day following the broadcast, Ed had a lunch date with Norman Corwin. As they walked out of the CBS building looking for a cab, Corwin recalled, "People reached out to touch him, they seized his hand. We got in a cab and the driver said, 'I saw your program last night and, let me tell you, I feel a lot easier today.'"

At the Century Club, the members thronged around Ed, slapping him on the back, shaking his hand, chorusing his praises. It seemed to Corwin that a dam of fear had broken and that resentment of Mc-Carthyism, so long repressed, was pouring out.

Over lunch Corwin asked Ed who had called. The sponsors had called, Ed reported, and said "they felt good about the program." What about the twentieth floor, Corwin asked? "They haven't said anything," Murrow answered. That same afternoon, Friendly rode the elevator with Jack Van Volkenburg, the CBS Television Network president. They exchanged pleasantries, a few words about Friendly moving to a new home, and parted with "So long, Fred," "So long, Jack." The McCarthy program went unmentioned. Nor had any word been heard from Bill Paley. Indeed, Paley had not seen the broadcast.[19]

The rest of the world continued more responsive. Murrow was bathed in an adulation that, to Sevareid, suggested "Lindbergh in 1927." He and Murrow were driving together through the Lincoln Tunnel and Sevareid remembered the police shouting, "Attaboy, Ed." If Murrow had the cops with him, Sevareid thought, he was all right. Messages piled up on Murrow's desk from CBS newswriters, researchers, and secretaries, the typical note reading, "You have made me proud and happy to work for CBS."

About a week after the broadcast, John Foster Dulles was sitting on the dais in the grand ballroom of the Waldorf-Astoria about to deliver a speech to the Overseas Press Club. An overflow audience of over 1,500 people started to stand and applaud. A smile came to the secretary of state's face until he realized that heads were turned in another direction. Ed Murrow was striding across the dais.

Ed and Janet went to serve as·godparents at the christening of Samuel Goldwyn Jr.'s son. Goldwyn was exclaiming over Murrow's courage in standing up to McCarthy. "Let's face it," Ed said. "McCarthy can't hurt me except economically. I was born with an outside toilet, and I can go out the same way."[20]

ALCOA received a telegram from McCarthy threatening the company with an investigation for subsidizing a subversive broadcast. ALCOA held fast, likely because the more than 4,000 letters and postcards that poured into the Pittsburgh headquarters favored Murrow by three to one. Still, ALCOA was a business, not a pulpit. As a company spokesman put it, "We originally bought the show for an institutional showcase, basically a prestige thing. If the day ever came when we go to sell products, we'd take another kind of show. If the day ever comes to quit, we'll quit."[21]

Radulovich had been the dress rehearsal. With the McCarthy broadcast, Murrow had synergized the words of journalism, the sounds of radio, and the images of television into the single most powerful political statement in television's brief life. His instincts about McCarthy had proved right when he had told Collingwood months before, "The thing to do is let him damn himself out of his own mouth." He had held up the face of a demagogue in front of a television screen for a half hour. When it was over, the country knew what Joe McCarthy was.

A few days later, Ben Shahn presented Murrow with a sketch. In it, a David-like Murrow is seen standing on a Goliath-like McCarthy. He has taken the giant's own sword and is holding it against the giant's throat. At the bottom, Shahn had penned a caption from the Bible, "And David ran and stood over the Philistine and took his sword and drew it out of the sheath thereof and slew him...." The metaphor was perfect, except that this Philistine was still very much alive, wounded and therefore all the more dangerous.[22]

McCarthy still had the standing offer of equal time from CBS. Thus far, he had not responded. Indeed, his staff put out the word that the senator had gone to bed early that Tuesday night and had not bothered to watch Murrow's broadcast.

The anger from the right was predictable. But there were also a few qualms among civil libertarians. Gilbert Seldes, who hated *Person to Person* and loved *See It Now*, did not quite see Shahn's David against Goliath. "I got the impression," Seldes wrote, that the giant Murrow had been fighting a pygmy. Intellectually this may be right; politically, I remain as frightened as if I had seen a ghost—the ghost of Hitler to be specific." *Newsweek* magazine, in a cover story on Murrow appearing shortly after the McCarthy program, asked, "Is it right in principle for television to take a clear stand on one side of a great issue?...how often would an individual or group that believed itself injured by editorialized television be able to come back with an equally effective dramatic presentation of its case?" Murrow responded, none too convincingly, "The last thing I want to do is to take the privileged opportunity I have five nights a week on radio and two on television to attack this man." He acknowledged that "...clever film cutters and trick shots can be distorted. It frightened me at first [but] we take extreme care in the editing of our film. I did him [McCarthy] no violence."[23]

CBS management felt it had to reconcile its vaunted policy of objectivity with Murrow's partisan assault. Frank Stanton and Richard Salant, a CBS attorney and vice president, wrestled with the contradiction and released a public statement: "In the production of such programs by CBS, it can and does at times delegate responsibility for the program content and for the expression of opinion, if any, to one of its staff members. It is careful, of course, not to delegate such responsibility except to one in whose integrity and devotion to demonstrated principles CBS reposes complete confidence." In other words, Murrow was an exception to the objectivity rule.[24]

The McCarthy broadcast was not objective reporting. It was subjective polemicizing. To those who would insist on purist rules governing even a fight with a barroom brawler, Murrow was wrong. But to millions, it had been satisfying to see the bully thrashed at last.

Joe McCarthy, the usually swift counterpuncher, had still not been heard from. To put the matter in the idiom the senator favored, "When you see someone coming at you, always kick the other guy first—in the balls." He had not yet kicked. Thus, the elation in the Murrow camp was tinged with anxiety.

Janet came back from Jamaica shortly after the broadcast, and Ed went out to the airport to meet her. The first thing he said was, "You've got to promise me you'll never let Casey out of your sight." Ed had received threatening phone calls. For the following year, a chagrined Casey was picked up and left off at the Buckley School by his mother or the maid.

West Point officials checked with the FBI before following through on an already-issued invitation to Murrow to address the cadets on national security. The Bureau sent the Army a long report of "background as well as derogatory data." To the Army's credit, the invitation stood, perhaps because the military also recently had its own taste of McCarthyism.[25]

Two days after the broadcast, McCarthy surfaced at another investigation by his subcommittee in the Senate Caucus Room. This time, his staff promised, he would deliver a Communist spy who had worked in the Pentagon code room. Murrow's favorite among the cameramen, Charley Mack, and reporter Joe Wershba were dispatched to cover the hearing.

The spy turned out to be a middle-aged black woman named Annie Lee Moss who indeed worked in the Pentagon with coded messages. Mrs. Moss, obviously frightened to death, faced the panel of senators in a frayed black coat, a tiny hat perched on her head.

McCarthy began, "Mrs. Moss, let me say for the record that you are not here because you are considered important in the Communist apparatus. We have the testimony that you are or have been a Communist. We are rather curious, however, to know how you suddenly were shifted from a worker in a cafeteria to the code room...."

Annie Lee Moss was asked to read the notice suspending her from her job and gave up after the word "adjudication" defeated her. Questioned if she had ever heard of Karl Marx, she answered, "Who's that?" Asked about espionage, her lawyer had to explain to her that the word meant spying. It further turned out that she did not work in the code room, and did not deal with encoding or decoding messages. She merely fed already coded tapes into a transmitting machine. A tier of U.S. senators arrayed against this pathetic-looking woman began to strike even

McCarthy as embarrassing. "I am afraid, I am going to have to excuse myself," he said. "I've got rather an important appointment tonight which I have got to work on right away...." Charley Mack continued to film, playing his camera from time to time over McCarthy's conspicuously empty chair.[26]

That evening, forty-eight hours after Murrow's broadcast, Joe McCarthy acknowledged the attack on him. He had been invited to appear with Fulton Lewis, Jr., over the Mutual Broadcasting System. McCarthy began lashing out at his critics, and when he reached Murrow's name, he pulled out the photostats of *The Pittsburgh Sun Telegraph* story. The article proved, he said, that Murrow was one of "the American advisors to a Communist propaganda school. This may explain why Edward Murrow, week after week, feels he must smear Senator McCarthy. Maybe he is worried about the exposure of some of his friends. I don't know."

Lewis asked him if he had seen the Murrow broadcast. "I may say, Fulton," McCarthy answered, "that I have a little difficulty answering the specific attack he made, because I never listen to the extreme left-wing, bleeding heart element of radio and television."

Murrow's nightly news followed on the heels of Lewis's program. But Ed had been caught off guard. He said only, "My personal reaction will have to wait for another time."

It was not long in coming. The following night, Murrow discussed the Moscow University seminar of 1935. He mentioned a few of the distinguished fellow members of the National Advisory Committee: John Dewey, Robert Hutchins, Frank Graham. "Some of the persons on that list are now dead," he added, "but presumably not yet immune from the senator's attentions. It was and is a rather distinguished list, and I plead neither ignorance nor youth as the reason for my name being on it." As for the seminar itself, he said, "The Russian authorities abruptly and without satisfactory explanation cancelled the proposed summer school before it began...." Since McCarthy had said nothing about the previous two sessions, which were held, neither did Murrow.[27]

Six days after the initial broadcast, McCarthy accepted CBS's offer of a full broadcast of *See It Now* to respond. However, he was too busy to make the broadcast himself he said. Instead, he was inviting an articulate young conservative author of a book, *McCarthy and His Enemies,* to speak for him. The young man, William F. Buckley, Jr., had agreed. Murrow's reply was immediate: "No stand-ins. The invitation is non-transferable." Thereupon, McCarthy sent Murrow a telegram reading, "...If I am correct in my position that you have consciously served the Communist cause, then it is very important for your listeners to have the clear-cut documented facts...." McCarthy would deliver his rebuttal personally on April 6.[28]

On March 16, *See It Now* devoted its full half hour to the Annie Lee Moss investigation. Murrow did not defend the woman. In his closing commentary, he said only, "You will notice that neither Senator McClellan, nor Senator Symington, nor this reporter know or claim that Mrs. Moss was or is not a Communist. Their claim was simply that she had the right to meet her accusers face to face." (Annie Lee Moss was reinstated in her job but again suspended some five months later on new information. In January of 1955, she was again reinstated, this time in a "nonsensitive" position. Three years later, the Subversive Activities Control Board issued a report stating that, in the 1940s, Annie Lee Moss had been a member of the Communist party.)

In the weeks before McCarthy was to deliver his reply, CBS researchers combed through every word that Ed Murrow had ever uttered over the air seeking out cracks in his armor. Ed hired his old NSFA roommate, Chet Williams, now running a research firm in Manhattan, to locate the records of that now defunct organization to determine if there was in them anything incriminating. The membership lists of a 1930s student organization would inevitably have contained the names of some Communists or sympathizers. Williams tracked the records to a demolished building in Seattle. He was able to report to a doubtless relieved Murrow that the records had been destroyed along with the building.

CBS hired a distinguished lawyer, Judge Bruce Bromley, of Cravath, Swaine, and Moore, to probe Murrow's past and that of his staff for grist for McCarthy's mill of character assassination. Rumors began to sweep through the network that there was indeed a Communist on the news staff. Don Hollenbeck and a few other names were bruited about. Actually, it was the former Communist, Winston Burdett, who had by then privately divulged his past to a congressional committee and the FBI.[29]

Even before the Bromley investigations, Howard K. Smith had written Murrow from London, "There's something of a grave nature that has happened to me." He did not want to discuss it in writing, Smith told Murrow, and asked if Ed might be coming to London soon. "I could be a weak point," Smith told Murrow. "I was very pro-Communist as an Oxford student. Then, I had joined the Labour Party and had been elected head of the Labour Party [at Oxford] by working with Communists." But Smith, in London, was never questioned in the Bromley sweep. Palmer Williams, in an unexpected turn of events, was.[30]

Williams was *See It Now*'s production chief, fiercely loyal to Murrow and determined not to be the cause of harm to him. He had mentioned during the *See It Now* confessional that his ex-wife had been a Communist. He now voluntarily went to one of Judge Bromley's lawyers and explained the matter. That was an end to it, Williams assumed. But later in the same day, he received a call to report to Daniel O'Shea, the network's chief of security and enforcer of the CBS blacklist. Judge Bromley's man was there too, and he and O'Shea had Williams repeat his story. O'Shea and the lawyer then disappeared for a private tête-à-tête. When they came back, they told Williams that he would have to sign a statement of the facts that they would prepare and then resign from CBS. "I was in a fog," Williams later recalled. "I wondered what was the difference between me and Milo Radulovich?" Still, Williams was ready to comply he said, "for the good of the service. But first I told them, I wanted to call Fred."

Friendly's response was immediate. He told Williams, "Don't sign anything. Don't do anything." Friendly called Murrow, who went directly to O'Shea's office and announced, "He's not signing anything and we're not accepting his resignation. Just forget about it." O'Shea backed off, and Palmer Williams's career was saved.[31]

Joe McCarthy informed ALCOA that since the company had paid for Murrow's attack on him, it should pay the production costs of his rebuttal. The company refused. ALCOA would pay only for the air time. McCarthy then went to CBS for the money. Murrow was angry. He had opposed giving McCarthy equal time in the first place. Now his own network was being asked to subsidize what could be his own destruction. He went to see Paley and urged him not to yield. Paley was adamant. "We will give him the money. I want him to have no excuses." In the end, CBS paid McCarthy $6,336.99 for production costs.

CBS was a news organization with long tentacles. Before long, word came filtering back of what McCarthy was supposedly up to—hard fact, surmise, rumor. George Sokolsky, the conservative syndicated columnist, was reportedly helping McCarthy to write the rebuttal. Louis B. Mayer was involved too, as was Carl Byoir, the public relations entrepreneur. (Byoir was later to say that his only connection with the program was to provide information on the Russian Revolution at Senator McCarthy's request.) Morris Ernst reported to Murrow that McCarthy planned to attack Paley along with him, a source of anxiety to Ed.

CBS managed to obtain a copy of a McCarthy memo which said that Murrow had been heavily influenced as a college student by Ida Lou Anderson, "a hump-backed lady" of leftist convictions. Jesse Zousmer learned that McCarthy's man, Don Surine, had contacted Wesley Price, author of *The Saturday Evening Post* article in which Murrow had erroneously been called a Wobbly. Surine wanted to know what else Price might have that proved Murrow's disloyalty. Price answered jokingly that he would probably break a leg wandering in the dark of his attic looking for his notes. Surine answered straight-faced, "We'll take care of any emergencies, all expenses."

What Murrow could not know for certain, but assumed, was that McCarthy had sources deep within the government security apparatus. Scott McLeod, McCarthy's hand-picked man running security for the State Department, did in fact order Mildred Smith, in State's Passport Office, to turn over her files on Murrow to Surine. The file was sown with raw, unverified derogatory material provided by the FBI. Mrs. Smith admirably fought off the order as improper.[32]

As the time for McCarthy's response drew near, Murrow became morose and withdrawn. Dewayne Kreager, a fellow alumnus of Washington State and former Truman administration official, had known Ed slightly at college, but became a closer friend of Ed's brother, Lacey. Shortly before McCarthy was to make his rebuttal, Lacey called Kreager and said, "Ed's got to get away and search his soul." Ed wanted Lacey to fly him down to a fishing camp that Lacey had on the St. Johns River in Florida. Lacey asked Kreager, whom Ed liked and admired, to come along.

The three men met in Washington, D.C., and flew in Lacey's plane to Florida. There, they stayed in a little fishing shack. As Kreager recalled the next two days, "All we did was drink and smoke. We barely ate, except that we whipped up a batch of eggs the first day and I went out for hamburgers the next day. Ed was in a foul mood. He seemed spiritually and mentally sick. At the same time, he was proud of what he had done to McCarthy. Ed brooded about what had happened to Larry Duggan. He worried about losing his sponsor. But mostly he talked about the system, what people like McCarthy had done to the country, what was wrong with television. He seemed more worried about the state of society than about himself. Lacey seemed to enjoy his role. He was patient and steady and understanding. For once he had the chance to play a proper big brother."

As Kreager summed up the episode, "We literally laid Ed out on the table, took his heart and soul out of his body, examined them, put them back and did it all over again and again. When we left, he seemed in somewhat better shape."[33]

Monday, the day before the McCarthy reply, tension in the Murrow camp was electric. As for the one certain charge, the Moscow seminar, Murrow took the position that he had served in an advisory capacity with an honorable body of men for a legitimate educational purpose. Furthermore, the 1935 seminar in question had never been held. But by now he knew that McCarthy knew that he had also served on the advisory committee in 1933 and 1934, when seminars had been held in Moscow. Additionally, there were the unknown reasons behind his occasional passport problems, the speculation about Communists in CBS news, and whatever other insinuations, innuendo, and half- and quarter-truths that could prove so damaging in McCarthy's hands. The strain lay in not knowing exactly what McCarthy had on him.

And then came a break. Late that Monday afternoon, Palmer Williams received a call from an employee of Hearst-Movietone Newsreels, the organization that provided Charlie Mack, Leo Rossi, and other film crews to *See It Now* under contract. The caller informed Williams that at that very moment, in the floor below the Hearst newsreel offices, in the De-Luxe film laboratories, the sound portion of the McCarthy broadcast was going through the lab bath. The caller offered to sell Williams a duplicate. How much would it cost, Williams wanted to know. One hundred dollars, he was told.

Williams immediately reported the conversation to Friendly. Friendly told Williams to draw $100 from the business office, but to give no reason. Within an hour, Williams was back with two cans of soundtrack. The film was threaded onto a moviola, and a stenotypist began transcribing it. By that evening, a complete transcript of McCarthy's rebuttal was in Murrow's hands. He worked throughout the night, with the network's lawyers, preparing his answer to McCarthy's charges.[34]

Since the McCarthy broadcast, over three weeks before, Murrow had still had no reaction from Bill Paley. He grumbled to friends that Paley was evidently unhappy with the program. He sent copies of complimentary letters on the broadcast from major figures, such as Chief Justice Earl Warren, up to Paley. The emotional hold was still strong. He needed Paley's approbation. He was uncomfortable when he sensed a distance between them. Though he had heard nothing from Paley about the broadcast, he went to him for advice on how he should respond to McCarthy.

Paley, in his autobiography, has described the encounter: "I suggested at some point that he say something to the effect that history would one day decide whether he or McCarthy had served the country better." Ed was delighted. "You gave me" he said, "the only answer I could properly make."[35]

On Tuesday, just hours before the program was to go on the air, McCarthy's lieutenants arrived at CBS with the filmed rebuttal. They had delivered it at the last possible minute so that CBS could not tamper with the film. Fred Friendly informed them that he wanted to run the film before it went on the air, but only to check its broadcast quality and to time it. He also informed McCarthy's people that Murrow would not be seeing the film before he announced it over the air. To the McCarthy people, such calm in the enemy camp on the eve of the counterattack was unsettling.

On screening the film, Friendly was shocked, not by the content, which he already knew, but by the quality. McCarthy was, Friendly said, "Caked in make-up that attempted to compensate for his deteriorating physical condition. The senator gave the appearance of a mask drawn by Herblock. His receding hairline was disguised by a botched mixture of false hair and eye brow pencil. At the beginning his voice was muted and flat, but eventually this gave way to the fanatical trumpeting that was his basic style."[36]

A huge audience was anticipated, since the program had the drawing power of a heavyweight rematch. Outside of Studio 41, reporters and cameramen thronged the hallway. They were assigned a rehearsal studio where they could watch the broadcast on a monitor.

Murrow arrived in time to go on camera live with a brief introduction. He made clear that no restrictions had been placed on McCarthy and that he, Murrow, would take up no further time. This half hour of *See It Now* belonged to Joe McCarthy.

McCarthy appeared on the screen seated at a desk looking somehow menacing yet ill at ease at the same time. He opened his mouth and a misstatement came out: "Mr. Edward R. Murrow, educational director of the Columbia Broadcasting System, devoted his program to an attack on the work of the United States Senate Investigation Committee and on me personally as its chairman...." Murrow had not held the educational post since 1936.

As television, the performance was plodding and unimaginative. With McCarthy using a pointer, maps, and pictures, the film had the quality of something produced by a college audiovisual arts department. But McCarthy had not achieved his successes by subtlety. He warmed to his theme: "Now, ordinarily, I would not take time out from the important work at hand to answer Murrow. However, in this case, I feel justified in doing so because Murrow is a symbol, the leader and the cleverest of the jackal pack which is always found at the throat of anyone who dares to expose individual Communists and traitors. I am compelled by the facts to say to you that Mr. Edward R. Murrow, as far back as twenty years ago, was engaged in propaganda for Communist causes. For example, the Institute of International Education, of which he was the acting director, was chosen to act as a representative by a Soviet agency to do a job which would normally be done by the Russian secret police. Mr. Murrow sponsored a Communist school in Moscow. In the selection of American students and teachers who were to attend, Mr. Murrow's organization acted for the Russian espionage and propaganda organization known as VOKS—V. O. K. S."

McCarthy then charged that "Mr. Murrow, by his own admission, was a member of the IWW—that's the Industrial Workers of the World—a terrorist organization cited as subversive by an attorney general of the United States."

McCarthy then traced a history of the Russian Revolution. He pointed to a map of the world. In 1917, he said, "There was not a single foot of ground under Communist control." He turned next to a contemporary map, noting that thirty-six years later, "Over one-third of the Earth's area" and some 800 million people were under Communist domination. They were delivered "by the jackal pack of Communist line propagandists, including the friends of Edward R. Murrow."

"If there were no Communists in government," McCarthy went on, "why did we delay for eighteen months, delay our research on the hydrogen bomb, even though our intelligence agencies were reporting day after day that the Russians were feverishly pushing their development of the H Bomb?...Was it loyal Americans or was it traitors in our government?" The unidentified traitor behind this fresh McCarthy charge would later be identified as J. Robert Oppenheimer.

McCarthy returned his attention to Murrow. He quoted from the March 9 issue of *The Daily Worker,* listing "Mr. Murrow's program as—

listen to this—'one of tonight's best bets on TV.'" He cited Murrow's defense of Owen Lattimore, "a conscious, articulate instrument of the Communist conspiracy." And to whom did "that greatest Communist propagandist of our time," Harold Laski, dedicate a book? To "My friends, E.R. Murrow and Lanham Tichener, with affection."

McCarthy looked as bad as Friendly had feared, made up like a corpse at a budget funeral home. His voice wavered between an insistent, nasal whine and peevish little shrieks. If one hated Joe McCarthy, he had given reason to hate him all the more. But for the true believers, he had told them what they needed to hear about Edward R. Murrow. The program also posed a danger to Murrow in that anyone who had missed his initial broadcast was now hearing only McCarthy's side.[37]

When it was over, a calm Murrow led the reporters to the ballroom of the adjacent Hotel Commodore for a press conference. They were handed a mimeographed, seven-page, point-by-point rebuttal of McCarthy's charges. A reporter from *The Daily Mirror* called out, "Ed, you said you never saw this film before tonight. So how come this hand-out?" Murrow fixed the man with a self-parody of the Murrow glower and deep voice and said, "Does Macy's tell Gimbels?"

He then read the statement. He denied that he had ever belonged to the IWW; he admitted only that he had known Wobblies in the lumber camps. In his original text he had written, "I was also sympathetic with their efforts to increase wages and improve working conditions, there's and mine." But he had crossed out this sentence. McCarthy, he apparently feared, was too crafty to be handed anything remotely exploitable.

As for the Institute of International Education being made out to be a tool of Soviet propaganda, Murrow pointed out that the Soviets called the organization "the center for international propaganda for American reaction." President Eisenhower, he said, had endorsed the organization's work. As for Harold Laski dedicating a book to him, Murrow said simply, "Laski was a friend of mine....He is a Socialist. I am not."

As for *The Daily Worker* approving his March 9 broadcast, Murrow's reply revealed his own instinct for the jugular: "I can say that I had no knowledge that I was to be the subject of notice by *The Daily Worker* or any other Communist publication. This is more than Senator McCarthy can say about the Communist support he accepted in aid of his 1946 campaign for the United States Senate...."

"When the record is finally written," he concluded, "as it will be one day, it will answer the question, who has helped the Communist cause and who has served his country better, Senator McCarthy or I? I would like to be remembered by the answer to that question." *Gratis*, Bill Paley. When it was all over, Ed called Paley and offered the warmest down-home tribute that he could summon. Bill Paley was the kind of man, as they said around Polecat Creek, "I'd go hunting with."

Two days later, *The New York Times* reported a tally of phone calls and telegrams to CBS and its affiliates on McCarthy's broadcast. The count showed 6,548 favoring Murrow and 3,654 favoring Joe McCarthy.[38]

Dwight Eisenhower had been President for nearly fourteen months at the time Murrow took on Joe McCarthy. During that period, Eisenhower had behaved toward McCarthy like a landlord with a crazy tenant who was afraid to throw him out for fear of what worse mayhem the man might commit. The way Eisenhower put it, he was not going to "get down in the gutter with that guy." Eisenhower held a press conference the day after McCarthy delivered his rebuttal, and Joe Harsch asked the President what he thought of Ed Murrow as a "loyal and patriotic American." Ike answered, "...First of all, I don't comment about people. I don't comment about things of which I know nothing. I will say this. I have known this man for many years. He has been one of the men I consider my friend among your profession...so far as indulging in philosophical discussion, I can't remember any instance...."

It was the patented Eisenhower smoke screen. But a story circulated that Ike had shared a dais with Murrow at a Washington banquet after the McCarthy rebuttal. At this event, a grinning Ike reportedly went up to Murrow, ran his hand over his back, and said with a grin, "Let me see if there are any marks where the knife went in." Murrow's equally smiling retort is supposed to have been, "Now, over to you, Mr. President."

More credible was what Fred Friendly reported several years later. Friendly had just published his broadcast memoir, *Due to Circumstances beyond Our Control,* and had sent Eisenhower a copy. He received a thank you from the former President. "He said he was glad to read about the McCarthy broadcasts that Murrow and I did," Friendly recalled of Ike's reply, "and that he never knew about it at the time, and he never knew he had such allies as Murrow and Friendly when he was fighting Joe McCarthy."[39]

Bill Shirer published his roman à clef, *Stranger Come Home,* at about the time of the Murrow-McCarthy affair. Shirer's cast included characters patterned after Murrow, Paley, McCarthy, and a composite of Shirer himself and John Carter Vincent, another McCarthy victim. In the book, Robert Fletcher, the Murrow character, rises to the top of the Federal Broadcasting Company. In a key scene, Fletcher/Murrow is called before the committee of Senator O'Brien/McCarthy to tell why he fired Raymond Whitehead from FBS. "Mr. Fletcher, the charges here are that Mr. Whitehead was a Communist and a Soviet agent. Having known him over many years, and having worked with him closely, would you say that either accusation—or both of them—was true?" Fletcher/Murrow answers, "Senator, I am not here to pass judgement. That sir, if I may so so, is your task."

The author's ear for Murrow's speech was dead right. But the characterization dead wrong, and the timing of the book unfortunate for Shirer. By the time *Stranger Come Home* came out, Murrow had not risen to the top of the network; he had cast that opportunity aside to become a broadcaster again. Murrow had not abandoned his friends to blacklisters and anti-Communist zealots; he had fought to save their careers. And, far from folding before McCarthy's intimidation, Murrow had taken the man head on. But the years since leaving CBS had not been kind to Bill Shirer; and he had not forgiven Ed Murrow.

The first reaction, after Murrow's March 9 broadcast on McCarthy, came from Don Hollenbeck on his 11 p.m. newscast. Hollenbeck was a bone in the throat of the Hearst chain. When he had done *CBS Reviews the Press* for Murrow, Hearst sensationalism was a favorite Hollenbeck target. William Randolph Hearst, Jr., had gone personally to Frank Stanton to try to have Hollenbeck fired.

After Hollenbeck's glowing remarks about the McCarthy program, Jack O'Brian, Hearst's television columnist, began a drumbeat of criticism. Hollenbeck was variously "a graduate of the demised pinko publication, *P.M.*" and, with Murrow, "the leading CBS leaners to the left" with "a peculiarly selective slant in their news work." O'Brian ran letters criticizing Hollenbeck in his column with the comment, "We'll print as many as we can."

Don Hollenbeck was a wreck of a man, emaciated, high strung, a heavy drinker, suffering from ulcers and obsessed by a failed marriage. He went to see Ed and told him that he could not take O'Brian's constant pounding. He was emotionally and physically sick and frightened of losing his job. Murrow was sympathetic, but he told Hollenbeck that the network could not be drawn into a shouting match with a Hearst columnist. Hollenbeck, he said, would simply have to ride out the storm. To his friends, Hollenbeck confessed, "O'Brian is driving me crazy."

On June 22, shortly after another O'Brian attack, Murrow and Friendly were in the cutting room editing that night's broadcast of *See It Now* when Jap Gude called. It was a point at which they were never to be interrupted. But Gude was insistent.

Murrow took the call. Friendly watched Ed sigh heavily and sink back in his chair. "Don Hollenbeck has just killed himself," he told Friendly after hanging up. The police had found Hollenbeck in his rooms at the Middletowne Hotel, dead of gas asphyxiation. "All that vilification, Jack O'Brian, it got to him," Ed said. That night on *See It Now* Murrow paid a tribute to "an honest reporter." A few days later, he was a pallbearer at Hollenbeck's funeral.

He was not done yet with Hollenbeck's tormenters. He did not see how he could continue doing business with a Hearst subsidiary. Yet, the fine camera crews used on *See It Now*, Charley Mack, Leo Rossi, and others, were contracted from Hearst-Movietone Newsreels. He and Friendly went to see Paley. They outlined a plan for buying their own equipment and hiring their own full-time camera crews. It would be expensive, they said. Paley heard them out without a word. When they finished, he said only, "How soon can you do it?" The Hearst employees who worked on

See It Now were given the choice of remaining where they were or coming over to CBS and chose CBS to a man.[40]

On December 2, 1954, nine months after the Murrow broadcast, the Senate of the United States declared that Joseph R. McCarthy "...tended to bring the Senate into dishonor and disrepute, to obstruct the constitutional processes of the Senate and to impair its dignity, and such conduct is hereby condemned." He was censured by a vote of 67 to 22.

His life, thereafter, became a steady slide into oblivion. At one point, he could not get his candidate for postmaster of his hometown approved. Reporters who had once scurried at his heels now took their coffee breaks on the rare occasions when he rose to speak in the Senate chamber. His political legacy was to make of his name an *ism* and a dirty word in the English language.[41]

To credit Edward R. Murrow with the fall of Joe McCarthy would be an exaggeration. The very day that Murrow had made his broadcast, courageous old Ralph Flanders of Vermont had risen on the Senate floor and heaped ridicule on McCarthy that approached poetry: "He dons war paint; he goes into his war dance; he emits his war whoops; he goes forth to battle and proudly returns with the scalp of a pink Army dentist."

The Army that McCarthy attacked had later counterattacked, charging that McCarthy and Roy Cohn had used improper influence to try to gain preferential treatment for the McCarthy aide, G. David Schine, whom the Army had dared induct as a lowly private. Thus, just weeks after Murrow's broadcast, the Senate conducted on television what history came to call the Army-McCarthy hearings. The public now saw Joe McCarthy unexpurgated, not for a half hour, but over thirty-six days. It was not a pretty sight. His Senate colleagues repudiated him and broke a slender reed of pride in this seemingly shameless man.

Murrow's contribution to the defeat of the demagogue was that he had had the courage to use television against McCarthy. He had taken a young medium, skittish over controversy, and plunged it into the hottest controversy of that era. His act demonstrated, for the first time on a grand scale, the awesome power of the medium for good or evil. Television's smaller-than-life images demonstrated a larger-than-life impact on the senses and a hypnotic hold over the viewer. Brave voices raised against McCarthy in the past in newspapers and over radio had faded for lack of amplification. But Murrow's presence, the voice, the demeanor, the authority, harnessed to this new phenomenon, achieved extraordinary magnification and penetration. March 9, 1954, did not mark the end of Joe McCarthy, but it can be counted the beginning of the end.

Murrow was sparing in his own praise. Years later he was to say: "The timing was right and the instrument powerful. We did it fairly well, with a degree of restraint and credibility. There was a great conspiracy of silence at the time. When there is such a conspiracy and somebody makes a loud noise, it attracts all the attention."[42]

That June, he received the Freedom House Award. The citation read:

"Free men were heartened by his courage in exposing those who would divide us by exploiting our fears." Sitting with Ed on the dais that night, beaming and looking like the proudest man in the room, was Bill Paley. Paley's place in the McCarthy affair is ambiguous. Those who like their moral melodramas in black and white can blacken him for a Pilate-like washing of his hands over the program, for presumably supporting the decision not to promote it, and in the end, for not seeing it. When Fred Friendly was asked if Paley had ever complimented Murrow for doing the broadcast, Friendly responded, "Not to my knowledge." But it was Paley's network. He knew that the program was going to be done. And, clearly, he could have stopped it at any time. He did not. His smile at the Freedom House ceremony was perhaps too broad, but not entirely unearned.[43]

As for Murrow, he had not known on the evening of the broadcast if he was moving toward a new height or risking a fall. In truth, he had reached the summit, which is simultaneously the high point and the beginning of the decline.

CHAPTER 26

Family Connections

The 1953–1954 season of *See It Now* had been successful but punishing. In early August, Ed escaped with the family to Heron Bay in Barbados where Ronnie and Marietta Tree had invited them to their tropical retreat.

The beaches were lovely and the surf inviting, but Marietta noticed that Ed shunned the water. At most he would put on his trunks and toss a beach ball back and forth with Casey in ankle-deep surf. Not knowing how to swim was another lost chapter of his youth, he said. There had been no time to learn when he was a boy. He spent most of the days in Barbados in his room reading Agatha Christie.[1]

By mid-August, the family was back at Quaker Hill. Casey was not feeling well. He seemed to have picked up a cold in Barbados that he could not shake. The boy's legs ached continuously. He could not sit up by himself. His mother had to carry him to the bathroom. Janet had a cousin who had been badly crippled by polio as a child. Thereafter, she had watched her aunt and uncle reconstruct their lives around their stricken child. Janet began to fear the worst.

Ed was away. He had begun work on the first broadcast of the 1954–1955 season. Janet called the doctor, and after he came down from Casey's bedroom, she said, "You think it's what I think, don't you, doctor?" "I'm afraid I do," he answered. A diagnosis of polio was confirmed by a second physician, and Casey was taken by ambulance to a hospital in nearby Poughkeepsie.

It turned out to be a mercifully mild case. He was out of the hospital in a week. Ed quietly asked officials at Casey's school not to make any great fuss, but to keep him out of too rigorous activities. For the next year, the boy complained, "Why do I always have to play goalie?" It had

395

been an unnervingly close call. But there was no residual damage. Casey Murrow was to grow up whole and healthy.[2]

The following March of 1955, Roscoe Murrow died. Dewey called to tell Ed that their father had passed away as peacefully as he had lived. The end came as no shock. The man had been half alive for the last nine years. Two strokes had left him imprisoned in a wheelchair, where he passed his days on the porch of a small, white frame house on a hillside overlooking the bay in Bellingham, Washington. He could speak only in short, barely understood phrases. Ethel tended him round the clock. Virtually his sole contact with the world was a 40-power telescope that Ed had brought him to look out over the water to the San Juan Islands and Olympic Mountains.[3]

Ed had been coming out to visit his father and mother almost every year in something of a filial rite. Often, Janet and Casey went on ahead and stayed longer. Ed came for a few days in between and was quickly restless. The house was small. His mother's chronic fussing and forced overfeeding of a man bored by food got on his nerves. He had traveled too far from this world to be patient in it for long. The sole remaining bond was a cord woven of Ethel's invisible hold over her boys and their sense of duty. "Ed was always," Janet observed, "trying to be the good little son."

His relations with his family were mellower at long distance. He phoned home often. Tales of Roscoe and Ethel were staples in his story-telling. He recounted a conversation between himself and his father to the broadcasting columnist, Ben Gross:

ROSCOE: I read a piece in a magazine that says you make $130,000 a year.

ED: Yes, sir.

ROSCOE: You reckon you're worth it?

ED: I don't know, sir.

ROSCOE: You get all that money just for talking?

ED: Yes, sir.

ROSCOE: Strange world, isn't it.[4]

One of Ethel's passions was trading in antiques, and during visits Ed and Janet occasionally drove her to dealers. She particularly prized her collection of pitchers. In her sweetly deceptive way, she was a shrewd negotiator. When she saw what she wanted, she would gaze at a pitcher, run her hand over it lovingly, and tell the dealer in her dainty southern accent, "I just love the pitcher. But my husband's been ill, don't you see, and we have only his pension. Now, I can understand it if you need that price. So I guess I can't...." Usually the dealer weakened, and the little old lady walked away with a bargain.

She never missed Ed's broadcasts. But she followed them as though her son had a permanent starring role in a school play. Janet Murrow had a sense that Ethel, given her constricted world, never fully grasped the size of the stage Ed played on. "Mother Murrow's concern," Janet recalled, "was mainly that Ed should be a good boy. That he not get into trouble." Ethel followed Ed's scrapes with the network brass, with Shirer, or with Joe McCarthy with the worried concern of a mother whose boy was being picked on by the playground bully. Her son's nemeses were her nemeses. A neighbor couple told Ethel that William L. Shirer was coming to lecture nearby, and they begged her to go with them to hear him. Ethel responded coldly, "I don't go out evenings."

Ed Murrow was generous to his parents. He set up a trust fund in case they outlived him. He sent them money from the trust from time to time. He paid for their health insurance and the considerable medical bills that Roscoe accumulated. But his generosity had to be dispensed with due regard for Murrow pride.[5]

The doctor bills occasioned a rare point of friction between Ed and Dewey. Dewey was a successful contractor, the middle son, stable, well adjusted, spared the pressures on the eldest or youngest child and seemingly free of envy over his brother's fame. He grew tired only of being referred to as "Dewey Murrow, Ed Murrow's brother." Even when he passed away, years after Ed, the local headline read "Famed Newscaster's Brother Dies."

In 1952, Ed received a letter from Dewey, who was miffed by the cavalier way in which Ed had taken over their parents' medical bills. The following exchange from subsequent letters reveals something of the Murrow fraternal style. From Ed: "Don't be so damned stuffy. I'm working seven days a week and don't have time for all the amenities of brotherly correspondence. Mother writes that she doesn't have the doctor bills; apparently you haven't either. Thanks for sending the ones you did." Dewey replies: "Yours of November 3 received. 1. So you're working seven days a week. I should send a medal? 2. To hell with your 'amenities.' 3. Enclosed find bill Dad's operation." Ed replies: "Don't send a medal, send aspirin. My bird dog died last week. Our brother was up three weeks ago, sober. The doctor's bill is being paid. Thanks."

The friction was unusual. To Ed, Dewey was the brother who had remained truest to himself. Dewey had roots. He found his values in his family, his church, his work. With Dewey, Ed was relaxed; they could play golf, sing the old logging songs, swap stories of their boyhood. Ed invested in an iron mine with Dewey. So uncertain were its prospects that they called it "The Drain." Ed told Dewey's wife, "You got the best of us." So unpretentious was Dewey that he could say of their boyhood, "Hell, we were just poor white trash." Ed, who was only too willing to exaggerate to his Upper East Side friends his impoverished childhood, bridled at this phrase. He did not want to hear it, he told Dewey.[6]

The line in Ed's letter, "Our brother was up three weeks ago, sober," went to the heart of Ed's relationship with Lacey.

After the war, Lacey Murrow had gone to work for the Association of American Railroads. When the Korean war broke out, Lacey was recalled to active duty and commissioned an Air Force brigadier general. After Korea, he joined a Washington-based construction firm that built airports, roads, and bridges around the world. He looked good on paper; and when sober, he performed well. But Lacey Murrow was an alcoholic.

Charles Collingwood recalled, "I had an office near Ed's for a while. Ed would suddenly ask me to substitute for him on the news for a day or two. When he'd get back, he'd tell me he had gone to find Lacey."

The calls might come from a desperate Marge, Lacey's wife, or from some hotel manager spotting the Murrow name on the register. However summoned, Ed would go, as he put it to Janet, "to pick up the pieces." Thus a famed newscaster found himself making the rounds of hotels in Chicago, Baltimore, or Atlanta looking for Lacey, who would eventually be found amid a clutter of empty bottles, senseless or in delirium. Ed would check him into a hospital to be dried out, and go back to work, until the next call. When Ed was not rescuing Lacey on the East Coast, Dewey was saving him on the West Coast.

Lacey Murrow's early life had been a chain of seemingly effortless successes. He was well on his way to fulfilling the classic southern expectations for the first-born son, to rise, achieve greatly, and bring honor and credit to the family name. He had been a hard drinker and carouser even as he was becoming the successful young state highway commissioner. But the destructive drinking began, his friends observed, at about the point when he was no longer Lacey Murrow and became Ed Murrow's brother. Dewayne Kreager recalled cohosting with Lacey a dinner of the Washington-Alaska Press Club in Seattle. As Lacey was being introduced as "the famous broadcaster's brother," Kreager remembered, "I could see the lines around Lacey's mouth tightening." The constant association with a famous brother wearied Dewey; it gnawed at Lacey's selfhood.

Thus, a man who had every reason to count himself a success felt diminished. He adopted a classic defense of certain insecure men. Lacey bragged, he swaggered, he exaggerated; he invented war stories, and appropriated Dewey's adventure in the gold fields of Colombia as his own. He inflated the help he had given Ed in college until Ed became angry.

The incident on the St. Johns River after the McCarthy broadcast had provided what Lacey Murrow wanted, the role of big brother, strong, wise, there when needed, the de facto head of the family. At that moment he had been at his best. But those two days were an all too rare exception. Lacey Murrow drank for no doubt commingled reasons, but one of them was a desire to blur the outcome of a family race he had expected to win as his birthright and had lost.[7]

It was rare for the entire Murrow clan to be together. In that March of 1955, Roscoe's death reunited them. Brothers, wives, and children stood together at his grave. Roscoe was buried in the Oddfellows Cemetery near Blanchard, where he had brought his family forty-three years before.

His legacy to his youngest son had not been ambition, or power, or love of wealth, since Roscoe possessed none of these. Roscoe's life was honest toil, simple pleasures, and peace of mind at the end of the day. "Do you think you're worth it?" Roscoe had asked Ed of his income. The question went deeper. What gnawed at Ed was whether his life was worth it. He could not have lived like his father. On the other hand, he had never found peace in the path he had chosen; but contentment was not in him. There was one undeniable legacy, however, from father to son. As Ed Murrow bagged game with a sure eye, rode horses, cut a tree, or plowed his Glen Arden fields, he had mastered the tests of manhood as a man was measured by his forebearers. His skills gave him a quiet satisfaction, a sense of primal worthiness. And he had been taught them by his father.

When the simple service was over, Ethel Murrow's sons took her back to the little house in Bellingham. She went inside, changed her clothes, and started to spade her garden. Ed went back to New York to a life that she could scarcely imagine. She had never seen the townhouse, or the apartment in Manhattan, or Rumblewood, or Glen Arden. Nor would she ever.[8]

Ed was back in the state of Washington a few months after his father's death, in July of that summer. He, Janet, and Casey boarded a Northwest Orient DC 3 flying from Seattle to Yakima. Ever the flying buff, Ed took Casey to the cockpit to meet the pilot. As the pilot explained the instrument panel to Casey, and the plane neared the airport, thunderheads blackened the sky. Still, the pilot said he expected an easy landing as they approached Yakima, and he let Ed and Casey stay in the cockpit.

Forty-mile-an-hour gusts were whipping across the runway as the pilot tried to touch down. The brakes could not hold the aircraft. Ed instinctively dropped to the floor, swung around so that his back was against the pilot's seat, and clutched Casey to him, as the plane careened toward the end of the strip. The pilot tried to lift off again but lacked the power. They were heading for high-tension wires. People were screaming. The pilot shut off the engine and the plane slammed back onto the runway. It slid off the end and struck a utility pole, shearing off six feet of wing before it came to a rest. The passengers were shaken, but no one was hurt.

Afterward, Ed jauntily told a reporter that he considered the landing beautiful. "I consider any landing that I walk away from beautiful." But a photograph, taken immediately after the crash shows a trusting little boy close to his father's side and a chagrined-looking Murrow walking past the partial wreck.[9]

He was away so often that he wanted time just for him and Casey, he said, "to get to know each other." The following summer of 1956, he and Casey drove across the country alone. He was a parent in the same way that he was a broadcaster. Whatever one did had to have a point, offer a lesson in living. On a Wisconsin lake, while Casey's attention wandered, a muskellunge hit and made off with a $60 rented rod in tow. From this experience, Casey was to learn responsibility. The full cost of the pole was extracted from his allowance over seemingly endless months.

Ed was furious when Casey spent money for a clock when there were all sorts of clocks around the house. The objective was to manufacture adversity where none existed. "I think my father felt he was bringing me up in an environment that was overprivileged," Casey later recalled. "He would tell me about his own boyhood. But he didn't make it negative. He'd talk about the advantages of having to solve problems yourself. He made a point of taking me to meet people who had not gone to college or made a lot of money, but who were happy and useful people."

When Casey erred, he was reprimanded in what he remembered as "staccato, machine gun bursts" that were "very effective." He was once playing Parcheesi with his father. Ed suddenly got up and broke off the game, saying he would not play with a cheater. Casey had not thought he cheated. But the lesson was not lost. Cheating was anathema. It had cost him what he prized most, his father's companionship. Marietta Tree observed this scene and was surprised by Ed's harshness toward a child on so trivial a matter. When he was older, Casey came to believe that the sternness had been a performance, a disciplinary tool of his father's that worked.

Casey was not allowed to watch television more than a half hour a night, and not until his homework was done. The single exception was *See It Now*. When he wanted a three-speed bike that cost $50, Ed told him he could have it when "You can explain—not recite—the Bill of Rights." When Casey came home announcing that he had learned the Pledge of Allegiance at school, Ed said that was fine, "Now tell me what it means." It was Ida Lou Anderson all over again. The point was to dig below the surface to find the essence.

They went to ball games together. They worked on the farm together. Jim Seward remembered Ed treating Casey "like a junior partner." Dan Schorr was invited to Quaker Hill for a weekend and drove up from New York with Ed and Casey. He was struck by a certain determined camaraderie between father and son. "Ed would say, 'Well, young man, what's the news from school this week?' And Casey would respond in kind, 'Well, Dad, what happened was....' I watched this manner over the entire weekend and it never changed," Schorr recalled.

If Ed was strict and impatient, if he was an incurable didactic, if he was not always spontaneous, Casey Murrow does not appear to have suffered. His memories were of a happy childhood, the happiest hours being those spent with his father. His single warmest memory of his youth, he has said, "was when my father would put his arm around me and try to tell me things to help me."[10]

During the mid-fifties, one person, outside his family, was admitted to the small circle of his intimates. In the years since the war, Ed had occasionally seen Pamela. She would call him at the office on her visits to America, and they would meet for lunch or drinks. The relationship remained for some time, as Charles Collingwood read it, "warm if no longer hot."

But another woman entered Ed's life. She was, in every imaginable respect, the antithesis of Pamela Churchill. Esther L. (a pseudonym—she has refused to be interviewed or identified) was plain, not glamorous; a friend more than a passion; a working woman, no patrician. And she toiled at a modest professional-level job in CBS radio news.

Palmer Williams remembered driving Ed to the airport one evening and having Ed tell him to wait in front of an apartment house on the Upper East Side. "He never said why," Williams said. "He was gone about a half an hour. And when he got back he never said a word either. I remembered asking myself, does Murrow have a girl friend?"

The affair, if it can be termed such, was conducted with utter discretion. Few people ever saw Ed and Esther L. together. The only one privy to the relationship was Charles Collingwood. "She was," Collingwood remembered, "considerably younger than Ed, maybe fifteen or twenty years. She was tall, no great beauty. And her job was not particularly elevated. But she was highly intelligent, easy to talk to, an undemanding, good natured woman. People were putting demands on Ed all day long. She didn't. She would cook him little meals in her apartment. Very rarely, he might stop somewhere with her for a drink. She was an escape from the pressure on him. He found some sort of solace in this anonymous, agreeable woman. I don't think there was any great passion on his part. To tell you the truth, I was surprised that he was attracted to her. But she was madly in love with him."[11]

CHAPTER 27

A Teacher, A Preacher

Casey's brush with polio the year before quickened Ed's interest in the work of a microbiologist at the University of Pittsburgh. In February of 1955, he invited Dr. Jonas Salk on *See It Now* to discuss his work. Field tests were still under way on Salk's killed-virus vaccine, but as Salk then knew, "The results were a foregone conclusion." A scourge that had twisted young bodies for centuries had at long last been vanquished. His achievement propelled Salk instantly from obscurity to the center of the world's gratitude. Two months later, Ed brought Salk back to *See It Now* again for a full hour.

"He was instantly a remarkable human being to me," Salk recalled of their first meeting. "You could see the depth of his soul, in a sense, through his eyes. He could draw out the essence of one's life. . . . I felt, in a spiritual sense, that I had met my match. I had come to discover a trivial manner in so many journalists. Ed Murrow was not trivial. I found myself responding at the level I like to respond to. I found him introspective, meditative, with a purity of thought. He had true pitch. Here was someone who in another age might have been a mystic. To me, Ed was a teacher, a preacher, a minister, a guide, but a teacher especially, in the best sense of the word, helping others to understand so that they might make better choices."

Salk enjoyed the Murrow wryness, the tendency to mock his own heroic image. "We were riding in a cab, one time," Salk recalled, "and as he got out at his studio, he turned to me and said, 'I'm off to poison the minds of the people.' He'd say to me, 'We all have prejudices. Mine are good prejudices.'"

After Salk first appeared on *See It Now,* Ed told him "a great tragedy has just befallen you, my friend." What was that? Salk wanted to know.

"You've just lost your anonymity." At the height of the cold war, Salk was invited to visit the Soviet Union. His opinion was sought on matters in which he felt not the slightest authority. Mayor Robert Wagner wanted to throw a ticker-tape parade for him in New York. "My life had been turned upside down," he said. "And I found myself turning to Ed Murrow." Murrow had a way of lighting a situation morally, he said, "so that you saw the way to doing the right thing for the right reason." He trusted Ed's judgment implicitly.

They were both self-made men, and they shared a common fear that their children had been deprived of the advantages of adversity. Murrow told Salk that unless a person had faced early adversity, "You are going out into the world unimmunized." The microbiologist savored the metaphor.

As much as he valued Murrow as a friend, there was one thing that Salk could not bring himself to do. He declined to appear on *Person to Person*. On *See It Now* he felt that he and Murrow were performing as teachers. But if he allowed himself to become part of the celebrity parade on *Person to Person*, it would confirm what his "envious" colleagues were already saying, "that I was a publicity seeker and all this was inspired, contrived and engineered by me."[1]

There was in the Murrow-Salk friendship what there was in so many Murrow relationships, something of the one-sided love affair. Ed's attentions tended to move on. Years before, Harold Laski had complained of Ed's declining attentiveness. Morris Ernst had felt it too. "Remember me?" he wrote. "The name is Ernst. I had been under the slight impression that I have even been of some aid to you and even at your beck and call when you wanted me. Tell me if the love affair is over and why it died?" Salk's devotion to Murrow, though not reciprocated at the same intensity, never waned. When talking about him twenty years after Murrow's death, he was still wearing the watch that Ed had given him after appearing on *See It Now*.[2]

The two Salk interviews were among forty-four broadcasts of *See It Now* during the 1954–1955 season. Light topics were few, a story on Roman ruins unearthed in London, a portrait of Las Vegas, Christmas aboard a Navy destroyer. For the most part, Murrow continued to plunge his audience into the political and moral thickets of the time.

In 1954, after the Supreme Court ruled public school segregation unconstitutional, he and Friendly sent their crews to two southern cities to find out what a lofty legal decision did when it reached down to people in their everyday lives. While producing "Report on Segregation," Ed made an unexpected admission to Joe Wershba. The young man who led the desegregation of a student conference in the Deep South in 1930, who deplored segregation among the troops in England in 1943, who did the first television documentary on *apartheid* in South Africa, confessed that, on race, he had had to struggle against his southern upbringing. "I had to learn my liberalism," he told Wershba. "You guys got it all in one piece. It takes me a little while."

In a business in which cigarette advertising revenues were one of the richest sources of income, and fully nine years before the surgeon general's report linked smoking to cancer, and certainly with no personal desire to know the truth, Ed Murrow did two broadcasts that season dealing with cigarettes and lung cancer. The controversy had never been touched by television. There was nothing to be gained by doing the documentary except that it satisfied his compulsion to bring a simmering issue out into the open.[3]

The cigarette in his own hand by now seemed as much a part of him as the hand itself. His son suffered from chronic bronchitis in the smoke-filled Murrow homes. The condition did not clear up until Casey went away to boarding school. Fred Friendly remembered sharing a room with Ed in the Hotel Connaught in London and being awakened by alarming noises. He saw Murrow sitting on the edge of the bed in a terrifying coughing spasm. "I was sure he was going to die," Friendly remembered, "and then he lit up." His habit was now over four packs a day. Jonas Salk offered to show Ed photographs of the lungs of smokers so that he could see that even those who had smoked for years benefited after they quit. As Janet remembered Salk's offer, "Ed would not look at the pictures." He did not need a famed medical researcher to rob him of his rationalizations for continuing a habit that he could not break. He smoked throughout both *See It Now* programs on cigarettes and lung cancer, though off camera.[4]

See It Now that season also dealt with book burning in a California school system, the United States' refusal to grant diplomatic recognition to Communist China, and the racist McCarran Immigration Act. CBS executives complained to Friendly, "Why does Murrow have to save the world every week?"[5]

He compensated for the superficial peeks into the lives of the famous on *Person to Person* by doing more probing portraits of people who fascinated him on *See It Now,* notably this season, Carl Sandburg. He went to Flat Rock, North Carolina, for a filmed visit with Sandburg at the poet's goat farm. The two men had been introduced earlier by Eric Sevareid, and it was affection at first sight. Ed immediately became "Brudda Murrow" to Sandburg. Ed was captivated by Sandburg's earthiness, the man's pure joy in being. On *See It Now,* Sandburg described his four essentials for the good life, "to be out of jail, to eat regular, to get what I write printed, and then a little love at home and a little outside."

While they were filming at Flat Rock, Ed asked, "Carl, is there an outhouse around here?" Sandburg, standing on a ledge, gestured expansively over what seemed the universe and said, "Ed, it's all one big outhouse."

The old man came to New York and usually stopped by Murrow's office, where they would sip from mason jars of moonshine that Sandburg brought up from North Carolina. "There are only three people who can tell me what to do," Sandburg once said. The three were his brother-in-law, the photographer Edward Steichen; Adlai Stevenson; and Ed Murrow.

Murrow occasionally expressed a bemused exasperation at the old man's intrusions. Don Hewitt took a call one day on the *See It Now* set from Sandburg, who asked to come by. "Don't have him come back here," Murrow groaned, "because the first thing you know, he'll write a poem." Here Murrow did an impersonation of the quavering Sandburg voice: "Don Hewitt sits in front of the big glass window...looking out on the cameras." The annoyance was feigned. Carl Sandburg entered the small, tight circle of people Ed Murrow genuinely cared about. He hung a photograph of Sandburg in his spartanly decorated office.[6]

In the fall of the 1954–1955 season, the FBI received a memo from its operative in New York reporting that Edward R. Murrow had been observed "in conference with Dr. J. Robert Oppenheimer of the Institute for Advanced Studies at Princeton, New Jersey, at the Institute for Advanced Studies on November 17, 1954. The nature of the conversation is unknown."

What the FBI made sound like a clandestine encounter between an enemy agent and his controller was the preparation for an Oppenheimer appearance on *See It Now*. Oppenheimer at the time was indeed under constant surveillance. The physicist who had led the Los Alamos scientists to the creation of the atomic bomb had been declared a "security risk" the previous year for his association with Communists and pro-Communist causes before the war. Oppenheimer had subsequently been removed as chairman of the advisory committee to the Atomic Energy Commission. Ten years before, his unhidden and undenied past flirtations with communism had not barred him from the most precious secret of World War II. But it was now the age of suspicion.[7]

Ed had gone to the Institute for Advanced Studies at Friendly's suggestion. His original intention was to film interviews at the institute, where, as Murrow put it, "You find a Nobel Prize winner every time you open a door." But his first choice, Albert Einstein, refused to be interviewed. Murrow then filmed a long conversation with the Danish physicist and Nobel laureate, Niels Bohr. Bohr proved incomprehensible to the layman. Ed told Friendly, "There isn't one usable foot of film in all that stuff."

Then Murrow spent two and a half hours with Oppenheimer. He felt that he could have run virtually all the film uncut and have produced gripping television. The problem was in choosing less than thirty minutes from the whole.

Daniel O'Shea, the CBS security chief, was outraged that Murrow wanted to put Oppenheimer on the network. After all of O'Shea's efforts to cleanse CBS of its Red taint, the appearance of a security risk, the man whom Joe McCarthy charged with deliberately stalling the development of the H-bomb for eighteen months, threatened to stain CBS all over again.

But Murrow was adamant, and Bill Paley backed him. Paley, in fact, agreed to let Oppenheimer run two minutes over. The material was too good to cut, Paley said. But the network's business staff again tried to distance CBS from the words and images it carried. Murrow and Friendly spent $1,500 of their own money to advertise the Oppenheimer broadcast.[8]

Oppenheimer appeared on *See It Now* in his office, surrounded by books, his desk a sea of paper, the blackboard covered with dizzying equations. Tall, ascetic, remotely mystical, his pepper and salt hair resembling a monk's skull cap, Oppenheimer spoke with a modest, almost hesitant manner. He continuously lit his pipe with quick, darting motions. He would suddenly leap from his chair to the blackboard on his egret legs to explain a principle. *The New Yorker* critic, Philip Hamburger, described Oppenheimer on *See It Now:* "tense, dedicated, deeper than deep, somewhat haunted, uncertain, calm, confident, and full, full, full of knowledge, not only of particles and things but of men and motives and of the basic humanity that may be the only savior we have in this strange world he and his colleagues have discovered."

The word "topology," new to Murrow and most of his audience, came up. "What exactly is that?" Murrow asked. Oppenheimer thought, then answered. "We had this year a Swiss [at the Institute], a French-Swiss psychologist—he's almost a philosopher, called Piaget, whose work has been on the way children learn to think, how they learn notions of cause, notions of time, notions of necessity, notions of number—all the things that Kant thought you were born with. Well, they—you, you are not born with them. You learn them. And he made one discovery which is not surprising, but a little odd. He found out those things which in normal mathematical instruction are the most highbrow are the things the children know first. Children know first whether objects are inside each other or separate, whether they can be deformed into each other, and these are the notions that topology deals with…the things that have to do with relatedness, the fact that a doughnut can't be turned into a sphere without tearing it, you see. This kind of thing the child knows, and these, these logical notions, I mentioned only trivial ones, are the basis of topology."[9]

The 1954–1955 *See It Now* season had been brilliant, winning three more broadcast awards. Awards brought esteem, but only ratings brought profits. The program had never won huge audiences by television standards. Its sponsor troubles can be dated from the point in 1955 that ALCOA introduced a new product, aluminum foil, and decided it wanted to woo, not an elite stratum of opinion makers, but housewives. For the previous five years, ALCOA had paid the bills virtually without a murmur while its salesmen were forever having to explain to certain customers, as Friendly put it, "why their company sponsored programs against McCarthy and for Oppenheimer, against cigarettes and for socialized medicine." The cost of air time kept rising, while the ratings softened. Surveys revealed that 53 percent of those who watched *See It Now* were college-educated, compared with 28 percent of all viewers. And 57 percent were professionals or white-collar workers, compared with 31 percent of all viewers. Here was a program clearly in trouble. Nearly 95 percent of the network radio affiliates carried Murrow's nightly news, and virtually all of the television affiliates carried *Person to Person*. But a third of the affiliates turned down *See It Now* for less controversial, more profitable fare.[10]

The last straw for ALCOA was one that Murrow could scarcely have anticipated. In May of 1955, *See It Now* did "The Power of the Press" on a favorite Murrow theme, the little guy standing up to evil and triumphing. Ken Tower was the editor of a Texas weekly, the *Cuero Record*, and Tower had exposed a land scandal whose taint reached the highest levels of Texas state government. For *See It Now*, the story had a real-life ending that could not have been improved upon by Frank Capra. The cameras were on Ken Tower when he received a phone call telling him that his series had won the Pulitzer Prize.

ALCOA, at that time, was embarked on a major expansion of its operations in Texas. The company needed the cooperation of state officials. Instead, it was getting outraged howls for sponsoring the defamation of the Lone Star State. The company had held fast through Radulovich, McCarthy, desegregation, Red China, Oppenheimer, and book burning. It had been content to bask in the reflected glory of Murrow's awards and the critics' praises. That was no longer enough. Unknown to Murrow, Chief Wilson, ALCOA's president, was meeting with Paley and Stanton. Wilson explained that *See It Now* had served its purpose. It had buffed ALCOA's once lusterless public image to an enlightened sheen. Now ALCOA wanted to sell aluminum foil to homemakers. It wanted serenity and a mass audience, not headaches and a handful of elitist admirers. Wilson informed Paley and Stanton that ALCOA was dropping *See It Now* for a dramatic series. The next day Murrow was told. The season had nine weeks to run. After that, *See It Now* and ALCOA would part forever.[11]

A second blow fell five weeks later. Ed was in the studio early, waiting to go on the air with a second broadcast on smoking and lung cancer. He was watching a new CBS program on the monitor, *The $64,000 Question*. The quiz show was a creation of Louis G. Cowan, who had produced the phenomenally popular radio quiz show, *Take It or Leave It*, the program that introduced the phrase the "$64 question" into the language. Cowan had bloated the rewards a thousandfold for television. The first contestant was a housewife who was supposed to be an authority on movies. When she stumbled, a policeman, a self-made expert on Shakespeare, followed her. The Bard-loving cop was up to $8,000 in winnings when time ran out. He would be back the following week to continue the climb toward $64,000. Murrow watched in fascinated horror.

The $64,000 Question was an instant sensation. The next week, Murrow was again watching this dollar bacchanal as he prepared to go on the air with *See It Now*, a program that had never made a dime for the network and had just lost its sponsor. He turned to Friendly and asked him how long he thought they would be able to hold on to their prime-time slot now.[12]

A few days after the last broadcast of the season, Paley asked Murrow and Friendly to come up to his office. Paley liked to think of himself, as indeed he was, a composite showman and statesman in the broadcast world. It would be foolish romanticism to suggest that Paley lived by ratings and profits, while Murrow somehow managed to achieve nobly on CBS television in spite of Paley. Murrow could not have produced *See It Now* for five weeks, much less five years, without Bill Paley's concurrence. Paley had never tried to censor *See It Now*. He had taken the sponsor threats, the political pressures, and stood by Murrow. When Murrow wanted to test new subjects for broadcasts, he skipped all the corporate layering and sought Bill Paley's advice directly. When Paley disliked an idea, Ed dropped it, not for fear of offending, but because he trusted the man's judgment completely. What had changed through the years in the hybrid showman-statesman Paley were the proportions.

The runaway success of *The $64,000 Question* had completely altered the economics of Tuesday night on CBS. In the new language of television, the success of the quiz show had increased the value of the program's "adjacencies." The expectation was that such a hit show would lead big audiences into the program that preceded it and out to the program that followed it.

Thus it might have seemed that *The $64,000 Question* should benefit *See It Now*. Paley was shrewd enough to recognize, however, that an audience dazzled by a shoemaker's knowledge of opera was not the same audience drawn to Murrow's pursuit of the meaning of topology with a Robert Oppenheimer. If he wanted to hold the huge audience of *The $64,000 Question* into the next hour, he needed something more to its taste than *See It Now*. Thus, in the theory and practice of scheduling, instead of *The $64,000 Question* helping *See It Now*, the hit show merely underscored Murrow's comparatively low ratings.

Even with a sponsor, *See It Now* had been bringing in only $50,000 per program from ALCOA, while the network had to pay more than that in production costs. But from the first broadcast, Revlon began paying $80,000 a week for *The $64,000 Question*. By the sixth week on the air, the program had the highest rating in television. And as the ratings soared, so, ultimately, would the sponsor's payment to the network rise, since the advertising fees were keyed to the ratings. *See It Now* became the equivalent of a cow pasture that finds itself one morning alongside a new shopping mall. The land was now very valuable, as long as it did not remain a cow pasture.

By 1955, CBS's overall ratings had become the highest in the industry, where they would stay for twenty-one years. That year alone, CBS earned $16 million after taxes. Surely the network could afford to sustain a small loss to keep on the air for a half hour every week the most prestigious, critically acclaimed, award-winning program on television. The decision, however, was no longer Paley's alone, or at least he had persuaded himself that it was not. Paley had not "owned" the network for years. It was no longer his cigar store. CBS was owned by thousands upon thousands of stockholders. And when a network produced a hit, like *The $64,000 Question,* or NBC's answer to it, *The Big Surprise,* or ABC's gangster chronicle, *The Untouchables,* that network's stock went up. The Nielsens, the Arbitrons, the Videodex ratings, had become the Dow-Jones averages of broadcasting.[13]

None of this was said, but it was the unspoken backdrop to the conversation between Paley, Murrow, and Friendly on that July day. They had come up from Ed's nondescript cubicle to Paley's stylish office with its Picasso, Dubuffet, and Rouault canvases, its antique furniture, and one wall adorned with old microphones from CBS's original affiliates.

Paley told them that he had good news. "I've got an idea for *See It Now,*" he said. "I don't think you can do justice to the kind of material you want to do in a half hour. I want you to have a full hour." The program, however, would not be weekly, but would instead appear eight to ten times a season at different times on the schedule. This irregular scheduling could even have its advantages. Documentaries were not noted for drawing huge audiences. But a documentary suddenly showing up along side a hit show might inherit part of the audience. Murrow and Friendly had gone upstairs with a program that had just lost its sponsor and that was slipping in the ratings. When Paley spoke, it was as though two soldiers expecting to be shot were told instead that they were to receive battlefield promotions. They allowed themselves to focus on the full-hour broadcast and tried to ignore the darker implications of losing a regular time on the network schedule. Indeed, their problems seemed over when, soon afterward, General Motors agreed to sponsor six to eight broadcasts of the 1955–1956 season.[14]

When *See It Now* finally came back on the air in its new incarnation three months later, it looked as if the Murrow luck was still holding. The program was "The Vice Presidency: The Great American Lottery," not on the face of it an irresistible topic. But between the time production began and before the program was finished, President Eisenhower suffered a heart attack. The question of presidential succession was hot, and there was Murrow, ready with an in-depth examination of the issue.

Unhappily for Murrow, General Motors saw the program as an attack on Richard Nixon's fitness for the presidency. The company canceled its contract, and *See It Now* lost its sponsor before the first broadcast went on the air. The aftershock for Murrow was the supine way in which CBS bowed to this unilateral abrogation of contract. The network made no attempt to hold GM to its word. CBS salesmen were now out in the street trying, with no great success, to peddle time to sponsors, a minute here, a minute there. The situation was coming more clearly into focus. Not only had Ed lost his regular place on the schedule, but CBS was not willing to fight for what was left.[15]

Still, Murrow and Friendly tried to make the best of the situation, and the hour-long format did enable them to achieve new depth in their broadcasts. One direction they took was to probe the life and work of American originals, people like Louis Armstrong and Grandma Moses.

The primitive artist from Eagle Bridge, New York, then in her ninety-fifth year, hardly proved primitive in the conduct of her business affairs. She was handled by "Grandma Moses Properties, Inc.," with offices at 46 West 57th Street in Manhattan. Two years of maddening negotiations with her agent had been required before the program was produced. When, at last, the visit with Grandma Moses emerged, the viewer was richly rewarded. The cameras caught the old woman at work, the knobbed, thickly veined hands moving with authority over her canvas. Murrow asked her, as she worked, "You had an ancestor who came over on the *Mayflower*, didn't you, Grandma Moses?"

MOSES: I came on it myself.

MURROW: What do you think of Winston Churchill as a painter?

MOSES: I think he's trying to copy me.

Murrow lead her to a childhood memory about the death of Lincoln. "I was going with my mother and aunt from Greenwich, coming down here toward Eagle Bridge to my Grandmother's," the old woman began, "and as we came near Coily above Cambridge, my mother says, why she says, 'I see everything is wrapped in black. What does this mean? The trees, the doors and the posts of the houses....I'm going into the store and find out what it's all about.' So she went into the store and they told her the President had been assassinated the night before...and mother came out and she felt so bad that she shed tears....That is the first I knew there was a president even."

History, for an instant, was not the stuff of textbooks; rather, it was sitting at a grandmother's knee and hearing her eyewitness account of the country on the saddest day in its history. It was television realizing its magic.[16]

That season also produced a new hero, a new love might be more accurate, in Ed Murrow's life, a younger rival for his old infatuation with England. In December of 1955, Sander Vanocur stopped by Ed's office. Vanocur had done some stringing for CBS and was waiting out a permanent job offer from the network. But, he told Ed, "I can't get CBS off the dime."

"What is it you really want to do?" Ed asked. "I want to go to Israel," Vanocur told him. "I think there's going to be a war there within a year." Murrow jumped up from his desk and pulled from his pants pocket "the fattest wad of bills I ever saw," Vanocur remembered. He started peeling off a thick sheaf. "Don't wait for CBS," Ed said. "I want you to go there as my personal stringer." Vanocur politely declined. He was willing to wait for something more durable.

Murrow went himself to Israel late in 1956 with a *See It Now* crew. John Foster Dulles had just outraged President Gamal Abdal Nasser by withdrawing American aid from the Egyptians for building the dam at Aswan. Egypt's response was to turn to the Soviet Union for comfort. Murrow's plan was to spend ten days on the Israeli side of the Suez Canal while Howard K. Smith worked in Egypt. Murrow would interview Ben Gurion while Smith talked to Nasser. At the end, the two reporters would join for a balanced report on the region.

Ed's party set out from Jerusalem on a twisting road toward Gaza. They drove past barren rock outcroppings and the red earth of the Wadi Sureik where Samson wooed Delilah. They crossed crumbling byways built by the Emperor Hadrian. Murrow, raised on Scripture, felt as though he were traveling through the Bible.

Twelve miles outside Kibbutz Nahaloz, his party was met by an escort of Israeli troops spilling from two jeeps. These sunburned men, assault rifles slung over their shoulders, moved with a casual air and lack of reverence for rank that reminded Ed of American GIs. As the party approached the kibbutz, they passed by tractors tilling the fields, each carrying three men, one to drive, the other two armed with rifles. They rode over slit trenches; past concrete bunkers, watch towers, and floodlights; through barbed wire; and finally into the kibbutz. Inside this desert fortress lived fifty-five families, fifty-five head of cattle, and 7,000 chickens.

Kibbutz Nahaloz was an island of self-sufficiency, growing its own food, generating its own power, pumping its own water, and defending it own existence. Ed was moved by the unity of the kibbutzim. Everything was "We"—"We are growing long staple cotton." "We brought in an oil well." He liked the selflessness and the way their lives were directly connected to the earth.

He traveled next to a kibbutz in the Negev, passing Beersheba, where Elijah fled the fury of Jezebel. They rode along a barren moonscape animated only by an occasional camel or goat. They arrived at Sde Bokar, a patch of green in the trackless sands. As Ed entered the gate, a short, powerfully built old man with a fringe of wild white hair, wearing British desert battle dress, emerged from a hut to greet him. The man was David Ben Gurion, the prime minister.

Murrow interviewed Ben Gurion for two hours. When they had finished with the prime minister's cool, confident exposition of Israel's side in the struggle with the Arabs, Murrow asked Ben Gurion why he spent his free time in this inhospitable backwater. Ben Gurion was slow to answer, and then said that what he liked about the desert was that there was "nothing there," a sentiment the solitary Murrow shared.

From the Negev, Ed and the crew journeyed north to an outpost on the Sea of Galilee, 400 yards from the Syrian border, the Kibbutz Dan. All talk here was of a recent raid. Three Syrians had slipped over the border and rustled 360 sheep. The secretary of the kibbutz took Ed to a rise and pointed out the hoofprints disappearing over the Syrian border. Ed asked the secretary if he was tempted to take his men, posse style, over the border to recover their sheep. "It could be done," the man said. "But it would disturb the tranquillity of the peace."

Murrow was entranced by the spirit of Israel. Until now, nothing in his life had so inspired him as England standing alone, a small country, battered by superior numbers, not only surviving but preserving her civilized values under direst provocation. In the plight of Israel, a tiny, beleaguered democracy, surrounded by enemies, he found another England.

At the end of the journey, he met with Howard K. Smith on the border between Egypt and Israel. "Ed was wildly enthusiastic about the Israelis," Smith remembered. "They could do no wrong. They were superhuman. That kind of got my goat." For Smith, as Murrow readily admitted, could make an equally strong case for the Arabs.[17]

See It Now's "The Arab-Israeli Crisis" aired in March of 1956. In July, Nasser nationalized the Suez Canal. By the fall, with another Arab-Israel clash imminent, Murrow happily went back to Israel. After he left, on October 29, Israel invaded Egypt, while Britain and France sent in troops to recover the canal. And so Ed flew to Israel for a third time. He described over the radio a ride in a six-by-six with Israeli soldiers who, forty-eight hours before, had been farming and clerking in offices. He watched a firefight in which four Israelis were killed. He congratulated their commander on the light casualties, and as he reported, "The man said—'small comfort for the mothers and fathers in Israel—or in Egypt.'"

On another occasion, a CBS stringer in Tel Aviv, Mike Elkins, cabled Ed in New York offering to do a tailpiece marking the anniversary of Israel's statehood. Ed turned to Kay Campbell and said, "I want to send a signal to Mr. Elkins thanking him for his offer. But decline. Advise him that if he were to do the analysis that he proposes on the anniversary of Israel that it would be 95 percent propaganda. I will do the analysis and it will be 100 percent propaganda." Don Hewitt once mentioned to Ed that "The Israelis must be worried now that the Saudis have got all those tanks." "Kid," Ed responded, "any good reform congregation could take on the Saudi Army."

David Schoenbrun, himself a Jew, told him, "Ed, everything that Israel does is not necessarily always right. You're prejudiced. Your credibility is in danger. And the credibility of an influential friend of Israel's like Ed Murrow, is important." He tried to be more balanced. But it did not come easily. Mary Warburg asked him at a dinner party how he felt about Israel. It was, he said, "the one place I would leave my typewriter and forty five, the last rampart that I'll fight on." He was not the objective journalist that he liked to imagine himself. He was the intuitive and subjective crusader that Smith had earlier identified. And now Israel was his crusade.[18]

That summer of 1956 Ed went off to do the thing he did not do best. It was an election year, and he went first to the Democratic Convention in Chicago. There, an ungainly battery pack was strapped to his back, with antennae sprouting from the top. He looked, one colleague said, "like a frogman in banker's grey." Bill Leonard was then a young CBS reporter and remembered seeing Murrow on the edge of the convention floor, looking decidedly uncomfortable. "I thought," Leonard said, "that's my beat. I belong there. But Murrow doesn't and he must hate every minute of it."

In Chicago, Ed wrote a footnote to the history of the presidency. Dore Schary was then heading MGM studios and had produced a campaign documentary written by Ed's friend Norman Corwin and Arthur Schlesinger, Jr. Schary was looking for a Democrat to narrate the film during the convention. Corwin offered to ask Murrow for his suggestions when they met for lunch. Ed ran through a list of possibilities with no great enthusiasm until he said, "I've got just the man for you. He's personable, photogenic, young. And I say he's going places—Jack Kennedy from Massachusetts."

Kennedy was indeed chosen to narrate the film, not only his first exposure before the full convention, but his debut over national television as a rising figure in the party. His performance boosted his bid later in the convention when Kennedy tried for the vice presidential nomination. He lost out to Estes Kefauver, but he had surfaced as a comer. It was the last political prize that would elude Jack Kennedy.[19]

The nominations of Stevenson at Chicago and later Eisenhower at San Francisco were foreordained. The surprise winners at the conventions were NBC's Chet Huntley and David Brinkley, who swept the early ratings.

Walter Cronkite had performed impressively as CBS's anchor at the 1952 convention. Thus, he had been confidently reassigned in 1956. But the unanticipated success of Huntley and Brinkley sowed panic at CBS. The Chicago papers carried stories that the network was sending in Murrow as co-anchor to shore up the beleaguered Cronkite. *The Chicago Sun Times* headlined a resulting Cronkite-Murrow feud. One columnist claimed that should Murrow be named co-anchor, Walter Cronkite threatened to walk out of the convention.

Cronkite called the network and asked if there was anything to the stories of Murrow coming to his rescue. "They told me," he later recalled, "there had been talk about Murrow but no decision yet. They wanted to know how I felt about the idea. I said fine."

Cronkite then called Murrow, who was staying in the same hotel, and asked, "Ed, are you mad at me about anything?" Murrow said that he was not. Cronkite then said, "Get the *Sun-Times* and call me back," which Murrow did. He told Cronkite, "This is crazy. There's nothing like this on my mind. Nobody has even talked to me about going on with you. And I don't want to do the daily business anyway. I don't intend to be a co-anchor." Cronkite thereupon suggested that they scotch the speculation about a feud "by having lunch at a conspicuous place," which they did, at the Pump Room.

As for actually sharing the anchor with Murrow, Cronkite later said, "I would have welcomed it. I would have basked in his sunshine." It was a gracious sentiment. But it seemed more generous than anyone had a right to expect. For all the civility between them, Murrow did resent Cronkite and Cronkite knew it. Ed was careful, however, to confine his opinions to the professional level. Of Cronkite's performance as anchorman, he told his friends only, "He talks too much."

During the 1956 campaign, Ed again quietly coached Adlai Stevenson on the use of television, as he had done in 1952. But he did not vote for Stevenson. Again, he did not vote for anyone. He simply did not vote, ever.[20]

He was overworking himself as usual, doing two television programs, the nightly radio news, and occasional specials, while he bombarded Paley with ideas for new programs. In one memo, he proposed, "As Others See Us," a series of views of America from abroad. "Who Made This Country" was to explore America's ethnic mosaic. He also wrote Paley, "If you have an old rusty fifteen minutes lying about that you would like shined and sharpened, where anecdotes, epigrams and just old-fashioned stories will fall like the gentle rain upon the parched earth, leave it to me." He had James Thurber in mind here as host of a program featuring storytellers, famous and obscure, who possessed the raconteur's art. The most original idea was for a series "to illustrate the consequences that have grown from apparently isolated incidents.... might turn out to be the most informative program on television."[21]

He worked compulsively, came home late, went to bed between two and four in the morning, was back in the office by ten, ate absently, smoked incessantly, and drank too much. In December, he again brought in the correspondents for the year-end wrap-up and then to his apartment for the buffet and poker game. Late in the evening, he disappeared from the table. Dan Schorr had to make a call and was randomly opening doors looking for a telephone when he stumbled on Murrow stretched out on a bed, bathed in sweat, gasping for air. "Ed," Schorr asked, "is there anything I can do to help?" "No, Dan, just go on back and I'll be in in a few minutes," Murrow answered in a voice weak but emphatic. "And it's not really necessary to say anything about this to the others." Schorr had inadvertently seen the Murrow that one was never to see. "The worst thing that could happen to him was for someone to find him in this condition," Schorr observed of this moment. "You must not see Ed Murrow vulnerable." Schorr also had a sense that this was not the first time Murrow had had these spells.[22]

His pace was so hectic that those who worked with him prized a rare idle moment to have him to themselves. For Palmer Williams, these were the times when he drove Ed to the airport. One Friday night, after fin-

ishing *Person to Person,* Williams was taking Ed out to Idlewild for a flight
to Berlin. Even the ride out was not to be wasted. Kay Campbell had scheduled a magazine writer, who had been trying for weeks to interview
Murrow, to ride with them.

The only flight available at that late hour was a Pan Am cargo aircraft. The staff had bought a bed for Ed at Sears and had had it installed
on the plane earlier. At 1 a.m, the reporter finished the interview and
left. But the aircraft had developed engine trouble and Murrow had to
wait. Williams happily agreed to keep Ed company until he left.

They settled into the operations room of the cargo area. Ed opened
his flight bag and pulled out one of the two flasks he carried on trips.
Williams found paper cups at the water cooler. And as they sipped scotch,
Ed began what seemed to Palmer Williams more a soliloquy than a conversation. "He seemed to be wondering out loud about how he had found
himself in a life where he was on the air all the time," Williams recalled.
"He felt he had taken on a great responsibility and he wondered if he was
worthy of it. Was anything he said worth listening to? It was the only time
I ever heard him say that *Person to Person* wasn't worth doing. He wasn't
putting any intellectual substance on the table with it. He asked if this was
what a grown man ought to be doing with his time. Yet, the program
bought him the farm, he said. It made his style of life possible. He felt
he'd gotten himself into a comfortable trap. He wasn't breast beating. His
attitude was kind of rueful as he looked back over his life."

At 3:30 in the morning, the plane was ready. Ed climbed into the
cargo hold to be greeted by crates of yelping dogs. He found it impossible to sleep. He took out his sleeping pills, gave one to each of the dogs,
took one himself, and woke up in Berlin. He later told friends that that
was what television was like—in a world full of barking discontent you
handed out tranquilizers.[23]

He was preparing for another trip abroad when something puzzling
happened. It was in the spring of 1955. He had gone over to the New
York City passport office at 630 Fifth Avenue to pick up his passport.
The clerk asked him to sign a form, a non-Communist affidavit. Was this
a new procedure, he asked? The clerk said no. Murrow then asked, "Were
all journalists going abroad asked to sign such an affidavit?" Again, the
clerk answered no. Then why, he wanted to know, did he have to sign it.
The clerk had no answer.

He went back to the office and fired off a letter to the redoubtable
Ruth Shipley, director of the Passport Office, demanding an explanation.
The response came from one of Shipley's aides, who informed Ed that
the affidavit was necessary "because of certain derogatory information
which the Department has received since the issue of your last passport."
In other words, since the McCarthy broadcast.

He went to Washington and managed at least to extract from close-
mouthed bureaucrats that the "derogatory information" was from an is-

sue of *Counterattack* that had appeared after the McCarthy broadcast, one devoted entirely to Murrow's presumed subversive activities. The sewage system of raw, unevaluated, unproven, anonymous accusations still flowed freely among the security agencies of the government. And these were *Counterattack*'s sources. McCarthy was finished, but not McCarthyism.

In the end, the bureaucracy beat Ed down. If he did not sign the affidavit, he would not be issued the passport. He signed it and sent it in with a protest that his signature was "not to be regarded as any recognition of the validity or accuracy of such derogatory information as may repose in your files."[24]

His own outrage over the witch hunters and his feeling that he had not done enough for the sick, persecuted Don Hollenbeck were on his mind when he was approached for help by another man.

John Henry Faulk did a country humor and music show, *Johnny's Front Porch*, over the CBS New York affiliate and other work for other stations. Faulk was a member of the American Federation of Television and Radio Artists. Faulk and Charles Collingwood had managed to oust a pro-blacklist leadership from the union. Thereafter, an organization called Aware Inc., another self-styled monitor of Americanism, had sent a bulletin to the networks reviving ten-year-old charges against Faulk that he had entertained before pro-Communist front organizations.

Lawrence Johnson, the supermarket owner who helped give birth to blacklisting five years before, now made Faulk the target of his patriotic zeal. Johnson went up and down Madison Avenue waving the *Aware* bulletin and threatening a boycott against any companies who dared sponsor Faulk. Faulk thereafter lost one of his shows and was on the point of losing another when he struck back. He filed a $3.5 million libel suit against *Aware* and Lawrence Johnson. Louis Nizer agreed to take Faulk's case for out-of-pocket expenses. However, for a lawyer in Nizer's class, expenses alone were estimated at $10,000.

Faulk had been able to scrape together $2,500 and was sitting in his office wondering where to get the rest of the money when his telephone rang. It was Ed Murrow. Carl Sandburg had tipped Ed off to Faulk's plight. Sandburg had said, "Whatever's the matter with America, Johnny ain't." Ed told Faulk that he was calling to say that his standing up to the *Aware* crowd was a fine and courageous act. "My door is always open to you, Johnny," he added. Whereupon Faulk answered, "Ed, I'm coming through it right now."

Faulk took the elevator to the seventeenth floor and laid out his dilemma to Murrow. Murrow said that he assumed CBS would take care of Faulk's legal expenses. Quite the contrary, Faulk informed him. CBS was putting pressure on him to drop the suit. "Tell Louis Nizer, Johnny," he said, "that he'll have the money tomorrow." Ed thereupon contacted Seward and had him make out a check to Nizer for $7,500. (While Faulk waited for his libel suit to come to trial, CBS fired him. He subsequently won the suit, although the judgment was reduced to $550,000 on appeal.

Ironically, in 1975, it was CBS that broadcast a two-hour dramatization of the Faulk case, entitled "Fear on Trial.")[25]

See It Now began its sixth season back where it had begun, in the Sunday afternoon ghetto. Murrow did nine broadcasts in the series that season and four special reports. In December of 1956, he and Friendly finished a beautifully crafted documentary that followed Danny Kaye on a round-the-world journey for UNICEF. It was called "The Secret Life of Danny Kaye." It was joyous, inspiring, and noncontroversial. The program should easily have found a sponsor. But the CBS sales department reported no takers. For months, *See It Now* had been like a foster child taken in for piecemeal stays by one-shot sponsors. Friendly was disbelieving and furious that the network could not sell the Kaye show. He could sell it himself he said, which he did after one phone call to Pan American Airways. Thereafter, Pan Am agreed to sponsor the remainder of the *See It Now* schedule for the season.[26]

It was a time in which Murrow sought to pierce the East-West veil of ignorance. Intellectual isolationism disturbed him. It smacked of fear and know-nothingism. It fostered McCarthyism. Murrow thought that Americans could hear an alien opinion without falling for it. In 1956, William Worthy, a reporter for the Baltimore *Afro-American*, managed to get into China. CBS radio thereafter carried a shortwave broadcast by Worthy. Undersecretary of State Robert Murphy was quickly on the phone to Bill Paley, persuading him not to expose Americans to such oral pollution in the future. After all, the United States did not recognize Red China.

Eric Sevareid wrote a commentary condemning the State Department for interfering with freedom of speech. The network killed Sevareid's commentary. Murrow then took up the cause. He did a tailpiece on America's right to know what was going on in the most populous nation on earth. Again, America was being made to look foolish and frightened, as though the land of Jefferson and the Bill of Rights could not survive five minutes of news about life under communism. Murrow was reprimanded by the CBS editorial board.[27]

In December of that year, he plunged directly into the maelstrom. Chou En-lai was visiting Rangoon. Murrow could not get State Department approval to travel to China, but he could go to Burma, where the Chinese premier was willing to be interviewed.

As a journalistic initiative, the Chou interview was historic. No one had yet delivered a leader of Red China to an American television audience. As communication, the broadcast was a flop. Chou did not answer Murrow's questions so much as use them as cues to recite copybook maxims from the teachings of Mao. But at least CBS management could not deny the historic significance of the encounter in Rangoon and allowed the interview to be broadcast. It was handled, however, like a case of leprosy, banished to the outermost fringe of the schedule, 11:15 on a Sunday night.[28]

Murrow then went to Yugoslavia and interviewed Marshall Tito. He tried but failed to penetrate the Soviet Union. Since 1952, he had attempted to get inside Russia to do a "Middletown USSR," a portrait of daily life in a world as remote to most Americans as the planets. First he had trouble getting the State Department to let him out of the country for that purpose, and then the Russians would not let him in.[29]

For all his thirst for information on the Communist bloc, he remained a conventional hard-liner, at least concerning Europe, a believer in the policy of containment and muscle to match muscle in the West's dealings with the Soviet Union—and an unlikely target for FBI probing and McCarthyite fears. He resisted, however, involvement in Asia. He particularly recoiled at the thought of America lifting the white man's burden from the backs of retreating British and French colonialists. Fifteen years before the words "Pleiku," "Khe San," and "Tet" entered the American vocabulary, on May 6, 1950, Murrow made a speech before the American Council on Education in Chicago. "I think," he said, "instead of attempting to converge a policy with the British and the French regarding Southeast Asia,...we should attempt to converge a policy with the people who live there....We have now committed ourselves in Indo-China. This, in the opinion of many, including myself, was a policy of doubtful wisdom. However, we are committed....By converging a policy with Britain and France, rather than attempting to get an agreement among the nations of Southeast Asia, may lead us into a disastrous situation...."[30]

By 1954, the question was no longer whether we should align ourselves with the old colonialists, but what to do when they hauled down the banners of empire. Here Murrow demonstrated an admirable prescience. The likelihood of a French defeat in Indo-China alarmed Washington that spring. Richard Nixon, as Vice President, favored sending in American troops to fill a power vacuum, if the French pulled out. Murrow said in a radio broadcast: "Advocates of intervention are unrealistic if they assume that the problem in Indo-China is primarily military. Actually, it is much more political. The victory in Indo-China is not to be won by more foreign ground troops or guns, be they French or American....it is to be won first of all in the realm of convictions. Only if the people of Indo-China believe that the fight against the Communists is the fight for their own freedom will they turn the present tide of the conflict." On May 7, Dienbienphu fell. For the time being, America did not rush into the morass. That was to be ten years and some 58,000 lost American lives in the future.[31]

At the end of the 1956–1957 season, *See It Now* had sponsor problems again. The program was on the air irregularly; thus it could not build up a loyal following; thus it could not win impressive ratings; thus it could not hold its sponsor. In June of 1957, Pan Am dropped out.[32]

Murrow now existed in two dimensions inside CBS. By doing *Person to Person* he was a joy to the network moneymen and an enigma even to himself. On *See It Now*, he was trouble to the network, a drain on profits, a suspiciously ticking package that sponsors held gingerly and briefly. But to his profession, he remained mythic. Harry Reasoner recalled coming to CBS-TV news in 1956 and being introduced to Murrow. It was, Reasoner said, "Something like a private audience with the Pope for a believing parish priest." A year later, Reasoner was summoned from "the ratty and depressing quarters of television news in the old Grand Central building," where he had been working as a "reporter-contact," to 485 Madison Avenue. There, a news executive, John Day, informed Reasoner that he was being promoted to "CBS correspondent." It was, Reasoner said, "the biggest day of my life. After all, that was Murrow's title."

Dan Schorr marked his initiation into the CBS fraternity from the moment he returned from a tour in Moscow and was invited to the year-end roundup, "with the names I idolized." After the broadcast, Murrow said to him only, "Brother Schorr, you'll do," and walked away. It was to Schorr perfect. Not gushing praise, but the Murrow understatement of broadcast legend, the highest compliment.

Marvin Kalb came to work as a CBS writer in 1957 and recalled the aura around the man: "Ed Murrow didn't stride into the newsroom. He walked in slowly, preoccupied, with his left hand in his pocket, right hand holding the cigarette, his head lowered, the weight of the world on his shoulders. He came in in his shirt sleeves. His pants rose to two points in the back where the suspenders buttoned, revealing the Savile Row tailoring. It was a noisy place, the newsroom. Everybody would be busy working, typing. When he came in, it was like the Red Sea parting. Everyone hushed and moved back as he walked through. It was not pomposity, just a presence, an awesome presence about the man. The spell was finally broken when he spoke to someone."

He remained the teacher. He liked to share with his younger colleagues his interviewing secrets. He told new correspondents, "If you put a direct question, the interviewee will answer it as he has probably answered the same question dozens of times before. Then begins the waiting game. He thinks he has given you the definitive answer. You manage a slightly uncomprehending, puzzled expression, and you can watch his mind work. 'You stupid oaf, if you didn't comprehend that, I'll put it in language you can understand' and proceeds to do so. Then, in the course of editing, you throw out the first answer and use the second one."

Murrow described his reporter's creed to Bernard Eismann, another youthful protegé: "You're a reporter and you're a special kind of reporter. The newspaper reporter has two and a half columns. You have sixty seconds or less. You have to paint in fine lines and broad colors so that while detail may be forgotten, the essence of the story will be remembered fully and clearly by the listener."

Eismann, 22 years old, was a free-lance broadcaster, and had been working out of Israel the first time Murrow asked him to do a story. Eismann remembered sitting in a broadcast booth in Jerusalem waiting for his cue and hearing Murrow in New York: "Now for an analysis of that story by my colleague, Bernard Eismann." "Colleague of Murrow?" Eismann remembered thinking. "I was overcome." He had a way of holding out his hand and pulling people up to share the pedestal where they placed him. It was very effective leadership.[33]

The sixth season of *See It Now* ended in the summer of 1957. Ed took his family out to the state of Washington for a vacation. They joined his old college mentor, Earl Foster, and Foster's family for a fishing trip on Sequin Bay. They were standing on the shore watching a smiling fisherman jump out of his boat and trot up the steps from the boat dock, holding aloft a salmon he had hooked. Suddenly the man stiffened and dropped dead. "When my time comes," Ed said later, "that's the way I want it." Earl Foster came close. The following morning, Foster was found dead in his bed.

When Ed returned to New York, he wrote Foster's widow, Katherine, a long letter about the friend they had both lost. "Someone wrote, there are no pockets in a shroud," he told Katherine Foster. "The dead hold in their hands only what they have given away." Earl, he said, had given much. The sentiment was a recurring theme when friends passed away. He used the same words when a more celebrated friend, Humphrey Bogart, died that year, when he wrote Bogey's widow, Lauren Bacall. The phrases about the shroud, he had picked up from Carl Sandburg. He liked to refer to life in his letters of condolence as, "This interlude between two mysteries."[34]

A third death that year affected him rather differently. On May 2, 1957, Ed was about to go on the air with the evening news when Ed Bliss informed him that Joe McCarthy was dead. As Bliss recalled the moment, "Ed showed no emotion, certainly no satisfaction." He said only, "Let me see what comes in on the ticker."

What he did say later on the news was, "Senator Joseph R. McCarthy died tonight at Bethesda Naval Hospital at the age of 47. The hospital announced that he succumbed to acute hepatitis, a disease of the liver, at 6:02 p.m. Washington time. The senator was admitted to the hospital last Sunday when his condition was reported serious. He is survived by his wife and an infant daughter they adopted early this year. McCarthy had been a Republican senator from Wisconsin since 1946."

"I think I have never been more objective in reporting anything," he was to say afterward. "Yet, in the morning, I found myself upbraided by hundreds for callousness, gloating and fraudulent compassion."[35]

See It Now continued to be plagued by controversy and sponsor problems. The State Department had sent the contralto, Marian Anderson, on a goodwill tour of Asian countries. *See It Now*'s cameras followed her. The product was a marriage of film art and travelogue. But several affiliates in the South did not want to air a program about a black singer traipsing around Asia at taxpayers' expense. The program was initially scheduled in the dead void of late Sunday afternoon, a time few sponsors would touch. Friendly had managed earlier to sign Pan Am as a sponsor. Murrow now tried his hand at hawking his own wares. He managed to sell the Marian Anderson broadcast to International Telephone and Telegraph for $150,000, enough to lift the "The Lady from Philadelphia" into prime time.

Earlier, in the fall of 1956, he ended the charade of membership on the CBS board of directors after nine years of near silent service. The given reason was that he was about to negotiate a new contract and wanted to do so without a conflict of interest. As Paley was later to describe the resignation, "He didn't, uh...make much of a contribution." It was a happy divorce for all parties.

To the network, he had become an ornament with sharp edges, a stirrer of controversy one day, a producer of profits the next. He continued to work himself into exhaustion, but he was handsomely rewarded for his labors. As a result of his renegotiated contract, he was, at the end of 1957, earning over $300,000 a year, the highest-paid figure in broadcast journalism, by far. When an investor asked Paley at a stockholders' meeting why Murrow was earning more than the chairman, Paley replied gallantly, "He's more valuable."[36]

CHAPTER 28

See It No More

If the best years of a man's professional life may be bracketed as by bookends, one, in Murrow's case, would be marked 1938 and the other 1958.

The latter year began with a triumph. Ed had been converted to television, in large part, because of the medium's potential to catch historic moments and figures on film and preserve them intact for future generations. Suppose television had been available to reporters asking Lincoln why he waited two years into the Civil War before freeing the slaves? Or how had the President felt about General Meade's failure to follow up his victory at Gettysburg? In pursuit of this kind of historical immediacy, Ed had been trying for three years to produce a six-part series of conversations with former President Harry Truman.

He first raised the subject with Truman in 1955. He later described to Paley Truman's response: "He wants money, although I refrained from discussing figures with him. When I suggested that the continuing sale of his film for educational purposes over decades, indeed centuries, would pay for the maintenance of the Truman library, he replied by saying the government would take care of that. He was interested in the maintenance of an old guy named Truman and his family."

The six-part series was never to be. As the salespeople put it, the reminiscences of an ex-President had "poor commercial prospects." Ed was reduced to a one-hour broadcast with Truman on *See It Now*. He went to Islamorada in the Florida Keys, Truman's favorite retreat, to film the show. There, they passed the time walking along the beach, sitting on the dock, and stretched out on deck chairs in front of Truman's cottage.

What emerged was "From Precinct to President," the contemporary equivalent of asking Lincoln why he had fought the Civil War. The President who dropped the atomic bomb told Murrow that this decision had not even been his most difficult. Dropping the bomb ended a war. The hard choice, Truman said, had been to intervene in Korea, which started a war. He told how he had almost accidentally strangled the atom bomb in its infancy. He was still a senator then, heading the Truman committee, tracking down wartime profiteers. He had become suspicious of enormous unexplained outlays at an obscure federal installation in Oak Ridge, Tennessee. The secretary of war, Henry Stimson, pleaded with him, "Harry, call off your dogs," but Stimson would not say another word about the matter. Truman agreed not to investigate Oak Ridge on the strength of the friendship between the two men, and the development of the bomb went on, with Congress in the dark.

Murrow clearly relished the conversation with this man who not only had made history, but was steeped in history. When he posed a question about the chronic crisis in the Middle East, Truman began with the Pax Romana and ancient tribal rivalries in Israel. As Murrow threw out names at random, Truman would lift the curtain on a hidden corner of the recent past. Of Eisenhower, Truman laughingly remembered how, at Potsdam, he cautioned the general that, of course, he could run for President, but it would damage his place in history. Truman then told Murrow that, shortly afterward, Eisenhower sent him a letter giving his own theory about why military men had no business pursuing the presidency. That this glimpse of living history would be available to Americans a hundred years later delighted Murrow, if not prospective sponsors.[1]

The Truman broadcast was followed on *See It Now* by "Statehood for Alaska and Hawaii?" a subject of such blandness that it seemed incapable of arousing any sizable audience, much less controversy. It was, however, to prove fateful.

The network's habit of caving in and granting equal time whenever a politician raised the cry of unfairness against *See It Now* infuriated Murrow. Equal time was a slur on his professional judgment. Equal time meant that the network was second-guessing him on his objectivity, his balance, his fairness as a reporter. The issue had first come up four years before when Ed did a program on the Bricker amendment. Conservative John Bricker of Ohio had introduced an amendment in the Senate to curb the treaty-making power of the President. Murrow had invited Bricker and Estes Kefauver, who opposed the amendment, along with other experts, to debate the issue on *See It Now*.

Bricker's aides actually used a stopwatch to compare the time given to each side. They complained that they received only eight minutes and fifty-three seconds, compared with eleven minutes and two seconds for the opponents. Murrow was shocked when CBS management forced him to give equal time to Bricker on a later program. Two months later, Paley compelled him to give over a full broadcast of *See It Now* to Joe McCarthy.[2]

In January of 1956, *See It Now* broadcast "The Farm Problem: Crisis in Abundance." The thrust of the story was that small farmers were being driven off the land by giant agribusinesses. For balance, Murrow and Friendly had Ezra Taft Benson, Eisenhower's secretary of agriculture, on the program to give the administration view.

Murrow and Friendly were in a Tel Aviv hotel lobby just returning from an all-night shooting session on the Sea of Galilee, grimy, unshaven, and exhausted, when Murrow was handed a message from New York. The Republican National Committee considered the farm broadcast biased and had demanded "equal time." The network, without consulting Murrow, had agreed. Secretary Benson was to go back on the air. Ed went to his room and drafted a cable announcing his resignation from CBS. Friendly persuaded him to sleep on it, and the cable was never sent.[3]

"Statehood for Alaska and Hawaii?" seemed controversy-proof. For years, the platforms of both political parties had supported statehood. Legislative inertia was the only serious obstacle to passage. Murrow and Friendly strained to pump life into an issue that offered all the contentiousness of sunshine and apple pie. And so, along with the supporters of statehood, they managed to unearth a near lunatic fringe of opponents. Senator Eastland was on the program, and the Mississippian warned, "Ed, the Communist Party controls the politics of the Islands, and if Hawaii were admitted to statehood, we would have in the American Congress two senators and representatives who, in my, judgment, would be influenced by the Communist Party."

The Red eminence who Jim Eastland feared was Harry Bridges, head of the International Longshoreman's Union. And so to further enliven the brew, Murrow also had Bridges say his piece on the broadcast. Bridges responded to Eastland and further mentioned a Republican congressman from upstate New York, John Pillion, who believed that statehood for Hawaii was "a major objective of the Soviet conspiracy." Bridges said of Pillion, "I think he's crazy."

"Statehood for Alaska and Hawaii?" was aired on a Sunday afternoon in March and aroused a profound silence. But among the trickle of letters that the program generated was one from Congressman John Pillion. He demanded equal time.[4]

Murrow could not take the request seriously. A crackpot view was a crackpot view, even in the mouth of a U.S. representative. But Pillion's request was on the agenda at the next meeting of the CBS editorial board. Sig Mickelson argued against granting the time. But one board member aggressively opposed Mickelson. That member insisted that Congressman Pillion be given his day in the court of public opinion. The member was Bill Paley. The hapless Mickelson faced one of his least pleasant duties, to deliver bad news to Ed Murrow. Mickelson was placed in the degrading position of a network news chief who could not protect his newsmen. It was 8:30 in the evening when he went to see Murrow. "He was drinking scotch," Mickelson remembered. "I explained what happened. I got no reaction. He barely noticed me, and I left."

Murrow had been overruled this time, not by a news bureaucrat like Mickelson, whose fiats he habitually ignored, or by a genuine power like Stanton, whom he could outflank, but by his friend, his champion, his hero. He wrote a memo to Paley, the gist of which was that if CBS was going to make decisions about his program without consulting him, he could not continue with *See It Now*.[5]

He had formed few deep attachments in his life. He was almost unnaturally self-contained. Paley was an exception. Murrow, who was the model to so many, needed someone to whom he could look up. He craved Paley's good opinion. He had always found a way to rationalize the bad corporate decisions before. They were the work of faceless, gutless corporate ciphers. But this time, Paley was undeniably to blame.

Ed had been warned by Aarons and Zousmer that a day would come when Paley would abandon him. "I don't care what Bill Paley or Babe Paley thinks about you socially," the streetwise Aarons had said. "When push comes to shove, Paley's got to back his management people, not you."

"You don't understand the relationship, Johnny," Murrow had responded. He and Paley had fought over the banned broadcast from Korea. Yet weeks later, Paley had stood by him when Campbell's Soup tried to take away Ed's evening news and replace it with a music show. Murrow surely jeopardized the network when he took on Joe McCarthy, and Bill Paley had not tried to stop him. He had made the break with Hearst-Movietone Newsreels after Don Hollenbeck's suicide. And Paley, without a second's hesitation, had approved hiring CBS's own camera crews at great cost. Oppenheimer's appearance on *See It Now* had revived the charge from the right that CBS was the Red Network. Not only had Paley approved the broadcast, he loved it. He had let it run overtime.

True, the social life between the Murrows and the Paleys, the exchange of country visits, had trailed off to an occasional lunch between Ed and Bill. That did not matter. What mattered was that the undergirding of mutual trust and admiration between the two men remained intact.[6]

What Murrow did not grasp, in his total absorption in his own world, was not so much the change in Paley as the change in CBS. Murrow still saw what he had seen on first joining the company in 1935, a medium of communication. But by 1958, what Bill Paley saw was a conglomerate. Yes, CBS was a broadcast network; it also made records, manufactured television parts, and backed Broadway shows (*My Fair Lady,* for one). It acquired a guitar factory and an amusement park, and would in the future buy a ball club. *See It Now* was a single strand in a vast corporate tapestry. Murrow saw CBS in only one strand. Paley saw the whole fabric.

Not all the company's diversifications had prospered. Hytron, a television manufacturing subsidiary, had been an expensive failure. After that debacle, Ralph Colin had detected a different Paley. "When he was young," Colin remembered, "he had been the quickest, most decisive executive I ever knew, because he had little to lose. Now he was cautious and conservative because he had so much to lose."

Paley was also a man of shifting passions. When he discovered art, collecting became his obsession. When he took up fishing, he became an avid angler. At another stage, it was golf, and at another, shooting. He brought the same waxing and waning attachment to the network's programming. He had a remarkable ability to get out when programs were peaking, while others only saw them at their peak. He had a similar touch with people. He had known precisely when to unload Ed Klauber and replace him with Paul Kesten. Paley's ex-wife, Dorothy, once remarked, "Ed had Bill on a pedestal." But as she knew from firsthand experience, Paley's interests were intense, but not necessarily permanent. McGeorge Bundy once observed of Paley, "He is not capable of permanent and total trust of anybody." With Bill Paley, everything and everyone had a season.

Paley now sensed a change in television news. Walter Cronkite was becoming phenomenally successful because, along with being a crack reporter, he was as comfortable as an old shoe. On NBC, people listening to David Brinkley felt they were hearing a tart, witty dinner guest. These men were cool in the McLuhan sense. Ed Murrow was hot. He had made of himself with *See It Now* a nagging conscience, a public scold, an irritant to the corporation. Bodies try either to digest irritants or to expel them.[7]

After sending his memo threatening to quit *See It Now,* Ed was invited up to the twentieth floor. Friendly went with him. Paley was sitting behind a leather-topped French provincial desk. He was, as always, impeccably groomed, wearing a blue shirt and stripped tie. Heavy, handsome cuff links poked from a well-tailored sleeve. His desk, in appropriate board chairman style, was not defiled by a single sheet of paper.

Paley remained seated. Murrow paced, one hand in his pocket, the other clutching his cigarette. Friendly watched. Murrow began telling Paley of his unhappiness over the handling of the Pillion affair. What he wanted, he said, was a say in any decisions by the editorial board affecting *See It Now.* The board's granting Pillion equal time without consulting him was intolerable.

Eric Sevareid had once observed of Bill Paley, "He was the kind of man to whom you say nothing carelessly," which Murrow was now to rediscover. He had earlier written the memo saying that *See It Now* could not continue under present conditions. Now, he was telling Paley, "I don't know whether I can work here."

When Murrow finished, Paley fired a shot as quietly and deadly as a bullet through a silencer. "But I thought," he said, "you and Fred didn't want to do *See It Now* anymore."

Murrow either did not grasp the import of what Paley was saying or disbelieved it, for he went on. He repeated that what he wanted was the chance to have a say in editorial board decisions that affected his program. "Of course we want the program to continue," he said.

It was, after twenty years of friendship and favored treatment, Murrow's turn to experience the killing frost of Paley's displeasure. "I thought we'd already decided about *See It Now*." Paley spoke with the flat finality of one unaccustomed to having to repeat his wishes.

Now it was Murrow, like Shirer twelve years before him, who could not accept what he was hearing. This time there was no buffer between Paley and the unpleasant truth, no news bureaucrat, no Frank Stanton to blame. It was Murrow and Paley debating Murrow's professional existence. They argued with cold intensity for forty-five minutes.

Paley was not about to be branded a broadcasting philistine. It was he who had given Murrow unparalleled freedom. He had never dictated or censored a single Murrow program. He had never balked at the millions of dollars the network had poured into *See It Now*. He, and yes, Frank Stanton too, Paley pointed out, had taken the political heat, while Murrow had gone dashing about on his white charger, the shining knight saving the world, while Paley and Stanton were cast as the heavies. It was Paley who had to hold onto the affiliates who wanted entertainment from the network, not civics lessons, who threatened to leave CBS for another network if they did not get the pop programming they preferred. It was he who had to protect CBS's government-granted license while Murrow offended the very elected officials, the Brickers, the McCarthys, the Eastlands, who could threaten that license.

Murrow was ready to grant Paley all the credit due for his indispensable role in the birth and survival of *See It Now*. And then he asked, "Are you going to destroy all this?"

Paley held his hands across his belly and said wearily, "I don't want this constant stomachache every time you do a controversial subject." With that, Murrow went one step too far. "I'm afraid," he said, "that's the price you have to be willing to pay. It goes with the job."

He was wrong, of course. The pain of controversy only had to be endured if one saw the network as a lectern instead of a cash register, as a classroom instead of a mint. Paley was in a position to make that choice. Indeed, in the matter of *See It Now*, he already had.

Looking back years later at the scene he had silently witnessed, Fred Friendly was to say, "I can't prove this, but, remember, Ed was the most famous and distinguished symbol in broadcasting. Ed Murrow *was* CBS. And I think there was on Paley's part the unspoken question, 'Whose company is this anyway?'"

When Murrow and Friendly left Paley's office that day, *See It Now* had two remaining broadcasts left for the season. Then it was dead. He and Friendly reluctantly began to let some of their people go.[8]

Paley was right on one point. Murrow had enjoyed unsurpassed freedom. With the death of *See It Now*, no single individual would ever again wield such unfettered power in television. The most discerning obituary for the program was John Crosby's in *The New York Herald Tribune:* "There were several historic occasions this week. One was the end of Edward R.

Murrow's *See It Now* after seven years of distinguished history. The other was the end of Elfrida von Nardoff after twenty-one weeks on *Twenty-One*. The events are more or less complementary.

"*See It Now* was born in the early days of television when it was thought that TV was a tremendous medium for the exchange of information and ideas. *Twenty-One* came along in the later phase when it was discovered that television was far better suited to play parlor games and give away money. *See It Now* enlightened us. *Twenty-One* stupefied us.

"There have been some dull *See It Now* shows, and some have been better than others, but it is by every criterion television's most brilliant, most decorated, most imaginative, most courageous and most important program. The fact that CBS cannot afford it but can afford *Beat the Clock* is shocking."[9]

See It Now was a first and a last. It had been television's first regularly scheduled documentary series, the first to elevate television journalism to the respectability of the printed word, and in a sense to go beyond, since it presented a fresh way of interpreting the world. What distinguished *See It Now* was the synergism of its combined visual and intellectual curiosity. In a program on Israel, a Buchenwald tattoo was visible on the arm of an Israel fighter pilot. In an investigation of African nationalism, a "rehabilitated" Mau Mau warrior was heard singing "Onward Christian Soldier." In an account of a M.A.S.H. unit in Korea, a nurse dropped a bullet taken from a soldier's spine into a metal bowl, and we heard the ping.

Nobody had done it better. Indeed, before *See It Now* nobody had done it at all. *See It Now* had achieved what thoughtful people had believed television was supposed to achieve all along. The program brought what was vital and significant in the world into the living room of Everyman, thus elevating him, instead of what the bulk of television was doing, giving mediocrity a wider stage and thus banalizing the viewers. Now, *See It Now* was over.[10]

Murrow, a man who could exude gloom in the best of times, now had something real for his pessimism to feed on. Friends who stopped by his office found him bitter. He retreated to the old fantasy, the college presidency in the small town. Janet had become a trustee of her alma mater, Mount Holyoke. She told Ed that she was going to the school for a weekend meeting and that she was going to note everything that a college president did. When she came back, she described the faculty teas, the reception lines, the prayer breakfasts. "You couldn't stand it for five minutes," she told her husband, "and I couldn't either."[11]

If a college presidency was not a realistic escape from his disillusionment, another possibility beckoned in the spring of 1958. Irving Ives was retiring that year as New York's Republican senator. Four years before, New York Democrats and the state's small, inordinately influential Liberal party had managed to elect Averell Harriman governor. Now, they wanted another eminent name, an incorruptible figure to run for Ives's seat.

In mid-March, Alex Rose, the clever hand behind the Liberal party, went to see Harriman in Albany. Coming out of the meeting, Rose issued a statement that Edward R. Murrow "would make a great United States senator....we hope he will exchange one brilliant career for another." Eleanor Roosevelt soon afterward told the East Side Democratic Club that Ed Murrow was on her list of Senate candidates because he had the requisite, "international viewpoint." Sam Rosenman, FDR's confidante, phrase maker and a kingmaker in the state Democratic party, favored Murrow as "a fresh face."

Harriman himself was cautiously encouraging. The governor told a press conference that he was "quite happy" to have Ed Murrow, a friend dating back to the Blitz, run with him on the Democratic ticket. And what of the prospective candidate? Murrow told a *New York Times* reporter, "The only thing I would like to say is that I have neither the intention nor the appetite to run for public office." He was not even enrolled in a political party, he said. The most he had ever admitted to, and then in private conversation, was that he considered himself "a Republican on national issues and a Democrat on international ones." And he did not even vote.

Nevertheless, his disclaimer was carefully scrutinized by experienced readers of political entrails. And they detected that he had not categorically ruled himself out.

It is evidence of Murrow's bruised but persistent faith in Bill Paley that only days after losing *See It Now*, he sought Paley's advice on the Senate race. "Do it," Paley told him. "I think you'll win." Indeed, Paley saw the Senate as a stepping-stone. "I don't think," he went on to say, "you'd be very far from the highest post in the land."

"I feel uncomfortable about it," Murrow answered. "I wasn't born here in New York and I don't feel I know this state well enough to represent it." "Ed," Paley said, "that's a lot of nonsense. You've lived here for years and you know what the problems are." Paley's encouragement can be read as genuine belief in Murrow's political prospects. It can also be seen as a happy solution, one that would preserve their friendship and remove a heavy cross from CBS. Among his confreres, Paley provided virtually the only encouragement Ed was to get. Correspondents who had covered Congress warned him that it would be ten years before he acquired real power. Collingwood told him, "I don't see you in that life. It's not just getting up and making speeches. It's meetings, which you hate, and putting up with constituents and their pleadings." Collingwood detected, however, that "Ed was tempted. No question about it. He told me he thought the Senate would be a bully platform." Indeed, when Eric Sevareid was quoted in the newspapers as saying he thought that Murrow would not make a good senator, "sitting in committee meetings and all that," he remembered, "I felt the Murrow chill for a while."

Ed sought the advice of someone who had served in the Senate. He went to see Harry Truman. Truman told him he would be lost in the Congress. "You'll have to figure out," Truman advised him, "if you want to be the junior senator from New York or Edward R. Murrow."

It quickly became apparent that the nomination would not be handed to him. Averell Harriman was a man who had believed all his life in experts, whether learning polo or politics, and his current political Svengali was the Tammany chief, Carmine G. De Sapio. What the Harriman ticket required, De Sapio was telling the governor, was not another WASP, but an Irish Catholic. If Murrow were serious about running for the Senate, he would have to fight for the nomination with the rest of the pack. Ed had no stomach for that. Talk of a Murrow candidacy faded before the summer was out. Ed would later say, "Politics was not for me. Politics requires a special appetite for public office, a desire for unlimited exposure and an undiscriminating liking for people. I don't have any of these qualifications." Collingwood was more to the point: "Ed Murrow was not a political animal. He was a moral animal."[12]

See It Now passed into history on July 7 with a report on West Germany's industrial rebirth, "Watch on the Ruhr." When it was over, Ed took Casey and went off trout fishing in the Rogue River in Oregon.

That fall, he faced the lightest workload since he had gone back into broadcasting in 1947, another season of *Person to Person* and the nightly news. The newscast, after eleven years, was beginning to pall. Ed Bliss did the newswriting. Ray Swing wrote most of the tailpieces. Ed Murrow read them.

But he had an idea, one that had been percolating in his imagination in various forms for years, one that would serve another end as well. Most of the *See It Now* crew had been dismantled and scattered. But the program he had in mind could keep the survivors working.

He explained his plan during something of a pub crawl with Lauren Bacall. They had seen each other a few months before at a party given in her honor, and she had been flattered to find Murrow among the guests. When her husband had been alive, she told Ed, "Bogey and I would never go out on Tuesday nights. We couldn't miss *See It Now*." Murrow for his part had been surprised by the seriousness and political passions of this smokily alluring woman.

She was rather astonished when he called, inviting her to go with him to a bar on Third Avenue. "One of those places with sawdust on the floor," she remembered. The talk at first was inconsequential. She was surprised at how much scotch he put away. Murrow for his part was favorably impressed at how Bacall handled her Jack Daniels. They adjourned to a restaurant for dinner and then went to the Gold Key, a private club on the East Side. "There was nothing romantic," she recalled. "We just liked and admired each other." At the club Ed finally broached the purpose of the meeting. He had an idea for a new program. He wanted to use the technology of television to juxtapose people, anywhere they might be on earth, people who would strike conversational sparks off each other. He proposed as an example Malcolm Muggeridge, who had retired as editor of *Punch,* and was in Australia; Eric Johnston, head of the Motion Picture Association of America from Washington; and Bacall, wherever she might be.

"I wondered," she said, "how this actress was supposed to keep up with these brains. But I was very flattered." Murrow told her he wanted her because "You care and you're involved."

As they drank and talked—"It seemed to me he put away a bottle of scotch and the only sign was that his voice got louder"—she made the point that he was "a big star." "He got angry," she said. "He hated to hear that. He snapped at me, 'I'm not a star. I'm a journalist.'"

She noticed that he never stopped smoking, that his fingers were tobacco-stained. She noticed too that he had the hands of a workman. And while it had been a stimulating evening, she found him wearyingly serious. Ed Murrow, she said, "was not particularly fun." She agreed to do the pilot. The series was to be called *Small World.*[13]

In selling the idea to the network, Ed happily gave all credit to Bill Paley. He sent Paley a memo saying that the seed of *Small World* was planted in 1938 with Paley's historic first radio roundup during the Austrian *Anschluss.* Paley was, he said, "the principal parent of *Small World.*"

In that pre-satellite era, Murrow's conversation with his guests was to be carried out over international telephone lines, while cameramen on location filmed each participant. The film would then be flown to New York and edited down to a half hour of conversation.[14]

Small World first went on the air in October 1958. The Bacall, Muggeridge, Johnston program was not the first, but rather the third broadcast. The maiden guests were Tom Dewey in Portland, Maine; Aldous Huxley in Turin; and Jawaharlal Nehru in New Delhi. For lovers of good conversation, the format worked. In a typical early broadcast, Murrow brought together James Thurber, Siobhan McKenna, and Noel Coward and directed the conversation to the nature of humor.

MURROW: What has happened to the whole field of political satire? It seems to me that's pretty well vanished from the whole English-speaking world.

COWARD: Only in the theater. It still goes on in government.

THURBER: …The thing that alarms me is that since the Black Age of McCarthy, political satire has become a glass of milk. It won't hurt anybody. But who likes it?

McKENNA: …Although I know humor must have a great deal of cruelty in it, I prefer the humor to be directed against themselves.

THURBER: ...Siobhan has just mentioned cruel humor....by definition, humor is gentle. The savage, the cruel, the harsh would
fall under the heading of wit and/or satire. The wit makes fun of
other persons; the satirist makes fun of the world; the humorist
makes fun of himself....

Murrow's pleasure in the repartee could be read in his face. His hopes
for *Small World* rose.[15]

In another broadcast, an imperious Maria Callas in Milan and Sir
Thomas Beecham in Nice formed an instant clique against the third participant, pianist-humorist, Victor Borge, in Connecticut. "Then, you're a
musician, sir," Beecham said to Borge, with disbelieving hauteur. When
Callas deigned to acknowledge Borge's existence, she did so lopping off
the last syllable of his name so that he emerged "Borg." Beecham launched
into a discussion of claques and then into the nature of artistic performance. "The supreme demonstration of art and accomplishment, whatever [the artist] is doing, is to leave the audience under the impression
that the performance could never be bettered in the world." To which
Borge added coolly, "And in this case the claque comes in handy some
times."[16]

In another *Small World* broadcast involving Senator Everett Dirksen,
Carl Sandburg, and C. Northcote Parkinson, Murrow asked if Lincoln
could be "nominated and elected today," and if so, would he run on the
Republican ticket. The sonorous Dirksen sought to hold onto the party's
patron saint: "I do sincerely believe that he would eschew the liberal
stance...." Sandburg, Lincoln's biographer, suggested that Lincoln "might
enjoy some success on television as a comedian of the Will Rogers school.
He would be doomed as a politician." Parkinson said, "An individualist
like Lincoln, an eccentric, simply wouldn't fit in." Dirksen began to ob-
ject, but Parkinson plowed on, "today that lonely man would be taken over
by psychoanalysis."[17]

Small World was, in a sense, Murrow's reward to himself for doing
Person to Person. Both dealt in famous names. But while on the latter the
conversation had all the bite of oatmeal, Murrow delighted in provoking
controversy on *Small World*. He was far better at probing minds than kitchens. But a half hour of stimulating conversation once a week was hardly
compensation for the loss of *See It Now*. If Paley and the CBS management believed that they had placated Murrow, they had only to wait three
days after the first appearance of *Small World* to learn otherwise.

The signs were there earlier. In September, Bernard Eismann had
attended a cocktail party that Paley gave for young people who had been
given CBS fellowships. Eismann had joined the usual circle hovering
around Murrow. He was astonished at Murrow's open bitterness. Ed was
telling the fellows that they were becoming "prisoners of an unwholesome
machine. Don't fool yourself that television is a medium of education and

elucidation. It's an advertising medium and don't forget it." All this was said by Murrow, Eismann recalled, with hard, sidelong glances at Paley and Stanton, who were mingling with the other guests. "I was shocked," Eismann recalled. Increasingly, Ed had been saying the same things to his colleagues. Bill Leonard had the impression that Murrow now "despised where he was working."[18]

On October 15, the dam burst. Kay Campbell went to Sig Mickelson's office and dropped off a long, double-spaced text. Attached to it was a memo from Murrow that read, "FYI. Here is a draft of what I am saying at the meeting of the Radio and Television News Directors in Chicago tonight." Copies had also gone out to the wire services and trade publications.

Mickelson read the speech with mounting horror. He rushed up to Stanton's office. Stanton was then in a meeting with Paley and several other company executives. Mickelson broke into the meeting.

What Paley read that afternoon, Murrow delivered that night to an audience of his peers at the Sheraton-Blackstone Hotel. His voice was firm, but his legs were trembling. "At the end of this discourse," he said, "a few people may accuse this reporter of fouling his own comfortable nest...[but] it is my desire, if not my duty, to try to talk to you journeymen with some candor about what is happening to radio and television....I am seized with an abiding fear regarding what these two instruments are doing to our society, our culture and our heritage. I invite your attention to the television schedules of all networks between the hours of 8 and 11 p.m. Eastern Time....Here you will find only fleeting and spasmodic reference to the fact that this nation is in mortal danger. There are, it is true, occasional informative programs presented in that intellectual ghetto on Sunday afternoons. But during the daily peak viewing periods, television, in the main, insulates us from the realities of the world in which we live....So far as radio—that most satisfying and rewarding instrument—is concerned, the diagnosis of its difficulties is rather easy....In order to progress, it need only go backward to the time when singing commercials were not allowed on news reports, when there was no middle commercial in a fifteen-minute news report, when radio was rather proud, alert and fast. I recently asked a network official, 'Why this great rash of five-minute news reports?' He replied, 'Because that seems to be the only thing we can sell.'...In this kind of complex and confusing world, you can't tell very much about the why of the news in broadcasts where only three minutes is available for news....The top management of the networks, with a few notable exceptions, has been trained in advertising, research, sales or show business. But by the nature of the corporate structure, they also make the final and crucial decisions having to do with news and public affairs. Frequently, they have neither the time nor the competence to do this.... Not so long ago the President of the United States delivered a television address to the nation. He was discoursing on the possibility or probability

of war between this nation and the Soviet Union and Communist China—
a reasonably compelling subject. Two networks, CBS and NBC, delayed
that broadcast for an hour and fifteen minutes. If this decision was dictated by anything other than financial reason, the networks didn't deign
to explain those reasons. That hour and fifteen minute delay, by the way,
is about twice the time required for an ICBM to travel from the Soviet
Union to major targets in the United States.... There is no suggestion here
that networks or individual stations should operate as philanthropies. But
I can find nothing in the Bill of Rights or the Communications Act which
says that they must increase their net profits each year, lest the Republic
collapse.... I am frightened by the imbalance, the constant striving to reach
the largest possible audience for everything; by the absence of a sustained
study of the state of the nation.... I would like television to produce some
itching pills rather than this endless outpouring of tranquilizers.... Let us
have a little competition. Not only in selling soap, cigarettes and automobiles, but in informing a troubled, apprehensive but receptive public. Why
should not each of the twenty or thirty big corporations which dominate
radio and television decide that they will give up one or two of their regularly scheduled programs each year, turn the time over to the networks
and say in effect: 'This is a tiny tithe, just a little bit of our profits. On this
particular night we aren't going to try to sell cigarettes or automobiles;
this is merely a gesture to indicate our belief in the importance of ideas.'
...Let us dream to the extent of saying that on a given Sunday night the
time normally occupied by Ed Sullivan is given over to a clinical survey of
the state of American education and a week or two later the time normally used by Steve Allen is devoted to American policy in the Middle
East.... Unless we get up off our fat surpluses and recognize that television in the main is being used to distract, delude, amuse and insulate us,
then television and those who finance it, those who look at it and those
who work at it, may see a totally different picture too late. I do not advocate that we turn television into a 27-inch wailing wall where longhairs
constantly moan about the state of our culture and our defense. But I
would just like to see it reflect occasionally the hard, unyielding realities
of the world in which we live.... This instrument can teach, it can illumi-
nate; yes, and it can even inspire. But it can do so only to the extent that
humans are determined to use it to those ends. Otherwise, it is merely
wires and lights in a box."

It was a scathing indictment rendered all the more devastating because it had been delivered, not by another carping social critic, but by
the most respected voice in the industry. Read on another level, the speech
is a remarkable piece of self-revelation. The essential Murrow is visible in
almost every line; a doomsday prophet who forever sees the world teetering on the edge of an abyss ("this nation is in mortal danger"); at the
same time, we see the skeptical idealist whose analysis is unerring, but
whose solution to the ills of television is astonishingly bland and safely

inside the bounds of the status quo. He does not propose a major over-haul of television, or a new structure for television, not public television or government financing of television to free it from dependence on commerce. Instead, he appeals to the conscience of big business. He asks sponsors to tithe themselves to support good works. The diagnosis had been far stronger than the prescription. Yet, unwittingly, he proved a man ahead of his time. While major corporate advertisers never did give up any of their regular programming on commercial networks for public affairs, their grants years later would become a mainstay of public television, which would produce much of the kind of television that Murrow preached.

Back in Paley's office, the cry was heresy. Dick Salant was there, working for Stanton at the time, doing the "odd jobs" that Joe Ream had once performed. "Paley," Salant recalled, "was furious. 'How could Ed do a thing like this after all I've done for him?' he kept saying. Ed was biting the hand that fed him. Ed *was* fouling his own nest."

As Paley himself later recalled that afternoon, "I made a very peculiar decision. I would never mention the speech to Ed. And I never did. I think my silence did more to impress him about the way I felt than if I had it out with him. Ed was bitter about the way he was being handled, and this was the way he got it off of his chest." Paley began this explanation to an interviewer with cool detachment. But as he went on, he became agitated, as though memory had torn open an old wound. His voice grew harsher. "I didn't want to know why he did it. I didn't want to discuss it. I didn't want to have a goddamned thing to do with it!"

As Salant, a discerning observer of the world in which he moved, read Paley's anger, "Bill Paley wanted to be number one in the ratings. He wanted to beat NBC. He wanted to show up Sarnoff. He wanted to make a lot of money. He also wanted to go down as the greatest broadcaster in history. Murrow's speech laid bare the contradictions."[19]

After he returned from delivering the speech, Murrow sagged visibly, as though he had emptied himself in Chicago. Friends found him chronically depressed, "beat from my youth" was the way he described himself. Blair Clark anchored another CBS newscast, and he and Ed often had a drink together before their broadcasts. Ed had once told Paley that Clark had "the best news judgment in CBS," words thereafter engraved in Clark's heart. Clark had known the later Murrow, and in all the years that Clark knew him, he remembered, "Ed seemed depressed the whole time. The energy level was not all that great. The flame was sputtering. He saw himself serving time."

At this low point, for one of the few times in his life, Ed turned to someone for help. He told Friendly that he was worried about himself. "He was suffering a combination of exhaustion, depression and frustration," Friendly said. "I sent him to see a doctor, a surgeon I respected very much. Not for surgery. Dr. Sam Standard was an older man, a father figure, a warm, marvelous man. I knew Ed could talk to him."

His health was suffering along with his spirits. Early in 1959, he was sitting in Studio 9 waiting to do the evening news. Ed Bliss watched from behind the plate glass in the control room. Murrow looked deathly pale. The script was shaking in his hand. With less than a minute before air time, he sprang up and bolted from the studio. He found Blair Clark in his cubicle and handed him the script. "Here, boy, you read it," he told Clark. "I can't."

Bliss followed Murrow into the hallway and watched him, shoulders bent, heading toward his office. Just outside, Ed folded his arms on the top of a filing cabinet and rested his head there. "His shoulders were heaving," Bliss recalled, "and he was sobbing like a child."

A doctor found a bronchospasm in Murrow's chest and feared that he may have had pulmonary emphysema. Ed went to the hospital for a battery of tests which uncovered nothing. Still, he was perpetually tired. "Ed's door was never closed before, even if a cabinet minister was in with him," Bliss noticed. "But now he had the door closed a half hour every day. He was supposed to be resting. But Ed just lay there and fumed and coughed."[20]

He saw Dr. Standard for several long visits and soon afterward told Friendly, "I'm going to take a year off. I'm going to take Janet and Casey on a trip around the world." His contract with CBS indeed allowed him a year's leave of absence, a sabbatical. He told Friendly that he intended to finish out the 1958–1959 season, leave the following summer, and be back by the summer of 1960.

When word leaked out that Murrow was planning a leave of absence, speculation in the industry was rife. Was he leaving television for good? Had he quit? Did CBS fire him? Was Murrow taking a leave of absence from CBS, or CBS from Murrow? Was he pushed, or did he jump? A visiting British lecturer hearing of the sabbatical said, "If we had Murrow in our country, we wouldn't permit his voice to be stilled. We'd put him in the House of Lords." Ed was astonished at the space the newspapers and magazines devoted to a reporter's temporary departure. The reaction itself was evidence of how deeply the medium had come to dominate the national consciousness. Those who reported the news on television had become news, as few print journalists ever had.

The last thing that CBS needed was to appear to have stilled the conscience of the network. And so it was arranged for Murrow and Stanton to set aside their personal animus and release to the press "Dear Frank" and "Dear Ed" letters in which Murrow formally requested the leave and Stanton granted it, adding, "We will all look forward to your return."[21]

Harry Reasoner, at the time with CBS television news, asked Murrow for an interview on the pending leave. In the studio, before the cameras rolled, Reasoner offered Murrow, "out of awe," something that he had never before given an interviewee. He asked Ed, "Would you like to know ahead of time what I'm going to ask you?" Murrow laughingly told him that it would be inappropriate: "That's your business."

Whereupon Reasoner proceeded to stun Murrow. As Reasoner later recalled the interview: "I asked him about the substance of his charges against television—that its programming was increasingly tawdry, that there seemed to be no room for thorough news programming, that it was, in effect, becoming a carnival. Then I asked him what he had done with his prestige and influence to change this? I asked him how he could criticize general entertainment programming and yet make a fortune from *Person to Person.*"

Murrow was clearly taken aback, but answered manfully if not satisfyingly. To Reasoner's point that *Person to Person* never achieved any depth, Murrow replied, "That is true to a very considerable extent." "Why was that the case?" Reasoner pressed on. "When you go into someone's home, at least I was brought up to believe, you do not start by asking a penetrating and embarrassing question."

Next, it was Reasoner's turn for surprises. After the interview aired, he began receiving phone calls and messages from people who wanted to know if the network had put him up to these questions in order to embarrass Murrow. Had he been made the tool of the network's money changers? Reasoner was sufficiently upset that he wrote Murrow hoping that Ed did not think he had "sold out to some vague anti-Murrow group." Murrow wrote back, "Anybody who agrees to sit in front of a camera for a free wheeling interview must expect to take what comes. I was mildly surprised by your line of questioning but sure as hell do not question your motives, harbor no resentment, have complained to no one and was due no explanation from you." Reasoner was much relieved, since, as he later said, "We all, in a professional and sentimental sense, walk in his shadow."[22]

That winter, Aarons and Zousmer managed to land a guest for *Person to Person* who promised something rather deeper than a house tour. The guest, at this point, did not yet have a home. He was staying in the Havana Hilton Hotel. He was Fidel Castro, fresh out of the Sierra Maestra and installed in power in Cuba only a month before. Landing the interview was a coup for *Person to Person.*

The debate had already begun about whether Castro was a knight in khaki who had rescued his country from the corrupt despot, Fulgencio Batista, or a clandestine Marxist. Only ten days before, his embryo regime had already been described in a CBS special broadcast as a "totalitarian dictatorship...rapidly becoming a Communist beachhead in the Caribbean." Castro had thus set one condition for the interview. Murrow was not to ask if he was a Communist.

Murrow, as was the custom on *Person to Person,* spoke from New York. Castro was in a suite in the hotel. His bearded corevolutionaries, packing pistols and rifles, milled around in front of the cameras. Johnny Aarons, who was the producer on the scene, suggested to Castro that he might make a better impression in American homes with a little less fire power in evidence. The troops were ordered out of camera range.

As the program opened, Castro was seen alone, sitting on a couch,

clad in ill-fitting pajamas looking uncomfortably as though the house detective had just caught him in an illicit union. Murrow asked him his first
question, "Tell me, Fidel Castro, are you concerned at all about Communist influence in Cuba?" Aarons blanched. Castro answered appealingly
in broken English, "Oh, I not worried because here not that amount Communism in Europe." Thereafter, the questions settled to the customary
Person to Person vapidity. Murrow asked if Castro's son, Fidelito, was with
him. On cue, an attractive little boy, clutching a puppy, came into view,
kissed his father, and presented Castro with the puppy as a gift.

Murrow asked Fidelito, "Do you have a dog of your own?" Then he
asked Castro, if he visited the United States, would it be "with the beard
or without it?" And "Were you as good-looking as your son when you
were his age?" Finally, as though he could stand it no longer, Murrow
asked Castro about the Batista aides whom Castro had executed after
drumhead trials. Castro answered, imploringly, "Our conditions now are
not normal. But you and all the people of the world can be sure, we are
just...."

Murrow asked Castro how he had obtained the arms and money to
carry out the revolution. Castro answered that he did not understand the
question. But after a translation, he answered that the money came from
Cubans of all classes and the arms "from enemy soldiers."

The program was awkward and contrived, justifying the gibes of the
harshest critics of *Person to Person*. But for Castro, it was an unmitigated
triumph. The leader, who in a sense was on trial in the court of American
public opinion, came across as the father of an adorable little boy, as a
lover of justice and puppies, and as an idealist who had faced unimaginable odds and lived to overthrow a sordid dictatorship. To Castro, something of a baseball player himself, Murrow had tossed tantalizing home-
run pitches for the most part, and the questions that did have an edge
were not followed up. To anyone reviewing an old kinescope of this performance with the clarity of hindsight, it is easy to see Murrow being manipulated by a clever demagogue. But in January of 1959, with Castro so
briefly in power, Murrow was not alone in his fear that American hostility
could drive the man into the arms of the Communists. He could not know
then that the man's soul was already there.[23]

In part, Murrow had been reduced to *Person to Person* and *Small World*
on television because the quiz shows had created an environment of profit
in which a program like *See It Now* could not survive. The shows became
a form of mass madness. On a single day, five new quiz shows debuted.
Lou Cowan, who started it all with *The $64,000 Question*, followed by *The
$64,000 Challenge*, imitated on other networks by *The Big Surprise, Twenty-
One,* and a dozen others, was so esteemed for his vision that he was named
president of the entire CBS Television Network. Cowan was now responsible not simply for entertainment, but for everything on the network,
including news and public affairs.

And then, one day, a Las Vegas chorus girl, billed as an astronomy expert on NBC's *The Big Surprise* (top prize, $100,000), sued the network. The young lady claimed that she had been dropped from the show for flunking a question in "rehearsal." Later, a contestant on *Dotto,* a CBS show, was waiting in the wings for his turn, watching a woman contestant then being asked a question worth $4,000. On her way on stage, she had dropped a notebook and the waiting contestant had picked it up. Thumbing through the notebook, he was stunned to find that the question the woman was answering at that instant was in it. Bill Golden, CBS's advertising chief, suggested confidentially that Murrow and Friendly take a look at the quiz shows. There might be, Golden told them, a story in it. Golden suspected that the shows were rigged.

Within months, the whole sordid empire of avarice began to collapse. Congress investigated. The prize exhibit of the quiz craze, the heir to one of the great literary names in America, a bookish, sensitive Columbia University instructor who had amassed $129,000 on NBC's *Twenty-One,* confessed. It had all been a fraud. From his very first appearance on the program, Charles Van Doren admitted that he had been coached so that he could dump a less appealing contestant, named Herbert Stempel, who had earlier been coached himself. The tin age of the quiz show was over. And the networks that battened on them were badly tarnished.[24]

In that spring of shame, Frank Stanton was invited to address his alma mater, Ohio State. He chose the occasion, May 6, 1959, to restore the good name of CBS with the most statesmanlike speech of his career. Stanton announced a new era. "Next year," he promised, "the CBS Television Network is scheduling regular hour long broadcasts once a month in prime time. We will report in depth on significant issues, events, and personalities in the news. In the following year, we propose to make this a bi-weekly and after that a weekly program...." Murrow, it seemed, was redeemed. The network had seen the folly of its ways. *See It Now,* or its moral equivalent, was coming back.[25]

But Fred Friendly had noticed something strange since the Pillion affair in Paley's office and the subsequent death of *See It Now.* Paley and Stanton "would talk to me more than Ed. It was embarrassing." Indeed, Murrow's name was nowhere heard in the executive reaches of the network following Stanton's Ohio proposal for reports "in depth" on significant issues.

Sig Mickelson had suffered Murrow's slights almost from the moment he had joined the network. For if, in Murrow's eyes, Frank Stanton represented the enemy, then Mickelson was the enemy's henchman for news and public affairs. Not necessarily a reasoned judgment, but a convenient one. For Mickelson, there were no Murrow invitations to lunch at the Century Club, no endearing nicknames, only disregard for Mickelson's authority in the news department and criticism of his performance. The dynamics of the relationship were well illustrated in an exchange of memos concerning a CBS television report on the World War II bombing of Schweinfurt. Murrow had had no part in the broadcast on "his war" and fired off a curt memo to Mickelson challenging the accuracy of the report. He offered no proof other than saying, in effect, "I was there. What could you know about it?" Whereupon Mickelson prepared a factual rebuttal defending the story, with copies scattered all over the network. Whereupon Stanton sent Mickelson a warm, handwritten note complimenting him on his handling of the matter.[26]

Sometime late in the spring of 1959, Mickelson was called in to Stanton's office to discuss who should produce the public affairs series Stanton had promised in his Ohio speech. Mickelson had his candidate, and he was surprised at how readily Stanton agreed.

Stanton also had a name in mind for the series. During *See It Now*'s heyday, the impression had somehow taken hold that the program was a thing apart, Murrow's property, with CBS an incidental air lane. The new series' parentage was to be made clear, Stanton said. It was to be called *CBS Reports*.

Friendly tells in his memoir of his CBS years that the Murrow-Friendly fortunes were so bleak at this point that when Mickelson asked him to interrupt his vacation and come in for a talk, "I examined my contract to find out when my next option could be dropped."

Instead, Mickelson offered him the position of executive producer for *CBS Reports*.

Friendly's response was, "I assume that this offer is made to the Friendly-Murrow unit." No, Mickelson said, the offer was being made to Fred Friendly. However, he could use whomever he wanted among the galaxy of CBS correspondents to anchor the program. Howard K. Smith was Mickelson's choice. Murrow could be used occasionally too. But *CBS Reports* was definitely not to be Murrow's vehicle, a point that he tried to make without too much obvious gloating. Mickelson also made the point that Murrow was not in good health, and he would soon be going off on his sabbatical anyway.

Friendly was too confused by the offer to answer immediately. Mickelson told him to take his time, but to consider the opportunity carefully.

Fred Friendly now faced "the hardest decision of my life." He went to see Murrow. If there was a single moment when Ed had to know that his marriage to CBS had finally failed, this was it. The captain in gleaming dress whites on the bridge had been rejected in favor of the sweat-streaked chief down in the engine room. If Murrow was shocked, angered, or hurt by the blow, he revealed little. As Friendly recalled his mood, Ed was "wistful."

Friendly asked what he should do. Ed said simply, "You ought to do it if they'll give you authority and leave you alone."

Friendly was torn. Howard K. Smith remembered Fred telling him at the time, "I will never take part in anything that goes against Murrow." Friendly prided himself not simply on his partnership with Murrow, but on his capacity virtually to disappear into Murrow's ego, "to see with Ed's eyes, to hear with his ears, to write with his fingers." He could still hear the delicious music of the time he had phoned Murrow in the midst of an interview and heard Murrow tell the reporter as he took the call, "That's my self-propelled man. We've been writing together so long now and re-writing each other that at times we don't know who wrote which lines."

Now he was being asked, in effect, to bump Murrow. Fred Friendly, for all his massive abilities, for all his monumental achievement, was an insecure man. What surer proof of his arrival at last than to be chosen over the master he idolized? And how more surely to be made to feel the ingrate than to leave Murrow behind? He was later to say that had it been the other way around, had the network offered Murrow *CBS Reports* mi-nus Friendly, that "Ed would have told them to stick it." But it had not been the other way around. Murrow told him, "Fred, you've got to do it, or it will fail." At the time, Fred answered, "I can't do it." He was to won-der "for the rest of my life," he later admitted, "if I meant it or not. I'm willing to have people judge me very harshly on that." In the end, he did accept.[27]

With word of the new series out, with Ed leaving the country for his sabbatical, and with knowledge that Friendly had the pick of the talent, the race was on at CBS for "the next Murrow."

Ed had already made known his choice. Friendly agreed. The man Murrow saw as his spiritual heir was Charles Collingwood, Bonnie Prince Charley. It was the grand total of the man's qualities that had always im-pressed Murrow, the marvelous Collingwood presence, the insightful anal-ysis, the graceful prose all resting on a classical education in history, politics, and philosophy. "Friendly told me," Collingwood later remarked, "that he'd made Ed Murrow and he could make Charles Collingwood."

The opportunity to become the next Murrow had come easily to Collingwood, too easily. Everything came too easily to Charles Colling-wood. Being able to achieve so much so effortlessly, he lacked the virus of consuming ambition. "I was something of a coward not to take on *CBS Reports,*" he was to remark long years afterward. "I was just not that driven." He was, as well as a superb broadcaster, a pursuer of the good life. He had served a CBS stint in Hollywood, married a beautiful actress, Louise Allbritton, and collected paintings and other fine things. As Seva-reid observed, "He put so much of his energy and talent into building a beautiful life that there was not enough left for his work."[28]

Instead of launching the next Murrow, *CBS Reports* was to be rotated among different correspondents. The first broadcast, "Biography of a Missile," would not air until the following fall when Ed would be away. But Friendly was determined that the first in the series must reunite the old team. Murrow and Friendly were to complete it before Ed's depar-ture.[29]

It was like old times again, except that now Ed Murrow was working for Fred Friendly.

CHAPTER 29

Leave of Absence

Early summer of 1959 was a time for tying up loose ends and cutting off stray ends before the sabbatical. Ed's motives for wanting to go away were mixed. Above all, he was burned out. He was suffering the deep fatigue of the soul that comes of fighting losing battles. He needed time to let the body rest and the soul heal. Then, renewed and healthy, he imagined he could come back and plan his future.

He maintained a frenzied pace right to the last minute. He and Friendly had gone on location for the first broadcast of *CBS Reports,* pursuing the fate of Explorer VI in the "Biography of a Missile." The launch vehicle, a Jupiter II rocket, blew up on the launch pad, consuming $5 million and eighteen months of work in six seconds and hurling flaming debris close enough to satisfy Murrow's love of danger. He also stockpiled five *Small World* broadcasts and continued with the nightly news and *Person to Person* before he left. *Person to Person* was one of the stray ends, rather a golden thread, that was about to be cut. After this season, he was finished with it. To his surprise, and disappointment, Collingwood, who turned down *CBS Reports,* was eager to inherit *Person to Person.* Collingwood was living the high life, trying futilely to keep up with Hollywood and society friends with five times his income. "I hankered after *Person to Person,*" he admitted. "It was a lucrative show, no heavy lifting, and I needed the money."

On the night of June 26, a Friday, Ed made his last newscast before the sabbatical. He used the occasion to end the wilder speculation about his leaving. "Tonight," he said, "this reporter departs this microphone for a year's leave of absence—a departure which has been rather overpublicized. Permit me a few words of personal explanation, I haven't been fired, haven't quit, my health is all right. For many years there has been

442

a clause in my long-term contract with CBS permitting me to take a year off. I asked for the year off, and the corporation granted it."[1]

He then went over to Studio 41 for his farewell broadcast of *Person to Person*. The show had been a phenomenal financial success, consistently drawing audiences of 15 and 20 million people who enjoyed watching Ed Murrow exchange pleasantries with their presumed betters. On the night he visited Elizabeth Taylor and Mike Todd, 36 million people, 22.7 percent of the entire population of the United States, watched. Through the years the show had made the Murrow countenance, enshrined in smoke and framed on a screen, a totem of the American pop scene, endlessly satirized and caricatured in cartoons, as stylized and familiar as a face on Mount Rushmore. The last two guests, actress Lee Remick and Hugh Baillie of the United Press, brought the total to 500 over six years. Baillie particularly had Murrow's gratitude. His UP provided an unintended farm system for Ed over the years, yielding up a half dozen of Murrow's Boys.

Ed had continued to defend *Person to Person* in public. He told Cleveland Amory, "If for every million people who watched a Hollywood star, I got one kid to practice the piano or violin a little harder—and try to be a Van Cliburn or Menuhin—then I feel the program was a success." Nevertheless, he was ditching it without a qualm.[2]

When he finished *Person to Person* that Friday night, he had to stop by Frank Stanton's office to tie up a few matters. In spite of the lateness of the hour, Stanton was in. He was always in. The man's appetite for work was legendary. Friendly once observed, "In two years, I never saw him take a day off, including Saturdays and Sundays." The man's life and his work appeared indistinguishable. Richard Salant observed of the childless Stantons, "They lavished their love and affection on a wire-haired airedale. Frank would bring it to the office on Saturdays. He took the dog to a psychiatrist."

Ed Murrow's attitude toward Stanton was an aberration. Blair Clark once remarked of Murrow, "His observations of people were rare, but acute." Stanton was the exception to the rule. Murrow referred to Stanton variously as "the foe," "a guy who knows which end of the horse he can play," "a man with a calculator for a mind," "a man with a computer instead of a heart." Frank Stanton had become an obsession.

After the *See It Now* broadcast on Danny Kaye's UNICEF tour, Murrow and Friendly had thrown a memorable party at Toots Shor's for Kaye and others who had appeared on the series over the years. Bill Paley and his wife were also there, even the CBS advertising director, Bill Golden. The president of CBS, Frank Stanton, was pointedly uninvited.

Murrow needed an embodiment of his quarrel with the network, a live target against which he could hurl his frustrations. He was incapable of making Paley the author of his unhappiness, even when merited. And so Stanton was assigned the role. "As the corporation grew and became more complicated, Paley had to have a Stanton," Eric Sevareid observed of the situation. "Before that, Ed and Bill had been close in making decisions. Then it became Paley and Stanton. I think this was the root of the problem between Ed and Frank." Collingwood put it more bluntly: "Part of Stanton's job was to do Paley's dirty work. Ed could not accept that." The dirty work had to be Stanton's doing.

Ironically, most of those who worshiped Murrow, his Boys, also admired Frank Stanton. "He was a staunch supporter of CBS News," Collingwood said. Howard K. Smith found Stanton a "supporter of Murrow and the news operation." In Sevareid's recollection, "Frank Stanton never tried to use any knives on Ed that I know of." Murrow remained adamant and almost alone in his antipathy. He disliked Frank Stanton intensely, and, rare for Murrow, vocally.

As for the workaholic with the computer for a heart, he had a secret side. Alexander Kendrick, when he was the CBS London correspondent, remembered, "Stanton at least twice showed up and asked me out to lunch. I was surprised that he seemed to have nothing on his mind. He didn't press me for anything. Only in casual conversation did it come out that the trip had nothing to do with CBS. He'd come to England to see the sculptor, Henry Moore."

When asked, Frank Stanton would say he "liked Ed Murrow," and given half a chance, he probably would have. Stanton's quarrel with Murrow was professional, not personal. Stanton was a man whose mind craved order and rationality. He was paid to impose these qualities on a sprawling and complex enterprise. Stanton was the chief executive of the corporation. Why should Murrow circumvent him? Stanton ran a conglomerate of diverse components. Why did Murrow behave as though only his piece existed? CBS had a policy of objectivity in the news. Why should Murrow be exempt from it? Stanton carried out Paley's wishes. Why was he, and not Paley, the back end of the horse?

That evening, after Ed and Stanton settled their business, Stanton made a rare gesture. He invited Ed back to his apartment for a drink. It may have been that both men looked on the sabbatical as a cease-fire, an end, at least temporarily, to having to contest each other. In any case, Ed accepted. They talked into the morning hours and finished off a bottle of Stanton's whiskey. "We settled all the problems of the world," Stanton remembered. It was as it should have been long before between two articulate men with curious, wide-ranging minds, who had grown up in the same company and loved broadcasting. On this night, it seemed that it could be different when Murrow returned; they could start again with a clean slate. Or maybe they had only been able to let their guard down temporarily, knowing that, for the next year, they would not be competing for Paley's favor.[3]

In July, Ed took a curious step. He applied for a commission in the Naval Reserve. He was 51 years old. He failed the first physical because he was erroneously given the examination for young recruits. He was eventually commissioned a commander in public information, the billet he had scorned during the war. He was close-mouthed about his motive. Even Friendly was not sure why he did it except that, "Ed always loved the military." The Reserve commission appears to have been an act of mutual self-interest. The commission would get him into parts of the new nuclear Navy faster than a press pass alone. And the Navy's public relations chief, Admiral Charles Kirkpatrick, believed that Commander Murrow "was even more advantageous to us than to himself. Murrow looked good for the Navy."[4]

The time for his leave of absence was fast approaching, a leave that the company had granted with unflattering speed. Nothing had been firmly settled about his future on his return. He was, in effect, taking off with no knowledge of where he was to land. Friendly, in their curious reversal of roles, was lobbying mightily for him. As Ed was about to begin the leave, Friendly arranged a literal eleventh-hour meeting for them with Stanton. For the next two hours, they hammered out a memorandum of agreement. Under it, Friendly was to be the executive producer of *CBS Reports* for the first year. The future arrangement would be decided after Murrow returned. Friendly left the meeting convinced that "reason and conciliation had prevailed." When Murrow came back, he expected that Ed would be his full partner in producing *CBS Reports* "automatically."

If anyone was aware of Murrow's physical and emotional exhaustion, it was Friendly. Still, his own indefatigable energy may have affected his judgment. He persuaded Ed to continue the weekly broadcasts of *Small World* during the sabbatical. The premise of the program was that people could be brought together electronically no matter where they were, and so Ed's travels presumably posed no obstacle. The sponsors would not accept anyone but Murrow as host. If the program went off the air, people would be out of work. The latter argument was one to which Murrow could never say no. He agreed to continue *Small World* as he traveled around the world.[5]

On August 26, Ed, Janet, and Casey boarded the Swedish American Line's *Gripsholm*, 631 feet long, carrying 842 passengers, a two-year-old namesake of the famous ancestor of the war era. Ed's Thunderbird was stowed in the hold. As the liner slipped from the dock, the Hetzels from Quaker Hill, Kay Campbell, Blair Clark, Larry Le Sueur, the Warburgs, and other friends waved from the shore, while the ship's band played "Over There."

The Murrows had taken two first-class cabins. Casey and Janet were to occupy one and Ed the other, since his cabin would be full of smoke all day and the grinding of his teeth all night. "I'll bet I inhaled more cigarette smoke than any 13-year-old kid in the country," Casey Murrow once observed.

Ed's mood as the voyage of renewal began, Janet remembered, was "nervous, jittery and despairing." The ship was soon enshrouded in fog, an apt metaphor for his state of mind. He rarely emerged from his cabin except for meals. He was a famous face seeking an impossible anonymity in the limited confines of a ship. And so he stayed alone.

The pace that the leave of absence was to take was set virtually the instant the *Gripsholm* docked in Göteborg, Sweden. As Ed came down the gangway at five o'clock in the morning, he was mobbed by Swedish journalists, radio reporters, and television cameramen.

The ship had lost a day crossing the Atlantic, and so Ed drove the T-Bird to Stockholm at breakneck speed to make a reception that the Swedish government was holding in his honor. To save time, he cut out a planned visit to the country place from which Janet's Grandfather Johnson emigrated to America. In Stockholm, Ed was swept up in an endless round of appointments. He met with the army chief of staff, and a parade of interviewers. Finally, as Casey recorded in his diary, "Dad (unhappy tourist) Mom and I started on a water tour of Stockholm."[6]

They drove on to Norway and Copenhagen, where Ed checked in by telephone with Friendly. He told a disbelieving Janet and Casey that he had to leave them at once. He had to go to Iran. He had originally been scheduled to interview the Shah in the fall for *CBS Reports*, but it had to be done immediately. It was as if he had been asked to weigh his need for a long rest against the insecurity that he felt at being away from the action. And insecurity had won.

Ed flew to Teheran, while Janet and Casey went to Switzerland to enroll an unhappy Casey in the Aiglon international boarding school near Zurich, where he was to stay until Christmas.[7]

Winston Burdett was CBS's man on the scene in Teheran. He later described the encounter of the heir to the peacock throne and the broadcaster: "When the cameramen had done with their arrangements, Murrow came in to be received by the Shah and as the two men faced each other on this little stage, in which all the pomp and panoply were on the Shah's side, I had the impression that it was the Shah who was meeting Murrow, and not Murrow being presented to the Shah. It was as though Murrow and not Reza Pahlavi were carrying the sword. The Shah himself it seemed, felt this.... Murrow's questions had a way of startling his interviewee and, indeed, they startled me, for they were questions I would never have thought of. I can recall only two of them. 'Your majesty,' Murrow said, 'during my two days in your country I have heard much criticism of you by your subjects.' (The Shah stiffened.) 'They say that you ride too hard, drive too fast, and fly too low.' (Relieved, the Shah expatiated freely on the amiable subject of his pastimes.) Then followed: 'On entering your palace I was impressed by the size of your bodyguard.... Are you afraid of assassination?' It was a lively and illuminating battle of wits, close sparring all the way."

As part of a briefing by the American Embassy, Murrow had been shown a film produced by Burnett Anderson of the U.S. Information

Agency that portrayed Iran as a crucial American ally. "Murrow kidded me unmercifully about 'that lying film,'" Anderson recalled. "Of course, he was proved right later."[8]

Ed and Janet were reunited in London, where they anticipated at long last a leisurely rest among old friends. So it was, briefly. They checked into the Connaught and spent some two weeks attending dinner parties and visiting the country homes they had known in their comparative youth. In the meantime, Ed worked on a speech he was to deliver in the Guildhall in mid-October on the influence of television on politics. After delivering the speech, he went to Manchester to do a film version of it for Granada TV. While he was there, he received a transatlantic telephone call from a much agitated Johnny Aarons and Jesse Zousmer.[9]

A year had passed since Ed had savaged the merchant princes of television with his speech before the Radio and Television News Directors in Chicago. With a nice sense of counterpoint, the news directors had invited Frank Stanton to address their annual convention this year.

Stanton had taken the opportunity to lift his network from the muck of scandal. By now the fraudulence of the quiz shows had been thoroughly exposed. Charles Van Doren and thirteen other contestants were about to be arrested for perjury. At the news director's speech in New Orleans, Stanton manfully accepted that the networks had been mistaken to make greed a chief ingredient of their schedules. He confessed that the networks, while not directly implicated in the rigged shows, had clearly been negligent. But he assured his listeners that CBS was clearing out any residual "hanky-panky" from its offerings. In the future, he promised, viewers would know that "what they see and hear on CBS is exactly what it purports to be."

And then a curious thing happened. Kidder Meade, CBS's public relations man, called Jack Gould, *The New York Times* television critic. The gist of the call was that Stanton might have something more to say about his New Orleans theme. Meade told Gould where he could reach Stanton in Texas. Gould called Stanton and wanted to know: What sort of hanky-panky was Stanton referring to? Stanton explained that he had meant such devices as canned applause and laugh tracks. He was also, Stanton said, talking about supposedly spontaneous interview shows that were actually rehearsed. Gould leaped at the bait. Could Dr. Stanton mean *Person to Person?* He did.

Gould's story appeared on page one of *The New York Times* under a headline, "CBS Revises Policy to End Program 'Deceits.'" "...*Person to Person,* which featured Edward R. Murrow last season and which now stars Charles Collingwood," the story read, "endeavored to create the illusion that it was spontaneous. In actuality, [Stanton] said guests have known in advance the questions that would be asked."

A night spent killing a bottle of whiskey with Murrow had apparently not mollified Frank Stanton. After years of playing the heavy to Murrow's stainless hero, Stanton, when asked about CBS's feet of clay, chose to hold up Murrow's. Asked later why he had chosen *Person to Person* to criticize in his interview with Gould, he said, "It bothered me to have the leading journalist on our network playing that kind of game. There were two Ed Murrows, you know. There was the journalist Murrow and the grease paint Murrow. When I pricked him for giving the *Person to Person* questions out in advance to make the show look spontaneous, he did not like it. He overreacted."

It was the Jack Gould story that had prompted Aarons and Zousmer to call Ed in London. Stanton had dumped them—and Murrow—into the same trash can with the people who rigged quiz shows. They were outraged. They wanted Ed to issue a statement rebutting Stanton to clear all their names.[10]

For a man of Murrow's thinly suppressed temper—Wershba once described the man's anger as "a terrible thing to behold"—he did not overreact to Stanton or react at all, not immediately. He had again worked himself into a frantic schedule. He was in the midst of doing *Small World* with Senator John F. Kennedy, Krishna Menon, and Lord Boothby. He was working on the Granada TV version of the Guildhall speech. He was filming still another broadcast for the BBC. He had imported Kay Campbell and wrote Jim Seward, "Neither of us has worked harder since the war days." The "sabbatical" was being made a mockery. He was also deluged with calls from reporters in America wanting his response to Stanton's remarks. Still, he kept his counsel.

Not only was he busy; there was another reason for his silence. He fully expected an official repudiation, at least a clarification, by the network of Stanton's statements. Surely, Stanton's offensive, off-hand remarks would not be left to stand as the last word. Certainly, Paley would come to his defense. But days passed. The reporters continued to badger him. And he heard nothing.

Four days after the Gould story appeared, Eric Sevareid was in the CBS London office when Murrow came in and dropped a cable on his desk. As Sevareid read it, he said, "Ed, you can't send this." Murrow answered, "I already have."[11]

On Sunday morning, October 25, Frank Stanton opened his *New York Times* to a front-page story headlined, "Murrow Says Stanton Criticism Shows Ignorance of TV Method." The story quoted Murrow's cable: "Dr. Frank Stanton has finally revealed his ignorance of both news and the requirements of production....He suggests that *Person to Person*, the program that I was associated with for six years, was not what it purported to be. Surely Stanton must know that cameras, lights and microphones do not just wander around a home. Producers must know who is going where and when for how long. They must know whether the individual will require twenty seconds or two minutes to answer a question. The alternative to a degree of rehearsal would be chaos. I am sorry Dr. Stanton feels that I have participated in perpetrating a fraud upon the public. My conscience is clear. His seems to be bothering him."[12]

If anyone was more furious than Stanton or Murrow over this public fight, it was Bill Paley. He had spent his life working to build an enterprise that performed a public service, entertained millions, earned money, and had made him a statesman in his industry. And now he picked up his paper to read about brickbats hurled across the Atlantic between his company's president and its brightest star.

Paley called in Stanton; his lawyer, Ralph Colin; and a public relations expert to consider how to defuse the situation and get the Stanton-Murrow row off the front pages. What Stanton had told Gould about Murrow, Paley said, was "off-base. But it wasn't a very serious thing." Murrow's reply, on the other hand, was unpardonable. It simply could not stand unchallenged. Paley wanted an apology from Murrow, one that could be issued to the press.

Ed Murrow and Ralph Colin had enjoyed something of a friendship through the years, visiting each other's homes and having occasional lunches at the Century Club. Colin was a small, sharp-featured, sharp-minded man of many parts, a founder of the Provincetown Players, a patron of the arts, and a collector of Impressionist paintings. He saw himself as a natural bridge between Paley and Murrow and volunteered to go to London. As Paley later recalled the day, Colin said, "I'll calm Ed down in no time flat."

Stanton was pessimistic: "I was not in favor of trying to get a statement from Ed because I knew he wouldn't be satisfied with anything that cast him in less than the superior role. That was the nature of Ed Murrow."

Colin was nevertheless optimistic. At nine o'clock that evening, he was on the London plane.[13]

After Ed had dispatched the cable attacking Stanton, he and Janet went to visit the Churchills. Four years before, after Churchill had left office as prime minister for the second time, Murrow had tried to get him to accept an offer of $100,000 for a five-part interview. The deal had fallen through. When he saw Churchill again this time at his home in Chartwell, Ed knew it was too late. The leader whom he once described as "perhaps the most considerable man to walk the stage of history in our time," a man for whom England was "never a large enough stage for him to play upon," had at last been defeated by time. He was in his eighty-fifth year, almost deaf, speaking little and with great difficulty, looking like a sagging pillow, the formidable spirit gone."[14]

After the visit to Chartwell, the Murrows had gone back to London for a party in their honor given by Thelma Cazalet-Keir. It was one of their best evenings since the leave began. Ed had been completely relaxed. He and Janet did not get back to the Connaught until the early hours. They planned to sleep late and have a champagne breakfast served in their room, since it was October 27, their twenty-fifth wedding anniversary. But there was a message waiting for Ed at the desk. Ralph Colin would be arriving within hours.

A sleepless and rumpled Colin went directly from his flight to the Connaught. Janet was not pleased, but she managed to remain graciously resigned. Colin found Murrow feisty. He told Ed, "It's not a good idea for two members of a company to be slamming each other in public, no matter where the merits lie." That was fine with him, Ed said. But he had not started the fight. Colin sensed that he was in for a long day. Whenever he mentioned Stanton's name, he remembered, "I could see Ed bristle."

He asked for some hotel stationery, and he and Ed settled down in the sitting room where Colin tried to draft a statement acceptable to all parties. "I knew, if I could come back with an apology," Colin recalled, "then that would be the end of it."

As a shrewd negotiator, Colin started out with a strong apology, but was prepared to back down—"Mr. Murrow's remarks were perhaps unduly vitriolic. Mr. Murrow not only applauds and vigorously supports, but has previously advocated the CBS basic policy of assuming responsibility for what appears on the network." Murrow rejected this naked surrender, and Colin backed off to the next level of contrition. He continued backing down, as the day wore on. Finally, at six o'clock, he took the best that he was able to wrest from Murrow and retired to Claridges, where at this late date, the only room available to him was in the servants' quarters. He called Paley and Stanton in New York from the hotel and read them the draft. It was utterly unacceptable. Its concluding phrase—"No suggestion was intended that either Mr. Murrow or his associates had been lacking in integrity in the past production of *Person to Person*"—virtually had Stanton apologizing to Murrow instead of Murrow to Stanton. As Fred Friendly later analyzed the antagonists at this point, "If it hadn't been for the weak position the network was in because of the quiz scandals, they would have dumped Murrow."

The Colin mission had failed. At the heart of the matter was that Stanton had wounded Murrow where he was proudest. If Ed Murrow believed one thing about himself, it was that he was a man of integrity. Stanton had questioned his integrity on the front page of *The New York Times*. As Colin told Paley when he returned to New York, "He'll never forgive Stanton for what he said."[15]

Ed and Janet slipped into the Cotswolds to escape this latest storm. At the end of November, they left England and motored through France to Switzerland, where they picked up Casey, happily sprung from the dreary Aiglon school.

In January, they left Switzerland for Italy. Ed decided to see what the T-Bird could do on a four-lane stretch of the *Autostrada* south of Milan. He pushed the car up to ninety miles an hour, then 100, then 105. The next day, he was doing 70 in a sleet storm on a narrow, two-lane road lined with pines between Florence and Rome, when he had a blowout. He struggled to keep the car under control and finally managed to bring it to a halt. "The Thunderbird held the road remarkably," he observed quietly. Janet was shaken and annoyed over his hot-rod antics.[16]

They sailed out of Naples on January 25 aboard the *Theodore Hertzl,* bound for Haifa. They were met on their arrival by a horde of press. Ed wrote Jim Seward that he was "being driven mad by well-meaning Hebrews who want lectures, interviews, articles, etc." He continued doing *Small World,* seven broadcasts from England, two from Switzerland, five from Italy. He interviewed Golda Meir, then Israel's foreign minister, for a pilot for a new program that Friendly wanted to produce. And he was hatching a new idea of his own. Werner Keller's *The Bible as History* had fired his imagination. Ed wrote Seward while still in Switzerland, "Am all steamed up about the possibility of doing a biblical series in modern dress...shot on the ground with someone like Glueck as guide and narrator." He was being practical, too, he said. He saw in the Bible the potential for a "truly great and *profitable* series."

Their arrival in Israel quickened his interest in the idea. The family toured the ruins of Hazor, destroyed by Joshua. They visited Megiddo, the presumed inspiration of Armageddon. They walked through the settlement's 2,000-year-old tunnels, while overhead the shriek of Israeli Mystere jet fighters split the sky. Back in Jerusalem, Ed met with a biblical scholar, Professor Yadin, to discuss a pilot program on the Bible.

There was a duality in his mood as they wound their way around the world. Janet was enjoying the journey, in spite of suffering a spate of bad colds, along with bouts of bursitis and rheumatism. Casey relished the longest uninterrupted attentions of his father thus far in his life. Janet had the sense that "Ed relaxed more as time went on." But the situation back in New York was never far from his mind. Jim Seward had emerged as Ed's chief confidante in absentia, and Ed had written Seward from Switzerland, "I do hope Stanton will not persist in his provocation about interview shows...for if he does I shall have to come back and have it out in public....have heard nothing from him or any of his colleagues on the twentieth floor....I am still determined that if there is a break they must fire me....after all they hired my services...not my silence." From Rome he had written Seward, "This leave just isn't working out. I can neither sleep nor relax. The complete exhaustion is worse than when we left. It's rather discouraging. Maybe things will improve with a bit of sunshine."

"I am tired beyond endurance," he wrote Seward from Israel, "and wish myself in some place but know not where...." He also told Seward that the trip was becoming expensive. He had cashed checks for over $10,000 and charged nearly another $5,000 for travel expenses.[17]

The T-Bird was shipped back from Israel, and the Murrows' odyssey continued by air to India, where Janet was sick and then Casey and then Ed, laid low by "Delhi belly." He was weary of being recognized and pestered by British and American tourists wherever they went. Virtually the only time he wrote in a positive vein was about the work he planned when he got back. From India he mailed Friendly an outline for the prospective Bible series, adding, "Believe me, that one will educate our grandchildren...and give us something to be proud of...also, it is something television needs at this juncture in its sordid history."[18]

He had talked vaguely of writing during the sabbatical. Blanche Knopf had pleaded with him for twenty years to write his memoirs. Another friend once asked him what had actually happened on that night of Pearl Harbor at the White House. "I expect to send Casey through college with that kind of material," he answered.

His most sustained prose effort thus far was a handful of articles and some book reviews, mostly about the war, one reviewing a book on Dunkirk for *The New York Times,* another reviewing Churchill's memoirs for the *Atlantic Monthly.* He told an interviewer, "It ain't false modesty to say I don't know enough to write a book. I can write the language of speech, but that's totally different. When I write a book review or a preface to somebody else's book, Janet has to go through it and scatter the commas." He still wrote with his ear. When he wrote to be read, the product was fairly mundane except for patches that leaped from the page because they had the vividness of speech. Whether on the sabbatical or afterward, he never wrote anything longer than a few pages.[19]

Seward kept him abreast of developments at home with a steady flow of newsclips and magazine articles. One pouch contained a speech that Stanton had delivered before an advertising association. After the congressional investigations of the quiz scandals, Stanton feared that the government might try to intrude itself into television programming, and he used the speech to warn against this evil. "Any control at all is repugnant to all our values," he said. "A society that sees one more Indian bite the dust on television is far safer than a society that sees one iota of its freedom given up to government." Commercial television, Stanton also made clear, had become an engine of national prosperity: "All of us here also have a special stake in a free television because we are all devoted to a free and expanding economy. The stimulative effect of television on that economy has been tremendous."

Murrow did not favor government interference in television programming any more than Stanton. But he read Stanton's words as a clever diversion of attention from the real issue. What had the networks done with the precious freedom they already possessed, except to kill his *See It Now* and pursue the greatest profits through the largest audiences? And Stanton's perception of television as an electronic pushcart appalled Murrow. He did not care what television did for sales; it was what it did to people that concerned him. He wrote Seward from Hong Kong, "As you know, I am in basic agreement with what Stanton is trying to do, but his last speech made me want to vomit."[20]

The travelers moved on to Japan. The stream of letters to Seward continued like a tether to a world from which Ed could never entirely free himself. Apart from Ralph Colin's visit, he had heard nothing official from the network about his status. He wrote Seward, "Unless I hear from someone in authority at CBS, I am likely to say that the last contact I had with the company was when they sent a man to London to tell me I was fired...and later I was told on the phone that they couldn't quite figure out a way to do it...."

Toward the end of the journey it seemed as if even the faithful Seward did not understand him. Seward sent Ed a letter suggesting how he might go about apologizing to Stanton. If reporters asked, Seward said, "You might say that you may well have been overcritical regarding Jack Gould's telephone interview with Stanton." Ed wrote Seward that if reporters asked, he would say, "I can think of nothing less important than what Dr. Stanton thinks of me, unless it's what I think of him."

The journey around the world took them next to Honolulu and then to Washington State for a visit with the family. Ed was back in New York on May 6, almost two months before his sabbatical was due to end.[21]

He had made this voyage to purge himself of bitterness, fatigue, and frustration, to nourish his body and spirit and return renewed. But the character had been molded and hardened long before. When he tried to relax, he felt guilty that he was not working. And when he worked, he exhausted himself and got no relaxation. As a boy, the enforced idleness of a single Quaker Sunday had left him restless. A year of self-indulgence was completely beyond him. To abandon himself even to therapeutic inactivity was not in him. He had often told his friends that he had not learned how to play as a child. He was not about to learn as a man.

Fred Friendly met Ed on his arrival. Friendly was full of ideas about the upcoming schedule of *CBS Reports*. Ed had been unavailable for the last seven broadcasts. But Friendly expected him to be heavily involved now. He assumed that Ed would anchor the series. That was the welcome news. But there had been another casualty. The sponsors of *Small World* preferred to switch their investment to the more resounding *CBS Reports*. The network had made no effort to find another sponsor. *Small World* was dead. Nor had there been any movement on the idea for the biblical series. Ed Murrow had returned to television without a program that he could call his own.[22]

CHAPTER 30

"Some Part of My Heart
Will Stay with CBS"

Ed had lunch with Paley three weeks after his return from the sabbatical. But according to Sig Mickelson, the conversation never extended beyond "guns," a surviving patch of common ground. Murrow's future was not discussed. "Sure, you can use Murrow on *CBS Reports,*" Mickelson told Friendly, "but let's keep our options open. Don't make Murrow the only one." Mickelson, so often overruled by the twentieth floor, felt utterly safe on this call. He knew what the executive suite now wanted.

Ed, however, did lead off the 1960–1961 season of *CBS Reports.* He anchored "The Year of the Polaris," and here the Navy commission paid off. He was granted a "secret" clearance and had been allowed into classified areas to do this report on the submarine-launched Polaris missile. The FBI duly noted this development in his dossier.

It was indeed like old times. Ed was soon in a row with the sponsor, a cigarette manufacturer. The company wanted to use a model of the Polaris missile in the commercials. Ed thought it unethical to exploit a project that the taxpayers had paid for to peddle cigarettes. He refused. The sponsor threatened to withdraw from the series. At the very least, the sponsor insisted on previewing the next program. A fundamental broadcasting issue had again been raised, sponsor interference in program content. In his first appearance since the sabbatical, Murrow had handed management another stomachache. This time, Paley and company bore the pain manfully and backed their broadcaster.[1]

His own smoking continued as heavy as ever, though he was given a jolting reason to quit that summer. In June, his brother Lacey had a cancerous lung removed. Like Ed, Lacey was a heavy smoker, and of Camels as well. Ed went on smoking. So did Lacey, for that matter.[2]

Ed had returned to television with the same ambivalence he had always felt toward the medium. Doing television had been rather like his marrying a rich woman while he was still in love with the girl next door. The marriage had brought him power, fame, and wealth, but his heart still belonged to his first love, radio. By now, however, commercial radio was no longer the spirited young thing that had so infatuated him. It had settled into what it is essentially today, a locally dominated, coin-free music box and news headline service. Network radio, beyond providing the headlines, was then already beginning to shrink into a vestigial member of the big networks. And so on his return from the sabbatical, Ed easily managed to find a place in a ghetto within a ghetto, a fifteen-minute program on radio on Sunday at noon. He called the program *Background.*

Background, at least, required no makeup artists, no lights, no cameras, no Hollywood-scale production, no budget battles, only Murrow and a microphone. As Ed described *Background,* "It won't be a rehash of what the listener has heard or read.... What we shall try to make it is this: a reasoned, rather leisurely analysis of the one, two or three news stories of the week, those that affect our national interest; what forces and individuals produced the event; and what consequences may reasonably be expected to flow from it...." He hoped to reach a discerning if small audience. No sponsor's millions were riding on a Sunday afternoon radio program.[3]

That fall of 1960, Nikita Khrushchev came to America to address the United Nations, and a State Department spokesman called the networks suggesting they downplay the Soviet premier's presence. On *Background,* Murrow said what he thought of that advice. "This is dangerous business," he said, "made more dangerous by the fact that only John Daley of ABC and the president of the Mutual Radio Network said in effect that they would decide what was news without any help or guidance from the State Department." His own CBS was not spared. The other networks, including CBS, "should have risen as one man and said, 'Thank you very much, period. We in the news business think we are competent to make our own decision....' The danger lies, not in Khrushchev's propaganda, or in the fact that the State Department improperly sought to bring pressure upon the networks, but rather that the networks did not seize the opportunity to defend not only their limited independence but one of the basic principles of a free society."

This time there were no howls from the twentieth floor. No one at CBS made so much as a whimper. The network executives so concerned over the effect of his television documentaries on sponsors and "adjacencies" were sailing on Long Island Sound or stirring martinis in Westchester patios on a Sunday afternoon. They were not listening to Ed Murrow on the radio.[4]

Background allowed Ed to repay a debt of conscience. He ran into Bill Shirer one day on Madison Avenue. The two men had scarcely seen each other since the wrenching experience in Paley's office thirteen years before. During most of that time, Shirer recalled, "I was broke and it was very discouraging." Finally, the world had turned around for Bill Shirer. Out of his profound knowledge of Germany, he had hewn a classic contemporary history, *The Rise and Fall of the Third Reich*. The book had been ten years in the writing, with publisher after publisher telling Shirer that nobody wanted to read about Germany and the war. But by the time he and Murrow bumped into each other, Shirer's book was near the top of the best-seller list.

Ed invited Bill to have a drink in a hotel bar. He complimented Shirer on the book. And then he told Shirer something that took him by surprise: "He told me all about his troubles with CBS," Shirer recalled, "and he said he had never forgotten what I had said, when I left CBS, that some day the same thing could happen to him."

For Murrow, the guilt over the Shirer affair of long ago lingered on. It was not an emotion that he could voice or erase easily. His style of contrition had been, rather, to see that Shirer was invited on *This I Believe*. On *Background,* after this chance encounter, he said, "From time to time this reporter will mention a book, for it is between hard covers that real background is to be found. The best of many books on that nightmare period 1933–1945 is *The Rise and Fall of the Third Reich* by William L. Shirer. No one interested in the personal, political and military phenomenon of our time can afford to ignore it." The author, however, was still unforgiving.[5]

Ed had returned to America in a presidential election year. The Democrats held their convention first in July in Los Angeles. CBS found itself in the rare position of underdog. Four years before, the network's habitual command of first place in news and public affairs had been jarred by the surfacing of Chet Huntley and David Brinkley at the party conventions. After 1956, Huntley and Brinkley had become coanchors of the NBC evening news, and an attractive pair they made. The manly authority of Huntley and the cool wit of Brinkley achieved an instant chemistry. They also tended to treat the news less awesomely and take themselves less somberly than CBS correspondents fashioned in the Murrow image. In 1960, they were again to anchor the conventions, facing Walter Cronkite for CBS.

Figuring out a place for Murrow at the Democratic Convention was Sig Mickelson's responsibility. Cronkite had the starring role, and Mickelson felt that "Murrow was too big to assign to one candidate or one caucus." Thus, Ed went to Los Angeles as "sort of a free spirit," as he himself put it. "I've been told I can rove around and speak whenever I feel like saying something. That's alright with me. I might not utter a damn word through the whole convention."

He also voiced the reflex pessimism that so wearied his friends. He told a *New York Post* reporter on arriving in Los Angeles, "I don't see that the outcome of the convention will make any difference in the important issues that face us, our position in relation to the rest of the world. I feel we are losing that position and I doubt if the choice of candidates will alter the trend to any extent."[6]

One of Jack Kennedy's operatives at the convention was Ken Galbraith. Galbraith later described an encounter with Ed to illustrate television's awesome power to magnify the merely trite to bloated significance: "I met Edward R. Murrow equipped like a space man with his own antennae. He asked me what was new.

"'Oh, everything's under control,' I replied without a thought.

"Conventions are hard on the feet, and shortly thereafter I went into a television monitoring room off the floor to rest mine for a few minutes. As I watched, Murrow appeared on the screen and sat down opposite Walter Cronkite.

"'Well, Ed, what's new?'

"'I just talked with Ken Galbraith, Walter.'

"'That's interesting, Ed. Professor Galbraith, eh? He usually has something interesting to say.'

"'Well, he did. He said that everything is under control, Walter.'

"'That's pretty important, Ed. So the Kennedy people think that everything's under control.'

"'That's the message, Walter. Under control.'

"'That's very interesting, Ed. As they see it, all under control.'"[7]

It quickly became evident that NBC was, as David Brinkley put it, "rolling up CBS like a rug." Mickelson came under intense pressure to reverse the rout.

Don Hewitt was an irrepressible idea man, some bizarre—as when he suggested that television reporters learn braille so that they would not have to look down at their copy—and some brilliant—notably CBS's *60 Minutes,* which was Hewitt's creation. Hewitt revived the idea that CBS still had two shining stars, both of greater magnitude than the opposition team, and that Murrow and Cronkite combined could overpower Huntley and Brinkley. The network brass agreed.

It was a doomed marriage from the start. Cronkite naturally resented the intrusion of Murrow. It was a vote of no-confidence in him before millions of viewers. But more deeply, as Hewitt later recognized, the two men were "single acts." Cronkite preferred to work alone. Murrow was accustomed to lead as a superior, not share as an equal. There was a near audible hollowness when they interacted. They were rather like two images on a split screen, seen simultaneously but not really together. The term most commonly seized upon by their fellow correspondents to describe the pairing of Murrow and Cronkite was "a disaster."

Thus, on the night of the balloting, Murrow returned to the floor, assigned to cover the Eastern Seaboard states. To younger CBS staffers, raised on the Murrow legend, the assignment was demeaning. Vern Diamond, a CBS director, remembered thinking, "This is God. What is God doing there with a clipboard reporting the delegate count from Delaware?"

When he left the convention for the street, Murrow was, however, as much as the candidates, a celebrity, constantly besieged by autograph seekers, most of them gushing that they never missed him on *Person to Person*.

He took his niece Nan, Dewey's daughter, out to dinner during the convention to the Bel Air Hotel. As she recalled the night, "The place was full of women with Hedda Hopper hats. Uncle Ed's first comment was 'I've seen better wine lists in Jerusalem.' At one of the tables some tipsy women were giggling and pointing at him. One of them got up and came over to our table and almost threw herself on him, babbling about how much she loved his programs. I thought he behaved gallantly. 'Thank you,' he said. 'You're so kind to say that.' After she left, I said, 'Uncle Ed, you were so gracious considering she was kind of obnoxious.' 'You have to understand' he told me, 'sometimes they even behave like that when they're sober.'"

John F. Kennedy won the nomination and chose to make his acceptance speech in the capacious arena of the Coliseum. Ed was assigned to do the remote from the stadium's press box with Vern Diamond directing. "We—Ed, Kay Campbell and me—had to lug our material up what seemed like six flights," Diamond recalled. "Then CBS decided not to do the remote from there and we lugged everything back down. They changed their mind again and decided to do it there after all. So up we went again. I was amazed at Ed's attitude. He muttered but really didn't complain. In fact, he was like a new correspondent, eager to make his mark. He was full of curiosity about how I intended to do the remote. Yet, I couldn't help thinking of what it said about his career, what it symbolized about what was happening to him at CBS to hear Murrow say, 'And now, back to you, Walter.'"[8]

In Chicago, late in July, the republicans nominated Richard Nixon. CBS was drubbed again in the ratings by Huntley and Brinkley.

Bernard Eismann was now the CBS Chicago Bureau chief. After the Republican Convention, Eismann invited the staff to his apartment for a late supper. Ed arrived, Eismann remembered, "exhausted and depressed." He took off his jacket, loosened his tie, stretched out on the Eismann's living room floor, and was soon asleep. He awoke at about 4 a.m. and asked where everybody had gone. Eismann told him that another party was under way at a strip joint on State Street. "They're over there," Murrow said bitterly, "dancing on the grave of CBS news with tarts and strippers. What an end to a noble endeavor." He was not about to separate his own fate from the fate of the network news operation. He was going down, so apparently must the news. Hadn't CBS been drubbed in the ratings?[9]

What Murrow thought of the Republican nominated at the convention was unequivocal. Richard Nixon would always be, to him, a member of the House Un-American Activities Committee whose investigations had driven an innocent Larry Duggan to his death. In his London Guildhall speech, Ed had praised Nixon with the back of his hand. Joe McCarthy, he said, "could not play upon the emotions with the same skill as his friend, Richard Nixon." Ed once took Casey to a movie where they ran into Nixon. After they sat down, Ed turned to Casey and said, "I can't believe that just happened, that I had to introduce you to that guy."[10]

Murrow's reaction to Jack Kennedy was more complicated. He had, to an extent, exploited the rich, handsome, youthful senator's star quality, first on an early broadcast of *Person to Person* and later on *Small World*. When Kennedy made a speech in 1958 on what was later to emerge as a major 1960 campaign theme, the "missile gap" between the American and Soviet nuclear arsenals, Murrow had written, "Dear Jack,...without doubt, it is one of the most penetrating and courageous speeches ever delivered on the floor of the Senate in a long time. It will not offend you for me to say that it was worthy of Senator Vandenburg in his better and enlightened days. More power to you." After Kennedy won the nomination, Ed said of him on *Background,* "Above everything else, he is confident. He is supremely convinced that he lacks none of the qualities or qualifications to be President of the Country. He appears to approach the prospect with no sense of awe...."

Privately, his judgments were harsh, even contemptuous. Jack Kennedy's most unpardonable failing, in Murrow's reckoning, was that he was Joe Kennedy's son. Ed's office neighbor, Blair Clark, had been a friend of Kennedy's at Harvard. Clark recalled, "Ed hated Joe Kennedy, felt contempt for him. It wasn't just that Joe Kennedy was all wrong about the British and the war. It had to do with Joe Kennedy and women. Joe Kennedy and bootlegging. Ed considered Joe Kennedy a buccaneer. Ed would say to me, 'Your friend, Jack, isn't he just a smartass kid?" Clark was "not all that idolatrous of Jack." But he found himself defending him. "I'd tell Ed that Jack Kennedy was better than he thought and that he was not in thrall to his father. Ed would say, 'Aahh, he's still Joe's kid.'"

To Murrow, Kennedy, like Nixon, also carried the McCarthy taint. The candidate's father had befriended McCarthy, contributed big money to his campaigns. The candidate's brother Bobby Kennedy had served as counsel on McCarthy's investigating subcommittee. Jack had been in the hospital recovering from spinal surgery when the Senate voted to censure Joe McCarthy, and thus was spared openly committing himself.[11]

In the middle of the campaign, Ed had lunch at the Century Club with Teddy White and Arthur Schlesinger, Jr. Schlesinger later wrote of their conversation, "He [Murrow] told us that if McCarthyism seemed to Kennedy's advantage, Kennedy would become a McCarthyite overnight. Nothing White or I said could dissuade him from this view." Schlesinger also described Murrow at this point in his life as "a harrowed, gloomy presence at New York dinners, punctuating his incessant cigarettes with brief and bitter cracks and leaving the impression that all the idealism in the world had vanished with the Battle of Britain."[12]

The first televised presidential debates in history had helped millions of viewers make up their minds between the two candidates. It was the kind of serious, educational, public-interest use of television that Murrow favored. But Ed, in a pessimism that now appeared to have metastasized to all subjects, felt that the American public had been the losers. He described the first debate as "a puny contribution—capsulized, homogenized, perhaps dangerous in its future implications." His disdain may have been influenced by the man who arranged the first debate, Frank Stanton.

The debate did, however, arouse one flicker of sympathy in him for Richard Nixon. In a *Background* broadcast, Ed said: "There has been considerable comment upon the obvious fact that Mr. Nixon perspired. It so happens that some people sweat mightily under those lights. And others don't. It is no proof of either nervousness or uncertainty." As he spoke, the sweat on his own hands was staining the pages of his script.[13]

The week before the election, Ed went out for the night with Bill and Roz Downs. He was again suffering from what appeared to be a bad cold. Colds, flu, respiratory infections, had become ritualized for him whenever winter approached. Before the night was over, he became sicker and developed a raging fever. The next day, he was in the hospital with pneumonia. Consequently, he missed taking part in the election night coverage. It was just as well. The man of moody withdrawals and sudden silences was not particularly suited for the impromptu banter that the long vigil required. He was never comfortable with, especially knowledgeable about, or particularly good at political reporting.[14]

What he did best he was now about to do, and incomparably. He and Friendly, and a gifted young producer named David Lowe, were creating, out of the genre of the television documentary, a lasting work of art.

The seed of "Harvest of Shame" was a radio commentary by Ed Morgan. Morgan's assistant had gone to the farm of Senator Harry Byrd in northern Virgina during the apple harvest and came back appalled by the conditions of migrant laborers he had seen there. Morgan chose the plight of these "stoop workers" as the text for a radio commentary. Friendly heard Morgan and knew instantly that here was a natural for *CBS Reports* and for Murrow who was congenitally compelled to come to the defense of the defenseless.

It was a Friday, November 25, 9:30 p.m., the day after Thanksgiving, when most Americans had finished off the last of the turkey and pumpkin pie leftovers.

CBS Reports opened with Aaron Copland's "Fanfare for the Common Man." A crowd of rural blacks was seen milling in front of a shed while a voice chanted, "Over here! Seventy cents a day. We pay more and longest hours. Seventy cents. Here we is today!" The men began clambering aboard a stake truck, jammed buttocks to buttocks while someone tied a rope across the back to keep them from falling out. Murrow came in, voiceover: "This scene is not taking place in the Congo. It has nothing to do with Johannesburg or Capetown. It is not Nyasaland or Nigeria. This is Florida. These are citizens of the United States, 1960. This is a shape-up for migrant workers....this is the way the humans who harvest the food for the best-fed people in the world get hired. One farmer looked at this and said, 'We used to own slaves. Now we just rent them.'" The film had been shot by Marty Bennet and Murrow's favorite cameraman, Charlie Mack, still using the more expensive, cumbersome 35-millimeter camera for finer results. For the next hour their cameras followed the migrants northward, American nomads, picking oranges in Florida, peaches in Georgia, beans in the Carolinas, corn in Virginia, lettuce on Long Island. Blacks had appeared in the opening frames. Subsequent scenes revealed that Hispanics and poor whites were migrant workers too.

After the commercial, Murrow appeared standing in a furrowed field that seemed to stretch off into infinity. He was wearing a sport shirt and slacks and looked like a motorist who had stumbled on a scene that he could not accept. He cut to an interview between his reporter and a migrant mother of nine children. The reporter asked, "Who works with you out of this family?"

WOMAN: Everybody but the baby.

REPORTER: Who takes care of them in the fields?

WOMAN: Well, they just kind of stay along with us, or take care of their self.

REPORTER: What's the usual dinner?

WOMAN: Well, I cook a pot of beans and fry some potatoes.

The reporter peered into a shack where the children slept and asked a 9-year-old boy about a hole in the wall. "How'd you get that hole?" "Rats," the boy answered.

The reporter talked with a woman who had picked beans for ten hours and said she had earned "a dollar." She had, she said, fourteen children.

The scene shifted to a white family standing in front of a jalopy in a scene lifted intact from *The Grapes of Wrath*. The family had spent the previous night sleeping in a field. The father said that he was looking for work. The reporter asked him how much money he had in the world, "A dollar forty-five cents," the man answered.

The camera followed the migrants to camps where workers slept outdoors on bales of hay, where fifty people shared two outside privies, and where there were no privies at all and the migrants had to relieve themselves in the fields.

In the midst of this squalor, the power of the human heart to hope was captured by the children. The reporter asked them what they wanted to be when they grew up? "Teacher," "nurse," "doctor," "dentist," they answered. Murrow noted that the federal government was spending $3.5

million a year for the education of these migrant children and $6.5 million to protect migrant wildlife.

For whom did these stoop laborers toil? The camera fixed on a stocky, good-natured farmer who hired migrants, and the reporter asked him what he thought of them. "Well," he answered, "I guess they got a little gypsy in their blood. They just like it. Lot of 'em wouldn't do anything else. Lot of 'em don't know anything different. That's all they want to do. They love it. They love to go from place to place. They don't have a worry in the world. They're happier than we are. Today they eat. Tomorrow they don't worry about. They're the happiest race of people on Earth." The man spoke amiably, without a trace of malice, contempt, or irony.

The power of "Harvest of Shame" rises from the dynamic of the visual images wedded to Murrow's commentary. At one point, the migrants are seen bouncing on the back of a truck as Murrow reports: "Produce en route to the tables of America by trailer is refrigerated and carefully packed to prevent bruising. Cattle carried to market, by Federal regulation, must be watered, fed and rested for five hours every twenty-eight hours. People—men, women, and children—are carried to the fields of the north in journeys as long as four days and three nights. They often ride ten hours without stopping for food or facilities." They work, he said, "the sweat shops of the soil....these are forgotten people....the soil has produced no Samuel Gompers or John L. Lewis...." The migrants were, in fact, specifically excluded from the law allowing workers in interstate commerce to organize and bargain collectively. Rootless, lacking a stable base, having no political muscle, they were as powerless as beasts of burden.

"Harvest of Shame" closed with the camera panning the faces we had come to know, the father with $1.45 to his name, the child who wanted to be a doctor, a mother who could afford milk for her children once a week. "The people you have seen," Murrow said in closing, "have the strength to harvest your fruit and vegetables. They do not have the strength to influence legislation. Maybe we do. Good night, and good luck."

"Harvest of Shame" is a work of passion and anger. It is to documentary film what Oscar Lewis's *The Children of Sanchez* is to prose. It plumbed American life at the bottom, and captured and distilled it into a harsh poetry. Decades later, the film would still be shown with none if its searing impact lost, and few of the ills it portrayed cured. As a work of television art and a cry for social justice it remains unsurpassed.[15]

The prospect of another, far different, yet intriguing, subject for *CBS Reports* surfaced that fall. Shortly after the presidential election, a reporter Ed had known during the war came to see him about a job. The man had come up from Florida, and he baited his hopes with a story of an invasion of Cuba that the CIA was supposedly mounting out of Florida. Murrow and Friendly were skeptical, but sent a producer to Miami to check out the story. Their man came back and reported that south Florida was a cauldron of invasion rumors, but he himself was skeptical. Murrow was not yet ready to reject the possibility out of hand, but he and Friendly had to wrestle with the ethics of the situation. As Friendly put it, "Suppose it is an invasion? Suppose we do a broadcast and it becomes a disaster because of the press we give it? It just seemed to us we were getting mixed up with something we couldn't handle." The rumors would force their way to the surface at another, and embarrassing, time for Murrow. But that was months off.[16]

Friendly had assumed all along that with Murrow back they would resurrect their old partnership full-time. Ed had, in fact, anchored less than half of the *CBS Reports* broadcasts from his return until the end of 1960. The program itself won every prize for which it was eligible, including three Peabodys. *See It Now* had metamorphosed into the new series in all but name.

In the final month of 1960, however, three factors converged like cross hairs in a gunsight to mark the end of a career and an era in broadcasting.

The first factor was a man named James Aubrey, now president of the CBS Television Network. Aubrey had replaced Lou Cowan, who had soared to the heights on his invention, the colossal-prize quiz show, and had crashed to earth in the same misguided missile.

Two years before, in Chicago, Murrow had said that he could find nothing in the Bill of Rights or the Communications Act requiring the networks to "increase their net profits each year, lest the Republic collapse." Jim Aubrey could imagine no other purpose for CBS. Mission houses save souls. Corporations make money, the more the better. The choice of Aubrey to succeed Cowan exposed a curious contradiction in CBS's soul. Stanton was carrying out damage repair to the network's reputation in the wake of the quiz show scandals by promising more public affairs programming in prime time. Yet Aubrey was the man chosen to control all of CBS's programming, a corporate clear-cutter who was ready to chop down profitless documentaries like so much dead wood in his cold-minded pursuit of profit.

Aubrey was in fact winning the ratings war for CBS almost every night of the week. But Thursday was hopeless. ABC had a phenomenal success on Thursdays at ten, the mobster series, *The Untouchables*, which, indeed, Aubrey could not touch. This hit program, on another network, was the second factor that combined to help bring about the end of the age of Murrow. Aubrey had to deliver on Stanton's promise of public affairs programming in prime time, and this promise indirectly became the third factor in Murrow's undoing. Since Aubrey had nothing to lose, he threw *CBS Reports* into the ten o'clock Thursday slot against the *Untouchables*, a shrewd sacrifice play.

Here, it seemed on the surface at least, was the opportunity Friendly had been waiting for. He had, for the first time in five years, a regularly scheduled place in prime time. His idea was to use this slot to alternate

CBS Reports with a series of high-level debates patterned after the presidential debates. Now was clearly the time to have Murrow designated the regular anchor and coproducer of *CBS Reports.*

The new schedule was to take effect in January of 1961. Friendly made his pitch for Murrow to Paley and Stanton in December. Paley's response was as chilling as a death knell: "What do you have against Howard Smith?" he wanted to know. To Friendly, the import of Paley's answer was unmistakable.

When Ed had first been denied the coproducership of *CBS Reports,* the year before, he had at least been left the face-saving rationale that he was going off on sabbatical and a final decision could be delayed until his return. Now he was back, and he had been rejected outright. He could follow, but he could no longer lead. He was being reduced, in effect, to one of his own Boys, another CBS correspondent.

He had reached the end of a twenty-five-year odyssey. He was down the far side of the slope. Since that day in March of 1938 when he had decided to go to Vienna, not to arrange for a broadcaster during the *Anschluss,* but to become a broadcaster, he had virtually created the profession of which he became the consummate practitioner. He had gone to the summit, but at some indefinable point after he had confronted McCarthy in 1954, he had suffered a slow, almost imperceptible, yet steady erosion of power and influence inside the network. As his bitterness grew, he tried to persuade himself, and told his wife, that the only reason he stayed on was to support the family.[17]

He still presided over the year-end wrap-up broadcast on December 2. Marvin Kalb remembered the mood. Kalb had been brought in from Moscow for his first year-ender. Afterward, beaming with pride, he went to Murrow and said, "Ed, I want to tell you how much it has meant to me to be on the show with you and I hope we can do many things like this in the future." He was met by "a pained, puzzled expression. Ed didn't say a word to me. I felt that I had stepped onto forbidden territory."[18]

And then, perilously close to earth, his parachute opened.

During the 1960 campaign, Frank Stanton had carried on a running battle with the Kennedy forces, the friction growing essentially out of Jack Kennedy's conviction that CBS had not covered him fairly. When, after the campaign, the President-elect asked Stanton to come to see him, Stanton pulled out all his old telephone notes and correspondence with Kennedy and went to Washington "prepared to have my balls cut off." Instead, Kennedy offered him a job.

They discussed Commerce and Education. But Kennedy offered Stanton one post outright, the U.S. Information Agency. Stanton declined. He thought his job at CBS was more important than running the government's overseas propaganda apparatus.

Kennedy then asked him to suggest other people for the post. Stanton mentioned several newspaper editors and publishers, and also suggested to Kennedy, "someone like Ed Murrow." Asked long afterward why he had not simply suggested Murrow outright, he said, "I never believed Ed would accept that job."[19]

Blair Clark had grown tired of CBS. Clark had hoped to use his friendship with Kennedy to land an embassy in the new administration. He went to Palm Beach to talk to Kennedy about the prospects. Later, on his return, Clark got a phone call from his old classmate. The President-elect was, however, not calling about an ambassadorship, but looking for guidance on the USIA appointment. Kennedy asked Clark, "What would you do if you were me, if you could choose between Frank Stanton and Ed Murrow for USIA?" Clark told him, "If you want a man extraordinarily well connected in Congress, an able, efficient administrator, Stanton is your man. But if you want a man with an international reputation, an honest communicator, then your man is Ed Murrow. I'd pick Murrow. But, I don't know what you're problems are." Clark reported Kennedy's interest to Murrow, without mentioning Stanton. Murrow, he recalled, typically gave no hint by word or expression of what he thought about the prospect.[20]

With only weeks remaining before the inauguration, Stanton was still Kennedy's first choice. The President-elect called again to offer Stanton the USIA position. He again refused.

The first feeler to Ed from the incoming administration was made by Chester Bowles, then in line for deputy undersecretary of state. Ed and Bowles met in Washington, where Bowles urged him to take the job, if offered, though Bowles was not in a position to offer it. It was an old Washington tactic. Bowles was trying to put Kennedy in the position of knowing that if he offered Murrow the job, Murrow would accept. Ed was not playing that game. He put Bowles off. If he were going to serve the President, he expected to be asked by the President.

On January 20, 1961, Ed climbed a 20-foot pine ladder to an improvised broadcast booth facing the steps of the Capitol. He looked out over a city swathed in a heavy fall of snow, the air biting cold with a temperature of 8 degrees. John F. Kennedy had just been sworn in as the country's thirty-fifth President, and Murrow was to make a radio commentary on the inaugural address. He was coughing and trembling when he reached the top, white with fatigue. Ed Bliss was with Ed that day and remembered thinking, "He looked awful, he wasn't well." But he would stand in no more frigid broadcast booths. His life as a working reporter was coming to an end.

He went to Alabama for a *CBS Reports* story on race relations, entitled "Who Speaks for Birmingham?" And the call finally came. The President asked him to become director of the USIA. Ed did not immediately accept. But he did go to Washington, and there he called Howard K. Smith and asked Smith to meet him at the Sheraton-Carlton. As Smith recalled their conversation, Ed said, "Look, that boy in the White House has offered me a job." "That boy," Smith reminded him, "is the President." Murrow then said, "I don't know whether to take it or not after all the things I've said about him." "Ed," Smith reassured him, "eating your words is the main diet in this town. Take the job."

His chief mentor, in the end, was Bill Paley. With some accuracy, Paley would later remark, "Even when he was not regarding me as highly as he might, he never took a step without coming to me for advice." Paley's advice, this time, might be expected to be enlightened self-interest. He could, in the same breath, remove a thorn from his side and give the country a distinguished public servant. But Bill Paley was never so transparent. "I assured him he could have a home at CBS as long as he wanted," Paley later recalled of their talk. "But it was a difficult decision for him to make and for me to advise him on." Paley did strongly suggest that he should make it a condition of taking the job that he be a member of the President's inner circle, attending all meetings of the cabinet, National Security Council, and any other serious policy discussions. "You have to tell Kennedy you have to be on the inside of the family," Paley warned. "You can't represent the country's viewpoint unless you know what's going on."

Murrow, Paley said, "agreed with me completely" and later told Paley that he had put these conditions to Kennedy, and that JFK had said, "Of course, absolutely."

Eight days later President Kennedy announced Ed's appointment as director of the U.S. Information Agency. Ed was spared the galling knowledge that Frank Stanton had been Kennedy's first choice. No one ever told him.

Instead of securing an embassy, Blair Clark had become CBS's general news manager. When the Murrow appointment became official, he stopped by Ed's office and said, "We'll have to put out a statement. What do you want us to say?" Murrow, seated at his desk, looked tired and pale. But his eyes suddenly brightened. He grinned like a boy and said, "Tell 'em I'm off to serve my country."[21]

His fellow journalists were unsure about the propriety of his appointment. Teddy White was "a little upset." Friendly opposed the move primarily because it pained him to see the finest journalist in broadcasting turned propagandist. Scotty Reston thought, "If you're a reporter, you don't get involved with the things you've reported. You have to go back to the separation of Church and State. It's that sacred to reporters." But when it was done, and Murrow, in effect, became the Voice of America, Reston wrote in *The New York Times* that it was a fine appointment: "He has the poetry of the nation in his bones."

The opportunity to serve his country was at considerable sacrifice. Ed had been earning between $200,000 and $300,000 a year in broadcasting. The director of the USIA was paid $22,750 annually.[22]

On January 31, wherever there was a monitor at CBS, knots of people gathered. Ed was in Washington, and a closed-circuit, in-house broadcast had been arranged for the New York offices and the affiliates. He was about to say goodbye.

He began in a strained jocular vein, telling one of his well-worn logging camp stories. He fidgeted with his cuff links. A pack of cigarettes was in sight on the desk. "It's naturally a little difficult to leave the shop after twenty-five years," he began, looking lost, the habitual self-assurance missing, his voice subdued, "...to leave a lot of good friends...." He stopped to regain his composure. "I think it's fair and honest to say that..."; again he halted as the words caught in his throat "...some part of my heart will stay with CBS." He went on to the end, fighting back the tears, more emotionally naked than any of them had ever seen this fiercely private man. "I wish you all good luck and good night," he said. And it was over.

Palmer Williams, watching on one of the monitors, remembered thinking, "I felt we had just lost the pilot." Joe Wershba described the reaction of a CBS news employee and a USIA official: The former: "I don't remember when morale around here has been any lower"; the latter: "Our morale has just shot up 2,000 percent!"

If there was sadness in the newsroom there was also undeniable relief on the executive floor. But what Bill Paley felt at that moment was locked inside that man's impenetrable soul. To the end, Ed remained faithful to the image of the first Paley he had known. The first letter he was to write from his new office was to Paley, "Had it not been for our last conversation," he wrote, "I doubt that I would have had the equanimity of mind or courage to undertake this task....I wanted you to know of my gratitude and abiding affections." Shortly before he had left CBS he told Blair Clark, "I think Bill's kind of given up." Ed had persuaded himself that both he and Paley were broadcasting victims, beaten down by the system.[23]

Over those twenty-five years, he had made more than 5,000 broadcasts. Within that body of work were to be found the mileposts of a new journalism born in the twentieth century and largely of his invention. The use of radio to paint events with sound—the Blitz, "Orchestrated Hell," Buchenwald—the now-forgotten classic radio documentaries of *Hear It Now,* the still valid, still honored works of *See It Now* and *CBS Reports—* Radulovich, McCarthy, Korea, "Harvest of Shame"—and nightly news reporting over twelve years of consistent quality, these were his legacy. *Person to Person* was his aberration, a performance neither as contemptible as his disappointed admirers found it, nor good enough, but for the wealth it brought him, to deserve his talents. All the work of his heart was marked by a respect for his audiences. He tended to treat adults as adults, capable of receiving hard truths and becoming the better for it. There was a sense of context in what he did, a relatedness to what had gone before and relevance to what would follow. And there was insight, virtually the trademark of a Murrow broadcast. The facts were never left alone. They were probed for the larger meaning they held, an inquisitiveness that Ida Lou Anderson had sown in him thirty years before.

He left behind a corps of broadcast journalists yet to be equaled, reporters, however individualistic, who were marked forever by the man who chose them, to the end Murrow's Boys. The gene was passed on to successive generations of correspondents and is still heard and seen in the mannerisms of a few and in the work of the best of the breed.

He had been, during that quarter century, not so much a journalist as a thinly veiled moralist. He would not leave the country alone. He brought it, sometimes dragged it, in front of the mirror. When he left CBS, Jack Gould wrote in *The Times*, "To whatever extent television has found its voice of conscience, purpose and integrity, it was as much the doing of Edward R. Murrow as any other single individual in one medium."

After he was gone, there followed at CBS what Harry Reasoner called, "The Great Correspondent Sweepstakes." Who was to be the next Murrow? There was no dearth of contenders. But there was, however, never to be another Murrow. The networks would never again risk giving so vast a grant of freedom to one figure. The man who had built the temple had, for all practical purposes, been driven from it. There was no place left for him in broadcasting to match his stature. And so the founder and then reigning master left. It was an irony wrapped in an absurdity.

When he left London in 1946, the BBC staff had given him the microphone he used in Studio B. Now, as he left CBS, the correspondents gave him a bust of FDR by Jo Davidson. The Peabodies and literally dozens of other awards he left in the attic at Glen Arden. He took the Roosevelt bust and installed it with the old BBC microphone in his new office at 1776 Pennsylvania Avenue in Washington.[24]

CHAPTER 31

The Minister of Truth

"I had the impression that Ed Murrow had lost interest in his old occupation, that he was burned out with broadcasting. It seemed he desperately needed something new in his life. He was very positive about the new job."

The speaker was Donald Wilson, the Kennedy administration's transition man at the USIA, and a proper New Frontiersman, young, lithe, clean-cut, Yale, former *Life* magazine reporter, and a touch-football-playing pal of the President and his brother Bobby.

Don Wilson picked up Ed and Janet at Union Station on a day early in February of 1961 and brought them to their suite at the Sheraton Carlton Hotel. Over the next several days, Wilson briefed Murrow on the organization he was about to inherit. Wilson was amused that Ed kept referring to his new boss as "that young man in the White House." That "boy" had evidently matured in recent weeks in Murrow's eyes.

The next agency official Ed met was Thomas Sorensen, another ex-journalist, now a career USIA foreign service officer. Sorensen had been asked by the White House to prepare an analysis of the USIA, its organization, programs, strengths, and the cure for its weaknesses. Of his first encounter with Murrow, Sorensen remembered thinking, "When you meet people you've only seen on television, they look either bigger or smaller in real life. Murrow looked bigger."

Murrow had read Sorensen's report, was much impressed, and told him, "I'd like you to be Deputy Director for Policy and Plans." Sorensen had just been offered his idea of the dream job in the Agency. He started to say something self-effacing when Murrow cut him off: "Well, do you want it or not?"

469

SORENSEN: I do.

MURROW: Fine. You've got it.

Murrow then added, "President Kennedy didn't tell me to appoint you. I asked him if it was all right." Sorensen was surprised by the man's brusqueness on the one hand and his sensitivity on the other to something that must be on Sorensen's mind. Tom Sorensen was the younger brother of Ted Sorensen, the President's special counsel and speechwriter, as close to JFK as anyone on the New Frontier, save JFK's brother Bobby. To Tom Sorensen, to be wanted by Murrow on his own merits was deeply gratifying.

Murrow had bargained for a free hand with the President in choosing his staff. He did not have to accept these two men whom he had never known before. But though a freshman bureaucrat, Ed was a life-long student of power. In Don Wilson and Tom Sorensen, he had inherited two capable men and two direct lines to the White House in one afternoon. He was content. Wilson became Murrow's chief deputy and Sorensen the number three man, forming with Murrow the troika that would run the USIA.

But they were all so young, these New Frontiersmen. Wilson was 35, Sorensen 34. It was Murrow who in his early career had been the boy wonder, adding years to his age to match the jobs he wanted. Now, at 53, he was nine years older than the President, the old man of the administration, except for Adlai Stevenson at the UN. He bridled visibly when he heard Kennedy people refer to 48-year-olds as "washed up," "too old for the job."[1]

The agency that he had inherited was hardly the jewel in the crown of American government. The U.S. Information Agency had its roots in the World War II Office of War Information. After the war, the propaganda functions had been scattered over a half-dozen government programs abroad. These activities had been consolidated in an independent agency, the USIA, only eight years before, in 1953. The director lacked cabinet rank. The agency's budget was anemic, its purpose ambiguous, even suspect. Propaganda had an alien ring in America. Its principle parent was the State Department, although as one observer put it, the USIA was treated there like "a bastard at a family reunion." In his early desire to make friends on Capitol Hill, Ed had stopped at the Senate to see the powerful Richard Russell of Georgia. Russell told him that the job he had taken on was "like a cat licking a grindstone."

Each incoming administration brought with it a fresh vision of the USIA's role. In one season, unvarnished truth was in style. Tell America's story, warts and all, and the world will admire us for it. In another season, it was trumpet America's successes, and the world will want to emulate us. In the shadow of McCarthyism, the agency, defensively, spent more effort telling what was wrong with the Soviet Union and communism than what was right with the United States and democracy.

As Murrow worked on the opening statement for his upcoming confirmation hearings, he began to formulate his own philosophy. Knee-jerk anticommunism was not enough. The United States, he believed, was engaged in a worldwide ideologic competition with communism, and "we will not be content to counter their lies and distortions. We shall constantly reiterate our faith in freedom." America must not appear smug and self-satisfied: "To the emerging nations, we shall try to make clear that we as a nation are not allergic to change and have no desire to sanctify the status quo." Above all, he accepted the limits of propaganda. America's good example was its best propaganda, "more important than its dollars or its words," he wrote.

He now headed an enterprise with 12,000 employees deployed in Washington and "U.S. Information Service" (USIS) posts in eighty-four countries. The agency operated libraries and binational friendship centers; exchanged students, teachers, leaders, and cultural figures with other countries; distributed films and magazines; circulated exhibits; attempted to place material in foreign newspapers and radio and television broadcasts; subsidized books favorable to the U.S. point of view; and ran the *Voice of America*.[2]

Word of Murrow's appointment had hit the USIA like a surge of adrenalin. Robert Sivard was a USIA officer posted to Paris at the time of the McCarthy broadcast. Some weeks afterward, he recalled being invited with a dozen other State and USIA people to a colleague's home to see a film of the program. It was, Sivard remembered, almost clandestine, "like watching an underground movie." After McCarthy's crude persecution of the *Voice of America* and Roy Cohn's and G. David Schine's bully-boy tour of USIS posts for McCarthy, it provided "a great sense of satisfaction to know that this man, Murrow, was now our boss." As another USIA veteran put it, "For the first time, USIA was seated above the salt."[3]

Ed took over the director's corner office on the fourth floor overlooking Pennsylvania Avenue and 18th Street Northwest. The few personal touches consisted of another stand-up desk for newspaper reading, his BBC microphone, and the bust of Roosevelt. There was a second phone on his desk, a white one that he answered himself, the direct line to the President.

He did not so much accept the furnishings—the drab government-issue drapes, desk, couch, conference table, and art—as appear oblivious to it all. Hewson Ryan, one of his Latin American deputies, found Murrow the least demanding of all the USIA directors. "The others," Ryan said, "always wanted everything redecorated, reupholstered. Murrow changed the room by his presence in it."

Another feature of the office was the constant cold. He had never overcome the English conviction that American buildings were overheated.

He kept his air conditioner on, winter and summer, and maintained a room temperature barely above 60 degrees.

In Washington, he had a new secretary for the first time in twenty-five years. Kay Campbell, who had gone to work for him as a young girl, now grown to stout middle age, was a British citizen and consequently could not work for the USIA director. "She could be tedious and maddening in her possessiveness towards Ed," Janet recalled, "and when Ed left New York, it was a devastating blow to Kay." She had made no other life for herself. To this man to whom she had given her spinster's love for a quarter of a century, it was still "Goodbye, Mr. Murrow" and "Goodbye, Miss Campbell" when they parted.

He had left another woman behind too, Esther L. She had provided a quiet harbor against the storms of his latter years in New York, a friend more than a great love. But when he went to Washington, it was over. She would wistfully talk of Ed when she ran into Charles Collingwood around CBS. But she would see him no more.

His new secretary in Washington was a quietly capable young woman named Dorothy Baas, who learned early that among her duties was to make sure that Mr. Murrow never ran out of cigarettes.[4]

As soon as his appointment was official, the FBI began to carry out its standard background investigation. After an embarrassing delay, a White House personnel officer asked the Bureau to speed up the clearances of Murrow and several other appointees. Hoover wrote across the bottom of the request, "Of course we will expedite them. But thoroughness is paramount especially as to such a character as Murrow." It is a measure of the fear and nonsense that J. Edgar Hoover could inspire in grown men that the FBI's mail to Murrow was addressed simply, "Director, U.S. Information Agency." It was done this way, an FBI man explained, because Hoover had ordered "that we have nothing to do with Murrow."[5]

At the USIA, Ed made clear by a simple, eloquent act that the age of paranoia had ended. He called a man whom he had never met and said, "I want you back here." At the next staff meeting, he turned to the gray-haired figure sitting next to him, a man pilloried and driven from his profession by Joe McCarthy, and said only, "Gentlemen, I just want to welcome Reed Harris back from eight year's leave." He also found a job at the *Voice of America* for William Hobson, a gifted radio dramatist who had been fired by CBS and thereafter spent ten years in the wilderness because his name had appeared in *Red Channels*.[6]

During the first six weeks on the job, Ed scrupulously signed his correspondence "Director-designate," while he awaited Senate confirmation. On March 14, J. William Fulbright, chairman of the Senate Foreign Relations Committee, opened his confirmation hearing. Murrow may as well never have seen a microphone in his life. He was uneasy and sweated heavily, spoke first too softly and then too loudly, and compounded his edginess by swearing off cigarettes during the hearing. He began giving his name and added, "I was christened Egbert but abandoned that name at the age of sixteen while working in logging camps in Western Washington." The laughter began to relax him. He was questioned for less than two hours. The next day the Senate unanimously voted confirmation. The date is important, because there was later to be speculation that he had truckled to special interests to ensure his confirmation.

On February 6, just days after Murrow had taken up his duties, Spessard Holland of Florida had risen on the Senate floor and denounced "Harvest of Shame" for "seven specific misrepresentations of fact in this film and its unfairness to Florida migrant agricultural workers and their employers." There were indeed inaccuracies. The migrant mother who claimed to have fourteen children had failed to mention that only seven were living. Murrow had said that there was no record of a Florida migrant child ever earning a college degree. Holland said he had a list of one hundred. There had been errors of fact and a degree of hyperbole. But to suggest that the film failed to capture the essence of the lives of these landless American serfs was untrue. The facts were not always right; the spirit, however, was unerring.[7]

But several days after Murrow's confirmation by the Senate, Holland had further reason to be upset. The Florida senator learned that his state, which he felt had been vilified at home, was now about to be held up to contempt abroad. CBS had sold the television rights to "Harvest of Shame" to the BBC. Holland made five calls to the State Department to try to kill the broadcast, only to be told that there was nothing State could do. The department, however, alerted the President's press secretary, Pierre Salinger, to Holland's unhappiness. Salinger called Richard Salant, now president of CBS news. Salinger was later to maintain that he had not tried to suppress the broadcast. His sole concern, he said, was that British viewers might think, since Murrow was now director of USIA, that "Harvest of Shame" must be an official U.S. government film. He managed to have CBS add disclaimers to the beginning and end of the film explaining that Murrow had been a private citizen when he made the documentary. Salinger then talked with Senator Holland, who was still apparently not satisfied, since, thereafter, Holland spoke twice with Murrow at the USIA about the BBC broadcast.[8]

Soon afterward, and coincidentally on the day on which the President swore him in as director of the USIA, Ed Murrow did something grossly out of character. He knew by now that Radio Moscow had already used a large chunk of a transcript of "Harvest of Shame" for a broadcast exposing poverty in America. He was learning, in the war for men's minds, that one man's truth was another's propaganda. After his conversations with Senator Holland, Ed placed a transatlantic call to Hugh Carlton Greene, director general of the BBC, a friend dating back to the war years. He asked Greene, as he later described the conversation, "Are you locked in or is a substitute possible?" Greene responded exactly as Murrow would have in like circumstances. Leonard Miall, the man in charge of BBC public affairs broadcasting, recalled the director general's response: "Greene had told him that he wouldn't dream of taking it off. And I think [Ed] was relieved."

Word of the call, however, leaked to the press. Jack Gould, whose admiration of Murrow so recently knew no bounds, was now swift to condemn: "...he should have resigned after twenty-four hours in office than concur in an incredible intrusion...." The American Civil Liberties Union made public a telegram it sent to Murrow declaring that the ACLU was "shocked" by his attempt to suppress his own broadcast. The disillusionment was perhaps best expressed in an editorial in the Harrisburg, Pennsylvania, *Patriot*, pleading, "Say it ain't so, Ed."

To the end, Murrow was loyally to deny that anyone, the President, Salinger, or Holland, had pressured him to make the call. "I did something that I have done for many years," he said. "I picked up the phone and called Hugh Carlton Greene, an old friend." Jack Gould was having none of it. In a subsequent column, he wrote, "...Murrow obviously was not acting alone, despite his sportsmanship in taking the blame and that there are others who should help him hold the bag."

He had already been confirmed by the Senate almost a week before this contretemps broke. To suggest, as some muttered, that Kennedy's official swearing-in of him depended on his making the phone call, is fatuous. But the call was a blunder and, at the very least, suggests the new kid on the block overly eager to become part of the neighborhood gang. The incident illuminated what happens, as a British reporter put it, to "a poacher turned gamekeeper."

He was also fast shedding his journalist's self-righteousness. He learned that virtue, like beauty, is in the eye of the beholder. "If I ever go back [to broadcasting]," he said, "I'll be far less dogmatic than I used to be." He was proud of "Harvest of Shame" as an unflinching examination of an American failure. But showing the film in Britain, he said, was like "sending an x-ray to a pen pal who wants to know how you look." Finally, the incident taught him that for a high-level public servant there were no casual acts, words, or phone calls. Everything he said or did now fell under high-power magnification.

Three days after he was formally sworn in, he spoke to over a thousand members of the USIA staff at the State Department auditorium in a meet-the-new-director program. He opened the meeting to questions and answers and was instantly hit with a query about the Carlton Greene call. He answered his questioner: "As was suggested in one of the editorials to which you referred, my telephone call was both foolish and futile....I did not become aware of which hat I was wearing....I still hope in spite of this I shall have a place to put the hat." The audience burst out in laughter and applause.[9]

The shakedown cruise had begun in rough waters. It was to get rougher. In the middle of April, Don Wilson burst into Murrow's office and told him that he had to break off an appointment. Wilson had disturbing news. He had just had breakfast with Tad Szulc of *The New York Times* and Szulc was urging the USIA to set up some sort of press briefing arrangement because Szulc knew "for a fact" that an invasion of Cuba, engineered by the CIA, was imminent.

On hearing this, Wilson recalled, "Ed was furious." He had taken Paley's advice—"You cannot represent your country unless you know what's going on behind the scenes." Kennedy had assured him he would know. Yet Ed knew nothing of what Szulc claimed. Within minutes, Murrow and Wilson were on their way to the office of the CIA director, Allen Dulles. Dulles refused to confirm or deny the invasion story. "Ed," he said, "there's nothing I can say about it at this time."

After Murrow left, Dulles alerted the White House to Ed's outrage at being excluded from an issue that his agency would have to explain to the world. When Ed got back to the office, he had a message that the President's national security adviser, McGeorge Bundy, wanted to see him.

Ed went to the White House to see Bundy, and when he got back to his own office, he told Wilson that a reporter indeed knew more about what was going on in the administration than the director of the U.S. Information Agency. Bundy had confirmed the invasion story.

Ed was livid, Wilson recalled. "What a stupid, stupid idea," he kept repeating. "He thought the invasion was not only foolish," Wilson remembered, "but immoral, wrong, even if it succeeded." To the world it would represent gunboat diplomacy of the most arrogant stripe.

The invasion was launched on April 17 in western Cuba at the Bay of Pigs. Three days later the 1,500 Cuban exiles who constituted Brigade 2506 were either dead or Castro's prisoners.

Had Murrow been privy to this secret earlier, his opposition might not have prevailed, but he could at least have pointed out the flawed premise in the strategy. The invasion's success was predicated on the CIA's assumption that a modest force landing at the Bay of Pigs would ignite a popular uprising against Castro throughout Cuba. But Murrow had had in his possession for months a poll conducted by the Institute for International Social Research revealing that the Cuban people, in overwhelming numbers, supported Castro. The report had never been forwarded to the White House because earlier rumors of an American-backed invasion were denied again and again.[10]

After what he regarded as this humiliating exclusion, Ed secured the President's promise that he not be left out of decisions that he would be expected to defend. He began attending meetings of the cabinet and the National Security Council, though by statute he was not a member of either. He cracked the NSC inner circle, sitting in on the meetings of its executive committee. He was named to a small body, Special Group (Augmented), with Bobby Kennedy, Dean Rusk, Robert McNamara, General

Maxwell Taylor, and a few others, to plan how now to undo Castro in the wake of the Bay of Pigs fiasco. One scheme involved assassinating Castro. Murrow heaped scorn on the idea and said that he hoped such foolishness would not even be made part of the committee's record.

His style in the inner sanctum was to speak rarely, and then usually only when his opinion was sought, a wise posture as it turned out. For JFK prized concision and, as McGeorge Bundy put it, "had a low tolerance for long expressions of wisdom as perceived by one individual."

When Ed did speak, his intent was unequivocal. And he was brutal in his estimation of those who were not. He told his CBS colleague, Bob Pierpoint, "You know what Dean Rusk does? He sits at cabinet meetings. The President goes around the table and asks everybody's opinion. Rusk doesn't give his until he's figured out what the President wants to hear."[11]

He proved a quick study in the image war, even displayed a touch of the gut fighter. As the Soviet Union prepared to put the first manned spacecraft in orbit, Ed sent a memo to the White House suggesting a course of action: "In the event of a Soviet manned space shot failure, we should express with all the sincerity we can muster the deep regret and distress of the President and the people of the United States....this reaction might take the form of a well publicized telegram from the President to Mr. Khrushchev....Simultaneously, one of our project Mercury astronauts might publicly express the regret of his group and extend sympathy to the Soviet astronaut's family and colleagues....covertly, the United States might encourage commentators in other countries to deplore the low regard for human life which prompted the Soviets to attempt a manned shot 'prematurely' despite their earlier assertion that their 'lofty humanism' demanded 'certainty of success.'" Nine days later, Yuri Gagarin soared safely into orbit.[12]

Murrow's stock with the President was tested that summer of 1961 when the Soviet Union broke the nuclear test ban. Kennedy was immediately under pressure from hard-liners in Congress to resume American testing at once. The Pentagon wanted a nuclear strike against a Soviet test site. Ted Sorensen later wrote, "The advice that JFK liked best was from USIA Director Murrow." As Ed himself described that advice, "I wanted maximum delay between their resumption of tests and our resumption of tests—assuming no overriding reasons for resuming at once. It is obvious that we had a tremendous propaganda advantage, that we should make the most of it as long as possible." Evelyn Lincoln, Kennedy's secretary, remembered the President telling her after the test ban issue, "He was sorry that he hadn't benefitted from Ed Murrow's advice on the Bay of Pigs."

His first sensation when he began sitting in the inner councils was chastening. He found himself suddenly awash in secrets any one of which a CBS correspondent would have killed for. And as he read news stories of matters that he was now privy to, he realized how much of the whole story that even the most aggressive reporter inevitably missed. At the first NSC meeting he attended, his reporter's reflex went off like an alarm clock and he started scribbling furiously what he heard. Back at his office, he briefed Wilson and Sorensen and tossed his notes into the waste basket. Sorensen dove for them. "You can't do that, Ed," he said. "That stuff's classified. It has to be burned!"[13]

He and Ken Galbraith had known each other for thirty years. Their wives had grown up together, and now the two men found themselves part of the same administration, with Galbraith rather uncertain about Murrow's right to be there. "Arthur Schlesinger and I," he later admitted, "had risen above friendship to urge against the appointment. We assumed that after his long years in radio and television, often passing along the Washington word, he would be another voice for the prevailing orthodoxy." Galbraith also feared that Ed was "too often inclined to act when he should think—and plays for effect."

Galbraith went to India as ambassador and soon after informed Murrow by memorandum that his USIS-India operation was "a devoted but pedestrian and spiritless organization." Galbraith had asked the USIS office to send some books to the ambassador's residence "to fill up some empty shelves." After looking them over, he wrote Murrow, "On balance, I prefer the shelves."

Galbraith's gift for mockery was particularly inspired by a column that came over the USIA wireless file, the material transmitted out of Washington which the post was supposed to try to place in foreign newspapers and newscasts. This column, bylined "Guy Sims Fitch," likened the United States to a great corporation. The people were the stockholders, the Congress the board of directors, and the President the chief executive officer. After reading Mr. Fitch's economic allegory, Galbraith sent a memo to the President. "I congratulated him warmly," he later recalled of this communication, "on being the head of this corporation and telling him how much I was impressed by this analogy and raised the question of whether there had not been a mistake. Obviously his old man was far better qualified than he was."

Soon afterward, Murrow's white telephone rang. The President was on the line and proceeded to read the Guy Sims Fitch column to Ed with malicious glee, blithely behaving as though Murrow himself had written it, interspersing his recital with questions: "What did you mean by this, Ed?" "Is this really true, Ed?"

A furious Murrow wrote back to Galbraith, "I appreciate your candor and the cutting edge of your language is refreshing…regarding your sarcasm on the matter of the books, those that you saw were of course in the pipeline before the new administration took over." In a second memo he wrote Galbraith, "The man who writes the GSF column is not an economist or a popularizer of economic theory to compare with John Kenneth Galbraith. If he were, he doubtless would be a professor at Harvard or even Ambassador to India rather than working as an underpaid USIA writer." Galbraith, commenting later on these acid exchanges, remarked that they were carried out "with high good humor."

How good-humoredly Murrow took the President's phone call is questionable. But Galbraith, in time, was to change his mind about Murrow's place in the administration. Ed, he said, "promptly made clear his opposition to the traditional litany," and "I soon became to think of him as the most effective of the New Frontier appointments."[14]

In their day-to-day operations, government agencies tend to run themselves. The difference that the politically appointed head hopes to make is to change the course of his lumbering vessel a few degrees and to get his appropriation approved by Congress. In the insider's Washington, it is the latter achievement, getting the money, that most impresses. To Murrow and his USIA predecessors, the most unpleasant, even demeaning, part of that task was John J. Rooney. Throughout the USIA, the name inspired fear and loathing. For if the USIA was treated like the bastard at a family reunion, Rooney was the mean-spirited stepfather.

John J. Rooney was a Brooklyn congressman who had risen to the chairmanship of the subcommittee that passed judgment on the appropriations of the State, Commerce, and Justice Departments and the USIA. He thus exercised virtual life-and-death power over the fortunes of these agencies. Rooney was an Irish-Catholic, a graduate of Fordham law school, a professional hard-nose who liked to greet the USIA chiefs before his subcommittee with a curled lip, an exaggerated Brooklyn accent, and phrases like "What's noooo...in Oagaduguuu?"

The USIA was a sitting duck for Rooney. As Stanley Plesent, the agency's counsel and lobbyist on Capitol Hill, put it, "We had no built-in domestic constituency, no postal workers union we could go to say, hey fellows your jobs are on the line. No one to send pressure mail."

Witnesses came before Rooney with their talk of global crises and the worldwide struggle for men's beliefs. But Rooney's world was Brooklyn. He had only to please the voters in his district to hold onto the power he wielded over the calling-card and canape crowd from State and the USIA. "Rooney's game," said Lewis Schmidt, the USIA's fiscal officer, "was to play the small-bore lawyer who catches the big boys squandering the taxpayers' money." Another of Rooney's obsessions was homosexuals in State and USIA. How many had been exposed and how many had been fired since the last fiscal year was his repeated query.

This was the man Ed Murrow faced in his first budget hearing in the spring of 1961. As he walked to the hearing room, he was faintly embarrassed by his fame. Tourists stared and asked for his autograph. Congressmen and senators came up to shake his hand. They had their pictures taken with him and invited him to appear with them on film clips that they would send to television stations back home. But John Rooney had seen them all come and go. He was not about to be bowled over by a USIA director, even Edward R. Murrow.

The budget that Murrow came in with was infinitesimal by federal standards. The entire agency could be run for a year for the cost of one Polaris missile. Murrow asked for $118.6 million, a $15.2 million increase over the year before, mostly to build up the agency's program in the two areas that the Kennedy administration considered vital, Latin America and Africa.

But Rooney was more interested in attacking a psychological testing program that the USIA had initiated to weed out employees who might be emotionally unsuited for living in foreign cultures. "You have not found more screwballs than the State Department, have you?" he asked Murrow. Rooney also learned that the agency had discovered eight homosexuals on the payroll, and wanted to know, "Of the eight, did you actually fire any one? I suppose the answer is no." Murrow asked for funds to open a USIA post in Kuwait, a country becoming increasingly critical since it held 60 percent of the world's known oil reserves. Rooney leaned forward and said, "Ku-what?"

Murrow had approached the committee believing in the power of reason. He thought that he could marshall the evidence and make a convincing case, and the subcommittee would then approve his budget. As McGeorge Bundy later observed, "Ed was not a political man. Rooney was only that. Ed thought that if you argued the case right, it would produce the right result. It doesn't work that way in Washington. Ed did not study the pressure points that would make Rooney do what he wanted." And he failed. he did not get his budget increase.[15]

It had been, with the BBC incident, the Bay of Pigs, and the budget defeat, a rough first semester. Washington, he was learning, was a more serpentine Byzantium even than broadcasting. On the other hand, he had won the President's confidence and a place in the inner councils beyond any of his predecessors. He had lifted the morale of a long demoralized staff and his own in the process. He appeared happy at the USIA.

Don Wilson and Tom Sorensen watched his reserve dissolve, slowly, cautiously. Now, at the end of a long day, they gathered in his office for a feet-on-the-desk hour of unwinding. The chauffeur would be sent out for a pint of scotch, and Murrow would review the victories and defeats of the day with a sardonic air. He trotted out his stories of dukes and dustmen and Churchill during the war. He did not, they noticed, speak often of CBS, of his more recent programs. It was as though he had put a fence around the last dozen years of his life.

He opened that tightly buttoned persona, however, to few others. To strangers, he was as spontaneous as a stone. The staff occasionally brought visiting dignitaries or new employees to meet the director, expecting a greeting, a well-turned pleasantry, and a goodbye. But "Ed had no gift for small talk," Wilson remembered. Hewson Ryan brought a party of Brazilian officials to Murrow's office where Ed sat with them in his classic elbows-on-knees pose and, after an excruciating silence, said, "So you're from Brazil," followed by another silence.

A magazine writer, familiar with Murrow's tactic of waiting out answers, recalled when he interviewed Ed in Washington, "I tried the same trick on him. But there is no outwaiting him. The silences between us sometimes lasted two minutes."

He and Janet sold the Park Avenue apartment when they left New York and bought a house in Washington. Ed wanted to give his new life a sense of rootedness. They rarely got away to Quaker Hill more than once a month. Yet they never plunged into the chic whirl of the New Frontier. They did not live in Georgetown. They entertained sparingly, old friends for the most part. They did not dance the twist, go on fifty-mile hikes, or get pushed into the pool at Bobby Kennedy's parties.[16]

That first summer, Ed took off with Casey, now 16, for a cross-country drive. He continued to try to peel away the cocoon of privilege that he feared would insulate his son from fundamental values. "He would still point out people to me," Casey remembered, "people who had been successful without a formal education, his cameraman, Charlie Mack, for example. He always stressed the point that a fancy job didn't make you happy or worthwhile."

Yet when the time came, he took his son on a tour of the most exclusive prep schools—Milton, Andover, Groton. A Groton admissions official took Ed aside and said, "You know, Mr. Murrow, if your son wants to go to Groton, there will be absolutely no problem." Ed was furious, Casey remembered. "Case," he said, "I won't pay for you to go to school here. You can pick any school, but not this one."

In the end, the boy chose Milton. "Dad was a little horrified that I went to such a snooty school," Casey recalled. "He was even more horrified when he found out that Milton sent most of its graduates to Harvard. The Eastern elitist image of these places bothered him." His son was also perceptive enough to say, "I think some of it was mock horror."

He could champion the lives of happy gas station owners and successes with high school diplomas. But his son went to Milton and eventually to Yale. It was the old ambivalence surfacing again, a compulsion to disparage privilege yet, at the same time, emulate the privileged. At least, Casey Murrow would never have to kite his education on a résumé.

Ed seized on what educators call the "teaching moment" to conduct Casey's sex education. There were at Glen Arden two prize Holstein Frisian bulls, and when the bulls serviced the cows, Ed explained to Casey the facts of reproduction. "When we talked about these things," Casey recalled, "his expression became very serious. When he talked to me about birth control, he talked about responsibility. He didn't just say 'you don't want to get the girl pregnant.' Instead, he'd say, 'You really have to want to take on the responsibility of being a father before you make love to someone.'" It was all very cool and clinical. But he clearly wanted to spare his son the painful school of personal experience in which he had learned these lessons long ago at Pullman.

That summer, they got as far as Salt Lake City. Then Ed checked in with his office by phone and decided that there was too much pressing business in Washington. He broke off the trip and went back.[17]

The USIA was essentially a field organization. Its cutting edge was the network of posts scattered throughout the world. That fall, after he felt that he had consolidated his grip on the home office, Ed took to the field. He made his first visit to Latin America. He also went to Europe and was in Berlin when the wall went up.

Staff members who traveled with him detected that he was not a well man. Tom Sorensen shared a hotel room with Ed at a run-down hotel on Cyprus where Ed warned him, "You may not like this. I'm told I gnash my teeth during my sleep." He gnashed his teeth, Sorensen remembered; he also "groaned, he muttered, he talked in his sleep, and he coughed all night long." At another point, Sorensen was searching a medicine cabinet for an aspirin and found that Murrow maintained a traveling pharmacy. He asked, "Are you ill?" "No," Ed told him. "It's just that I have trouble sleeping, so I take sleeping pills at night. Then I want to be alert during the day, so I take something else." For the chronic cough, Hew Ryan remembered, "He was always swigging codeine."[18]

As Christmas approached in that first year in Washington, Lacey Murrow, an irrepressible collector of properties, announced that he wanted the whole family to meet for a holiday reunion at his latest acquisition, a resort home in Wickenburg, Arizona, sixty miles northwest of Phoenix. Their mother, who had not made a long trip since she left North Carolina in 1913, was going to be there.

Ed was uneasy. His contacts with Lacey were a scar tissue of unpleasantness and embarrassment. But there was no way out. Ethel was now 85, "like a small, gnarled oak," Janet remembered, failing in health, and there would not likely be another gathering of the Murrow clan in Ethel's lifetime.

Failing health or not, she was still fiercely independent. Her daughters-in-law would find someone to keep house for her, and Ethel would fire the housekeeper as soon as she was alone again. During one visit, Ed and Janet bought Ethel a grandfather clock. Later, the dealer wrote a worried letter to Ed. He had not been able to persuade Ethel that she had placed the clock in an unsafe corner where it might topple over on her. Ed wrote the man, "I'm afraid there is little either of us could do about the position of the clock....my mother is a very opinionated person."

The Wickenburg reunion was a classic family encounter in which everyone was there to please someone else, with the net effect that no one was really pleased. Lacey was drunk most of the time. "We all hoped that Mother Murrow wouldn't notice," Janet remembered, "but Ed was heartsick." Dewey left early. Ethel took to her bed and refused to eat. Lacey's wife, Marge, called a doctor, who examined the old woman and said, "It seems she just doesn't want to live anymore."

Ed arranged to fly with his mother back to Washington State. She was so weak that he arranged to have an ambulance pick her up at the other end of the flight. On the plane, Ethel refused to buckle her seat belt. She had to be able to get out of the plane if anything went wrong, she said. A lengthy scene ensued with the stewardess. "Dad was very embarrassed," Casey remembered.

She was taking heart medication, and Ed had given her a pill on takeoff. On their arrival in Seattle, they put her aboard the ambulance and then went to pick up a car. Suddenly, Ed remembered that Ethel was due for another pill and that he still had them. As Casey recalled, "She probably could have missed one dosage, but we got into the car and Dad tore after that ambulance at a speed I found thrilling." They caught up with the ambulance and eventually got Ethel back to the little house in Bellingham. Ed stayed for a few days until he knew that Dewey and his wife were coming, in effect, to relieve him of the watch; then he flew back to the East.

A few days later, Dewey called to tell him that their mother was dead. "I think it broke her heart about Lacey," Donnie Murrow later remarked of her mother-in-law's death. "She just stopped eating. I think she willed herself to die."

After the funeral, the three brothers went back to the little white house and took down the bottle of medicinal whiskey that had been on the shelf for as long as they could remember and finished it off.[19]

This tiny, iron-willed figure had been the chief author of the complex, driven character of her youngest son. Her principal gift, if such it can be called, was the conscience that drove him, cajoled him, haunted him, never let him believe that he had done enough, never granted him peace. She had taught him how to work, but not how to play, too much about life's duties and not enough about life's joys. She had also bequeathed to him, fortunately, the saving grace of wry humor.

He returned to Washington early in January as the second year of the Kennedy administration opened. It also might have been his last year, since New York Democrats were again urging Ed to consider a Senate race, this time against Jack Javits. The President had other ideas.

Ed and Janet were invited to dinner with JFK and Jackie in the family dining room upstairs at the White House. The third couple present was Ed's deputy, Don Wilson, and Wilson's wife, Susan. As social arrival was measured along the New Frontier, these intimate little dinners represented the deepest point of penetration. That night, a high-spirited Jack Kennedy did most of the talking, and late in the evening he asked, "Ed, did you ever consider running for office?" The Republican that JFK had feared most in 1960 was Nelson Rockefeller, governor of New York, a man still hungering for the presidency. Rockefeller was up for reelection in 1962. If Murrow could beat him for governor of New York, Rockefeller would virtually be dead as a presidential prospect in 1964. Kennedy asked if Murrow was interested in the New York race. "I'd make a terrible candidate," Ed answered. Kennedy did not press the issue.[20]

He rarely spoke of his last years at the network. But under the influence of drink, he revealed his still smoldering disillusionment. After the 1962 White House Correspondents Dinner, he went out for a night on the town, with three other journalists that ended in a Baltimore strip joint. As dawn approached, the quartet was back in Washington and banged on the door of columnist Mary McGrory, who let them in for breakfast. One of the party was Bernard Eismann, and he remembered how Murrow, his tongue thick with drink, launched into a funereal monologue on the failure of his career. To Eismann it was painful to hear his idol's dreary plaint. "Everything he had accomplished in broadcasting was in vain. It was all being destroyed," Eismann recalled Ed saying again and again.[21]

But when he had slept that mood off, he put it behind him and plunged back into eleven-hour days at 1776 Pennsylvania Avenue.

He told a panel of reporters on ABC's *Issues and Answers* that the greatest obstacle to telling America's story abroad was racial bigotry at home. Washington in 1962 was, in its soul, still southern, still a Jim Crow town. Murrow described the futility of trying to win over newly emerging black nations when their diplomats in Washington found that "Landlords will not rent to them; schools refuse their children; stores will not let them try on clothes; beaches bar their families."

His old colleague, Ray Swing, put up Ed and Carl Rowan for membership in the Cosmos Club. What Ed liked about the prestigious Cosmos was that it based its membership not on some vapid notion of social status, but on professional achievement. Rowan was a Pulitzer Prize-winning journalist, assistant secretary of state for public affairs, and the highest-ranking black in the Kennedy administration.

Rowan and Murrow had become friendly at State Department staff meetings. Rowan recalled, "He brought a more liberal view of foreign policy to those meetings, more sensitivity to people in Africa and Latin America and Asia. He and I were almost always on the same side. We thought it was ludicrous in terms of American foreign policy that black American sailors had to stay aboard ship when the Navy put into South African ports. We fought it and we won." The Cosmos Club rejected Rowan. Murrow immediately withdrew his application for membership.

Ed made a long tour of USIA operations in black Africa. He advised the President to direct NASA to start training black astronauts. His USIA film director, George Stevens, Jr., produced a film entitled *March*, on Martin Luther King's march on Washington in 1963 that ended with King before the Lincoln monument declaring, "I have a dream...." Powerful southern congressmen did not like *March*. They did not want it shown abroad. Stan Plesent, as Murrow's man on the Hill, reported their muttered warnings—"If you only knew what the FBI has on King"—to Ed. Ed's response was, "Tell 'em to go to hell." *March* was exhibited.[22]

When he returned from the African sojourn, his secretary, Dorothy

Baas, could see that he was not well. Almost every time he went abroad, he came back sick. In his first eighteen months at the USIA, he lost 8 pounds that his lank frame could ill afford. He was still smoking heavily, taking pills, and seeing doctors often. Larry Le Sueur reminded him of the mounting evidence that smoking could cause cancer. Ed told him, "By the time I get cancer, they'll have a cure for it."

In the fall of 1962, he left for a trip that was to include Paris, Berlin, Teheran, and ultimately India. He felt unwell on his arrival in Paris, and worse in Berlin. In Teheran, on October 2, he collapsed. He spent a week in an Army hospital, where the initial diagnosis was pleurisy. A week later, he was flown back to the States and went home to Quaker Hill to recuperate. His family doctor told him to get himself into a good hospital. He thereafter entered the Naval Hospital in Bethesda, where Navy doctors found a spot on his left lung. They concluded, however, that the spot was an old scar dating back to the time when he had been caught in the forest fire as a college student. He was out of work a month. He came back, still smoking heavily, and relievedly telling his staff that he did not have cancer. It had been, nevertheless, a punishing illness. "We had a sense after that," McGeorge Bundy remembered, "that he was not a well man, that he was flying on one wing."[23]

His sickness also cost him his place in the most intense drama in the country's history since Pearl Harbor. For while Ed was out ill and Don Wilson was running the USIA, the country went to the brink of the nuclear abyss. On October 14, a U-2 flying a routine reconnaissance over western Cuba filmed what was identified as missile-launching sites under construction. On October 22, the President went before the nation on television and announced that the sites were Soviet-inspired and that "the purpose of these bases can be none other than to provide a nuclear strike capability against the Western Hemisphere." During the succeeding thirteen days of the Cuban missile crisis, Ed Murrow was flat on his back. It was, he said, "the most frustrating experience of my life."[24]

The missile crisis, nevertheless, marked his full conversion from skeptic to an open admirer of the President. In Kennedy's handling of the Cuban crisis, he had been impressed by the delicate balance achieved, firmness coupled with restraint, the readiness to use force and the wisdom to reason before using it. "He's become quite a President," Ed told Don Wilson when he returned to work. He had also long since stopped referring to Kennedy as "that young man in the White House."

Murrow's relationship with the President was becoming easy, even chummy. Before departing on one holiday, he wrote, "I will be in touch with the office by telephone daily and will file you an occasional brief report of what folks in the gas stations and motels think of your foreign policy."

He remained resistant, however, to the appeal of Robert F. Kennedy. Ordinarily, an attorney general and a director of the USIA would have little traffic with each other anyway. But Bobby Kennedy roved over the New Frontier as his brother's troubleshooter, particularly in the foreign policy area. Murrow found the 36-year-old Bobby "brash and immature."

Bobby had started what came to be called, after his country place, the Hickory Hill seminars, the intellectually chic place to be on the New Frontier. The seminars rotated among the top-level appointees' homes, with experts, usually recruited by Arthur Schlesinger, Jr., presiding over an informal colloquy. Murrow was usually invited and usually attended. But he rarely spoke and never asked a question. He had gone through these intellectual calisthenics thirty years ago in the NSFA and later with the refugee professors when he worked with the Emergency Committee. Ed found the seminars self-conscious and sophomoric, as he put it, "Bobby's way of educating himself."

Bobby Kennedy's most ineradicable sin in Murrow's eyes was that he had worked for Joe McCarthy. Ed did not forget an incident nine months after the McCarthy broadcast. He had gone to Louisville, Kentucky, to speak at a U.S. Chamber of Commerce banquet honoring "the nation's ten outstanding young men," among them, Robert F. Kennedy, then 29, "Chief Counsel of the Sub-Committee on Investigations." Murrow's text that night was the abuses of congressional investigations, and as Murrow began, Bobby Kennedy walked out. The wariness was mutual. Even after JFK appointed Ed USIA director, Bobby feared that he was one of those "reflex liberals" he so much disliked and distrusted.

Ed came back to the office after one NSC meeting and confided to his finance man, Lew Schmidt, "Thank God, there's little of Bobby in the President. I don't like to say this. But I think that man could be dangerous in a position of authority."[25]

Murrow's tutor in Washington during the first year had been hard experience. In the summer of 1963, he was to learn one more lesson the hard way. He had gone to what he regarded as almost demeaning lengths to cultivate John Rooney. He believed that he had finally wooed and won the obstreperous chairman. Yet, for the third year in a row, Rooney slashed USIA's appropriations request.

After this defeat, Ed called in his staff. He was furious. One small mind, he said, must not be allowed to frustrate the international information policy of an entire government. He was going over the head of this Brooklyn pol and take his case directly to the people. Old Washington hands on his staff eyed each other uneasily. But they kept their counsel. Here was the foremost communicator in America, and they were loath to tell him that he should not try to communicate with the country.

In mid-June he was to speak before the Advertising Federation of America in Atlanta. The USIA press office began promoting the speech early, getting advance copies to editors, softening up the Washington bureau chiefs of the major newspapers, the wire services, and the networks with personal visits.

The speech shook with a righteous wrath: "Either the House of Representatives believes in the potency of ideas and the importance of information or it does not. On the record, it does not so believe....We are being outspent, outpublished and outbroadcast. We are a first rate power. We must speak with a first-rate voice abroad." Ed repeated a variation on the theme weeks later in a blistering speech in Detroit. The result of his exercise in pure democracy was a thick sheaf of admiring news clippings, and virtual ostracism on Capitol Hill. As Lew Schmidt recalled, "When Ed realized what he had done, he tried to get an appointment to see Rooney. But every attempt failed."[26]

It was also a time when the march into the Vietnamese quagmire began. Murrow had always been skeptical about Asia as a place to invest American life and treasure. He was preeminently a man of Europe, convinced that here was where America's vital interests lay. He had once called for a pullout from Korea. After the French defeat at Dienbienphu, he virtually dripped scorn for American leaders, like Nixon, who wanted to take up France's falling banner of colonialism in Indochina. Above all, he was convinced that the struggle in South Vietnam was a national concern. It was essentially political and domestic, not military and international.

But now, as an administration official, particularly in his position, his situation was anomalous. He headed the agency charged with selling U.S. policy in South Vietnam. The embassy spokesmen who briefed American newsmen in Saigon were USIA officials. The anti-Communist films, leaflets, and magazines distributed in South Vietnam were USIA products. The U.S. military was expanding its presence in South Vietnam, and so was the USIA. And when the administration debated its Vietnam policy, Murrow was a participant.

The Kennedy administration itself was badly riven over that policy. By 1963, the United States was caught between the future possibility of a Communist takeover and the present reality of a dictatorship in South Vietnam. The regime of Prime Minister Ngo Dinh Diem had grown corrupt and repressive, a hard partner for the United States, professing its faith in democracy, to defend. Sentiment within the administration had split roughly between those ready to dump Diem for a more respectable Vietnamese leader and those prepared to stick with him on the at-least-he's-our-son-of-a-bitch theory of international alliances.

Murrow supported the President's increase of armed American "advisers" in Vietnam from 8,000 to 16,000; but he did so when others in the administration, General Maxwell Taylor and Walt W. Rostow among them, were urging the President to send in as many as 300,000 combat troops. When the use of a new chemical defoliant was debated to expose enemy supply trails and deny rice crops to the Viet Cong, Murrow strenuously opposed using Agent Orange. He told the President that this was not the kind of war Americans should be fighting. Had the shorthand labels of hawks and doves been in vogue that early, Murrow was clearly a dove.[27]

The situation in South Vietnam had come to a head, and Diem was about to be overthrown in the coup that cost him his life, when Murrow was diverted from that conflict abroad to a battle raging within his own body.

He went in September to Philadelphia for a heavy schedule of speeches and interviews. He barely managed to get through them. His voice had become raspy, and he complained of pains in his throat. A few days later, he had to ask Tom Sorensen to take over another speaking engagement. He entered Washington Hospital Center, where his condition was diagnosed initially as a blocked bronchial tube. When the surgeons went to remove it, they found a cancer in his left lung. The lung was removed in a three-hour operation on October 6.

When Don Wison learned of Murrow's condition, he asked the USIA library to send him a medical encyclopedia. The odds of surviving lung cancer, he discovered, "were grim." Still Ed himself felt optimistic. Lacey had had a lung removed three years before and appeared to have made a successful recovery.

From the moment of the diagnosis, he never smoked another cigarette. It was as though now, when it was too late, he had to prove his mastery over himself. The deprivation was achieved, nevertheless, at a heavy psychic price. Cigarettes had tranquilized him, had pacified his nervous system for forty years. "He still gestured with his hand when he talked," Janet remembered, "as though he was holding a cigarette."[28]

He was at home late in November waiting for his brother Dewey to come to Washington to help take him back to Quaker Hill to complete his recovery. He and Janet were having lunch in the library. "We had a young black maid at the time," Janet recalled. "She had been watching television and she came to the door and motioned for me to come out. She told me President Kennedy had been shot and she didn't want to alarm Ed. I got Ed back into bed and then I told him."

Ed appeared stunned, and then he said, "We've known people who've been shot and lived. Let's hope he'll be one of them." In the ensuing hours, while Americans were riveted to their television sets, Ed listened on radio. It was still his medium. Radio was so much faster with the news, he said.

When the President's death was confirmed, he called Don Wilson at the office. "It's awful," he told Wilson. "I want to come in. But, I'm too weak."

"He called me because he seemed to need to connect with somebody over what had happened," Wilson recalled. "He was crying. That was so uncharacteristic of him. I think it was an accumulation of things. His own sickness had thrown him into a deep depression, and now the death of the President. But, the open emotionalism was certainly not his style."

The following day, a Saturday, broke cold and drizzly over the nation's capital. The President was lying in state in the East Room of the

White House. Ed left his bed and had his chauffeur drive him and Janet there. He was taken to the wrong entrance and consequently faced a long flight of stairs. A Marine guard reminded him that there was an elevator nearby. "No," Ed said, "that's not necessary."

"He almost collapsed going up those stairs," Janet remembered. "He didn't have the strength to walk by the coffin. He had to sit down in a corner, while people fussed over him. It was just the sort of scene he had hoped to avoid."[29]

He tried to return to work early in December. The President was now Lyndon Johnson, a source of some uneasiness to Murrow. Johnson was well known throughout the USIA. He had made several trips abroad in the make-work vice presidential role of goodwill ambassador. He was regarded within the agency as a bully and a prima donna. Wherever Lyndon Johnson traveled, he demanded his brand of scotch, his type of shower head, his size bed. If crowds were large, it was because of his pulling power. If crowds were small, it was the USIA's fault. If he won headlines, it was because he was a great man. If he failed to get heavy news coverage, the USIA was to blame. He insisted on his own clipping service and "deluxe, gold-engraved, leather-bound" photo albums of all his encounters with world figures. At Sam Rayburn's funeral, he berated Murrow out loud for not assigning him the USIA's best photographer, Yoichi Okamoto. Most galling were Johnson's remarks to reporters at the National Press Club after a visit to Asia. Johnson told them, "I wish that you would resign and go over to Ed Murrow and tell him you'd like to go out to one of those posts and take charge. We need some good people and some extra effort in most fields. All I saw wasn't good, and there's no use kidding you about it."

The people at the USIA feared that, as President, Lyndon Johnson would now convert their agency into a crude instrument for his own glorification and use the agency to project to the world a vulgar American chauvinism.[30]

Murrow's unhappiness with the new order was to be short-lived. He was only coming in for a few hours a day, but even this effort exhausted him. Within a few weeks he confided to Wilson and Sorensen what was hardest for Ed Murrow to admit, that something was beyond him. "I can't do this job anymore," he said. "The doctors tell me I have to quit."

On December 19, he sent Johnson a letter saying, "As you know, I was separated from a cancerous lung in early October...." He went on to ask that the President accept his resignation effective in mid-January. And then he went to see Johnson personally.

Lyndon Johnson was an accidental President, a regional figure until now, an unlovable man suddenly thrust into the place of a beloved and martyred predecessor. His first objective was to preserve an appearance of continuity with the Kennedy presidency. The heart of this strategy was to hold on to Kennedy's people. Ed Murrow, while not the most powerful man in the administration, was the most famous. His departure, Johnson feared, could be read as a vote of no-confidence in Lyndon Johnson. He told Murrow that he did not want him to leave. He needed him. Ed Murrow was his strong right arm. He used this argument on so many Kennedy appointees, McGeorge Bundy recalled, "that one had the sense we were dealing with an octopus."

Murrow held firm. He knew that the exertion of staying on would threaten his recovery, possibly kill him. And so he went back to his office expecting his resignation to be announced momentarily.

The cold, damp Washington winter was hell for a sick man with one lung. Jonas Salk had urged Ed, as soon as Johnson freed him, to come to southern California to recuperate. Ed waited for agonizing weeks with no word. He tried to get another appointment. He tried to phone Johnson. His calls were not taken. He was mystified, humiliated, and in pain. Finally, he could wait no longer. He and Janet were at Dulles Airport preparing to fly to California when an airport official located him and asked him to come to an office to take an urgent call. The President came on the line. Johnson thanked Ed for his service to his country. He had found a replacement, he said. Carl Rowan was to become the new director of the USIA. LBJ would now accept Ed's resignation. Just eighteen days short of three years, Ed Murrow's career in public service ended.

Shortly afterward, he wrote a letter to J. Robert Oppenheimer contrasting the two Presidents he had served. Of Kennedy, he wrote, "I have had great difficulty in trying to reach some judgment regarding that young man's relation to his time. I saw him at fairly close range under a variety of circumstances, and there remains for me a considerable element of mystery—and maybe that is good. I always knew where his mind was, but I was not always sure where his heart was. My experience with Lyndon Johnson was rather the reverse. I was never in doubt where his heart was, as he was generally beating me over the head with it." (LBJ proved no less unforgiving toward Murrow. In 1967, after Murrow's death, when Johnson was preparing to sign the Public Broadcasting Act, an aide, Douglas Cater, suggested that Johnson quote from Murrow's 1958 Chicago speech. LBJ scrawled across Cater's memo, "No Murrow for me.")[31]

And what of his own tenure in government? Murrow was frustrated by the federal bureaucracy. Like many people who arrive in Washington from the private sector, he had been stunned to discover that incompetence was insufficient cause for firing even high-level officials protected by Civil Service. "I'm talking into a dead mike," he once complained. "I make a decision, everybody says 'fine.' And then I find, six months later, that nothing has happened."

Yet almost all of those who saw him during this time—fellow officials, old broadcast friends, his family—were convinced that he was as happy at the USIA as Ed Murrow was capable of being. The ironic exception was the one man who could have kept Murrow in broadcasting.

"He never complained to me when I saw him," Bill Paley was later to remark, "but he made you understand he was not happy down there." It
may well be that Murrow did give Paley that impression. It may have been
his way, even unconsciously, of saying that he belonged at CBS, of reminding Paley that he had been driven from his true métier.

His budget defeats on Capitol Hill were neither more nor less than
those of his predecessors. Indeed, midway through Ed's government service, while John Rooney was happily lopping off his requests, he told a
reporter that Murrow was "the best USIA director we've ever had."

Given an undernourished agency with an amorphous mandate and
no domestic constituency, he had managed a creditable record. He steered
the agency onto the new ideological battlefields. He opened twenty new
USIA posts in Africa, vastly expanded Spanish and Portuguese broadcasting to Latin America, and increased by six-fold the total of American
books translated and distributed abroad. He had been appalled at the virtually snow-white coloration of the top USIA staff. When he left, the number of top-ranking blacks in the agency matched their proportion in the
nation's population. He was the first USIA director to sit in the deliber-
ation of the cabinet and National Security Council. He never cracked the
Kennedy inner circle, however. He was in the next outward ring, valued,
but not invaluable.

Ultimately, his tenure has to be measured by the direction in which
he took America in the nebulous warfare of ideas. The question was perhaps best answered by Arthur Schlesinger, Jr.: "Before this administration, our own propaganda reinforced the idea that we were conservative,
dogmatic, committed to free enterprise in the sense that every country
should have it. This didn't reflect the reality. The truth about us proves
to be more attractive to the world. Under Murrow, we have told the truth."

Eight days after Ed left Washington, Jackie Kennedy sent him a message in an album put together by the administration, marking his departure. It read in part, "For Edward R. Murrow, who made the President so
proud. You will never know how many hours of joy and pride you gave
him—so many evenings, the minute we finished dinner, he would say
'Come, we'll go down to the movie room for half an hour—there is a film
of Ed Murrow's I want you to see.' He must have seen them all—and I
often wondered if you knew how devotedly he followed what you were
doing.... Jack was only allowed to be President for such a brief time. But
look at all that he did in those thousand days. And the greatest thing of
all he did was inspiring men like you—to leave comfortable lives and come
to serve your country."

He had come to Washington in the winter of his discontent, driven
from his true calling, to serve a man in whom he had scant faith. The
Kennedy appointment had been, frankly, a life ring seized by a drowning
man. Yet he was to find deep and unexpected fulfillment in the work and
develop respect for the man. Then, suddenly, it was over, the new career
and the life of the man he had come to serve.[32]

CHAPTER 32

Good Night and Good Luck

He began an odyssey that was to take him to California, Washington, Quaker Hill, New York City, and back to Quaker Hill, a journey careening between hope and despair.

Jonas Salk found Ed and Janet a cliffside house in La Jolla overlooking the Pacific near the Salk Institute for Biological Sciences. During the four months that he stayed there, Ed tried to play golf, but he tired after two or three holes. The weather was cold and drizzly, and he caught pneumonia. When he recovered, he restricted himself to slow walks. Most of all, he craved rest.

Salk was a man of boundless energy, utterly devoted to Murrow, eager to heal Ed's body by reviving his interest in living. Salk wanted Ed to become involved with the circle of intellectuals gathered at his institute. Ed did not respond. Janet wrote a friend that Salk had "the Friendly touch," by which she meant an aggressive desire to be helpful.

Salk understood what the battle with cancer had done to Ed spiritually as well as physically. Before, Ed Murrow had looked on adversity as a test that had strengthened him like the flames that turn iron to steel. The conquest of adversity gave him a sense of power and of control over his life. But the test of cancer had left him weaker, not stronger, feeling powerless instead of in control. He had made the struggle more difficult, Salk believed, by giving up smoking. It was too late for cigarettes to make much difference now. But the self-denial, Salk thought, "exacted a tremendous price, emotionally and physically." Ed kept a pack of cigarettes at his bedside "as a security blanket." Being able to resist smoking became psychologically important. "It showed that he still had control over himself," Salk said, "that he was not helpless." But he had denied himself a crutch that he had leaned on all his adult life, at the time when it was hardest for him to stand alone.[1]

His spirits did lift when he learned that Bill Paley was coming to see him in March. He insisted on picking Paley up at the airport, showing him around, and having him meet Jonas Salk. Paley's visit was not to be allowed to become a sick call. They spent the day together, and Paley remembered, "Ed was so attentive, so concerned about everything I was doing. He made me know his feelings toward me better that day than ever before." Ed's condition was too visibly weak for them to talk seriously about his coming back to the network. But Paley said he wanted Ed to become his consultant, to help him locate good programming.

Friendly had written him, "I think it's time for you to come back here.... I am going to cause the company to make you a specific offer.... you may be learning to get along with one lung, but I've been limping along with only a half a heart and half a gut and a quarter of an intellect and I am asking to be rescued." Friendly too came out to La Jolla. He had recently taken over the CBS news division, and was bursting with creative energy, arriving like a whirlwind through a sick ward, telling the wan, hollow-eyed Murrow that he knew he would soon be back at the network.[2]

By May, Ed was back in Washington briefly to close out his life there. He was feeling stronger and talking about going back to work. He had had feelers from the other two networks too. He saw Bill Downs and warned him not to let his wife "sign up for life" in her job at *National Geographic*. He wanted Roz Downs to work for him on some program ideas as soon as he finished his convalescence, he said. Ed looked thin to Downs, but a man clearly on the mend.

Henry Loomis, head of the *Voice of America,* and John McKnight, another USIA colleague, stopped to see Ed at the house he would soon be leaving in Washington and found him excited about a new arena. He talked about doing a documentary series in public television, "where I can spend six months on one show."[3]

He went back to Quaker Hill and told Friendly that he might ask him to send up Charlie Mack "to see how I look on camera. I think I'm ready."

He had a steady stream of visitors. Joe Wershba came with his wife, Shirley, and Ed took them on a jolting jeep tour of the property. "Ed, you shouldn't be doing this," Wershba said uneasily. Murrow responded with a grin, "Never complain, never explain." He waved grandly toward the main house. "Paid for," he said contentedly.[4]

That July, he did his first CBS broadcast since leaving the network. Studio 9, on the seventeenth floor of 485 Madison Avenue, was shutting down after serving essentially as the larynx of CBS news since 1933. The news operation was being moved to a new broadcast center on West 57th Street. The staff planned a final broadcast, "A Farewell to Studio Nine," distilling the history that had passed over the microphones there: H.V. Kaltenborn, describing people carrying the first portable radios, the size of small suitcases, during the Sudeten crisis; Eric Sevareid reporting on the fall of France, "The life just ran out of Paris like a beautiful woman lying in a coma"; John Daley, "interrupting this program to bring you a special news bulletin. The Japanese have bombed Pearl Harbor by air"; Murrow intoning, "I'm standing again on a rooftop in London feeling rather large and lonesome"; Allan Jackson reporting, "President Kennedy and Governor John Connally of Texas were both hit by a would-be assassin's bullets as they toured downtown Dallas."

The farewell closed with a reminiscence between Ed and Bob Trout recalling the old days, including Murrow's first tipsy debut when he had taken the microphone away from Trout. There was in his speech an unconvincing lightheartedness. His voice had a thin, dry quality as though the resonance had been hollowed out and only the husk was left. When the red light went off for the last time in Studio 9, it went off as well for Murrow. It was his last broadcast.[5]

He would become excited over an idea, and just as quickly, his enthusiasm would flag. Toward the end of summer, he told Janet something she found foreboding. He wanted to see Bill Shirer. Janet called Tess Shirer and invited her and Bill to Glen Arden for lunch. There had been so little contact between these once close men during the past nineteen years. Ed had read the roman à clef, *Stranger Come Home*, in which he figured so unflatteringly. Afterward, all that he had said to Janet was, "Bill had a big hurt. He suffered and he's written it out."

The tone at the lunch was coolly cordial. At the end, Ed invited Bill to go for a ride with him. They drove around Pawling on a sweltering upstate summer day. Ed was sweating and coughing. Shirer thought, "He looked terrible." As Shirer later described their conversation, "Once or twice he would start to bring up the past, but I would change the subject. I did not want to talk about it. It had happened. It had threatened to destroy me, but I had survived. That was that." Was not Murrow's invitation to Shirer, after all these years, clearly the gesture of a man who saw himself at the end of his life, who wanted to make amends, unburden his soul, and seek the forgiveness of a friend whom he feared he had wronged? Shirer was asked long afterward if this was probably the reason that Murrow had reached out to him. "It may have crossed my mind," Shirer said. "But I just didn't want to get into it." They returned to the house and said polite goodbyes, and the Shirers drove home, as Tess recalled, "in almost total silence." Bill Shirer had tried to cut the memory out of his heart, and forgiveness had gone with it.[6]

Ed was clearly inventorying his life, including his marriage. Bob Dixon had always found Ed and Janet reserved and undemonstrative with each other. Now Ed showed Janet open affection, hugging her and freely admitting how much he needed her. He had lost his own religious faith long ago. When he filled out forms that asked his religion, he would write "No preference." But he told Janet that her unwavering faith "has always been a source of strength to me."

The marriage had come full circle. Close in the beginning, they had grown so far apart in mid-passage that the bond almost snapped. Now they were close again. At this point Ed finally confessed to Janet what he had held back for over thirty years. He admitted to her that when he had gone to New Hampshire to see her in summer stock playing the lead in *The Late Christopher Bean*, he had never uttered a word to her about how good she was because he feared she might have chosen a life in the theater instead of him. He had found a woman for his partner in life who could tolerate both his negligence and his demons and provide a secure anchorage for the storms of his spirit. He had married wisely and luckily. He had always known it, but rarely said it. But now it was easier to tell her.[7]

That fall, Jonas Salk and Sander Vanocur happened to visit Ed on the same day. He took the two men for a walk through his favorite spot along the stream that ran through the glen. He was telling them a story about Harry Truman when, suddenly, he lost the thread of it. They thought nothing of it until he started telling a story about Bobby Kennedy and again became confused. The other two men now eyed each other uneasily. "I felt a cold sweat," Jonas Salk recalled. "I knew instantly what his stumbling probably meant." When they got back to the house, Salk took Janet aside and told her to get Ed to a neurologist.[8]

On November 8, he entered New York Hospital. Ten days later a tumor was removed from near his brain. After the operation, the surgeon told Janet, "I removed as much as I possibly could. If I had removed any more, I would have left him without speech. I couldn't do it to that man."

Still, for a time, they were hopeful. Janet took a furnished apartment on East 66th Street, where Ed came when he was discharged from the hospital the day before Christmas. The Galbraiths came to visit and found Ed in surprisingly good spirits. Janet told them, "We're through with this business. From now on, Ed's going to be better." They felt optimistic enough to buy an apartment in the old Dakota on West 72nd Street for $60,000. Ed wanted something on the West Side where he could reach the new CBS studios easily.

He looked cadaverous, his voice now like a rustling parchment. His head had been shaved for the operation, and he received his visitors in a wool cap. All his life, he had bridled at the attention given to his good looks. He had been like the rich man who could afford to disdain wealth. But now he was self-conscious about his appearance. His visitors tried to conceal their shock that this beautifully made man had wasted away to a shell of what he had been. Yet he was stubbornly genial, his wit as mordant as ever. His smile became a wry mask to hide the pain. He talked about everything, except his condition.

His spirits rose one day and plunged the next. They struck bottom, it seemed, when Winston Churchill died. Marietta Tree visited the day of Churchill's funeral and sat with Ed as he watched the coverage from a special club chair fitted with radio and television remote controls in the arm rest. She saw a strange smile cross his lips when she informed him that every detail of the pageantry they were watching had been worked out by Churchill before his death.

Ed spoke, she said, "as though Churchill's death marked the end of an age, his age too."

He and Janet did not speak of death, as though each was trying to protect the other. But Ed told Charles Collingwood, "I know I'm dying." Throughout this ordeal, now in its fifteenth month, their friends marveled at Janet's quiet strength. She was unfailingly cheerful around him, and buried her private grief in the consuming demands of looking after a mortally ill man.[9]

Why he was dying at age 56 could be explained in detached, clinical terms. But in the poorly understood places where the mind, the spirit, and the physical processes of human life intersect, other forces may have been at work. "As we see patients who are experiencing bereavement," Jonas Salk observed later, "we are seeing a higher incidence of serious disease, including cancer, within a short time afterwards....Ed suffered a form of professional bereavement in that his career had died."[10]

They were in the Dakota only seventeen days when Ed had to reenter New York Hospital. The cancer had reached the brain.

Bob Dixon was having lunch at Louis and Armand's when Victor, the maître d', told him that he had a phone call. "It was Janet," Dixon recalled. "She told me that Casey was at the hospital with his father, and Ed was saying he had to see me. I took a cab and Casey met me at the third floor. I went to Ed's room and when he saw me he grabbed me by the arm with both hands with incredible strength. His eyes were ablaze."

Ed told him, "They're trying to keep me here. I want to go home to Quaker Hill. I want you to go to those goddamned doctors and tell them you want me out of here. If they say no, I want you to make me a promise." He was squeezing Dixon's arms so hard, Dixon said, "that I thought he'd cut off the circulation." "I want you to promise me" Ed went on, "that you'll carry me out on your back if you have to."

Dixon placated him. He then led Casey out of the room and told him, "The man wants to go home to die, Casey. You'd better face up to it." Dixon then called Janet. She arranged to have a hospital bed installed at Glen Arden and hired three nurses to look after Ed around the clock.[11]

By April 6, he was back in his own room in the country. He was heavily medicated. When awake, he was reasonably cheerful, but he was increasingly slipping in and out of consciousness. The words of one of his old broadcasts seemed poignantly apt: "The names and faces of friends who are dead, and those who were lucky, are all a little vague. The door of memory is only slightly ajar, and it is necessary to close it completely when the red light goes on, lest one remember too much of the past." What was left of his life was now measured in hours. In that last hazy reverie, what ghosts from the past flickered through his failing consciousness—from childhood, from logging camps, from the campus at Pullman, from the pyres of London in 1940?[12]

He had lived a modern saga. In the birth of broadcast journalism, he had been present at the creation—indeed more than anyone else, was the creator. He had had the advantage of writing on the slate when it was virtually clean. As Marvin Kalb put it, "Murrow was a meteor in a fairly empty sky." He was no comet, however. His like would not come back. He was sui generis, partly because of what he was and partly because when he left broadcasting, the door closed on the kind of freedom he had known.

The whole of the man was more than the sum of the parts. Savareid and Howard K. Smith were better writers; Trout, Collingwood, and Cronkite more facile talkers; Quincy Howe and Shirer keener analysts; Hottelet a tougher reporter. But the composite man, they agreed, was unsurpassed. Oddly, he did not possess the cardinal virtues of the journalist, objectivity and balance. His power lay rather in his subjectivity, in the passionate moral biases, however coolly concealed, that he brought to his work. He is conceded by those who worked with him, and those who competed against him, and by their heirs, to be the patron saint of the profession. He might have shown a little more magnanimity toward Walter Cronkite; yet Cronkite happily agreed that "Murrow established the norms by which we in the profession pretty well live today." It had ended badly between him and Shirer; yet Shirer would say, "More than anyone, Ed Murrow realized the potential in radio and television for serious journalism." Harry Reasoner may well have perceived his most enduring contribution: "You get a tradition established and you have made it difficult for small people to corrupt it." To Reasoner, Murrow was the tradition.[13]

He won every award that his profession had to offer, most of them more than once. In the last months of his life he was given the Medal of Freedom, the country's highest civilian honor. Queen Elizabeth knighted him. If British, he would have been Sir Edward, and in a corner of his soul, he always was. England was where, he said, "this reporter left all of his youth and much of his heart."

The honors heaped on him by others failed to silence the small, nagging voice that whispered within that he had never done well enough. His chronic discontent drove him to succeed, yet robbed him of the capacity to enjoy success. He liked to quote Mark Twain: "It is not likely that any complete life has ever been lived which was not a failure in the secret judgment of the person who lived it."[14]

His own departure from broadcasting coincided with the waning of television's golden age. The phrase is perhaps too casually employed. But in commercial network television, that period roughly from 1953 to 1961 can fairly be called golden. Not all of it certainly. But the proportion of what was good then was greater than what is good now. It was the period when Murrow's medium, the documentary, flourished on commercial television as it has not since. It was a time when serious theater was attempted and often realized on *Playhouse 90, Studio One, The Philco Television Playhouse*. In watching these dramas today—the work of A.E. Hotchner, Abby Mann, Paddy Chayevsky, Rod Serling, Reginald Rose, and others—one is stunned. Work of that stature debuted on television? And was shown once?[15]

What had happened to the golden age is best understood in something Bill Paley said in the spring of 1965, while Ed Murrow lay dying. Paley told a CBS stockholders' meeting that net income for the first quarter had dropped. The cost of unscheduled news coverage—Winston Churchill's death, space exploration, civil rights stories—had cut earnings by 6 cents per share. If Paley could be thinking and publicly expressing himself in these terms, the location of television's soul at that point could be fixed with absolute precision. As Fred Friendly described what had happened, "Television can make so much money doing its worst it often cannot afford to do its best." As for Bill Paley's place in the pantheon of broadcasting, it is secure. But it rests more securely on how it began than where it ended.[16]

To berate broadcasting, particularly television, for succumbing to tawdry commercialism, to the tyranny of ratings, to the triumph of raw numbers, is to flog a dead horse. Murrow had already said it all in Chicago in 1958. Critics have repeated it virtually every season since, and nothing really changes. To expect a corporation, which is, by its very nature, a device for earning profits, to behave with more enlightenment for less profit, is to expect the beast to go against its nature.

Where would Murrow fit into television today? Had he lived longer, had he come along later, what would he think of contemporary broadcasting? It is a futile, yet tantalizing, speculation. While he was with the USIA, he did draft a proposal for the Ford Foundation for a "fourth network," a public-style broadcasting channel that could challenge the networks where they were weakest, in public affairs. After his first operation, when he talked of going back into television, he spoke often of the greater maneuverability and freedom that he would enjoy in public television, where, indeed, Fred Friendly went on to new triumphs and awards when he could no longer stomach commercial television's accounting mentality. Murrow might well have done likewise.[17]

One imagines that Ed Murrow, as a viewer, would watch with pleasure and pride his lineal descendants on the network news, clearly the finest continuing work done on contemporary commercial television. He would no doubt beam with a paternal pleasure at CBS's *Sunday Morning* and *60 Minutes* and stay up for intelligent discourse on a program like *Nightline*. He would envy the technical resources that enable correspondents to follow stories almost instantaneously to virtually the ends of the earth. He would probably applaud the choice offered, if not always the content offered, by all-news channels. But he would likely miss the bite and idiosyncratic perspectives of that virtually vanished breed, the broadcast commentator, an Elmer Davis, a Raymond Swing, a Quincy Howe, an Eric Sevareid. One is left with a sense that when the news and public affairs ended on the commercial networks, Ed Murrow would be listening to NPR and watching PBS, when he was not reading a good book.

Before the broadcaster was the man. To the end of his days, he kept that piece of redwood with his initials carved on it, a permanent memento of his roots. His values were suspended between two worlds, the one in which he was raised and the one to which he rose. His impulses were those of a populist reformer. Yet he lived like an English squire. He had a congenital attraction to underdogs—working people, Britain during the war, Israel, Radulovich, McCarthy's victims. And in his romantic imagination, he saw himself as an underdog, up from poverty. He prided himself on his capacity to mix with cowboys, lumberjacks, and farmers. But he was honestly more at home with an intellectual Harold Laski, a social Ronnie Tree, a powerful Bill Paley. His character remained forever contradictory, uncapturable. He could be, in Eric Sevareid's phrase, "an engaging boy one moment and an unknowable recluse the next."

His friend Larry Le Sueur sketched his several faces in a few deft strokes: "There's Murrow the Southern gentleman—he was born down South, you know—with his code. He almost never gossips, and shrinks from real crudity. He's got an intense sense of honor and integrity. There's Murrow the Westerner, breezy, open, confident, fiercely loyal to his friends, the man of action....There's Murrow the brooding pessimist—I'm not sure, I believe he's as pessimistic as he makes out....There's Murrow the patriot, with his love of country and feeling of responsibility for it. In his own way he's almost as complicated as the American image is and made up of the same stuff."

"He had no real political ideas," Collingwood believed. "I couldn't place him on the political spectrum. His politics were based on old-fashioned notions of morality and honor, not ideology. He had character, and that is something you just can not fake."

Shirer had him just about right. Murrow, he said was "a skeptical idealist." The idealism was his moral fuel, the skepticism his armor.

His friends talked unabashedly about a man they loved. Howard K. Smith called Murrow, "A prince, the most impressive man I ever met." "Not a day of my life goes by," Sevareid said long after Murrow was gone, "that I don't think in some way of Ed." Friendly had a framed sketch of Murrow hung in the staircase of his home and said he could not pass it without feeling the man judging him. "I loved him as much as I did any man except my father and brother," Charles Collingwood admitted. Yet he echoed a reaction common among even those closest to Murrow: "I never presumed to think I had penetrated his nature. I never really understood the man."

Janet could not recall anyone her husband could or would turn to, to open his heart. Asked who his best friends were, Ed might answer with an enigmatic smile, "Casey," or say on another occasion that he had "only colleagues and acquaintances." The emotional self-sufficiency was almost total. The way he spoke, in finished phrases, suggested a man editing his thoughts as he spoke, screening out spontaneous effusions that might reveal too much of the inner self. The withdrawals, the long silences, revealed a man able to walk away from the world even as he stood in the midst of it, a man unafraid to think his own thoughts in front of other people.

Sevareid wondered "how a man could attract so many who came to love him yet lack the capacity to give much of himself." In his final tribute to Murrow, Sevareid provided his own answer: "What is it in some human spirits that makes men remember them long after they are gone. It is not the sound and stable virtues; it is not their industriousness or their steady goodness. It is the intensity with which they lived. It is the magic in them that makes their presence a moment of magic, their simplest gestures somehow remarkable, their most casual words extraordinary and to be remembered. It is the incandescence within them that illuminates their way and gathers to them, like moths to the light, friends, strangers, the curious, the hangers-on, all those who need the light and magic in their lives."[18]

He was an American original, as Scotty Reston put it, with "the poetry of the country in his bones." The irony of his life is that he was driven by the servants of profit from the thing he loved. Murrow wanted the world to be a better place than it is, and he wanted television to serve that end. He credited adults with adult minds, and so he wanted them to face hard truths. He wanted television to storm the beaches of ignorance and injustice, instead of wallowing in a mind-numbing sea of mediocrity and easy profits. Perhaps therefore he was doomed from the outset. If so, he made a noble misjudgment. It is no small tribute to a man that he may have judged his fellow man too highly.

Ed Murrow died, unconscious, with Janet at his side, on April 27, 1965, two days past his fifty-seventh birthday. He was cremated, and his ashes were scattered in the glen at Glen Arden farm.

Acknowledgments

In the course of writing the life of Edward R. Murrow, I had indispensable help from people whose contributions I gratefully acknowledge here. Chief among my creditors is Mrs. Edward R. Murrow. Not only was Janet Murrow unstinting in the time she gave me for interviews, but she generously allowed me access to the Murrow family papers, letters, and the wartime diaries she kept. She paved the way for numerous key interviews that I might otherwise not have obtained.

The chief repository of the Murrow papers is at the Edward R. Murrow Center of the Fletcher School of Law and Diplomacy, at Tufts University. There I enjoyed invaluable assistance from Barbara Boyce and Hewson Ryan.

The CBS Archive possesses an important collection of Murrow material. I am grateful for the attention given my requests there by the CBS archivist, Samuel T. Suratt, and his capable assistants, particularly Laura Kapnick and Carol Parnes. I am indebted to Joseph Bellon and Kris Slavik also of CBS for helping me acquire photographs from the CBS collection.

A key part of my research was carried out at Ed Murrow's alma mater, Washington State University, in Pullman, Washington. There I not only had the inestimable help of Eugene H. Semingson of the WSC film center, but enjoyed the warm hospitality of Gene and his wife, Freda. My work at Pullman was carried out at the WSU library, where I first had the help of Terry Abraham, and later of John Guido and Lawrence R. Stark, a fine archivist who unfailingly fulfilled my many requests.

In the Library of Congress, I received critical assistance from the staff of the manuscript division and on countless occasions from Mark Matucci, Margrit Krewson, Kay Blair, David McGhee, and Sybil Pike.

I thank Dr. Robert Batscha of the Museum of Broadcasting in New York City for the use of the museum's collection of Murrow films and tapes. Catherine Frances Heinz was most helpful in providing materials from the Broadcast Pioneers Library in Washington, D.C.

I was aided in certain important phases of my research by Dr. Kathleen Kendall, chairman of the Department of Communications, State University of New York at Albany, and her students, Suzanne Carr, Dorothy D'Amico, Richard Hanlon, Myriam Pedro, and Joseph A. Zangri.

Vivian V. Light of the U.S. Information Agency led me through the Murrow papers relating to his government career. Lawrence Hall of the U.S. Information Agency Alumni Association helped me locate key interviewees. Jo Ann La Verde Curcio of Nielsen Media Research provided invaluable data to me. Robert Kasmire and Tanya Melich were generous in explaining to me certain inner workings of the television industry. Hollis Humphreys Cannon also helped me with key information in locating interviewees.

I benefited from the help of Dr. Santiago Pavlovsky of Washington, D.C., and Dr. John Horton, of Albany, New York, oncologists who explained to me the implications of Ed Murrow's illness. I am much indebted as well to Dr. Leslie Sanders, who shared with me psychological insights that helped me to understand my subject better.

Not only were Fred Friendly's interviews critical, but Fred steered my research and interviewing along highly rewarding avenues. Natalie Foster Paine, Fred Friendly's assistant, invariably came through on my numerous requests for help, for which I am deeply in her debt.

I thank the members of Ed Murrow's family for sharing both their memories and just as often their hospitality with me; these include his son, Casey Murrow; his sisters-in-law, Margaret Murrow and Donna Jean Murrow; his nieces, Helen Murrow Best and Nancy Murrow Gruelich; and his cousins, Nell Murrow Shuping and Louise Lamb Dennis.

I am especially grateful to Gladys Justin Carr, vice president and publisher of McGraw-Hill, for her early enthusiasm and support for the project and to my editor, Thomas Ward Miller, for shepherding my manuscript through to publication.

I save a special expression of gratitude for Clyde Taylor, of Curtis Brown Ltd., my literary agent and a staunch and understanding friend of this writer.

I also benefited from a careful reading of two fine Murrow biographies that preceded my own, Alexander Kendrick's *Prime Time: The Life of Edward R. Murrow* and A.M. Sperber's *Murrow: His Life and Times.*

I thank my family, my wife, Sylvia, my daughters, Vanya and Andrea, and my mother, Blanche Persico, not alone for inexhaustible patience, but for their help with the research and for preparation of the manuscript.

Finally, this book is the product in immeasurable degree of those people who shared with me their memories of Ed Murrow. Beyond those already mentioned above, they include Betsy Aaron, Burnett Anderson, Lauren Bacall, Edward Bliss, Jr., David Brinkley, McGeorge Bundy, Winston Burdett, Louis Cioffi, Blair Clark, Katherine Foster Clodius, Paul Coie, Ralph Colin, Charles Collingwood, Norman Corwin, Dorothy Baas Cox, Walter Cronkite, John Charles Daley, Hermine Duthie Decker, Gene DePoris, Vernon Diamond, Robert Dixon, Rosalind Downs, Douglas Edwards, Bernard Eismann, Robert Evans, Robert Foster, Jack Friel, Catherine Galbraith, John Kenneth Galbraith, Frank Gervasi, Georgia Gibbs, Samuel Goldwyn, Jr., John G. Gude, Ralph Hetzel, Don Hewitt, Willma Dudley Hill, Dorothy Hirshon, Ann Hottelet, Richard Hottelet, Marvin Kalb, Kay Fulton Katterle, Alexander Kendrick, Charles Kirkpatrick, Dewayne Kreager, William Leonard, Larry Le Sueur, Evelyn Lincoln, Henry Loomis, Deirdre Mason (pseudonym), John McKnight, Kidder Meade, Sig Mickelson, Edward P. Morgan, John Murrow, Josh Nelson, William S. Paley, Robert Pierpoint, Stanley Plesent, Lewis Powell, Joseph Ream, Harry Reasoner, James Reston, Carl Rowan, Charlotte Ramsay Rubin, Helen Hazen Rymond, Richard Salant, Jonas Salk, Richard Salvatierra, Robert Sandberg, Franklin Schaffner, Lewis Schmidt, David Schoenbrun, Daniel Schorr, Eric Sevareid, James Seward, Stewart Sheftel, Teresa Shirer, William L. Shirer, Helen Sioussat, Robert Sivard, Howard K. Smith, Thomas Sorensen, Frank Stanton, Marietta Tree, Robert Trout, Sander Vanocur, Edward M.M. Warburg, Mary Warburg, Joseph Wershba, Theodore White, Jerome Wiesner, Chester Williams, Palmer Williams, Donald M. Wilson, Walter Wyrick, Barry Zorthian, and Steven Zousmer.

Notes

The chapter notes provide the full name and title of a given work only the first time it is cited. Thereafter, only the author and page numbers where appropriate are cited. Full listings are available in the bibliography. If more than one work of an author is listed in the bibliography, the title will also be mentioned in the note. Edward R. Murrow is referred to in the notes as ERM.

The footnote number at the end of a paragraph in the text pertains to material in that paragraph and all preceding paragraphs following the previous footnote.

Chapter 1: The Peak or the Precipice

1. *The New York Times,* Mar. 9, 1954.
2. *See It Now,* Mar. 9, 1954.
3. Joseph Wershba, *The Senator and the Broadcaster;* interview, Joseph Wershba.
4. Fred J. Cook, *The Nightmare Decade,* 78, 79; Richard H. Rovere, *Senator Joe McCarthy,* 79.
5. Cook, 78, 79, 99; Rovere, 79, 98–100.
6. Rovere, 122, 123; Cook, 139–141.
7. Cook, 148, 149.
8. Cook, 433.
9. Cook, 151, 152, 172, 173; Rovere, 116; interview, Joseph Wershba.
10. Cook, 305, 308, 391; Rovere, 36–38.
11. Rovere, 185, 186.
12. Cook, 149, 150, 399–403, 420, 421; Rovere, 15.
13. Cook, 65; Rovere, 75.

14. Cook, 142; Rovere, 138.

15. Interview, Janet Murrow.

16. *Edward R. Murrow with the News,* Oct. 27, 1947; Owen Lattimore, *Ordeal by Slander,* 211; interview, Rosalind Downs.

17. Edward Bliss, Jr., *In Search of Light,* 5; Wershba, 16.

18. William Bragg Ewald, Jr., *Who Killed Joe McCarthy?* 230, 231.

19. Jimmy Breslin, *The New York Herald Tribune,* Apr. 28, 1965.

20. Interview, Samuel Goldwyn, Jr.

21. Rovere, 137, 166.

22. *Look,* August 1954.

23. Fred W. Friendly, *Due to Circumstances Beyond Our Control,* 21; interview, Charles Collingwood.

24. Interview, Charles Collingwood.

25. Cook, 405, 465; Rovere, 30.

26. Wershba, 70.

27. Rovere, 4.

28. Interview, Fred Friendly.

29. Interview, Fred Friendly.

30. Interview, Sig Mickelson.

31. Interview, Fred Friendly.

32. Steve Neal, "Why We Were Right to Like Ike," *American Heritage;* Wershba, 17.

33. Cook, 116, 130; Rovere, 42, 53, 54, 87, 95, 121.

34. Cook, 534; Rovere, 13.

35. Interviews, Janet Murrow, William S. Paley.

36. William S. Paley, *As It Happened,* 284; interview, William S. Paley; Alexander Kendrick, *Prime Time,* 42. James L. Baughman, "See It Now and Television's Golden Age," *Journal of Popular Culture.*

37. Interview, Janet Murrow.

38. Interview, Frank Stanton.

39. *Edward R. Murrow with the News,* Mar. 9, 1954.

40. Wershba, 83; interview, Joseph Wershba.

41. Kendrick, 49.

42. Interviews, Don Hewitt, Fred Friendly.

43. R. Franklin Smith, *Edward R. Murrow: The War Years,* 85; interview, Howard K. Smith.

44. *Time,* Sept. 30, 1957; interview, Edward Bliss, Jr.

Chapter 2: A Child of Polecat Creek

1. Family Bible, Nell Murrow Shuping; Kendrick, 77, 78.

2. Kendrick, 74, 79; ERM and Maria Schell, "A *Redbook* Dialogue" *Redbook;* interview, Janet Murrow.

3. Blackwell R. Robinson and Alexander P. Stoesen, *The History of Guilford County, North Carolina, USA to 1980,* 10; William Clogswell, ed.; *New England Historical and Genealogical Register;* Kendrick, 74, 75.

4. Interview, Nell Murrow Shuping; Kendrick, 72.

5. Interview, Nell Murrow Shuping; Charles Wertenbaker, "Profiles: The World on His Back," *The New Yorker;* Kendrick, 76, 77.

6. Louise Lamb Dennis to author, Aug. 21, 1985; interviews, Janet Murrow, Nancy Murrow Gruelich; General Aid Committee, *Those Murrow Boys,* 2; interview, Howard K. Smith.

7. Family Bible, Nell Murrow Shuping; Louise Lamb Dennis to author, Aug. 18, 1985; Hortense Myers and Ruth Burnett, *Edward R. Murrow: Young Newscaster;* Wertenbaker.

8. Interview, Janet Murrow; Willma Hill to author, Mar. 24, 1985.

9. Interview, Nell Murrow Shuping; interview, Margaret Murrow.

10. Interview, John Murrow; *Greensboro (North Carolina) Daily News,* Jan. 23, 1985; Sallie W. Stockard, *The History of Guilford County, North Carolina,* iii; Robinson and Stoesen, 1; Kendrick, 73, 74.

11. Interview, John Murrow; Meyers and Burnett, 17; Kendrick, 77.

12. Robinson and Stoesen, 16, 187; Kendrick, 79; Stockard, iii; *Newsweek,* Mar. 23, 1953.

13. Louise Lamb Dennis to author, Aug. 21, 1985; CBS Publicity Release, biographic sketch of ERM, Dec. 18, 1953; Stockard, iv, 52, 53; *Time,* Sept. 30, 1957; *Greensboro Daily News,* Oct. 2, 1982; Kendrick, 72, 75.

14. Wertenbaker.

15. Interviews, Janet Murrow, Donna Jean Murrow, Margaret Murrow, Edward Bliss, Jr.; Kendrick, 79, 105; Wertenbaker.

16. Interviews, Donna Jean Murrow, Janet Murrow.

17. Myers and Burnett, 21, 22–25.

18. ERM speech, Guildhall, London, Oct. 19, 1959; Kendrick, 76, 78; CBS Publicity Release, ERM, Dec. 18, 1953; Myers and Burnett, 11, 12.

19. Interviews, Donna Jean Murrow, Helen Murrow Best, Nancy Murrow Gruelich; Kendrick, 78, 79.

20. General Aid Program Committee, 2; interview, Nell Murrow Shuping.

21. ERM to Murray Yaeger, August 1956; Kendrick, 81.

22. Myers and Burnett, 14; Kendrick, 83.

23. Louise Lamb Dennis to author, Aug. 18, 1985; Myers and Burnett, 45–51, 59, 60; CBS Publicity Release, ERM, Dec. 18, 1953; *Broadcasting Magazine,* May 3, 1965; interviews, Donna Jean Murrow, Helen Murrow Best.

Chapter 3: A Northwest Passage

1. Interview, Casey Murrow; Myers and Burnett, 86–88; General Aid Program Committee, 9.
2. Interview, Casey Murrow; Cleveland Amory, "First of the Month," *Saturday Review.*
3. Interview, Janet Murrow; Wertenbaker; Kendrick, 82.
4. General Aid Program Committee, 3; interviews, Donna Jean Murrow, Janet Murrow.
5. Interview, Casey Murrow; Myers and Burnett, 66, 67.
6. Interviews, Casey Murrow, Janet Murrow, Donna Jean Murrow, Robert Evans.
7. General Aid Program Committee, 3; *Time,* Sept. 30, 1957; Isabella Taves, "A Personal Story, Edward R. Murrow," *McCall's;* interview, Janet Murrow.
8. General Aid Program Committee, 4.
9. Interview, Janet Murrow; Myers and Burnett, 77–79; CBS Publicity Release on ERM, Dec. 18, 1953.
10. Thomas Russell Woolley, Jr., *A Rhetorical Study: The Radio Speaking of Edward R. Murrow,* a doctoral dissertation; General Aid Program Committee, 13; Ethel Murrow to Casey Murrow, undated.
11. Interview, Josh Nelson; ERM file, Federal Bureau of Investigation; Myers and Burnett, 69.
12. General Aid Program Committee, 14; interview, Janet Murrow.
13. Interviews, Casey Murrow, Donna Jean Murrow; CBS Publicity Release on ERM, Dec. 18, 1953.
14. Interviews, Janet Murrow, Nancy Murrow Gruelich; Myers and Burnett, 107–111.
15. Interview, Casey Murrow; General Aid Program Committee, 9; Myers and Burnett, 98, 113, 114.
16. General Aid Program Committee, 14; Kendrick, 95.
17. Myers and Burnett, 108.
18. CBS Publicity Release on ERM, Dec. 18, 1953; General Aid Program Committee, 14; *Time,* May 7, 1965; Myers and Burnett, 103.
19. Interviews, Kay Fulton Katterle, Edward P. Morgan, Donna Jean Murrow; Kendrick, 96.
20. Interviews, Donna Jean Murrow, Josh Nelson.
21. Interview, Donna Jean Murrow; ERM file, FBI; Kendrick, 99, 100.
22. Willma Hill to author, Mar. 24, 1985; Kendrick, 100.
23. Interviews, Robert Evans, Casey Murrow; ERM to W.K. Meredith, Aug. 11, 1941; ERM and Maria Schell, *Redbook*; Myers and Burnett, 120–126.
24. Interviews, Casey Murrow, Donna Jean Murrow.
25. General Aid Program Committee, 4.
26. Ethel Murrow to ERM, undated; interview, Nancy Murrow Gruelich.

27. Interviews, Casey Murrow, Janet Murrow.

28. Interviews, Jack Friel, Donna Jean Murrow, Janet Murrow; ERM to parents, Apr. 1, 1941; General Aid Program Committee, 3, 23; Kendrick, 96, 97.

29. Interview, Dewayne Kreager; General Aid Program Committee, 15; Kendrick, 100.

Chapter 4: The Undergraduate

1. *Chinook* (Washington State college yearbook), 1926; interview, Kay Fulton Katterle.

2. *Historic Resource Survey and Analysis,* Washington State University, undated report; interview, Kay Fulton Katterle.

3. Paul Coie Remarks at ERM Symposium, April 1983, Washington State University; *Chinook,* 1926.

4. A. McCarron to ERM, Apr. 5, 1945.

5. Wertenbaker, *The Evergreen* (Washington State College newspaper), Feb. 13, 1929.

6. Edward R. Murrow Symposium, *Pioneering a Legacy;* interview, Donna Jean Murrow.

7. ERM college transcript, Washington State College, June 2, 1930.

8. *Chinook,* 1926.

9. *Chinook,* 1926; General Aid Program Committee, 4; interviews, Paul Coie, Jack Friel, Dewayne Kreager, Donna Jean Murrow, Helen Hazen Rymond.

10. Interview, Paul Coie.

11. General Aid Program Committee, 15; CBS Publicity Release on ERM, Dec. 18, 1953.

12. Interview, Janet Murrow; ERM college transcript, Washington State College.

13. Kendrick, 100; Edward R. Murrow Symposium, *Pioneering a Legacy.*

14. *Ida Lou Anderson Memorial Booklet,* Sept. 21, 1941, Washington State University Archives; interviews, Paul Coie, Kay Fulton Katterle, Janet Murrow, Helen Hazen Rymond.

15. Murray Russell Yaeger, *An Analysis of Edward R. Murrow's "See It Now" Television Program,* doctoral dissertation; Myers and Burnett, 130, 131; *Ida Lou Anderson Memorial Booklet.*

16. Ida Lou Anderson Papers, Notebooks; interviews, Kay Fulton Katterle, Helen Hazen Rymond.

17. Interview, Paul Coie.

18. Robert A. Sandberg, "A Man and His Teacher," speech; *Ida Lou Anderson Memorial Booklet;* Ida Lou Anderson Notebooks.

19. "Ed Murrow: The Man and His Legend," *Caduceus,* August 1973; *The Evergreen,* Jan. 26, 1927.

20. Interviews, Nancy Murrow Gruelich, Donna Jean Murrow, Josh Nelson; Donna Jean Murrow to author, Sept. 4, 1985.

21. ERM college transcript, Washington State College.

22. Interview, Donna Jean Murrow.

23. Interview, Chester Williams; ERM Press Statement Rebutting Senator Joseph R. McCarthy, Apr. 5, 1954, CBS Archives; ERM file, FBI; Kendrick, 89–93.

24. *The Seattle Times*, Sept. 9, 1940; interview, Paul Coie.

25. Interviews, Donna Jean Murrow, Hermine Duthie Decker, Kay Fulton Katterle, Helen Hazen Rymond; "Ed Murrow: The Man and His Legend," *Caduceus*.

26. *Chinook*, 1928; interviews, Willma Dudley Hill, Paul Coie, Helen Hazen Rymond; *The Seattle Times*, Sept. 9, 1940; Willma Dudley Hill to author, Mar. 24, 1985.

27. ERM college transcript, Washington State College; interviews, Kay Fulton, Paul Coie; C.C. Todd to E.O. Holland, Dec. 15, 1927; Murray Bundy to C. C. Todd, Nov. 14, 1928.

28. Interview, Willma Dudley Hill; Willma Dudley Hill to author, Mar. 24, 1985.

29. Interviews, Paul Coie, Kay Fulton Katterle, Dewayne Kreager, Helen Hazen Rymond.

30. *The Evergreen*, Jan. 28, 1928.

31. Interviews, Janet Murrow, Walter Wyrick; *Time*, Sept. 30, 1957.

32. Interviews, Paul Coie, Hermine Duthie Decker; *The Evergreen*, Jan. 18, Mar., 19, 1928; Kendrick, 105.

33. Interview, Willma Dudley Hill; Willma Dudley Hill to author, Mar. 24, 1985.

Chapter 5: "We All Knew He'd Make a Name For Himself"

1. Interview, Willma Dudley Hill.

2. Willma Dudley Hill to author, Mar. 24, 1985.

3. *The Evergreen*, Oct. 28, Nov. 16, 1928.

4. *The Evergreen*, Oct. 1, Nov. 2, 1928; *Chinook*, 1929.

5. *Washington State College Catalogue*, 1928–1929; interviews, Willma Dudley Hill, Margaret Murrow; Willma Dudley Hill to author, Mar. 24, 1985.

6. Interview, Kay Fulton Katterle.

7. Interview, Hermine Duthie Decker.

8. Yaeger, 29; interview, Helen Hazen Rymond.

9. Interviews, Willma Dudley Hill, Margaret Murrow; General Aid Program Committee, 5; ERM to Lacey Murrow, June 11, 1947.

10. ERM to Ed Sullivan, May 11, 1959.

11. Yaeger, 29, 30; Woolley, *A Rhetorical Study: The Radio Speaking of Edward R. Murrow*, doctoral dissertation; August *Chinook*, 1929.

12. *Chinook*, 1929; interviews, Hermine Duthie Decker, Helen Hazen Rymond.

13. *The Evergreen*, May 1, May 18, 1929; interview, Hermine Duthie Decker.

14. ERM to Willma Dudley, October 1929; Willma Dudley Hill to author, Mar. 24, 1985.

15. The *Evergreen,* Sept. 30, 1929.

16. *Yearbook,* National Student Federation of America, 1930.

17. Interviews, Dewayne Kreager, Katherine Foster Clodius.

18. Interviews, Deirdre Mason (requested pseudonym), Lewis Powell, Chester Williams; Chester S. Williams, "To Casey Murrow: Memories of Your Father."

19. *The Evergreen,* Jan. 8, Jan. 22, 1930.

20. *The Evergreen,* Jan. 8, 1930; interview, Kay Fulton Katterle.

21. *Chinook,* 1930; interview, Deirdre Mason.

22. Myers and Burnett, 127; *The Evergreen,* Feb. 13, 1929, Feb. 3, 1930; *Chinook,* 1926–1930; Edward R. Murrow Symposium, *Pioneering a Legacy;* Yaeger, 18; *Washington State College Catalogue,* 1930; ERM college transcript, Washington State College.

23. *The Evergreen,* Mar. 24, 1930.

24. Interview, Paul Coie; *The Evergreen,* Apr. 3, 1929; CBS Publicity Release on ERM, Dec. 18, 1953.

25. Interview, Kay Fulton Katterle.

26. Sandberg, "A Man and His Teacher"; interviews, Kay Fulton Katterle, Helen Hazen Rymond.

27. Willma Dudley Hill to author, Mar. 24, 1985.

28. Interview, Samuel Goldwyn, Jr.; ERM to Janet Murrow, undated.

29. "Ed Murrow: The Man and His Legend," *Caduceus.*

30. *The Evergreen,* Apr. 23, 1930, May 28, 1930; Williams, "To Casey Murrow"; *Chinook,* 1930.

31. Interviews, Hermine Duthie Decker, Kay Fulton Katterle.

32. Edward Bliss, Jr., "He's Johnny on the Spot," *Argosy;* Kendrick, 104, 105.

33. Interviews, Paul Coie, Janet Murrow; *Time,* Sept. 30, 1957; Kendrick, 109.

Chapter 6:　A New York Apprenticeship

1. Interview, Chester Williams; ERM passport application, July 10, 1930.

2. Williams, "To Casey Murrow"; interviews, Lewis Powell, Chester Williams; Wertenbaker.

3. Interview, Paul Coie.

4. ERM passport application, July 10, 1930.

5. Interview, Lewis Powell.

6. Bliss, *In Search of Light,* 3.

7. Interviews, Deirdre Mason, Lewis Powell.

8. Interview, Lewis Powell.

9. ERM to E.O. Holland, July 19, 1930; Williams, "To Casey Murrow."

10. Interview, Chester Williams; Williams, "To Casey Murrow."

11. Williams, "To Casey Murrow"; interview, Lewis Powell.

12. Interview, Chester Williams; Williams, "To Casey Murrow"; *The Statistical History of the United States from Colonial Times to the Present.*

13. *The New York Times,* Dec. 12, 1930; Erik Barnouw, *The Golden Web: A History of Broadcasting in the United States* vol. II, 1933–1953; Ben Gross in *The New York Sunday News,* June 28, 1953; Williams, "To Casey Murrow"; ERM to E.O. Holland, Sept. 18, 1931.

14. Interview, Chester Williams; Williams, "To Casey Murrow."

15. ERM to E.O. Holland, Sept. 18, 1931; CBS Publicity Release on ERM, Dec. 18, 1953.

16. ERM to (addressee blanked out), June 6, 1932, in ERM FBI file; Frederick Vanderbilt Field, *From Right to Left,* Lawrence Hill and Company, Westport, Conn., 1983; Corliss Lamont, *Memoirs of Corliss Lamont,* Horizon Press, 1981.

17. James T. Shotwell to Frank Stanton, Apr. 6, 1954; Westbrook Pegler, column, King Features Syndicate Inc., Mar. 19, 1954; *The New Columbia Encyclopedia,* Columbia University Press, New York, 1975.

18. Interview, Hermine Duthie Decker.

19. Interview, Lewis Powell.

20. Kendrick, 113; Wertenbaker; ERM to E.O. Holland, Aug. 29, 1932; Williams, "To Casey Murrow."

21. CBS Publicity Release on ERM, Dec. 18, 1953.

22. Kendrick, 113.

Chapter 7: Janet

1. Interview, Nell Murrow Shuping.

2. Interviews, Janet Murrow, Edward Bliss, Jr.

3. Interview, Janet Murrow.

4. ERM draft article for *Cosmopolitan* magazine, 1942.

5. Interview, Janet Murrow; Kendrick, 127–129.

6. Interview, Catherine Galbraith.

7. Interview, Janet Murrow.

8. Kendrick, 119.

9. John Toland, *Adolf Hitler,* 311; Kendrick, 121.

10. *The New York Mirror,* Feb. 27, 1953; *Report of the Emergency Committee of Displaced Foreign Scholars,* June 1, 1941; ERM address, award ceremony honoring Albert Einstein, May 5, 1957.

11. Interview, Janet Murrow; Myers and Burnett, 134; Wertenbaker.

12. *Report of the Emergency Committee of Displaced Foreign Scholars.*

13. Interview, Janet Murrow; R. Franklin Smith, 140; Yaeger, 21. ERM handwritten inscription, *Report of the Emergency Committee of Displaced Foreign Scholars.*

14. Interviews, Janet Murrow, Catherine Galbraith; David Holbrook Culbert, *News for Everyman: Radio and Foreign Affairs in Thirties America,* 183.

15. Interview, Janet Murrow.

16. Kendrick, 126–128.

17. Interview, Janet Murrow; Kendrick, 104.

18. Interview, Janet Murrow; Kendrick, 124–127.

19. Interview, Janet Murrow; Kendrick, 120, 124, 125.

20. Kendrick, 65, 66, 121, 127.

21. Interview, Janet Murrow.

22. General Aid Program Committee, 21; interviews, Janet Murrow, Donna Jean Murrow.

23. Interview, Janet Murrow.

24. Alfred Cohn, *Minerva's Progress: Tradition and Dissent in American Culture;* Joseph Lash, ed., *From the Diaries of Felix Frankfurter,* interviews, Dorothy Paley Hirshon, Janet Murrow.

25. Interview, Janet Murrow; Wertenbaker; Kendrick, 129.

Chapter 8: An Empire Built on Air

1. History of radio drawn from Barnouw, *A Tower in Babel,* 19–27, 36, 64–81; Culbert, 27–31, 91.

1. Barnouw, *The Golden Web,* 4–6, 16.

2. Early Paley biographical material from: Interviews, William S. Paley, Ralph Colin; Paley, *As It Happened,* pp. 4–37; Robert Metz, *CBS Reflections in a Blood-shot Eye,* 10–22; Barnouw, *The Golden Web,* 55, 56; *Variety,* Jan. 6, 1927.

3. Metz, xvi, 3.

4. Paley *As It Happened,* 41, 42; Barnouw, *A Tower in Babel,* 64–72, 81; interview, William S. Paley.

5. Paley, *As It Happened,* 62–102.

6. Metz, 10, 32.

7. Interview, Ralph Colin; Paley, *As It Happened,* 2, 86.

8. Interviews, Helen Sioussat, James Seward; Gore Vidal, "See It Later," *The New York Review of Books;* Kendrick, 132.

9. ERM passport application, June 25, 1935; Janet Murrow diary, August–September 1935.

10. Interviews, Robert Trout, James Seward, Ralph Colin; Metz, 37.

11. *The New York Times,* Nov. 26, 1943; David H. Hosley, *As Good As Any: Foreign Correspondence on American Radio, 1930–1940,* 14; David Halberstam, *The Powers That Be,* 34–38; John G. Gude to author, June 11, 1984; Paley *As It Happened,* 63; Metz, 38, 39; interviews, Helen Sioussat, John Daley.

12. Interview, Janet Murrow; John G. Gude to author, June 11, 1984; Raymond Swing, *Good Evening: A Professional Memoir,* 139, 191–195; Barnouw, *The Golden Web,* 76.

13. Culbert, 183; Hosley, 35, 36; Fred Cordova to author, Oct. 23, 1984; Ernestine M. Jones to author, Nov. 13, 1984; interview, Janet Murrow; CBS Press Release announcing appointment of ERM, Sept. 20, 1935.

Chapter 9: A CBS Apprenticeship

1. Interview, Helen Sioussat; Helen Sioussat, *Mikes Don't Bite*, 15.
2. Interviews, Helen Sioussat, Charles Collingwood; Kendrick, 134, 137; CBS Press Release, Murrow on talks, Dec. 31, 1936.
3. John G. Gude to author, June 11, 1984; "Press Book," Columbia Lecture Bureau, undated; Sioussat, 149.
4. Interview, Robert Trout.
5. Swing, 193; Hosley, 41.
6. Interview, John Daley.
7. Interview, Helen Sioussat
8. Interviews, Helen Sioussat, Janet Murrow, Ralph Colin.
9. Interviews, William S. Paley, Dorothy Paley Hirshon; Hosley, 30.
10. Interviews, Helen Sioussat, Janet Murrow.
11. Interviews, Edward Bliss, Jr., John Daley, Richard Hottelet, Janet Murrow, Helen Sioussat, Frank Stanton, Robert Trout; John G. Gude to author, Sept. 1, 1984; Barnouw, *The Golden Web*, 186; Hosley, 16; Metz, 43.
12. Interview, John Daley.
13. Interview, Robert Trout.
14. Interview, Robert Trout; Hosley, 33.
15. ERM to Ethel Murrow, undated.
16. Kendrick, 142.

Chapter 10: The Last Tranquil Year

1. Cesar Saerchinger, *Hello America: Radio Adventures in Europe;* Swing, 157; Robert Landry, "Edward R. Murrow," *Scribner's Magazine;* Kendrick, 139, 141; Hosley, 30.
2. Interview, James Seward; Barnouw, *The Golden Web*, 76; Halberstam, 38.
3. Interviews, Janet Murrow, Helen Sioussat; Culbert, 184.
4. Interview, James Seward; ERM to James Seward, Dec. 17, 1937; James M. Seward, "Reflections on Ed Murrow," unpublished manuscript.
5. Leonore Silvian, "This Is Murrow," *Look;* CBS Press Release, ERM appointment to European post, Apr. 20, 1937.
6. Janet Murrow to parents, Apr. 1, Apr. 27, 1937.
7. R. Franklin Smith, 7; interview, Janet Murrow; Janet Murrow to parents, May 2, July 4, 1937.
8. Janet Murrow to parents, May 2, 1937; interview, Janet Murrow.

9. Janet Murrow to parents, May 7, 1937.

10. Janet Murrow to parents, May 16, May 31, June 9, 1937.

11. Janet Murrow to parents, July 14, 1937.

12. William L. Shirer, *Berlin Diary*, 18, 19.

13. R. Franklin Smith, 8, 9; Saerchinger, 17, 18.

14. Saerchinger, x; Hosley, 37; interview, Howard K. Smith; Janet Murrow to parents, Dec. 7, 1940; Kathryn Campbell to Janet Murrow, Apr. 12, 1960.

15. R. Franklin Smith, 9, 61, 62; Janet Murrow to parents, June 9, 1937.

16. R. Franklin Smith, 8; Kendrick, 138, 143.

17. Culbert, 17.

18. Interview, Janet Murrow.

19. Kingsley Martin, *Harold Laski*, 63; 1. Janet Murrow to parents, June 9, July 6, 1937; interviews, Janet Murrow, Charles Collingwood.

20. Interviews, John Kenneth Galbraith, Janet Murrow.

21. Janet Murrow to parents, June 9, 1937.

22. R. Franklin Smith, 9, 10.

23. Janet Murrow to parents, May 14, 1937.

24. Interview, Janet Murrow; Janet Murrow to parents, May 25, 1937.

25. Interviews, James Reston, Ralph Hetzel.

26. Janet Murrow to parents, Oct. 19, 1937, Jan. 21, 1938; Hosley, 37.

27. Janet Murrow to parents, Nov. 8, 1937.

28. Interview, Eric Sevareid; Eric Sevareid, *Not So Wild a Dream;* R. Franklin Smith, 19, 20, 82.

Chapter 11: This Is London

1. Paley, *As It Happened*, 118, 119, 120.

2. Barnouw, *A Tower in Babel*, 277; Culbert, 16; Friendly, xiv.

3. Metz, 42; Paley, 122; Sioussat, 150.

4. Paley, *As It Happened*, 122.

5. Barnouw, *The Golden Web*, 19–22; Metz, 45; Paley, 25.

6. Paley, 116; Sioussat, 29; Barnouw, *The Golden Web*, 135.

7. Barnouw, 17.

8. Saerchinger, 4, 6.

9. Culbert, 72.

10. Shirer, *Berlin Diary*, 3, 4, 77–82; interviews, William L. Shirer, Teresa Shirer; Hosley, 39.

11. William L. Shirer, *Stranger Come Home;* interview, William L. Shirer.

12. Shirer, *Berlin Diary*, 87; Janet Murrow to parents, Oct. 5, 1937.

13. Interview, Janet Murrow; Janet Murrow to parents, Feb. 17, 1939; ERM to parents, undated.

14. Janet Murrow diary, Feb. 8, 1938; Janet Murrow to parents, Feb. 15, 1938.

15. Shirer, *Berlin Diary*, 94; Janet Murrow diary, Feb. 28, 1938.

16. Shirer, *Berlin Diary*, 95–99.

17. Interview, William S. Paley; Paley, *As It Happened*, 130–134.

18. Paul W. White, *News on the Air*, 45; Shirer, *Berlin Diary*, 95–99.

19. CBS Radio Biographic Service (ERM biography), Apr. 30, 1952; Janet Murrow diary, Apr. 20, 1938.

20. Interview, William S. Paley.

21. Interview, Frank Gervasi.

22. Shirer, *Berlin Diary*, 41; Paley, *As It Happened*, 130–134.

23. Kendrick, 158.

24. Bliss, *In Search of Light*, 4, 5; Kendrick, 159.

25. Interview, Howard K. Smith.

26. Interview, Lewis Powell.

27. Interview, William L. Shirer; Shirer, *Berlin Diary*, 94–99.

28. R. Franklin Smith, 91.

29. R. Franklin Smith, 15.

30. Janet Murrow diary, Mar. 17, 1938; interview, John Kenneth Galbraith.

31. Interview, William L. Shirer; Shirer, *Berlin Diary*, 118; interview, Janet Murrow.

32. Interview, James Seward; Janet Murrow diary, Aug. 30, 1938.

33. Janet Murrow diary, Sept. 10, 1938.

34. Kendrick, 150, 163.

35. Interview, Larry Le Sueur; Saerchinger, 102.

36. Bliss, *In Search of Light*, 6, 8, 10; Shirer, *Berlin Diary*, 132–146.

37. R. Franklin Smith, 24; Bliss, *In Search of Light*, 122–124; Edward P. Morgan, ed., *This I Believe*, viii; Kendrick, 165; Janet Murrow to parents, Oct. 5, 1938; CBS Press Release (ERM on Czech Crisis), Oct. 5, 1938.

38. Interview, William L. Shirer; Shirer, *Berlin Diary*, 112, 149–160.

39. Interview, Robert Trout; William Manchester, *The Glory and the Dream: A Narrative History of America*, 181, 182.

40. Landry; Culbert, 4; CBS Biography of ERM, Apr. 21, 1937; CBS Press Release on ERM, Aug. 28, 1937.

41. Interview, Janet Murrow; William Slocum, CBS Press Department, to Herbert Jenkins, Washington State College, Oct. 14, 1938.

42. Interview, Janet Murrow; Bliss, *In Search of Light*, 6, 7; Myers and Burnett, 150.

Chapter 12: "A State of War Exists"

1. Janet Murrow letters to parents, Mar. 14, July 11, July 15, 1939; Paley, *As It Happened*, 105; Hosley, 65, 67; Shirer, *Berlin Diary*, 169.

2. Interviews, Charles Collingwood, Janet Murrow, William L. Shirer, Charlotte Ramsay Rubin; Janet Murrow to parents, July 3, 1939, May 10, 1943; Janet Murrow diary, June 13, 1938, June 22, 1941; Fred Bate to ERM, Oct. 1, 1944; *Time*, Sept. 30, 1957; Vincent Sheean, *Between the Thunder and the Sun*, Random House, New York, 1943, 237–239, 327.

3. Kendrick, 174, 195; ERM to parents, Oct. 5, 1938, Apr. 5, 1939.

4. R. Franklin Smith, 30; interview, Hewson Ryan.

5. Janet Murrow to parents, Oct. 12, 1939; Kendrick, 193; Culbert, 192.

6. Interview, Eric Sevareid; Sevareid, 3, 4, 31, 60, 71, 85–107.

7. Interview, Larry Le Sueur.

8. Interview, Robert Trout; CBS Radio News, "Farewell to Studio 9," July 25, 1964; Culbert, 67.

9. Interviews, Janet Murrow, Robert Trout; Janet Murrow to parents, July 26, 1939; R. Franklin Smith, 131.

10. Interview, William L. Shirer; Shirer, *Berlin Diary*, 181–184.

11. R. Franklin Smith, 23, 24; Bliss, *In Search of Light*, 16.

12. Bliss, *In Search of Light*, 17.

13. Interview, Robert Trout; Bliss, "He's Johnny on the Spot," *Argosy*, September 1949; Woolley, 101.

14. Interviews, Janet Murrow, Leslie Sanders; Bliss, 17.

15. Shirer, *Berlin Diary*, 205, 206.

16. Wertenbaker.

17. Interview is, Mary Marvin Breckenridge Patterson; Janet Murrow to parents, Apr. 27, 1937; Hosley, 93, 94, 118.

18. Kendrick, 190.

19. Interview, Janet Murrow; Janet Murrow to parents, July 31, Nov. 27, 1939.

20. Bliss, *In Search of Light*, 20.

21. ERM will, Dec. 14, 1939.

22. Edward R. Murrow, *This Is London*, 53.

23. Interview, Janet Murrow.

24. Shirer, *Berlin Diary*, 277, 278.

25. Interview, Eric Sevareid; Janet Murrow to family, Feb. 7, 1940; Janet Murrow diary, Feb. 3, 1940.

26. Janet Murrow diary, Apr. 11, 1940.

27. Bliss, *In Search of Light*, 24; Janet Murrow diary, May 18, 1940.

28. Interview, Janet Murrow; Janet Murrow to Florence Clement, 1939, undated.

29. Winston Burdett to author, Dec. 18, 1984; Barnouw, *The Golden Web*, 150.

Chapter 13: The Blitz

1. Janet Murrow diary, May 19, May 23, May 28, 1940.

2. Janet Murrow diary, May 31, 1940; ERM, "Stable Boy," notes on preface probably for ERM book, *This Is London;* Bliss, *In Search of Light,* 27, 28.

3. Janet Murrow diary, June 10, 1940; ERM speech, Testimonial dinner, Waldorf Astoria, New York City, Dec. 2, 1941.

4. Janet Murrow to parents, July 3, 1940; Janet Murrow to ERM's parents, June 11, 1940; Janet Murrow diary, June 13, 1941; interview, Eric Sevareid; Vincent "Jimmy" Sheean to ERM, Nov. 5, 1940; Sheean, 62, 238–243, 296.

5. Bliss, *In Search of Light,* 28; Janet Murrow diary, June 14, 1940; Richard J. Whalen, *The Founding Father: The Story of Joseph P. Kennedy,* 292, 300.

6. Robert Goralski, *World War II Almanac: 1931–1945,* 116.

7. Interview, Janet Murrow; Janet Murrow to parents, June 11, July 3, 1940; Janet Murrow diary, June 13, 1940; ERM to Ed Dakin, July 9, 1940; ERM, *This Is London,* 131.

8. Interview, Janet Murrow; Janet Murrow diary, Jan. 19, June 4, 1940.

9. ERM to Ed Dakin, July 9, 1940; ERM to Charles Siepmann, May 6, 1940; ERM to John Russel, June 15, 1940; R. Franklin Smith, 31; interview, Mary Warburg; Sheean, 210; Janet Murrow diary, June 22, 1940.

10. Janet Murrow diary, Apr. 28, Oct. 5, 1940; Lady Milner to ERM, June 29, 1940; interviews, Marietta Tree, James Reston, Eric Sevareid.

11. Sheean, 203; Kendrick, 197–203.

12. Sheean, 212–214, 220–229; Bliss, *In Search of Light,* 31, 32; Janet Murrow to parents, Apr. 12, 1939; Janet Murrow diary, Sept. 6, 1940; interview, Janet Murrow.

13. ERM, *This Is London,* 149; interview, Janet Murrow.

14. *BBC Yearbook,* 1943; BBC-TV Production, "Goodnight and Good Luck"; Kathryn Campbell memo to ERM, undated; Friendly, *Due to Circumstances Beyond Our Control,* xv; Hosley, 139, 140; Woodrow Wirsig, "This Is Murrow," *Coronet Magazine,* Kendrick, 206, 207, 219; interview, Janet Murrow; "This Is Edward R. Murrow," CBS recording, undated; Bliss, "He's Johnny on the Spot"; John Hohenberg, *Foreign Correspondence: The Great Reporters and Their Times;* ERM, *This Is London,* 149, 162; Barnouw, *The Golden Web,* 141.

15. Hosley, 142.

16. Janet Murrow to parents, June 11, 1940; Hosley, 65, 123; Sevareid, 155–163; R. Franklin Smith, 137.

17. Interview, Larry Le Sueur.

18. Woolley, 25; *Washington Evening Star,* Apr. 30, 1965; ERM to Kenneth Merredith, undated; Sevareid, 159, 179, 251; Janet Murrow to parents, Oct. 22, 1940; R. Franklin Smith, 46.

19. Janet Murrow diary, Oct. 15, 1940; Kendrick, 206; Pete Martin, *Edward R. Murrow: An Intimate Portrait,* privately published, 18; Sheean, 212.

20. Janet Murrow diary, Oct. 24, 1940; Janet Murrow to parents, undated.

21. Bliss, *In Search of Light,* 30; ERM, *This Is London,* 182, 188.

22. Whalen, 324.

23. Interview, Robert Dixon; Bliss, *In Search of Light,* 47; General Aid Program Committee, 19; ERM, *This Is London,* 187; Sheean, 231, 236; interview, Stuart Sheftel.

24. ERM to parents, September 1940; ERM, *This Is London,* 214; Larry Le Sueur "The Most Unforgettable Character I've Met," *Reader's Digest;* Wirsig, 110; interview, Eric Sevareid.

25. Janet Murrow diary, May 4, 1940; interviews, Larry Le Sueur, James Reston; ERM speech, National Press Club, Washington, D.C., 1961.

26. Interviews, Janet Murrow, Larry Le Sueur; Janet Murrow diary, Apr. 13, 1940; Le Sueur; Hosley, 141; R. Franklin Smith, 39, 40.

27. Janet Murrow diary, Jan. 8, Apr. 3, 1940; ERM to Ed Dakin, July 9, 1940.

28. Hosley, 128; Sheean, 263; ERM to Sheean, Dec. 3, 1940; Whalen, 328–330; Culbert, 19; H.V. Kaltenborn to ERM, Aug. 20, 1940; Shirer, *Berlin Diary,* 600–604.

29. Janet Murrow, Dec. 8, 1940; Asa Briggs, *The History of Broadcasting in the United Kingdom, Vol. III, The War of Words.*

30. Janet Murrow to parents, Oct. 9, 1940; interview, Janet Murrow; ERM to Vincent Sheean, Dec. 3, 1940; *The New York World Telegram & Sun,* Apr. 3, 1954.

31. Shirer, *Berlin Diary,* 515, 516; ERM, *This Is London,* 214; Sheean, 248; Hosley, 141; Lucille Elliot Fox to ERM, May 1941.

Chapter 14:   America at War

1. Janet Murrow diary, Apr. 28, May 30, July 7, Nov. 15, Dec. 29, Dec. 31, 1940, Apr. 1, 1941; Janet Murrow to parents, Nov. 18, 1941; interview, Janet Murrow.

2. Interviews, Larry Le Sueur, Janet Murrow, William L. Shirer; Janet Murrow diary, June 11, Dec. 19, 1940; Jan. 14, 1941.

3. Interview, Janet Murrow; Janet Murrow diary, May 25, Sept. 7, Sept. 8, 1940; Janet Murrow to parents, Aug. 8, 1940.

4. Hosley, 27, 58; Philip Jordan, *Jordan's Tunis Diary,* Collins, London, 1943, 10, 11; Landry; Janet Murrow diary, Oct. 2, 1938; interviews, Charles Collingwood, Larry Le Sueur, Margaret Murrow, Eric Sevareid.

5. Janet Murrow diary, Apr. 14, July 14, July 16, July 26, 1941.

6. ERM to E.O. Holland, June 30, 1941; Wesley Price, "Murrow Sticks to the News," *Saturday Evening Post;* Kendrick, 234.

7. Interview, Janet Murrow; Janet Murrow diary, Apr. 16, 1941, May 10, 1941; draft of ERM article for *Cosmopolitan* magazine, undated.

8. Sheean, 294–296; *The Daily Telegraph,* Feb. 26, 1946; Culbert, 192.

9. ERM to Alfred Cohn, Mar. 18, 1941; ERM to parents, Apr. 1, 1941; ERM to Chester Williams, May 15, 1941; Vincent Sheean to ERM, Nov. 5, 1940.

10. Interview, Charles Collingwood; Barnouw, *The Golden Web,* 185; R. Franklin Smith, 18, 19, 42, 67, 69; Taves, "A Personal Story: Edward R. Murrow."

11. Interviews, Charles Collingwood, Eric Sevareid, Helen Sioussat.

12. Bliss, *In Search of Light,* 44; James Seward to Ida Lou Anderson, Dec. 24, 1940; Ida Lou Anderson to ERM, Dec. 23, Dec. 28, 1940; Ida Lou Anderson to E.O. Holland, Feb. 18, 1941; Robert Sandberg to author, Apr. 22, 1984; Ida Lou Anderson to Ethel Murrow, undated; interview, Janet Murrow; E. O. Holland to ERM, Sept. 19, 1941; ERM to E.O. Holland, Dec. 8, 1943; Yaeger, 16, 17.

13. Interviews, Janet Murrow, Robert Trout; ERM to John Marshall, Sept. 9, 1941; CBS Press Release on ERM's return to U.S., Nov. 17, 1941; ERM to Stephen Duggan, Oct. 25, 1941.

14. Sevareid, 185; Paley, *As It Happened,* 143; Barnouw, *The Golden Web,* 151; R. Franklin Smith, 111; Wirsig, 108; ERM speech, Waldorf Astoria, Dec. 2, 1941; James Seward to author, July 14, 1984; Janet Murrow diary, Jan. 11, 1941.

15. Interviews, Janet Murrow, Eric Sevareid; Louis Gimbel, Jr., to ERM, Aug. 22, 1941; Manchester, 251; ERM broadcast on the death of Harry Hopkins, Feb. 3, 1946; Grace Tully, *FDR, My Boss,* 76, 56, 254–256; James MacGregor Burns, *Roosevelt: The Soldier of Freedom,* 165; Price; Sevareid, 205; Nathan Miller, *FDR: An Intimate Biography,* 79, 80; Bliss, 108, 109; Robert Trout, in *Broadcasting Magazine,* May 3, 1965; R. Franklin Smith, 114.

16. Interviews, Helen Murrow Best, Donna Jean Murrow, Eric Sevareid, William L. Shirer, Helen Sioussat, Mary Warburg; speech, E.O. Holland, introducing ERM at Washington State College, Jan. 29, 1942; ERM broadcast over BBC, June 14, 1942; R. Franklin Smith, 73; *The New York Times,* Apr. 18, 1943; Janet Murrow to parents, Dec. 18, 1941; ERM to Harold Laski, Dec. 6, 1941; ERM to parents, Dec. 18, 1941; ERM to Lacey Murrow, Jan. 10, 1942; ERM to E.O. Holland, Apr. 13, Apr. 27, 1942; Ann Gillis to ERM, May 29, 1942; Franklin D. Roosevelt to ERM, June 24, 1942; ERM to Sir Philip Joubert, May 4, 1943; ERM to Earl Foster, Jan. 17, 1944.

17. Interviews, Donna Jean Murrow, Janet Murrow; ERM to parents, Apr. 1, 1941; Janet Murrow to parents, Nov. 4, 1939, Apr. 23, 1942; U.S. Navy, Bureau of Personnel; Lacey Murrow to ERM, Jan. 8, 1942; General Aid Program Committee, 10–12; Kendrick, 251; ERM, *This Is London,* 90.

18. ERM broadcast, Nov. 22, 1942.

19. R. Franklin Smith, 107; Woolley, 238; Harry C. Butcher, *My Three Years with Eisenhower,* 6, 7, 14, 21.

20. Butcher, 19–21; R. Franklin Smith, 143; interview, Norman Corwin; Joseph Julian, *This Was Radio: A Personal Memoir,* 98–100.

21. Interviews, Charles Collingwood, Eric Sevareid, Burt Harrison; Kendrick, 256; ERM to Ed Dakin, Jan. 6, 1943; ERM broadcast, Nov. 15, 1942.

22. Winston Burdett to author, Dec. 18, 1984.

23. Janet Murrow diary, Mar. 19, 1940; Janet Murrow to parents, Mar. 20, 1940, June 9, 1942, May 16, 1943; R. Franklin Smith, 57, 135; ERM to Ann Gillis, July 1, 1940; ERM to parents, Sept. 20, 1941, Nov. 18, 1941, July 9, 1942, July 3, 1944; ERM to Alfred Cohn, Jan. 26, Dec. 29, 1943; Harold Laski to

ERM, Oct. 27, 1941, Aug. 8, 1942, Dec. 12, 1943; Lanham Titchener to ERM, Sept. 15, 1943.

24. Interviews, Edward Bliss, Jr., Charles Collingwood; Janet Murrow to ERM's parents, Jan. 10, 1943; R. Franklin Smith, 102; Ann Gillis to ERM, May 29, 1942.

25. Bliss, *In Search of Light,* 56, 57.

Chapter 15: Unnecessary Risks

1. Earl Foster to ERM, Feb. 16, 1944; ERM to Earl Foster, Mar. 21, 1944.

2. Interviews, William S. Paley, Frank Stanton; Hosley, 145; Joseph P. Lash, *From the Diaries of Felix Frankfurter,* 256, 257; Butcher, 708.

3. ERM file, FBI.

4. Bliss, *In Search of Light,* 65.

5. ERM to Paul White, Feb. 17, 1944; Paley, *As It Happened,* 64, 153; Metz, 49, 50, 89; *The New York Times,* Oct. 26, 1943; ERM eulogy for Edward Klauber.

6. Interviews, Charles Collingwood, Dorothy Paley Hirshon, William S. Paley; Paley, *As It Happened,* 144, 149, 151–154; William S. Paley, "The New Journalism: A Case History," unpublished, undated manuscript; Lucille Singleton to ERM, May 5, 1944.

7. Interviews, Charles Collingwood, Janet Murrow, Larry Le Sueur; R. Franklin Smith, 45; Wirsig, 107; Collingwood to ERM, undated; Janet Murrow to parents, Jan. 17, 1943; ERM to Wells Church, Jan. 22, 1943; Lowell Bennet to Edward Bliss, Jr., Sept. 15, 1966; Group Captain Peter Johnson to ERM, Dec. 15, 1943; ERM broadcast, "Orchestrated Hell," Dec. 5, 1943.

8. Interviews, Charles Collingwood, Dorothy Paley Hirshon, Janet Murrow, Eric Sevareid, William L. Shirer, Mary Warburg; R. Franklin Smith, 137.

9. Interviews, Rosalind Downs, Eric Sevareid, Richard Hottelet; Howard K. Smith, *Last Train from Berlin,* 3, 80; Edward Bliss, Jr., "Edward R. Murrow and Today's News." *Television Quarterly.*

10. Interviews, Charles Collingwood, Walter Cronkite.

11. Interviews, Eric Sevareid, William L. Shirer; Hosley, 137–139; *The New York World Telegram & Sun,* Apr. 3, 1954; William Stott, *Documentary Expression in Thirties America,* 89; ERM, "Stable Boy." Barnouw, *The Golden Web,* 241.

12. Bliss, "He's Johnny on the Spot."

13. Interviews, John Kenneth Galbraith, William S. Paley, Lewis Powell, Charlotte Ramsay Rubin, Robert Trout; Paley, *As It Happened,* 151, 152; Bliss, *In Search of Light,* 142; Flight Lieutenant Jack Howard to ERM, undated; Brendan Bracken to ERM, Dec. 21, 1943; Barnouw, *The Golden Web,* 185, 186; BBC-TV production, "Goodnight and Good Luck"; Wertenbaker; ERM to Remsen Bird, Jan. 31, 1944; ERM to Donna Jean Murrow, Aug. 24, 1944; R. Franklin Smith, 47.

14. Interviews, Charles Collingwood, Richard Hottelet, Larry Le Sueur, Janet Murrow, Eric Sevareid; CBS News on D-Day; White, 332; ERM to ED Dakin,

Aug. 10, 1942; Bliss, *In Search of Light,* 81; ERM to Janet Murrow, 1944; Hosley, 139.

15. ERM broadcast, Nov. 12, 1944; Bliss, *In Search of Light,* 88, 89.

16. ERM to parents, Nov. 7, 1944.

17. William Schramm, State University of Iowa, to ERM, Oct. 7, 1943; E.O. Holland to ERM, May 13, 1944; ERM to E.O. Holland, July 17, 1944.

18. Interviews, Janet Murrow, William S. Paley; ERM to E.O. Holland, Sept. 26, 1944; ERM to parents, Dec. 7, 1944.

19. Interviews, Charles Collingwood, Janet Murrow, Dorothy Hirshon Paley, Mary Warburg; ERM to Janet Murrow's parents, May 6, 1945; ERM to parents, June 3, 1944.

Chapter 16: Goodbye to All That

1. Interviews, Charles Collingwood, Douglas Edwards; R. Franklin Smith, 87–89; Ben Gross, in *The New York Sunday News,* June 28, 1953; ERM broadcast, Apr. 15, 1945.

2. Interviews, Douglas Edwards, Janet Murrow; Bliss, *In Search of Light,* 97; *PM,* Feb. 24, 1943.

3. ERM to Janet Murrow, June 12, July 15, 1945; ERM broadcast, Mar. 3, 1946.

4. ERM to E.O. Holland, June 7, 1945; Bliss, *In Search of Light,* 102.

5. ERM, *This I Believe,* viii; Kendrick, 258.

6. ERM, "Peace Means Revolution," *Look;* R. Franklin Smith, 146; ERM to Elmer Davis, Dec. 15, 1943; Sevareid, 173, 174; Kendrick, 282.

7. ERM and Maria Schell; ERM, in *Atlantic Monthly,* Nov. 10, 1950.

8. Interview, Eric Sevareid; Kingsley Martin, 128, 163; Harold Laski to Kathryn Campbell, Sept. 7, 1945.

9. Interviews, Richard Hottelet, Eric Sevareid; Wells Church to ERM, Aug. 8, 1944.

10. Interview, Janet Murrow; Isabella Taves, "Ed Murrow and Son," *Parents Magazine;* ERM to Janet Murrow's parents, Nov. 9, Nov. 19, 1945.

11. ERM to Janet Murrow, Dec. 8, 1945; interview, William S. Paley; Metz, 109; John G. Gude to author, Sept. 1, 1984.

12. ERM to Janet Murrow, Dec. 10, Dec. 13, Dec. 31, 1945, Jan. 16, 1946.

13. John G. Gude to author, Sept. 1, 1984.

14. ERM to Janet Murrow, Dec. 8, Dec. 10, Dec. 11, Dec. 12, Dec. 13, Dec. 21, Dec. 22, 1945; John G. Gude to author, Sept. 1, 1984; interview, William S. Paley.

15. Paley, *As It Happened,* 180; interviews, Janet Murrow, Eric Sevareid; ERM to Janet Murrow, Jan. 19, Jan. 25, 1946.

16. ERM to Janet Murrow, Dec. 24, 1945, Jan. 4, Jan. 9, Jan. 13, Jan. 25, 1946; Eleanor Roosevelt syndicated column, *My Day,* Jan. 15, 1946.

17. Interview, Howard K. Smith; Janet Murrow appointment book, Mar. 10, 1946.

18. David Schoenbrun, *America Inside Out: At Home and Abroad from Roosevelt to Reagan*, 28, 160.

19. Interviews, Robert Dixon, Douglas Edwards, William Leonard, James Reston, Daniel Schorr, Palmer Williams; Elmer Davis, introduction to ERM, *This Is London*, viii; CBS Radio News, "Farewell to Studio 9," Sheean, 211; *The Daily Mail*, Feb. 11, 1946; Culbert, 185–187; ERM broadcast, June 14, 1942; Price; Sevareid, 178, 179; R. Franklin Smith, 91; Barnouw, *The Golden Web*, 140.

20. Interviews, Winston Burdett, Eric Sevareid, Theodore White; ERM to John Marshall, June 4, 1940; R. Franklin Smith, 17, 70, 131; Sheean, 216.

21. Interviews, John Daley, Howard K. Smith; ERM, *This Is London*, 105; Bliss, 3, 173; ERM broadcast, Mar. 10, 1946; R. Franklin Smith, 75, 139; Woolley, 285.

Chapter 17: The Reluctant Executive

1. Friendly, 286; Paley, *As It Happened*, 173, 174; Vidal.

2. Paley, *As It Happened*, 75, 108, 272, 273; Halberstam, 128.

3. Metz, 5; Barnouw, *The Golden Web*, 241.

4. Loren Ghiglione, "Don Hollenbeck: Broadcasting the First Stone," *The News*, Southbridge, Mass.; Kendrick, 286, 299.

5. Schoenbrun, 160, 161, 186, 199, 465.

6. Interviews, Douglas Edwards, Casey Murrow, Janet Murrow, Eric Sevareid, Teresa Shirer; ERM to Janet Murrow, Jan. 19, 1946; ERM to E.O. Holland, Nov. 5, 1946; Wertenbaker; Daniel J. Leab, "See It Now: A Legend Reassessed," *American Television: Reinterpreting the Video Past*.

7. Interviews, Donna Jean Murrow, Helen Murrow Best, Janet Murrow, Margaret Murrow; R. Franklin Smith, 102; ERM to E.O. Holland, July 5, 1946; interview, Robert Sandberg.

8. Interviews, Dorothy Paley Hirshon, Janet Murrow.

9. Interviews, Janet Murrow, Howard K. Smith; *Cue*, Feb. 21, 1953.

10. Paul White to ERM, Jan. 27, 1948; White, 49; Kendrick, 295.

11. *Newsweek*, Apr. 15, 1946; Hosley, 36; R. Franklin Smith, 130; interviews, Charles Collingwood, Janet Murrow, Eric Sevareid, William L. Shirer, Howard K. Smith, James Seward; ERM to Janet Murrow, Dec. 30, 1945.

12. Interviews, Charles Collingwood, Rosalind Downs, Richard Hottelet, Edith Katz Lieber, Janet Murrow, Eric Sevareid, Teresa Shirer, William L. Shirer, Helen Sioussat, Howard K. Smith; *The New York Herald Tribune*, Mar. 24, Mar. 25, 1946; *The New York Times*, Jan. 5, Jan. 26, Mar. 24, Mar. 25, Mar. 31, 1947; Howard K. Smith to ERM, Sept. 27, 1947; Halberstam, 132, 133; ERM speech (draft) Overseas Press Club, Apr. 16, 1947; John Cogley, *Report on Blacklisting*, 26, 27; Shirer, *Stranger Come Home*.

13. Interview, William S. Paley; Paley, *As It Happened,* 179; CBS News, Biographical Sketch, ERM, Dec. 18, 1953; BBC-TV production, "Goodnight and Good Luck."

Chapter 18: Listen to Murrow Tomorrow

1. Interviews, Edward P. Morgan, James Seward, Robert Trout; *Newsweek,* Apr. 15, 1946; ERM to Janet Murrow, Feb. 3, 1946; Ward Wheelock to ERM, May 4, 1946.

2. Interview, Eric Sevareid; R. Franklin Smith, 132.

3. Interview, Robert Trout.

4. *Variety,* July 23, 1947.

5. Interviews, Edward Bliss, Jr., James Seward; *Variety,* July 16, 1947; Taves, "A Personal Story: Edward R. Murrow."

6. Interview, Palmer Williams; *Apartment Life* magazine, February 1953.

7. Interviews, Edward R. Bliss, Jr., Louis Cioffi, Robert Dixon, Robert Trout, Howard K. Smith, Steven Zousmer; Bliss, *In Search of Light,* 115.

8. Interviews, Edward Bliss, Jr., Robert Dixon.

9. Interviews, Robert Trout, Janet Murrow; John Crosby, *Out of the Blue,* 177: *Edward R. Murrow with the News,* Dec. 1, 1947.

10. Interviews, Norman Corwin, Janet Murrow; Taves, "A Personal Story: Edward R. Murrow"; *The Hartford Times,* Oct. 10, 1949.

11. Taves, "Ed Murrow and Son"; John Cooper, *International News Service,* Dec. 22, 1948.

12. Interviews, Janet Murrow, Robert Dixon, James Seward, Frank Stanton; Jerome Beatty, "Hot Time in Tom Dewey's Home Town," *The American Magazine,* Marilyn Bender, "Quaker Hill: Where Lowell Thomas Is Patriarch of the Quiet Celebrities," *New York Times,* Nov. 10, 1968; Wertenbaker; Lord Salisbury to ERM, Oct. 20, 1949.

Chapter 19: Enter Stanton

1. Interviews, Janet Murrow, Howard K. Smith, Frank Stanton; Bliss, *In Search of Light,* 136; *ERM with the News,* Nov. 5, 1948.

2. Interview, Frank Stanton.

3. Interview, Frank Stanton; Metz, 5; Paley, *As It Happened,* 119.

4. Interviews, Ralph Colin, Fred Friendly, Frank Stanton; Paley, *As It Happened,* 177–178; *Time,* Apr. 15, 1946.

5. Interviews, Ralph Colin, Fred Friendly; Metz, 115–116; Paley, *As It Happened,* 187.

6. Interviews, Ralph Colin, William L. Shirer, Frank Stanton.

7. Interviews, Ralph Colin, Joseph Ream, Richard Salant, Frank Stanton; Metz, 110; ERM to Joseph C. Harsch, May 6, 1949; CBS Press Release on ERM appointment to Board of Directors, Apr. 20, 1949.

8. Bliss, *In Search of Light*, 146; Kendrick, 258; ERM speech, Smith College Commencement, June 1947; ERM speech, National Council of Public Relations Executives, Feb. 6, 1947.

9. Bliss, *In Search of Light*, 122–124; interviews, Lewis Powell, Larry Le Sueur.

10. *Time*, Mar. 29, 1948; Bliss, *In Search of Light*, 130–131; interview, Howard K. Smith.

11. Myers and Burnett, 170; Bliss, 133–135; Wertenbaker.

12. Interviews, Edward Bliss, Jr., Blair Clark, Robert Dixon, William Gehron, Marvin Kalb, William Leonard, Mary Warburg, Palmer Williams; Taves, "A Personal Story: Edward R. Murrow"; Cabell Greet to ERM, Feb. 21, 1949; Isabella Taves, "Ed Murrow: Fighter with a Soft Heart," *McCall's;* Friendly, 102; Price, 152; Woolley, 141, 152; Wertenbaker.

13. Interviews, John Daley, Howard K. Smith, Robert Trout; Metz, 92; Taves, "A Personal Story: Edward R. Murrow"; Wertenbaker.

14. *Time*, Mar. 29, 1948; Harrison B. Sommers, *Radio Programs Carried on National Networks: 1926–1956*, Ohio State University, 1958; Kendrick, 317; Paley, *As It Happened*, 191; interview, Franklin Schaffner; Price.

Chapter 20:   Enter Friendly

1. Interview, Edward Bliss, Jr.

2. Interview, Fred W. Friendly; Barnouw, *The Golden Web*, 204; Yaeger, 47, 237; Harvey Swados, *Radical at Large*, 131; Friendly, *Due to Circumstances Beyond Our Control*, xvii, xviii; Marjorie Dent Candee, ed.: *Current Biography*, 1957, 196, 197; Metz, 182, 183; Crosby, 237; Wertenbaker.

3. Interviews, Blair Clark, Sig Mickelson, Harry Reasoner; Axel Madsen, *60 Minutes*, 66, 67.

4. Interviews, Janet Murrow, Louis Cioffi, Larry Le Sueur, Eric Sevareid; Bliss, *In Search of Light*, 164.

5. Kendrick, 328.

6. Bliss, 167–169.

7. Interviews, William S. Paley, Frank Stanton; CBS Internal Memorandum, ERM/Korea, Aug. 14, 1950; Fred Friendly, Columbia University Oral History Project.

8. Interview, Edward Bliss, Jr.; *Variety*, Aug. 2, 1950.

9. Schoenbrun, 257; Paley, *As It Happened*, 216; Madsen, 61; ERM draft article for *The New York Times* (unpublished), February 1949; Jack Gould to ERM, Apr. 7, 1949.

10. Isabella Taves, "Ed Murrow: Fighter with a Soft Heart"; interview, Edward P. Morgan; ERM Foreword, Edward P. Morgan, ed. *This I Believe*, ix–xi; Wertenbaker; Kay Salz, CBS Archives, to author, July 15, 1986.

11. Interviews, Betsy Aarons, Norman Corwin, Casey Murrow, Janet Murrow, Marietta Tree; R. Franklin Smith, 104; Taves, "Ed Murrow: Fighter with a Soft Heart"; Llewellyn Miller, "Ed Murrow: Favorite Newscaster," *Today's Woman; The New York World Telegram & Sun,* Mar. 23, 1948, Apr. 3, 1954; Taves, "Ed Murrow and Son"; Wershba, 61.

Chapter 21: "The Most Important Program on Television"

1. Archibald MacLeish to ERM, Oct. 5, 1951, Jan. 6, 1952.

2. Ben Gross, "Looking and Listening," *New York Sunday News,* June 28, 1953; Kendrick, 349.

3. Interviews, John Kenneth Galbraith, Sig Mickelson, Harry Reasoner.

4. Manchester, 601.

5. Interview, Robert Sandberg; Alan Rogers (WSU Selection Committee) to ERM, July 5, 1951; ERM to Alan Rogers, July 11, 1951; ERM to John F. Camp, Jr. (WSU Selection Committee), Oct. 4, 1951.

6. Interview, Palmer Williams.

7. Interviews, Edward Bliss, Jr., Fred Friendly, Joseph Wershba, Palmer Williams; Wershba, 48, 49; Madsen, 63; Ghiglione, 13.

8. Interviews, Charles Collingwood, Fred Friendly; Barnouw, *The Golden Web,* 42; *Times,* Sept. 30, 1957.

9. O'Connor, 7; Kendrick, 333–335; interviews, Robert Dixon, Don Hewitt, Natalie Foster Paine, Howard K. Smith; *Newsweek,* Mar. 23, 1953; *Time,* Sept. 30, 1957; Wertenbaker.

10. Interviews, Fred Friendly, Don Hewitt, Palmer Williams.

11. *Variety,* Apr. 9, 1952; Paley, 240; Barnouw, *The Golden Web,* 54; interview, David Brinkley; Swados, 136.

12. Interview, Fred Friendly; *Business Week,* Dec. 19, 1953; Llewellyn Miller.

13. Interviews, Fred Friendly, Janet Murrow, James Seward, Palmer Williams; Candee, ed., *Current Biography,* 1957, 198; *Time,* Sept. 30, 1957; Yaeger, 37; *Newsweek,* Mar. 9, 1953.

14. Interviews, Edward Bliss, Jr., Douglas Edwards, Don Hewitt, Sig Mickelson, Daniel Schorr, Palmer Williams.

15. Interviews, Betsy Aarons, Edward Bliss, Jr., Fred Friendly, William Leonard, Harry Reasoner, Richard Salant, David Schoenbrun, James Seward, Palmer Williams; Halberstam, 135, 136; Swados, 130–135, 143; Wershba, 58, 59, 64–66; Yaeger, 36; Metz, 208, 279.

16. Interviews, Don Hewitt, William Leonard, Howard K. Smith, Palmer Williams; Howard K. Smith to ERM, Mar. 17, 1953.

17. Sig Mickelson, *The Electric Mirror: Politics in an Age of Television,* Dodd, Mead and Company, New York, 1972, 220; Madsen, 64; Sig Mickelson to ERM, Apr. 2, 1952; ERM to Sig Mickelson, Apr. 8, 1952.

18. Interviews, Walter Cronkite, Bernard Eismann, Sig Mickelson; Madsen, 67, 68.

19. Interviews, Walter Cronkite, Rosalind Downs.

20. Schoenbrun, 264, 265.

21. Barnouw, *The Golden Web*, 155.

22. Interviews, Janet Murrow, Howard K. Smith; ERM speech, Guildhall, London, Oct. 19, 1959; George W. Ball, *The Past Has Another Pattern*, 144.

23. Paley, *As It Happened*, 312

24. Interviews, William Leonard, Eric Sevareid, Howard K. Smith.

25. ERM speech, Guildhall.

26. Interview, Robert Pierpoint; Madsen, 153–155; Robert Pierpoint, *At the White House: Assignment to Six Presidents*, 154, 155.

27. *ERM with the News*, Dec. 10, 1952; ERM in *Saturday Review* Apr. 21, 1951; *Birmingham News* (date unknown, apparently late 1952).

28. Interviews, Louis Cioffi, Robert Pierpoint, Robert Trout; ERM Memo to Staff, Dec. 2, 1952; Harriet Van Horne column, Dec. 27, 1952; *ERM with the News*, Dec. 16, 1952; Crosby, 248, 249; *The New York Times*, Dec. 29, 1952; Kendrick, 354.

29. Ben Gross, "Looking and Listening," *New York Sunday News*, June. 28, 1953; *The New York Herald Tribune*, Jan. 20, 1952; Fred Friendly, Columbia University Oral History; Barnouw, *The Golden Web*, 42; *The New York Times*, May 4, 1952; interviews, Edward Bliss, Jr., William Leonard, Palmer Williams.

30. Wertenbaker; interview, Palmer Williams; Bliss, *In Search of Light*, 199, 200; Clementine Churchill to Janet Murrow, May 4, 1948, Jan. 1, Jan. 30, 1949; *The New York Herald Tribune*, Mar. 16, 1952; interview, Samuel Goldwyn, Jr.; Samuel Goldwyn to ERM, Feb. 14, 1952; ERM to Sam Goldwyn, Mar. 17, 1953.

31. Wertenbaker; interviews, Fred Friendly, Sig Mickelson, Palmer Williams; Friendly, *Due to Circumstances Beyond Our Control*, 154.

32. Interview, Don Hewitt; Paley, *As It Happened*, 216; Kendrick, 343, 349. Yaeger, 2.

Chapter 22: The Age of Suspicion

1. Interview, Deirdre Mason.

2. Friendly, *Due to Circumstances Beyond Our Control*, 23; interview, Janet Murrow.

3. ERM to Harold Laski, June 5, 1947; Bliss, *In Search of Light*, 118–120, 126–129.

4. Woolley, 400; Bliss, *In Search of Light*, 172, 173.

5. *ERM with the News*, Dec. 21, 1948; Kendrick, 44; ERM memo to file, Dec. 22, 1948.

6. Lattimore, 211; Cook, 210, 376; Rovere, 151; *ERM with the News*, May 2, 1950.

7. ERM to Harold Laski, Feb. 18, 1948; interview, Janet Murrow; ERM file, FBI.

8. ERM file, Passport Services, U.S. Department of State; ERM file, FBI; Price, 152.

9. ERM file, FBI; *ERM with the News,* Nov. 9, 1953; Paley, *As It Happened,* 73, 74.

10. Kendrick, 66, 67; Cogley, 80.

11. *The New York Times,* Apr. 16, 1951; Kendrick, 331, 332.

12. Bliss, *In Search of Light,* 234.

13. Interview, Sig Mickelson.

14. Cogley, 1; Barnouw, *The Golden Web,* 253, 254, 265–267.

15. Cogley, 62, 63, 104, 122; Barnouw, 273–276.

16. Julian, 169, 178, 179.

17. *Counterattack,* American Business Consultants, Inc., Feb. 22, 1952.

18. Interview, David Schoenbrun; Schoenbrun, 280–283.

19. Hosley, 118; *The New York Times,* June 30, 1955; Cogley, 126, 127; ERM file, FBI; interviews, Charles Collingwood, Rosalind Downs, Eric Sevareid.

20. Interviews, William S. Paley, Joseph Ream; memorandum, Joseph Ream to "the Organization (CBS)," Dec. 19, 1950; Metz, 281; Paley, 281.

21. Interviews, Michael Bessie, Charles Collingwood, Rosalind Downs, Alexander Kendrick, Joseph Ream, David Schoenbrun, Eric Sevareid, Howard K. Smith.

Chapter 23: Person to Person: Another Murrow

1. Pete Martin, "I Call on Edward R. Murrow," *Saturday Evening Post; See It Now,* Feb. 24, June 28, 1952.

2. Interviews, Betsy Aarons, Fred Friendly, James Reston, Steven Zousmer; Price, 152.

3. ERM to J. Edgar Hoover and others, Sept. 8, 1953; Amory; William S. Paley to ERM, Oct. 8, 1953.

4. Interview, Theodore White; Joseph Doyle, "Murrow: The Man, the Myth, and the McCarthy Fighter," *Look.*

5. Pete Martin, "I Call on Edward R. Murrow."

6. *Cue,* Oct. 24, 1953; *Time,* Oct. 5, 1953; Gilbert Seldes, "At Home with Edward R. Murrow," *Saturday Review.*

7. *Time,* Sept. 30, 1957.

8. Amory; "I Call on Edward R. Murrow"; interviews, Georgia Gibbs, Betsy Aarons; Pete Martin, *The New York World Telegram & Sun,* Apr. 3, 1954; *The New York Times,* Dec. 20, 1953.

9. *Person to Person,* Oct. 30, 1953.

10. *Person to Person,* Feb. 12, Mar. 12, 1954, Apr. 8, 1955.

11. Pete Martin, "I Call on Edward R. Murrow"; interview, Betsy Aarons; ERM to J. Edgar Hoover, Sept. 18, 1953; Barnouw, *The Golden Web,* 51; *Time,* Sept. 30, 1957.

12. *The New York Post,* Mar. 20, 1957; Kendrick, 399.

13. Pete Martin "I Call on Edward R. Murrow"; *Person to Person*, Dec. 4, 1953, Jan. 5, Oct. 19, 1956, June 28, 1957; interview, Robert Dixon.

14. Jesse Zousmer, John Aarons to Gilbert Seldes, Feb. 26, 1958; Seldes.

15. John Lardner, "The Air," *The New Yorker*, Jan. 11, 1958.

16. ERM and Maria Schell; interview, Fred Friendly.

17. Interview, Don Hewitt.

18. *Person to Person*, Apr. 8, 1955.

19. Interviews, Edward Bliss, Jr., Rosalind Downs, Fred Friendly, Dorothy Paley Hirshon, Daniel Schorr, Helen Sioussat, Frank Stanton.

20. Interviews, William S. Paley, James Seward; Yaeger, 28.

21. Baughman.

22. Interviews, Paul Coie, William S. Paley, Frank Stanton; ERM to James Seward, June 29, 1955; Halberstam, 140; William S. Paley, "The New Journalism—A Case History."

23. Interview, Edward Bliss, Jr.

Chapter 24: At His Ease

1. Interviews, Janet Murrow, James Seward; "Ed Murrow: The Man, and His Legend"; sales prospectus, Glen Arden Farm.

2. Interviews, Robert Dixon, Janet Murrow, James Seward, Eric Sevareid; Taves, "A Visit with Edward R. Murrow"; Pete Martin, *Edward R. Murrow, An Intimate Portrait*, 11; *TV Guide*, Feb. 5, 1955.

3. Taves, "A Visit with Edward R. Murrow"; Bliss, "The Meaning of Murrow"; interviews, Edward Bliss, Jr., Fred Friendly.

4. Interviews, Robert Dixon.

5. Interviews, Ralph Hetzel, Eric Sevareid.

6. Interviews, Palmer Williams.

7. Interviews, Rosalind Downs, Robert Pierpoint; ERM to William Costello, undated.

8. Interview, Janet Murrow, Ralph Colin, Marietta Tree.

9. Interview, Janet Murrow; ERM to Tadeusz Kaczorowski, May 1, 1956.

10. Interviews, Robert Dixon, Fred Friendly, Janet Murrow, Howard K. Smith, Marietta Tree, Mary Warburg; Taves, "A Personal Story, Edward R. Murrow"; *St. Petersburg Times*, Apr. 15, 1956.

11. Interviews, Robert Dixon, Ralph Hetzel, Casey Murrow, Janet Murrow, Steven Zousmer; Pete Martin, *Edward R. Murrow: An Intimate Portrait*, 5; ERM and Maria Schell.

12. Interviews, Robert Dixon, Steven Zousmer.

13. Interviews, Edward Bliss, Jr., Robert Dixon, Theodore White.

14. Interviews, John Kenneth Galbraith, Eric Sevareid; Wertenbaker; Taves, "A Personal Story, Edward R. Murrow."

15. Interviews, Robert Dixon, Don Hewitt, Mary Warburg; Taves, "Ed Murrow: Fighter with a Soft Heart."

16. Interviews, Dorothy Paley Hirshon, Richard Hottelet, Marietta Tree, Mary Warburg; *Time*, Sept. 31, 1957; CBS Biography, ERM, Dec. 18, 1953.

17. Interviews, Edward Bliss, Jr., Marvin Kalb, Janet Murrow, Robert Pierpoint; Schoenbrun, 255, 256.

18. Interviews, Robert Dixon, Bernard Eismann, Robert Evans, Robert Pierpoint, Joseph Wershba.

19. Interviews, Edward Bliss, Jr., Howard K. Smith.

20. Interviews, Louis Cioffi; Katherine Foster Clodius, Janet Murrow, Eric Sevareid, James Seward, Joseph Wershba; James Seward to author, July 14, 1984; Vincent Sheean to ERM, Nov. 18, 1953; ERM to Alfred Cohn, Oct. 26, 1945.

21. Interviews, Edward P. Morgan, David Schoenbrun; ERM eulogy for Edward Klauber; John Sharnik, quoted in ERM Symposium, *Pioneering a Legacy*.

Chapter 25: The Broadcaster and the Demagogue

1. Interview, Fred Friendly; Friendly, *Due to Circumstances beyond Our Control*, 5.

2. Ben Gross, "Looking and Listening," *The New York Sunday News*, June 28, 1953.

3. Baughman; Yaeger, 52; *See It Now*, Oct. 20, 1953.

4. Harriet Van Horne to ERM, Nov. 21, 1953; Kendrick, 39; Friendly, *Due to Circumstances Beyond Our Control*, 16.

5. Interview, Fred Friendly; *See It Now*, Oct. 27, 1953.

6. Kendrick, 47; Friendly, *Due to Circumstances Beyond Our Control*, 28, 29; John E. O'Connor, *American History/American Television: Interpreting the Video Past*, ed., 22; *See It Now*, Dec. 16, 1951.

7. ERM file, FBI; Wershba, 18–23.

8. *See It Now*, Mar. 2, 1954; interview, Janet Murrow.

9. Interview, Fred Friendly.

10. Interview, Fred Friendly; Friendly, *Due to Circumstances Beyond Our Control*, 33; Kendrick, 50, 51.

11. Interview, Fred Friendly.

12. Interview, Howard K. Smith.

13. Friendly, *Due to Circumstances Beyond Our Control*, 35–37.

14. Interview, Edward Bliss, Jr.

15. Interview, Fred Friendly.

16. *See It Now*, Mar. 9, 1954.

17. Friendly, *Due to Circumstances Beyond Our Control*, 37.

18. Kendrick, 54.

19. Interviews, Norman Corwin, Fred Friendly.

20. Interviews, Samuel Goldwyn, Jr., Kidder Meade, Eric Sevareid; Wershba, 105.

21. Thomas C. Reeves, *The Life and Times of Joe McCarthy*, 566; *The New York World Telegram & Sun*, Mar. 27, 1954; *Newsweek*, Mar. 29, 1954.

22. Interview, Fred Friendly.

23. Vidal; *Newsweek*, Mar. 29, 1954; Yaeger, 163.

24. Interview, Richard Salant; Yaeger, 162.

25. Wershba, 32; Friendly, *Due to Circumstances Beyond Our Control*, 51; ERM file, FBI.

26. Friendly, *Due to Circumstances Beyond Our Control*, 45–51; Wershba, 99; *See It Now*, Mar. 16, 1954.

27. *The New York Times*, Mar. 12, Mar. 13, 1954; *ERM with the News*, Mar. 11, 1954.

28. Friendly, *Due to Circumstances Beyond Our Control*, 50; Joseph McCarthy to ERM, Mar. 15, 1954.

29. *See It Now*, Mar. 16, 1954; interview, Chester Williams; Williams; Friendly, *Due to Circumstances Beyond Our Control*, 50.

30. Interview, Howard K. Smith; Howard K. Smith to ERM, Mar. 9, 1954.

31. Interview, Palmer Williams.

32. *The New York Times*, Apr. 7, 1954; Morris Ernst to ERM, Apr. 1, 1954; Jessie Zousmer memo to ERM, Apr. 13, 1954; ERM file, FBI.

33. Interview, Dewayne Kreager.

34. Interview, Palmer Williams.

35. ERM memo to William S. Paley, Mar. 30, 1954; Paley, *As It Happened*, 285.

36. Interview, Fred Friendly; Friendly, *Due to Circumstances Beyond Our Control*, 53–58.

37. *See It Now*, Apr. 6, 1954.

38. ERM statement rebutting Senator Joseph McCarthy, Apr. 6, 1961; *The New York Times*, Apr. 7, Apr. 8, 1954; Friendly, *Due to Circumstances Beyond Our Control*, 58, 59; interview, Palmer Williams.

39. President Dwight David Eisenhower, Press Conference, Apr. 7, 1954; Friendly, *Due to Circumstances Beyond Our Control*, 51, 109; Friendly, Columbia University Oral History Project.

40. Interview, Fred Friendly; Wershba, 49, 50; Ghiglione; Friendly, *Due to Circumstances Beyond Our Control*, 62, 63, 66; John G. Gude to author, Aug. 21, 1984; Metz, 288; Barnouw, *The Golden Web*, 56.

41. Rovere, 222, 239.

42. O'Connor, 22.

43. Interview, Fred Friendly; Friendly, *Due to Circumstances Beyond Our Control*, 68; Bliss, *In Search of Light*, 349; Edward R. Murrow and Fred Friendly, eds., *See It Now*.

Chapter 26: Family Connections

1. Interview, Marietta Tree; Marietta Tree to author, May 1, 1985.

2. Interview, Janet Murrow; Associated Press item on Casey Murrow, Aug. 27, 1954.

3. Interviews, Casey Murrow, Janet Murrow; ERM to father, Dec. 26, 1951.

4. Interviews, Casey Murrow, Janet Murrow; Ben Gross, in *The New York Sunday News*, June 21, 1953.

5. Interviews, Fred Friendly, Nancy Murrow Gruelich, Donna Jean Murrow, Ethel Murrow to ERM family, undated letters, approximately mid-fifties.

6. Interviews, Casey Murrow, Donna Jean Murrow, James Seward; Dewey Murrow to ERM, Oct. 8, 1947, Oct. 28, Nov. 14, 1952; ERM to Dewey Murrow, Nov. 3, 1952.

7. Interviews, Charles Collingwood, Dewayne Kreager, Larry Le Sueur, Donna Jean Murrow, Janet Murrow, Margaret Murrow.

8. Kendrick, 400.

9. Interview, Casey Murrow; *The New York Herald Tribune*, July 17, 1955.

10. Interviews, Casey Murrow, Janet Murrow, Daniel Schorr, James Seward; Taves, "Ed Murrow and Son."

11. Interviews, Charles Collingwood, Fred Friendly, Palmer Williams.

Chapter 27: A Teacher, A Preacher

1. Interviews, Janet Murrow, Jonas Salk.

2. Morris Ernst to ERM, Nov. 13, 1957.

3. Interviews, Fred Friendly, Joseph Wershba; Wershba, 52; *See It Now*, May 25, 1954, May 31, June 7, 1955.

4. Interviews, Fred Friendly, Janet Murrow.

5. Friendly, *Due to Circumstances Beyond Our Control*, 69; *See It Now*, Sept. 10, 1954.

6. Interviews, Edward Bliss, Jr., Blair Clark, Don Hewitt, Eric Sevareid, Joseph Wershba; *See It Now*, Oct. 5, 1954; Taves, "Ed Murrow and Son."

7. ERM file, FBI; Bliss, *In Search of Light*, 259.

8. Cogley, 127; Kendrick, 377.

9. Philip Hamburger in *The New Yorker*, Jan. 15, 1955; Friendly, *Due to Circumstances Beyond Our Control*, 69–75; *See It Now*, Jan. 4, 1955.

10. Yaeger, 112; Baughman, 109, 112; Friendly, *Due to Circumstances Beyond Our Control*, 62, 75.

11. *The New York Herald Tribune*, Apr. 16, 1954; interviews, Fred Friendly, Frank Stanton; Friendly, *Due to Circumstances Beyond Our Control*, 75, 76.

12. Barnouw, *The Golden Web*, 161; Paley, *As It Happened*, 244; Friendly, *Due to Circumstances Beyond Our Control*, 77.

13. Friendly, *Due to Circumstances Beyond Our Control*, 162; BBC-TV production, "Good Night and Good Luck"; Barnouw, *The Golden Web*, 150; interview, Frank Stanton; Paley, *As It Happened*, 242.

14. Friendly, *Due to Circumstances Beyond Our Control*, xxiii, 78; O'Connor, 7, *The New York Times*, May 1, 1985; interview, Fred Friendly.

15. *See It Now*, Oct. 26, 1955; interviews, Fred Friendly, Frank Stanton.

16. Otto Kallir to ERM, Jan. 6, 1956; *See It Now*, Dec. 13, 1955.

17. Interviews, Robert Evans, Howard K. Smith, Sander Vanocur; ERM draft radio scripts, undated; *See It Now*, Mar. 13, 1956.

18. *ERM with the News*, Nov. 6, 1956; interviews, Bernard Eismann, Don Hewitt, David Schoenbrun, Daniel Schorr, Mary Warburg.

19. Interviews, Norman Corwin, William Leonard; Barnouw, *The Golden Web*, 78.

20. Interviews, David Brinkley, Walter Cronkite, Fred Friendly, William Leonard, Eric Sevareid.

21. Wertenbaker; ERM memos to William Paley, June 15, 1955, Apr. 17, 1956.

22. Interview, Daniel Schorr.

23. Friendly, *Due to Circumstances Beyond Our Control*, xix; interview, Palmer Williams.

24. ERM file, Passport Services, U.S. Department of State; Willis H. Young, Deputy Director of the Passport Office, to ERM, Apr. 21, 1955; ERM file, FBI.

25. John Henry Faulk, *Fear on Trial*, 4, 5, 12, 29, 37, 38, 42; *Look*, May 7, 1963; Barnouw, *The Golden Web*, 76; Friendly, *Due to Circumstances Beyond Our Control*, 65.

26. Friendly, *Due to Circumstances Beyond Our Control*, 85; *See It Now*, Dec. 2, 1956.

27. Barnouw, *The Golden Web*, 99, 100.

28. CBS Special: "Conversation with Chou En-lai," Dec. 31, 1956; Friendly, *Due to Circumstances Beyond Our Control*, 86, 87.

29. Kendrick, 403; ERM to Department of State, Sept. 1, 1956.

30. ERM speech to American Council on Education, May 6, 1950.

31. Charles Kuralt, "Edward R. Murrow," *The North Carolina Historical Review;* Bliss, *In Search of Light*, 249, 254, 255.

32. Friendly, *Due to Circumstances Beyond Our Control*, 87.

33. Interviews, Bernard Eismann, Marvin Kalb, Harry Reasoner, Daniel Schorr; Harry Reasoner, *Before the Colors Fade*, 20, 23, 84; ERM speech, Guildhall, London, Oct. 19, 1959; Taves, "A Personal Story: Edward R. Murrow."

34. Interviews, Katherine Foster Clodius, Lauren Bacall.

35. Bliss, "Remembering Edward R. Murrow"; Bliss, *In Search of Light*, 307; Rovere, 248, 249; *ERM with the News*, May 2, 1957.

36. Friendly, *Due to Circumstances Beyond Our Control*, 88; interview, William S. Paley; *The Washington Post and Times Herald*, Oct. 11, 1956; *Time*, Sept. 30, 1957; CBS Press Release, ERM resigns from Board of Directors, Oct. 10, 1956; John Sharnik, quoted in ERM Symposium, *Pioneering a Legend*.

Chapter 28:   See It No More

1. ERM memo to William S. Paley, Oct. 4, 1955; *See It Now,* Feb. 2, 1958.

2. Friendly, *Due to Circumstances Beyond Our Control,* 26, 27.

3. Interview, Sig Mickelson; Friendly, *Due to Circumstances Beyond Our Control,* 80, 81.

4. *See It Now,* Mar. 2, 1958.

5. Interview, Sig Mickelson; Friendly, *Due to Circumstances Beyond Our Control,* 91.

6. Interviews, Betsy Aarons, Samuel Goldwyn, Jr.

7. Interviews, McGeorge Bundy, Ralph Colin, Dorothy Paley Hirshon, Sig Mickelson; Paley, *As It Happened,* 335; White, 169; Baughman, 111; Robert Lewis Shayon, "The Two Men Who Were Edward R. Murrow," *Columbia Journalism Review.*

8. Interviews, Fred Friendly, William S. Paley, Eric Sevareid; Friendly, *Due to Circumstances Beyond Our Control,* 89–93.

9. Friendly, *Due to Circumstances Beyond Our Control,* 87, 88, 94, 95.

10. *Time,* Sept. 30, 1957; Wershba, 90; *See It Now,* Nov. 30, 1954.

11. Interviews, Fred Friendly, Janet Murrow.

12. Interviews, McGeorge Bundy, Charles Collingwood, Janet Murrow, Eric Sevareid; *The New York Daily Mirror,* June 2, 1957; *The New York Times,* Mar. 11, 1958; *The New York Herald Tribune,* Mar. 11, Mar. 14, 1958; *The New York Post,* Mar. 12, Mar. 17, 1958; Paley, *As It Happened,* 180; *The Chicago American,* June 16, 1959; Paley, "The New Journalism—A Case History"; Arthur Herzog, "The Voice of Uncle Sam," *True.*

13. Interviews, Lauren Bacall, Fred Friendly, Howard K. Smith.

14. Interview, Fred Friendly; Friendly, *Due to Circumstances Beyond Our Control,* 93, 94; ERM memo to William S. Paley, Oct. 2, 1958.

15. *Small World,* Mar. 22, 1959.

16. *Small World,* Jan. 4, 1959.

17. *Small World,* Feb. 18, 1959.

18. Interviews, Bernard Eismann, William Leonard.

19. ERM speech to Radio-Television News Directors Association, Oct. 15, 1958; interviews, William S. Paley, Richard Salant, Sig Mickelson; Paley, *As It Happened,* 295.

20. Friendly, *Due to Circumstances Beyond Our Control,* 102; interviews, Edward Bliss, Jr., Blair Clark, Fred Friendly.

21. Interview, Fred Friendly; *The New York Herald Tribune,* Feb. 20, 1959; CBS Press Release, ERM leave of absence, Feb. 16, 1959.

22. Interview, Harry Reasoner; Reasoner, 84–86; transcript, Harry Reasoner Interview, ERM Feb. 17, 1959; Harry Reasoner, memo to ERM, Feb. 18, 1959; ERM memo to Harry Reasoner, Feb. 20, 1959.

23. *Person to Person,* Feb. 6, 1959; interview, Betsy Aarons.

24. Friendly, *Due to Circumstances Beyond Our Control*, 97; Barnouw, *The Image Empire*, 123, 124; Kendrick, 375, 400, 401, 409.

25. Friendly, *Due to Circumstances Beyond Our Control*, 104; Paley, *As It Happened*, 248.

26. Interviews, Fred Friendly, Sig Mickelson.

27. Interviews, Fred Friendly, Richard Salant, Sig Mickelson, Howard K. Smith; Friendly, *Due to Circumstances Beyond Our Control*, 105–108; Margaret McManus, "Edward R. Murrow Newscaster," *Waterbury Sunday Republican*, Apr. 17, 1955.

28. Interviews, Charles Collingwood, Fred Friendly, Eric Sevareid.

29. Friendly, *Due to Circumstances Beyond Our Control*, 110.

Chapter 29: Leave of Absence

1. Friendly, *Due to Circumstances Beyond Our Control*, 110, 111; interview, Charles Collingwood; Metz, 291; Bliss, *In Search of Light*, 337.

2. Amory.

3. Interviews, Blair Clark, Charles Collingwood, Fred Friendly, Dewayne Kreager, Sig Mickelson, Richard Salant, Eric Sevareid, Howard K. Smith, Frank Stanton; Seward, "Reflections on Ed Murrow"; Friendly, *Due to Circumstances Beyond Our Control*, xxi, 85.

4. Secretary of the Navy to ERM, May 5, 1959; *The New York Times*, July 28, 1959; interviews, Fred Friendly, Charles Kirkpatrick.

5. Friendly, *Due to Circumstances Beyond Our Control*, 104, 108.

6. Casey Murrow diary, Aug. 25, 1959; interview, Janet Murrow; Kendrick, 426.

7. Casey Murrow diary, Sept. 5, 1959; interview, Janet Murrow.

8. Winston Burdett to author, Dec. 18, 1984; interview, Burnett Anderson.

9. ERM speech, Guildhall; Janet Murrow to parents, Oct. 25, 1959.

10. Interview, Frank Stanton; Friendly, *Due to Circumstances Beyond Our Control*, 108–110; *The New York Times*, Oct. 20, 1959.

11. Wershba, 64; ERM to James Seward, Oct. 21, Oct. 26, 1959; interview, Eric Sevareid.

12. *The New York Times*, Oct. 25, 1959.

13. Interviews, Ralph Colin, William S. Paley, Frank Stanton; *Avenue Magazine*, February 1984.

14. Janet Murrow to parents, Oct. 25, 1959; ERM to Winston Churchill, June 25, 1955; Winston Churchill to ERM, Aug. 6, 1955; Bliss, *In Search of Light*, 275.

15. Janet Murrow to parents, Oct. 4, 1959; interview, Ralph Colin; Ralph Colin, draft statements re Murrow-Stanton dispute, from files of James Seward.

16. Janet Murrow to parents, Sept. 26, 1959; Casey Murrow diary, Jan. 11, 1960; interview, Casey Murrow; ERM to James Seward, Jan. 15, 1960.

17. Casey Murrow diary, Sept. 16, 1959, Jan. 25, Jan. 26, Jan. 28, Feb. 7, Feb. 23, 1960; ERM to James Seward, Dec. 12, 1959, Feb. 2, Feb. 16, Feb. 21, 1960; Janet Murrow to parents, Feb. 19, 1960.

18. ERM to James Seward, Mar. 1, 1959.

19. Bliss, *In Search of Light*, dedication page; Friendly, *Due to Circumstances Beyond Our Control*, xx; *The New York Times Book Review*, May 30, 1948; Wertenbaker.

20. Frank Stanton, speech, *Printers Ink* Magazine Gold Medal Award Dinner, Feb. 18, 1960; ERM to James Seward, Mar. 20, 1960.

21. Casey Murrow diary, Mar. 14, Mar. 22, 1960; James Seward to ERM, Mar. 26, 1960; ERM to James Seward, Mar. 20, Apr. 6, 1960.

22. James Seward to ERM, Mar. 26, 1960; interview, Fred Friendly.

Chapter 30: "Some Part of My Heart Will Stay with CBS"

1. Interview, Sig Mickelson; Janet Murrow appointment book, May 31, 1960; Kendrick, 448; ERM file, FBI; *CBS Reports*, Oct. 27, 1959.

2. Interview, Margaret Murrow; Janet Murrow to author, Sept. 20, 1984.

3. ERM statement on *Background*, Apr. 1, 1960.

4. Bliss, "Edward R. Murrow and Today's News."

5. Interview, William L. Shirer; *Background*, Dec. 4, 1960.

6. Interview, Sig Mickelson; Barnouw, *The Golden Web*, 78; *The New York Post*, July 7, 1960.

7. John Kenneth Galbraith, *A Life in Our Times: Memoirs*, 382.

8. Interviews, David Brinkley, Vernon Diamond, Don Hewitt, Harry Reasoner; Madsen, 65; Friendly, *Due to Circumstances Beyond Our Control*, 120; Reasoner, 100.

9. Interview, Bernard Eismann.

10. ERM speech, Guildhall; Paley, *As It Happened*, 312; interview, Casey Murrow.

11. ERM to John F. Kennedy, Sept. 8, 1958; *Background*, July 17, 1960; interview, Blair Clark.

12. Arthur M. Schlesinger, Jr., *A Thousand Days: John F. Kennedy in the White House*.

13. ERM speech, Radio-Television Executives Society.

14. Interviews, Rosalind Downs, Eric Sevareid; *The New York Post*, Nov. 9, 1960.

15. Interview, Edward P. Morgan; Friendly, *Due to Circumstances Beyond Our Control*, 121; *CBS Reports:* "Harvest of Shame," Nov. 25, 1960.

16. Barnouw, *The Image Empire*, 174; Fred Friendly, Columbia University Oral History Project.

17. Friendly, *Due to Circumstances Beyond Our Control*, 112, 122–123.

18. Interview, Marvin Kalb.

19. Interview, Frank Stanton.

20. Interview, Blair Clark.

21. Interviews, Edward Bliss, Jr., Blair Clark, William S. Paley, Howard K. Smith; Paley, *As It Happened*, 296; Seward, "Reflections on Ed Murrow"; Barnouw, *The Image Empire*, 178.

22. Interviews, Fred Friendly, James Reston, Theodore White, *The New York Times*, Jan. 29, 1961.

23. Friendly, *Due to Circumstances Beyond Our Control*, 125; ERM Farewell to CBS, videotape in the Fred Friendly Collection, Jan. 31, 1961; Joseph Wershba, *New York Post Magazine*, Feb. 5, 1961; interviews, Palmer Williams, Robert Pierpoint.

24. Friendly, *Due to Circumstances Beyond Our Control*, xi; Reasoner, 93; interview, Janet Murrow.

Chapter 31: The Minister of Truth

1. Interviews, Donald Wilson, Thomas Sorensen; Committee on Foreign Relations, *Hearings, Confirmation of Edward R. Murrow;* Thomas Sorensen, *The Word War*, 119.

2. Thomas Sorensen, 21–46, 66, 71; Barnouw, *The Image Empire*, 85; Stewart Dyke, "USIA: The Murrow Years"; *The New York Post*, Feb. 27, 1961.

3. Interviews, Robert Sivard, Barry Zorthian.

4. Interviews, Charles Collingwood, Dorothy Baas Cox, Janet Murrow, Hewson Ryan; *Newsweek*, Sept. 18, 1961.

5. ERM file, FBI.

6. Interview, Stanley Plesent; *The New York Herald Tribune*, Apr. 28, 1965; Barnouw, *The Golden Web*, 280; 281.

7. Committee on Foreign Relations, *Hearings, Confirmation of Edward R. Murrow;* Thomas Sorensen, 136; *Indianapolis News*, Mar. 15, 1961; *The New York Times*, Mar. 15, 1961.

8. Kendrick, 458; *The New York Times*, Feb. 23, 1961; CBS Press Release, "Harvest of Shame," BBC Broadcast, Mar. 22, 1961.

9. Committee on Foreign Relations, *Hearings, Confirmation of Edward R. Murrow;* Paul Sanker, American Committee for Liberation, to ERM, Feb. 28, 1961; R. Franklin Smith, 144; Press Release, Office of U.S. Senator Spessard Holland, Mar. 22, 1961; *The New York Times*, Mar. 23, 1961; American Civil Liberties Union, telegram to ERM, Mar. 23, 1961; ERM speech, Radio-Television Executives Society, Apr. 4, 1961; Jack Gould, *The New York Times*, Mar. 28, 1961; Gillespie Evans, USIA, memo to Mr. Payne, USIA, Mar. 23, 1961; Pierre Salinger, transcript, press briefing, Mar. 28, 1961; ERM to Patrick Murphy Malin, ACLU, Mar. 24, 1961; ERM remarks to USIA Staff Meeting, Mar. 24, 1961.

10. Interviews, McGeorge Bundy, Hewson Ryan, Donald Wilson; Thomas Sorenson, 139, 140.

11. Herzog; Collier and David Horowitz, *The Kennedys: An American Drama*, 294, 295; interviews, McGeorge Bundy, Robert Pierpoint.

12. ERM memo to McGeorge Bundy, Apr. 3, 1961.

13. Interviews, Evelyn Lincoln, Thomas Sorensen; Theodore C. Sorensen, *Kennedy,* 619; *Newsweek,* Sept. 18, 1961; *The New York Times,* May 21, 1961; Thomas Sorensen, 137.

14. Interviews, John Kenneth Galbraith; John Kenneth Galbraith to ERM, Apr. 25, 1961; Galbraith, *A Life in Our Times: Memoirs,* 413, 414; ERM to John Kenneth Galbraith, May 6, 1961; John Kenneth Galbraith, *Ambassador's Journal: A Personal Account of the Kennedy Years.*

15. Interviews, McGeorge Bundy, Hewson Ryan, Stanley Plesent, Lewis Schmidt, Donald Wilson; *The Washington Post,* May 25, 1961; *Hearings before the Subcommittee, Departments of State, Justice, the Judiciary and Related Agencies Appropriations,* Mar. 27–28, 1961, Government Printing Office.

16. Interviews, McGeorge Bundy, Dorothy Baas Cox, Janet Murrow, Hewson Ryan, Thomas Sorensen, Donald Wilson; Herzog; Joseph Kraft, "Uncle Sam's Interpreter Abroad," *Show, The Washington Post,* Feb. 18, 1962.

17. Interview, Casey Murrow.

18. Interview, Thomas Sorensen.

19. Interviews, Casey Murrow, Donna Jean Murrow, Janet Murrow, Margaret Murrow; ERM to Eric Pointer, Aug. 24, 1957.

20. Interviews, McGeorge Bundy, Donald Wilson.

21. Interview, Bernard Eismann.

22. *Issues and Answers,* ABC, Aug. 4, 1963; ERM speech, National Press Club, Washington, D.C., May 24, 1961; Galbraith, *Ambassador's Journal,* 297, 298; Raymond Swing to Kathryn Campbell, Feb. 1, 1961; *Time,* Jan. 19, 1962; interviews, Stanley Plesent, Carl Rowan; Barnouw, *The Image Empire,* 222; ERM to President John F. Kennedy, Apr. 23, 1962; Thomas Sorensen, 108; *The Washington Daily News,* Sept. 17, 1962.

23. Interviews, McGeorge Bundy, Dorothy Baas Cox, Janet Murrow, Donald Wilson; Le Sueur; *The New York Times,* Oct. 3, 1962.

24. Sorensen, 198; Barnouw, *The Golden Web,* 211, 214; interview, Donald Wilson; Herzog.

25. Interviews, McGeorge Bundy, Lewis Schmidt, Donald Wilson; ERM memo to President John F. Kennedy, June 21, 1962; Thomas Sorensen, 129, 130; David Burner and Thomas West, *The Torch Is Passed;* CBS Press Release, ERM speech to U.S. Chamber of Commerce, Jan. 22, 1955.

26. Interview, Lewis Schmidt; ERM speech to the Advertising Federation of America, June 19, 1963; Thomas Sorensen, 220.

27. Interviews, Robert Pierpoint, Donald Wilson; Thomas Sorensen, 190; ERM memo to President John F. Kennedy.

28. Interviews, Janet Murrow, Stanley Plesent, Thomas Sorensen, Donald Wilson.

29. Interviews, Janet Murrow, Donald Wilson.

30. Interview, Thomas Sorensen; Thomas Sorensen, 131, 132; ERM to Roger Tubby, Sept. 15, 1961; ERM memo to Lyman L. Lemnitzer; Vice President Lyndon B. Johnson, Speech and Questions and Answers, National Press Club, May 26, 1961; Manchester, 516.

31. Interviews, McGeorge Bundy, Dorothy Baas Cox, Janet Murrow, Jonas Salk, Thomas Sorensen; Kendrick, 500.

32. Interviews, Rosalind Downs, Fred Friendly, Janet Murrow, William S. Paley; Thomas Sorensen, 142, 171; *The Washington Daily News*, Sept. 17, 1962; Herzog, "The Voice of Uncle Sam"; Jacqueline Kennedy to ERM, Jan. 28, 1964.

Chapter 32: Good Night and Good Luck

1. Interviews, Janet Murrow, Jonas Salk.
2. Interview, William S. Paley; ERM to James Seward, 1964, undated; Fred Friendly to ERM, Oct. 10, 1963.
3. Interviews, Rosalind Downs, Henry Loomis, John McKnight; Thomas Sorensen, 222.
4. Interviews, Fred Friendly, Joseph Wershba.
5. "Farewell to Studio Nine," CBS Broadcast, July 25, 1964; *The New York Herald Tribune*, May 1, 1964; Fred Friendly to author, May 21, 1985.
6. Interviews, Janet Murrow, Teresa Shirer, William L. Shirer.
7. Interviews, Robert Dixon, Janet Murrow; ERM personnel record, U.S. Navy.
8. Interviews, Jonas Salk, Sander Vanocur.
9. Interviews, Charles Collingwood, John Kenneth Galbraith, Janet Murrow, James Seward, Marietta Tree, Donald Wilson.
10. Interview, Jonas Salk.
11. Interview, Robert Dixon.
12. Interview, Janet Murrow; "Person to Person," *Cosmopolitan*, April 1956.
13. Interviews, Walter Cronkite, Marvin Kalb, William L. Shirer; *Time*, Sept. 30, 1957; Reasoner, 82.
14. Yaeger, 246–251; *Broadcasting* magazine, May 3, 1965; Bliss, *In Search of Light*, 160.
15. Paley, *As It Happened*, 240–241.
16. Friendly, *Due to Circumstances Beyond Our Control*, xii, 170.
17. Interview, Henry Loomis.
18. Interviews, Charles Collingwood, Janet Murrow, Daniel Schorr, Eric Sevareid, William L. Shirer, Howard K. Smith; Herzog; Wershba, 43; Sevareid, 176, 177; *The Washington Evening Star*, Apr. 30, 1965; John Sharnik, quoted in ERM Symposium, *Pioneering a Legacy; Taves*, "A Personal Story, Edward R. Murrow."

Bibliography

The principal documentary sources used in this work are:

The Edward R. Murrow Collection, Fletcher School of Law and Diplomacy, Tufts University, Medford, Massachusetts

Columbia University Broadcast System Archives, New York City

The private papers of Mrs. Edward R. Murrow

The Library of Congress, Washington, D.C.

The Archives of Washington State University, Pullman, Washington.

Archives of the U.S. Information Agency, Washington, D.C.

Other written sources used include:

BOOKS

Ball, George W.: *The Past Has Another Pattern*, W. W. Norton & Company, New York, 1982.

Barnouw, Erik: *A Tower in Babel, A History of Broadcasting in the United States*, Vol. I, Oxford University Press, New York, 1966.

_____: *The Golden Web: A History of Broadcasting in the United States*, Vol. II, *1933–1953*, Oxford University Press, New York, 1968.

_____: *The Image Empire: A History of Broadcasting in the United States*, Vol. III, *From 1953*, Oxford University Press, New York, 1970.

Bliss, Edward, Jr., ed.: *In Search of Light, The Broadcasts of Edward R. Murrow, 1938–1961*, Alfred A. Knopf, Inc., New York, 1967.

Block, Maxine, ed.: *Current Biography,* The H.W. Wilson Company, New York, 1942.

Bogart, Leo: *The Age of Television,* Frederick Ungar Publishing Company, New York, 1972.

Briggs, Asa: *The History of Broadcasting in the United Kingdom, Vol. III, The War of Words,* Oxford University Press, London, 1970.

Burner, David, and Thomas West: *The Torch Is Passed,* Atheneum Publishers, New York, 1984.

Burns, James MacGregor: *Roosevelt: The Soldier of Freedom,* Harcourt Brace Jovanovich, Inc., New York, 1970.

Butcher, Harry C.: *My Three Years with Eisenhower,* Simon & Schuster, New York, 1946.

Candee, Marjorie Dent, ed.: *Current Biography,* H. W. Wilson Company, New York, 1953.

_____: *Current Biography,* H. W. Wilson Company, New York, 1956.

_____: *Current Biography,* H. W. Wilson Company, New York, 1957.

Clogswell, William D.D., ed.: *New England Historical and Genealogical Register,* New England Historical Genealogical Society, vol. I, Boston, Samuel D. Drake, Publisher, 1847.

Cogley, John: *Report on Blacklisting,* The Fund for the Republic Inc., 1956.

Cohn, Alfred: *Minerva's Progress: Tradition and Dissent in American Culture,* Harcourt Brace & Company, New York, 1946.

Collier, Peter, and David Horowitz: *The Kennedys: An American Drama,* Summit Books, New York, 1984.

Cook, Fred J.: *The Nightmare Decade: The Life and Times of Senator Joe McCarthy,* Random House, New York, 1971.

Crosby, John: *Out of the Blue,* Simon & Schuster, New York, 1952.

Culbert, David Holbrook: *News for Everyman: Radio and Foreign Affairs in Thirties America,* Greenwood Press, Westport, Conn., 1976.

Ewald, William Bragg, Jr.: *Who Killed Joe McCarthy?* Simon & Schuster, New York, 1984.

Faulk, John Henry: *Fear on Trial,* Grosset & Dunlap, New York, 1976.

Friendly, Fred W.: *Due to Circumstances Beyond Our Control,* Vintage Books (Division of Harcourt Brace), 1968.

Galbraith, John Kenneth: *Ambassador's Journal, A Personal Account of the Kennedy Years,* 1979.

_____: *A Life in Our Times: Memoirs,* Houghton Mifflin Company, Boston, 1981.

Goldman, Eric F.: *The Crucial Decade and After: America, 1945–1960,* Alfred A. Knopf, Inc., New York, 1956.

Goralski, Robert: *World War II Almanac: 1931–1945,* G. P. Putnam's Sons, New York, 1981.

Halberstam, David: *The Powers That Be,* Alfred A. Knopf, Inc., New York, 1979.

Hayward, Brooke: *Haywire,* Alfred A. Knopf, Inc., New York, 1977.

Hohenberg, John: *Foreign Correspondence: The Great Reporters and Their Times,* Columbia University Press, New York, 1964.

Hosley, David H.: *As Good as Any: Foreign Correspondence on American Radio, 1930–1940,* Greenwood Press, Westport, Conn., 1984.

Jordan, Philip, *Jordan's Tunis Diary,* Collins, London, 1943.

Julian, Joseph: *This Was Radio: A Personal Memoir,* The Viking Press, New York, 1975.

Kendrick, Alexander: *Prime Time: The Life of Edward R. Murrow,* Little, Brown and Company, Boston, 1969.

Lamont, Corliss: *Memoirs of Corliss Lamont,* Horizon Press, New York, 1981.

Lash, Joseph P., ed.: *From the Diaries of Felix Frankfurter,* W. W. Norton & Company, New York, 1975.

Laski, Harold J.: *The American Democracy,* The Viking Press, New York, 1948.

Lattimore, Owen: *Ordeal by Slander,* Greenwood Press, Westport, Conn., 1950.

Leab, Daniel J.: "See It Now: A Legend Reassessed," *American Television: Reinterpreting the Video Past,* John E. O'Connor, ed., Frederick Ungar Publishing Company, New York, 1983.

MacVane, William: *On the Air in World War II,* William Morrow & Company, New York, 1979.

Madsen, Axel: *60 Minutes,* Dodd, Mead & Company, New York, 1984.

Manchester, William: *The Glory and the Dream: A Narrative History of America,* Bantam Books, New York, 1975.

Marconi, Degna: *My Father Marconi,* McGraw-Hill Book Company, Inc., New York, 1962.

Martin, Kingsley: *Harold Laski,* The Viking Press, New York, 1953.

Metz, Robert: *CBS: Reflections in a Bloodshot Eye,* New American Library, New York, 1975.

Michelmore, Peter: *The Swift Years,* Dodd, Mead & Company, New York, 1969.

Mickelson, Sig: *The Electronic Mirror: Politics in an Age of Television,* Dodd, Mead & Company, New York, 1972.

Miller, Nathan: *FDR: An Intimate Biography,* Doubleday & Company, Inc., Garden City, N.Y., 1983.

Morgan, Edward P., ed.: *This I Believe,* Foreword by Edward R. Murrow, Simon & Schuster, New York, 1952.

Morgan, Ted: *Maughm,* Simon & Schuster, New York, 1980.

Murrow, Edward R.: *This Is London,* Elmer Davis, ed., Simon & Schuster, New York, 1941.

———and Fred Friendly, eds.: *See It Now,* Simon & Schuster, New York, 1955.

Myers, Hortense, and Ruth Burnett: *Edward R. Murrow: Young Newscaster,* The Bobbs-Merrill Company, Inc., New York, 1969.

O'Connor, John E., ed.: *American History/American Television: Interpreting the Video Past,* Frederick Ungar Publishing Company, New York, 1983.

Paley, William S.: *As It Happened,* Doubleday & Company, Garden City, N.Y., 1979.

Pierpoint, Robert: *At the White House: Assignment to Six Presidents,* G. P. Putnam's Sons, New York, 1981.

Reasoner, Harry, *Before the Colors Fade,* Alfred A. Knopf, Inc., New York, 1981.

Reeves, Thomas C., *The Life and Times of Joe McCarthy,* Stein and Day, New York, 1982.

Robinson, Blackwell P., and Alexander K. Stoesen: *The History of Guilford County North Carolina, USA to 1980 AD,* Guilford County Bicentennial Commission, 1981.

Rovere, Richard H.: *Senator Joe McCarthy,* Harcourt, Brace and Company, New York, 1959.

Saerchinger, Caesar: *Hello America: Radio Adventures in Europe,* Houghton Mifflin Company, Boston 1938.

Schlesinger, Arthur M., Jr.: *A Thousand Days: John F. Kennedy in the White House,* Houghton Mifflin Company, Boston, 1965.

Schoenbrun, David: *America Inside Out: At Home and Abroad from Roosevelt to Reagan,* McGraw-Hill Book Company, New York, 1984.

Sevareid, Eric: *Not So Wild a Dream,* Atheneum Publishers, New York, 1976.

Sheean, Vincent: *Between the Thunder and the Sun,* Random House, New York, 1943.

Shirer, William L.: *Berlin Diary,* Alfred A. Knopf, Inc., New York, 1941.

_____: *Stranger Come Home,* Little, Brown and Company, Boston, 1954.

Sioussat, Helen: *Mikes Don't Bite,* L. B. Fischer, New York, 1943.

Smith, Howard K.: *Last Train from Berlin,* Alfred A. Knopf, Inc., New York, 1942.

Smith, R. Franklin: *Edward R. Murrow: The War Years,* New Issues Press, Western Michigan University, Kalamazoo, Mich., 1978.

Sorensen, Theodore C.: *Kennedy,* Harper & Row, Publishers, Inc., New York, 1965.

Sorensen, Thomas C.: *The Word War,* Harper & Row, Publishers, Inc., New York, 1968.

The Statistical History of the United States from Colonial Times to the Present, Fairfield Publishers, Inc., Stamford, Conn., 1965.

Stockard, Sallie W.: *The History of Guilford County, North Carolina,* republished by the Guilford County Genealogical Society, 1983.

Stott, William: *Documentary Expression and Thirties America,* Oxford University Press, New York, 1973.

Summers, Harrison B.: *Radio Programs Carried on National Networks, 1926–1956,* Ohio State University, Columbus, January 1958.

Swados, Harvey: *Radical at Large,* Robert Hart-Davis, London, 1968.

Swing, Raymond: *Good Evening: A Professional Memoir,* Harcourt, Brace & World, Inc., New York, 1964.

Toland, John: *Adolf Hitler,* Doubleday & Company, Inc., Garden City, N.Y., 1976.

Tully, Grace: *FDR, My Boss,* Charles Scribner's Sons, New York, 1949.

Whalen, Richard J.: *The Founding Father: The Story of Joseph P. Kennedy,* New American Library, New York, 1964.

White, Paul W.: *News on the Air,* Harcourt, Brace and Company, New York, 1947.

PERIODICALS

Amory, Cleveland: "First of the Month," *Saturday Review,* July 5, 1959.

Baughman, James L.: "See It Now and Television's Golden Age," *Journal of Popular Culture,* vol. 15, Fall 1981.

Beatty, Jerome: "Hot Time in Tom Dewey's Home Town," *The American Magazine,* October 1948.

Bliss, Edward, Jr.: "He's Johnny on the Spot," *Argosy,* September 1949.

_____: "Edward R. Murrow and Today's News," *Television Quarterly,* Fall 1970.

_____: "Remembering Edward R. Murrow," *Saturday Review,* May 31, 1975.

_____: "The Meaning of Murrow," *Feedback,* published by The Broadcast Education Association, Winter 1983–1984.

Doyle, Joseph: "Murrow: The Man, the Myth and the McCarthy Fighter," *Look,* Aug. 24, 1954.

Dudar, Helen: "A Post Portrait: Ed Murrow," *The New York Post,* Feb. 24, Feb. 26, Feb. 27, Mar. 1, 1959.

Dyke, Stewart: "USIA: The Murrow Years," School of Journalism, University of Missouri, Freedom of Information Center, Publication 127, July 1964.

"Ed Murrow: The Man and His Legend," *Caduceus,* magazine of Kappa Sigma International Fraternity, August 1973.

"Fine Careless Rapture," *The New Yorker,* Jan. 20, 1940,

Ghiglione, Loren: "Don Hollenback: Broadcasting the First Stone," *The News,* Southbridge, Mass., Dec. 19, 1976.

Herzog, Arthur: "The Voice of Uncle Sam," *True,* June 1963.

"If You Weren't Yourself, Who Would You Like to Be?" *Look,* October 1943.

Kamm, Herbert: "Murrow: Person to Person," *World Telegram & Sun Saturday Magazine,* Apr. 3, 1954.

Kraft, Joseph: "Uncle Sam's Interpreter Abroad," *Show,* June 1963.

Kuralt, Charles: "Edward R. Murrow," *The North Carolina Historical Review,* April 1971.

Landry, Robert: "Edward R. Murrow," *Scribner's Magazine,* December 1938.

Lardner, John: "The Air," *The New Yorker,* Jan. 11, 1958.

_____: "The Air," *The New Yorker,* Apr. 18, 1959.

Le Sueur, Larry: "The Most Unforgettable Character I've Met," *Reader's Digest,* May 1969.

Martin, Pete: "I Call on Edward R. Murrow," *Saturday Evening Post,* Jan. 18, 1958.

Miller, Llewellyn: "Ed Murrow: Favorite Newscaster," *Today's Woman,* March 1952.

Murrow, Edward: "Peace Means Revolution," *Look,* May 18, 1943.

_____and Maria Schell: "A Redbook Dialogue," *Redbook,* July 1961.

Neal, Steve: "Why We Were Right to Like Ike," *American Heritage,* December 1985.

Price, Wesley: "Murrow Sticks to the News," *Saturday Evening Post,* Dec. 10, 1949.

Seldes, Gilbert: "At Home with Edward Murrow," *Saturday Review,* Nov. 7, 1953.

Shayon, Robert Lewis: "The Two Men Who Were Murrow," *Columbia Journalism Review,* Fall 1969.

Silvian, Leonore: "This Is Murrow," *Look,* Mar. 11, 1952.

Taves, Isabella: "A Personal Story, Edward R. Murrow," *McCall's,* February 1954.

———: "Ed Murrow: Fighter with a Soft Heart," *McCall's,* April 1954.

———: "Ed Murrow and Son," *Parents Magazine,* September 1956.

———: "A Visit with Edward R. Murrow," *Look,* Aug. 18, 1959.

"This Is Murrow," *TV Guide,* Feb. 5, 1955.

Vidal, Gore: "See It Later," *The New York Review of Books,* Dec. 7, 1967.

Wertenbaker, Charles: "Profiles: The World on His Back," *The New Yorker,* Dec. 26, 1953.

Wirsig, Woodrow: "This Is Murrow," *Coronet Magazine,* September 1943.

"Wooing the Eggheads for ALCOA," *Business Week,* Dec. 19, 1953, pp. 115–118.

OTHER SOURCES

Anderson, Ida Lou: Papers, Washington State University Archives, Pullman, Wash.

BBC-TV Production, "Good Night and Good Luck," 1975.

CBS News on D-Day, New York, 1945.

CBS Radio Network broadcast, "Murrow Remembered," *Newsmark,* produced by Frank Devine and narrated by Dan Rather.

CBS Radio News, "Farewell to Studio Nine," July 25, 1964.

Committee on Foreign Relations, U.S. Senate, hearing, Mar. 14, 1961.

Dixon, Robert: "Reminiscences of ERM," unpublished manuscript.

Edward R. Murrow Symposium, *Pioneering a Legacy,* report prepared for the ninth program in the series, Apr. 21–23, 1983, Washington State University, Pullman, Wash.

Friendly, Fred: Columbia University Oral History Project, Dec. 27, 1968 (Eric Barnouw, interviewer).

General Aid Program Committee: "Those Murrow Boys," Bellingham, Wash., undated, unpublished.

Lyons, Louis M.: Interview of Edward R. Murrow on WGBH-TV, Boston, 1959, sponsored by Fund for the Republic.

Martin, Pete: *Edward R. Murrow: An Intimate Portrait,* published by the author, 1981, P.O. Box 375, Belvedere Island, Cal.

Meet the Press, transcript, June 4, 1961.

Murrow, Casey: Diary, 1959–1960.

Murrow, Charles Havland: "The Murrow Family of Virginia, Kentucky, Indiana, Iowa and Kansas," unpublished typescript, 1940, Des Moines, Iowa.

Murrow, Edward R.: Statement before the U.S. Senate Subcommittee on Overseas Information Programs, Mar. 26, 1953.

——: Hearings before the Subcommittee, Departments of State and Justice, U.S. Senate, the Judiciary and related agencies appropriations, Mar. 14, 1961.

——: Speech, Guildhall, London, Oct. 19, 1959.

——: Eulogy, Edward Klauber Memorial Service, September 1954.

——: Address, award ceremony honoring Albert Einstein, May 5, 1957.

——: Farewell Broadcast to CBS, Jan. 31, 1961.

——: Speech, Radio-Television Executives Association, Jan. 12, 1961.

——: Commencement Address, Washington State University, Pullman, Wash., 1962.

Paley, William S.: "The New Journalism—A Case History," unpublished manuscript.

Sandberg, Robert A.: "A Man and His Teacher," Apr. 22, 1983, delivered at Edward R. Murrow Symposium, *Pioneering a Legacy,* Washington State University, Pullman, Wash.

Seward, James M.: "Reflections on Ed Murrow," Feb. 15, 1978, unpublished typescript.

Smith, J. Walker, and Renee Keever Davis: "A Shadow Cast by Sound," May 1981, unpublished manuscript.

U.S. Navy, Bureau of Personnel, Officer's Selection Board Jacket, Edward R. Murrow.

Wershba, Joseph: "The Senator and the Broadcaster," undated, unpublished manuscript.

Williams, Chester S.: "To Casey Murrow: Memories of Your Father," June 1965, unpublished manuscript.

Woolley, Thomas Russell, Jr.: *A Rhetorical Study: The Radio Speaking of Edward R. Murrow,* doctoral dissertation, Northwestern University, Evanston, Ill., August 1957.

Yaeger, Murray Russell: *An Analysis of Edward R. Murrow's "See It Now" Television Program,* doctoral dissertation, State University of Iowa, August 1956.

Yearbook, National Student Federation of the United States of America, New York, 1930.

Index